SO-CEY-722

The A+ Cram Sheet

1. The power supply brings in 110 volts (AC) and typically puts out 12, 5, and 3.x volts (DC). Sometimes jumpers can set a voltage regulator module (VRM) on the system board to provide other voltages. Many processors use 3.3 volts or less. Mobile technology CPUs use just above 1 volt. Intel "Centrino" is a branded name for mobile technology.

2. **ESD** is **electro**static discharge. **EMI** is **electro-magnetic** interference.

3. A good circuit (for example, working fuse) shows close to 0 Ohms on a **multimeter**. Capacitors store an electrical charge and are used in power supplies.

4. BIOS chips come in PROM (programmable ROM), EPROM (erasable programmable ROM), and EEPROM (electrically erasable PROM). Flash memory is used on things like Compact Flash and SmartMedia cards. Flash memory is built like an EEPROM chip, but uses different write/erase.

5. CMOS is a battery-backed chip that contains system settings, configured from a hot-key combination at bootup. CMOS stores passwords. The best way to recover from a forgotten CMOS password is to disconnect the chip's power supply and clear all settings. A badly configured CMOS (where the hardware attached is set with the wrong name) usually generates a "device mismatch" error.

6. Slot 1, Slot 2, Socket 7, Socket 8, and Socket 370 are Intel processor mountings. **Slot A** and **Socket A** are **AMD** processor mounts.

7. Pentium chips have a 32-bit address bus, and a 64-bit processor bus, for the most part. Hyper Threading technology is an Intel-specific technology. Net Burst is also Intel's name for new Pentium 4 features.

8. **IDE** is a **type of hard drive** with integrated electronics. EIDE is the extended IDE. **ATA** is a **specification** for how data transfers from a disk to the motherboard. ATA comes in Fast-ATA and Ultra-ATA. UDMA is just another name for the ATA specification. So is ATA/ATAPI. ATA is like SCSI, and both are specifications. SCSI is also a bus architecture like PCI.

9. If a keyed connector doesn't have a physical notch, the red stripe refers to Pin 1.

10. **Sectors** are **512 bytes**. Clusters change sizes and must completely fill a logical drive (volume).

11. The **Master Boot Record** (**MBR**) is in Sector 0, Track 0, Head 0, Cylinder 0 of the Active, Primary partition. FAT32 uses smaller clusters and can address more than the FAT16 2GB drive limit. NTFS is the Windows NT File System.

12. SIMM stands for Single Inline Memory Module. DIMM stands for Dual Inline Memory Module. Parity tests RAM chips for structural integrity. Thermal changes can affect the RAM chips and cause parity errors. Parity comes in Odd or Even parity.

13. DRAM is Dynamic RAM and isn't timed. SDRAM is Synchronous DRAM and is timed. SRAM is Static RAM and is very fast. RDRAM is Rambus RAM, licensed by Intel. DDR SDRAM is Double-Data Rate SDRAM and uses half-ticks.

14. **Parallel** cables usually have a **DB25** 25-pin male connector on one end and a **Centronics 36-pin** male connector at the other end. The Parallel port on the back panel of the PC is usually a 25-pin female socket.

15. **Serial** cables usually have a **DB9** 9-pin connector. **Video** cables use a **15-pin** connector.

16. PS/2 connectors are 6-pin circular connectors. DIN connectors (or AT connectors) use a 5-pin connector larger than PS/2 connectors. USB and FireWire connectors look like rectangles.

17. RJ-45 is a network connector. RJ-11 is usually a telephone connector.

18. **SCSI** uses **50-pin** ribbon cables. SCSI chains have 1 Host Adapter, and up to 7 additional devices (8 total devices). SCSI cables must be **terminated** at both ends, and are used for devices outside the box. Host adapters are usually inside the box (expansion cards).

19. IDE controllers can have up to 2 devices on each controller. Motherboards usually have 2 IDE connectors (also known as controllers). SCSI and USB are used for external devices such as CDROMs, DVD drives, and scanners. IDE doesn't connect to devices outside the box.

70. **MSINFO32.EXE** provides hardware and **system information**. **MSCONFIG.EXE** provides **startup** information and system services. TASKMAN.EXE (Task Manager) shows all programs running in memory.

71. **Recovery Console** is in the **\i386** folder. Install to the hard drive with the **winnt.exe /cmdcons** switch. It's a separate, text-based application, not a DOS environment.

72. Event Viewer is part of a Control Panel applet (console) that reports problems with system events, such as loading an application or service, printing, and security. DRWATSON.EXE loads into memory, watches the system, and can run a report of a system snapshot at the time of the error.

73. **XP Startup failures**: "Missing NTLDR" system can't find kernel. "Missing NTDETECT" can't find hardware and devices. "Can't find this or that file." Bad BOOT.INI file, and system can't find system files.

47. **DOS** and Windows 9x **bootable floppies** must have **COMMAND.COM**, **IO.SYS**, and **MSDOS.SYS**.

48. **Windows NT/2000/XP** ERD **(Emergency Repair Disk)** must have **NTLDR**, **NTDETECT.COM** (hardware detection), and **BOOT.INI** (NT configuration file). SCSI disks must also have NTBOOTDD.SYS.

49. **Executable** file extensions are mostly .EXE, .COM, .BAT, and .PIF. System initialization (configuration) files are .INI and aren't executable.

50. The **first 1MB** of physical memory is called **conventional memory** (640KB) and can be split into low memory (IRQ tables), application memory (640KB), upper memory blocks, and high memory (together, around 370KB). UMB stands for Upper Memory Blocks, where DOS places certain things such as parts of COMMAND.COM.

51. **Real Mode** originates with the 8086 processor, when the chip could address only 1MB of real memory addresses. Protected Mode allows for virtual memory by swapping memory images to disk. Both are CPU-based events. Windows uses virtual memory.

52. Windows 9x creates a Real Mode virtual machine (VM) to run 16-bit applications and device drivers. Windows NT/2000/XP use the hardware abstraction layer (HAL) to control devices. Windows NT/XP do not support Real Mode.

53. **EMS** is **expanded** memory. **XMS** is **extended** memory ("**X**-10-ded"). EMM386.EXE is never used in Windows 9x, and is commented out if found in a CONFIG.SYS file.

54. **HIMEM.SYS** loads from **MSDOS.SYS** (Windows 9x) and is a **required extended memory manager** in Windows 9x, Windows NT, Windows 2000, and Windows XP.

55. The three critical **DOS system** files are **IO.SYS**, **MSDOS.SYS**, and **COMMAND.COM** (in that order). An operating system is a command line, a command interpreter (COMMAND.COM), and a user interface.

56. The DOS load order is BIOS, POST, IO.SYS, CONFIG.SYS, MSDOS.SYS, COMMAND.COM, and AUTOEXEC.BAT. Beep codes are POST-level error codes, using the internal speaker.

57. **CONFIG.SYS** loads Real Mode device drivers (DEVICE=). **AUTOEXEC.BAT** executes commands at startup. Device drivers usually have a .SYS extension. LASTDRIVE= tells the system how many logical drive letters have been assigned, and is a directive in CONFIG.SYS. The original default was 5 drives. LASTDRIVE=Z is now the default.

58. RAMDRIVE.SYS is a driver that creates a virtual disk in memory (a RAM drive). MSCDEX.EXE is a Microsoft generic CDROM driver.

59. **DEFRAG.EXE** is a way to move parts of files (**clusters**) next to each other and speed up access times on a hard drive. Defrag optimizes disk reads (**performance**). **SCANDISK.EXE** checks and **repairs** a disk with bad **sectors** and file allocation problems.

60. **SMARTDRV.EXE** is a software **cache** for reading hard drives. SmartDrive optimizes performance. Windows 9x removes SMARTDRV from a CONFIG.SYS file. Windows XP installs faster with SmartDrive loaded into memory.

61. **REM** (remark) goes at the beginning of the line in batch files. The **semi-colon** (;) remarks out lines in an .INI (initialization) file.

62. Windows 9x uses ScanDisk to clean and repair problems on disks. Windows NT/2000/XP use **CHKDSK.EXE** (Check Disk) to do the same thing for a "dirty" disk.

63. **Safe Mode** keys: **F8** for Windows **98**. **NT/2000/XP** also use F8 from the "Which operating system" menu prior to the Welcome screen's appearance. (Windows 95 uses F5.) Windows 98/Me can also use the CTRL key for Safe Mode. Safe Mode loads VGA drivers and keyboard drivers, but no network drivers.

64. WIN.COM starts Windows. **SYSTEM.INI** contains **device drivers** and program configurations. **WIN.INI** holds **user options**, LOAD= and RUN= startup lines, and environment configurations. WIN.INI is not necessary, but it is created if it doesn't exist. (Registry: **System.dat** stores **system settings**, and **User.dat** stores **user settings**). Windows XP/2000 use "hives" to store settings.

65. All versions of Windows may use an optional CONFIG.SYS and AUTOEXEC.BAT file. Windows 9x loads IO.SYS, CONFIG.SYS, and MSDOS.SYS.

66. SYSTEM.DAT and USER.DAT are the **Registry files**. Windows 9x uses the REGEDIT.EXE editor. Windows NT and Windows 2000 also use REGEDT32.EXE editor. Windows XP goes back to using REGEDIT.EXE. The Registry Editor gathers together files under **HKeys**.

67. **ERU.EXE** (Emergency Repair Utility) **backs up** the Windows 9x Registry. **SCANREGW.EXE checks** the 9x Registry for structural integrity and makes daily backups, named RB000.cab through RB004.CAB. SCANREG.INI determines how many days Windows will make a new backup before over-writing. Windows XP/2000 uses **System Restore**.

68. LOGVIEW.EXE (Windows 9x) shows startup log files. BOOTLOG.TXT contains startup error conditions. SYSEDIT.EXE opens startup configuration files.

69. **Registry keys**: HKEY_LOCAL_MACHINE, HKEY_CLASSES_ROOT, HKEY_CURRENT_CONFIG, HKEY_CURRENT_USER, and HKEY_USERS.

20. COM1 and COM3 are logically joined, whereas COM2 and COM4 are logically joined. **COM1 and 3 use IRQ 4**, whereas **COM2 and 4 use IRQ 3**.

21. COM port addresses: com1=03F8; com3=03E8; com2=02F8; com4=02E8

22. LPT1 uses **IRQ 7**, and LPT2 uses IRQ 5.

23. **IRQ 14** is the **primary** (first) drive controller. **IRQ 15** is the **secondary** drive controller. Floppy controllers use IRQ 6. **IRQ 9** cannot be used when it **cascades** to **IRQ 2**. The PCI bus provides IRQ sharing, and several PCI devices can use an available IRQ.

24. There are **8 DMA** channels and **16 IRQ** lines (2 four-channel DMA controllers, 2 eight-channel IRQ controllers).

25. **Interlaced** monitors scan odd lines, then even lines, in a **two-step** process. **Non-interlaced** monitors scan every line in one pass.

26. Dots per inch is written as **dpi** (printers and scanners). Pixels measure graphics resolutions.

27. Standard **VGA (Safe Mode)** is 640x480x16 colors. SVGA is *super* VGA and provides resolutions up to 1,600x1,200x16-million colors.

28. The **Primary corona** wire charges the EP drum. The drum is cleaned, charged, and written to. The image develops (by the charge) and pulls toner to the drum. Charged paper pulls toner from the drum. The **fuser rollers** fuse toner. If the heat sensor on the fuser rollers shuts down, the toner will fail to stick to the paper. A bad **separator pad** usually causes paper jams.

29. **FAT16** uses 16-bit addressing, in 16KB, and limits at 2GB. FAT32 uses adjustable cluster sizes and limits at 8GB. NTFS uses a relational database type of file system for better security.

30. USB supports hot-swapping. Devices can be changed without the power being turned off. USB 1.1 supports speeds up to 12Mbps. USB 2.0 provides 480Mbps throughput. 1 USB controller can support 127 devices, using hubs.

31. Plug and Play requires three things: a PnP operating system, PnP BIOS, and PnP devices. Windows can use a non-PnP device, but it won't allocate dynamic resources to them.

32. The **IEEE-1394** (Sony i.Link or **FireWire**) controller can support speeds up to 400Mbps (now 800Mbps) and 63 daisy-chained devices. Sony uses 4 wires; FireWire uses 6 (two for power).

33. IEEE **802.11b** is **wireless** networking and uses Frequency Hopping Spread Spectrum broadcasting (FHSS). The **SSID** is the **Service Set ID** number used for security. **WEP** is **Wireless Equivalency Privacy**, and is used for wireless data encryption.

34. **Ethernet** is a **bus** (wire) network. It can be wired in a *star* or *bus* topology. Token ring networks can be wired in a *star* or *ring* topology. Star topology uses hubs. USB uses hubs in a tiered-star topology. USB is not a networking protocol.

35. **Bridges segment** a congested network into parts. **Routers connect** and direct traffic between networks. **PING** tests a connection. **TRACEROUTE** reports segment hops.

36. Ethernet cables are 10Base5, 10Base2, and **10Base-T**. The "2" and "5" are 200 and 500 **meter limits**. The "T" stands for twisted-pair wire and comes in **Cat-5** (category 5) and other categories. Twisted pair comes in Shielded twisted pair (STP) and Unshielded twisted pair (UTP).

37. **OSI** Layers: #7—Application. #6—Presentation. #5—Session. #4—Transport. #3—Network. #2—Data Link. #1—Physical. (Physical layer is wire. Network layer connects to networks. Application layer is for programs.)

38. Network Interface Cards (**NICs**) usually include a link-status light to show whether they're working.

39. Email uses the Internet TCP/IP networking protocol. An email address (aplus@jamesgjones.com) requires a *username* (aplus) and a *domain name* (jamesgjones.com). A Domain Name Systems (DNS) server converts the IP address to a readable name. An IP address consists of many numbers and periods.

OPERATING SYSTEMS TECHNOLOGIES EXAM

40. **FDISK.EXE** is used to create **partitions**. **FORMAT.COM** is used to create **logical drives** (volumes).

41. **FORMAT C: /S** transfers **system files** to Drive C:, making that drive bootable.

42. **SYS C:** (SYS.COM) is used to transfer **system files** to a corrupted Drive C: showing a "Missing or bad system files" error.

43. Physical disks can have a maximum of 24 logical drives (A: and B: are floppies). When a Drive C: has been partitioned, the largest Extended partition can have 23 drive letters. Bootable hard drives must have a Primary, Active partition.

44. **DIR *.*** lists all files with any extension. **DIR *.* /S** lists all files in all subfolders. **DIR *.SYS** lists all files with a .SYS extension. **DIR *.* /A:H** lists all hidden files.

45. **Wildcards** are * and ?. The * finds any number of characters to the right and ? finds only one character per question mark. DIR *.DLL will find all .DLL files in a folder. DIR *.DLL /S will search all **subfolders**.

46. **ATTRIB.EXE** is used to set file attributes such as Hidden, Read-only, System, Archive. The Hidden or System attribute prevents DOS from showing a file when using the DIR command.

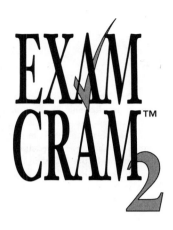

A+

Second Edition

James G. Jones

Craig Landes

A+ Exam Cram 2, Second Edition

Copyright © 2004 by Que Publishing

International Standard Book Number: 0-7897-3043-X

Library of Congress Catalog Card Number: 2003109249

Printed in the United States of America

First Printing: December 2003

06   05   04   4   3

Trademarks

All terms mentioned in this book that are known to be trademarks or service marks have been appropriately capitalized. Que Publishing cannot attest to the accuracy of this information. Use of a term in this book should not be regarded as affecting the validity of any trademark or service mark.

Warning and Disclaimer

Every effort has been made to make this book as complete and as accurate as possible, but no warranty or fitness is implied. The information provided is on an "as is" basis. The author(s) and the publisher shall have neither liability nor responsibility to any person or entity with respect to any loss or damages arising from the information contained in this book or from the use of the CD or programs accompanying it.

Bulk Sales

Que Publishing offers excellent discounts on this book when ordered in quantity for bulk purchases or special sales. For more information, please contact

U.S. Corporate and Government Sales

1-800-382-3419

corpsales@pearsontechgroup.com

For sales outside of the U.S., please contact

International Sales

1-317-428-3341

international@pearsontechgroup.com

Publisher
Paul Boger

Executive Editor
Jeff Riley

Acquisitions Editor
Jeff Riley

Development Editor
Steve Rowe

Managing Editor
Charlotte Clapp

Project Editor
Tricia Liebig

Copy Editor
Margo Catts

Indexer
Ken Johnson

Technical Editors
David Eytchison
Marc Savage

Team Coordinator
Pamalee Nelson

Multimedia Developer
Dan Scherf

Interior Designer
Gary Adair

Cover Designer
Anne Jones

CERTIFICATION

Que Certification • 800 East 96th Street • Indianapolis, Indiana 46240

A Note from Series Editor Ed Tittel

You know better than to trust your certification preparation to just anybody. That's why you, and more than two million others, have purchased an Exam Cram book. As Series Editor for the new and improved Exam Cram 2 series, I have worked with the staff at Que Certification to ensure you won't be disappointed. That's why we've taken the world's best-selling certification product—a finalist for "Best Study Guide" in a CertCities reader poll in 2002—and made it even better.

As a "Favorite Study Guide Author" finalist in a 2002 poll of CertCities readers, I know the value of good books. You'll be impressed with Que Certification's stringent review process, which ensures the books are high-quality, relevant, and technically accurate. Rest assured that at least a dozen industry experts—including the panel of certification experts at CramSession—have reviewed this material, helping us deliver an excellent solution to your exam preparation needs.

Best Study Guides

We've also added a preview edition of PrepLogic's powerful, full-featured test engine, which is trusted by certification students throughout the world.

As a 20-year-plus veteran of the computing industry and the original creator and editor of the Exam Cram series, I've brought my IT experience to bear on these books. During my tenure at Novell from 1989 to 1994, I worked with and around its excellent education and certification department. This experience helped push my writing and teaching activities heavily in the certification direction. Since then, I've worked on more than 70 certification-related books, and I write about certification topics for numerous Web sites and for *Certification* magazine.

In 1996, while studying for various MCP exams, I became frustrated with the huge, unwieldy study guides that were the only preparation tools available. As an experienced IT professional and former instructor, I wanted "nothing but the facts" necessary to prepare for the exams. From this impetus, Exam Cram emerged in 1997. It quickly became the best-selling computer book series since "...*For Dummies*," and the best-selling certification book series ever. By maintaining an intense focus on subject matter, tracking errata and updates quickly, and following the certification market closely, Exam Cram was able to establish the dominant position in cert prep books.

You will not be disappointed in your decision to purchase this book. If you are, please contact me at etittel@jump.net. All suggestions, ideas, input, or constructive criticism are welcome!

Ed Tittel

About the Authors

James G. Jones

With over 30 years in the information technology and communications industry, Jim has held numerous positions from technician to senior vice president of a Fortune 500 multinational corporation. With a B.S. in Education, and an M.B.A. from Michigan State University, Jim is also Microsoft MCSE certified, Novell CNE certified, and Cisco CCNA and CCDA certified. Additionally, Jim holds certificates in A+, network cabling, fiber optics, and microwave transmission, to name a few. Jim is the president of JGJ & Associates, a consulting firm providing executive seminars pertaining to technology, sales, and marketing to some of the world's largest IT corporations, including (among others): IBM, Microsoft, Oracle, Hewlett Packard, Compaq, and Siemens. Jim has been deeply involved with the A+ program since its inception, and can be reached by email at jim@jamesgjones.com.

Craig Landes

Craig Landes has over 18 years experience in information technology, holding numerous positions from database programming to Management Information Systems in the field of health care. Craig is A+ certified, and has worked with some of today's largest consulting firms, developing technical and educational programs for clients and employees at all levels. Currently, Craig Landes is the president of Triax Corporation, a consulting business providing freelance technical writing, help systems, and educational materials development. Craig can be reached by email at CLandesAPlus@aol.com.

We Want to Hear from You!

As the reader of this book, *you* are our most important critic and commentator. We value your opinion and want to know what we're doing right, what we could do better, what areas you'd like to see us publish in, and any other words of wisdom you're willing to pass our way.

As an executive editor for Que, I welcome your comments. You can email or write me directly to let me know what you did or didn't like about this book—as well as what we can do to make our books better.

Please note that I cannot help you with technical problems related to the topic of this book. We do have a User Services group, however, where I will forward specific technical questions related to the book.

When you write, please be sure to include this book's title and author as well as your name, email address, and phone number. I will carefully review your comments and share them with the author and editors who worked on the book.

Email: feedback@quepublishing.com

Mail: Jeff Riley
         Executive Editor
         Que Publishing
         800 East 96th Street
         Indianapolis, IN 46240 USA

For information about the Exam Cram 2 series, visit www.examcram2.com. Type the ISBN (excluding hyphens) or the title of a book in the Search field to find the page you're looking for.

Contents at a Glance

Table of Contents

Introduction

Welcome to *A+ Exam Cram, Second Edition*! This introduction is a lot like the "Quick Setup" reference section for a software application. Chapter 1 describes the testing environment and provides a discussion of test-taking strategies. Chapters 2–16 are designed to remind you of everything you'll need to know in order to take—and pass—the **220-301** and **220-302** Computing Technology Industry Association's (CompTIA) A+ certification exam.

The A+ exam is actually made up of two components: the Core Hardware exam and the Operating System Technologies exam. Both components are related, and we recommend taking them both on the same day. The first half of this book (Chapters 2–11) covers the hardware objectives. Following Chapter 11, we've developed a sample hardware test, much like the actual test. The second half of the book (Chapters 12–16) covers the software objectives. Following Chapter 16 you'll find a sample software test.

The two sample tests should give you an accurate assessment of how well you'll do on the actual exam. And yes, we've provided the answers and their explanations for each test. We strongly encourage you to read Chapter 1, either before you read the rest of the book, or before you take the sample tests. Chapter 1 is where we discuss the exam environment and various strategies for taking tests.

We also recommend that you read the introductory text to the sample hardware test at the end of the first section. CompTIA will ask many questions that are ambiguous or that call on your memory of details. Rather than trying to remember every detail, we provide many strategies and methods for analyzing the questions themselves for the correct answers. The answer keys for both sample tests go into further detail, in terms of how to analyze a question.

What This Book Will Not Do

This book will *not* teach you everything you need to know about computers, or even about a given topic. This book is *not* an introduction to computer technology. If you're new to computers and looking for an initial preparation guide, there are a number of books on the market for that purpose. This is a final review of what you'll need to know before you take the test. Although we sometimes refer to the latest-and-greatest trends in technology, our main purpose is to review the CompTIA A+ certification exam objectives—what the organization has listed as test subjects.

This is not a "cheat book." We do not list every question on the exam, and then follow it with a discussion of that specific topic. Instead, we've tried to drive home the conceptual fundamentals that led to the development of each exam objective. We expect you to have a significant amount of experience with PCs and Windows before you read this book. Then, as you read each chapter, we try to "bring it all together" and show you how to make sense of that experience.

If you aren't already comfortable with command-line operations and getting under the hood of a computer, you should start with a comprehensive A+ preparation course or manual. Otherwise, this book uses a variety of teaching principles and memorization techniques to analyze the exam-related topics, and provide you with ways to input, index, and retrieve everything you'll need to know to pass the test. Once again, it is *not* an introduction to computers.

What This Book Is Designed to Do

This book is designed specifically around the areas of knowledge on which you're going to be tested. In other words, you may want to read the book one time to get an insight into your knowledge of computers. Then, do a fast pass-through before you go for the actual test, to get a distillation of the entire field of PCs, Windows, and basic networking. Use the Table of Contents to remember the topics, and skim-read for study alerts, bullet points, summaries, and topic headings.

We've drawn on material from CompTIA's listing of its objectives, from other preparation guides, and from the exams themselves. We've also drawn from a battery of third-party test preparation tools, numerous technical Web sites, and from our own experience with PCs, going all the way back to the Altair. Our aim is to walk you through PCs and simple networking, looking over your shoulder, so to speak, and pointing out those things that are important for you to remember (for example, by providing exam alerts, practice questions, and so on).

The certification test makes a basic assumption that you already have a *very* strong background in PC hardware and software. On the other hand, we think the technology is changing so quickly that no one can be a total expert. We've tried to de-mystify the jargon, acronyms, terms, and concepts. Wherever we think you're likely to "blur past" an important concept, we've defined the assumptions and premises behind that concept.

Our Teaching Methodology

You'll find many books on the market that are designed to teach you how to do something. Subjects range from Access databases to Zip files and archives. We've found that the majority of "How To" books are essentially hardcopy duplicates of online references and help files. We think that the best way to learn anything is to understand why it was developed, and the surrounding context of how it fits in with the rest of the world. In other words, if you can't build a picture, or model in your mind, you won't really learn it.

Most books about Microsoft Word, for example, have a section on styles. The authors simply explain how to create and modify a style. But unless you know why you would ever want to use styles, so what? Likewise, every book has a reference to bold typeface. You'll find an explanation of how to make some text bold, but you won't find an explanation of why anyone would want to highlight text.

We know there are plenty of books about A+ that go into great detail for every exam objective. Our intent isn't to duplicate those books, but to provide you with a companion book to summarize all those details. We've tried to provide you with a sort of tree, or framework, on which to hang the myriad of technical details you've learned from all those other books. You should always test your assumptions before you build an entire edifice of knowledge on those assumptions. Our philosophy is to help you check what you know from the ground up.

Formatting and Organization

Each chapter follows a regular structure, along with graphical cues about especially important or useful material. The structure of a typical chapter includes

➤ *Opening Hotlists*—Lists of the terms you'll need to understand and the concepts you'll need to master before you can be fully conversant with the chapter's subject matter. We follow the hotlists with a few introductory paragraphs, setting the stage for the rest of the chapter.

➤ *Topical Coverage*—After the opening hotlists, each chapter covers at least four topics related to the chapter's subject.

➤ *Exam Alerts*—Highlighted material most likely to appear on the exam. An Exam Alert looks like this:

 An Exam Alert stresses concepts, terms, software, or activities that are most likely to appear in one or more certification exam questions. For that reason, we think any information found offset in this format is worthy of unusual attentiveness on your part.

Even if material isn't flagged as an Exam Alert, *all* the content in this book is associated in some way with test-related material. What appears in the chapter content is also important.

➤ *Sidebars*—When we discuss an exam topic that may be based on common knowledge among people in the IT industry, we use sidebars to examine the underlying assumptions of the discussion. You may have many years of experience with PCs, or you may be just starting out. Your certification shouldn't depend on "secret knowledge" that you're supposed to "just know" somehow.

Something You May Not Know

A sidebar like this steps outside the flow of the discussion to provide you with "insider" information that you may not have heard before. A sidebar is a way to increase the saturation level of your knowledge and apply some "glue" to help keep topical facts from slipping out of your ears.

➤ *Notes*—Where something is outside the main scope of the book, we use Notes to indicate areas of concern or specialty training.

 Cramming for an exam will get you through a test. It won't make you a competent IT professional. Although you can memorize just the facts you need to become certified, your daily work in the field will rapidly put you in water over your head if you don't know the underlying principles of computers.

➤ *Tips*—We provide tips to help you to build a better foundation of knowledge, or to refer to things that reappear later in the book. We also use tips to refer to information that won't necessarily be on the exam, but that you should know if you want to understand a topic more completely.

You should read Chapter 1 for helpful strategies to use when taking a test. The introduction to the hardware sample test contains additional tips on how to figure out the correct response to a question, or what to do if you draw a complete blank. Finally, each explanation in the answer key points out how certain questions are designed to mess with your head.

➤ *Supplementary Information*—In some cases, the exam-specific material covered in a topic section may be outdated or limited. Where we think it would be helpful to understand the real-world market technology, we've included supplemental information. This type of information is more than you'd find in a simple sidebar, but is beyond the scope of the exam.

➤ *Category Summaries*—In many instances, the topic under discussion is so filled with details, numbers, acronyms, trouble spots, and alerts, that you may become lost in the jumble of words. We've tried to put some breathing space at the end of each generally related category, as a sort of reality check in terms of what ought to be the focus of your memorization efforts.

➤ *Exam Prep Questions*—This section presents a short list of exam-like questions related to the overall chapter topic. Each question has a following explanation of both correct and incorrect answers. The practice questions are similar in format to those found on the A+ exams. Knowing an answer is only part of being prepared. Being familiar with how CompTIA asks questions is also very important.

➤ *Need to Know More?*—Every chapter ends with a section titled "Need to Know More?" This section provides pointers to resources that we found to be helpful in offering further details on the chapter's subject matter. If you find a resource you like in this collection, use it, but don't feel compelled to use all these resources. We use this section to recommend resources that we have used on a regular basis, so none of the recommendations will be a waste of your time or money. These resources may go out of print, or be taken down (in the case of Web sites), so we've tried to reference widely accepted resources.

The bulk of the book follows this chapter structure, but there are a few other elements that we would like to point out:

➤ *Practice Exams*—A very close approximation of the types of questions you're likely to see on the current A+ exam.

➤ *Answer Keys*—The answers to both practice exams, with a following explanation of both the correct response and the incorrect responses. Each practice exam has its own answer key.

➤ *Acronym Glossary*—An extensive glossary of acronyms. We've tried to include every acronym used in the book.

➤ *The Cram Sheet*—This is a tear-away sheet, inside the front cover of this book. It represents a collection of the most difficult-to-remember facts and numbers we think you should memorize before taking the test. You can dump this information out of your head onto the provided paper as soon as you enter the testing room. You only need to remember this information long enough to write it down when you walk into the test room. (Be advised that you will be asked to surrender all personal belongings before you enter the exam room itself.)

You might want to look at the Cram Sheet in the car or in the lobby of the testing center, just before you walk in to take the exam. Keep in mind that if you take both tests together, there is a break between the Core Hardware and the Operating Systems Technologies exam.

Codes and Commands

In most cases, program commands that are to be issued at a command-line prompt are in bold. For example, if we tell you to type DIR /P at a command line, the "DIR /P" is an actual command. When you encounter an instruction about a command, the command will not be bold, and will be surrounded in quotes. The quotes are not part of the command. For example, we might say that people often type "DIR /P" at a command line to get a directory listing.

Margin limitations will often introduce false line breaks in programming code, character strings, pathnames, and other related text. We make every effort to ensure that a line break, or line wrap generated by the page margins, does not change the meaning of the information. In some cases, a hyphen may be inserted into the string by mistake. Where there may be some ambiguity, we try to clarify the intent immediately following the text. If an erroneous hyphen appears in print, we hope you'll understand that these things happen, but do feel free to call it to our attention.

For example, a very long pathname might be: C:\WINDOWS\SYSTEM\CatRoot\ {127D0A1D-4EF2-11D1-8608-00C04FC295EE}. Note that the first characters in the string are "C:\WI..." and the last characters of the same string, on the same line, are "...5EE}" (without the quotes).

Contacting the Authors

We've tried to create a real-world tool that you can use to prepare for and pass both of the A+ certification exams. We are interested in any feedback you would care to share about the book, especially if you have ideas about how we can improve it for future test takers. We will consider everything you say carefully and will respond to all reasonable suggestions and comments. You can reach us via email at `aplus@jamesgjones.com`.

Let us know if you found this book to be helpful in your preparation efforts. We'd also like to know how you felt about your chances of passing the exam *before* you read the book and then *after* you read the book. Of course, we'd love to hear that you passed the exam, and even if you just want to share your triumph, we'd be happy to hear from you.

Thanks for choosing us as your personal trainers, and enjoy the book. We would wish you luck on the exam, but we know that if you read through all the chapters, you won't need luck—you'll ace the test on the strength of real knowledge!

Self-Assessment

The reason we included a Self-Assessment in this *Exam Cram* book is to help you evaluate your readiness to tackle A+ certification. But before you tackle this Self-Assessment, let's talk about concerns you may face when pursuing A+ certification and what an ideal candidate might look like.

CompTIA-Certified Computer Technicians in the Real World

Most people will take the two modules of the A+ certification exam in order to serve in the PC hardware and software repair field. Others might see these tests as a great starting point for gaining the basic PC knowledge that can be used in many other fields. You can get all the real-world motivation you need from knowing that many others have gone before, so you'll be able to follow in their footsteps. If you're willing to tackle the process seriously and do what it takes to obtain the necessary experience and knowledge, you can take—and pass—the certification modules involved in obtaining A+ certification. In fact, the entire *Exam Cram* series is designed to make it as easy as possible for you to prepare for certification exams. But prepare you must!

The same, of course, is true for other CompTIA certifications, including the following:

➤ CompTIA's Certified Document Imaging Architect (CDIA) certification is a nationally recognized credential acknowledging competency and professionalism in the document imaging industry. CDIA candidates possess critical knowledge of all major areas and technologies used to plan, design, and specify an imaging system.

➤ Network+ certifies the knowledge of networking technicians with 18 to 24 months of experience in the IT industry.

➤ i-Net+ certification is designed specifically for any individual interested in demonstrating baseline technical knowledge that would allow him or her to pursue a variety of Internet-related careers.

Put Yourself to the Test

The following series of questions and observations is designed to help you figure out how much work you must do to pursue A+ certification and what kinds of resources you might consult on your quest. Be absolutely honest in your answers; otherwise, you'll end up wasting money on exams you're not yet ready to take. There are no right or wrong answers, only steps along the path to certification. Only you can decide where you really belong in the broad spectrum of aspiring candidates.

Two things should be clear from the outset, however:

➤ Even a modest background in computer science will be helpful.

➤ Hands-on experience with personal computers is an essential ingredient of certification success.

Educational Background

1. Have you ever taken any computer-related classes? [Yes or No]

   If Yes, proceed to question 2; if No, proceed to question 4.

2. Have you taken any classes on computer operating systems? [Yes or No]

   If Yes, you'll probably be able to handle operating system architecture and system component discussions. If you're rusty, brush up on basic operating system concepts, especially virtual memory, multitasking regimes, user-mode versus kernel-mode operation, and general computer security topics.

   If No, consider some basic reading in this area. A good place to start is *A+ Certification Training Guide, Fifth Edition* by Charles Brooks (Que Publishing, 2003, ISBN 0-7897-3044-8). This book covers A+ topics in far more detail than the *Exam Cram* series. If this title doesn't appeal to you, check out www.examcram2.com. This site has a whole section dedicated to A+ and offers a wealth of information. CompTIA's Web site (www.comptia.org) is also a good location to find all kinds of A+-related material.

3. Have you taken any networking concepts or technologies classes? [Yes or No]

   If Yes, you'll probably be able to handle the A+ certification networking terminology, concepts, and technologies. If you're rusty, Scott Muller's *Upgrading and Repairing Networks* (Que Publishing, 2002, ISBN 0-7897-2557-6) will help you brush up on basic networking concepts and terminology, especially networking media, transmission types, the OSI Reference Model, and networking technologies such as Ethernet, Token Ring, FDDI, and WAN links.

If No, you might want to supplement the material available in this book with other good works. The three best books that we know of are *Computer Networks, Third Edition*, by Andrew S. Tanenbaum (Prentice-Hall, 1996, ISBN 0-133-49945-6), *Computer Networks and Internets*, by Douglas E. Comer (Prentice-Hall, 1997, ISBN 0-132-39070-1), and *Encyclopedia of Networking*, by Tom Sheldon (Osborne/McGraw-Hill, 1998, ISBN 0-07-882333-1). Don't forget Scott Muller's *Upgrading and Repairing Networks* mentioned in the previous paragraph. This is a great book to have for reference both now and in the future.

Skip to the next section, "Hands-On Experience."

4. Have you done any reading on operating systems or networks? [Yes or No]

   If Yes, review the requirements stated in the first paragraphs after questions 2 and 3. If you meet those requirements, move on to the next section, "Hands-On Experience." If No, you'll find the *A+ Certification Training Guide, Fifth Edition*, by Charles Brooks (Que Publishing, 2002, ISBN 0-7897-3044-8) very helpful.

Hands-On Experience

The most important key to success on all the CompTIA tests is hands-on experience, especially with basic computer hardware, as well as Windows 95, Windows 98, Windows NT Workstation, Windows 2000 Professional, and, to a lesser degree, MS-DOS. If we leave you with only one realization after taking this Self-Assessment, it should be that there's no substitute for time spent installing, configuring, and using PC hardware and software.

Before you even think about taking any exam, make sure you've spent enough time with the related hardware and software to understand how it can be installed and configured, how to maintain such an installation, and how to troubleshoot when things go wrong. This will help you in the exam, and in real life.

Testing Your Exam-Readiness

Whether you attend a formal class on a specific topic to get ready for an exam or use written materials to study on your own, some preparation for the A+ certification exams is essential. At more than $100 a try (pass or fail) you want to do everything you can to pass on your first try. That's where studying comes in.

For any given subject, consider taking a class if you've tackled self-study materials, taken the test, and failed anyway. The opportunity to interact with an instructor and fellow students can make all the difference in the world, if you can afford that privilege. For information about CompTIA classes, visit the CompTIA Web site at www.comptia.org (follow the Certification link to find training).

If you can't afford to take a class, visit the Web page anyway, because it also includes a detailed breakdown of the objectives for both modules of the A+ certification exam. This will serve as a good roadmap for your studies.

Even if you can't afford to spend much, you should use practice exams to their fullest. Practice exams can help you assess your readiness to pass a test better than any other tool. We have included some very good practice exams in the *Exam Cram* book and also on the CD accompanying the book. However, if you feel you need more help in this area, there are numerous practice exams available from commercial vendors. The CompTIA Web site (www.comptia.org) is a good place to start looking for additional exams.

5. Have you taken a practice exam on your chosen test subject? [Yes or No]

If Yes, and you scored 75% or better, you're probably ready to tackle the real thing. If your score isn't above that crucial threshold, keep at it until you break that barrier.

If No, obtain all the free and low-budget practice tests you can find and get to work. Keep at it until you can break the passing threshold comfortably.

When it comes to assessing your test readiness, there's no better way than to take a good-quality practice exam and pass with a score of 75% or better. When we're preparing ourselves, we shoot for 80+%, just to leave room for the "weirdness factor" that sometimes shows up on exams.

One last note: We can't stress enough the importance of hands-on experience in the context of both modules of the A+ certification exam. As you review the material, you'll realize that hands-on experience with basic PC hardware, operating system commands, tools, and utilities is invaluable.

Onward!

After you've assessed your readiness, undertaken the right background studies, and obtained some hands-on experience, you're ready to go after the real thing. So pick up the phone and set up a test time at your favorite testing facility. We have even included a coupon with this book to help you with the cost.

PART 1

A+ Core Hardware Exam

1

A+ Certification Tests

As an experience in life, taking a test is usually about as exciting as root canal work. Hardly anyone eagerly anticipates a test, no matter how well they're prepared. On the other hand, familiarity usually helps reduce anxiety. What this means is that you probably wouldn't be as nervous taking a second exam as you would be before taking a test you've never seen before. We've taken lots of exams, and this book is about helping you to get rid of some of your anxiety.

It doesn't matter whether this is your first or your tenth try. Understanding the setting you'll be in, how much time to spend on questions, and the testing software itself will help you concentrate on the material. Don't worry about the environment. We'll show you some basic test-taking skills in this chapter, which should help you recognize—and perhaps out-fox—a lot of the tricks and "gotchas" you're bound to encounter. Reading this book should go a long way toward making the A+ certification exam a familiar experience. Understanding how to take tests should also help you with every other type of written exam you'll run into over the course of your life.

Are You Certifiable?

Perhaps a quick way for you to decide where you stand in relation to the current certification is to leaf through this book and see how well you do with the practice questions at the end of each chapter. Try not to sneak a peek at the sample test at the end of each section, because you should consider it to be a final run at the actual exam. If you haven't looked at the sample test until you're ready to schedule the real exam, you'll have a more accurate sense of your readiness. Take the sample tests a couple of days before you decide to schedule your exam and commit your money.

We recommend that you begin your studies with a visit to the CompTIA Web site (http://www.comptia.org) for a definition of what it means to be A+ certified. As far as we're concerned, the only reason you might not be certifiable would be if you believe that the exam is a simple evaluation of entry-level skills. Don't make that assumption! A+ certification means that you have a comprehensive understanding of first-tier tech support. The CompTIA exam-development team has gone to great lengths to weed out dilettantes and "hot shots."

We *strongly* recommend that you've previously installed, configured, and generally "fooled around" with at least one example of both the Windows 9x environment and the Windows 2000/XP environment. Sometimes the only way to effectively do this is through classroom training. In addition, you should be familiar with the underlying DOS operating environment you'll find on most Windows 9x systems. Keep in mind that Windows 9x runs on top of DOS 7.x, and that the Windows 2000/XP Recovery Console uses many utilities that originally came out of DOS.

Windows NT/2000/XP are based on the NT kernel and do not use DOS at all. The command-line environment uses many commands that look a lot like DOS, but they aren't the same. Although the current versions of Windows aren't running "over" DOS, you'll have to know a substantial amount about those DOS-like commands.

The A+ Certification Exams

You will be required to pass both the *Core Hardware* test and the *Operating Systems Technologies* test. These tests are available in Spanish, German, French, and Japanese; however, you should call CompTIA directly at (630)268-1818 for more information if you plan to take the test in a language other than English.

The Core Hardware exam tests your knowledge of PC hardware. CompTIA means "hardware" to include the following:

➤ Motherboards

➤ Processors

➤ Memory

➤ Peripherals (input, output, and storage)

➤ IRQs and DMA channels

➤ Port addresses

➤ Electronics

➤ Buses

➤ Networking

➤ Cables and connectors

The Operating Systems Technologies exam tests your knowledge of the three most widely used operating systems in the current market. By "operating systems," CompTIA means the following:

➤ DOS

➤ Windows 9x and Me

➤ Windows NT, 2000, and XP (built on Windows NT)

Both the Core Hardware test and the Operating Systems Technologies test are designed to uncover not only your understanding of the technology, but also how to solve problems related to each area. Troubleshooting is an important aspect of the exam, as most certified A+ individuals will be working in the field as tech support personnel. Chapter 16 is particularly devoted to areas of troubleshooting.

Where Do I Sign Up?

Many people think that the two components are so closely related that they should be combined into a single exam. We recommend you treat the two components as one exam. If you study all of the material before taking either exam, your probability of success will definitely be increased. In fact, we've organized this book on that basis, and we urge you to read all the way through the book prior to taking either exam. You'll be charged $145 for each test whether you take them at the same time or separately. There are no refunds if you fail the exam but you can retake the test at a later date. Of course, you will be charged another $145, so it is best to be prepared the first time.

CompTIA is continually evaluating the pricing of these tests, and it may change prior to your enrollment in the exam. We are sure the price will not go down, so the sooner you sign up, the better.

Tests are administered by two organizations: Vue Testing Services and Thomson Prometric. Both services provide the same tests, and you should be able to find a testing location near your home. Additional information can be obtained at the CompTIA Web site (http://www.comptia.org) or by contacting the testing services directly:

➤ VUE Testing Service
   www.vue.com
   (877)551-7587

➤ Thomson Prometric
   http://www.prometric.com
   (800)776-4276

How Do I Schedule the Test?

To schedule an exam, you must call at least one day in advance. When calling, have the following information ready for the sales representative who handles your call:

➤ Your name, your organization, and your mailing address

➤ The name of the exam(s) you wish to take and the exam(s) ID number(s)

➤ Your method of payment

Cancellations

Payment must be received before a test can be scheduled. *To cancel or reschedule an exam without a cost penalty*, you must call at least 12 hours before the scheduled test time. The most convenient payment method is to provide a valid credit card number with sufficient available credit. Otherwise, payments are accepted by check, money order, or purchase order (P.O.).

 If you are paying by purchase order, ask the testing service's sales representative for more details.

Keep in mind that if your payment involves the postal service and banking system (that is, check, purchase order, and so on), you'll have to call to schedule your exam much earlier than one day in advance.

Current Exam Requirements

The A+ certification exam is constantly being updated to reflect the ever-progressive developments in the PC industry. Although we have gone to great lengths to ensure that this book is the most up-to-date text available, it is still a good idea to check with CompTIA for any last-minute changes. The best source of current exam information is CompTIA's Web site at http://www.comptia.org. If you don't have access to the Internet, you can call or write CompTIA directly at

Computing Technology Industry Association
1815 S. Meyers Road, Suite 300
Oakbrook Terrace, IL 60181-5228
Phone: (630)678-8300
Fax: (630)268-1384

Additional Resources

Self-study candidates may use many individual reference books that, taken together, cover most of the required material on the exam. This is one approach, and a good professional should always have a solid reference library. See the "Need to Know More?" sections at the end of each chapter for lists of some of our recommended references.

If you like a little more structure, there are several good preparation programs available in both a self-paced and classroom format. However, you must be sure the program you select has been developed for the current A+ requirements, released in November 2003. Consider, too, that the cost of a structured class environment is significantly higher than the price of this book.

The Certificate

When you've passed both of the certification exams, you will be A+ certified. Save the test results you are given at the conclusion of the tests, as they are your immediate proof of certification before you receive your certification package. Official certification normally takes anywhere from four to six weeks. When the package arrives, it will include a Welcome Kit, a certificate (suitable for framing), and an identification lapel pin. As an official recognition of hard work and broad-based knowledge, A+ certification is a badge of honor.

The Test Site

On the day of your exam, try to arrive at least 15 minutes before the scheduled time. You must bring *two* forms of identification, one of which *must* be a photo ID. Typically, a driver's license and credit card are valid forms of identification. You may also use an insurance card, birth certificate, State ID card, employee identification card, or any other form of legal identification. If you're not sure whether your identification is acceptable, ask the person with whom you schedule your exam.

After you've signed in at the exam site and your time slot arrives, you'll be asked to deposit any books, bags, or other items you brought with you. You'll then be escorted into a closed room. Typically, the testing room will be furnished with anywhere from one to six computers. Each workstation will be separated from the others by dividers, designed to keep you from seeing what's happening on someone else's computer.

The exam room features a wall with a large pane of glass or a video camera. This is to permit the test coordinator to monitor the room, to prevent test-takers from talking to one another, and to observe anything out of the ordinary that might take place. The exam coordinator will have preloaded the A+ certification test and you'll be permitted to start as soon as you're seated in front of the machine.

NOTE Remember that you're not required to start as soon as you're seated. You may use a reasonable amount of time to spew (technical term) out those critical facts you memorized just before you entered the room.

Taking the Exam

We suggest that when you enter the exam room you *immediately write down the most critical information* about the test you're taking on your blank sheet of paper. We have provided a tear-away Cram Sheet, located in the front of the book, listing the most essential, last-minute information you'll want to remember before you enter the exam room.

Both A+ tests use traditional multiple-choice questions. In most cases there will be only one correct answer. However, a few questions will have multiple answers. Fortunately, you will be instructed when this is the case by a message like "choose two" or "select the three best answers." Each question will also have a check box for you to identify those questions you want to review prior to submitting your test for grading.

Each test will have 80 questions and you have only 90 minutes to complete them all. A timer showing the remaining time will be viewable on the computer screen, but it is your responsibility to manage your time. We recommend you answer each question the first time through even if it is only a guess. This way, if you run out of time, at least you have a chance of getting the question right. However, if you do guess, or are unsure of your answer, mark it for review.

When you answer the last question, a summary screen will come up showing your answers for all the questions, along with those questions marked for review. When you click on one of the questions, you will be taken back to that question and given an opportunity to review or change your answer. When you indicate you are finished, or run out of time, the test will be scored and you will be shown your score along with the required score for the test (percentages).

Keep in mind that if you've registered for both exams, you can take a break between the Core Hardware and the Operating Systems Technologies exams. If you jam the hardware details into your head just before the first exam, you'll have some time to step out of the testing room, take a break, and jam the software details into your head in a separate process.

After the Exam

The administrator will give you a report with your overall score. Your score will be broken out into several topical areas when you leave the exam room. Even if you fail, we suggest that you keep a printed copy of the report. If necessary, you can use the printout to help you prepare for another attempt. If you pass (and we are sure you will) *be sure to keep the printout*. The printout is your only proof of passing the test in the unlikely event that there is a mixup between CompTIA and the testing agency.

Preparing for an Exam

Network certification, aerobics certification, and even driving certification (a driver's license) tests are probably simpler than passing a comprehensive, broad-based examination of everything having to do with PCs, operating systems, and basic networking. In those other situations, the area in which you're being certified is a limited subset of only that field. A+ certification, on the other hand, has no boundaries. Anything at all about a PC is a valid subject for testing—even multimeter readings and COM port IRQs!

We've made no assumptions, whatsoever, about your current knowledge. We've tried to cram between the covers of this book as much information as possible about PCs. However, our main focus is to get you through the exam. You might consider us as virtual tutors, coming to your site, at your convenience, and stuffing facts between your ears.

We've "been there, done that," so to speak, and we'll point you in the right direction for your studies. We've also tried to provide a context for the information we're covering, with summaries, sidebars, tips, notes, and supplemental information. Our philosophy is that if you can form a picture of something, you can better remember it.

We continue to believe that one of the best tools we can provide you with are the questions we've created. As we've said, these questions are designed partly to test your knowledge and partly to demonstrate the kinds of mind games you're almost surely going to encounter on the exam. Once again: If you can get through our test and questions, we're confident that you'll be well prepared for the CompTIA exams.

Questions and Language

The most important advice we can give you about taking any test is this: *Read each question carefully*! Some questions are deliberately ambiguous, offering several possibilities that could be correct, depending on your reading of the question. We use Exam Alerts and Tips throughout the book, as well as the Exam Prep Questions at the end of each chapter, to point out where you may run into these types of questions.

Double Negatives

Some questions use double negatives, such as, "Which of the following files is *not unnecessary* during the boot process?" Observe how easily you could read this as "not necessary" and miss the double negative. This is one of those psychological tricks we've mentioned.

Precision Language

Other questions use terminology in *incredibly* precise ways. We've taken numerous practice and real tests, and in nearly every case we've missed at least one question because *we didn't read it closely or carefully enough*. Are you getting the idea, here? The use of the word "required" is a favorite way to make questions that mess you up. For example, you might be asked which list of items is required in a CONFIG.SYS file. Each response may offer you a list where all but one of the items is required. Only in one response will *every* item be required.

Here's another example of a precision question. "Windows 95 and 98 require the WIN.INI and SYSTEM.INI files during the startup process to load device drivers and user options." The responses are True or False.

The correct answer is False, because the WIN.INI file isn't *required*. Windows creates a WIN.INI file if one is not found, but because the file can be created on the fly, that file is, therefore, not required. Neither does 32-bit Windows use the WIN.INI file in the same manner as 16-bit Windows. Watch how easily you can skip past "require" in the question. Don't do it!

Here are some suggestions on how to deal with the tendency to jump to an answer too quickly:

➤ Make sure you *read every word in the question*! If you find yourself jumping ahead impatiently, go back and start over. Don't schedule your exam on a day when you have lots of other appointments and errands. Take your time!

➤ As you read, try to rephrase the question in your own terms. If you can do this, it should make it easier to pick the correct answer.

➤ Don't second-guess the examiners. Try to puzzle out what specific fact or event you're being tested on. Don't try to figure out what could possibly apply in the entire field of the topic. Stay focused! Each question has more to do with troubleshooting a specific problem than the overall theory of the problem area.

➤ *Trust your subconscious*! If you've studied the book, and if you feel you're ready to take the exam, then you probably *are* ready to take the exam. The subconscious mind never forgets anything. Every perception, memory, event, fact, or situation you've ever experienced is written to your subconscious database. The problem is getting the data out again. If you just relax and use your imagination, your intuition can come through and often provide you with the answer. Chances are, if the answer you choose feels right, it is right.

Above all, try to deal with each question by thinking through what you know about hardware and software systems. Then use your imagination and try to picture the page on which you saw the answer. By reviewing what you know (and what you've written down on your scratch sheet), you'll often recall or understand things sufficiently to determine the answer to the question.

Neurolinguistic Programming (NLP)

Not long ago, a couple of very clever guys—a psychiatrist and a computer programmer—got together to develop a new psychoanalytic tool. In the course of the process, they used modern neurological research, biofeedback systems, electronic imaging machines, and other research to find out some interesting things about how our minds work. The result became the foundation for inspirational seminars, psychological counseling, new learning systems, and emotive therapy. In fact, one of the NLP techniques was demonstrated in the film, *The Negotiator*.

Here's something you can use to further check your preparedness for the exam. When you recall properly stored information, your eyes move to your left. When you're *creating* new information, prior to storing it, your eyes move to your right. Visual recall tends to move your eyes to the upper left, and auditory recall tends to move your eyes to the lower left. In other words, if you "hear" an answer to a question in your mind, you'll tend to glance left and down. If you "see" the answer in your memory, you'll tend to glance left and up (approximately 5% of the population responds in the reverse manner).

Studies conducted in school systems have repeatedly shown that students with poor reading skills almost always look to the upper right as they try to read. They're trying to "create" the sounds of words, the shapes of letters, or the visual recognition of sentences at the same time as they're reading. They aren't storing the information. In other words, they're learning how to read over and over again, and not remembering what they're learning. It's continually new information to them. However, students who know how to read well and have learned the skill, invariably glance to their left (except those few who are reversed). They're recalling words and the sounds of those words from their memory.

You can check your "group" by having a friend ask you for your street address or some other bit of information you have to recall. Most people will quickly glance to their left. Ask your friend to watch which way your eyes move and tell you. When you've determined your group, have your friend ask you questions you had problems with, taken from the sample tests and practice questions. If you're glancing to the right, then you probably haven't stored the facts and data as solidly as you can.

The solution is to read the answer key for each question you're having trouble with. As you read, imagine the data stream entering the right side of your head and forming a pool of data. Clearly visualize the pool of correct information. Pause; then close your eyes and willfully imagine that data slowly poring over to the left side of your head. You may think this is ridiculous, but numerous studies have shown that it works. You don't have to worry about what's taking place in your mind: The visualization process is sufficient. Do the same for each particular area of information with which you're having trouble.

Question-Handling Strategies

Based on the tests we've taken, a couple of interesting trends in the responses have become apparent. Usually, some responses will be obviously incorrect, and two of the remaining answers will be plausible. Remember that unless otherwise stated, only one response can be correct. If the answer leaps out at you, reread the question to look for a trick—just in case.

Things to look for in the "obviously wrong" category include weird menu choices or utility names, nonexistent software options, and terminology you've never seen before. If you've done your homework for the exam, *nothing should be completely new* to you. In that case, unfamiliar or bizarre terminology probably indicates a totally bogus answer. As long as you're sure of what's wrong, it's easier to figure out what's right.

Bogus Choices

Our best advice regarding responses that are totally wrong would be to once again rely on your intuition. Nothing on the exam should come as a surprise to you if you've read this book and taken the sample tests. If you see something totally unfamiliar, the chances are high that it's a made-up word.

The following question tries to throw you off this way:

> Which is the most useful tool for checking a circuit?
>
> ○ A. Differentiometer
>
> ○ B. Analytic Resistance Meter
>
> ○ C. Multimeter
>
> ○ D. Integrity Probe

Chances are that you've at least heard of a *multimeter* before. The remaining options sound plausible, but they don't exist.

Duplicate False Responses

Another trend you can use to your advantage is a tendency to give you two possible responses that say the same thing, but reversed, or in slightly different order. When you see duplicate choices, there's a high probability that those two choices are wrong. We play off of this on our own Sample Tests, and make this trick work against you. If you get through our test, you'll be able to spot duplicate, false responses just fine.

An example of a repeating wrong answer would be in the responses to the following question:

> Which of the following files make up the Windows core files?
>
> ○ A. user.exe, core.exe, gdi.exe
>
> ○ B. core.exe, krnl386.exe, gdi.exe
>
> ○ C. user.exe, gdi.exe, core.exe
>
> ○ D. gdi.exe, kern386.exe, user.exe

Examine the preceding question closely, and observe that core.exe repeats in all three responses. Also note that answers A and C are exactly the same, in a different order. Right off the bat you can probably eliminate A and C. That leaves B and D. Now why do you suppose that "core.exe " shows up in three, but not all four of the responses?

The only response that does *not* repeat core.exe is the last choice. Using this particular strategy, you don't necessarily have to know what the core files are to begin guessing that response D is probably the right one.

Caution: Hazardous Grammar Conditions

These kinds of questions can be divided into two problem categories: arguable grammar and tricky logic. Consider the following logic question, which has an absolute answer. You should be able to piece together the correct response from only the internal parts of the question and your own experience.

How many people live in the State of Illinois and Indiana?

The correct response is zero. Although many people might have an address or own a home in both Illinois and Indiana, it isn't possible for anyone to live in both states at the same time. The entire question revolves around the AND operator, and the definition of "live." You might want to make a case that living is an ongoing process, taking place over time, in which case many people might be alive in both states at *different* times. However, if CompTIA is trying to test your logic capabilities, they will most likely make an assumption of the *same* time.

A second problem we found on the exam has to do with improper or debatable use of language. You might find a word combination in either a question or a response that causes you some difficulties. Generally, you should try to imagine yourself in the position of the people who created the question, and try to determine what overall concept of technology they're trying to test. In other words, ask yourself, "What are they trying to test me on?"

The boot sequence is a primary function of which of the following:

○ A. Booting up a computer

○ B. Configuring the system settings

○ C. Boot management software

○ D. Loading an operating system

This is a very difficult question to answer. Each of the responses has a legitimate connection with the boot sequence. Upon closer inspection, we would suggest that "sequence" is the critical term in the question. If we were to remove the word, we'd be left with: "The boot is a primary function of which of the following."

The second necessary part of the question has to do with "function of." Presumably, this means we're talking about cause and effect. Logically, we could try replacing the words with "part of." In that case, the question would read: "Boot is a primary part of which of the following?"

Finally, business-type people are so caught up in using passive voice that many questions are reversed on the basis of simple language. Try rephrasing the question as a direct statement. Replace each response with an absolute, definitive statement of fact. For example:

➤ Booting up a computer is a primary part of boot.

➤ Configuring the system settings is a primary part of boot.

➤ Boot management software is a primary part of boot.

➤ Loading the operating system is a primary part of boot.

The first response is basically circular logic and makes little sense: "Booting is part of booting." The second response could be construed to be technically correct. However, you're being tested on the boot *sequence*, not the overall system configuration. CMOS has a lot to do with system configuration, and there's no reference to CMOS in the responses.

The third response is also something that could possibly be proven in court. On the other hand, very few people ever refer to boot management software. You might make a case that the BASIC bootstrap loader programming is software, but the more appropriate term would be "firmware." If you still have doubts, compare the third response to the fourth response. Of all the responses, the fourth is really the best way to state the facts. The boot sequence loads an operating system.

This type of grammatical hair-splitting will give you plenty of headaches. In fact, you might want to bring along a couple of aspirin for after the exam. Is it fair? No, it's not. But then, life isn't fair. If anyone could be a computer technician, then it wouldn't be mysterious, would it?

Mastering the Inner Game

In the final analysis, knowledge breeds confidence, and confidence breeds success. Study the materials in this book carefully. Review the questions at the end of each chapter, and take the Sample Tests following Chapters 11 and 16. When you're finished, you should be aware of all the areas where you'll need additional studying. Pay attention to all the troubleshooting topics and the "Troubleshooting" chapter. If you find yourself scratching your head over any of the problem-description terms, then you're not ready to take the final exam.

We've been privileged to combine our efforts with those of Scott Mueller, an acknowledged expert in all things hardware. You'll find some of his lectures on the accompanying CD at the back of this book. Many of the A+ hardware questions have been developed from his book, *Upgrading and Repairing PCs, 14th Edition*. As such, we've listed a number of topics in the hardware section of this book as summaries of what you're surely going to be tested on.

When you've worked your way through the Exam Cram, take the practice tests. They'll provide you with a very realistic trial run, and help you identify areas you need to study further. You'll find additional, interactive practice exams on the second CD at the back of this book. Make sure you follow up and review materials related to the questions you miss before scheduling a real test. Only when you've covered all the ground and *feel comfortable* with the whole scope of the practice test should you take a real test. It's not an easy test!

Always remember that it's a part of human nature to want to make specialized knowledge the key to a special club of mysterious people. Be confident! You've worked with computers, and you know how to fix them. Otherwise, you wouldn't be taking this test. Most of the anxiety you'll feel will be based on the natural anxiety we all feel when we're called on the carpet, so to speak, and have to prove that we know what we know. The rest of your anxiety will most likely be psychological in nature. Let it go. Don't worry; be happy. Take your time and read the questions backwards and forwards. Then read them sideways. After you're certified, you won't have to go through the process anymore. You'll be part of the *Illuminati*!

Motherboards

Terms you'll need to understand:

✓ Signal trace, circuit trace, integrated circuit
✓ Motherboard, form factor
✓ Input/Output (I/O)
✓ Data path, data signals, signal traces
✓ Printed circuit, integrated circuit (IC), and IC boards
✓ Bus (expansion bus), expansion slots, add-on or expansion cards
✓ Bits and bytes, kilo (1-thousand), mega (1-million), and giga (1-billion)
✓ Horizontal (sideways), vertical (up and down), riser cards
✓ Cycles, frequency, and megahertz (MHz)

Concepts you'll need to master:

✓ Form factors (XT, AT, ATX, LPX, NLX)
✓ Bus types (ISA, EISA, VESA, MCA, PCI, and PC Card)
✓ Keyed connectors, connectivity, and interfaces
✓ Throughput and bandwidth
✓ Bus mastering
✓ North-South Bridge architecture

The motherboard, or main board, is sometimes called the system board, *planar* board, or just "the board." Motherboards may also be referred to as "the mobo" in jargon-speak, but never that way on the exam. The motherboard is the basic foundation of a computer and connects all the system components. Aside from the central processing unit (CPU) and its supporting chipset, the motherboard holds the expansion bus, Input/Output (I/O) interfaces, drive controllers, and system memory.

Nowadays, almost all the electronic components in a personal computer (PC) have been consolidated onto the motherboard. The system board provides *connectivity* for all these components. Essentially, it's the underlying foundation, providing the following capabilities:

➤ Distributing power from the power supply

➤ Providing data paths for control signals and data

➤ Offering various sockets and pads for mounting components

➤ Providing expansion slots for add-on *integrated circuits (ICs)*, or *printed circuit boards (PCBs)*

Generally speaking, the motherboard has three basic attributes or technical specifications. The *form factor* determines the actual physical shape and dimensions of the board. A form factor is the physical shape and construction (sometimes called the "implementation") of a design specification. The *bus structure* determines the actual design of the circuit traces on the board, and the *chipset* describes the chips on the board, used to support the attached components. The chipset manages the electrical signals flowing across the circuit traces. We'll examine buses at length, later in this chapter, and chipsets in Chapter 5, "Processors and Chipsets."

System Boards: A Brief History

In 1981, International Business Machines (IBM) released the first personal computer, designed mostly for electronics enthusiasts. The original motherboard had five expansion slots, designed so as to allow additional components to be added on to the basic system. Back then, almost everything we now consider standard was an add-on product. The original slots were configured much like the later Industry Standard Architecture (ISA) slots, and the underlying bus structure could handle only 8 bits of information at a time. In other words, data moved through the motherboard's circuit traces 8 bits at a time.

ISA is also an acronym for the Instruction Set Architecture (ISA), defined by the IA-64 specifications. EPIC is an acronym for Explicitly Parallel Instruction Computing, and is a set of techniques used in compiling programs and moving instructions around in a CPU. EPIC evolved from the Reduced Instruction Set Computer (RISC), and Complex Instruction Set Computer (CISC) methodologies. IA-64 specifies a computing architecture. ISA, in the CompTIA exam, refers to the Industry Standard Architecture bus architecture.

The original PCs supported between 64KB (kilobytes) and 256KB of memory, and had two connectors on the back of the board. The first was a keyboard connector: the second, a cassette tape connector. At the time, floppy disks were too expensive to include in these machines, so cassette tape was used for programming and running software.

In 1983, IBM released the eXtended Technology (XT) computer, having three additional expansion slots. The XT kept the keyboard connector (which became standard on all later motherboards), but the cassette tape deck quickly gave way to floppy drives and the newly released 10MB fixed disks (generally synonymous with "hard drives"). The primary memory capacity was increased to a maximum of 640KB, which became the basis of almost all the complications, confusion, and frustration associated with DOS and Real Mode. We discuss memory in Chapter 3, "Memory: Types and Forms," and how the operating system uses memory in Chapter 13, "Booting, Startup Files, and Memory."

Signal Traces and Integrated Circuits

A *trace* is a solid-state replacement for wire. A printed circuit board starts as a sheet of copper, bonded to a board made up of insulating material. Manufacturers use wax to lay out circuit pathways on the copper, after which the board is dipped in acid. This is much like the etching process used in the art world: Wherever the copper isn't protected by wax, it gets eaten away by the acid. The remaining "traces" of copper perform in the same way as wire. A circuit trace and a *signal trace* are the same thing. Modern motherboards are often made up of multi-layer boards (*strata*), meaning that one etched board is bonded on top of others. The original AT boards (discussed in a moment) used this method to reduce the size of previous boards.

When a device is plugged into a socket or soldered onto a board, we refer to it as being *integrated*. In other words, it is joined together, or combined with the underlying board—its foundation. These boards and their onboard electronics may be referred to as IC cards, but most professionals call them IC boards.

An *integrated circuit* refers to a chip that replaces multiple separate components. It is integrated because of the many devices etched on its strata. A signal trace is the piece of circuitry that allows for the flow of electricity.

For example, a CPU has thousands of transistors, capacitors, and resistors integrated onto a single chip. An integrated circuit can itself be mounted on a board, as can a component such as a resistor. The network interface card (NIC, pronounced "nick"), shown in Figure 2.2, is variously called a circuit board, an expansion board, or a printed circuit board. It can also be called an ISA card, if it uses an ISA bus, or a PCI card, if it uses the PCI bus. Both of these bus architectures are discussed in this chapter.

If you produce eight pulses of electricity in a synchronized fashion, you can call those combined pulses an 8-bit piece of information. One 8-bit combination can also be called 1 byte of information. A bus is a way to move that information around a circuit board. Therefore, if you want to move an 8-bit piece of information, you need eight signal traces—an 8-bit bus.

Dated Names and Technology

Early technical developments never took into consideration how fast the computer industry would develop. Each introduction of a new device or advancement was considered the ultimate and final development. When the first 10MB hard drive was introduced, industry experts couldn't imagine that anyone would ever need more drive space. As such, many acronyms dating from the past—and even some of today's names and labels—seem a bit silly.

The NT acronym in Windows NT stood for "New Technology." Many years later, Microsoft had to completely change its entire marketing strategy in order to get away from what had become stone-age technology. "Advanced Technology" is now obsolete, and "Industry Standard Architecture" hasn't been an industry standard for years. But in those days, nobody envisioned the degree to which computers would change the world. Naming processors after their speeds, using version numbers and dates in software, and trademark law all had a significant impact on the way today's corporations name their products.

The Advanced Technology (AT) Form Factor

By 1984, the microcomputer was catching on. One of the most influential changes was IBM's release of the then-new, Advanced Technology (AT) form factor. The company was primarily focused on developing technology and upgrading the motherboard, and wasn't thinking about the physical size of the components. Nor were engineers concerned with the amount of space a PC would take up on a desk. PCs, after all, were supposed to be for hobbyists, not "regular people." A full-size AT system—designed around the XT, and often referred to simply as an AT—took up a lot of space. Tower cases were vertically oriented, usually standing a couple of feet high on the floor. Desktop machines (horizontally oriented) were the size of a small suitcase.

The AT used a 16-bit data path, meaning that information could travel across the motherboard in 16-bit rows. This underlying 16-bit bus meant that the 8-bit ISA slots had to be modified to handle the wider data bits. Most of the ISA slots were changed, but one or two kept the 8-bit configuration for backward compatibility with XT expansion boards. The first processor to use the AT form factor was the Intel 80286, with a 16-bit internal and a 16-bit external memory bus. The wider 16-bit slots were also designed to match the wider processor bus.

 Information moves in and out of a processor on a small bus. That bus is some number of bits wide. Constant competition between the width of the processor data and the movement of that data across other motherboard buses at the same path width has been a determining factor in changing bus architectures and system designs. Processors generally move information much faster than their attached buses. Modern technology is an ongoing race, with the buses trying to catch up to the processors.

The ISA slots were laid flat on the motherboards, with expansion cards inserted perpendicular (at a right angle) and standing straight up. In a desktop machine, vertical add-on cards meant a taller profile (height of the machine). Later motherboards introduced a riser card, which allowed the expansion cards to be inserted parallel to the board, making the outer casing thinner and giving it a lower profile. We discuss riser cards under "Low-Profile Extensions (LPX)."

IBM, the exclusive manufacturer of the AT form factor, used a large, 5-pin DIN connector for the keyboard. (See Chapter 11, "Cables and Connectors," for illustrations of typical keyboard connectors.) The DIN connector became known as the AT connector, following the widespread acceptance of the motherboard. IBM then introduced the PS/2 line of computers, which introduced a smaller keyboard and mouse connector, along with Micro Channel technology. The PS/2, or mini-DIN connector, was targeted to replace the AT, and so the keyboard connector was quickly replaced. Although gradually giving way to USB or wireless keyboard and mouse connectors, many computers still use PS/2 connectors for both the keyboard and mouse.

Bits and Bytes

Everyone throws around terms like bits, bytes, kilobytes, megabytes, and ever-larger numbers referring to larger amounts of storage. You need to know that a 1KB file isn't exactly 1,000 bytes, but 1,024 bytes. We discuss binary and hexadecimal numbering systems in Chapter 4, and why technology doesn't use nicely rounded numbers. A typical page of writing from a word processor generates a file approximately 2KB in size. To avoid any possibility of confusion, Table 2.1 lists the exact number of bits and bytes in single units of each category. Note that a bit uses a lowercase *b*, whereas a byte uses an uppercase *B*.

Table 2.1 Standard Terminology for Bits and Bytes	
Term	**Number of Bits**
Bit	Single 0 or 1
Kilobit (Kb)	1 bit×1,024—1,024 bits
Megabit (Mb)	1 bit×1,024^2 (or 1,024×1,024)—1,048,576 bits (millions)
Gigabit (Gb)	1 bit×1,024^3—1,073,741,824 bits (billions)
Terabit (Tb)	1 bit×1,024^4—1,099,511,627,776 bits (trillions)
Byte	8 bits
Kilobyte (KB)	1 byte×1,024—1,024 bytes (8,192 bits, or 1,024×8) (thousands)
Megabyte (MB)	1 byte×1,024^2—1,048,576 bytes (millions)
Gigabyte (GB)	1 byte×1,024^3—1,073,741,824 bytes (billions)
Terabyte (TB)	1 byte×1,024^4—1,099,511,627,776 bytes (trillions)

Figure 2.1 is a stylized diagram (not a schematic) of a typical AT motherboard. The diagram is for your general reference, showing an outlined representation of typical motherboard components. Note that the rear panel is to the *left* of the diagram. Although ATX and NLX boards (discussed later in this chapter) can be laid out quite differently, the relative size and shape of the various components are easy to see on an AT board.

You will be required to visually recognize various form factors on the exam, by either the back panel or the layout of the most important components. You will be shown a series of graphics and asked to assign a correct form factor from a list of question responses.

We sometimes found it difficult to differentiate a power supply from a possible keyboard connector or power connector on the exam graphics. Because there are so many motherboards on the market, it is also difficult to present a universal layout. Generally, a power supply is off to the rear of a motherboard representation, but you should look at various examples of motherboard layouts before you take the exam. It's possible that the exam may reference a power *connector* as being the power supply.

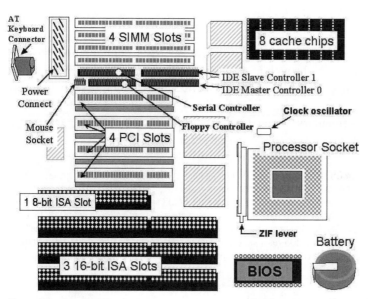

Figure 2.1 A basic AT motherboard.

Designers added an extension to the original slots to make the new 16-bit ISA slots backward compatible with the original 8-bit XT slots. The extension used additional edge connectors, separated by a small space. The boards themselves acted somewhat like a bridge across the original XT slot to the secondary AT extension. Figure 2.2 shows a typical ISA network interface card, often found in a PC. Observe the gap in the slot, separating the original section from the added extension. ISA eventually gave way to PCI bus technology, discussed later in this chapter.

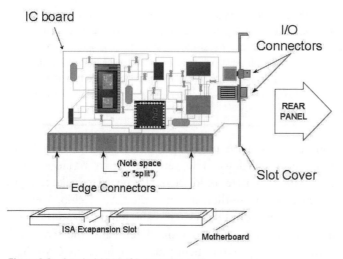

Figure 2.2 A typical 16-bit ISA expansion card.

CMOS

XT motherboards were relatively simple, so basic configuration changes were done manually through jumpers and DIP switches. Another important change introduced in the AT was ROM BIOS and CMOS. Essentially, these are two types of memory used for configuring the basic elements of a computer. Complementary Metal Oxide Semiconductor (CMOS) is a small memory bank that stores configuration settings.

CMOS settings are maintained for as long as any electrical current is available. Even when the PC is disconnected from a wall outlet, a small battery on the motherboard provides enough current to maintain the CMOS settings. In the event that those settings become corrupted, or if someone changes the settings, a common way to reset the CMOS is to remove the battery and wait a few minutes. Another common method is to use a CMOS-reset jumper, found on many motherboards. Using a screwdriver to short-circuit the system is considered inelegant.

Jumpers and DIP Switches

Consider a circuit path, where electricity comes to a sort of fork in the road. Two different outcomes depend upon which direction the current takes. One outcome might be a certain setting, with the other outcome meaning a different setting. The original jumper was a small piece of plastic with two holes connected by a wire. A circuit trace on the motherboard would be broken, with each side of the trace ending in a vertical pin rising up from the motherboard. "Setting" the jumper involved pushing the plastic jumper over the two pins, reconnecting the circuit with the wire.

Without a jumper, electric current flowing through the circuit would stop at the pins. Setting a jumper enables current to flow through the completed circuit. Although primitive, jumpers were highly reliable and inexpensive.

A *dual inline package (DIP)* switch is a very small slide switch or rocker switch, usually moved with the tip of a pen or pencil. DIP switches are typically aligned in sets of two or more, but sometimes you'll see a single switch. They're easier to see and set than jumpers, but are not as reliable. Most manufacturers try to avoid DIP switches in favor of software configurable parameters. One place where you'll often find a set of DIP switches is on the back of an IDE drive. By changing the DIP switches, you tell the controller whether to "see" the drive as a master or slave (primary or secondary drive).

At first, the AT and PS/2 computers used a special configuration diskette to change basic configuration settings. The setup program would provide access to the CMOS, where the user could use the keyboard to make changes to the system. Those changes were then stored to the CMOS chip. Memory chips moved computers away from DIP switches and jumpers, and provided the AT with many more configuration options. Eventually, the setup disk was eliminated, with the setup program being stored right in the CMOS.

NOTE These setup disks should not be confused with emergency startup disks or bootable floppies. Neither should they be confused with a Recovery CD, which usually contains an image of an entire system—including installed software. Rather, the setup disks were often the only way to access the machine's basic configuration settings. Nowadays, you can usually access these settings through the CMOS by pressing a key such as F1, F2, Esc, or Del during the initial boot sequence.

Baby AT and ATX

It wasn't long before IBM lost its dominance in the PC industry (because of pricing, proprietary technology, and missed marketing opportunities). Some companies were designing computers using technologies different from IBM's, whereas other companies were producing machines that were exactly compatible with IBM machines. These exact copies were called *clones*, and whenever IBM came up with a new idea, the clone manufacturers produced a copy. Compaq was one of the first clone manufacturers leading the microprocessor revolution that swept across the world in the late 1980s.

The terms "IBM-compatible" and "IBM clone" came to mean that a system matched a set of emerging standards based on IBM design specs. Even though 16-bit expansion cards could still fit on a cloned XT board, the clone companies didn't want to market old technology. Instead, they retrofitted the new cards to a smaller motherboard, and called their design the *Baby AT* board. In the process, they accidentally produced a smaller, more streamlined PC that used less desktop space. With motherboards directly related to processors, it didn't take long before Intel, the leading chip manufacturer, got directly involved with motherboard design.

In 1995, Intel released its specifications for the Advanced Technology eXtension (ATX) form factor, calling for an open standard in the design of future motherboards. An *open standard* means that anyone can use the design freely. Apple Computer (and IBM, many times) chose to use a *proprietary standard*, meaning that anyone who wanted to build an Apple-compatible computer or device had to pay a licensing fee to Apple Computer.

Figure 2.3 shows a simplified outline of a typical ATX motherboard. Note that the rear panel is toward the *top* of the picture. Note also that the drawing shows a vertically mounted CPU. Chapter 5, "Processors and Chipsets" discusses slot and socket technology. In short, slots are used to attach a CPU vertically and sockets are used for mounting a CPU horizontally. Figure 2.1 showed a socket-mounted CPU, and Figure 2.3 shows a slot-mounted chip.

The slot-mounting shown in Figure 2.3 isn't exactly accurate. We've left off the outer casing for the fan to show the CPU heat sink. In reality, that heat sink is in direct contact with the CPU. In our drawing, we've left a slight space to differentiate the sink from the IC board and chip circuitry. The other heat sink, with the more recognizable square and "fin" shape, is used to cool the secondary supporting chipset. Modern machines have returned to the flat CPU form factor with the finned heat sink directly over the flat CPU.

Changes in form factor are typically designed to reduce the cost of manufacturing, and to provide for faster, easier maintenance. Competition in the processor manufacturing sector was heating up as Advanced Micro Devices (AMD) and Cyrix began selling their own brands of processor chips. When Intel released the original ATX specification, AMD's K-5 and K-6 chips were plug compatible. AMD later released its own open standard, which was different from Intel's and required a different corresponding chipset.

AMD was originally organized as a secondary backup source of processor chips. IBM didn't want to have the entire chip supply tied up in a single company. Intel and AMD began a friendly competition at the time, with AMD choosing a different way of speeding up the CPU. Over the years, AMD grew to become Intel's main competition.

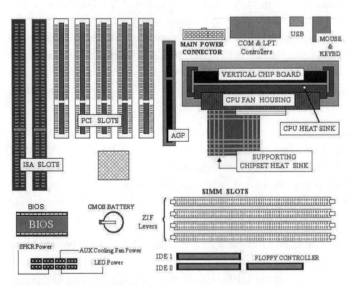

Figure 2.3   The ATX form factor.

The ATX specification called for several important improvements. One of the changes was the built-in, double-high, external I/O connector panel shown in Figure 2.4. (Note that different machines have a different number of expansion slots.) Along with changes in the panel, the location of the connectors was changed to allow for shorter cables between devices such as hard drives and floppy drives. The CPU and memory banks were relocated toward the rear, allowing for easier accessibility and cooling. Another change was the standardization of single-keyed power connectors.

 The ATX uses a single-keyed, 20-pin power supply connector. A so-called *keyed connector* can be connected to its opposite connection in only one direction. Usually, this is done by a molded notch or groove in the plastic connector casing, or by color coding the ribbon cable attached to the connector. Keying a connector means designing the plug and the socket with matching notches. If the notches don't line up, the plug can't fit into the socket. Keyed connectors inspired the use of keyed expansion cards, often found on a PCI bus.

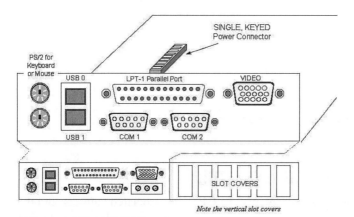

Figure 2.4   The ATX double-high I/O rear panel.

The ATX form factor featured I/O ports built right into the board (as opposed to just their connectors being on AT boards). They also featured an integrated PS/2 mouse connector, to go along with the keyboard connector. The board was rotated 90 degrees, for access to the entire surface, and used better cooling circulation to reduce heat. Air blows into rather than out of the case, and so the CPU was placed closer to the power supply with its cooling fan. Modern systems often provide connectors for additional fans. Auxiliary cooling fans should not be confused with chip cooling fans, dedicated to cooling the CPU.

 The design of a computer's case is engineered to provide an even flow of air around the inside of the machine. Keeping unused expansion slots covered maintains this flow of air. Therefore, an expansion slot should either have an expansion card installed in it, or the slot cover should be in place.

With the orientation rotated 90 degrees from the Baby AT design, the drive connector cables could be placed closer to the drives themselves. The more efficient use of space allowed for the CPU to be moved back toward the power supply and cooling fan. Figure 2.5 demonstrates this change, which then carried forward to the NLX form factors.

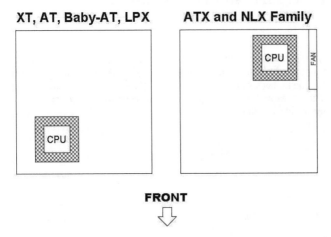

Figure 2.5 CPU moves to the back near the cooling fan on ATX and NLX boards.

Internal Cooling Systems

Increasing the power requirements of a CPU, its associated chipsets, and the expansion boards means a bigger power supply and more electricity flowing through the circuits. More current means more heat; and as components became smaller, the need to dissipate that heat became critical. The 486DX2, running at 66MHz—and all subsequent processors—required additional cooling of some type. In fact, the Pentium line of processors generated so much heat that an onboard chip-cooling fan and heat sink were developed to maintain acceptable operating temperatures. Each additional (auxiliary) fan requires more power, which, in turn, generates even more heat, not to mention noise.

Any given area of air contains only so many molecules. When those air molecules take on energy, the temperature of the air increases. Air is not a very good conductor of heat, so as the heat increases, we need more and more air to dissipate that heat. *Dissipation* means that we reduce a concentrated amount of something by scattering its parts to many different locations. For example, your paycheck dollars are concentrated in your pocket, but those dollars become dissipated when you go shopping at a mall.

One principle of physics refers to *radiation* and radiant heat. This involves a process by which energy transfers to a surrounding area using molecular energy. Radiation would be where the heat inside a monitor casing simply moves to the air outside the vents. In early computers, the amount of radiant heat from the electronic components was negligible. However, multiple processors, secondary graphics processors, and more system components produce more heat than can be radiated away.

Another law of physics involves *conduction*. Essentially, this process involves energy transfers between moving particles. You've seen this on a pool table, where a moving ball hits a stationary ball and transfers its energy. The stationary ball takes on energy and begins to move, whereas the moving ball loses energy and slows down. When faster-moving heated molecules transfer some of their energy to slower-moving cooler molecules, heat is conducted from the faster to the slower molecules. A group of molecules, all hitting each other this way, would conduct heat away from a source like a processor.

On a molecular level, electricity moving through a conductor transfers energy to the surrounding air molecules. Those air molecules begin moving faster (heating up) and start hitting surrounding molecules, which in turn speeds up the surrounding molecules. The air surrounding the electrical components heats up because of convection; then radiation takes care of dissipating to the general air flow inside the case.

We can make this process more efficient by using a fan to pull heated air out of the case and then replacing it with cooler air. Even so, Pentium chips generate heat so quickly that the main cooling fan can't keep up. The chips are also so small that they don't have enough surface area for the slow radiation process. Engineers needed to find a way to increase the surface area of the chips, giving them more contact with the air circulation inside the main case. The solution was a *heat sink*.

A heat sink is typically made of an aluminum alloy, which is a great heat conductor. Its surface includes many tiny fins, and it looks like a dark-colored plate resting on top of the chip. One surface, with no fins, is in direct, physical contact with the chip. The physical contact means the surface area of the CPU takes on the additional area of the heat sink. The aluminum absorbs heat from the chip, and more air passes over the larger combined surface area.

Microscopic flaws on the surface of both the processor and the heat sink keep the two from making a perfect fit, no matter how well they're manufactured. If we use a sort of paste made up of conductive materials to fill in the flaws, we can increase the conductive efficiency between the surfaces. This paste is called a *thermal coupling*, and is used to join (couple) the heat sink to the CPU.

Liquid Cooling Technology

Controlling heat has become so important to modern systems that many motherboards now include heat sensors. These sensors, primarily attached to CPUs, allow software diagnostics applications to monitor critical temperatures inside the box. The problem is that air cooling has pretty much reached its limit. Continually shrinking components and their smaller surface areas make it more and more difficult to dissipate heat. Even low-voltage and ultra-low-voltage processors are pushing the limits of the traditional air-cooling process.

The next step in cooling technology seems to be coming from automobile technology. Once again, we have a central component (the engine) producing a tremendous amount of heat. A small engine might simply radiate away the extra heat, but most vehicles use a radiator filled with water or antifreeze. Similarly, new heat sinks are designed to have hollow fins filled with some kind of liquid (antifreeze being the primary candidate).

Liquid is a better heat conductor than either metal or air. So if we can pass liquid over a heat sink, we can quickly move the heated liquid away from the processor. If we quickly cool the liquid, we might then re-circulate the same liquid over the heat sink. This is exactly how we cool nuclear reactors, large internal combustion engines, and even everyday automobile engines.

 A CPU is not a nuclear reactor, and should never be confused with one.

Déjà vu All Over Again

Liquid cooling is hardly new to the computer industry. Some of the big IBM mainframes, such as the Model 168, were liquid cooled. The pretty-looking fountains and pools outside many corporate offices were actually part of the computer cooling systems. Cray computers generate an enormous amount of heat, and were cooled with liquid nitrogen. Liquid cooling systems available for today's PCs aren't all that different from these earlier examples.

When we intervene to improve the convection process, we refer to an active heat sink. Without intervention, we refer to a passive heat sink. Some of the less expensive systems today use passive convection to move liquid coolant over the chip. Much like warm air rising from your monitor, these systems rely on warm liquid rising through rubber tubes. When the liquid has been cooled, it descends through adjacent tubes. However, most of liquid cooling systems are more active, using a small propeller (called an impeller) to move the liquid from the base near the chip, up to a radiator where a fan, or fans, push air over the fins to aid in dissipating the heat.

The biggest problem with liquid cooling, for the moment, seems to be engineering design hurdles and installation. Not long ago, size was an issue, with the cooling system taking up a lot of internal space. Smaller designs seem to require additional fans at the top of the radiator. So although liquid cooling systems provide for a very quiet environment, add-on costs for secondary fans and relatively complex installation schemes are delaying acceptance of the technology in the mass market.

Low Profile Extensions (LPX)

When Lotus released the 1-2-3 spreadsheet, it quickly became a "must-have" application. Corporate America began buying personal computers in very large quantities, and desk space became a problem. In 1987, Western Digital Corporation released an even smaller form factor than the ATX. This Low Profile eXtensions (LPX) design introduced the *bus riser card*. The riser card was mounted in the center of the motherboard, and was narrower than a typical expansion card. By installing the expansion cards parallel to the motherboard, the LPX form factor significantly lowered the overall height of the outer casing. This "low profile" is signified by the "LP" in LPX. We'll discuss the NLX boards in a moment, but Figure 2.6 shows the movement of the riser card.

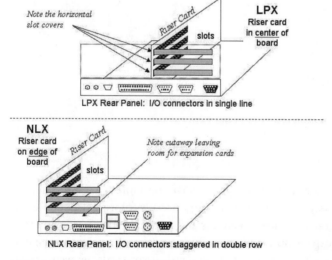

Figure 2.6 Riser card location in LPX and NLX motherboards.

Typically when you look at the back of an AT or Baby AT computer, you'll see that the slot covers are in an up-and-down, vertical orientation. However, on the back of an LPX machine, the slot covers are in a left-right, horizontal orientation. The AT, Baby AT, and LPX form factors have largely been replaced by the ATX and NLX family of motherboards.

NLX

When the LPX form factor was updated to the NLX form factor (refer to Figure 2.6), the new design moved the riser card to the outer edge of the motherboard. This provided more room on the board for expansion slots, along with greater accessibility to system components. Both the LPX and NLX retain the parallel (horizontal) slot orientation, with the NLX having a sort of L-shaped profile, or step shape, where the riser card sits on the edge of the motherboard.

An easily recognizable feature of the NLX board is the sort of step shape of the back panel, as shown in Figure 2.7. Some of the connectors are in a single line, whereas others are one above the other in a double line. The step shape leaves room for expansion cards.

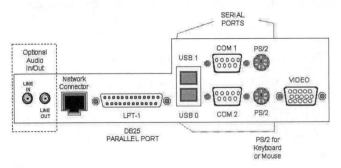

Figure 2.7   NLX step configuration.

Riser Cards

We all know that mobile computing and small, portable (handheld) devices are changing the way we live our lives. Additionally, more peripheral components and integrated devices mean less and less real estate inside any type of box. Installing expansion cards vertically means that the height of the case (its profile) must be at least as tall as the card. Riser cards, as we've mentioned, are a workaround that allow several cards to use the same vertical space as a single card.

Modern riser cards are now capable of handling simple bus mastering. Bus mastering is discussed in the "Peripheral Component Interconnect (PCI)" section later in this chapter, but essentially, a bus riser card can allow any of its secondary cards to use a single slot. Much of this technology is an out-growth of the PCI specification, and the market now provides for riser cards where a single slot can be used to install three PCI expansion cards.

Naturally there's a trade-off based on how far apart the main slots are locat-ed on the motherboard, but with nominal changes to that space, we could eventually see boards with four slots using four riser cards, each supporting three secondary cards, meaning twelve PCI cards. Something like this idea can be found in Intel's *server blades*, where entire file servers can be built onto an IC board and installed in rows.

Summary—Form Factors

The preceding section covers motherboards, CMOS, and the basic shape and design (form factor) of typical motherboards. Be sure that you under-stand how the AT form factor evolved into the Baby AT, and eventually became the ATX, LPX, and NLX form factors. Remember the concept of riser cards, and the step design shown in Figure 2.7. The exam doesn't ask you for dates and history, but rather tests you on whether you can recognize various types of motherboards and back panels by their shape and slot orien-tation.

Most importantly, you should examine the diagrams of a basic motherboard and learn the relative sizes and shapes of the various components. We've tried to keep the illustrations as simple as possible, knowing that mother-boards vary greatly. The critical knowledge you must have is how to distin-guish an ISA slot from a PCI slot, an AGP slot, or a DIMM slot. You should be able to see a CPU and distinguish it from a BIOS chip. You should be able to separate a CMOS chip from a backup battery. If you're not comfortable with our diagram, be sure that you study some physical motherboards, or use additional preparation guides and hardware manuals until you reach a solid comfort level.

Many of today's computers come with a modified tower configuration or mini-tower design. Whether they're called mini-desktops, vertical form factors, or anything else, the exam tests you only on the horizontal motherboards we've included in this book. You won't see *mobo* on the exam, but you might see the term *planar board*. Remember that acquiring knowledge is a lifelong process, but passing an exam is a one-time event. Whether exam terminology is current or not, your A+ certification depends upon your knowing the correct responses to the questions on that specific exam.

Data Transfers—The Bus

New peripheral devices, such as printers, drives, monitors, and so forth, are being developed all the time. To take advantage of these new developments, systems must have a common way of connecting them to the motherboard. Each of these common connection points is called an *expansion bus*, or sometimes an *I/O bus*. A bus is simply a way to move electrical signals from one place to another on a circuit board. In this case, the circuit board we're talking about is the motherboard. When the bus is an additional part—connected to, and often controlled by the board—it expands the capabilities of the motherboard, which is why it's called an expansion bus.

The bus structure provides a number of long, narrow connection *slots* so that circuit boards can be pushed into them edgewise. The slots, located on the motherboard, provide connectivity between the data path and the device. A video card is a typical circuit board designed to expand the capabilities of the system video.

Expansion cards are designed to work with specific bus architectures (designs), and have become known as ISA cards, PCI cards, and so forth. In other words, although you might see four ISA slots on a system board, they're all being controlled by a single ISA bus. All four cards are attached to the same bus and controlled by one controller (chip).

NOTE Be careful that you don't confuse a PCI card with a PC Card that is designed for a notebook computer. Additionally, you may have to ask for clarification if someone is speaking about a printed circuit card (PC Card) or the small expansion card for a notebook computer. The two cards use the same name. Acronyms are not unique in the technology industry, so PC can stand for personal computer or printed circuit, depending on the context.

Throughput and Data Path

Throughput is essentially how much data we can move through a bus. If you think of horses at the racetrack, then an 8-bit bus would be like eight starting gates. Each horse (a bit) has its own gate. Eight horses in a row would constitute one byte. Suppose you have ten rows of horses, and the gates open and close one time for each row. Every time the gates open, a row of horses goes through, and then the gates close. That's one *cycle*. The *bus clock* tells the gates when to open and shut. The number of times that they open and shut in a given time is the cycle *frequency*. Early PCs used the motherboard oscillator as the bus clock.

When everything in a given data path is timed directly to the main oscillator, it's referred to as being a synchronous operation. Asynchronous (not synchronized) operation usually applies to longer distances, where there is no timing. When you connect to the Internet through a modem you are using asynchronous communication. A letter or number is sent down the line only when you type that letter or number. No one times your keystrokes and makes you type a letter every half second. You type as fast or as slow as you want. That being said, you'll often find references to timed events inside a computer as being synchronous or asynchronous. If the events are timed to a single clock, they're synchronous; if they're timed to separate clocks, they're asynchronous.

Although we say a bus is some number of bits, that doesn't mean that there are only 8, or 16, or some other number of connectors on the bus. A bus has additional connectors used for such things as addressing, interrupt requests (IRQs), or other functions within the bus itself. However, we always refer to the size of the bus in terms of how many bits of data can move across that bus—the *data path*.

The data path is like a highway, with the bus being a toll plaza. Eight tollbooths on an eight-lane highway allow traffic to move fairly smoothly. However, a sixteen-lane highway with only eight tollbooths causes traffic jams (bottlenecks) as cars funnel down from sixteen to eight lanes. Some cars have to wait (in a buffer) while other cars pass through the toll gate. This is what happens when a 16-bit processor is connected to an 8-bit bus (see Figure 2.8). The processor is pumping out "cars" of data on a motherboard data path sixteen lanes wide. The memory bus or an expansion card bus has to reduce the flow of information down to that bus width.

By the way, you may have heard of the poor government worker whose tollbooth was constantly being demolished by large trucks. He would run out with some kind of compound and quickly glue the broken pieces back together. Finally, his co-workers asked what kind of compound he was using, and he told them it was *toll gate booth paste*. (Badda-bump!)

Clock Ticks and Information Cycles

We'll discuss clock ticks and cycles in the "Cycles and Frequencies" section of Chapter 3, but you should have a sense of how the motherboard clock and various bus clocks relate to information. Have you ever seen one of those old movies where a Roman galleon had to be moved with oars? A nasty-looking guy stood in the back of the boat, pounding out a rhythm on a big drum. One rowing *cycle* breaks down into steps: dropping the blade, setting the oar, pulling the handle, lifting the blade, and preparing for the next cycle. The cycle is directly related to how fast the drummer beats the drum.

The rhythm of the drum is the *frequency*. The process of rowing is a cycle of information movement. Each step in the cycle is broken into its separate steps. In some cases, it would take two drumbeats for each step. In other instances, it might take only one beat per step. If the galleon were manned by a bunch of supermen, they could possibly complete an entire cycle—all five steps—in only a single drumbeat. This relationship is very much like the link between increased processor speeds, lagging bus speeds, and how various systems use ticks coming from different clocks. Another limit is the strength, or composition, of the men moving the oars. Building stronger men would be like writing a more powerful operating system.

The motherboard oscillator is like the guy in the back of the boat. He and it are the main timers. If the boat were very long, it would make sense to have additional guys stationed along the way toward the front of the boat. These additional drummers are like secondary clocks, synchronized to the main guy in the back of the boat. Carrying the analogy further, if there were smaller boats moving around the main vessel, and each one had its own drummer, they would row in a different rhythm. They still would work together to protect the galleon in a common purpose. This is how asynchronous operations use separate clocks that aren't synchronized to the main clock.

Cycles per Second—Hertz (Hz)

Throughput indicates the amount of information per cycle moving across a bus. Throughput usually refers to an amount of data moved per second. As the cycle frequency increases, the throughput increases. We can move more than one bit of data per cycle. If the frequency stays the same, the throughput will then increase.

Frequency (in computer terminology) is the number of cycles per second. A clock cycle means the time between the start of a tick (up-tick, or leading edge) and the end of that tick (down-tick, or trailing edge). We use one second as a standard measure for frequency timing. The number of cycles in a given second is written as cycles per second, and expressed in hertz (Hz). Therefore, 1 cycle in 1 second is 1Hz.

Suppose it takes ten seconds to complete a single cycle of something. For example, it takes ten seconds to open the starting gates, let a row of eight horses through, and then close the gates. The eight horses represent eight bits—a single byte. In this case the throughput is eight bits per ten seconds. Another way of saying the same thing would be one byte per ten seconds. If we divide eight bits by ten seconds, we have 0.8 bits per second, or 0.8bps throughput.

Now imagine a wave of water, where you slice through the wave every fraction of an inch, cutting it into slices. Each slice, from one end to the other, is some number of bits wide. A slice might be eight bits wide, or sixteen, or thirty-two, or sixty-four, or wider. Wave after wave is hitting a flood gate, which is analogous to data hitting the bus. When we open the gate, a whole bunch (technical term) of water goes rushing through. Depending on when the gate closes, either the whole wave or only some part of the wave gets through.

The bus clock manages the opening and closing of the gate—the imaginary flood gate. If the gate is the same width as the slices of water, then a lot of water gets through. But if the bus is narrower than the wave, everything has to slow down as parts of the wave funnel through the gate. The expansion bus provides exceptional flexibility, but it can also be a bottleneck as processor speeds increase. Figure 2.8 shows the bottleneck taking place when the data path is wider than the bus.

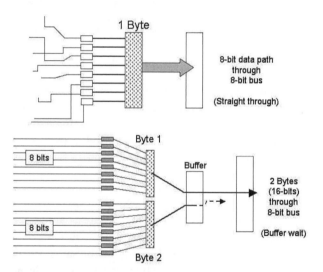

Figure 2.8   Throughput bottlenecks.

Suppose we have waves of water (data) 8 bits wide. Therefore, each slice of the wave is also 1 byte wide (a byte being eight bits). Let's make the wave 100 slices thick. We'll say that it takes one second to open and close the flood gate. Therefore, in that single second, all 100 slices of water go zooming through. In this story, one hundred 8-bit rows have moved per second. The throughput is 800 bits per second (100 slices times 8 bits in a slice). Divide this by eight to find the bytes, then by 1,000 to find the kilobytes, and we have roughly 0.09KB/s (kilobytes per second).

In this example, the timer is running at 1Hz (one event per second). We could either put more pressure on the water and push, say, 1,000 slices through the gates in that second (1KB/s), or we could make the gates wider. If we make the gate twice as wide, we can move 16-bit slices of water through, every second, thereby doubling the throughput. In this way, widening a bus increases throughput even though the timing frequency remains the same.

Now suppose we move down to the electronic level, where bits and bytes are flying around like laser beams at a rock concert. If you could make the cycles go faster, then you could also move more bits. If we could "compress" the frequency, we might even be able to open and close the gates two, five, ten, or more times per second. A PCI bus, running at 33MHz, generates 33,000,000 cycles per second. Imagine how many waves of water could sneak through that kind of gate in a single second!

 Speed increases in new computers often are linked to increasing bus speeds. The PCI specification continues to change, as do processor and memory bus speeds. Revised PCI-X specifications call for 533–800MHz bus speeds. That's around eight-hundred million cycles per second.

Expansion bus design has changed almost as fast as processor development in the quest for performance improvements. These efforts have led to 32-bit, 64-bit, and 128-bit bus widths, as well as faster data signals movement. Modern buses have their own clocks, sometimes synchronized to the motherboard clock. But no matter how fast or wide the bus, its entire reason for living is to move bits and bytes of data.

Operating systems involve many instructions, composed of bits and bytes of programming information. This is what we mean when we speak about 32-bit operating systems, 64-bit operating systems, and the underlying data paths and buses. All parts of the data path should ideally be the same width, which means that even the operating system must be written to take advantage of bus architecture. Add in multiple processors, all sending 128-bit data streams, and you can see some awesome bottleneck problems developing.

Bandwidth

Bandwidth is the total potential of a medium to move information. Potential refers to something that might be possible, as opposed to what actually is happening. Throughput is the actual amount of data being moved. Technically, we rarely refer to bandwidth in terms of moving data through a bus. Usually, bandwidth refers to radio (such as wireless networking) or a cable of some kind (such as coaxial cable), regardless of today's references to increased "bandwidth" in a bus. Baseband Ethernet bandwidth has the capability of moving only one signal at a time, with that signal taking up the entire bandwidth.

Bandwidth is the difference between the highest and the lowest frequency being transmitted. High bandwidth allows for the transmission of a lot of information in a high frequency (many cycles per second). Low bandwidth allows for less information to move at a lower frequency. Generally, the bigger this difference, the more signal we can pass.

For example, video (television) signals require a difference of over a million cycles per second (1MHz). Morse code requires a difference of only 500 cycles (500Hz). Video and TV require high bandwidth to transmit signals. Morse code, being a far simpler type of signal, requires less "room." We could pass more than 2,000 individual Morse code conversations in the 1,000,000-cycle bandwidth required by a TV signal. A difference of 2MHz (two million cycles) would mean we could pass two TV signals, or 4,000 conversations in code.

Don't confuse bandwidth "capacity" with electrical capacitance, discussed in Chapter 6, "Basic Electronics." For instance, a racetrack might be capable of handling a burst of eight horses going through the gates. Part of that capability, or bandwidth, is defined by the dirt on the track. Another part involves the weather and the nature of the track. The "something" through which the data is moving could be a bus, an Ethernet cable, or even air.

The Bandwidth Bandwagon

Computer jargon tends to forget the link between bandwidth and frequency, making bandwidth synonymous with capacity. For instance, you might hear that "We don't have the bandwidth for that type of file transfer," or "We have more than enough bandwidth to do both payroll accounting and the market analysis." The term is also used for things completely unrelated to information flow or frequency. "I just don't have enough bandwidth to complete the report and to meet with Sid." Be aware of what bandwidth really means, but understand how it's used to mean capacity or capability. You'll probably find the term used both ways on the test.

People use the term *bandwidth*, nowadays, to mean all sorts of things. The measurement of bandwidth is a complex calculation, involving various factors such as packet size and types of information. If a water pipe is like a cable, then increasing the diameter of the pipe allows more water to pass through (throughput). But the diameter of the pipe is only part of the bandwidth calculation. Bandwidth can also be like the difference between digging a trench in soft dirt, versus laying a length of plastic pipe. The pipe has less friction than the dirt, and so water flows not only faster, but in greater volume.

Modern linguistics and political correctness are having the continuing effect of degrading the English language. We hear high-level government officials talk about "nucular" as opposed to nuclear threats, and even the dictionary includes the improper spelling and pronunciation. Just so, even Microsoft speaks of the "bandwidth" of a Front Side Bus, or how increased "bandwidth" in a PCI bus can improve performance. Go ahead and accept the term to mean something similar to bus width or throughput, but try to remember that words often have both a proper and irregular usage.

Broadband and Baseband

Broadband allows many signals to simultaneously travel over a transmission medium by using a different frequency for each signal. In other words, it parcels out the bandwidth in frequency blocks so that each signal can have a portion of the bandwidth for the length of the transmission. Until recently, the most common example of broadband technology was radio, where many different stations transmit at the same time, using different frequencies.

When you hear station WAEC at 890 on your dial, that station is transmitting at a frequency of 890KHz. If you want to hear the station, you must tune your radio to the 890KHz frequency. Although there are hundreds of other stations transmitting in the same medium, you will pick up only the information assigned that particular frequency.

Broadband uses a "broad" range of frequencies, moving continuously. Any given signal gets only one frequency. Broadband takes the entire range of frequencies and slices them up into channels. Each channel only has a fraction of the bandwidth available, but it has that channel all the time. If two signals are being transmitted, each signal remains continuous and uses its own channel.

Baseband also allows for many signals to share the same media, but only one at a time. Baseband transmissions take up the entire bandwidth for each signal. However, each signal takes the total bandwidth for only a fraction of a second. When that time *slice* ends, the entire bandwidth is given over to another signal. If the signals are switched fast enough it will seem like any one signal has a continuous circuit. It's all very confusing, but baseband is typically used in networking, so you should know the terms and what they mean.

Until recently, fiber optics required a dedicated circuit, and used neither broadband nor baseband technologies. However, a new type of fiber signaling called *Dense Wave Multiplexing* sends light at different frequencies down the same cable. This is essentially frequency-division multiplexing, another name for broadband.

Expansion Bus Architecture

PCs use different types of buses, including processor buses, memory buses, address buses, and expansion buses. The first three relate to moving data in or out of various chips and are discussed further in Chapter 4, but you need to be able to distinguish the various types of expansion buses. You'll be asked to identify an expansion bus on the basis of its name, shape, and general location on the board.

 An expansion bus commonly indicates a number of slots designed for add-on cards that will control different types of peripheral devices. The bus is designed to "expand" the capabilities of the overall system. That being said, the AGP also takes an add-on card: specifically a video accelerator card. CompTIA may call the AGP an expansion bus, and offer it as a response possibility. Technically, the AGP is the Accelerated Graphics Port and is not an expansion bus. If you have to include the AGP to reach a correct answer, then let CompTIA call it an expansion bus. Never let technical truth interfere with what the exam calls a correct response.

Bus configurations can be 8-bit, 16-bit, 32-bit, 64-bit, and so on. The more bits of information that can be processed simultaneously, the faster the throughput at a given clock speed. The earliest computers used an 8-bit signal track. The fundamental change in the AT boards was to use a 16-bit bus (although the proper term is *path*, as in 8 separate signal paths). This allowed the AT motherboards to move far more complex information across the system. Much of this information was in the form of a 16-bit operating system (DOS) and 16-bit application software.

Today's motherboards have at least three different buses and several memory buses. These buses include (but aren't limited to)

➤ *ISA bus*—This bus is typically a 16-bit bus for compatibility with older machines using legacy cards.

➤ *PCI bus*—This bus provides a bridge between the processor, the slower ISA bus, and connected peripherals.

➤ *Accelerated Graphics Port (AGP) bus*—This bus is dedicated to high-speed video processing.

➤ *L-2 Cache processor bus*—This Level 2 bus (the backside bus) helps the CPU store and retrieve data.

Industry Standard Architecture (ISA)

The original 8086 and 8088 processors could address only 1MB of memory. The original 8-bit ISA bus was designed to use the edge of an IC card—an *edge connector* (sometimes called a "paddle board," in jargon-speak). It used 62 contacts, providing 8 data lines and 20 address lines. This allowed every card installed in the system to be addressed within the first megabyte of memory (discussed in Chapter 13). Although the CPU in earlier machines ran at various clock speeds, the original ISA buses ran at only 4.77MHz.

As processor speeds increased, new devices and applications required moving more information through the buses. At 4.77MHz, the original throughput for an ISA bus was 39 megabits (Mb)—not megabytes (MB)—per second. Faster throughput demanded larger buses, so the AT form factor used a 16-bit bus. Originally, the 16-bit buses ran at 6MHz. Not long after, they sped up to 8MHz, and the industry soon decided it needed a standard speed. The ISA bus was eventually set to 8.33MHz, allowing for a theoretical maximum throughput of 8MB/s. The more realistic throughput was approximately 1.25MB/s, but that was still much faster than the previous buses.

The 16-bit bus continued to be the standard far beyond the introduction of 32-bit microprocessors. As is typical of the computer industry, no new standard was provided for changing technology. To take advantage of the faster processors, many companies began using proprietary (not open) technology in their own buses. Different types of cards were coming out, such as memory and video cards, but each card had to match a particular bus technology on the motherboard. Chaos was king!

 The Small Computer System Interface (SCSI) bus is discussed separately in Chapter 8, "Peripherals: Storage Devices." The SCSI bus was a way for IBM-compatible microcomputers to work with devices intended for completely different platforms, such as Apple computers.

MCA and EISA

IBM developed the Micro Channel Architecture (MCA) bus in an attempt to standardize a 32-bit bus. MCA took full advantage of 32-bit processing, providing a much faster data path. However, the MCA bus wasn't backward compatible with ISA. For example, if you had a tape backup unit that used a 16-bit bus, you couldn't use it in a new IBM machine. Instead, you had to buy a whole new card connector, based on MCA technology, and you'd often have to buy a whole new backup machine to go along with it.

Meanwhile, the clone manufacturers, spearheaded by Compaq, came up with their own standard. They called it the Extended Industry Standard Architecture (EISA) bus. IBM was demanding a license fee from any manufacturer that wanted to install the MCA bus on their motherboards, and the clone manufacturers didn't want to pay for a license. Because of the incompatibility, licensing fee, and the rapidly expanding clone machine market, the MCA bus never caught on and died a quiet death.

The EISA bus added 90 new connections and 55 new signal paths, making the slot and card much larger. However, rather than putting the connectors in a single row on one side of the card (as the ISA cards did), the EISA cards used two lines of connectors running along both sides of the card's edge. This enabled an ISA card to fit in an EISA connector and work just fine. However, you couldn't put an EISA card into an older ISA connector (no contacts for the second side of the card).

 This idea of using both sides of an edge connector inspired the change in architecture between a SIMM and a DIMM, both memory modules that are discussed in Chapter 3.

Although the EISA bus ran at 8.33MHz, the bus width was increased to 32 bits of information, making for a theoretical maximum transfer rate (throughput) of 33.32MB/s. More signal paths meant more data could pass the "gates." Although MCA and EISA were superior technologies, the EISA bus was significantly more expensive to purchase. It didn't require a licensing fee, but the high cost meant it never really caught on for anything other than network servers and high-end PCs. The EISA bus and the VESA bus (discussed next) were eventually replaced by the PCI bus.

VESA Local Bus—32-Bit

As you can imagine, a real bottleneck began to develop as processors got faster and faster, and the ISA bus continued to limit throughput. To fix the problem, an organization called the Video Electronics Standard Association (VESA) developed the VESA Local (VL) bus. It was "local" in the sense that it attached directly to a 32-bit processor, using what's called a local processor bus. This meant that data didn't have to funnel through the 16-bit ISA bus, but could come right out of the processor and move off to whatever device it was targeted for, keeping a continuous 32-bit pathway. These devices were generally memory and graphics cards.

 VESA continues to be an important player in the standards-setting arena. Although modern flat-panel LCD monitor connectors haven't yet been standardized (digital versus analog), the VESA standard seems to be the front-runner.

Windows was entering the market in 1992, designed to take advantage of CPUs with 32-bit internal and external processor buses. The new graphical user interface (GUI) moved tremendous amounts of information, and the local bus came in handy for speeding up graphics processing. However, although it connected with newer chipsets and was inexpensive to produce, the VL-Bus had problems. It was more of an extension of the 80486 processor bus, and didn't work well with other bus types. There were also numerous glitches in connecting with other chips, along with timing problems.

Peripheral Component Interconnect (PCI)

The VL-Bus was an important step in the development of graphics accelerator cards. It inspired the idea of off-loading processing from the CPU to an auxiliary card; in this case, one with integrated graphics processors and video RAM. Because of its intermittent problems, the VL-Bus quickly lost market share when the PCI specification was released in 1993. PCI was developed by Intel, and had the advantages of better technology and some basic standardization, not to mention the heavy marketing influence of a leading hardware manufacturer.

We've seen that the VESA specification called for an entirely new bus, separate from the main bus, and dedicated exclusively to the CPU. Keep in mind that the main bus controlled a number of ISA slots and their cards. Prior to the VESA bus, a video card would have to be inserted into one of the slots on the motherboard's main expansion bus. This led to competition with other cards for the CPU's attention.

The PCI specification, like the VESA specification, called for an additional bus and placed it between the central processor and the ISA bus. However, unlike the VL-Bus, the PCI bus was not tied directly to the processor. The original PCI Local bus used various bridges to avoid timing issues, and its main features included the following:

➤ *Burst Mode*—A way to send a data stream without having to constantly search for a destination address.

➤ *Bus Mastering*—A way for devices to take on some control over how a particular bus is used, reducing conflicts and competition.

➤ *Additional Expansion Slots*—More expansion slots than the VL-Bus; typically three or four, with some versions offering even more.

> *Configurable Bandwidth*—Originally designed as a 32-bit bus running at 33/66MHz; then changing to 64 bits at 133HMz. PCI-X revisions call for increasing clock speeds (233, 566, and 800MHz) and wider data paths, with PCI Express being the next set of evolving specifications.

Bus Mastering

One of the primary benefits of the PCI/PCI-X bus is its bus-mastering capability. The older ISA bus would take all incoming information, from all its attached devices, and try to send that data to the proper destinations in whatever order. If one device was trying to move a large amount of data, the transfer would often be held up while the ISA bus tried to move low-priority information. This would be like a hospital emergency room without a triage nurse making decisions on the relative importance of incoming injuries.

The capability of both the bus and its attached devices to communicate with each other led to a change in the way the system uses Interrupt ReQuests (IRQs). We'll be discussing IRQs and DMAs in Chapter 4, but essentially, an interrupt (INT) is a request for the CPU's attention. These interrupts can come from either hardware or software. Early systems assigned a specific IRQ line, or *channel*, to each device.

The PCI bus is capable of monitoring each request and assigning changing (dynamic) IRQs to each request. The bus then works with the underlying IRQ controllers to take an open IRQ line and move the instructions.

 Bus mastering means that a particular device can take over the entire bus throughput, at any given time, to move priority information across the bus. We'll see throughout this book how concepts and ideas coming from one area of advancing technology find their way into the much smaller environment of the microcomputer. Keep an eye on how distributed processing and networking principles (found in Chapter 10, "Basic Networking") show up in memory modules, chipset architectures, and even the PCI bus.

To differentiate between the actual—or "real"—interrupt requests on each controller and chip from dynamic interrupts, the PCI bus uses a different, internal, system of assigning its own IRQs. Usually, these are called A, B, C, and D. The typical PCI bus has four slots, and therefore, four primary IRQs. That being said, you may still see PCI interrupts listed as numbers 1–4. We'll discuss the DMI Pool later in this chapter under "Supplementary Information," but you can see the way the typical four slots are assigned if you press the Pause key during an initial boot sequence.

PCI interrupts almost always take IRQ 9 through IRQ 12. This will be a problem in the real world of troubleshooting, but you should know the standard IRQ table (found in Chapter 4) for the exam.

An interesting problem with the PCI bus is that Windows (versions later than Windows 95 OS/A) might show many more than the traditional 16 IRQs. This has a lot to do with foundational changes in the Pentium family chip architecture, and goes beyond the scope of this book. Understand that although the PCI bus is managing many interrupt requests, CompTIA's motherboards continue to use only two IRQ controllers, with a total of 16 "real" IRQ lines.

Finally, you should know, in terms of general knowledge, that the PCI bus and bus mastering enable several devices to share a single expansion slot's IRQ. This applies to the PCI bus, but not to the ISA bus. Often you might see IRQ 9 being shared by multiple devices. Remember that this is handled by the bus, even though it might appear to result in IRQ conflicts. In the past, when multiple devices tried to interrupt the CPU at the same time, the system would crash. Arbitration (conflict resolution) circuitry, in today's chipsets and buses, generally manage to keep this from happening.

Older (legacy) devices, such as parallel ports (LPT) and serial ports (COM), rarely have Plug and Play technology included. As a result, you're still likely to see these ports connected to an ISA bus. The ISA slots may be slowly vanishing, but the underlying bus continues to exist as a hard-wired solution. Likewise, although a PCI bus can handle a video card, most systems include an accelerated graphics port (AGP) for video processing. Even SCSI host adapters and IDE controllers can connect with a PCI bus, but motherboards still tend to use an onboard set of IDE controllers for IDE drives, including many CD and DVD drives.

North Bridge and South Bridge

The original PCI bus was a sort of bridge between the processor and ISA bus. Actually, it introduced two new components called the *North Bridge* and the *South Bridge*. The North Bridge is generally used for high-speed interface cards, such as video accelerators, Synchronous RAM (SRAM), and memory. The South Bridge is generally used for slower devices such as USB ports, IDE drives, and ISA slots. As you can see in Figure 2.9, data flows from the CPU to the North Bridge, then out to the South Bridge in a sort of daisy chain. We discuss hub architecture in Chapter 5, but bridge architecture is more closely related to buses, and so we've included it here.

Pay attention to the L-1 and L-2 cache locations in Figure 2.9. Note the 400MHz processor bus connecting with the North Bridge. This bus is also referred to as the System Bus, or Front Side Bus (FSB). Also note the connection between the CPU and the L-2 cache. This is a Backside Bus. We also discuss the L-1 and L-2 cache in Chapter 3. Keep in mind that speeds aren't the important point; the concepts are what matter.

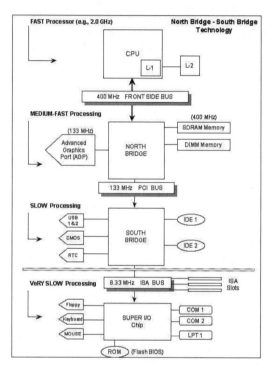

Figure 2.9   North Bridge, South Bridge, and Super I/O chip.

The South Bridge works in conjunction with what's called a Super I/O chip. The original Input/Output (I/O) ports—like the COMmunications (COM ports), as well as the Line Printer Terminal, or Line PrinTer (LPT ports)— were all separate devices on the motherboard. The Super I/O chip brought them all together onto one chip, reducing the space required. Usually, a manufacturer orders the Super I/O chip from a third-party manufacturer, and so many people don't consider it part of the chipset.

Older Pentium machines, in particular, reference the North Bridge and South Bridge of the PCI bus. Remember that the North Bridge is connected to the CPU for high-speed components. Data coming out of the North Bridge passes through to the South Bridge, which is used for "S"lower components (South and Slow start with "S"). On a map, North is usually on top, whereas South is usually on the bottom. It may help you if you think of "top" being top speed, or higher speed, with South being lower and slower.

North Bridge components are usually an accelerated graphics port (AGP), SRAM, and other memory chips. South Bridge components are usually the Universal Serial Buses (USB), IDE drives, ISA slots, the Super I/O chip with COM1, COM2, LPT1, and the floppy drives (A: and B:).

You should be careful to keep two concepts separate in your mind: The PCI bus is one thing, whereas PCI slots are something else. The bus is divided into the North and South Bridge. PCI slots connect expansion cards to the system. The bus is a set of specifications, but the actual slot holding the card is a component of that specification and bus. When you see a number of PCI slots on the motherboard, you can assume they all use a PCI bus.

The main difference between a PCI bus and a VL-Bus is that the PCI bus is a specifically designed, high-speed main expansion bus shared by multiple devices. The VL-Bus was a separate bus dedicated to a single device. Remember that the VLB ran at the same speed as the processor, making it useful for fast video data transfers. It was tied to the CPU's processor bus—almost as an extension. The PCI bus is entirely independent.

The PCI bus ran at 33MHz, which made it much faster than the older 8.3MHz ISA bus. Many computers have both a PCI and an ISA bus available on the motherboard. However, the ISA bus is gradually falling into disuse. You may see references to PCI-32 or PCI-64, referring to the width of different PCI buses. PCI-X specifies a 64-bit bus and uses clock speeds of 133MHz, 266MHz, and 533MHz.

Supplementary Information

At this time, we want to point out that technology is moving so quickly, with so many changes, that no book can hope to contain the latest and greatest, up-to-the-minute, bleeding-edge technology. You'll have plenty of time in your career to go out and find machines that far outstrip whatever specifications and capabilities we discuss in these chapters. However, keep in mind that passing the A+ certification exam is a one-time event, and you'll be required to give the correct response to whatever questions you find on the exam—not whatever questions you think *ought* to be on the exam! Whether or not those questions deal with today's technology, you have the choice of focusing on what you know is happening in the field, or focusing on what response CompTIA is asking for to a particular question. Remember: *The concept is important, not the current examples of how that concept is implemented.*

We include references under these "Supplementary Information" headings that point to the direction technology is moving at press time. Obviously, some of the information will either become obsolete very quickly, or never catch on in the open market. Chipsets and bus technology are a particular example of this problem. As such, we start with what is most likely to be on the actual exam, then include pointers on topics you can explore on your own. Preparation for the exam can be as minimal as you want, or you can choose to understand the entire surrounding field of whatever matches your interests. It's up to you.

Conventional PCI

The original PCI specification (and revisions 2.0, 2.1, and 2.2) was designed for fifth- and sixth-generation Pentiums, partly to take advantage of the chip's Virtual Mode Extensions (VME). Although there may be a link to the VME bus, there isn't any law that says a particular acronym must mean only one thing. In a nutshell, these (programming) extensions are particularly useful when running virtual DOS sessions under Windows (and the concept of dynamic interrupts). Remember that the VL-Bus was, for the most part, an extension of the processor's memory bus, which tied the bus to the chip. The PCI bus broke that link, handing over flow-control decisions to the bus and chipset. But the PCI bus was still directly tied to the underlying chipset, which is part of the reason Intel tried to move to hub architecture. Hub architecture, discussed in Chapter 5, gave independent control to low-level process management controllers.

Aside from the specific features of the PCI bus, the fact that it's a set of standard specifications allows the bus to be used in environments other than a PC. When VESA introduced the VL-Bus, expansion bus architecture began to split into different directions. The SCSI bus was providing connectivity with devices designed for the Macintosh, and another type of bus was the VME bus (IEEE-1014). VME, meaning VERSA Module Eurocard, had a throughput of 40–50MB/s, and was, at the time, the fastest bus around. When the PCI specification changed to a 64-bit architecture, the CompactPCI bus could generate throughputs higher than 200MB/s. (VME was developed in 1980, by a consortium including Motorola, Mostek, and Signetics corporations.)

The Peripheral Component Interface was originally called the PCI Local Bus, and developed as a bridge-type workaround for the slow ISA bus. When it first came out, it was configured as a 32-bit bus, running at 33MHz, with a throughput of 133MB/s. The specifications changed, following rapid increases in CPU speeds, to become a 64-bit bus, running at 66MHz and changing throughputs. PCI is implemented as PCI (Rev 2.2), PCI-X (64-bit, 133MHz), cPCI (Compact PCI using a VME form factor), and PC104-Plus (an add-on to the ISA form factor).

PCI was designed around 5.0V (volts), but as the overall industry moved toward lower voltages, later PCI specifications call for 3.3V signaling. This helps the bus to better integrate with laptops and other portable devices. Keep in mind that a bus must integrate with the underlying motherboard and chipset. If the main board is running at one voltage, any integrated peripherals must run at about the same voltage. With modern processors capable of high performance at lower voltages, the main PCI bus had to change to run with a lower overall voltage. During the transition, there was a "universal card," which was an expansion card running at both 3.3 and 5.0 volts.

NOTE We've mentioned the CompactPCI bus, but you should know that this is not a PCI-SIG specification. Instead, cPCI is a specification developed and promoted by the PCI Industrial Computer Manufacturers Group (PCIMG).

Low-Profile PCI, Mini PCI

We've mentioned riser cards, which make it possible to insert a vertically oriented card into a slot and attach additional horizontally oriented cards. For the most part, this is purely a way to save space inside a system box. The Low-Profile PCI specification describes cards that are the same as standard PCI cards, but use a shorter form factor and include a different type of mounting bracket. Low-Profile PCI is primarily designed for desktop and server boxes, and is short enough to possibly eliminate the need for a riser card.

Mini PCI is yet another modification of the PCI specification, designed more for the mobile computing environment and small devices. The Mini PCI was originally developed for integrated peripherals such as modems and network cards. These cards and buses are primarily available to original equipment manufacturers (OEMs) and aren't designed to be used by the typical PC owner. You'll see the Mini PCI specification implemented in such things as laptop and notebook computers, docking stations, and printers. Low-Profile PCI uses much of the existing motherboard design, whereas Mini PCI requires an entirely different interface.

Although Low-Profile PCI was originally backward compatible with the standard PCI brackets, the industry movement toward the lower voltages makes newer cards incompatible with 5.0V systems. One of the places where

Low-Profile PCI is entering the market is with 10/100 Fast Ethernet adapter cards.

PCI Revision 2.3

The PCI specification is a living standard, changing as quickly as possible to meet evolving systems. Revision 2.3 no longer supports the 5.0V original standard, moving, instead, toward the newer 3.3V power requirements. Additionally, PCI 2.3 also provided for support of 3.3V universally keyed cards, meaning they could be inserted into a slot only one way—the correct way. PCI 66, PCI-X, Mini PCI, and Low-Profile PCI support only 3.3V signaling on 3.3V keyed system board connectors and 3.3V and Universal keyed add-in cards.

PCI-X (Revision 1.0b)

We've said that PCI was a 32-bit bus, clocked at 33/66MHz, with a 133MB/s throughput. PCI-X was a response to faster CPUs with wider processor buses and greater throughput. The new version took on the "X" (extended) description and the older specification became known as Conventional PCI. PCI-X initially provided for a 133MHz clock speed, allowing for 1GB/s throughput. Additionally, the constant movement toward greater efficiency allows for better use of bandwidth, regardless of the clock frequency.

When PCI-X is installed on an older system, it's backward compatible with the original clock speeds. Because of the built-in intelligence of the bus, even when a conventional PCI card is installed on a newer bus, PCI-X is smart enough to run the older card at either 33MHz or 66MHx, depending on the needs of the device. The downside, much like with IDE controllers, is that the overall bus then restricts other bus devices to the lower frequency. When two drives with different speeds are placed on an IDE controller, the controller limits throughput to the slowest drive (which is why you should put a CD or DVD drive on its own controller).

PCI-X (Revision 2.0)

The first version of PCI-X, sometimes called PCI-X66 and PCI-X133, refers to the two supported bus clock speeds. With a 64-bit configuration, the bus allowed for 1GB/s throughput. The second major revision specified 266MHz and 533MHz clock speeds, and can produce upwards of 4.3GB/s throughput. Note that although the bandwidth is capable of these numbers, that doesn't necessarily mean the bus produces the actual throughput.

We discuss parity checking and ECC memory in Chapter 3, but the PCI-X 2.0 standard introduces ECC support to the bus. This makes for better reliability as data moves through the bus, with single-bit repairs to faulty data and a capability to detect, at least, double-bit errors. This revision takes on support for 10GB Fibre Channel, 10GB Ethernet, RAID controllers, SCSI and iSCSI, InfiniBand Architecture, and other high-speed transfer architectures.

InfiniBand Architecture is a set of specifications under construction by yet another industry group. Currently, file servers connect to many different systems using proprietary interfaces and designs for each connection. The result is a mess (technical term) of cables and management problems. InfiniBand will provide a unified architecture for these many separate connections (**http://www.infinibandta.org**).

Desktop Management Interface (DMI)

We'll be discussing the Plug and Play standard later in this book, but it comes down to a set of standards by which hardware devices, system BIOS, and the operating system can communicate. Much of the communication involved centers around configuration and data movement. When you install Windows, the OS examines the hardware connected to the motherboard and puts together a list of drivers in the Device Manager. Windows also installs the correct configuration settings (you hope) for whatever devices it finds and understands. DMI is designed to give Windows (or other operating systems) those configuration settings.

The DMI standard provides for a "layer" of software between the system components and the rest of the overall system. Management of the standard is done by the Desktop Management Task Force (DMTF), an industry group that includes Hewlett-Packard, IBM, Intel, Microsoft, Apple, and Novell, to name only a few of the hundreds of vendors and developers involved. DMI is a sort of sideways evolution of PnP, designed to help manage individual PCs, file servers, peripherals, and applications all the way from the network level to the desktop. One of the goals is to put DMI on all microcomputers and network components, across multiple platforms.

Chapter 10, "Basic Networking," takes a short look at the OSI model—a set of instruction standards, layered one above another, each of which helps to explain all the parts of a network and how they interact. DMI is similar to the OSI model, but works on the BIOS and system level. Manufacturers can use DMI standards to ensure that each PnP device can store configuration information in Management Information Format (MIF) files. The DMI Service Layer stores the information to an MIF database. If it all works, DMI also provides software diagnostics tools to help systems administrators troubleshoot configuration problems.

Any intelligent component of a standalone system or network can use DMI to access the MIF database, then configure devices either during the startup process or on the fly. One of the reasons hot-swapping is possible is that this active communication between components keeps the entire system always aware of itself. In other words, if computers are supposed to be so smart, why can't they fix themselves on their own? (Don't answer that: We need a constant supply of A+ technicians!) For more information about DMI 2.0 compliance, visit `http://www.dmtf.org`.

Another way to think of DMI is to relate it somewhat to ActiveX controls or the JavaScript language. As a computer logs on to a Web site, increasing intelligence coming from both software and hardware enables the computers to "speak" with each other and move information or application software back and forth. If a site requires a particular multimedia tool, for example, it can query your system to find out whether or not the necessary components exist.

You won't need to know this for the exam, but it might help you to understand a system hang at the "Verifying DMI Pool..." message. The Desktop Management Interface includes the following layers:

Service Layer—Collects and manages information from products in the management information format database (MIFD).

Management Applications—Remote or local programs for changing, interrogating, controlling, tracking, and listing the elements of a desktop system.

Management Interface (MI)—The boundary between the Service Layer and Management Applications.

Manageable Products—Hardware, software, or peripherals that occupy or are attached to a desktop computer or network server.

Component Interface (CI)—The boundary between the Service Layer and Manageable Products, such as hardware peripherals and software components (word processors, spreadsheets, and so on).

Management Information Format Database—Contains the information about the products on the system, coming from the MIF files provided with each manageable product.

Verifying DMI Pool

One of the more aggravating problems with system startups is the inexplicable crash that leaves the DMI pool verification message on the screen. Keep in mind that we're still in the infancy stages of computer technology, so although everyone is trying to make PCs easier to work with and fix, not everything works as well as it eventually will. DMI problems are so compli-cated that few people have any real solution. We'll include some of the diag-nostics steps here, but we'll also encourage you to do some research into DMI on your own.

> These ideas are meant as suggestions only, and carry no guarantees at all as to whether they will work on your system. Nor do we recommend even attempting some of these suggestions unless you have a total backup and a current emergency start disk. Working at this level of the system is always extremely dangerous in terms of completely disabling the entire system. If you don't know what you're doing, don't even try it.

Hard drives are a common cause of DMI crashes, so you might disconnect the drive and tell the CMOS that nothing is installed. Set the BIOS to its default setting and restart the machine. Sometimes the BIOS must be upgraded, or there might be a problem with the chip itself. Another annoy-ing problem can show up with internal and external caches, or even with Shadow RAM. Go into the BIOS and disable any caching. Make sure you write down the original setting; then try booting to a floppy disk.

DMI pool crashes can often be linked to incorrect information coming from any device in the system. Hard drives might have a failed Master Boot Record (MBR), in which case reinstalling the system files or running the FDISK /MBR switch might help. We discuss SYS.COM and FDISK.EXE in the Operating System section of this book. In some instances, resetting the CMOS might be all that's necessary.

Finally, electrostatic discharge (ESD) is a good candidate for the source of a DMI crash. Quality components almost always come with a sealed, slivery anti-static bag. If the bag is opened, punctured, or missing, you stand a good chance of having a damaged component. We'll examine ESD in Chapter 6, "Basic Electronics," but you should weigh the advantages of bargain-basement parts against DMI pool problems.

Memory Buses

We measure memory speed in *nanoseconds* (billionths of a second), abbrev-iated as the lowercase "ns." On the other hand, we measure CPU speeds in megahertz (millions of cycles per second) or gigahertz (billions of cycles per second). Blending the two, we come up with how many *million instructions per second (MIPS)* a processor can complete. Disk speed is measured in millisec-onds (thousandths of a second), and a hard disk typically reads information at around 100 *reads per second*—not to be confused with Revolutions Per

Minute (RPM). A floppy disk generally performs 10 reads per second, whereas RAM can make a billion reads per second. So moving data in and out of RAM is extremely fast—much faster than moving it to and from a disk.

Using North-South Bridge architecture, the CPU no longer directly connects with the system memory. Instead, it works in combination with the North Bridge and the memory controller to move data bits in and out of main memory. In Figure 2.10 you can see how the CPU uses additional buses to connect with the L-1 cache inside the processor housing, and the L-2 cache outside the housing. In modern computers, the L-2 cache is usually internal to the housing, and you might find an external Level 3 (L-3) cache using the backside bus.

 The A+ exam generally expects the Level 2 cache to be external. When in doubt, check the various responses and see whether you can isolate the correct assumption from your choices. Be aware that with so many modern CPUs having built-in L-2 caches, you might also find a set of responses indicating that the L-3 cache is external and the L-1 and L-2 are both internal.

A CPU has a number of very small places inside the housing where it stores bits and bytes of data. Technically speaking, the storage places inside a CPU are called *registers*. The data storage locations on a DIMM are called *cells*. In Chapter 3 we'll discuss how memory modules store bits of data in capacitors or transistors. For now, understand that data is constantly moving in and out of registers and is being temporarily stored in main memory or cache memory.

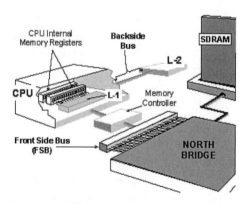

Figure 2.10 The Front Side Bus.

Front Side Bus

The North Bridge handles fast data transfers into and out of system memory, working with the memory controller over a bus. This bus is the subject of fair amount of controversy, with some people calling it the system bus and others calling it the Front Side Bus (FSB). You also may find references to a processor bus or a memory bus. We'll refer to it as the front side bus. System performance is based on a timing relationship between the CPU and the FSB, with the bus being clocked at a reduced multiple of the processor.

In other words, if you have an 800MHz Pentium 4, with an FSB clocked at 133MHz, the FSB is running at one sixth the speed of the chip. Doubling the speed of the FSB to 266MHz increases the bus to one third of the chip speed. Many of today's performance ratings are based on increasing the clock speed of the front side bus.

NOTE

Technical design and developments are constantly focusing on the FSB and how to increase its throughput. Wider processor buses and faster CPUs continually demand upgrades to all the other buses on the motherboard. We've tried to capture a moving set of standards in this book, but you can assume that whatever speeds we're using will be out of date—probably by the time you read this. That being said, the underlying principles and concepts are what you'll find on the A+ exam, and what you'll be tested on.

Once again: Don't confuse specific details of throughput and clock speeds with an understanding of the components and their function. Some of our speed examples use numbers that are more easily calculated in your head, while you're reading, and aren't a reflection of actual processor speeds in a modern machine.

Here's another example of FSB speed in relation to CPU speed. Suppose you have an 800MHz Celeron processor in a machine with a front side bus clocked at 3:1, or a third of the processor speed. Data transfers take place at 266MHz. Now suppose you have a machine with a 1GHz Pentium 4 and an FSB clocked at 4:1, or a quarter of the processor speed. In this instance, data transfers take place at 250MHz (1,000÷4). Which is the better system: the 800MHz or 1GHz machine? Can we say that a Pentium 4 is always better than a Celeron?

You begin to see that performance is very much tied to the speed of the front side bus. This isn't to say that the entire system is hanging on the FSB, but to point out that performance is becoming a combined measure of many different components—much like bandwidth is a combined calculation of many variables.

The backside bus, shown in Figure 2.10, connects the CPU with an external L-2 cache. Because the data path is extremely short and Level 2 caches usually use SRAM, data transfers take place at about the same speed as the CPU.

Chapter 3 discusses the L-1 and L-2 caches, as well as how a cache operates, but you should have a picture of how the various components of memory are connected.

PC Card (PCMCIA)

The Personal Computer Memory Card Industry Association (PCMCIA) card was introduced in 1990 to give laptop and notebook computers an expansion capability similar to that of desktop computers. Originally, the PC Card was designed to store memory on a card, but many manufacturers of peripherals came to realize it could be used to connect other I/O devices. Because no one could remember the acronym PCMCIA, it became known as the PC Card. One way to remember the acronym is that "People Can't Memorize Computer Industry Acronyms." These credit card–size expansion boards have the following features:

➤ They're produced in four types: Types I, II, III, and IV.

➤ They're differentiated into types according to card thickness in millimeters: Type I, 3.3mm; Type II, 5mm; Type III, 10.5mm; and Type IV, thicker than 10.5mm, but not yet standardized.

➤ They're included in the plug-and-play (PnP) specification.

➤ PC cards introduced the concept of combining the device and its I/O card on the card itself.

➤ Type I, II, and III form factors share an identical bus connector. Therefore, thinner cards can be installed in computer slots designed for thicker card formats.

➤ They're hot-swappable, meaning that you can remove one card and insert another without turning off the machine.

The PC Card specification eventually was upgraded to include something called CardBus. This redefined and enhanced the PCMCIA bus structure, with backward compatibility to PCMCIA Release 1 and 2. CardBus provided higher speeds than the PCMCIA bus, supporting a 32-bit data flow and memory paths. Note that CardBus cards do not plug into Release 2.x or earlier PCMCIA slots. Windows, for the most part, includes PnP recognition for most PC Cards.

Most newer laptops, using PC Card slots, use both Card software and Socket Services software. Card software, together with Socket Services software, is similar to the BIOS and underlying operating system found on desktop machines. Taken together, the software provides a standardized interface between the computer and the PC Card itself.

With the standardization of PC Cards, they can now be used not only in laptop and notebook computers, but also in personal digital assistants (PDAs) and other handheld devices. PC Cards are used for many things, including several types of RAM, pre-programmed ROM cards containing software applications, modems, sound cards, floppy disk controllers, portable hard drives, CDROM and SCSI controllers, Global Positioning System (GPS) cards, local area network (LAN) cards, and pagers, to name a few. A fascinating development in the world of physics indicates that today's nanotechnology has reached a point where an entire device can be added directly to a piece of wire. This is not something found on the exam, but we thought we'd pass the news along.

Summary—Bus Architectures

Buses, slots, transfer rates, throughput, and bandwidth are all very complicated concepts to master. Try not to get too worked up about remembering every single thing we've talked about in the previous segment. Remember that CompTIA is trying to test your knowledge of the basic concepts and how they apply to troubleshooting and repairing common PC problems. You'll have to be able to pull up certain details in the exam room, but many times you'll be able to use some of our test-taking strategies to help with names and numbers.

The exam is geared toward troubleshooting and problem-solving skills. Most of the trouble spots involving motherboards have to do with power supplies, over-clocking, and burnt-out boards. Bus problems typically mean IRQ conflicts and resolutions. We'll discuss interrupts in Chapter 4, so don't worry about them now. There is a small chance you may have to know about backward compatibility, and the main areas to watch are the ISA legacy slots and how PCI-X supports conventional PCI.

The important thing to remember regarding bus architecture and technology is that most of the developments have centered on how quickly we can move large amounts of information, coming from fast processors, back and forth between various other devices running at slower speeds. You already know that a CPU and memory module process data extremely fast. Likewise, a hard drive or printer port is going to move a whole lot slower. Make an effort to remember the following points:

➤ Throughput is measured in bytes per second (B/s), generally in megabytes or gigabytes. Bandwidth, the overall capability of a bus, takes into account the clock speed (in MHz), the data path (32-bit, 64-bit, 128-bit), transfer rates, and the physical composition of the electronic components.

➤ The main expansion buses you'll see on the exam are the ISA bus (16-bit) and the PCI bus (32-bit and 64-bit). Remember that ISA is clocked at about 8.33MHz, and PCI is clocked at 33/66MHz (PCI). PCI-X is clocked at 133/266/533MHz.

➤ PCI questions are likely to hit you for clock speeds, based on specification names and possibly revision numbers. Aside from changes to the clock speeds, the main thing to remember is the 32-bit and 64-bit data path expansion. Know which is which.

➤ Don't worry about the AGP in this chapter, as you'll see it discussed again, at length, in Chapter 9.

➤ MCA stands for IBM's Micro Channel architecture, and EISA (pronounced "ee-suh") represents the Extended ISA bus developed by the clone manufacturers. Both MCA and EISA had a 32-bit data path (as opposed to the 16-bit ISA bus), and EISA ended up being used in high-end file servers. MCA went away.

➤ The VESA organization developed the VESA Local Bus (32-bit), also called the VL-Bus, or VLB. It was tied to the central processor's memory bus and had timing problems. The main idea was to offload some of the video processing from the CPU and assign it to a separate graphics card. VLB was replaced by the more sophisticated PCI bus.

➤ You'll likely see a couple of questions having to do with North-South Bridge architecture. Remember which Bridge handles what components, and that slower devices are connected to the South Bridge. Bridge architecture has been replaced by hub architecture, which we discuss in Chapter 5.

➤ Make a note of the four main PCMCIA (PC Card) types. You'll most likely be able to take the millimeter sizes from responses to questions, but you should know how to relate the types to their thickness measurements. Remember that PC Cards all use the same bus architecture, and they're hot-swappable. Make a note of CardBus and Socket Services configuration software.

Exam Prep Questions

Question 1

Which one of the following designs and form factors will ensure that a device is not damaged when it is attached to a motherboard?

- O A. ATX riser
- O B. Baby AT DIN connector
- O C. Colored ribbon cable
- O D. Keyed connector

Answer D is correct. Keyed connectors have a notch or groove in the molded plastic connector casing that allow the connector only a correct orientation. Older computers often had problems with power connectors, expansion cards, and other connectors being inserted backwards or upside down. Answer A is incorrect because an ATX riser might refer to a riser card, used to install expansion cards horizontally, but it isn't a real term. Answer B is incorrect because a DIN connector is a keyboard connection and has no bearing on damaging the system. DIN connectors were used with Baby AT and AT systems. Answer C is incorrect because there's no such thing, technically, as a colored ribbon cable. A single wire or edge of a ribbon cable might be color-coded to provide orientation, but not the entire cable.

Question 2

The PCI64 bus supports which of the following clock speeds? (Choose all that apply)

- ❏ A. 66MHz
- ❏ B. 512MHz
- ❏ C. 133MHz
- ❏ D. 332MHz

Answers A and C are correct. Answer B is incorrect because none of the buses are clocked at 512MHz, although the number is often used in computer terminology. Answer D is incorrect because neither is any bus clocked at 332MHz. The number is thrown in for our dyslexic friends and readers. Be on the lookout for reversed numbers that may take advantage of the way your particular brain works.

Question 3

Many expansion slots can support multiple clock speeds, which are set with the DOS **Time** command.

○ A. True

○ B. False

Answer B, false, is correct. Motherboards and expansion buses use oscillators to define the overall timing for components. Although many boards and buses do support multiple clock speeds, those speeds are usually set through jumpers or internal manufacturing design. Answer A is incorrect because the DOS Time command is used to set or display the time of day, and that time is derived from the motherboard clock.

Question 4

What type of expansion bus is included on most system boards? (Choose all that apply)

❑ A. MCA

❑ B. ISA

❑ C. PCI

❑ D. EISA

❑ E. VESA

Answers B and C are correct. Most system boards include both the PCI bus and the ISA bus for compatibility, although this is changing. Answer A is incorrect because the MCA bus, developed by IBM, never really caught on. Answer E is incorrect because the VL-Buses (VESA) were predominantly used for video controllers prior to the adoption of the PCI bus. Answer D is incorrect because the EISA bus became primarily a network file server niche-market bus, not used on "most" system boards.

Question 5

> Which of the following components are usually connected to the South Bridge of a 440-series chipset? (Choose all that apply)
>
> ❑ A. L-2 cache
>
> ❑ B. SDRAM
>
> ❑ C. USB 0
>
> ❑ D. Master IDE drive
>
> ❑ E. AGP

Answers C and D are correct. The North Bridge is for high-speed devices such as SDRAM memory chips and an applied graphics port (AGP), making answers B and E incorrect. The South Bridge connects lower-speed devices such as the USB ports, IDE drive controllers, and CMOS. The Super I/O chip is for very slow COM and LPT ports. Answer A is incorrect because the L-2 cache is usually part of the chip die, or very close to the CPU and connecting with its own backside bus.

Question 6

> The Device Manager shows that two devices are successfully installed and working with a single IRQ. Which of the following is taking place?
>
> ○ A. Dynamic Interrupt Management
>
> ○ B. Bus mastering
>
> ○ C. Bus management
>
> ○ D. IRQ Controller Mastering

Answer B is correct. Bus mastering is where a device can take control of a bus and manage how data passes across that bus. Answer A is incorrect because there's no such term as "dynamic interrupt management." Answer C is incorrect because although a device is managing the bus, the correct term is "mastering" the bus. Answer D is incorrect because an IRQ controller is incapable of controlling device data.

Need to Know More?

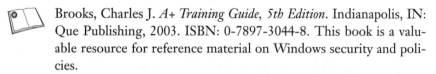 Brooks, Charles J. *A+ Training Guide, 5th Edition*. Indianapolis, IN: Que Publishing, 2003. ISBN: 0-7897-3044-8. This book is a valuable resource for reference material on Windows security and policies.

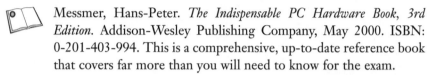 Messmer, Hans-Peter. *The Indispensable PC Hardware Book, 3rd Edition*. Addison-Wesley Publishing Company, May 2000. ISBN: 0-201-403-994. This is a comprehensive, up-to-date reference book that covers far more than you will need to know for the exam.

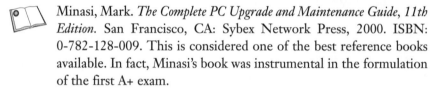 Minasi, Mark. *The Complete PC Upgrade and Maintenance Guide, 11th Edition*. San Francisco, CA: Sybex Network Press, 2000. ISBN: 0-782-128-009. This is considered one of the best reference books available. In fact, Minasi's book was instrumental in the formulation of the first A+ exam.

Rosch, Winn. *Hardware Bible, 5th Edition*. Indianapolis, IN: Sams Publishing, 1999. ISBN: 0-789-717-433. This is a well-organized reference book that covers software issues as well as hardware.

Mueller, Scott. *Upgrading and Repairing PCs, 14th Edition*. Indianapolis, IN: Que Publishing, 2000. ISBN: 0-7897-2745-5. This is one of our favorites! If you are only going to have one reference book, give this one serious consideration.

Mueller, Scott. *Upgrading and Repairing PCs: A+ Certification Study Guide, Second Edition*. Indianapolis, IN: Que Publishing, 2001. ISBN: 0-7897-2453-7.

Freedman, Alan. *Computer Desktop Encyclopedia, 2nd Edition*. AMACOM, 1999. ISBN: 0-814-479-855. Great for a fast look-up or refresher.

Memory: Types and Forms

Terms you'll need to understand:

- ✓ Volatile and nonvolatile
- ✓ Memory register and memory cell
- ✓ BIOS and CMOS
- ✓ Synchronous (synchronized), and asynchronous (not synchronized)
- ✓ Cache hierachy, cache, buffer
- ✓ Fast Page Mode (FPM), Extended Data Out (EDO) memory
- ✓ RAM, DRAM, SRAM, SDRAM, RDRAM, DDR-SDRAM, VRAM
- ✓ DIP, SIMM, DIMM, RIMM
- ✓ Parity, ECC

Concepts you'll need to master:

- ✓ Read-only memory (ROM), Programmable ROM (PROM), and Random Access Memory (RAM)
- ✓ Memory address, grids, and matrix
- ✓ Memory refresh and wait states
- ✓ Clock multipliers
- ✓ Secondary memory caching, internal and external memory
- ✓ Memory pages
- ✓ Chip packaging and modular manufacturing
- ✓ Odd and even parity, error detection

Perhaps the most familiar parts of a computer are the central processing unit and the main memory. The main memory is the same as the "computer's memory," also commonly referred to as system memory, or RAM. In this chapter we examine memory chips and how they're packaged. In Chapter 5, "Processors and Chipsets," we then look at different types of processors.

Memory is only a temporary place to store information until a device can get to it. Essentially, the CPU uses memory to move program instructions and data in and out of that temporary storage area. A typical instruction might be a request to store a data bit somewhere. Another instruction might be to retrieve that bit from a particular place—an *address*. Data might be a number, a letter, or any other bit of information. Remember that a data bit is also a small charge of electricity.

Data becomes information when it takes on context (surrounding circumstances). 76 means nothing on its own, other than the fact that it's a number. Surround that number with context: "Tomorrow, the temperature is expected to reach 76," and it becomes information. RAM is like a holding tank for data on its way to becoming information.

Storage is any location where information can be placed and retained for some amount of time. Computer memory is temporary storage, in that it generally requires the presence of electrical current. *Volatile* memory can hold information only when a normal electrical current is present. *Nonvolatile* memory can hold information in the absence of an electrical current. System memory is, for the most part, volatile.

Compact memory cards, smart memory cards, and memory sticks used in digital photography are examples of nonvolatile memory. Although some amount of current is necessary to change information, that information then remains stored even when there is no further current. Remember that volatile memory requires a continuing supply of current.

Volatile, from the Latin "to fly," means that information "flies away" when there's no electricity to keep it in place. Television reporters often refer to an explosive situation as a volatile situation, meaning that it could change at any second. Volatile memory will lose all of its data when electricity is removed. Nonvolatile memory will maintain its data even without electricity.

Floppy disks, fixed disks, optical disks, and card media are all nonvolatile. However, although disks retain information without electrical current, we refer to them as permanent storage, not "memory." The terms *volatile* and *nonvolatile* are generally assigned to memory chips.

Permanence is a relative word. A burst of static electricity can completely wipe out any information on a magnetic storage device or in a memory chip. Optical disks store data in structural changes to the media, and so even ESD or close proximity to a magnet (electromagnetic interference) rarely affect that information. Chapter 6, "Basic Electronics," examines both ESD and EMI.

Conceptual Overview

Computer memory is fairly easy to remember when you've grasped the basic concepts. In a nutshell, a CPU uses transistors to handle bits of data. These transistors are grouped together into registers, making for small storage places inside the processor housing (the chip die). At some point, either the registers fill up or the instructions are completed. The CPU then works together with a memory controller to move data bits out to memory *cells*. Memory cells are typically capacitors that form small storage places on a memory chip. Both processor registers and memory cells have addresses. Every time a bit of data goes somewhere, it crosses a bus of some kind. That's it; now go pass the exam!

All right, so it's a bit—so to speak—more complicated than that. Most memory began as *dynamic random access memory (DRAM)*. The main engineering changes that have taken place have all been attempts to find ways of either speeding up the memory to match CPU speeds, or to speed up the CPU to match memory speeds. The rest of memory technology relates to moving bits of information across buses more quickly.

When we refer to speeding up memory, we usually mean increasing the speed of the memory chips, increasing the clock speed of associated buses, or handling larger pieces of data.

To understand memory addresses, you should first understand a grid or *matrix*. We're therefore going to use Table 3.1 to a slightly different fashion, making it into a sort of "mind map." If you can see the way the overall types of memory break down on a grid, then perhaps they'll be easier to remember.

A matrix is nothing more than an arrangement of columns and rows, like a spreadsheet or an Etch-a-Sketch. Columns go up and down across the page, and rows go left and right across the page. Remember the word "page." Column addresses are at the top; row addresses are along the side.

Cells going left to right (horizontally) in a row have an X coordinate. Cells going up and down (vertically) in a column have a Y coordinate. The direction of rows is called the X axis, and columns are called the Y axis. Combining X and Y coordinates gives us an *address* in the grid, like a cell address in a spreadsheet. A *memory page* is a range (group) of cell addresses within a row.

Table 3.1 Mind Map of Basic Memory Concepts		
Permanent Storage/Nonvolatile Memory		
Magnetic disks Optical disks Printed paper	Permanent	
Swap files	Temporary	
ROM BIOS Programmable ROM (Flash BIOS)	Nonvolatile	
Memory cards	Nonvolatile	
Volatile Memory	**Acronym**	**Packaging**
Random Access Memory	RAM	
Dynamic RAM—main memory	DRAM	DIP

Static RAM
  Cache Memory (L-1 and L-2)
  CMOS—(uses trickle charge battery)
	SRAM	SIMM or
		chip

Synchronous DRAM—main memory	SDRAM	DIMM
Rambus DRAM—main memory	RDRAM	RIMM
Double Data Rate SDRAM—main memory	DDR SDRAM	DIMM

We discuss several additional types of memory in this chapter, but the A+ exam is focused primarily on the types listed in Table 3.1.

Read-Only Memory (ROM)

Every computer uses both read-write (RW) memory and read-only (R) memory. We see these same designations applied to CD-RW and CD-R, or DVD-RW and DVD-R optical disks. "Writing to" memory is the same as placing information in a memory address. "Reading from" memory is the same as retrieving information from an address. Information can be temporarily stored (written) in RAM, then a moment later, taken out (read). New information can then be written to the same place. Although the acronym RAM stands for *random access memory*, think of it, for the moment, as read/write memory: It can be both written to and read from.

ROM is *read-only memory*, and typically, doesn't allow changes. ROM can have information written into it only one time. From that point on, all we can do is read whatever was put there. Imagine a bulletin board under glass at the back of a classroom. ROM information is like hard-copy notes placed under the glass. At the end of the day, we turn out the lights and everyone goes home. The words on the paper remain unchanged. The next day, the notes are exactly the way they were the day before.

ROM is nonvolatile because no electrical current is required for the information to remain stored. ROM chips are mostly used for BIOS, although the same concept and acronym applies to commercial pre-recorded compact disks. The *ROM* in CDROM stands for read-only memory. Although CD-RW and DVD-RW can be changed, they're referred to as permanent storage media.

In some instances, ROM can be changed through the use of certain tools. Flash ROM is nonvolatile memory that occasionally can be changed, such as when a BIOS chip must be updated.

A single letter can really mess you up on the exam if you don't pay close attention. We've seen questions like, "RAM BIOS is used to permanently store instructions for a hardware device: True or False?" (The answer is false.) Keep your eyes peeled, and remember that RAM sounds like RANdom. RAM is never used in BIOS. Because the BIOS instructions are permanent, they almost always use ROM.

RAM, on the other hand, is like a blackboard. It starts out empty, then during the day, information is written on it, read from it, and maybe even erased. When something is erased, new information is then written to the same place on the blackboard. At the end of the day, we turn off the lights and wash off the blackboard. Whatever data was on the board goes away forever. When you turn off the power to a computer, RAM no longer has the necessary electrical current to sustain the data in its memory cells. Once again, RAM is volatile because it can't store information without using electricity.

Windows sets aside (allocates) some amount of memory as resource memory. When we write and erase many times on a blackboard, we get a chalk build-up. Similarly, resource memory can sometimes become disorganized and confusing for Windows to read. You can repair this memory fragmentation either by re-starting the machine or by using specialized third-party software utilities.

RAM Versus ROM

RAM is to a computer as your attention span is to your mind. When you cram for this exam, you'll focus your attention on facts and figures, placing them into short-term memory just long enough to write them out to a piece of paper in the exam room. After the data is stored to the sheet of paper, you can "erase" the information in your attention area and bring in new data. New data might be an exam question, on which you can then perform calculations such as determining a correct answer. When you require the information you wrote to the paper, you can return it to your attention by reading the page.

The tear-away Cram Sheet on the front cover of this book is designed to give you the minimal basics of those difficult-to-remember facts you'll likely want to have handy during the exam. Although you can't bring the sheet into the exam room, you can try to remember them long enough to write them on the blank piece of paper you'll be given when you've entered the exam room.

The piece of paper in the example is similar to a floppy disk. There isn't a lot of room on the paper, but you can carry it easily in your shirt pocket. A loose-leaf binder or notebook would be more like a hard disk. Depending upon the size of the binder, you can store a lot more information than on a single piece of paper. If you were to engrave the information on the desk in the exam room (not allowed), it would be analogous to authoring a CDROM.

ROM is like your long-term memory, holding the things you remember from your past. This is also like the information stored in BIOS and CMOS. When the computer "wakes up," ROM settings provide an awareness of the size of the hard disk, the presence of a sound card, whether or not any memory exists (and how to use it), and simple access routines to permanent hardware.

Basic Input/Output System (BIOS)

When you turn on a PC, the processor first looks at the *basic input/output system* to determine the machine's fundamental configuration and environment. This information is stored in a ROM chip and largely determines what peripherals the system can support. BIOS instructions are updated regularly by the manufacturer, not by the end user. If the chip is made to be updated (re-programmed) by the end user, it is often called *Flash BIOS*, or sometimes, *Flash ROM*. These programmable chips are often referred to as EEPROM (pronounced *ee-prom*) chips, discussed in a moment.

In a human being, BIOS would be like waking up and learning that you have a head, two arms, and two legs. The POST would be like a quick self-assessment as to whether or not you can move your arms and legs, and how bad a headache you have. CMOS would be like knowing your name, your address, and that you were last configured as a drinking machine.

Shadow RAM

In Chapter 2, "Motherboards," we pointed out that memory speed has usually been measured in *nanoseconds* (billionths of a second). We measure processor speeds in megahertz (millions of cycles per second) or gigahertz (billions of cycles per second). Although gigahertz CPUs operate in billionths of a second, instructions executing out of other processors, such as BIOS chips, execute quite a bit slower. The CPU and other devices may have to repeatedly query the BIOS chip for simple but permanent instructions, thereby reducing system performance. Shadow RAM is a method of storing a copy of certain BIOS instructions in main memory, rather than leaving them in a chip. The process improves execution speed and avoids constant calls to the slower chip. Many computers provide an option to shadow both the BIOS and certain video functions.

DRAM, fast page mode (FPM), and extended data output (EDO) mode all measured memory access times in nanoseconds. A 70ns unit would be labeled a "7." A 60ns unit would be labeled a "6," and so on. The lower the number, the faster the memory (shorter access time). With the introduction of SDRAM, these time measurements became less accurate. At such short intervals, fractions began to lose any real meaning. Instead, it began to make more sense to use speed measurements in the same way as CPUs. For this reason, SRAM and SDRAM modules use ratings such as 66MHz, 100MHz, 133MHz, or 800MHz.

Programmable ROM

Here's an example of one-time, read-only memory: storing a book on CDROM. Technically, write-once, read-many (times) is written as WORM. A magnetic disk is write-many, read-many, but you won't see a WMRM acronym. Instead, we speak of re-writeable optical disks. CD-RW changed the way that we use CDs and DVDs, just as programmable ROM chips changed the BIOS.

A manufacturing mask is the photographic blueprint for the given chip. It's used to etch the complex circuitry into a piece (chip) of silicon. The overall combination of silicon wafers, circuits, and microscopic components making up a CPU is called the *die* (like one of a pair of dice). The formal name for a chip that cannot be modified is *mask ROM* (from the manufacturing mask). The following types of chips offer varying degrees of programmability:

➤ *Programmable ROM (PROM)*—Requires a special type of machine called a PROM programmer or PROM burner (like a CD burner) and can be changed only one time. The original chip is blank, and the programmer burns in specific instructions. From that point, it cannot be changed.

➤ *Erasable programmable ROM (EPROM)*—Uses the PROM burner, but can be erased by shining ultraviolet (UV) light through a window in the top of the chip. Normal room light contains very little UV light.

➤ *Electrically erasable programmable ROM (EEPROM)*—Can be erased by an electrical charge, then written to by using higher-than-normal voltage. EEPROM can be erased one byte at a time, rather than erasing the entire chip with UV light. Because these chips can be changed without opening a casing, they're often used to store programmable instructions in devices such as printers and other peripherals.

Flash BIOS

With advances in technology, most BIOS chips became Flash EEPROM. These chips make it easier to change the BIOS. Rather than pulling out an actual chip and replacing it with a newer one, upgraded programming can be downloaded through the Internet or a bulletin board service (BBS). A small installation program changes the actual program instructions, eliminating the need for opening the computer case.

These types of chips are sometimes called *Flash ROM* or *Flash memory*, and store data much as EEPROM does. They use a super-voltage charge to erase a block of data. However, as we said earlier, EEPROM can be erased only one byte at a time. Although both Flash ROM and EEPROM can perform unlimited read/write operations, they can be erased only a certain number of times. (Be aware that Flash memory is not the same thing as nonvolatile memory cards used in such devices as digital cameras.)

CMOS Memory

As you know, basic motherboards vary in components such as CD or DVD drives, hard drives, memory, and so forth. The CMOS chip is a particular type of memory (static RAM) used to store optional system settings for those components. For example, the board might have a floppy drive and some memory chips. The BIOS stores instructions as to how to reach those components, and the fact that they exist. The CMOS stores variable settings, such as the disk size, the number of platters, and how much memory happens to be installed.

CMOS tends to store information about "unexpected" devices, and settings are held in memory through the use of a small electrical charge. Although CMOS is technically volatile memory, a *trickle charge* comes from a battery installed on the motherboard. Even when the main power is turned off, the charge continues to maintain the settings. However, if the battery power fails, all CMOS information vanishes.

BIOS determines compatibility. Some modern BIOS settings are often stored in the CMOS chip. Older BIOS was completely stored in nonvolatile ROM chips, often soldered right onto the motherboard. Remember that the CMOS is almost always where the computer's configuration settings are stored. BIOS is where basic input/output routines for the computer are stored.

CMOS is different from ROM BIOS in that the CMOS settings require some source of electrical power. Nonvolatile memory doesn't require electricity at all. CMOS settings are essential to the configuration of a specific computer. BIOS instructions typically work with a generic type of motherboard and its chipset.

A symptom of a fading CMOS battery is that the system date begins to fluctuate, sometimes by months at a time. Backing up files and software are a standard part of keeping a current backup, but you should also have a report of the current CMOS settings. On many PCs, turning on a local printer, restarting the machine (as opposed to a first-time boot), and going into the CMOS settings can generate this type of report. Press the Print Screen key at each screen.

When you exit out of the CMOS setup, the machine will most likely restart. From within Windows, open a text editor (for example, Notepad) and print a blank page. The stored page in the printer comes out as part of the print job. From a DOS command line, you can send an end-of-form page request to the printer to print the last page in the printer's memory. The following ^L is actually created by pressing the Ctrl+L key. Type `echo ^L > prn`.

Most computers cannot access the PRN device before a successful boot process. Therefore, the Print Screen function may not work. However, a warm reset, as opposed to a power-down and cold reboot, often allows the Print Screen function to remain in low memory. If the Print Screen function doesn't remain loaded on a particular machine, the only other way to store the CMOS settings is to manually write them down on a piece of paper. We discuss other problems with CMOS in Chapter 16, "Troubleshooting."

Random Access Memory (RAM)

The memory experts over at Crucial Technology, a division of Micron Technology, Inc. (http://www.crucial.com) have created a great illustration of memory. We're going to modify their original inspiration, and expand it to include some of the related concepts discussed throughout this book. Imagine a motherboard as being like a printing business. Originally, there was only "the guy in charge" and a few employees. They all worked in a small building, and things were pretty disorganized. The CPU—the boss—is in charge of getting things done. The other components on the board all have been developed to lend a helping hand.

When the CPU finishes a processing job, it uses the address bus to set up memory locations for the results of its processing. It then sends the data to the memory controller, where each bit in every byte is stored in a memory cell. At some point, if the CPU needs the results again, it orders the memory controller to find the stored bits and send them back.

Dynamic RAM (DRAM)

In the old days, when the boss took in a print job, he'd have to go running back to the pressman to have it printed. The pressman is the memory controller, and the printing press is a memory chip. (The print job is a set of bits the CPU needs to move out of its registers.) The pressman would examine each document he got from the boss, character by character, and grab matching lead blocks, individually carved with each letter. He would then place each block of lead into a form, one by one. In other words, each bit gets its own address in a matrix.

After the form was typeset (filled with letters), the pressman slopped on ink and put a piece of paper under the press. He would crank down a handle and print a copy of the document. Then he had to re-ink the grid to get it ready to print another copy. This is much like the process where a memory controller takes bits from the CPU, examines them, then assigns each one a memory address. The "printing" step is the moment the storage takes place in the memory cells. Keep an eye on that moment, because the re-inking step relates to a memory refresh.

NOTE

A controller is a small device, usually a single chip, that controls data flow for a particular piece of hardware. A memory chip is also a device, and the memory controller executes various instructions as to how to use the chip. A disk drive controller contains instructions to operate the drive mechanics. Most PC motherboards use simple controllers for the basic I/O ports, as well as having two controllers for IDE drives.

Nowadays you can buy a toy printing kit, with many letters engraved on pieces of rubber. You slide each piece of rubber into a rail, one by one. After you've inserted a complete line of letters, you apply some ink and stamp the line onto a piece of paper. When you're finished, you remove each letter, one by one, and start all over again. Suppose you could insert an entire line of rubber letters all at once? Wouldn't that be a whole lot faster? That was the idea behind FPM and EDO memory, which we'll look at later in this chapter.

NOTE

Here's a bit of trivia: The space above and below a line of printing is called the leading—pronounced as "led-ding." This space was the extra room on a lead block surrounding each carved letter on those original printing presses.

Memory Refresh and Wait States

DRAM cells are made up of many capacitors that can either hold a charge (1) or not hold a charge (0). One of the problems with capacitors is that they leak (their charge fades). This is somewhat similar to ink coming off each letter block during a print job. A memory refresh is when the memory controller checks with the CPU for a correct data bit, then re-charges a specific capacitor. While a memory refresh is taking place, the memory controller is busy and can't work with other data. (Remember that "moment," earlier?)

 When two devices attempt to exchange information, but one of them is busy doing something else, we speak of a *wait state*. The CPU is often the fastest device in a system, and so it often has to wait for other devices. The more wait states, the less efficiency and the slower the performance of the overall system.

One of the big problems with DRAM, to follow the story, was that at any given time, the boss wouldn't know what the pressman was doing. Neither did the pressman have any idea of what the boss was doing. If the boss ran in with a new document while the pressman was re-inking the press, he'd have to wait until the guy was done before they could talk. This is like the CPU waiting for the memory controller to complete a memory *refresh*.

If there were some way to avoid the capacitor leakage, the CPU and memory controller wouldn't have to constantly waste time recharging memory cells. Fewer wait states would mean faster throughput. Without the recharging cycle, the controller could also avoid interrupting the CPU for copies of data bit information.

Refreshing a Bit Charge

Technically speaking, a *bit* is a pulse of electrical current. When the CPU moves a bit out to memory, it sends a pulse over a signal trace (like a very tiny wire). The pulse moves through the memory controller, which directs the charge to a small capacitor. The charge trips a switch in the controller, indicating that the capacitor is in use. The controller then "remembers" which capacitor stored that pulse.

The memory controller recharges the capacitors on a cyclical basis, whether or not they really need it. The timing for the recharge is designed to be well before significant leakage would take place. Note that Static RAM (SRAM) works with transistors, rather than capacitors. Transistors are switches—either on or off. Unlike capacitors, transistors don't leak, but remain switched on or off, as long as a small amount of current remains present.

Transistors provide a performance increase over capacitors when they're used in memory chips. Because the transistors in SRAM don't require constant refreshes to prevent leakage, data changes only when the CPU sends out an instruction pulse. This makes SRAM a lot faster than DRAM and SDRAM.

Static RAM (SRAM)

Be careful that you don't confuse *Static* RAM (SRAM) with Synchronous DRAM (SDRAM). SRAM is referred to as being static, because when its transistors are set, they remain that way until actively changed. *Static* comes from the Latin *staticus*, meaning unchanging. It relates to a Greek word meaning to make a stand. *Dynamic* comes from the Greek *dynamikós*, meaning force or power. In a manner of speaking, dynamic RAM requires memory refresh logic to "force" the capacitors to remember their stored data.

SRAM is *static memory*. SDRAM is *synchronous dynamic memory*. Both chips require electrical current to retain information, but DRAM and SDRAM also require memory refreshes to prevent the capacitors from leaking their charge. SRAM uses power to switch a transistor on or off, and doesn't require additional current to refresh the switch's state.

Transistors can be built onto a chip either close together or far apart. In the same way we refer to trees growing closely together or farther apart as the *density* of the forest, so, too, do we refer to SRAM *densities*. Depending upon how many transistors are used in a given area, SRAM is categorized as either *fast* SRAM (high-density), or *low-density* SRAM (slower).

Fast SRAM is more expensive to manufacture, and uses significantly more power than low-density chips (watts versus microwatts, respectively). Because transistors are also usually placed farther apart than capacitors, SRAM uses more chips than DRAM to produce the same amount of memory. Higher manufacturing costs and less memory per chip mean that fast SRAM is typically used in Level 1 and Level 2 caches, where speed is critical. Low-density SRAM chips are more often used on less important devices, or for battery-powered backup memory such as CMOS.

Secondary memory caches (L-1 and L-2) are usually SRAM chips, which are extremely fast (as fast as 7–9ns, and 2–5ns for *ultra-fast* SRAM). Level 2 cache is usually installed in sizes of 256KB or 512KB.

SRAM is also used for CMOS configuration setups and requires a small amount of electricity. This current is provided by a backup battery on the system board. SRAM comes on credit-card-sized memory cards, available in 128KB, 256KB, 512KB, 1MB, 2MB, and 4MB sizes. Typical CMOS battery life is 10 or more years.

Asynchronous Memory

Getting back to the story, DRAM has another problem. Each time the pressman finished a job and was ready to take it back to the boss, he'd come running into the front office and interrupt whatever was going on. If the boss was busy with a customer, then the pressman would stand there and shout, "Hey boss! Hey boss! Hey boss!" until eventually he was heard (or punched in the face—an IRQ conflict). Once in awhile, just by luck, the pressman would run into the office when there weren't any customers and the boss was free to talk.

The CPU only sends a request to the memory controller on a clock tick. The clock is always ticking, and the CPU tries to do something with every clock tick. Meanwhile, the controller has run off to track down the necessary bits to send back to the CPU, taking time to do so. Think of the clock pulses as a pendulum, always swinging back and forth (positive and negative polarity). The CPU can't connect with the controller again until the clock's pendulum swings back its way, opening up another "tick." The CPU in Figure 3.1 can attach and send off a request, or take back a bit only when the clock ticks— when the pendulum is on its side. Meanwhile, with asynchronous memory, the controller isn't paying any attention to the clock at all.

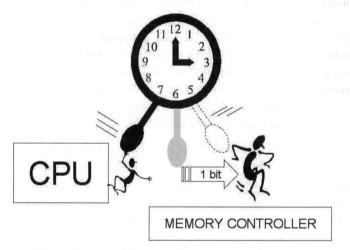

Figure 3.1 Moving data on the clock tick.

In a DRAM setup—unsynchronized memory—only the CPU transmits and receives according to a clock tick. The memory controller has no idea a clock is ticking, and tries to send data back to the CPU, unaware of the swinging pendulum.

Synchronized DRAM (SDRAM)

Interruptions are known as *Interrupt Requests (IRQs)* and, to mix metaphors, they are like a two-year-old demanding attention. One way to handle them is to repeat "not now...not now...not now" until it's a good time to listen. Another way to handle an interruption is to say, "Come back in a minute and I'll be ready to respond then." The problem is explaining to the two-year-old what you mean by "a minute." We'll discuss IRQs in Chapter 4, "Processor Mechanics, IRQs, and DMA."

One day the boss had a great idea. There was a big clock in the front office (the motherboard oscillator) and he proposed that both he and the pressman wear a watch. That way, both of them could tell time. It was a novel idea: The boss would then be able to call out to the pressman that he had a job to run, and the pressman could holler back, "I'll be ready in a minute."

This could also work the other way around. When the pressman finished a job, he could call out to the boss that he was ready to deliver the goods. The boss could then shout back that he needed another minute because he was busy with a customer. Either one of them could watch the clock for a minute to go by, doing something else until the other one was ready to talk.

Another way to think of clock ticks is to imagine a ski lift. Regardless of whether anyone takes a seat, an endless chain goes up and down the slope. Each seat is a clock tick, and either the CPU or the memory controller can put a data bit on a seat. Synchronization is sort of like waiting until a seat comes by before putting a data bit on it. Asynchronous is something like trying to shove a data bit toward the ski lift without paying any attention at all to whether or not there's a seat nearby. Usually, the bit goes nowhere and the device has to try again, hoping a seat just happens to show up.

An interesting feature of SRAM is that it allows for timing and synchronization with the CPU. The same idea was retrofitted to DRAM chips, and synchronized memory was born. DRAM is called *asynchronous* because it reacts immediately and on its own, to any given instruction. SDRAM is *synchronous* because it waits for a clock tick before responding to instructions.

 SDRAM provides a way for the memory controller and CPU to both understand clock ticks, and to adjust their actions according to the same clock.

Cycles and Frequencies

Any business can make more money by choosing different growth paths. One path is to move the product along faster. Speeding things up means that in a given time period, we can ship out more stuff (technical term). More stuff means more money, and the business grows. System performance is no different in a computer, and some improvements have come about by simply making things go faster.

Taking half as long to move a byte means moving twice as many bytes in a given time. If it takes 10 ticks to move one byte, then using 5 ticks to move the same byte means faster throughput. In other words, we can keep the byte the same size and move it in less time. This is essentially the underlying principle of multipliers and half ticks, and gave rise to *double data rate (DDR)* memory.

The power supply converts alternating current (AC) to direct current (DC), but that doesn't mean we never see alternating current again. Consider the oscillator, vibrating back and forth very quickly. How would that be possible, unless the associated electrical charges were moving back and forth? In fact, some components in a computer re-convert the incoming direct current to very low amperage alternating current. This isn't ordinary AC power, but means that small amounts of electricity reverse direction (polarity) for the purposes of timing and signaling.

Timing cycles are represented as waves moving up and down through a midpoint. The height between the top (peak) and bottom (trough) of a single wave cycle is called the *amplitude*. The number of waves being generated in a single second is called the *frequency*. We mentioned frequency in Chapter 2, in our discussion of bandwidth and broadband, but let's take a closer look at the specific concept.

Signal information moves at some frequency number. In Chapter 11, "Cables and Connectors," we reference various types of wire specifications, but as an example, Category 4 low-grade cable specifies a transmission rate of 20MHz. This means signals are passing through the wire at a cycle rate of twenty million waves per second. To produce both the timing of the cycles, and the characteristic up-reverse-down pattern of a wave, the electrical current must be moving in an alternating, cyclical flow pattern. (Think of your hand moving back and forth at one end of a tub of water. Although your arm is moving horizontally, the pulses of water are measured vertically.) The reversing directions of alternating current produce pulses of electricity that we see as waves on an oscilloscope.

Clock Speed and Megahertz

Clock speed is a frequency measurement, referring to cycles per second. It's usually written in *megahertz (MHz)*, where "mega" refers to 1 million cycles per second and "giga" refers to one billion cycles per second. One cycle per second is 1Hz. The motherboard oscillator—a sort of electronic clock—is configured through jumpers to produce a specific frequency. Once again, the number of waves passing a given point in one second, from the start to finish of each wave, is the frequency of the cycle.

A single clock tick (wave cycle) is measured from the point where a wave begins to move upwards, all the way down and through a midline, to the point where the wave moves back up and touches the midline again. Figure 3.2 is a *sine* wave, with smooth up and down movements very similar to waves you see in water. Waves come in various shapes, but the two we'll be concerned with are the sine wave and the square or *pulse* wave. When you look at any signal wave on an oscilloscope, you'll see that the name refers to its actual shape.

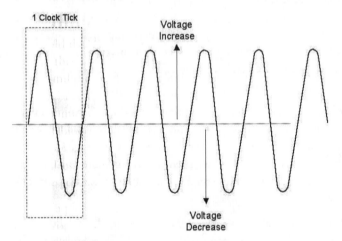

Figure 3.2 A sine wave.

When you hear a sine wave generated on a synthesizer oscillator (not so different from a computer oscillator), it sounds very smooth, like a flute. The many steps taking place as the wave moves up and down make it an analog signal. We'll discuss the difference between analog and digital in Chapter 6, "Basic Electronics." A pulse wave, on the other hand, sounds very harsh, like a motorcycle engine. Pulse waves have three components we're interested in: the midline, the peak, and the trough. Figure 3.3 shows a pulse or square wave.

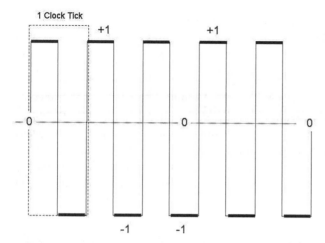

Figure 3.3 A square wave.

Note that in Figure 3.3, we've highlighted the top and bottom of the wave with a heavier, thicker line. The actual wave is the same signal strength, but we want you to see how a pulse wave is much like the on/off concept of any binary system. When we speak of the leading edge of a wave, we can also speak of the immediate-on, top of a pulse. Likewise, the trailing edge can be the immediate-on, bottom of the wave. The top is one polarity and can take on a +1 setting, whereas the bottom is the reversed polarity and can take on a -1 setting. When the wave is at the immediate-off centerline, it has a 0 setting.

Clock Multipliers

A computer timing oscillator is a piece of crystal. When it's connected to an electrical current, the crystal begins to vibrate, sending out very fast pulses of current. Pulses from the oscillator enter a frequency synthesizer, where the main frequency can be changed and directed to different components. The various fractional speeds are set with jumpers. Generally, the motherboard uses one fraction of the crystal's vibration, which constitutes the motherboard speed. The CPU uses a different fraction, usually faster than the motherboard.

This is highly simplified for the purpose of creating an example only.

Suppose the crystal vibrates at 660MHz, and the motherboard speed is one twentieth of that: 33MHz (660/20). If the CPU uses one fifth of the crystal's frequency, it runs at 133MHz (660/5). That means the CPU is also running four times faster than the motherboard (33×4), making it a 4X processor.

The original XT machines used the same timing frequency for all the components on the motherboard. The 80486 introduced the concept of multipliers and frequency synthesizers. Nowadays, we see various frequencies being assigned to such things as the processor, the front-side bus, the memory bus, memory caches, the expansion bus, and so forth. The frequency assigned to the CPU's internal processing can also be sent to a high-speed L-1 cache.

 When you hear that a memory controller is synchronized to a processor bus, it means a certain timing frequency is being derived from the main oscillator and "sent" to both devices.

Have you ever watched a group of children playing with a jump rope? Part of the game is to move the arc of the rope around a cylinder of space at some speed. At the high end of the arc, the rope passes over the jumper's head. At the low end of the arc, the jumper has to jump up and create a gap for the rope to pass between his feet and the ground. Each jump is like a 1-bit data transfer. The speed of the rope is the timing frequency.

Suppose we have two groups of children, where the pair on the left is twirling their rope in one direction. Their friends on the right are twirling a second rope, twice as fast, in the opposite direction. Let's not worry about the jumping kids, but instead, watch each rope in slow motion. Figure 3.4 shows the centers of each rope as they come close together. (Note that the following physics and math are incorrect, but we're using an example.)

The rope to the left, in Figure 3.4, is producing one cycle for every two cycles on the right. The CPU typically attaches a bit of information (represented by the cylinder on the rope) to each of its own cycles (the high end of the arc). Notice that a transfer to the memory controller takes place in one cycle, but the "rope" in the CPU passes by twice. For every two ticks taking place inside the CPU, the components working with the motherboard clock "hear" only a single tick. When the CPU attaches a bit to each wave (each turn of its rope), it has to wait until the memory cycle is ready for that second bit.

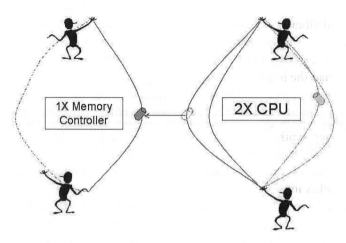

Figure 3.4   Relative cycle speeds and one missed transfer.

We can improve performance in the CPU by adding a small buffer, or *cache*, to the motherboard, close to the CPU. When the processor and memory controller's timing cycles are synchronized, the processor can offload a bit directly to memory. When their cycles are out of sync, the CPU can still move its second bit into the buffer and get on with something else. Figure 3.5 shows how a small buffer (the little guy in the middle), synchronized to the processor, can temporarily store bits until the memory controller is ready for a transfer.

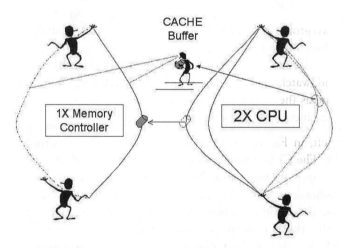

Figure 3.5   CPU transfers buffered to a "holding tank."

The small buffer we're talking about is the *L-1 cache*. In CPU-memory transfers, a buffer is the same as a cache. A critical difference is that memory caches do not work with probabilities. Each bit going into the cache is absolutely going to be sent to memory. When the L-1 cache fills up, the L-2 cache takes the overflow. If both the L-1 and L-2 buffers become filled, a Level 3 cache might be helpful. The goal is to ensure that bits are transferred for every single processor clock tick. Understand that the CPU can also recall bits from memory and use the caches. However, at twice the speed of memory, the CPU more often is ready, willing, and able to take bits while the memory controller is still searching.

To bring this together: Imagine installing a Pentium processor on a 66MHz motherboard, using a 4X clock multiplier. Internally, the Pentium moves data at 264MHz (call it 266Mhz). The memory controller runs at 66MHz (the speed of the motherboard). When the Pentium "hangs" a byte onto a clock tick, it may have to wait for up to four of its own cycles before the memory controller is ready to handle the transfer. This assumes we're using SDRAM and the controller "hears" the same ticks as the processor. Remember that DRAM had no timing link between the processor and CPU, and each component had to wait until the other wasn't busy before it could accomplish a transfer.

The PC100 Standard

Motherboard speeds eventually increased to 100MHz, and CPU speeds went beyond 500MHz. The industry decided that SDRAM modules should be synchronized at 100MHz. Someone had to set the standards for the way memory modules were clocked, so Intel developed the PC100 standard as part of the overall PCI standard. The initial standard made sure that a 100MHz module was really capable of, and really did run at 100MHz. Naturally, this created headaches for memory manufacturing companies, but the standard helped in determining system performance.

At 100MHz and higher, timing is absolutely critical, and everything from the length of the signal traces to the construction of the memory chips themselves is a factor. The shorter the distance the signal needs to travel, the faster it runs. Non-compliant modules—those that didn't meet the PC100 specification—could significantly reduce the performance and reliability of the system. The standard caught on, although unscrupulous vendors would sometimes label 100MHz memory chips as PC100 compliant. (This didn't necessarily do any harm, but it did leave people who built their own systems wondering why their computer didn't run as they expected.)

We evaluate memory speed partly on the basis of the actual memory chips in a module, and partly on the underlying printed circuit board and buses.

Because of the physics of electricity, a module designed with individual parts running at 100MHz rarely reaches that overall speed. It takes time for the signals to move through the wire, and the wire itself can slow things down. This led to ratings problems similar to those involving processors, which are covered in Chapter 5.

PC66 Versus PC100

PC100 SDRAM modules required 8 ns DRAM chips, capable of operating at 125MHz. The extra twenty-five megahertz provides a margin of error, to make sure that the overall module will be able to run at 100MHz. The standard also called for a correctly programmed EEPROM, on a properly designed circuit board.

SDRAM modules prior to the PC100 standard used either 83MHz chips (12 ns) or 100MHz chips at 10 ns. They ran on systems using only a 66MHz bus. It happens that these slightly slower 100MHz chips could produce a module that would operate reliably at about 83MHz. These slower SDRAM modules are now called PC66, to differentiate them from the PC100 specification (with 8 ns chips).

As memory speeds increased, the PC100 standard was upgraded to keep pace with new modules. Intel released a PC133 specification, synchronized to a 133MHz chipset, and so it went. PC800 RDRAM was released to coincide with Intel's 800 series chipset, running at 800MHz. These days, we see a PC1066 specification, designed for even higher-speed memory. As bus speeds and module designs change, so too does the specification.

MHz to Nanosecond

SDRAM modules are rated in megahertz, so as to link the chip speed to the bus speed. To find the speed in nanoseconds, divide 1 second (1 billion nanoseconds) by the output frequency of the chip. For example, a 67MHz chip runs at 67-million cycles per second. If you divide one billion by 67 million, the result is 14.9, which rounds off to 15 ns.

You can use this same formula to make a loose comparison between processor speeds and memory modules. For example, we can take a 900MHz Pentium and divide one billion by 900 million. The result shows a CPU running at 0.9 nanoseconds. Compare a 12 ns SDRAM chip with this CPU and you can see how much faster the processor is running. Even when we take ultra-fast SRAM running at 2 ns, we can see a significant difference in speed. Understand that nanosecond timing numbers don't tell the whole story when it comes to performance.

NRZI and DDR

Instructions can be designed to begin from exact points in a wave cycle. This is another way of improving processor performance. When the cycle is going up, we refer to an "up tick." When the cycle is going down, we refer to a "down tick." Using an analog sine wave, we can use the midpoint for a 0 setting, and some amount of signal (other than zero) as a 1. This is the concept of *Non-Return-to-Zero-Inverted (NRZI)* encoding. NRZI encoding means that any variation in the voltage level produces a change in state. A steady voltage represents a 1, and *any change at all* in voltage represents a 0.

If we use a pulse wave, we can clearly differentiate between a zero, and two additional numbers: the +1 and the -1. Pipelining and double-data rate (DDR) memory both take advantage of the square design of a pulse wave to send two signals per clock tick.

Pipelining

Suppose your friend asks you to go buy a soda. Right as you turn to the door, he then asks you to hand him a pencil. Both instructions are mixed together, and you'll have to make a processing decision as to which takes priority. That decision moment slows down your overall actions. Essentially, when an asynchronous DRAM chip receives an instruction to store something, it runs into the same problem. It takes the first instruction, then processes it until it finishes. At that point, it "looks up," so to speak, to get another instruction.

On the other hand, when we're aware of our surroundings, someone can ask us to do something and also ask us to do something else when we're done. Although we're busy with the first task, we store the second task in a cache, knowing that as soon as we're finished with the first, we can begin the second. In other words, we don't have to be told a second time. This type of buffering (a very small memory cache) saves time for the person issuing the instructions.

Instead of being constantly interrupted, the clock and a pipeline cache in a memory module allows instructions to be organized one after the other. The process is called a *pipeline* system. Pipelining is a little like the way a CPU uses IRQ lines to make some sense out of the data stream chaos flying around in electronic space.

Using regular pipelining, a memory controller can write a bit to memory at the same time as it's "hearing" the next call from the CPU. Likewise, when it reads a bit from memory, it can have the next bit ready to go before the CPU asks for it. We'll encounter the concept of pipelining again when we take a look at Pentium processors in the next chapter. Dual-pipeline architecture means a chip can listen to a new instruction while it's completing the first instruction. This is yet another way to speed up any system or subsystem.

Pseudo Static RAM (PSRAM)

Synchronous DRAM takes into account interrupt timing and the motherboard clock, and works just like SRAM. Capacitors allow for higher density (and lower cost) of a DRAM chip, as opposed to the more expensive transistors on SRAM chips. Most SDRAM controllers are built into the North Bridge of the motherboard chipset.

Another type of memory is called Pseudo Static RAM (PSRAM). This is DRAM with built-in refresh and address-control circuitry to make it behave similarly to SRAM. It combines the high density of DRAM capacitors with the speed of SRAM, but instead of having to rely on the CPU for an accuracy check of the original "send," the built-in circuitry "remembers" the data correctly.

Larger Bytes and Wider Buses

The other way to improve performance is by increasing the size of the information packet (combining bytes) and moving everything at the original time. This is similar to increasing bus widths. For example, a piece of paper four inches wide and eight inches long can hold some number of words. Handing you a piece of paper still takes only one movement. But if the paper changes to eight inches wide, it can store a lot more words. In the same single movement, you receive much more information.

Summary—Basic Memory

We've seen that memory can be broadly divided into two categories: memory that the system can change, and that which the system cannot change. RAM and ROM, respectively, are the beginning concepts for understanding memory. The ROM BIOS is where the motherboard remembers the most basic instructions about the hardware of a particular chipset. CMOS stores system configuration settings, as well as settings for additional hardware connected to the basic chipset. BIOS and CMOS are different in that CMOS requires a small amount of electricity to maintain its settings.

BIOS and CMOS can be changed, but not without some effort. Make sure you know the acronyms associated with these chips and the ways in which they can be updated. Additionally, you should have a comfortable understanding about the following points having to do with memory:

➤ The central processing unit, the memory controller, and the system clock

➤ Clock cycles and multipliers, and how electrical data pulses are "pushed" along by clock pulses

➤ How timing affects performance, and the difference between asynchronous and synchronous data transfers

➤ The North Bridge and South Bridge architecture (see Chapter 2), and how the front side bus stands between the CPU and the North Bridge

We've talked about the original DRAM chips, and how they became SDRAM chips. The important change was when the memory controllers began to use timing frequencies to perform reads, writes, and refreshes. We've also examined the concept of timing oscillators and how their frequency can be divided into multipliers. Notice how we refer to the CPU speed as a multiple of slowest speed, and rarely as a fraction of a faster speed (a good marketing technique).

DRAM and SDRAM are both different from BIOS and CMOS. Be sure you know the acronyms, because you'll find them on the exam. SIMMs and DIMMs are modules, and we'll be discussing them shortly. Memory chips use different components as storage cells. After the chip has been manufactured, it's packaged onto a module. The individual chips fit onto a small IC board to form a module.

Cache Memory

Do you remember the printing business? Well, the company expanded, meaning there was more and more paperwork. Between print jobs, they had to send copies of financial statements and records off to the accounting department and the government. So the boss hired a secretary. At first, they sent these small jobs to the press room—after all, they were a printing company—but that was costing too much money. Finally, he bought a laser printer for himself (L-1 cache), and one for his secretary (L-2 cache) so they could do these quick little jobs themselves.

Whenever the boss was working up a price quote for a customer, he could set up various calculations and have his secretary print them off. Because they didn't have to go all the way to the press room (main memory), these temporary jobs were extremely quick. The CPU uses Level 1 and Level 2 caching in a similar fashion.

Level 1 (primary) cache memory is like the boss's own personal printer, right there by his desk. Level 2 (secondary) cache memory is like the secretary's printer in the next room. It takes a bit longer for the secretary to print a job and carry it back to the boss's office, but it's still much faster than having to run the job through the entire building.

> Remember that the CPU uses memory caches to store data from registers that it will be using again soon. It also uses memory caches to store data on the way to memory, where the memory controller is too slow to capture each bit in relation to the CPU's timing speed. L-1 and L-2 caches run at the speed of the processor bus (also known as the front side bus). This allows the caches to capture a bit every time (clock tick) the processor sends a bit, or the reverse.

Memory Caches

Cache (pronounced "cash") is derived from the French word *cacher*, meaning to hide. Two types of caching are commonly used in personal computers: *memory caching* and *disk caching*. A memory cache (sometimes called a cache store, a memory buffer, or a RAM cache) is a portion of memory made up of high-speed static RAM (SRAM) instead of the slower and cheaper dynamic RAM (DRAM). Memory caching is effective because most programs access the same instructions over and over. By keeping as much of this information as possible in SRAM, the computer avoids having to access the slower DRAM.

The *memory hierarchy* is a way to handle differences in speed. "Hierarchy" is a fancy way of saying "the order of things; from top to bottom, fast to slow, or most important to least important." Going from fastest to slowest, the memory hierarchy is made up of registers, caches, main memory, and disks.

When the processor needs information, it looks at the top of the hierarchy (the fastest memory). If the data is there, it wins. Otherwise, a so-called miss occurs, and the processor has to look in the next, lower level of hierarchy. When a miss occurs, the whole block of memory containing the requested missing information is brought in from a lower, slower hierarchical level. Some existing blocks or pages must be removed for a new one to be brought in.

Disk caching is different from memory caching, in that it uses a formula based on probabilities. If you are editing page one of a text you are probably going to request page two. So even if page two has not been requested, it is retrieved and placed in a disk cache on the assumption it will be required in the near future. Disk caches use main memory or in some cases additional memory included with the disk itself.

Memory caching is based on things the CPU has already used. When data or an instruction has been used once, the chances are very good the same instruction or data will be used again. Processing speed can be dramatically increased if the CPU can grab needed instructions or data from a high-speed memory cache rather than going to slower main memory or an even slower hard disk. The L1, L2, and L3 cache are made up of extremely high-speed memory and provide a place to store instructions and data that may be used again.

Using Memory Levels

Here's another way to understand the different levels of a hierarchy. Think of the answer to the following questions, and then watch what happens in your mind. What's your name? This information is immediately available to you from something like the ROM BIOS in a computer. What day is it? This information is somewhat less available and requires a quick calculation, or "remembering" process. This is vaguely like the CMOS settings in the system.

What's your address? Once again you have a fairly quick access to your long-term memory, and quickly call the information into RAM (your attention span). What's the address of the White House? Now, for the first time, you're likely to draw a blank. In that case you have two options: The first is that you might remember a particular murder-mystery movie and the title, which acts somewhat like an index pointer to retrieve "1600 Pennsylvania Avenue" from your internal hard drive. In other instances, you'll likely have to access process instructions, which point you to a research tool like the Internet or a phone book.

You should be able to see how it takes longer to retrieve something when you're less likely to use the information on a regular basis. Not only that, but an entire body of information can be stored in your mind, or you may have only a "stub." The stub then calls up a process by which you can load an entire application, which goes out and finds the information. If you expect to need something, you keep it handy, so to speak. A cache is a way of keeping information handy.

Understand that a cache is just a predefined place to store data. It can be fast or slow, large or small, and can be used in different ways.

L-1 and L-2 Cache Memory

The Intel 486 and early Pentium chips had a small, built-in, 16KB cache on the CPU called a Level 1 (L-1), or *primary cache*. Another cache is the Level 2 (L-2), or *secondary cache*. The L-2 cache was generally (not very often, anymore) a separate memory chip, one step slower than the L-1 cache in the memory hierarchy. L-2 cache almost always uses a dedicated *memory bus*, also known as a backside bus (see Figure 2.10 in Chapter 2).

A *die*, sometimes called the chip *package*, is essentially the foundation for a multitude of circuit traces making up a microprocessor. Today, we have *internal* caches (inside the CPU housing) and *external* caches (outside the die). When Intel came up with the idea of a small amount of cache memory (Level 1), engineers were able to fit it right on the die. The 80486 used this process and it worked very well. Then the designers decided that if one cache was good, two would be better. However, that secondary cache (Level 2) couldn't fit on the die, so the company had to purchase separate memory chips from someone else.

Don't confuse a chip package with a chipset—the entire set of chips used on a motherboard to support a CPU.

These separate memory chips came pre-packaged from other companies, so Intel developed a small IC board to combine their own chips with the separate cache memory. They mounted the cards vertically, and changed the mounts from sockets to slots. It wasn't until later that evolving engineering techniques and smaller transistors allowed them to move the L-2 cache onto the die. In other words, not every design change is due to more efficient manufacturing.

For the purposes of the exam, you should remember that the primary (L-1) cache is internal to the processor chip itself, and the secondary (L-2) cache is almost always external. Modern systems may have the L-1 and L-2 cache combined in an integrated package, but the exam may easily differentiate an L-2 cache as being external. Up until the 486 family of chips, the CPU had no internal cache, so any external cache was designated as the "primary" memory cache. The 80486 introduced an 8KB internal L-1 cache, which was later increased to 16KB. The Pentium family added a 256KB or 512KB external, secondary L-2 cache.

Larger memory storage means more memory addresses, which, in turn, means larger numbers. A CPU register can store only a certain size byte, and larger numbers mean wider registers, as well as wider address buses. Note that registers (discussed again in Chapter 4) are usually designed around the number of bits a CPU can process simultaneously. A 16-bit processor usually has 16-bit registers; a 32-bit processor has 32-bit registers, and so forth. These larger numbers require a correspondingly wider data bus to move a complete address out of the processor.

You should be getting a sense of how larger and faster CPUs generate a chain of events that lead to whole new chipsets and motherboards. Not only does the chip run faster, but the internal registers grow larger, or new ways to move instructions more quickly demand faster bus speeds. Although we can always add cells to a memory chip, it isn't so easy to add registers to a microprocessor.

Larger numbers mean the memory controller takes more time to decode the addresses and to find stored information. Faster processing requires more efficient memory storage, faster memory chips, and better bus technology. Everything associated with timing, transfers, and interruptions must be upgraded to support the new central processor.

L-3 Caches

You may see references to an L-3—or a Level 3—cache. Tertiary (third) caches originated out of server technology, where high-end systems use more than a single processor. One way to add an L-3 cache is to build some additional memory chips directly into the North Bridge. Another way is to place the cache into a controller sub-system between the CPU and its dependent devices. These small I/O managers are part of hub architecture, discussed in Chapter 5. Newer Pentium 4 processors use up to 20-level pipelining operations; an L-3 cache would also be a way to offload next-due instructions from a memory controller.

Simply put: More and more CPUs have both the L-1 and L-2 cache built right onto the die. If a third cache remains outside the die, many people refer to it as a Level 3 cache. Level 3 caches are usually larger than L-2 caches, more often in the 1MB size range. All three types of cache usually run at the processor speed, rather than the speed of a slower memory bus. (Benchmark tests on single-processor systems have shown that an L-2 cache peaks out at about 512KB, so adding more memory to a third-level cache isn't always going to increase system performance.)

Memory Pages

The CPU sends data to memory in order to empty its registers and make room for more calculations. In other words, the CPU has some information it wants to get rid of, and sends that information out to the memory controller. The memory controller shoves it into whichever capacitors are available and keeps track of where it put everything. Each bit is assigned a memory address for as long as the controller is in charge of it (no pun intended).

When the CPU wants to empty a register, it waits for one of its internal electrical pulses (processor clock tick). When the pulse arrives, it sends out a data bit, usually to a memory cache. Very quickly, a stream of bits generates bytes in multiples of eight (8-bit byte, 16-bit bytes, and so on). The cache waits for the slower pulses of the motherboard clock, and then sends each bit over to the memory controller. The controller then directs each electrical charge into a memory cell. The cell might be a capacitor, in which case it has to be recharged. Or, it might be a transistor, in which case a switch opens or closes. Regardless of how wide a register or an address is, each bit ends up in its own cell, somewhere in the memory chip.

Page Ranges

Typically, memory is divided into blocks. At the main memory level, a block of memory is referred to as a *memory page*. A page is a related group of bytes (and their bits). It can vary in size from 512 bits to several kilobytes, depending on the way the operating system is set up. Understand that physical memory is fixed, with the amount of memory identified in the BIOS. However, the operating system dictates much of how the memory is being used. For example, a 32-bit operating system will structure memory pages in multiples of thirty-two bits; a 64-bit operating system will use pages that are multiples of sixty-four.

DRAM cells are usually accessed through *paging*. The controller keeps track of the electrical charges, their location, and the state (condition) of each capacitor and/or transistors of each memory chip. This combination of states and locations is the actual address.

Pages are similar to named ranges in a spreadsheet. Without ranges, a spreadsheet formula must include every necessary cell in a calculation. We might have a formula something like =SUM(A1+B1+C1+D1+E1). Now suppose we assign cells C1, D1, and E1 to a range, and call that range "LastWeek." We can now change the formula to include the range name: =SUM(A1+B1+"LastWeek"). The range name includes a set of cells.

A named range is analogous to the memory controller giving a unique name to part of a row of charges. This range of charges is called a *page address*. A memory page is some part of a row in a grid. A page address means that the controller doesn't have to go looking for every single capacitor or transistor containing particular data bits.

Do you remember that cheap little printing toy we talked about earlier—the one with the rubber letters and the rail? One way to think of memory addressing is as if we were trying to locate every single piece of rubber in the rail. The memory controller has to ask, "Get me letter 1, at the left end. Now get me letter 2, next to letter 1. Now get me letter 3, the third one in from the left," and so on. But suppose we don't worry about each letter, and think instead of the whole rail. Now the controller has only to ask, "Get me everything in the rail right now." This is more like memory paging.

Burst Mode

A *burst* of information is when a sub-system stores up pieces of information, and then sends them all out at once. Back in World War II, submarines were at risk every time they surfaced to send radio messages to headquarters. To reduce the time on the surface, people would record a message at a slow speed, and then play it back during the transmission in a single high-speed burst. To anyone listening, the message would sound like a quick stream of unintelligible noise.

"Bursting" is a rapid data-transfer technique that automatically generates a series of consecutive addresses every time the processor requests only a single address. In other words, although the processor is asking for only one address, bursting creates a block of more than that one. The assumption is that the additional addresses will be located adjacent to the previous data in the same row. Bursting can be applied both to read operations (from memory) and write operations (to memory).

On a system bus, burst mode is more like taking control of the phone line and not allowing anyone else to interrupt until the end of the conversation. However, memory systems use burst mode to mean something more like caching: The next-expected information is prepared before the CPU actually makes a request. Neither process is really a burst, but rather an *uninterrupted transmission* of information. Setting aside the semantics, burst mode takes place for only limited amounts of time, because otherwise no other subsystems would be able to request an interruption.

Fast Page Mode (FPM)

Dynamic RAM originally began with Fast Page Mode (FPM), back in the late 1980s. Even now, many technical references refer to FPM DRAM or EDO memory (discussed next). In many situations, the CPU transfers data back and forth between memory, in bursts of consecutive addresses. Fast page mode simplifies the process by providing an automatic column counter. Keep in mind that addresses are held in a matrix, and that a given row is a page of memory. Each bit in the page also has a row-column number (address).

In plain DRAM, the controller not only had to find a row of bits (the page), it also had to go up and "manually" look at each column heading. Fast Page Mode automatically increments the column address, when the controller selects a memory page. It can then access the next cell without having to go get another column address. The controller uses fast page mode to make an assumption that the data read/write following a CPU request will be in the next three columns of the page row. This is somewhat like having a line of letters all ready to go in the toy stamp.

Using FPM, the controller doesn't have to waste time looking for a range address for at least three more times: It can read-assume-assume-assume. The three assumptions are *burst cycles*. The process saves time, and increases speed when reading or writing bursts of data.

 NOTE | Fast Page Mode is capable of processing commands at up to 50 ns. Fifty nanoseconds is fifty billionths of a second, which used to be considered very fast. Remember that the controller first moves to a row, then to a column, then retrieves the information. The row and column number is a matrix address.

The Data Output Buffer

Suppose the CPU wants back 16 bits of data (two bytes). Figure 3.6 illustrates what happens next. Note that the controller has stored the data in what it calls Page 12, in the cell range 1–16. It passes through the memory chip, looking for Page 12, bit 1 (Cell A12). It then moves each bit into the *data output buffer* cell at the top of each column. Remember: The controller doesn't have to look again at the page number for bits number 2, 3, or 4. It's already read "page 12," and assumes-assumes-assumes. For the fifth bit, it quickly re-reads the page address, and then goes and gets bits 5, 6, 7, and 8. Notice that in two reads, the controller has picked up one byte: half of a 16-bit address.

After the controller completes its pass through the entire page (four reads: one complete number), it validates the information and hands it back to the CPU. The controller then turns off the data output buffer (above the columns, in Figure 3.6). This takes approximately 10 nanoseconds. Finally, each cell in the page is prepared for the next transmission from the CPU. The memory enters a 10 ns wait state while the capacitors are pre-charged for the next cycle. In other words, that part of the row is given a zero charge (wiped out) and prepared for the next transmission.

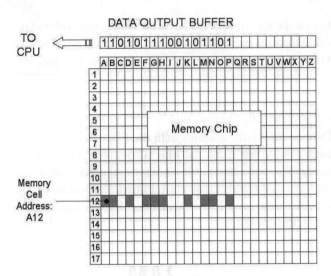

Figure 3.6 Memory controller retrieves cell data.

> **NOTE**
>
> Understand that FPM has a 20 ns wait state: 10 ns to turn off the data output buffer, plus 10 ns to recharge specific cells in a page.

Extended Data Output (EDO) RAM

FPM evolved into Extended Data Out (EDO) memory. The big improvement in EDO was that column cell addresses were merely deactivated, not wiped out. The data remained valid until the next call from the CPU. In other words, Fast Page Mode deactivated the data output buffer (10 ns), and then removed the data bits in the column cells (10 ns). EDO, on the other hand, kept the data output buffer active until the beginning of the next cycle, leaving the data bits alone. One less step means a faster process.

EDO memory is sometimes referred to as *hyper-page mode*, and allows a *timing overlap* between successive read/writes. Remember that the data output buffers aren't turned off when the memory controller finishes reading a page. Instead, the CPU (not the memory controller) determines the start of the deactivation process by sending a new request. The result of this overlap in the process is that EDO eliminates 10 ns per cycle delay of fast page mode, generating faster throughput.

Here's another way to look at it. When you delete a file, the operating system has two ways to go about the process. It can either write a series of zeroes over every bit of data pertaining to that file, everywhere they exist, or it can simply cancel the FAT index reference. Obviously it's a lot faster to just cancel the first letter of the file's index name than it is to spend time clean-ing out every data bit. Utility software applications allow you to "undelete" a file by resetting the first letter of a recoverable file. These applications also provide a way to wipe out a disk by writing all zeros to the file area. In the latter case, nobody can recover the information. FPM is like writing all zeros to a disk, and EDO is like changing only the first letter of the index name.

Both FPM and EDO memory are *asynchronous*. (In the English language, the "a" in front of synchronous is called a prefix. The "a" prefix generally means "not," or "the opposite.") In asynchronous memory, the memory controller is not working with any other clocks. DRAM is asynchronous memory. In asynchronous mode, the CPU and memory controller have to wait for each other to be ready before they can transfer data.

Rambus Memory (RDRAM)

All the memory systems that we've talked about so far are known as *wide channel* systems because the memory channel is equal to the width of the processor bus. RDRAM is known as a *narrow channel* system because data is transferred only 2 bytes (16 bits) at a time. This might seem small, but those 2 bytes move extremely fast! The Rambus data bus is 16 bits wide, as opposed to the more typical 32 or 64 bits wide. Additionally, Rambus memory sends data more frequently. It reads data on both the rising and falling edges of the clock signal.

RDRAM

Rambus dynamic RAM comes out of technology developed originally by Rambus, Inc., for the Nintendo 64 gaming system. It's not that new, but it seems new because Intel started to use it with its Pentium 4 processors and 800-series chipset. Rambus memory is integrated onto Rambus Inline Memory Modules (RIMMs). The modules use Rambus DRAM (RDRAM) chips. We discuss memory modules (packaging) later in this chapter.

RDRAM chips use the processor's memory bus timing frequency, not the motherboard clock. Therefore, the processor won't request something at mid tick (the reverse of an interrupt). On the other hand, SRAM and SDRAM are synced to the CPU at a multiple closer to the motherboard clock. In other words, SDRAM, running at 100MHz, might be three times the speed of a 33MHz board.

RDRAM starts with the CPU speed, multiplied from a 66MHz board. A 10X processor on the same board would now be running at 660MHz. RDRAM then sets the memory bus to one half or one third of the CPU speed. 660 divided by two sets the memory bus at 330MHz. Divide by three, and the memory bus transfers at 220MHz. Both are faster than SDRAM. Remember that speed alone doesn't account for total performance.

Earlier Pentiums used a 64-bit bus and transferred data in parallel. The corresponding memory module bus was also 64 bits wide, which meant that data could be moved across the memory bus in 64-bit (8-byte) chunks. Another way of looking at it is that a bit is one-eighth of a byte. Therefore, 64 bits divided by 8 equals 8 bytes.

SLDRAM

Earlier memory chips used separate address, data, and control lines. This separation tended to limit speed. Engineers decided that joining the three types of data into a single packet and moving it across a single bus would improve efficiency. Along the way, they came up with two different methods, or protocols, for doing so. The protocol-based designs we'll mention are SyncLink DRAM (SLDRAM) and Rambus DRAM, sometimes called Direct Rambus DRAM (DRDRAM).

Intel eventually bought Rambus and began licensing the technology for a fee. SLDRAM, on the other hand, was an open industry standard. You may remember the problems IBM had with their micro-channel architecture buses. In the same way, memory manufacturers moved more toward SLDRAM. A secondary benefit of SLDRAM was that it doesn't require that existing RAM chips be redesigned. RDRAM, with its narrow channel bus, is a whole new architecture.

The original SLDRAM used a 200Mhz bus, making it faster than standard SDRAM. Double Data Rate SDRAM (DDR SDRAM) and SLDRAM both use the rising and falling edge of the clock to move twice the amount of information as SDRAM. As such, the overall transfer started out at 400MHz and quickly moved up to 800MHz.

Prior to Rambus memory, the fastest chips had a throughput of 100MHz. SDRAM with a 64-bit bus (to match the Pentium) transfers data in 8-byte chunks. Eight megabytes moving in parallel means an 8MB transfer every second. RDRAM chips transfer data in 2-byte chunks, twice per cycle (one on the up tick, one on the down tick). At 800MHz, RIMMs move 1,600MB per second (2 transfers per cycle times 800), which translates to 1.66 gigabytes (GB) or a billion bytes—about twice as fast as SDRAM.

Double Data Rate SDRAM (DDR SDRAM)

SLDRAM generated DDR SDRAM and DDR-II. Both use a newer version of the Intel i845E chipset. Double Data Rate (DDR) came about as a response to Intel's RDRAM changed architecture and licensing fees. AMD was developing faster processing by using a double-speed bus. Instead of using a full clock tick to run an event, they used a "half-tick" cycle, which is the voltage change during a clock cycle. As the clock begins a tick, the voltage goes up (an up tick) and an event takes place. When the clock ends the tick, the voltage goes down (a down tick) and a second event takes place. Every clock cycle has two memory cycle events. The AMD Athlon and Duron use the DDR specification with the double-speed bus.

DDR and Rambus memory are not backward compatible with SDRAM. The big difference between DDR and SDRAM memory is that DDR reads data on both the rising and falling edges of the clock tick. SDRAM only carries information on the rising edge of a signal. Basically, this allows the DDR module to transfer twice as much data as SDRAM in the same time period. For example, instead of a data rate of 133MB/s, DDR memory transfers data at 266MB/s.

DDR is packaged in dual inline memory modules (DIMMs) like their SDRAM predecessors. They connect to the motherboard in a similar way as SDRAM. DDR memory supports both ECC (error correction code, typically used in servers) and non-parity (used on desktops/laptops). We discuss parity at the end of this chapter.

 NOTE RDRAM also developed a different type of chip packaging called Fine Pitch Ball Grid Array (FPBGA). Rambus chips are much larger than SDRAM or DDR die, which means that fewer parts can be produced on a wafer. Most DDR SDRAM uses a Thin Small Outline Package (TSOP). TSOP chips have fairly long contact pins on each side. FPBGA chips have tiny ball contacts on the underside. The very small soldered balls have a much lower capacitive load than the TSOP pins. DDR SDRAM using FPBGA packaging runs at 200–266MHz, whereas the same chips in a TSOP package are limited to 150–180MHz.

DDR-II

The current PC1066 RDRAM can reach 667MHz speeds (which is really PC1333), so Samsung and Elpida have announced that they are studying 1,333MHz RDRAM and 800MHz memory (PC1600). These systems would most likely be used in high-end network systems, but that doesn't mean that RDRAM would be completely removed from the home consumer market.

Rambus has already developed a new technology, codenamed "Yellowstone," which should lead to 3.2GHz memory, with a 12.4GB/s throughput. With a 128-bit interface, Rambus promises to achieve 100GB/s throughput. Yellowstone technology is expected to arrive in game boxes first, with PC memory scheduled for sometime around 2005.

DDR-II may be the end of Rambus memory, although people have previously speculated that RDRAM wouldn't last. DDR-II extends the original DDR concept, taking on some of the advantages developed by Rambus. DDR-II uses FPBGA packaging for faster connection to the system, and reduces some of the signal reflection problems (collisions) of the original DDR. However, latency problems increase with higher bus speeds. DDR-II is entering the consumer market, but RDRAM is expected to continue, although with limited chipset support.

Serial Transfers and Latency

One of the problems with Rambus memory is that the RIMMs are connected to the bus in a series. A data item has to pass through all the other modules before it reaches the memory bus. The signal has to travel a lot farther than it does on a DIMM, where the bus uses parallel transfers. The longer distance introduces a time lag, called *latency*. The longer the delay before the signal reaches the bus, the higher the latency. In a Nintendo game, data generally moves in long streams, so serial transfers aren't a problem. But in a typical PC, data routinely moves in short bursts, and latency becomes a problem.

To understand latency, take a look at the difference between serial and parallel transfers. Think of a train in a movie scene. The hero is at one end of the train and has to chase the bad guy, using a serial process. He goes from one end of a car, along all the seats, and then leaves by a door at the other end, which is connected to the next car in the train. Then the process starts all over again, until he either reaches the end of the train or someone gets killed.

Now take that same train, but this time there isn't a hero chasing a bad guy. Instead, imagine a train full of people on their way to work. If there was only one door at the back of the train, it would take forever to let everyone off at the train station. To fix that problem, each car has its own door. When the train comes to a stop, everyone turns to the side facing the platform: The doors in each car open up, and people leave each car simultaneously. This is a parallel transfer.

RDRAM uses a 16-bit bus for the data signals. This narrow 2-byte path is the main reason why RDRAM can run at higher speeds than SDRAM. Keep in mind that transfers are not only faster, but there are two of them per cycle. On the other hand, one of the problems with parallel transfers at high speeds is something called *skew*. The longer and faster the bus gets, the more likely it is that some data signals will arrive too soon or too late: not in a perfect line. It would be as if sixty-four people started to leave the train at the same time, but each one stepped onto the platform at a different time.

SLDRAM uses a lower clock speed, which reduces signal problems. With no licensing fees, it's also cheaper to produce. Another useful feature is that it has a higher bandwidth than DRDRAM, allowing for a potential transfer of 3.2GB/s, as opposed to Rambus's 1.6GB/s. (Note that modern Intel chipsets use two parallel Rambus channels to reach 3.2GB/s.)

Intel went the Rambus course, and released the 800 series chipset to work only with RDRAM. Soon after, Via released a chipset that would run DDR memory, an outgrowth of the SLDRAM technology. AMD wasn't going to be limited to an Intel board, so much of the market jumped on the Via chipset. This put pressure on Intel to come up with a modified 840-series chipset that would also support DDR memory. It appears as though Rambus may have a hard battle to win market share, but it continues to hang on in high-end desktops and workstations.

In a nutshell, fast and long may not be the same as slow and short. For instance, suppose you want to go two miles to the store. If you go the long way, using a highway, it's a ten-mile drive. However, you can drive 60 mph on the highway. If you go directly to the store, you're stuck driving 30 mph on local roads. Using the highway, you arrive in six minutes (60 mph/10 miles). The other way, you arrive in four minutes (30 mph/2 miles). You might drive a whole lot faster on the highway, but you'll get to the store faster on the straight-line route. In this example, the store is the memory controller. The different roads represent different types of bus architectures.

Video RAM (VRAM)

VRAM (Video RAM) and WRAM (Windows RAM) have been mostly supplanted by DDR memory chips, but you may find a question about VRAM (pronounced "vee-ram") on the exam. Video RAM was designed to provide two access paths to the same memory address. It's as if VRAM were a café that has two doors: one in the front and one in the back. Information comes in one "entrance" at the same time that other information flows out the other "exit." When the video controller reads the memory for information, it accesses an address with one of the paths. When the CPU writes data to that memory, it accesses the address via the other path. Because of these two access paths, we say that VRAM is *dual-ported*.

Manipulating graphics is processing-intensive, and so this capability to push data in and out of the chip at the same time helps a moving image appear continuous. In a way, the concept is similar to pipelining, but dual-porting uses one channel for "in" and the other channel for "out." Pipelining uses only one channel, but doesn't have to ask for instructions twice. VRAM chips are about 20% larger than DRAM chips because of extra circuitry requirements. (Modern computers usually have basic graphics processing integrated right onto the motherboard, with the AGP providing for faster video processing.)

VRAM, WRAM, and AGP

The AGP acronym stands for Accelerated Graphics Port. Most computers include this accelerated port, which is an integrated part of the I/O system. An AGP is not the same thing as VRAM or a video accelerator card, nor is it the same thing as today's integrated graphics. Although some video cards still use the main expansion bus, most connect with the AGP.

To say that a computer has "AGP memory" or "comes with AGP" can be confusing at best. At worst, it can demonstrate a faulty knowledge of the distinction between video memory and I/O subsystems. AGP is discussed in the "Accelerated Graphics Port (AGP)" section of Chapter 9, "Peripherals: Output Devices."

WRAM is short for Windows RAM, and has no connection with Microsoft, even though the acronym includes the word "Windows." WRAM, like VRAM, is dual-ported, but uses large block addressing to achieve higher bandwidth. Additional features provided better performance than video RAM at lower manufacturing costs. With the advent of AGP and DDR memory, both VRAM and Windows RAM have faded from the marketplace. That's not to say that add-on graphics accelerator cards have vanished.

Supplemental Information

VRAM has been superseded by DDR SDRAM and Synchronous Graphics RAM (SGRAM). This is a specialized form of SDRAM that uses bit masking (writing to a specified bit plane without affecting the others) and block writes (filling a block of memory with a single color). Synchronous Graphics RAM uses very fast memory transfers. It also incorporates specific design changes for certain acceleration features built into video cards. SGRAM is still single-ported, unlike VRAM or WRAM, but offers performance similar to VRAM. SGRAM is typically used in moderate to high-end cards where performance is important, but very high resolution isn't required.

Multibank DRAM (MDRAM)

Multibank DRAM was invented by MoSys, specifically for use in graphics cards, and differs substantially in design from other types of video memory. Conventional memory designs use a single block of memory for the frame buffer. MDRAM breaks its memory up into multiple 32KB banks that can be accessed independently. This means that instead of the entire bandwidth being devoted to a single frame, smaller pieces can be processed in an overlapped system. This overlapping is called interleaving, and isn't the same as interlaced monitors, which we discuss in Chapter 9.

Given that other forms of video memory use these single blocks, video cards tend to be manufactured with increments of whole megabytes of memory, typically in 1MB, 2MB, 4MB, or 8MB, and so forth. A monitor running 1,024×768 resolution in true color (24 bits) uses 2.25MB of video memory for the frame buffer. That's more than 2MB, but the next step up is 4MB, leaving 1.75MB of wasted memory. MDRAM has no such restriction, allowing video cards to be manufactured with any amount of RAM, even exactly 2.25MB.

Earlier, we mentioned that VRAM and WRAM are dual-ported. Table 3.2 lists the various types of memory, along with the way they're ported. You probably won't need to know single or dual, but this may help put all the types of memory in one place.

Table 3.2 Types of Memory Used for Video Processing	
Memory Type	**Ports**
Standard (FPM) DRAM	Single
EDO DRAM	Single
VRAM	Dual
WRAM	Dual
SGRAM	Single
MDRAM	Single

Packaging Modules

We've discussed how memory chips work on the inside, but you'll need to know how these chips are installed on a motherboard. Most of the changes in form came about either to make maintenance easier or to avoid bad connections. Keep in mind that installing a combined unit or module of some kind is less expensive than having many individual units to install. (This is one reason why Intel wanted to get the Level 2 cache onto the die, rather than onto a separate processor IC board.)

Everything about the packaging of memory chips rests on the concept of modules. These modules are vaguely like tiny motherboards within a motherboard, in that they, too, are integrated circuit boards. The big difference between DRAM and SDRAM is the synchronization feature. Be sure you understand how SDRAM uses timing cycles to more efficiently interrupt the CPU. Remember, SRAM is extremely fast and is used in secondary caches; SDRAM is a type of main memory.

It's all well and good to know how SDRAM differs from Rambus RAM, but you're also going to have to be able to differentiate between SIMMs and DIMMs. Inline memory modules are the small IC cards you install in your machine when you upgrade your memory. You won't have to remember clock speeds and the exact number of pins, but you'll definitely be tested on the different types of modules. (That being said, keep in mind that SIMMs are usually 30-pin or 72-pin modules, and DIMMs often use a 168-pin configuration.)

Dual Inline Package (DIP)

Originally, DRAM came in individual chips called *dual inline packages (DIPs)*. XT and AT systems had 36 sockets on the motherboard, each with one DIP per socket. Later, a number of DIPs were mounted on a memory board that plugged into an expansion slot. It was very time consuming to change memory, and there were problems with *chip creep* (thermal cycling), where the chips would work their way out of the sockets as the PC turned on and off. Heat expanded and contracted the sockets, and you'd have to push the chips back in with your fingers.

To solve this problem, manufacturers finally soldered the first 640 kilobytes of memory right onto the board. Then the problem was trying to replace a bad chip. Finally, chips went onto their own card, called a *single inline memory module* or SIMM. On a SIMM, each individual chip is soldered onto a small circuit board with an edge connector. Prices had fallen, so it was cost effective to simply replace the whole module if a memory chip failed.

Connectors: Gold Versus Tin

SIMMs and DIMMs come with either tin (silver-colored) or gold edge connectors. Although you may assume that gold is always better, that's not true. You'll want to match the metal of the edge connectors to the metal in the board's socket. If the motherboard uses gold sockets, use a gold SIMM. Tin sockets (or slots) should use tin edge connectors. The cost difference is minimal, but matching the metal type is critical.

Although it's true that gold won't corrode, a gold SIMM in a tin connector will produce much faster corrosion in the tin connectors. This quickly leads to random glitches and problems, so look at the board and match the color of the metal.

It's important to note, too, that each module is rated for the number of installations, or *insertions*. Each insertion causes scratches, and the more metal that is scratched off, the worse the connection becomes. In flea market exchanges and corporate environments, modules are subjected to constant wear and tear, and nobody is looking at the rated number of insertions.

Single Inline Memory Modules (SIMMs)

When DRAM chips were placed in a line on their own circuit board, it gave rise to the term *inline* memory. After the chips were formed into a *module*, the entire module would fit into a socket on the board. These modules and sockets are referred to as *memory banks*. Depending on how the chips are connected on their own little circuit board, the module is called either a single or dual inline memory module (SIMM or DIMM).

 Remember that SIMM, with an *S*, is a Single inline memory module. *D* is for double, and DIMM is a dual (two) inline memory module, with connectors on two sides, making it a double-edged connector. DIP is a dual inline package, but refers to single chips.

SIMMs come in both 30-pin and 72-pin versions. The 30-pin module is an 8-bit chip, with 1 optional *parity* bit. The 72-pin SIMM is a 32-bit chip, with 4 optional parity bits.

The memory bus grew from 8 bits to 16 bits, and then from 32 bits to 64 bits wide. The 32-bit bus coincided with the development of the SIMM, which meant that the 32-bit-wide data bus could connect directly to one SIMM (4 sets of 8 bits). However, when the bus widened to 64 bits, rather than making a gigantic SIMM, boards started using two SIMMs in paired memory banks. The 64-bit-wide DIMM was developed after the SIMMs, and went back to using only one module per socket again.

 SIMMs and DIMMs are sometimes referred to as chips, but they are really series of chips (modules). DRAM itself is a chip, and many chips are grouped together to form SIMMs and DIMMs. SIMMs can come with a varying number of pins, including 30-pin and 72-pin. (Even though the 72-pin module could have chips on both sides, it was still a SIMM.)

Be careful when you read a question on the exam that you don't accidentally agree that a SIMM is a memory chip. A good way to keep alert is that chips have RAM in their name: DRAM, SRAM, SDRAM, RDRAM, and so forth.

Dual Inline Memory Modules (DIMMs)

Dual inline memory modules are very similar to SIMMs in that they install vertically into sockets on the system board. DIMMs are also a line of DRAM chips, combined on a circuit board. The main difference is that a dual module has two different *signal pins*, one on each side of the module. This is why they are *dual* inline modules.

The differences between SIMMs and DIMMs are as follows:

➤ A DIMM has opposing pins on either side of its board. The pins remain electrically isolated to form two separate contacts—a dual set of electrical contacts (sort of like a parallel circuit).

➤ A SIMM also has opposing pins on either side of the board. However, the pins are connected, tying them together. The connection forms a single electrical contact (sort of like a series circuit).

DIMMs began to be used in computers that supported a 64-bit or wider memory bus. Pentium MMX, Pentium Pro, and Pentium II boards use 168-pin modules. They are 1 inch longer than 72-pin SIMMs, with a secondary *keying notch* so they'll fit into their slots only one way.

Don't Mix Different Types of Memory

Mixing different types of SIMMs or DIMMs within the same memory bank prevents the CPU from accurately detecting how much memory it has. In this case, the system will either fail to boot, or will boot and fail to recognize or use some of the memory.

➤ You can, however, substitute a SIMM with a different speed within the same memory bank, but only if the replacement is equal to or faster than the replaced module.

➤ All memory taken together (from all memory banks) will be set to the speed of the slowest SIMM.

Rambus Inline Memory Modules (RIMMs)

Rambus inline memory modules (RIMMs) use Rambus memory chips. On a standard bi-directional bus, prior to Rambus memory, data traveled down the bus in one direction, with returning data moving back up the same bus in the opposite direction. This same process took place for each bank of memory, with each module being addressed separately. As a result, the system entered a wait state until the bus was ready for either type of transfer.

RIMMs use a *looped* system, where everything is going in one direction (unidirectional) all the time. In a looped system, data moves forward from chip to chip and module to module. Data goes down the line, and then the *results* data continues forward on the wire in the same direction. The results data doesn't have to wait for downstream data to finish being sent.

Continuity Modules

Because Rambus memory works with serial transfers, there must be a memory module in every motherboard memory slot. Even if all the memory is contained in a single module, the unused sockets must have an installed printed circuit board, known as a *continuity module*, to complete the circuit. This is similar to a string of lights, wired in series, where every socket requires a bulb.

RDRAM chips are set on their modules contiguously (next to each other in a chain) and are connected to each other in a series. This means that if an empty memory bank socket is in between two RIMM chips, you must install a continuity module. These are low-cost circuit boards that look like a RIMM, but with no memory chips. All the continuity module does is allow the current to move through the chain of RDRAM chips.

 RDRAM is fast for two reasons: It doesn't have to wait for the bus to turn around, and the cycle time is running at a fast 800MHz, so it doesn't have to wait very long for the next cycle. Using RDRAM chips, signals go from one module to the next to the next, and the throughput is triple that of 100MHz SDRAM. There can also be four RDRAM channels (narrow channel memory) at the same time. This can increase throughput to either 3.2GB (dual channel) or 6.4GB (all four channels).

Memory Diagnostics—Parity

The first thing a PC tests when it runs through the POST (Power On Self-Test) is the memory integrity. On many machines we can see this taking place as a rapidly increasing number displayed on the monitor before anything else happens. The testing is designed to verify the structural fitness of each cell (usually capacitors) in every main memory module. When all the cells have been checked, the boot process continues. The POST test is a simple, one-time test, and may not uncover a bad memory module.

 A bad memory module can cause strange, intermittent errors having to do with read failures, page faults, or even more obscure error messages. Before you tear apart Windows in an attempt to diagnose a possible operating system problem, run a comprehensive hardware diagnostics program on the machine. These applications do a much more exhaustive test of each memory cell, and produce a report of a failed module by its location in the memory banks.

Memory modules may or may not use parity checking, depending on how they're manufactured. The circuitry must be built into the module for it to be capable of parity checking. Keep in mind that parity checking is not the same as the initial test of the cells. Parity checking takes place only after the machine is up and running, and is used to check read/write operations.

Originally, parity checking was a major development in data protection. At the time, memory chips were nowhere near as reliable as they are today, and the process went a long way toward keeping data accurate. Parity checking is still the most common (and least expensive) way to check whether a memory cell can accurately hold data. A more sophisticated (and expensive) method uses Error Correcting Code (ECC) parity.

 Most DRAM chips in SIMMs or DIMMs require a parity bit because memory can be corrupted even if the computer hasn't actually been bashed with a hammer. Alpha particles can disturb memory cells with ionizing radiation, resulting in lost data. Electromagnetic interference (EMI) also can change stored information.

Even or Odd Parity

In odd and even parity, every byte gets 1 parity bit attached, making a combined 9-bit byte. Therefore, a 16-bit byte has 2 parity bits, a 32-bit byte has 4 parity bits, and so forth. This produces extra pins on the memory module, and this is one of the reasons why various DIMMs and SIMMs have a different number of pins.

Again, parity adds 1 bit to every 8-bit byte going into memory. If parity is set to odd, the circuit totals the number of binary "1s" in the byte and then adds a 1 or a 0 in the ninth place to make the total odd. When the same byte is read from memory, the circuit totals up all eight bits to ensure the total is still odd. If the total has changed to even, an error has occurred and a parity error message is generated. Figure 3.7 shows various bytes of data with their additional parity bit.

Even parity checking is where the total of all the 1 bits in a byte must equal an even number. If five of the bits are set to 1, the parity bit will also be set to 1 to total six (an even number). If 6 bits were set to 1, the parity bit would be set to 0 to maintain the even number six.

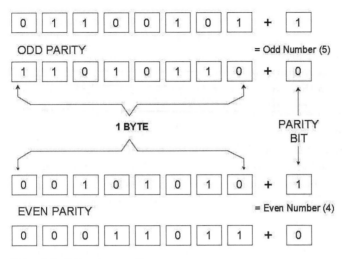

Figure 3.7   Odd and even parity.

Fake or Disabled Parity

Some computer manufacturers install a less expensive "fake" parity chip that simply sends a 1 or a 0 to the parity circuit to supply parity on the basis of which parity state is expected. Regardless of whether the parity is valid, the computer is fooled into thinking that everything is valid. This method means no connection whatsoever exists between the parity bit being sent and the associated byte of data.

A more common way for manufacturers to reduce the cost of SIMMs is to simply disable the parity completely, or to build a computer without any parity checking capability installed. Some of today's PCs are being shipped this way, and they make no reference to the disabled or missing parity. The purchaser must ensure that the SIMMs have parity capabilities, and must configure the motherboard to turn parity on.

Error Correction Code (ECC)

Parity checking is limited in the sense that it can only detect an error—it can't repair or correct the error. The circuit can't tell which one of the eight bits is invalid. Additionally, if multiple bits are wrong but the result according to the parity is correct, the circuit passes the invalid data as okay.

You'll receive a *parity error* if the parity is odd and the circuit gets an even number, or if the parity is even and the parity circuit gets an odd number. The circuit can't correct the error, but it can detect that the data is wrong.

Error correction code (ECC) uses a special algorithm to work with the memory controller, adding error correction code bits to data bytes when they're sent to memory. When the CPU calls for data, the memory controller decodes the error correction bits and determines the validity of its attached data. Depending on the system, a 32-bit word (4 bytes) might use four bits for the overall accuracy test, and another two bits for specific errors. This example uses 6 ECC bits, but there may be more.

ECC requires more bits for each byte, but the benefit is that it can correct single-bit errors, rather than only the entire word. (We discuss bytes and words in the next chapter.) Because approximately 90% of data errors are single-bit errors, ECC does a very good job. On the other hand, ECC costs a lot more, because of the additional number of bits.

Remember that ECC can correct single-bit errors. However, like odd-even parity, it can also detect (not correct) multi-bit errors. Regular parity checking understands only that the overall byte coming out of memory doesn't match what was sent into memory: It cannot correct *anything.*

Usually, whoever is buying the computer decides which type of data integrity checking he or she wants, depending mainly on cost benefits. The buyer can choose ECC, parity checking, or nothing. High-end computers (file servers, for example) typically use an ECC-capable memory controller. Midrange desktop business computers typically are configured with parity checking. Low-cost home computers often have non-parity memory (no parity checking or "fake" parity).

Exam Prep Questions

Question 1

> Part of a computer's RAM chip is dedicated to storing key system settings required for boot-up.
>
> ○ A. True
> ○ B. False

Answer B, false, is correct. Random access memory (RAM) is volatile and loses all its data without a source of power. RAM comes in modules and is almost never referred to as a chip. System boards commonly use nonvolatile CMOS to store system settings. CMOS memory uses very little current (a trickle charge) and continues to be powered for extended periods of inactivity by a small battery on the system board.

Question 2

> Over-clocking allows a microprocessor to run considerably faster than motherboard components. What type of memory structure was developed to minimize the delay of accessing RAM on the motherboard?
>
> ○ A. Processor resident pipeline
> ○ B. L-2 cache
> ○ C. CMOS memory
> ○ D. Duplex memory

Answer B is correct. Intel 486 and Pentium processors have a small amount of memory integrated in the chip called an L-1 cache. However, as processor speeds increased, additional high-speed memory was needed. This second block of memory was called an L-2 cache and was located on a special high-speed bus. Later designs include the L-2 cache on the processor cartridge or the die itself. Duplex memory and a processor resident pipeline do not exist. Answers A and D are incorrect because they're imaginary terms. Answer C is incorrect because CMOS is used to store settings information and has no effect on processor speed.

Question 3

> DIMMs and SIMMs are interchangeable, provided speed and capacity require-
> ments are observed.
>
> ○ A. True
> ○ B. False

Answer B, false, is correct. SIMMs and DIMMs look similar, and both use
edge connectors. However, DIMMs use both sides of the connector to support a 64-bit or wider memory bus, and they have two separate connector
pins, one on each side of the module board. SIMMs also have two separate
connector pins, but they are wired together.

Question 4

> Parity chips on SIMMs no longer provide a useful purpose and have been large-
> ly removed.
>
> ○ A. True
> ○ B. False

Answer B, false, is correct. Parity chips allow memory to be tested during the
POST, and they also monitor memory during computer operations. Some
manufacturers have eliminated them or bypassed their function to cut costs.
This allows less expensive SIMMs to be used, but at the expense of reliability.

Question 5

> Which of the following choices best describes what is meant by cache memory?
>
> ○ A. A place where instructions are stored about the operations of a device
>   or application
> ○ B. Extended memory that can be made accessible with the **SMARTDRV**
>   **/ON** command
> ○ C. Memory that holds applications and data that the CPU isn't running
> ○ D. Memory that holds data that the CPU will search first

Answer D is correct. The CPU looks in cache memory first. If it fails to find
the necessary data, it looks in main memory. If it fails to find what it needs
in main memory, the CPU looks on the disk. Answer A is incorrect because

hardware instructions are handled at a bus level, not in system memory. Answer B is incorrect because cache memory is a small amount of specialized memory. Extended memory is part of main memory. Answer C is incorrect because a cache is used to speed up memory usage. If the CPU isn't running an application it has no need for speed.

Question 6

Which of the following types of memory operate on a principle similar to serial transfers running through a cable? (Choose all that apply)

❑ A. SDRAM

❑ B. SRAM

❑ C. RDRAM

❑ D. DDR SDRAM

Answer C is correct. This is a trick question, not in the types of memory but in the misleading suggestion that there is more than one answer. Rambus memory (RDRAM) is different from other forms of memory in that not only are the chips on the RIMMs running in series, but the memory slots on the board also are in series, requiring a continuity module. Answer D is incorrect because DDR memory is particularly designed around a parallel transfer structure. Answers A and B are incorrect because SRAM and SDRAM move bytes across the memory bus in whatever width the system can support.

Need to Know More?

 Freedman, Alan. *Computer Desktop Encyclopedia, 2nd Edition.* AMACOM, 1999. ISBN: 0-814-479-855. This is great for a fast look-up or refresher.

 Messmer, Hans-Peter. *The Indispensable PC Hardware Book, 3rd Edition.* Reading, MA: Addison-Wesley Publishing Company, 2000. ISBN: 0-201-403-994. This is a comprehensive, up-to-date reference book that covers far more than you will need to know for the exam.

 Minasi, Mark. *The Complete PC Upgrade and Maintenance Guide, 11th Edition.* San Francisco, CA: Sybex Network Press, 2000. ISBN: 0-782-128-009. This is considered one of the best reference books available. In fact, Minasi's book was instrumental in the formulation of the first A+ exam.

 Mueller, Scott. *Upgrading and Repairing PCs, 14th Edition.* Indianapolis, IN: Que, 2000. ISBN: 0-7897-2745-5. This is one of our favorites. If you are going to have only one reference book, give this one serious consideration.

 Rosch, Winn. *Hardware Bible, 5th Edition.* Indianapolis, IN: Sams Publishing, 1999. ISBN: 0-789-717-433. This is a well-organized reference book that covers software issues as well as hardware.

 http://www.aceshardware.com: Ace's Hardware—Technical Information for the Masters and the Novices. A comprehensive site covering everything you would ever want to know about memory.

Brian Neal—Publisher, Webmaster
All Content is Copyright © 1998-2002 Ace's Hardware. All Rights Reserved.

Processor Mechanics, IRQs, and DMA

. . . .

Terms you'll need to understand:

✓ Microprocessor, processor, chip
✓ Hex, binary
✓ Vanilla ASCII, text file, text editor
✓ Floating point unit (FPU), also known as a math coprocessor
✓ Signal trace, interconnect, transistor

✓ Micron, millimeter, nanometer
✓ Register, microcode, instruction
✓ Clocking, multipliers, dividers
✓ Interrupt Requests (IRQ), Direct Memory Access (DMA)
✓ Port, address

Concepts you'll need to master:

✓ Base-numbering systems
✓ Bytes and words
✓ Micron manufacturing process
✓ On-die versus external central processing unit (CPU) functions (internal and external bus)
✓ Buses and transfers

✓ PCI specifications
✓ Address bus, processor bus, memory bus, system bus (also called the front-side bus)
✓ Instruction pipelines
✓ Write and read operations
✓ CPU interruptions, PCI steering

The CPU, also known as the central processor, is the heart of the system. We've found that the biggest cause of "glaze factor" in learning about computers is first, the overwhelming amount of jargon involved, and second, the lack of any single reliable source of explanation or translations. Preparation guides are loaded with specs and acronyms, but give very little context. On the other hand, a good gamer or hacker can give you plenty of CPU details, but generally in jargon-speak. Aside from fixing computers, we believe that A+ certified technicians should also be able to hold up their end of a conversation having to do with over-clocking and what makes a powerful machine.

We've tried to use this chapter to focus on context. Throughout our own careers, we've found that when people understand the ideas that originally went into building a device, they can more easily piggy-back the changing details of new technology onto what they already know. Technology follows evolutionary lines, after all, just like everything else. Scott Mueller's *Upgrading and Repairing PCs* is now in its 14th edition, and is a superb source for the many details of PC hardware. We've listed the book at the end of the chapter. However, this book is both a combination of specific details and the broader context you'll need to make those details stick in your head before you take the exam.

Chapters 3, 4, and 5 are all interconnected. Everything related to how processors differ rests on your knowledge of certain principal ideas. This chapter lays the groundwork for specifics of CPUs and chipsets discussed in the next chapter. Processors are complicated pieces of electronic wizardry, and sorting through these concepts may be a little confusing. However, each segment helps to define the way processors work—from the original processors, all the way through to Pentium 4 and Athlon chips. If you already know how a CPU works, then skim the headings and proceed to Chapter 5, "Processors and Chipsets." Otherwise, we believe the terms and definitions in this chapter will build a "tree" on which you can hang the myriad of numbers and specifications you'll want to remember when you read the next chapter.

Finally, few people seem to agree on terminology as it applies to processors. We've examined the Intel and AMD Web sites, read numerous white papers, looked at countless other sites and documents, and drawn from our own experience. Our conclusion: You may find a significant difference between the way various terms are used on the exam, and how they're used in the real world. As such, we've made every effort to distinguish between terms, their definitions, and their usage. Our thinking is that if you know how something works, you'll be able to understand the point of a conversation, regardless of how particular terms are being used in any specific context. Now let's begin.

Numbers, Symbols, and Words

We all draw numbers by using symbols and pictures. Those drawings have a direct relationship with underlying patterns. From the time our brains evolved, we've been able to recognize pattern sets. We choose to make pictures of those patterns, in whatever way we want. For example, the Romans used an "I" for a one, a "V" for a five, and an "X" for a ten. They started with a simple, incremental listing: I, II, III, until they came to IIII and IIIII. Maybe they looked at their hands, seeing that their thumb had a different shape, and decided that "V" would mean a whole hand. Or maybe they got tired of carving so many 1s into stone. Either way, the "V" was a single symbol that could represent five other symbols—five fingers, or units.

In the decimal numbering system, a "9" is a single symbol that replaces 1+1+1+1+1+1+1+1+1. It could also replace 111111111, sort of the way the Romans were headed. A group of 1s can represent a number using a different numbering system entirely. In binary, for instance, 111111111 is a 9-bit representation of decimal 511. When we include the 0 in our counting, we actually have 512 combinations of ones and zeros. Interestingly enough, a fixed disk sector contains 512 bytes.

Everything was working fairly well for the Romans, but nobody bothered to make a symbol for "nothing." After all, if there wasn't a mark, it was nothing—so why pretend it was something? Meanwhile, the Arabians were figuring out all sorts of interesting things to do with numbers. They were busy people, and didn't have time to play around with carving wide pictures into stone. So they chose different, simpler symbols that took up less room. They still used the 1 (maybe because it looked like a finger), but they drew a 2, 3, 5, 8, 9, and so forth. In order to represent "nothing," they chose the 0. (Possibly, because it looked like the circle of life and these guys had no life: They were busy inventing mathematics.)

Equal To and Same As

Nobody can teach you how to recognize that something is the "same as" something else. It's a built-in (innate) function of a normal brain. Someone can teach you how to put into words what you automatically understand, but she can't teach you pattern recognition. Either you "see" it or you don't. In the same way, nobody can teach you what "add" or "subtract" means. Children must first grasp the idea of "more" and "less" on their own, before they can relate the ideas to words involving "add" and "subtract." First we learn three words: the-same-as. Then we replace them with a single word: equals. Finally, we translate "equals" into the "=" symbol.

How does a computer know that 1 is the same as 1 (1 = 1)? How does a CPU know that 00 has more zeros than 0, or that 1 has less ones than 11? These are instructions built into the microcode. Microcode is stored right on the chip die. The three concepts of "equal to," "make more," and "take some away," are part of simple arithmetic, and are programmed into the arithmetic logic unit. The ALU also contains simple logic instructions that determine whether something is true or not true, and other Boolean logic operations.

Irish mathematician George Boole (1815–1864) developed Boolean logic. He reduced all search logic to three operators: AND, NOT, and OR. Each operator was assigned True or False, which can be represented by a binary 1 or 0. Modern transistors, computers, flash memory, and search engines continue to use Boolean logic.

Bytes and Words

Suppose we have a theater filled with rows of seats (see Figure 4.2, later in this chapter). Each row has an address, much the way a memory page has an address on a DRAM chip. Each seat within the row also has a column address. (When you stand at the front looking toward the back of the theater, the seats are lined up in columns.) For example, one address might be the twelfth seat in row thirty-one. What if you had a ticket that told you to go to seat 3112? Is that row 3, seat 112; or row 311, seat 2? Maybe it's seat 31 in row 12? (Imagine what a Roman ticket to the Coliseum would look like!)

We can divide numbers with a hyphen, and make up a rule: The first numbers will always be the row; the second numbers will always be the seat (a column address in a row). Now your ticket would be printed with 31-12. All you would need to know is the rule (and how to count). Binary and hexadecimal numbers are often divided into smaller pieces with a hyphen or a comma, primarily for better readability. (The computer doesn't care whether there's a hyphen. It looks only at 1s and 0s.)

People tend to talk about 8-bit bytes, but we could just as easily have 16-bit, 32-bit, 64-bit bytes, or even larger bytes. A "byte" is whatever someone says it is. Traditionally, a byte is the largest bit-unit the CPU can work with in a given time frame. Generally, we speak of bytes as moving around the system, external to the CPU. On the other hand, we tend to reference data moving around inside the processor itself as "words. "

NOTE   Anything taking place inside the chip housing, on the chip die, is "internal" to the processor. When data crosses the processor bus and moves to any other device, including the North-South bridge and memory controller, that data becomes "external" to the processor (outside) .

A "word" is essentially the number of bits a CPU can combine into a working unit. In many cases, the word is the same thing as a byte. We can take a 16-bit binary number with a hyphen inserted between two groups of eight characters, and it's still a 16-bit byte. In that case, we could say we have a two-word byte. On the other hand, if the CPU can handle sixteen bits at a time in its registers, we could call the entire 16-bit number a word. Again, the hyphen is just for people of the human being persuasion.

 A byte is the largest binary number a bus outside the CPU can transfer. Bytes also move around over a CPU's internal buses. A register is usually as wide as the byte, and a byte is as wide as the CPU's registers. The registers are usually as wide as the CPU's internal bus structure. In other words, the number of wires (signal traces) making up the internal bus is the same as the number of transistors in a register. When a byte is inside a CPU, we often distinguish it by calling it a "word." In our opinion, CompTIA defines a byte as being eight bits.

Binary Numbers

It would be nice if 10 millivolts would mean a one, 20 millivolts would mean a two, and 30 millivolts would mean a three, going up to nine. But it would be almost impossible to condition the electrical current in any wire to such an exact degree that it would never vary unless we said it should. Analog computers tried using this principle, but PCs use a digital, on/off system.

Computers use binary numbers—regardless of what we type on a keyboard, or how we use language in a program. The last step of the process is always to convert whatever people have been doing into 1s and 0s (on and off). The area inside a CPU that does this is the *decode unit*, or the *instruction decoder* (not on the exam). There are several translation tables between binary numbers and "regular" characters (letters, numbers, and punctuation marks). The one we're interested in is the *American Standard Code for Information Interchange (ASCII)* character set.

 You probably won't need to know the names of the specific internal processing areas on the exam. However, you'll most likely have to know the common terms for features that differentiate processor families. To distinguish certain terms, we'll specify that they're not on the exam by saying so in parentheses, as we did in the preceding paragraph, or we'll use the "Tip" feature.

Everyone in the world pretty much agrees that the first 128 numbers in the ASCII table represent the same characters. IBM created an additional 128 *extended* ASCII character set, but many people use extended character sets as code pages for different language symbols. It happens that we can have 256 combinations of 1s and 0s in an 8-bit binary number (eight places wide). The 8080 processor (first in the "80-something" family of chips) had an 8-bit internal bus, so it made sense for IBM to use numbers that could move along that bus. They created the extended character set at about the same time.

The extended ASCII table has 256 combinations of 1s and 0s, but the highest decimal number in the list is 255. Why? Because the first number is 0. An eight-bit binary zero is **00000000**. If we fill every placeholder with a 1, we end up with **11111111**, which translates to decimal 255. Count up every number in the entire list and you'll see that there are 256 numbers when you include the eight-bit 0.

Vanilla ASCII (Plain Text)

Batch files, AUTOEXEC.BAT, CONFIG.SYS, and many generic reference files must contain *only* characters from ASCII 0032 through 0126. (The numbers 0001 through 0031 are used as control signal characters, like the "bell" code or "carriage return.") These generic characters are called *plain* or *vanilla* ASCII characters (from plain-old vanilla ice cream). Reference books often mention using a text editor or your favorite word processor to create these files. A *text editor* is a simple word processing program that allows only plain ASCII characters, and no additional formatting codes. Commercial word processors routinely used special characters and formatting codes (taken from entirely separate code tables).

Creating Text Files

EDLIN.COM was the original DOS text editor (for "edit line"), and drove most early PC users insane. DOS 5.0 introduced EDIT.COM, which still exists and works like a simple word processor. The DOS Editor allows Cut & Paste, Find, and other conveniences. Upscale word processors provide the File | Save As feature, and you can choose to save a file as a *.TXT file type rather than the default, proprietary, binary format. Plain-vanilla ASCII files almost always have the .TXT extension. Be very careful that you never open a critical text file, and then save it again in a proprietary word processor format. CONFIG.SYS, AUTOEXEC.BAT, and SYSTEM.INI are examples of files that will fail if they're not in pure text format.

Windows introduced NOTEPAD.EXE as a graphical text editor, and it's still available in most later versions of Windows. WORDPAD.EXE is the Windows 9x replacement for Notepad. If you have a copy of it, you can copy NOTEPAD.EXE to the Windows 9x Windows\Send To folder. It will then show up as an option on the Context menu (the right-click pop-up menu). This allows you to highlight a file in the Explorer, right-click for the Context menu, and send the file to a text "viewer." Simply seeing a file's contents in Notepad can often give you an idea of what the file does. This is particularly useful if a file extension isn't registered in the Explorer's File Associations (for example, shareware documentation).

Microsoft has been around from the beginning, and so another common format is their Rich Text Format (.RTF). The format isn't as widespread as plain ASCII text, and neither can critical DOS files use it. Windows 9x ships with WordPad, which allows you to use basic formatting tools to make a document visually interesting. In fact, you can save a fully formatted Word document as a .RTF file, then open it in WordPad. Someone reading the file may not be able to make many formatting changes, but they at least can see something more sophisticated than a plain-text Notepad file.

Numbering Systems

Let's quickly review three different numbering systems. Our habit is to think of the "first" of something as being number 1. In the world of computer technology, the first something is always 0. The decimal, hexadecimal, and binary numbering systems all start with zero. If you remember your grade school arithmetic, the number of digits that can fit into the units (ones) column is called the *base*. Decimal numbering is *base-10* numbering. The word "decimal" comes from the Latin "ten," which means you're allowed a maximum of ten digits in the ones column (0–9). Remember, we start with zero, not one!

Always remember that computer numbering begins with 0 before moving higher. There are sixteen IRQ lines, but the largest number is IRQ-15. There are eight DMA channels, but the largest number is 7. We're speaking of the physical lines, built into the interrupt controllers on the motherboard, and the actual channels provided by the two DMA controllers. Don't worry about virtual IRQs, in terms of the exam.

There's actually no symbol for "ten" in decimal numbering. The word *ten* describes only a 0 in the ones (units) column and a 1 in the tens column. "Ten" is the same word in any base numbering, but we get there by a different maximum in the units column. Regardless of the numbering system, we count out the allowable numbers until we have to add one more. Then we stand up and shout, "TEN!" Base-3 counting would be: zero, one, two, TEN! Base-7 numbers would be: zero, one, two, three, four, five, six, TEN!

In base-10 numbering, we start counting with 0 and are allowed to go up to 9. Any more digits and we've reached the end of the line and have to go back to the beginning again (0). But where will we keep track of our first ten numbers? Fortunately, someone invented the tens column. We "carry the one" and put a 1 in the tens column. The 1 means we've already accounted for ten numbers and want to go higher.

Binary Numbers—Base-2

Someone once said that there are only ten kinds of people in the world: those who understand binary, and those who don't. *Binary* refers to base-2 numbers, in that we can use only two units—zero and one—before we have to "carry the one." In base-2 numbering, there's no such thing as "2." After we've accounted for our two allowed numbers, we put a one in the tens column and shout, "TEN!" It's just like base-10, only different.

Binary counting would be: zero, one, TEN! We then move on with eleven, one hundred, one hundred and one, and so forth. (There's no "eleventy-one.") The binary sequence in symbols would be 0, 1, 10, 11, 100, 101. Notice the increasing number of placeholders? Binary numbers use only ones and zeros, so the "2" is replaced by what we think of as a 10. Confusing? Of course—that's what computers are all about! The exam won't have any binary or hexadecimal math conversions, but you must be able to recognize the concept.

Hexadecimal Numbers—Base-16

Hexadecimal (*base-16* numbering) is where numbers in the ones column go beyond ten digits, all the way to 16 places. For that, we use letters. Decimal numbering has only ten available digits—0, 1, 2, 3, 4, 5, 6, 7, 8, and 9— before we make a TEN. Hexadecimal (often abbreviated as Hex, H, or h) includes an additional A, B, C, D, E, and F. Fortunately, computers were invented a few years after we stopped using Roman numerals. Come to think of it, though, wasn't a Chinese abacus a computer, or at least a calculator?

In hexadecimal, "F" is the sixteenth digit, and therefore, the last allowable number that can fit in the ones column. (Don't forget that zero is the first digit.) Counting a full, hexadecimal sequence would be: 0, 1, 2, 3, 4, 5, 6, 7, 8, 9, A (not ten), B, C, D, E, F; then we would shout, "TEN!" Note how the A replaces the 10. The F represents the crossover point—where we "carry the one." In decimal numbers, the 9 represents the same crossover point.

Following F (in Hex) we arrive at our carry-the-one process. So the next number after F is 10h. Pay attention to the small "h" following the number. This indicates that the number is a hexadecimal number. It is *not* a third symbol in the number itself. The sequence continues as 11, 12, 13, 14, 15, 16, 17, 18, 19, 1A, 1B, 1C, 1D, 1E, 1F, and then another tens unit, making 20.

Be sure to remember that human beings typically specify computer memory addresses in hexadecimal notation. Hex notation can appear as **10h**, **10H**, **&H10**, or **&h10**. The first two formats are the most common. Therefore, decimal 255 is typically written as **FFh** in hexadecimal format. The actual hex address is **FF** with the **h**, letting the reader know that this is a hexadecimal number.

16-bit hexadecimal numbers are usually divided into two eight-bit "words" separated by a comma. For example, decimal 23,505 is written as **5B,D1h**. When you examine the contents of a binary file, you may see the hex addresses as groups of four numbers, or listed with a space: **5BD1** or **5B D1** and no "h" indicator.

So what would the number A0h be—one hundred? Actually, it would be decimal 160. In any base system, 100 means we've reached our maximum in the "tens" column and have to cross over to the "hundreds" column. Decimal

100 is hexadecimal 64. On the other hand, hexadecimal 100 (100h) is decimal 256, which would require a 9-bit binary number. The last allowable, two-place number in hexadecimal is FF, which is decimal 255. (Hey, we said it was confusing!)

Hexadecimal numbering allows us to cram more information into a smaller space when we're writing programs (in Assembler, for example). For example, 255 uses three placeholders (bits) in decimal numbering. The same number is 11111111 in binary numbering, taking up eight places. It becomes FF in Hex, using only two places. Understand that a computer couldn't care less what we human beings draw on paper. Computers always work with binary numbers. Only the fact of how ridiculous it is to read binary numbers accounts for why we use hexadecimal. It's a lot easier to write (and read) 00,9E than to write 0000000010011110. (That being said, low-level programming works with the CPU and certain registers to almost directly use hexadecimal numbers.)

Most programming languages work with character symbols before a *compiler* changes those symbols into machine language. Finally, the decode unit inside the CPU translates the machine language into binary numbers. Most of the binary numbers inside the CPU represent internal or external memory addresses.

Logic and Numbers

Have you ever seen a movie where a submarine sinks and divers come to the rescue? The divers can't talk underwater, so they bang on the hull of the boat. Anyone hearing the noise bangs back. If there's noise, then someone inside is alive. This is a basic logical proposition. *If noise, then life: else, no life.* We all use logic, all the time. *If lights on, someone home: else, empty house.*

As long as we know the condition we want to test, we can set a 1 to mean "True," and a 0 to mean "False." For example, we might want to test a password someone enters. The password is "Bob." Of course, when the user types B o b, the keyboard controller translates the letters to binary numbers. The keyboard sends a 01000010 (capital *B*) to the CPU, which stores each digit in a separate transistor. In an 8-bit CPU, eight transistors make up one register. Then we send 01101111 (*o*) and finally 01100010 (lowercase *b*), filling three registers. The CPU stores 01000010-01101111-01100010.

Meanwhile, Windows has the same number stored in a configuration file. The operating system loads into memory and knows which file contains the password number. (The file would probably contain hexadecimal 426F 6200.) The CPU doesn't know what to do with the numbers in its registers, so it looks in the microcode for instructions. When it fails to find instructions, it sends a request to main memory. Main memory contains instructions as part of Windows, and loads information from the password file. The memory controller then sends 01000010-01101111-01100010 back to the CPU.

The CPU stores the number in three additional registers (making a total of six registers). Once again the CPU looks in microcode for instructions. Logic instructions check the voltage in each transistor of the first three registers, to see whether it's the "same as" the voltage in the transistors making up the other three registers. When all twenty-four transistors match, the logic instructions send a 1 for "True." The password matches, and the CPU then works with Windows to move on to the next step.

Interesting Areas Inside a CPU

When a string of bits enters the CPU, they swing by the control unit to say hello. The control unit can do several basic things, four of which are fetch, decode, execute, or store (not on the exam). If the control unit doesn't know what to do with the arriving bits, they go to the pre-fetch waiting area (like a cache, sort of). The control unit then tries to find instructions somewhere in the memory hierarchy (instruction cache, L-1, L-2, or main memory). If a software application has placed some useful instructions into main memory, the address for a particular "sentence" of instructions is sent over the processor bus to the address bus. The control unit's fetch operation then takes apart the address for each word in the arriving instruction. Next, it sends each word to a specific address location in the instruction cache.

 This may seem like "way too much information," but the Intel Marketing Department has invented terms like Advanced Dynamic Execution, Execution Trace Cache, and Rapid Execution Engine, along with other esoteric names, for the Pentium 4 chip. You'll have a much better time understanding these so-called features if you have an overall sense of what takes place inside a CPU. For example, instruction words are broken down even further, using pipeline architecture and predictive branch logic. Finally, Windows XP waits a certain length of time to load or shut down while it sets up or clears the pre-fetch buffer. The concept arose out of the same CPU pre-fetch area. Understanding the concept applies to all sorts of interesting things.

The control unit tells the pre-fetch unit to move the bits it's holding to the instruction cache. There, they join the newly arrived instructions. The bits and their instructions can finally move to the decode unit. The decode unit translates the data into binary numbers, along with its address and instructions. It then sends the entire data package back to the control unit. The control unit reads the data and instructions. The execute operation initiates the *arithmetic logic unit* (ALU, not on the exam). The store operation then makes sure that all the results are given addresses and stored in certain registers.

NOTE

The L-1 cache was originally used to store overall instructions on the chip die, before they arrived at the decode unit. Because of pipeline architecture, Intel now uses what used to be the L-1 to cache data fragments for the decode unit. On a Pentium 4, this is now the Execution Trace Cache. With the L-2 cache running at processor speeds, it has now taken over the work previously done by the Level 1 cache. In other words, a Pentium 4 doesn't have an L-1 cache by that name. AMD was the first to build the L-2 cache onto the chip die, with late-model Pentium 4 soon to follow. Remember that CompTIA may propose that the L-2 cache is still an entirely separate chip. Realistically, an L-3 cache is more often a separate cache chip, or at least outside the chip die.

The FPU

The ALU performs simple arithmetic operations on whole numbers, and doesn't deal with fractions directly. Prior to the 80486, Intel added a separate floating point unit (FPU) processor chip to the system. This so-called math co-processor works directly on fractions (calculated as decimal numbers). The FPU went onto the chip die in the 486. Modern chips incorporate the FPU to handle sophisticated mathematical calculations used in computer-aided design programs (CAD) and gaming software. Today's games use incredibly complicated numbers, and seventh-generation chips have to take those calculations into account.

Microcode

Processors work with instructions, arriving from some type of memory. Instructions are like sentences that can be broken down into individual words. Instructions may be either internal to the CPU and a permanent part of the chip, or external. External instructions typically originate in software programs, like the operating system, for example. Internal instructions are the chip's *microcode* (not on the exam). Some microcode instructions have to do with arithmetic, and others have to do with logic and taking care of business. (Microcode instructions are to a CPU vaguely similar to what BIOS instructions are to a motherboard. We refer to programming built into a controller or hardware device as *firmware*.)

Software programs contain many more instructions than could possibly fit inside a CPU. To get around this, the processor works with individual instructions in sequences, very quickly. Microprocessors are way too fast to work with anything other than memory chips. As a result, software applications place whole blocks of instructions into memory and some of the CPU's microcode is in charge of moving individual instructions in and out of that memory. (A memory cache is an area, smaller than main memory, where the next-up instructions are waiting to be processed.)

 Although processors are working with instructions and parts of instructions, most of the binary numbers moving around inside the CPU are addresses.

Originally, we measured a CPU in terms of its capability to handle some millions of instructions per second (MIPS). Later measurements tended to be based on the CPU's capability to execute FLoating-point-unit OPerations per Second (FLOPS). You may hear of Mega-FLOPS and Giga-FLOPS; this has nothing to do with Broadway productions or movies.

Pipelines and Micro-ops

Intel's Net Burst technology, used in the Pentium 4, is like the approach Henry Ford used to build a Model-T. Mr. Ford proposed that the key to production was to use an assembly line, and reduce the number of tasks assigned to any one worker. Producing a finished car is like processing a complete set of instructions. Each particular instruction is like putting together a piece of the car.

Assigning multiple tasks to a single worker slows down the production of a car. A person on the assembly line would have to switch tasks and fetch new tools to perform each different set of instructions. A better idea would be to have each worker perform only one task, and then outfit each station in the line with only the tools necessary for that task. So if there are 100 tasks involved in building a Model-T, the assembly line would ideally have 100 workers and 100 stations. Each station would use only the tools necessary to complete a specific task, and the overall manufacturing process would be faster.

Net Burst mimics this approach to building a car. A task is like a line of instructions coming from memory. Each task can be broken down into specific steps, which is like a single word in an instruction. Then each individual step can be further broken apart into particular movements and a single tool. This is like a fragment of a word, individual bits and bytes.

 Word fragments are called micro-operations, or sometimes, instruction fragments. Micro-operations are abbreviated as "micro-ops," μ-ops, or μops.

The pipeline in a Pentium 4 functions exactly like an assembly line, with a single pipeline for each task. The Pentium III performed branch prediction in 12 stages. The Pentium 4 uses a 20-stage branch-predictive pipeline to accomplish the same function. Generally, more stages in a pipeline mean faster execution, and the more pipelines in a CPU, the faster the overall throughput. Net Burst increases both the number of stages and the number of pipelines to enable development of high-speed processors.

Branch Prediction

Suppose we want to bolt an alternator onto an engine. We need two hands, the alternator, the bolts, the nuts, and a wrench to tighten the nuts. When we see the engine come along the assembly line, we can predict we'll need to fetch an alternator from the available pile. We can also predict we'll need our first bolt and then a nut to go with it. Finally, we can predict we'll require the wrench. Each prediction has a high probability of being true, because what we're trying to predict is such a small event. One of the internal bottlenecks in faster processors has to do with the size of instructions and words. AMD opted to reduce the size of the instructions moving around inside the CPU, and to use fewer processing steps. Intel chose pipeline architecture, and added extra steps in breaking apart larger instructions.

The smaller we can break down an operation (task), the higher the accuracy of our predictions becomes concerning each piece. However, there's a flaw in the logic. When the task is to "Install the alternator" and the assembly line fails, there's only one step between noticing the failure and our decision to do something else. But when the task is to "Insert the fourth bolt" and something fails, we then have to make a number of decisions returning all the way back to when the engine showed up in the first place.

Branch prediction has to do with examining an incoming instruction and "grabbing" the parts that can be executed more quickly than other parts. In a sense, the CPU predicts which "branch" of a line of instructions it can handle immediately. Because the technique tends to break apart instructions, the CPU must also keep track of all the related fragments of instruction lines. Intel's Advanced Dynamic Execution technology (part of Net Burst) has to do with how many fragments the CPU can track.

Branch-predictive logic provides a substantial performance increase only for as long as there are no failures within the pipeline. When something in a 20-stage pipeline fails, then the CPU must take extra time to cancel the entire process and empty the pipeline to make room for a new instruction line. Even when nothing fails, all twenty stages must take place, regardless of how many times the same instruction executes. To help speed the process of converting an instruction to binary, the L-1 cache was assigned to helping the decoding unit, and now contains already-converted numbers. Intel renamed it to become the Execution Trace Cache.

The x86 Instruction Set

Processor instructions generally come in two flavors. The processors we're concerned with use instructions written for a *complex instruction set computer (CISC)*. The other flavor is used with a *reduced instruction set computer (RISC)*. As the name implies, the two systems are based on the complexity of the instructions a CPU can handle. RISC instructions are a set length, whereas CISC instructions are variable length. One step in pipeline architecture is to figure out the length of a particular instruction. The number, type, and length of instructions a processor can execute is determined by its instruction set (microcode) and clock speed.

IBM and Intel decided to use CISC architecture in the original 8086. Later processors, such as the 80286, 80386, 80486, and so on, all had an "86" in their name, making them all part of the "something-86" family. Jargon shortened the "something" to an "x" and so we have the x86 family of processors. These include the Pentiums and Celerons, as well as chips used in any IBM-compatible computer. AMD's Athlon and Duron processors are part of the generic x86 family, and all these chips use the x86 instruction set in their microcode.

Until now, PC-type processors used the IA-32 instruction set (Intel Architecture 32-bit), commonly referred to as x86. Intel 64-bit processors (for example, Itanium and Pentium 4) use the IA-64 instruction set. However, AMD 64-bit chips use a new instruction set that retains backward compatibility with the IA-32 set. It isn't really CISC, nor is it really RISC. The AMD instruction set has come to be known as the x86-64 set, referring to the x86 backward compatibility of the Opteron and Athlon-64 processors.

CPU Manufacturing

Microprocessors begin with a silicon bar called an ingot. A machine slices off a thin piece of silicon called a wafer. The thinner the wafer, the more slices per ingot. Signal traces, technically called *interconnects*, are etched onto a wafer by lithography—a sort of photographic process. You can think of signal traces as tiny wires (although they're not). Until recently, CPUs used aluminum for the traces. IBM developed a way to use copper—a better conductor—and in 1998, fast CPUs began using copper interconnects.

 Western Electric developed a process, in 1950, of growing large single crystals of silicon that could be sliced into wafers. In 1958, both Texas Instruments (TI) and Fairchild Semiconductor developed the integrated circuit, with TI arriving just ahead of Fairchild in the patent process. Wafers and transistors used to be built from something called *germanium* until Fairchild Semiconductors introduced a process using less-expensive silicon.

Everything placed on the various wafers is part of the chip *die*. The wafers are then enclosed within the chip *housing*. The manufacturing process "yields" some number of wafers, which in turn yield some number of processor chips. Thinner wafers mean more chips per ingot and reduced manufacturing costs. A more complex, larger CPU uses more wafers per ingot, thereby increasing manufacturing costs. The smaller we can make the signal traces, transistors, and components, the more we can fit onto a wafer. (Modern chips use between seven and nine layers of wafers.)

Signal Traces and Wafers

The lithographic process works with ultra-violet light and a *mask*, which is sort of like a photographic negative. The wavelength of the light sets a limit to how small the interconnects and transistors can be (approximately 100 nanometers). Until recently, most manufacturers used Deep Ultra Violet (DUV) lithography to etch the wafers. Evolving technology is moving to Extreme Ultra Violet (EUV) light, with shorter wavelengths. EUV allows for traces as small as 10 nm (nanometers) to accommodate some seriously small transistors.

Modern transistors and signal traces run into problems at an atomic level. "Electromigration" is essentially electrons "bumping into" atoms along the path of the trace and "falling out of" the conductor. Over time, enough conductive electrons migrate away from the traces so that the CPU begins to fail. IBM's Silicon-on-insulator (SOI) manufacturing process is one way to reduce heat, which is an important source of electromigration. AMD has chosen the SOI process and copper interconnects.

IBM has recently announced that they've successfully tested silicon-germanium transistors running at 210GHz and using 50% less power than today's transistors. The company predicts this could lead to 100GHz processors by around 2005, although they would be used in limited areas such as networking and communications hardware.

Always remember that smaller devices mean shorter travel distances and faster speeds. On the other hand, high-speed current in a small device also usually means more heat. It took a long time to develop copper trace technology because of problems with insulation, heat, electromigration, and bonding the copper to silicon. SOI uses a pure-crystal silicon insulator to resolve the bonding problem.

The Processor Core

Microprocessors have many parts, not all of which are directly responsible for calculations and handling instructions. The *processor core* is the area within a chip that particularly deals with event processing. Although we speak of registers, these are more like small regions inside a processor, organized into related tasks. There aren't any real divisions on a wafer, and so the core is a way to reference the components inside the housing. In other words, we speak of the core speed (internal) as being separate from the processor bus speed, which connects the CPU to the "outside world."

Given that almost all processors, nowadays, are called a Pentium or an "AMD chip," people have begun to reference the code name for the processor core used by design engineers. When you hear about a Pentium "Northwood" or "Prescott," or an AMD "Thunderbird" or "Thoroughbred" (T-bred), the terms refer to the microcode changes built into new processor cores.

The Micron Manufacturing Processes

Micron manufacturing (not the same as Micron, Inc.) refers to how closely together signal traces can be etched onto a wafer. Suppose we want ten traces running alongside each other, and each trace is one inch wide. For the sake of argument, let's say each trace must be separated by 50% of its diameter—half an inch, in this example—so as to prevent a short circuit. There are only nine spaces between ten wires. If we lay all the traces on a piece of cardboard, we end up with a wafer 14.5 inches wide (10×1) + (9×0.5).

What if we could shrink the wire to half an inch wide? Each wire can now be separated by only a quarter of an inch. Our wafer becomes (10×0.5) + (9×0.25), making it seven and a quarter inches wide. It's half as wide, but do we still need it to be ten inches long? Why bother, given that we cut the width in half? We can also cut the length in half, making for shorter wires (five inches long). Shorter traces mean that signals don't have to travel as far, and so everything moves faster.

Microns (mu) and Nanometers (nm)

We all know that computers work in a whole different world of measurements. Speed measurements are based on cycles per second, and we describe numbers using the metric system. The average human hair is about 150 microns thick. A micron (also called a micrometer) is one millionth of a meter. A meter is slightly longer than a U.S. yard, coming in at 39.37 inches. Why such a weird number? Well, back in 1889, the International Bureau of Weights and Measures decided a meter should be one ten-millionth of the distance to the North Pole, straight up from the equator over the curved surface of the planet (a meridian).

People got tired of always having to pace off the distance to one of the poles, so The Authorities (the famous "They") etched two lines on a platinum-iridium bar and called the distance between them the International Prototype Meter. By 1960, nobody had time to fly to Paris for a copy of the distance, so a meter became 1,650,763.73 wavelengths of the orange-red radiation of krypton 86. Obviously, Superman was involved and, back then, everyone could easily see wavelengths without their glasses. Nowadays, we're far more sophisticated, but we don't see as well as people used to. Today, a meter is 1/299,792,458 of the distance light travels in a vacuum in one second. If you have very small feet, you can pace off the distance yourself.

A nanometer, also called a millimicron, is one billionth of a meter: a thousand times smaller than a micron. Remember: An average human hair is 150 microns thick, which is the same as 150,000 nanometers. Intel started out with signal traces being 10 microns apart, which works out to 10,000 nanometers. Lately, they've been using a 90 nm process, down from 130 nanometers. 130 nm is the same as 0.13 microns. 90 nm is half the separation of yesterday's chips, at 0.09 microns. Get out your glasses and compare a modern silicon wafer to one of your hairs: You'll see. Manufacturing numbers are moving to nanometers because, let's face it, microns are just way too big!

Intel recently announced a new 45-nanometer manufacturing process (0.045 microns) to allow for 20 nm transistors in CPUs by 2007. The transistors are 30% smaller and run 25% faster than today's transistors. CPUs have already crossed the 2GHz mark, and by 2007 Intel expects to produce chips running at 20GHz speeds. (That's almost as fast as Superman!)

The Original Microprocessor—4004

Intel introduced the 4004 on November 15, 1971. The world's first micro-processor had a 4-bit internal bus, with 2,300 transistors on a single chip (not on the exam). Designed for the Busicom calculator, the chip could address 640 bytes (5,120 bits) of internal memory, and 4,096 bytes (4KB) of external, system memory. The chip ran at 740KHz—0.037% as fast as a 2GHz Pentium. Still, everyone thought it astonishing. Another way of saying it is that the Pentium runs 2,700 times faster than that original 4004—a 2,700% increase in speed. On a highway, your car would go from 60 mph to 162,100 miles per hour. (There's a speeding ticket waiting to happen!)

What we're going to attempt to do in this chapter (don't try this at home) is to get from 2,300 transistors to the 40-million-plus transistors on a Pentium (over 100 million in 64-bit processors). We're starting with 740,000 cycles per second, and expect to end up at 2,048,000,000 cycles per second. The 4004 used a 10 micron process, as opposed to our Pentium's 0.18 mu process (10,000 nm down to 180 nm). Along the way (in the next chapter), we'll watch the L-1 and L-2 cache move onto the die, and check out MMX, SIMD, SSE, and other changes to the microcode. The 80286 and 80386 processors introduced something called Protected Mode and Virtual Real Mode, both of which are necessary concepts to understanding Windows. Each of these features rests on the ideas in the following sections.

Inside the CPU

The wafers making up a CPU are divided into many areas, based on related tasks. As we've said, we can put imaginary boundaries around these areas, and think of them as "neighborhoods." A *register* is a group of related transistors. To keep things simple, we'll say that the main building blocks of a CPU are its transistors and signal traces. Transistors are special types of switches, and without getting technical, they're made up of two charged terminals separated by a "middle place." The electrical charge in this middle place is the opposite of the two charged terminals—it has the opposite *polarity*.

Transistor mechanics aren't on the exam. However, understanding modern processors rests on your understanding of the transistors in a register. Parts of a transistor may be referred to as a "gate," giving rise to the term "gated logic."

The magic of transistors lies in their tiny control lead (the base), connected to the middle section. Figure 4.1 shows how a transistor acts like a break in a circuit by either amplifying or impeding the charge in the middle. We can add to or reduce this charge, allowing current in the main circuit to flow through the transistor, or be stopped from flowing through. (For a discussion on how removing negative charge increases positive charge, see Chapter 6, "Basic Electronics.")

Figure 4.1 illustrates a PNP transistor, manufactured as positive-negative-positive. The two charged terminals are positive, separated by a negative charge in the middle place. Transistors may be the reverse, or NPN, where two negative charges are separated by a positive charge. Transistors have different characteristics, according to their being either PNP or NPN. Our illustration is highly simplified, for the purpose of demonstration only, and you won't have to know about transistors for the exam. Semiconductor transistors are not "little tubes," as depicted, but rather small areas on a silicon wafer that contain added impurities (called "doping").

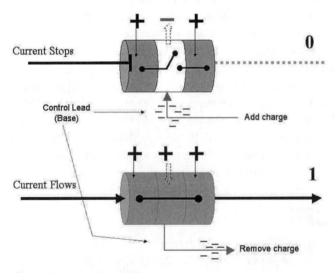

Figure 4.1   A transistor switch.

Transistors are obviously more complex than what we're depicting, but understand the concept of the separating charge. The main circuit has some amount of voltage in a particular polarity. The "break in the circuit" (the middle place) is the opposite polarity, which prevents current flow. The control lead changes the polarity in the middle until it matches the two outer terminals. When the charges match, current then flows through the main circuit. When current flows, the computer understands a 1. When no current flows, the computer understands a 0.

Earlier processors sent a 5V pulse to change a bit. Later processors worked with approximately 3.3V. Modern and mobile processors, as well as Low-Voltage and Ultra-Low-Voltage processors, work with pulses of about 1 volt or less. "Battery Optimization Mode" is related to assigning power to areas within the CPU based on activity. With no activity, the area "shuts down" until it's needed again. Mobile chips usually have an "M" in the name (for "M"obile), as with the Pentium M line of processors. "Centrino" is an Intel brand name for a group of technologies working together in mobile computers.

The Internal CPU Bus and Registers

People speak of registers, and how registers are so-many-bits wide. As we've said, a register is just an imaginary neighborhood of some number of transistors all working together. There are many types of registers inside a CPU, all handling different tasks. Some work with the built-in microcode, and others act as small amounts of memory—storage areas. The registers we're interested in are the ones having to do with moving bits and bytes of information, and the ones involved with storage.

Let's suppose we have an 8-bit processor. It has miniature "highways" or interconnects running between its registers. The highways make up the CPU's internal bus. Data moving inside the processor travels in eight-bit-wide words, along these tiny wire roads. We tend to think in terms of 8-bit bytes, so we'll say that eight "wires" make up one lane.

Remember the Chinese abacus? It's made up of a frame with wires strung like a bus. Beads travel back and forth over individual wires, and each bead is like a bit. We can look at the bead patterns (bytes) in the whole framework (a register) and see a number. (At least some people can.)

When we have only an 8-bit bus, it's like moving traffic back and forth on a one-lane road. Cars (bits) going in one direction must wait until there's a break in the traffic going the opposite direction. If we widen the road to a 16-bit bus width, we can use each lane to move traffic in both directions simultaneously, 8 bits at a time. We could say we're moving two 8-bit words in opposite directions. (Or, we could move all 16 bits in one direction.) When the 16-bit "road" inside the CPU reaches the narrower 8-bit processor bus, we end up with a traffic jam. Most current desktop processors have a 32-bit internal bus (like a 4-lane highway). 64-bit processors have a full, 64-bit internal bus and also can handle 64-bit bytes.

 It costs money to extend a bus all around a motherboard. An 8-bit bus is cheaper to produce than a 16-bit system bus. The main difference between the 8088 and 8086 processor was that the 8088 was retro-engineered to use a narrower motherboard bus. The 8088 was a 16-bit 8086 designed to connect to an 8-bit motherboard bus, using an 8-bit processor bus. Otherwise, they were the same chips.

The Address Bus

We said earlier that "the 4004 chip could address 640 bytes (5,120 bits) of internal memory, and 4KB (4,096 bytes) of external, system memory." What, exactly, does that mean? Sure, a CPU has small areas of memory inside the housing, and processors work with addresses rather than specific bits, but keep in mind that the chip had only 2,300 transistors, some of which had to store microcode. The 4004 must have been able to address 32,768 transistors (4KB) for memory storage—somewhere. *Something* inside the processor had to be able to put together a unique, binary address for each of those transistors. That something is the address bus (sometimes incorrectly referred to as the memory bus).

The address bus is arguably one of the most confounding parts of a CPU. And yet, we could say that how the processor uses the address bus is a key factor in distinguishing chip families. Simply put, the address bus

➤ Is where the CPU puts together memory addresses

➤ Assigns those addresses to data bits

 You won't be required to know *exactly* how the address bus works for the exam. However, you will have to be able to differentiate processors based on the various amounts of memory they can address. Internal and external memory capabilities refer to the address bus. "Addressable memory" is specifically related to the width of the chip's address bus.

Scott Mueller has an excellent example of how addresses differ from bus widths. We've said that buses are like roads and highways. A one-lane road with a lot of traffic is going to have traffic jams. When we widen the road to two lanes, we can move a lot more traffic before we run into a jam.

Regardless of how wide the road might be, let's suppose there are houses alongside. Each house must have its own unique address. When we use a single digit for each house address, we can build a maximum of ten houses

(0–9). Using two digits for the address, we can build a maximum of 100 houses (00–99). The houses may be in a neighborhood with four-lane roads, but we still can have only one hundred houses. What if we add one additional digit? Now we jump from a hundred to a thousand houses (000–999). A four-digit address allows us to use 10,000 cells (houses) in a memory chip. The house address has nothing to do with the width of the road, other than the fact that rush hour might create a traffic jam as more people try to get to their houses.

> Each time we add another place for a digit in a number, we increase the allowable addresses by a factor of the base. For example, a single place multiplied by the 10 in base-10 allows for ten addresses. Four places, using base-10, would be 10×10×10×10, or 10 to the fourth power (10,000). The same four places, using base-2, would be 2×2×2×2, or 2 to the fourth power (16). Eight binary placeholders would be 2 to the eighth power—256. (You can use the **POWER** function in Excel to figure out these numbers in any base-numbering.)

Row-Column Addresses

Let's use the theater example again. (Remember? We talked about it a year ago, at the top of this chapter.) Suppose we have 32 rows, each with 8 seats. This is like having a 256-bit memory chip (each seat is a capacitor). The theater can hold a total of 256 seats (32×8). Our DRAM chip has 256 capacitors. Figure 4.2 may help you visualize rows of seats. We'll use a CPU with 4-bit registers. Each seat has its own addresses. Each row is a memory page and it, too (the whole page row), has its own address. The example shows Row 5, Seat 4. How can we put "5-4" into two binary numbers? We can't.

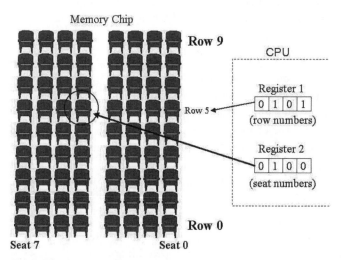

Figure 4.2   Rows of registers (theater seats).

Binary 1111 can generate 16 address combinations (2×2×2×2). But using only one register, we still have to split our "theater ticket" to show both rows and seats. It would look like 11-11. So we really can store only enough locations for four rows of four seats (2×2, and 2×2) in each half of the address. That means our last ticket would show only the fourth seat in the fourth row. But we want 32 rows of 8 seats! (*Please make a whining sound at this point to demonstrate multimedia being used in a hardcopy book. Thank you.*)

Now…suppose we assign the row numbers to one register. We'll assign the seat numbers to a second register. Finally, we'll put someone in the last possible seat. That ticket will read 1111-1111. The seat is in the sixteenth row and it's the sixteenth seat. Our problem is that we want our rows to be only eight seats wide. Better that we should use a 5-bit number for the rows, and a 3-bit number for the seats. That way, our last ticket would be 11111-111, which translates to Row 31 (thirty-second row), Seat 7 (eighth seat).

Sadly, we can't squeeze five bits (row numbers) into four transistors. Not only that, but even though we're only using three bits for our seat numbers, the register still has four transistors. That leaves an extra transistor, and you can bet some sneaky pulse of electricity is going to come along to change that fourth switch to a 1 or a 0 when we're not looking!

Processor Bus Bottleneck

Here's something else to consider. Address numbers break apart in clock ticks as they cross the narrower processor bus. The processor bus is the point where, one way or another, the CPU connects to the motherboard and the outside world, including the memory chip and its own bus. (We'll examine all the bus connections in the next section.) Only a portion of the address number can typically move across the processor bus at a given time. The remaining bits must wait for the next clock tick.

After all the parts of an address have crossed the processor bus, the memory controller takes them across the memory bus and reassembles the complete address. It then opens a channel to the required memory cells. When the controller tells the CPU the channel is open, the CPU sends through a data bit. Each event in this little dance takes place on some number of clock ticks—a clock *cycle*. Some of the clock cycles are at the core speed; other cycles are at system bus speeds. (Nowadays, CPU clocking derives from the front-side bus.)

Synchronous DRAM allows both the memory controller and the CPU to "discuss" the status of a given channel without wasting time. Asynchronous (not synchronized) DRAM means that the CPU has to waste clock ticks checking to see whether the memory controller has opened a channel yet. (Isochronous means "performed in equal amounts of time" and applies to multi-processing systems.)

Figure 4.3 shows a highly stylized illustration of data moving across the processor bus, coming from the address bus. Control lines determine whether the address bus is writing data out to memory, or reading data in from memory. Either way, the address bus controls the process. The CPU either orders the memory controller to accept data or it orders the controller to send out data. The CPU is the boss of the bus and the remaining bits must wait for the next clock tick!

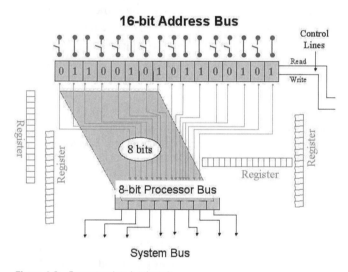

Figure 4.3 Processor bus bottleneck.

When the CPU wants to read a bit from memory, it sends the controller an address. Once again, the processor bus splits the segments. The memory controller then re-assembles the segments and opens a channel to a cell. The memory controller sends the data back to the CPU, and the incoming data goes back over the address bus into one of the CPU's data registers. The remaining bits must wait for the next clock tick.

16-Bit and 32-Bit Systems

Effectively, the processor bus determines how many data bits can transfer into and out of memory at one time. An 8-bit processor bus moves eight bits at a time, and works with eight-bit memory pages. The "time" is a clock cycle. A clock cycle is the combination of some number of clock ticks. A 16-bit processor with a 16-bit processor bus can move sixteen bits per cycle across the bus, in 16-bit memory page addresses. (1MB of RAM requires a 20-bit address bus.) Carrying through the logic, a 32-bit processor bus works with 32-bit memory pages and 32-bit bytes in a cycle (using a 36-bit address bus).

The size of the processor bus helps determine the width of the address bus, and the amount of system memory any given CPU can address.

64-bit systems don't necessarily have a 64-bit internal bus. Instead, a 32-bit Pentium chip might generate two 32-bit words at the same time, sending them both across a 64-bit processor bus. This would be like having two virtual 32-bit processors built into the same chip. Pentium III and Pentium 4 processors do this, using pipeline architecture to work with a 64-bit processor bus. In other words, the internal highway is narrower than the external processor bus.

Superscalar architecture, referring to pipelines, means that a chip uses multiple pipelines to move smaller internal words through a larger processor bus. The remaining bits must wait for the next clock tick.

Split Transfers

A CPU is a really fast gizmo (new technical term). We human beings might think it's a little stupid to send a row address, then a seat address, and then a data bit, but the CPU does things so quickly that the sequence is almost instantaneous. All that matters is that a controller understands pulses of electricity in a programmed order. When the first set of pulses arrives, the controller finds a row of cells in memory. When the second set of pulses arrives, the controller finds a column. It then opens up a channel to a specific transistor at the row-column location (a specific seat in the theater). Finally, the CPU sends a data pulse and the memory cell turns on or off.

If you think about it, doesn't the same process take place when you and seven of your friends go to see a movie? You show up at the ticket counter (address bus). The clerk, using an abacus, moves twelve beads, one at a time, until they form a pattern. He or she then writes down a seat address on a piece of paper and hands it to you. You hand your ticket to an usher (this is back in the old days). The "usher" is a control instruction. Both of you walk into the theater (the memory controller) and start counting rows. When you arrive at your row, the usher tells you to count every seat until you find your own. When you tell the usher you're seated, he or she then goes back to tell the ticket clerk to let the next person into the theater. Now suppose each step took place in a millionth of a second!

Memory Write

What if we use three registers, and send a third of an address to the address bus every clock tick? With a little microcode programming, we could combine the three pieces of data into a useful binary number: 1111-1111-1111. Then we could program the CPU to say that the first three numbers are the row address. The next number (not part of the binary address) will be a control instruction. The control instruction tells the memory controller that the number coming after it will be a seat address (we've used five clock ticks, going one way only). Our only problem is we need an address bus wide enough to store 12 digits, using twelve transistors.

Having read Chapter 3, "Memory: Types and Forms," you should know that a row in memory is called a memory page. The address bus can send a page address, then the address of a specific column (a cell) within the page, and finally, the bit pulse.

"Internal memory" or "addressable memory" means that the address bus is wide enough to handle a particular binary number. It doesn't mean how much memory is built onto the chip die. Neither does it mean the total number of all available memory cells in RAM. Rather, it describes how many row addresses, or column addresses the address bus can handle. Note that we're speaking of either rows or columns, not the combination of both row and column addresses.

Figure 4.4 shows how separate registers can be used to store a memory address. The address bus is sort of like a train station, combining the contents of several registers before sending them on their way. Understand that even with only 2,300 transistors, the 4004 could set aside a mere forty or so transistors to accomplish what we've laid out in our examples.

Memory Read

Because the CPU controls the address bus, we can run the same process backwards. Combining three 4-bit numbers gives us a 12-bit page address, which the CPU then sends to the memory controller. After the CPU gets back a "go" signal, it sends a column address (a simple 4-bit number). Once again, it gets back a "go" signal from the controller, and the CPU opens a channel to one of its internal data registers. With the channel open, the CPU then slurps up (different technical term) the data bit coming from the memory controller. (This time, we've used eight clock ticks for data going in both directions.)

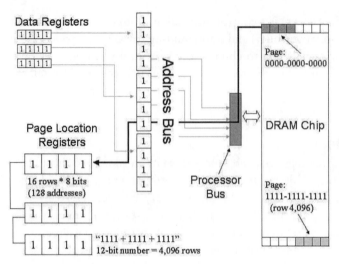

Figure 4.4 Memory pages and addressable memory.

The address bus is a special bus inside the CPU, designed to handle binary address numbers. Each address is the location of either a memory page (row), or a specific memory cell (a transistor or capacitor). Memory cells can be inside the processor, as well as on an external memory chip. After the CPU assigns an address, a channel opens up to a specified memory cell. When the channel opens, a pulse of electricity crosses the channel and changes the state of the cell to a 1 or a 0.

Addressable Memory

Think back to the 4004 with its 4KB of addressable memory. If we send three 4-bit signals for an address (using three clock ticks), we can work with any one of 4,096 row addresses (memory pages). One tick later, and we can send another 4-bit number to locate one of eight cells in a particular row—a column address. Now we have 4,096×8 to give us 32,768 possible locations.

Hey, wait a minute! Didn't we say the 4004 could address 32,768 bits of "programmable" memory? We've had to use several clock ticks, but so what? The limit comes from the 4-bit processor bus, but the CPU has clock ticks to spare.

Internal addresses are usually the size of the internal bus (in this case 4-bit addresses), and move very fast. External addresses use combinations of registers and take longer to move.

The important thing to understand is that the CPU sends a page address, then a bit address, and then the actual bit control pulse. By using this process, a 4-bit system, with an 8-bit address bus and 8-bit memory pages, can rapidly develop some very large numbers. A single 4-bit page register can store 16 page addresses (128 cells). Two registers (8 transistors) can store 256 pages (for 2,048 cells); three registers can store 4,096 pages (for 32,768 cells); and four registers (16 transistors) can store 65,536 pages (524,288 cells).

We don't particularly care whether a CPU uses 4-bit, 7-bit, 29-bit, or 73-bit registers. What we're interested in is the width of the address bus. Whatever memory chip we connect to the CPU, that chip will have some number of cells. All the cells, taken together, form a grid. Each cell in the grid has a unique address. However many cells there are in the entire grid, the address bus must be able to store the number of the largest row address (memory page) as a binary number. The column addresses will always be smaller than the row addresses.

 The 8086 and 8088 processors used a 20-bit internal address bus to address 1MB of memory (1,024,000 bytes of page addresses). This process is called Real Mode addressing (discussed in the next chapter).

Micro Buses

To finish up our discussion of how a CPU works, let's expand a little on the topic of buses. We first introduced them in Chapter 2, "Motherboards," but it's important for you to see how the CPU uses a number of small buses. As you saw in the password example, each time we send a letter from the keyboard, eight bits go zooming across the motherboard's system bus. Understand that the CPU is the *Master of All That Is*, and can't waste time talking directly with the lowly keyboard. Instead, the CPU works with system RAM and cache memory chips. It's all a question of speed. The CPU is extremely fast, with memory chips being the only components fast enough to keep up their end of a conversation.

We know that we can increase performance with wider data paths and faster transfer rates. With the 80486, there was a growing gap between the core speed and the processor bus speed. Keep in mind that although the CPU mostly talks with memory chips, the rest of the motherboard is still an essential part of the system. Everything on the motherboard is getting data from the CPU. The processor bus connects the CPU directly to the overall motherboard, and the motherboard's bus was being left behind in the cosmic dust. Intel realized that some sort of "traffic control" center was necessary.

North-South Bridge architecture acts like this control center. The idea was to have high-speed lanes for fast traffic (memory), and slower lanes for traffic moving back and forth between expansion cards, the keyboard, and the mouse. The CPU would use its processor bus to connect to the "front side" of this control center. The rest of the surrounding devices could then connect to other areas of the center. Each connecting bus, handling particular types of traffic, could then be clocked according to the needs of its particular devices.

The System Bus—Motherboard

Up until the 80486 processor, the motherboard's and processor's bus speeds were reasonably matched. The ISA bus had an 8.33MHz clock, but Intel was able to give it a 4× multiplier to bring it up to 33MHz (a 3× multiplier generated 25MHz). With the introduction of the Pentium, Intel also released the specifications for the PCI bus, which we covered in Chapter 2. What matters now is that the PCI specification proposed a fast North Bridge and a slower South Bridge to be connected by the new bus—the traffic control center. The Super I/O chip would manage the slow ISA bus speed, and connect to the South Bridge.

The ISA bus was first-generation input-output management, and the PCI specification was second-generation I/O. Intel has been designing a third-generation protocol, referring to it as 3GIO (3rd Generation I/O). This evolution recently became formalized as *PCI Express*. Be sure you don't confuse it with PCI-X, which is version 2.x of the second-generation specification, and called for a 100MHz, then 133MHz clock. The 800MHz FSB in a Pentium 4 is presumably a 100MHz clock with an 8× multiplier. The 533MHz bus is a 133MHz clock with a 4× multiplier. PCI Express is expected to be as much as six times faster than PCI-X, reaching speeds of 6.6GB/s.

We've seen many confusing references to a "system bus" applied to who-knows-what actual bus. Technically speaking, the system bus is the data transfer path on the actual motherboard. When a keyboard sends its bits of information, they travel through the signal traces that make up the motherboard's system bus. Only when they arrive at the South Bridge do they become part of the "crowd" of other buses.

Regardless of who calls which bus the system bus, we refer to the system bus as the motherboard's primary data transfer path. Technically, the "system bus" is the data pathway laid down on the motherboard itself, where information crosses to the North-South Bridge structure. That being said, we've seen references to the system bus as connecting memory to the FSB, connecting the FSB to the processor bus, connecting the CPU to memory, and even being the processor bus itself.

Figure 4.5 shows the many different buses connecting the North-South Bridge with the CPU. Each micro bus in the picture has a letter (for the sake of reducing clutter in the graphic). The important thing to understand is that various companies use different names for each particular bus, but the relative location of each type of bus is correct. Table 4.1 is the key to each letter and the bus it represents. For example, the PCI bus is listed as letter F, and shows the actual bus connecting the two bridges. PCI slots are connected to the bus (some distance away), but you should be able to see that the PCI *specification* is more than a simple bus. The entire specification determines how all the various micro buses function.

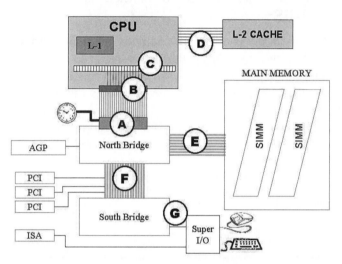

Figure 4.5 How the CPU connects to the overall system.

Table 4.1	Letter Key for Figure 4.5
Letter	**Bus Name**
A	Front-side bus (FSB). Specified as being timed by the main timing clock oscillator.
B	Processor bus, also called the Processor Side Bus (PSB), and sometimes the Data bus.
C	Address bus.
D	Backside bus, used to connect an off-die memory cache to the CPU.
E	Memory bus, connecting system RAM clocked at a multiplier of the FSB. PCI800 SDRAM uses an 8× multiplier of 100MHz to reach 800MHz memory "speed."
F	PCI bus; originally clocked at 33MHz, then 66MHz. The bus itself is not the PCI-specified "system clock."
G	ISA bus, clocked at 8.3MHz using a 1/8× or 1/12× divider. The ISA bus is always present for legacy I/O, but the motherboard may not have ISA expansion slots anymore.

F—The PCI (Conventional) Bus

Intel originally specified that CPU timing, as well as bridge and memory timing, would derive from a 66MHz clock. The clock is assigned to a bus at the front side of the North Bridge. This front-side bus—the FSB—is the connection between the central processor and the high-speed North Bridge. By splitting off the front-side bus timing from the CPU's processor bus timing, Intel could then manipulate the speed of the new bus to increase throughput rates.

The PCI bus itself connects the two bridges, and is timed to the specified system clock. The PCI specification changed the location and designation of the system clock to be an integral part of the North-South Bridge architecture. In other words, the motherboard clock moved. Clocks can be multiplied and speeded up, or they can be "divided" and slowed down. The original PCI bus (PCI Conventional) was a 33MHz bus, and the front-side bus ran at 33MHz. Soon after its release, the bus went up to 66MHz.

 CompTIA may very well refer to the FSB as the "system bus," and use those references to indicate overall clock speeds. After you've passed the exam, never confuse the memory bus with the FSB or the processor bus.

The System Clock

A system clock is a complicated little gizmo with several output channels. Some channels are fixed at 66MHz or 100MHz, and other channels may be "stepped down" with some set of clock dividers. 386 machines had stabilized many devices at 33MHz, but Intel was already looking at clock doubling and the PCI concept. As such, the first PCI specification called for a 66MHz clock that could be divided down to 33MHz, 25MHz, and 8.3MHz, to match existing device speeds. The actual PCI expansion bus was clocked at 33MHz, to match standard expansion cards and devices.

The second specification still calls for 66MHz, but has fixed output channels stepped up 1/3 to 100MHz. Current FSBs, running at 133, 200, 400, 533, and 800MHz, all use a multiplier of the 66MHz clock. Still, many PCI bus devices expect a 33MHz clock, whereas the AGP port expects a 66MHz clock. Although PCI devices are fairly restrictive in their timing needs, the AGP can often handle a fair amount of over-clocking.

PCI Sig (**www.pcisig.org**) states the following: "There are 4 speed grades in the PCI-X 2.0 specification: PCI-XTM 66, PCI-XTM 133, PCI-XTM 266, and PCI-XTM 533. The PCI-X 66 and PCI-X 133 speed grades were included in the PCI-X 1.0 specification; they support 66MHz and 133MHz PCI-X respectively. 100MHz PCI-X has been implemented in the market by using PCI-X 133 adapter cards. Both PCI-X 266 and PCI-X 533 are new to PCI-X 2.0; they are the 266MHz and 533MHz versions of the specification. All four speed grades are included in the PCI-X 2.0 specification."

A—The Front-Side Bus

Figure 4.5 shows the FSB as letter "A." All the chipset components derive their speeds from the front-side bus. A 266MHz Pentium means the chip is using a 4× multiple of the original 66MHz clock. As we've said, that clock is part of the PCI Bus specification. Intel licenses the PCI bus architecture to chipset manufacturers, and with each major change in architecture, the chipset companies must renew their licenses. (At one point, Intel sued VIA over licensing issues, which were later resolved.)

Let's suppose we have a front-side bus clocked at 100MHz and a 2GHz processor. The CPU is using a 20× multiplier to define the core speed. However, the PCI bus is using a 1/2× divider of the actual clock to stay at 33MHz. An AGP bus is supposed to run at 66MHz, and so it uses 1:1 clock synchronized to the system clock. Understand that "system clock" often refers to the front-side bus clock, and not that actual clock oscillator. Therefore, people may say that the PCI bus, with a 100MHz FSB, is actually using a 1/3× divider, and the AGP is using a 2/3× divider. It's not exactly true, but you should be aware of what's going on.

 Regardless of whether we're talking about the AGP, PCI expansion slots, the CPU speed, or memory speed, today's specifications say that everything connected to the North-South Bridge derives its speed from the front-side bus clock. Because almost everything is connected to the North-South Bridge, many people tend to call the front-side bus the "system bus," or simply "the bus." Only when we understand the purpose of the FSB do we begin to understand CPU and memory speed ratings.

B—The Processor Bus

We've said that data transfers move from the address bus across another bus to get to the outside world. The processor bus is the specific point where electrical pulses move in and out of the CPU. Although the pulses are generated during core-speed clock cycles, the width of the processor bus may or may not cause a traffic jam. The outside buses each can only accept some number of pulses according to the number of clock ticks they use for data transfers (their own bus speeds). Remember that Pentium chips use a processor bus that's wider than the address bus, and so there wasn't a bottleneck issue until the Pentium 4 chips.

 Pentiums use a 36-bit address bus and a 64-bit processor bus. The 36-bit address bus allows for 64GB of addressable memory. Pentiums used in laptops are not necessarily the same as mobile Pentium "M" chips. Laptop Pentiums often use a 31-bit address bus to address 2GB of main memory. (We'll discuss this again in the next chapter.)

C and D—The Address and Backside Bus

We've already discussed the address bus, but you can see that the entire unit is internal to the CPU. Signal traces going to and from the address bus are part of the processor's internal bus.

On the other hand, the backside bus, letter "D," is a separate bus that connects memory cache chips directly to the central processor. Because of the separation, L-2 and L-3 caches can be set to transfer data at the same speed as the CPU. In other words, it isn't that the capacitors in an L-2 cache switch back and forth at some speed. Rather, data transfers take place across a dedicated bus, timed to a much higher speed than the main memory bus. Additionally, separating the backside bus allows for it to be made wider than any other bus. Intel's Advanced Transfer Cache (ATC) features a very wide, 256-bit backside bus.

 Pentium III Mobile Technology laptops use an ATC cache with a Celeron processor. Desktop PIIIs use an older L-2 cache with a narrower bus.

E—The Memory Bus

The PCI specification called for standard ratings to apply to memory modules, as we discussed in Chapter 3. Main memory connects to the North Bridge using its own, separate bus, which can be clocked at some multiplier of the FSB clock. The principal difference of DDR memory is that the memory controller can transfer data on the "half-tick." For example, PCI800 DDR memory might use a 400MHz memory bus speed, but with two transfers per clock tick. 400×2 = 800, which generates the 800MHz speed rating. Also understand that the 400MHz memory bus is first using a 4× multiplier of a 100MHz FSB clock.

AMD's 64-bit Opteron processor uses a completely new idea, installing the memory controller as an integral part of the chip itself. This enables the memory bus to run at core speeds. In addition to the integrated memory controller, AMD is introducing yet another new bus: the Hyper-Transport bus (discussed later in the next chapter). Essentially, this is an even smaller bus that connects multiple CPUs to each other. Intel is moving toward multiple processors, but each processor continues to connect through the North Bridge.

Intel tried to make the North-South Bridge architecture more efficient by introducing Hub architecture. However, it seems that market acceptance of the idea hasn't been very enthusiastic. Pentium 4s and Athlons continue to use chipsets designed with the bridge architecture.

Summary—How CPUs Work

Relax! Much of what we've discussed up until this point isn't specifically going to be on the exam. So what was the point? First of all, you should understand how a CPU works, and how it handles data addresses. Secondly, and more importantly, the entire x86 family of processors has changed in certain categorical ways. Back when A+ certification was getting started, we could easily point to a 486 and say that it was different from a 386 in that it had a built-in FPU and L-1 cache. But how do you explain the difference between a Pentium Pro and a Pentium III—or a P-4, for that matter?

Because we laid the groundwork in the previous section, we can "cut to the chase," so to speak, and highlight in the next chapter what we think you're most likely to find on the current exam. Chapter 5, presents only the changes to any given chip: the ones we think you can be tested on. Most modern chips generally differ in the following ways:

➤ Changes to the microcode—new instructions for multimedia and graphics processing

➤ Manufacturing process, number of transistors, and register sizes

➤ Internal bus width and word sizes

➤ Address bus width and addressable memory

➤ Front-side bus speed, which generates CPU speed

➤ Location and amount of Level 1 and Level 2 memory

Remember that processors work only with binary numbers, and each number must cross various buses. Then remember that simple calculations and logic work with whole numbers. More complex calculations usually require fractions. A floating point unit (FPU, or math coprocessor) is simply a way for a CPU to work directly with decimal points. Also remember that we can speed things up by either adjusting clock speeds or by making wider transfer buses. Early processors had a narrow 16-bit processor bus. Modern Pentiums and Athlons have 64-bit processor buses.

When we speak of a 32-bit processor or a 64-bit processor, we're referring to how many bits a processor can work with according to clock cycles. A clock cycle may be more than a single clock tick. Understand that however many ticks it takes to complete a specific task, the total number of ticks is a clock cycle. The cycle is defined by the number of ticks it takes to complete a task.

Although we often talk about bytes having eight bits, a processor handles some number of bits as "words," which are usually, but not necessarily, the same size as bytes. A byte is whatever number of bits the processor can handle in a single clock tick. A 32-bit processor can move 32 bits around at a time. When data leaves the processor, it does so over the processor bus, typically using additional clock ticks (more than the CPU needs for the same movement).

NOTE   A 32-bit processor, with a 16-bit processor bus, performs more slowly than the same processor with a 32-bit PSB. However, a 64-bit processor with a 32-bit processor bus may move each word in a "half tick." Modern processors typically move more than one byte per clock tick.

Interrupt Requests (IRQs)

We saw in Chapter 3 that when the CPU is busy with a process, any request by the memory controller must interrupt what the CPU is doing. The specific instructions for these interruptions are provided by the ROM BIOS on both the motherboard and on many devices. The operating system also understands interrupts, and uses part of low memory to store something called the *interrupt vector table*. Low memory is discussed in Chapter 13, "Booting, Startup Files, and Memory."

If you think of the CPU as the Wizard of Oz, then an IRQ line is like an 8- or a 16-lane yellow brick road. An IRQ is a signal coming from a piece of hardware (such as a mouse) indicating that it needs the CPU to do something. To take pressure off the CPU, IBM created a chip called an *interrupt controller*, which is analogous to that weird gatekeeper to the Emerald City.

When a piece of hardware sends a demand to the busy CPU, it tries to interrupt the processing by sending an IRQ down its own, assigned IRQ line. The IRQ signals (Dorothy and pals) run along the IRQ lines (yellow brick road) to an interrupt controller (that bizarre gatekeeper), which assigns *priorities* to incoming IRQs (puts them in the waiting room) and then delivers them to the CPU (the Wizard).

Because the interrupt controller (different from the memory controller) expects signals from only one hardware device per IRQ line, an *IRQ conflict* occurs when two devices try to use the same IRQ line at the same time. It's like two people trying to get through a gate at the same time. When that happens, computers usually crash, the gatekeeper loses his mind, and you're left in the poppy fields! This is why assigning IRQs to new hardware, prior to Plug 'n' Play, was so important—and why it was such a pain to diagnose when things went wrong. (One technical term for this pain is *major aggravation*.)

IRQ 2 Cascades to IRQ 9

The single, original XT interrupt controller chip could handle only eight IRQs, using eight lines. Starting with the AT and continuing through to modern PCs, motherboards began using two controllers. Each controller handles eight lines (0–7 and 8–15). To get the two controllers working together, IRQ 9 on the second controller was set aside to pass certain requests to IRQ 2 on the original controller. This is known as *cascading*.

The AT controllers began using interrupts 8–15 but kept the original XT lines 0–7. Therefore, the newer IRQ 9 often borrowed the old IRQ 2 in a process called "cascading." Be sure to know the term *cascading* for the exam.

Make a note that if IRQ 2 is being used, IRQ 9 is also being used. IRQ 9 is *cascading*, *vectoring*, or *redirecting* to IRQ 2. All three words refer to the same process of pointing to somewhere else. This concept typically shows up in a question on the exam. When source information is *redirected* to a destination, the destination receives *cascaded* information from that source.

By daisy-chaining the two controller chips (running them in series), the AT motherboard could handle 16 IRQs (14, really, when you consider the cascading between IRQ 9 and IRQ 2). Again, IRQ controllers support 16 interrupt request lines—IRQ 0 through IRQ 15. The concept of daisy-chaining spread throughout the hardware industry, beginning with IRQ and SCSI controllers, and continuing forward with USB and FireWire devices. (USB and FireWire are discussed in Chapter 10, "Basic Networking.")

PCI Steering

An interrupt controller is also known as a Programmable Interrupt Controller (PIC). Be very careful that you don't confuse PIC with PCI! The PCI specification, together with the DMI pool and PnP, introduced a system by which the PCI bus can "lock" one or more IRQs. A programmable interrupt controller is a chip, not a specification. Depending upon which device is active, the PCI bus can allow or disallow the use of that "locked" IRQ. In other words, the PCI bus "steers" a device to the interrupt controller and a specific IRQ—it *programs* the PIC. The concept evolved, and now Windows

XP shows such listings as IRQ 70 or IRQ 64. These are virtual IRQs (not on the exam). Virtual IRQs can range from 16 to 255.

 CompTIA will reference the standard sixteen hardware IRQs (0–15) found on the two controllers. Windows XP and the PCI bus can assign virtual IRQs to more than sixteen devices. The Device Manager still shows the underlying hardware IRQ through its virtual IRQ. This isn't an easy problem to diagnose and resolve, but the exam will focus only on the main hardware IRQs.

IRQ steering was designed to work with the Plug and Play feature that arrived in Windows 95. This is one of the reasons why the PnP specification requires a compatible BIOS, operating system, and device controllers. (Remember those three things!) Bus mastering is where a device takes control of a bus during a throughput operation. PCI steering, on the other hand, is where the bus itself directs data traffic to specific IRQs, based on their availability. The underlying hardware is still two programmable interrupt controllers with 16 IRQs (0 through 15).

IRQ Reports and MSINFO32.EXE

DOS platforms shipped with the *Microsoft System Diagnostics* tool, MSD.EXE. The utility (also called an accessory or tool) generated a report of the various devices in the system, along with the IRQ each was using. MSD went on to become MSINFO32 (Microsoft System Information) in Windows 98/Me and Windows XP. The program wasn't available in Windows 95 or Windows NT; however, Microsoft Office 7.0, 97, and Office 2000 shipped with the utility. Windows NT used a program called WINMSD.EXE (Windows MSD), but the Office version of MSINFO32 works just fine.

To use the accessory, right-click on My Computer, and then choose Properties | Device Manager | "System Devices." Another way is to click Start | Run | type msinfo32, and press Enter. If your version of Windows doesn't have the utility, but you have one of the Microsoft Office products, you can click on Help | About Microsoft Word | "System Information." (See Chapter 14, "Windows 9x," for more on MSInfo and a freeware replacement.)

You can't add an IRQ line to a system. The available IRQ lines are limited to the original sixteen. However, if you add a SCSI controller, the controller can take one IRQ line and assign separate SCSI ID numbers (LUNs) to six devices on the SCSI bus. This idea is similar to how USB hubs are designed to assign 247 devices to a single IRQ. The USB specification handles traffic management. The PCI bus evolved between SCSI and USB, and allows us to use many more than the few devices older motherboards could support.

Because some devices reserve USB bandwidth, the practical maximum of devices is less than the theoretical maximum of 247. Realistically, you can connect only 127 devices with USB hubs.

Windows IRQ Listings

When you run Microsoft Information (MSInfo), you'll see that it looks much like any Explorer tree structure. "Hardware Resources" is one of the main branches, which you can expand to show the IRQs. This report shows the actual IRQs and how they're assigned. When you run the Device Manager, you'll see the "PCI Bus" under "System Devices." Expanding this branch shows you the actual devices and their IRQs. This is where you'll often see several devices using the same IRQ. Don't be confused! The PCI bus is steering those devices, based on their activity. When two devices try to use the same IRQ at the same time and the bus fails to control them, that's when you have an IRQ conflict.

When Windows develops an IRQ conflict, one way to try and resolve it is to examine the Device Manager to see which two devices may be using the same underlying IRQ. One solution would be to disconnect devices sharing IRQ lines until there is only one left. Each time you add a disconnected device back into the system and restart, Windows and the PCI bus should (hopefully) reassign them to different IRQs. In some cases, system vendors ship a device with a limited set of IRQ options written into the PnP instructions. In a situation like this, if the PCI bus can't assign the device, then you must manually assign the device to an IRQ. For this reason you should always have a reference manual that explicitly details the device's IRQ options.

Default IRQ Listing

Table 4.2 lists the original IRQs. Another way of looking at the information is to think of the original design specifications built into the two original IRQ controllers. From what we've seen in the past, CompTIA may expect you to have the most important IRQs in your head, and we've listed them with an asterisk to the right of the IRQ numbers.

Be sure to remember that technical numbering begins with 00. The master IDE hard drive IRQ is number 14, but it's the fifteenth line. If you remember that there are two 8-line controllers, and then make the mistake of thinking of them as going from one to eight, you're likely to make the worse mistake of assigning a secondary hard drive to IRQ 16. There's no such number!

Table 4.2 Original IRQ Lines	
IRQ Line	**Device**
0	System Timer
1	Keyboard
2 *	Cascaded from IRQ 9
3 *	COM 2 or COM 4
4 *	COM 1 or COM 3
5 *	LPT2 or Sound Card (original XT hard drive controller)
6	Floppy Drive Controller
7 *	LPT1
8	Real Time Clock
9 *	Redirected Cascade to IRQ 2 (also used for PCI steering)
10	Open
11	Open
12	Mouse (PS/2 port)
13	Math Co-processor
14 *	Primary Hard Drive Controller
15 *	Secondary Hard Drive Controller (often used for CD or DVD drives)

Typically, IRQ 7 is always taken (LPT1). IRQ 5 shows as being available with a PCI bus, or it might be used as the default IRQ for a sound card.

IRQ 14 and Secondary Controllers

IRQ 14 is set aside for the primary IDE (ATA) drive controller. 14 comes before 15: Remember that! The primary controller is often referred to as the master controller, the master drive, Drive 0, the primary hard drive, or the first hard disk. Note that the device is Drive 0, but the IRQ is 14. Most motherboards have two IDE drive controllers, and each controller can have two devices. The second controller (not the drives themselves) uses IRQ 15.

Each IDE or EIDE controller can have two devices chained to it. The first device is usually the *master*, with the second device being the *slave*. A slave is typically a second hard drive. IRQ 15 (the last IRQ) is set aside for the secondary IDE drive controller, *not a second drive*. Remember that IDE controllers let you daisy-chain two devices, so a master and slave can connect to a single controller. The secondary controller is then open for a CDROM or DVD drive (or two).

Remember that the default IRQ 14 is used for the primary hard disk IDE controller. IRQ 15 most likely is used for either a *third* physical disk, or another type of slower drive. Often, two physical disks use the primary controller on IRQ 14. Adding a third disk requires using a second IDE controller, which then uses IRQ 15. Pay close attention to a question that asks about a master *controller* versus a secondary *drive*. IRQ 14 and 15 are the two important IRQs, but there can be four IDE drives.

Direct Memory Access (DMA)

No matter how fast the CPU runs, it can easily be loaded down if it wants to send data to something like a very slow (relative to the CPU) hard drive. If this is the case, the CPU then has to wait around for the drive to report back. This movement of data from slow disk to fast memory used to have to pass through some very small memory registers in the CPU. The DMA controller was developed to offload this sort of drudge work and to avoid bottlenecks in processing.

A number of semi-intelligent chips work together with the CPU. The interrupt controllers are two of these chips. The DMA controllers handle Direct Memory Access (DMA), and are also part of the *chipset*. When the CPU agrees, certain operations can bypass the ordinary processing channels and access RAM directly. For example, when a hard drive needs to access system memory for addresses or instructions, those interrupt requests don't have to interrupt the CPU. Fewer interruptions means more work gets done (just like in real life) and better system performance. The ATA specification and UDMA (Ultra DMA) are an outgrowth of this idea.

An evolving technology is to use Serial ATA transfers (SATA). We'll examine this technology in Chapter 8, "Peripherals: Storage Devices," where we discuss storage peripherals.

The DMA controller is like a highway bypass going around a city so that you don't have to deal with traffic congestion. It bypasses the CPU registers and moves information directly into and out of RAM. Oddly enough, that's why it's called "*direct* memory" access. A DMA controller chip is allowed to take control of the system, but it must first request control from the microprocessor. If it gets permission, the CPU makes itself look as if it's been removed from the circuit.

Originally, a motherboard had only one DMA controller. The system worked so well that a second DMA controller was added. Each controller allows four channels, so today we have 8 DMA channels (0–7) available on most systems. Again: two controllers, with eight channels.

DMA Channels

The original 8088/86 (8-bit/16-bit) processors had 4 DMA channels capable of supporting both 8- and 16-bit expansion cards. The 80286 added four more channels, but only for 16-bit cards. Table 4.3 lists the DMA channels and the most common devices configured to use them.

 DMA channels and IRQ lines interconnect devices, the CPU, and memory. You should document the current devices and their IRQs and DMA settings before you install and configure a new device. Keep the information in a dedicated system binder.

Table 4.3 Direct Memory Accessing Channels		
DMA Channel	**Bus Width**	**Common Device**
0	8- or 16-bit	Reserved (open)
1	8- or 16-bit	SDLC controller, Audio sound card, or LAN
2	8- or 16-bit	Floppy Drive controller
3	8- or 16-bit	Sound card, Hard Disk controller, ECP/EPP Parallel port, (or sometimes open)
4	16-bit	Cascade to channels 0–3
5	16-bit	Reserved (LAN)
6	16-bit	Reserved
7	16-bit	Reserved (Sound card)

Port IRQs and Addresses

The word "port" is derived from "portal," which is an entranceway to something. A door is a physical portal, but a computer interface is a logical port. Because we carry things through a doorway, another use of the word carry is "portage," which also reduces to "port." When an application can be carried (ported) over to another platform, we say it is portable. Adobe uses the *portable* document format (.PDF) to carry formatted text across different platforms.

Certain physical port interfaces, like the COM and LPT ports, can be divided into logical ports with separate memory addresses. The Internet (TCP/IP) often uses virtual ports as the final entryway into a destination computer. If this all sounds impossible, implausible, or immaterial, remember that it's imPORTant!

COM Ports

Each logical port has its own default memory address. Most modern computers have several physical I/O interfaces built into the motherboard. The two physical serial interfaces are broken up into four logical COM *ports*. ("COM" is a DOS device name.) COM1 and COM3 go together with the first physical interface. COM2 and COM4 go together with a second serial interface. USB ports, discussed in Chapter 10, are also serial ports, designed for fast serial transfers. However, USB ports use their own controllers and are not part of the COM ports.

In the real world, you'll be able to research memory addresses such as those of the COM and LPT ports on a given PC. However, the exam contains questions about ports and memory addresses. Even on an old DOS machine, MSD.EXE prints out whether a device is attached to either serial port, and which address the device is using. For the purposes of the exam, Table 4.4 lists the default memory addresses assigned to each COM port.

Table 4.4 Default COM Port Addresses and IRQs			
I/O Serial Interface	Port	Address (Hexadecimal)	IRQ
Controller 1	COM 1 (physical)	03F8	4
Controller 1	COM 3 (logical)	03E8	4
Controller 2	COM 2 (physical)	02F8	3
Controller 2	COM 4 (logical)	02E8	3

Here's a mnemonic that might help you build COM addresses during the exam. Observe that the only changing address values are "2–3" and "F–E." All four default addresses begin with 0 and end with 8. The only IRQ choices are 4 and 3.

It might help to think of COM3 and COM4 as "Extra," with an "E" hex address. COM1 and COM2 are "First," with an "F" hex address. The exam is multiple choice, so you won't really need to remember the 0 or the 8.

Using an odd/even trick, COM1 and 3 use the "3" (odd address) and COM2 and 4 the "2" (even address). In other words

➤ Port 1 (odd), COM1 and 3, use odd "03" (03F8).

➤ Port 2 (even), COM2 and 4, use even "02" (02E8).

➤ First (Ph)ysical interfaces 1 and 2 use "F" for First (xxF8).

➤ Extra logical interfaces 3 and 4 use an "E" for Extra (xxE8).

➤ The even ports (2 and 4) use odd IRQ 3. The odd ports (1 and 3) use even IRQ 4.

LPT Ports

Aside from the COM ports, the default printer (LPT) ports and their IRQs are also considered testable knowledge. The good news is that although the default COM port memory addresses are considered common knowledge, the LPT addresses aren't. LPT ports have a range of addresses, though they commonly try for a default address. Table 4.5 lists the two LPT ports and their default IRQs.

Table 4.5 LPT2 and LPT1 and Their Default IRQ Lines	
Parallel Interface	**IRQ**
LPT2 (parallel port)	5
LPT1 (parallel port)	7

LPT2 is rarely used these days, except on network print servers (PCs under the control of a network operating system and dedicated to managing a shared printer). IRQ 5 is much more often assigned to PCI steering. That being said, IRQ 5 is often the default for Sound Blaster cards, with LPT1 going to IRQ 7. If LPT2 is being used, it is usually assigned to IRQ 5 and 278h.

LPT2 comes first because IRQ 5 was originally the XT hard drive controller's IRQ. Later PCs had a normal configuration of two parallel ports, so LPT2 took over from the obsolete XT controller. Nowadays, you will most likely never see a workstation with more than one parallel port.

We've tried to come up with some ways to help you remember the proper order of the LPT ports and their default IRQs. Here are some suggestions, though you might have your own method:

➤ "There's only 1 God and only 1 heaven, and LPT1 uses IRQ 7."

➤ P-R-I-N-T-E-R has 7 letters.

➤ You have two hands with five fingers (each). LPT2 uses IRQ 5.

➤ 1 (LPT1) and 2 (LPT2) make "12." In the same way, 7 + 5 = 12.

Exam Prep Questions

Question 1

> You have a mouse connected to a PS/2 connector, and an external modem con-
> nected to a serial port. The mouse is using _____ and the modem is
> therefore using _____.
>
> ○ A. COM1, COM2
> ○ B. COM2, COM1
> ○ C. COM1, LPT1
> ○ D. COM2, LPT1

Answer A is correct. In most cases, the PS/2 connector is using one of the
motherboard's serial interfaces. The modem then uses the second interface.
One way to get rid of at least two of the responses is to remember that neither a mouse nor a modem use the LPT ports, which are parallel interfaces
and often used by printers. You'll have to use rote memory to select the right
answer from the remaining two.

Question 2

> Both hardware serial ports are in use, and the system has a serial bus mouse
> installed on COM3. Which IRQ and address are assigned to the logical serial
> port?
>
> ○ A. 3, 03E8
> ○ B. 3, 03F8
> ○ C. 4, 03E8
> ○ D. 4, 03F8

Answer C is correct. Don't get fooled into freaking out about a serial bus
mouse. All that matters is that something is using COM3. IRQ 4 uses odd
numbers for the leading numbers, and 03E8 is the correct address for COM
3, the logical port. Always remember that COM1 and 2 are physical ports,
and COM3 and 4 are logical ports.

Question 3

A local laser printer is attached to a Pentium III system, in a typical configuration, using _____ and _____.
○ A. LPT2, IRQ 7
○ B. LPT1, IRQ 5
○ C. LPT2, IRQ 5
○ D. LPT1, IRQ 7

Answer D is correct. Once again, the type of printer and CPU are irrelevant. This is a "scenario" question, designed to distract you from the fundamental problem. A printer is using some port and IRQ, based on the responses. Modern computers mostly come with a single parallel port (LPT1), which uses the default IRQ 7. The question indicates a local printer being attached directly to the computer. LPT2 would be more likely used for a network printer.

Question 4

The high-bit color 3D graphics taking place on the monitor are managed by the video card and the _____.
○ A. ALU
○ B. FPU
○ C. CPU
○ D. MMU

Answer B is correct. This question is one of those "deer-in-the-headlights" kinds of mind games you'll find on multiple choice tests. Before you run away and hide, remember that graphics require number-crunching. FPU should be a readily recognizable acronym for the math coprocessor. If you can't remember what the others do, take the guess. You'll probably be right. The floating point unit is designed to offload decimal fractions and complex numbers used in gaming and multimedia. The ALU is the arithmetic logic unit inside the central processing unit (CPU), so answer A is incorrect. Answer D is incorrect because the memory management unit is designed to handle virtual machines. Answer C is incorrect because the CPU is the overall central processing unit. Although it's technically true that the CPU handles graphics, the other responses all have something to do with an area inside the CPU. If the answer looks like a complete giveaway, chances are it's the wrong answer.

Question 5

The L-1 cache is composed of 2,000 transistors on a wafer inside the CPU.

○ A. True

○ B. False

Answer B is correct. L-1 cache is composed of some number of transistors, but not a set number such as 2,000.

Question 6

Which of the following buses is responsible for taking up extra clock ticks during a data transfer between the CPU and RAM?

○ A. FSB

○ B. PSB

○ C. PCI

○ D. PIC

Answer B is correct. The odds are even as to whether you'll see a reference to the Processor bus, Processor Side Bus, or PSB. Examine the question and see that you're being asked about some kind of slowdown in the system. Answer D is wrong, and you should be able to see that it's a play on the PCI bus. It's the programmable interrupt controller. Answer A is incorrect because the Front-Side Bus generally has to do with more than RAM. That leaves answers B and C to choose from. The PCI bus is a slow bus used to connect the North and South bridge. It's usually assigned to the AGP and to expansion cards, not memory. If you couldn't remember what "PSB" stands for, then the process of elimination should help.

Question 7

You're looking at a spec sheet for a new computer and you see that the CPU is capable of addressing 64GB of programmable memory. How many registers in the CPU are used to store that memory data?

○ A. Several thousand

○ B. More than half

○ C. A few hundred

○ D. None

Answer D is correct. This is a nicely tricky question because it implies that the CPU stores memory. Add in the idea of programmable memory, and the concept of the CPU being responsible for something, and you could easily forget that the CPU has no way to store 64GB of data. The clue to the right answer is in the "memory data." Not memory alone—the data. Answers A, B, and C are all wrong because programmable memory means that the CPU can generate numbers on an address bus that will be large enough to address memory outside the chip die—system memory.

Question 8

> You decide to buy a used 1.3GHz Pentium 4 system with a 533MHz front-side bus to use as a test machine. The system is using _____ together with the _____.
>
> ○ A. A clock divider, motherboard clock
> ○ B. The system oscillator, FSB
> ○ C. A clock multiplier, FSB
> ○ D. A fast CPU, multiplied FSB

Answer C is correct. Once again, this is a scenario question designed to confuse you with gobblety-gook about CPU and FSB ratings. Before you try to figure out the answer, look at all the responses to see whether you can work out what concept you're being tested for. Three of the responses include a reference to multipliers and the FSB. Answer A is incorrect because the CPU and FSB don't work with dividers, which make for slow speeds. Answer B is incorrect because you'll probably never hear about a "system oscillator." That leaves C and D to choose between. Answer D could technically be right, but it uses a personal judgement call to say that a 1.3GHz processor is "fast." Answer C could also be right, and simply states the facts. Between the two, go with the objective facts, and say that answer D is wrong.

Question 9

> How many DMA controllers are used on a system with 16 IRQ lines?
> ○ A. 2
> ○ B. 8
> ○ C. 4
> ○ D. 1

Answer A is correct. The essence of the question is to ask how many DMA controllers are in a computer. It doesn't matter that there are 16 IRQ lines; the question could just as easily ask about 25 IRQ lines. Answers B and C are incorrect, but both of them are designed to get you thinking about 8 DMA channels (answer B), or the original 4 channels in the XT machines (answer C). The real choice is between answers A and D. Answer D is wrong, and you'll just have to remember that PCs have two DMA controllers and two IRQ controllers.

Question 10

Choose the largest binary number from the following list of numbers:

- ○ A. 1101012
- ○ B. A0,F9
- ○ C. 16
- ○ D. 11

Answer D is correct. When CompTIA proposes an objective having to do with knowing about numbering systems, this is an example of how a multiple-choice question can nicely give you a lower score. At first you might think you should've remembered all that binary conversion math. Not true! You don't need to do a single math operation to correctly answer this question. Read the question carefully! If we drill into one thing, it's that: Read the question! You're being asked about a binary number. Who cares how large? Answer B is clearly wrong because it's a hexadecimal number. Answer C is wrong because there's no "6" in binary numbers. Answer A is likewise wrong, because there's no "2" in binary numbers. However, "binary" means "2," and binary numbers are usually a string of 1s and 0s, so it might look right if you don't think about it. Of all the response options, only answer D is a true binary number, even if eleven doesn't look like a very large number.

Need to Know More?

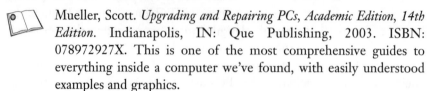 Mueller, Scott. *Upgrading and Repairing PCs, Academic Edition, 14th Edition.* Indianapolis, IN: Que Publishing, 2003. ISBN: 078972927X. This is one of the most comprehensive guides to everything inside a computer we've found, with easily understood examples and graphics.

Karney, James. *Upgrade and Maintain Your PC.* New York, NY: MIS Press, 1998. ISBN: 1-55828-460-5.

Messmer, Hans-Peter. *The Indispensable PC Hardware Book.* Reading, MA: Addison-Wesley, 1995. ISBN: 0-201-87697-3. This is the resource to consult if you are unclear on any aspect of memory or CPUs.

Rosch, Winn. *Hardware Bible, Premier Edition.* Indianapolis, IN: Sams Publishing, 2003. ISBN 0-672-30954-8.

5

Processors and Chipsets

· ·

Terms you'll need to understand:

✓ Net Burst, Hyper-Threading technology

✓ Real Mode, Protected Mode

✓ Virtual Machine (VM)

✓ Virtual DOS Machine (VDM), DOS session

✓ MMX, SIMD, SEE

✓ Socket, slot

Concepts you'll need to master:

✓ Swap files

✓ Real Mode, 32-bit Protected Mode

✓ Hyper-Threading multi-processing

✓ Microcode multimedia enhancements

✓ Slot technology and CPU cartridges

The CPU, often referred to as the *chip* or the *processor*, is the microprocessor that lies at the heart of every PC. For the most part, the CPU is in charge of executing program instructions, math, and logic calculations. A number of companies make processor chips, including Intel, Advanced Micro Devices (AMD), IBM, and Motorola, to name a few. These days, AMD has taken a significant share of the market, and so in this chapter, we'll focus on the Intel and AMD processors you're likely to encounter on the A+ exam.

When you open up a PC and look at the motherboard, the central processing unit is typically the largest chip you'll see. Although it may be hiding under a heat sink, it's typically inserted into a plastic holder—a *socket* or *slot*—making it easy to spot. We'll discuss sockets and slots after we look at types of processors. At the end of the chapter, we'll also provide an overview of chipsets and motherboards.

Original Processors

Historians generally point to the Altair 8800 as the first microcomputer. It used the Intel 8080 processor, clocked at 2MHz, with 6,000 transistors in a 6-micron process. The chip was released in April 1974, with an 8-bit processor bus, designed to work on an 8-bit system bus. Microsoft's first big sale was a version of the BASIC programming language, designed to work with the Altair. CP/M was the first operating system. This *Control Program for Microcomputers* was the granddaddy of DOS, and we'll mention it again in Chapter 12, "DOS."

In July 1976, the Zilog corporation released a clone of the 8080, calling it the Z-80. It included an integrated memory interface and memory refresh circuitry, making it more sophisticated than the Intel chip. The Z-80 used a different set of instructions, but included a sub-set of the 8080 microcode so it could run many of the software programs that were springing up everywhere. It was such a popular chip that Radio Shack used it in the TRS-80, one of the computers that began the home PC revolution. The Z-80 became the standard processor for computers using the CP/M operating system.

NOTE

When something is integrated, in terms of chip manufacturing, we mean it's built onto the chip die. Engineers usually come up with a new idea and produce a separate chip as part of the chipset. The L-1 cache is a good example of an invention that became integrated onto the central processor die. Mobile computing and server technology often lead the way in developing closer integration with the CPU.

Although Intel had already released the 8085 in March of that year, it never caught on the way the Z-80 did. However, the 8085 was clocked at 5MHz, and used a 3-micron process to yield 6,500 transistors. Computers were the talk of the town, but they were all using an 8-bit system bus, so both the Z-80 and 8085 used an 8-bit processor bus.

MOS, a company formed by former Motorola engineers, was marketing a 6502 chip, using a completely different architecture. At $25, it was much less expensive than the $300 Intel chips, and in the right price range for Steve Wozniak to use in the Apple I and Apple II. Motorola chips developed into the 68000 series, and their descendents are used in Apple Macintosh computers.

Commodore computers used the 6502, as did various computer games, including the original Nintendo Entertainment System. The Justice Department tells us that Windows is nothing at all like the Macintosh interface. And so we'll say that Intel's Rambus RAM is entirely different from the memory designs used in Nintendo games.

Intel 8086 and 8088

In June 1978, Intel introduced the chip that became the ancestor of every IBM-compatible PC we know today: the 8086, and its x86 instruction set. As you'll see in a moment, it wasn't the chip used in the IBM XT, but it was the starting point. For the first time, a chip used 16-bit registers and a 16-bit internal bus. It also had a matching 16-bit processor bus, but it used a 20-bit address bus. 1MB is a thousand kilobytes, which works out to 1,024,000 bytes. The 20-bit address bus could handle a binary number representing 1MB of memory pages.

The 8086 came in three clock speeds (5MHz, 8MHz, and 10MHz), and used a 3-micron process to yield 29,000 transistors. It was an expensive chip, in a market where many pre-existing motherboards still used an 8-bit system bus. As a result, Intel released a hybrid version of the chip in 1979. The 8088 had the same *core* as the 8086, but used an 8-bit processor bus and had only two clock speeds (5MHz and 8MHz).

Beginning with the 16-bit 8086, motherboards took on a separate, high-speed memory cache, running at the same speed as the processor. This cache was the original Level 1 cache, and only moved onto the chip die in the 80486 processor. The memory cache chip had its own connection to the CPU, which allowed transfers as fast as the CPU core speed. This separate connection is known as the backside bus. When the L-1 moved onto the die, the L-2 cache took the backside bus. L-3 caches usually work with multiple processors and have their own bus connection. However, with L-2 cache moving onto the die, L-3 caches may end up using the traditional backside bus.

Keep in mind that any CPU will have a supporting set of chips (the chipset) on the underlying motherboard. The 8088's processor bus connected with the same chipset as the 8080 and 8085, but used the more advanced internal architecture of the 8086. The chip could generate an internal address in one clock tick, but used two ticks to transfer the address across the processor bus. Although it was a slower chip, its price and the historical times were right, and so the 8088 helped launch the IBM/Intel platform. (This same type of limitation took place again in the 32-bit 386-SX chips.)

 The 8086 used the original microcode from the 8080, along with additional instructions. As a result, it could run software designed for the earlier chip, making it backward compatible with many software programs on the market. Much of this software used the CP/M operating system, which later became DOS. The microcode became the x86 instruction set, and "backward compatibility" became the rallying cry for all future chips and operating systems. The Pentium Itanium chips may be Intel's final break from the long tradition of backward compatibility, whereas AMD is betting on a continuing market for backward compatibility with the x86-64 Opteron and Athlon 64.

Real Mode

Both the 8088 and 8086 processors used a 20-bit address bus to directly address one megabyte of memory. Both chips could process any row address in 1MB of memory. DOS is a 16-bit operating system, meaning that it uses 16-bit instructions, and matched the internal register and bus widths of the early chips. When a CPU uses 16-bit words to process instructions and store exact locations in memory, we say it's using Real Mode. In a moment we'll discuss the 80286, which introduced Protected Mode.

Real Mode means that a processor uses 16-bit registers and a 16-bit internal bus to process 16-bit instructions. The operating system typically sends the majority of instructions to the CPU, and software applications are typically written with instructions the same size as the OS. Windows 3.x ran on top of the 16-bit DOS operating system. The 8086, and the less expensive 8088, were both 16-bit processors. When Windows creates a virtual DOS machine, it mimics the operations of a 16-bit processor. "Virtual 86 Mode" refers all the way back to the original 8086 chip.

The 16-Bit 80286

Personal computers were catching on and Intel was working toward higher-speed processors with smaller transistors. By 1981, the company had developed the 80186, which was mostly used in controller devices. Then in February 1982, they demonstrated a new 1.5-micron process with 134,000 transistors: the 80286. The new chip could run at three speeds (6MHz, 8MHz, and 12.5MHz), but continued using the 16-bit processor bus. However, one interesting feature was its 24-bit address bus. Another interesting feature was that it could use 1GB of *virtual memory*.

 A virtual device is an "idea" of a device that acts the same as a real device would in the physical world. An idea can be programmed into a set of instructions, and so virtual devices can be created out of thin air, so to speak. Pentium processors include microcode to create virtual computers inside the chip. This idea shows up in VxDs, the Hardware Abstraction Layer, and many other areas of computer technology.

A 24-bit bus allows for 16,384,000 memory pages, which means the 80286 could address 16MB of system memory. Now, it happens that 1GB of memory is 1,024,000,000 bytes (one billion). So how could the 80286 work with one gigabyte of virtual memory? The answer lies in some tricky maneuvering taking place inside the chip.

Swap Files (Memory "Snapshots")

When we speak of *single-tasking*, we mean that a processor can run only as many 16-bit applications (including the operating system) as will fit into 1MB of memory. Back then, users were usually stuck with the operating system and one additional program. However, with more than that megabyte available, the 80286 could "borrow" some memory to store a sort of "snapshot" of whatever was taking place in the first megabyte of RAM. The snapshot could be either stored in real memory or saved to a disk file (swapped to disk). This file became known as a swap file, and later became known as Windows virtual memory.

 The first 1MB of memory is also known as conventional memory. Applications can use about 640KB, and the system uses the remainder. We'll discuss software memory usage in Chapter 13, "Booting, Startup Files, and Memory."

Understand that the 80286 continued to run 16-bit applications, with their largest memory page addresses being only a 20-bit number. On the other hand, the chip used the larger 24-bit numbers as a sort of camera lens, to take "memory pictures." This technique provided 15MB of extra memory to play with. Using the extra memory, the 286 could pretend it was an entirely different machine, fooling applications into believing they were running on their own. It could store multiple snapshots of 1MB "chunks" and tell the operating system the first megabyte of memory was empty. When the Real Mode application used up all the 20-bit memory addresses, the 286 could store an entire 1MB chunk to disk, using 24-bit page addresses to keep track of where it put everything. This sort of daisy-chaining is how the chip could keep track of 1GB of virtual memory addresses.

16-bit Real Mode applications run the same way as they would in an 8086, but everything in the 286 took place more quickly. According to the marketing department, everything was running "faster." According to the engineering department, the user could boot up into 16-bit DOS, and then run as many applications as would fit into one megabyte of memory. Using the snapshot feature, the user was then supposed to be able to start a whole additional set of applications, each of which would use up to one megabyte of memory. These multiple sessions became known as *DOS sessions*, and the snapshot feature was called *protected mode*.

video

For more information on memory, see the Memory video by Scott Mueller on the accompanying CD.

Original Protected Mode

In theory, the 80286 would write information to a specific megabyte of addresses for each individual DOS session. Then it would use an entirely different megabyte for separate sessions. Each area of memory was supposed to be *protected* from any overwrite operations. Two things went wrong. In the first place, the processor had to start in the same manner as previous 16-bit processors: in Real Mode. It then had to switch to Protected Mode in order to take advantage of all the fancy memory tricks. Unfortunately, it couldn't go back to Real Mode unless the user rebooted the computer to get out of Protected Mode (often forgetting to save everything).

NOTE

All Intel-compatible processors begin in 16-bit Real Mode (including AMD and Cyrix). When a 32-bit application (like the operating system) accesses the processor for the first time, it switches the CPU into 32-bit Protected Mode (discussed in a moment). The problem with the 286 was that when a 16-bit application requested Real Mode again, the chip couldn't switch back.

The second problem was worse. Instead of guaranteeing that any instruction addresses in some stored megabyte of RAM would stay untouchable, the 286 would often overwrite addresses with instructions that were supposed to be taking place in another megabyte's session. In other words, users would start a DOS session and run some applications. They would then "switch" to a different session, and the 286 would store its snapshot. But instead of keeping that snapshot protected, the chip would send information from the second session to locations inside the snapshot. The net result was a total system crash.

The 80286 and Windows

Bill Gates is said to have told IBM that the 286 was a "brain dead" processor and that they should work with the 386 to develop a multi-tasking operating system. Multi-tasking, in this instance, means that more than one DOS session can run at the "same" time. More properly, what they were talking about was task-switching. Either way, both IBM and Microsoft were working together to build an operating system that would provide the same flexibility as Macintosh users had. This "second" operating system was OS/2 (DOS being the first operating system, "OS/1"). IBM was falling behind schedule, because of the problems in the 286, but corporate policy said that when the company made a promise, it would deliver on that promise, no matter what.

IBM continued to develop OS/2 for the 286, leaving Microsoft to develop the graphic user interface. When Intel showed the plans for the 80386, Microsoft stopped work on the GUI for the 286. Both companies shared all development code, and so when the 386 entered the market, Microsoft released what it had, calling it "Windows." This new "operating system" was actually only a flashy interface running on top of DOS, but it captured the world's imagination. IBM sued Microsoft over the pre-release of what was only a partially finished product, and the two companies went their separate ways. Some people say that, nowadays, Microsoft releases only fully developed products.

Microsoft gained the rights to all operating system code developed by IBM, and IBM gained the rights to the interface code Microsoft had developed. OS/2 Warp was IBM's product, and Windows NT was Microsoft's version of the "new technology." However, NT was a 32-bit operating system, and the vast majority of PC owners were using the 16-bit DOS. From that point forward, Microsoft wanted to bring together the networking and true multi-tasking capabilities of NT with the GUI of Windows and the backward compatibility of DOS. Everything from Windows 3.0 to Windows Me has been geared toward shifting home PC users away from DOS. Windows 2000 was the first really workable 32-bit home-user product, and Windows XP is the first really stable product.

Third Generation: The 32-Bit 80386

The 80386 entered the market in October 1985 and resolved the two problems with the 286. Users could move back and forth between Real and Protected Mode without rebooting, and the CPU would no longer overwrite protected memory locations. A new 1.0-micron process yielded 275,000 transistors, with four system clock speeds (16MHz, 20MHz, 25MHz, and 33MHz). For the first time, the processor bus expanded to 32 bits, and the chip included a built-in floating point unit (math coprocessor).

The AT form factor motherboards used a 33MHz system bus. The 386/33-DX was the first CPU to run at the same speed as the system bus. Keep in mind that the ISA bus was still set to 8.3MHz for older expansion cards and basic I/O.

People were discussing millions of instructions per second, and at 33MHz, the 386 could process 11.4 MIPS, scanning the entire Encyclopedia Britannica in 12.5 seconds. The chip was 32 bits all the way through: registers, internal bus, processor bus, and a 32-bit address bus. The expanded address bus meant the processor could work with 4GB of memory page addresses (which works out to 4,294,967,296 bytes, or FF,FF FF,FFh). Using the same swapping scheme as the 286, the 80386 could also work with 64 terabytes (TB) of virtual memory. (1TB is one thousand gigabytes, or one trillion bytes.) With a 32-bit core, the 386 was ready for a real 32-bit operating system.

DOS (together with the Windows 3.x shell) is a 16-bit operating system. Windows 9x and Me are hybrid mixtures of 16-bit and 32-bit instructions, but the core is a 16-bit OS. Windows NT and OS/2 are complete, 32-bit operating systems. Novell NetWare is also a 32-bit network operating system. Windows 2000 and Windows XP evolved from Windows NT, and are 32-bit operating systems.

Backward compatibility means the operating system can emulate 16-bit DOS and older Windows 3.x applications. (Microsoft currently sells a 64-bit version of Windows XP, optimized and written for the Intel Itanium chip, mostly used in high-end corporate settings. In all probability, that version is the underlying basis for the 64-bit consumer version of XP, code named "Longhorn," which is slated for release sometime in 2005.)

32-Bit Protected Mode (386 Mode)

Perhaps the most significant development in the 80386 was its capability to switch between Protected Mode and Real Mode without requiring the user to reboot the system. For the first time, 16-bit applications could run alongside each other in completely separate 1MB chunks of memory. At the same time, Windows memory management worked with the CPU to take care of handling all those memory "snapshots" taking place. As you know, computer-type people invent new words and terms as easily as breathing, and so the Virtual DOS Machine (VDM) and Virtual Machine (VM) were born.

A "Wintel" machine is a personal computer using Windows with an Intel, or Intel-compatible processor. In almost all cases, a Wintel machine is also an IBM-compatible machine.

Virtual Machines and Virtual Real Mode

A *virtual machine (VM)* is where a CPU creates a secondary 8088 *machine process* inside the chip. The chip empties its registers and resets itself as though it had just booted up. On the other hand, when Windows moves everything around in memory to make room for a 16-bit session, it creates a Virtual DOS Machine (VDM). The Windows VDM is really just a way for Windows to keep track of everything that was taking place during a particular machine process.

To provide driver instructions across multiple virtual machines, Windows works with Virtual Device Drivers, or VxDs. We replace the "x" with the actual device name because it sounds tacky to refer to Windows and VD in the same sentence. (If you thought the Enron accounting system was complicated, imagine what's going on between Windows and the CPU!)

 Virtual Real Mode is the method by which Windows emulates (mimics) a 16-bit DOS operating system so as to run older applications. A CPU creates Virtual Machines (the VM) to handle 16-bit instructions coming from memory. When both the CPU and Windows are working together to run older applications, Windows is running in Virtual Real Mode. Windows generates an "image" of everything an IBM XT would have, including BIOS, CMOS settings, and device instructions.

Here's what happens: The CPU uses microcode to create a 16-bit process called a virtual machine. (The area inside the chip is the memory management unit, or MMU.) Windows sends 16-bit instructions to the CPU, and between the two of them, they pretend they're running an 8088 computer. Remember that Windows uses only 1MB of memory for each 16-bit session, and the CPU makes it seem as if it's the first megabyte of memory. (We discuss conventional and extended memory in Chapter 13.)

Now the user wants to start another DOS application—another session. Windows takes a snapshot of 1MB of memory and sends a set of addresses to the CPU. The CPU moves everything in its registers to the set aside memory pages, and then launches a new 16-bit virtual machine. It then tells Windows the first megabyte of conventional memory is free. Windows opens up the new application, using the processor as though nothing had been going on previously.

 32-bit Protected Mode allows for running a protected 16-bit process inside a 32-bit process. Protected 16-bit virtual machines can run alongside 32-bit processes, as long as there is enough memory. Modern processors are easily capable of this type of multi-tasking. Note that a 16-bit session runs almost exactly the same as it would have with an 8088 chip, which means it runs just as slow.

Applications and hardware devices may have 16-bit drivers, but Microsoft continually develops virtual device driver replacements. We've said that older applications will try to switch the CPU to slow 8088 mode, so wherever possible, try to use a replacement 32-bit VxD. Virtual drivers aren't limited to Real Mode, so the application may run faster. Note, however, that some applications can't run "faster," and so either require a patch to run on a fast CPU, or won't run at all. These patches act in the reverse of Turbo mode, causing the virtual machine to slow down to earlier CPU speeds.

Troubleshooting and Diagnostics Software

Many hardware and system diagnostics programs won't work in anything other than Real Mode. Understand that when any chip starts up, it begins in Real Mode until a 32-bit application switches it into Protected Mode. Windows 9x is mostly a 32-bit operating system, with a 16-bit subset of instructions to allow for backward compatibility. Windows 2000 and XP are 32-bit operating systems. So how do we keep the CPU in Real Mode when the system is booting into a 32-bit operating system?

Although it's becoming more and more difficult, all versions of Windows provide for a way to boot the computer into a 16-bit command-line environment. Windows 2000 and XP provide a separate application called "The Windows Recovery Console," which presents a command-line interface that uses most of the same commands and syntax as DOS. Windows 95 and 98 provide a bypass keystroke to bring up the Startup Menu with an option to start in a 16-bit command-line setting. Windows Me removed the bypass keystroke, but you can still boot to DOS from a Windows 98 Emergency Boot Disk (EBD).

You should know how to boot a PC into 16-bit Real Mode regardless of what operating system is installed. You should also know how to create a Windows 9x bootable floppy disk, and what to do when a system doesn't come with a floppy drive. Finally, you should know how to test for a bootable CDROM, how to change CMOS settings to allow booting from the CD, and how to install software drivers for CDROM support. You'll have to know how to get around in a command-line environment so you that can run these diagnostics software programs.

Although CompTIA may refer to a Windows NT/2000/XP start disk as a "bootable" disk, you should know that the diskette isn't actually bootable. NTLDR is the Windows NT Loader, used to begin the overall Startup process for NT/2000/XP. If the basic operating system load files are unavailable on the hard drive, the so-called bootable disk will try to find the system files on a mounted CDROM. If the CD is unavailable, the boot process either halts or seeks out another operating system somewhere on a visible partition.

The Fourth Generation 80486, DX, SX, and SL

In 1985, the 386 brought PCs into the mainstream, with all the heavy processing demands of Windows, networking, online communications, color video, graphics, computer games, sound, and complex mathematics. Having solved the protection problem, Intel began focusing on making faster chips and developing multi-level price ranges. To get more computers into the market place, the company began producing different versions of each new type of chip. The complete, fully loaded CPU added a "DX" to the 80*x*86 name (for example, 80386-DX). Less expensive versions added "SX."

When Intel discovered it couldn't copyright a number, it started using actual words for names, as in Pentium, Pentium Pro, Xeon, and Itanium. However, at the time, a 386-DX meant a full-featured processor in the Intel-compatible 80386 family.

Perhaps the best-known characteristic of an SX processor is that it doesn't have a companion math coprocessor (the FPU). A lesser-known difference is in the size of the address bus. New lines of chips almost always require a new motherboard and supporting chipset. On the other hand, when the new chip can be retro-fitted to a previous motherboard, the overall computer ends up with a lower price tag.

386-SX

In 1988, three years after the 80386 was introduced, Intel produced the 386-SX. It had the same clock speeds as the 386-DX, and the same 32-bit core. However, it had a 24-bit address bus, like the 286, limiting it to only 16MB of addressable memory. It also used the 16-bit processor bus supported by older chipsets. With the reduced address bus, the chip could address only 256GB of virtual memory, rather than the 64 terabytes of the DX version. The narrower processor bus was the main cause of performance reduction, but at the same time, the reason for a less expensive computer.

The 80386-SX was mostly used for "value" desktop machines, and the emerging portable computing industry (laptop and notebook computers). It kept the 32-bit internal processing and Protected Mode multi-tasking, but did not come with a coprocessor. People could "upgrade" their machine by adding a coprocessor later, as a separate chip. To differentiate the "real" chip from the coprocessor, Intel created the 80387 chip and provided a secondary upgrade socket on the motherboard.

The 486 primarily differed from the 386 and 286 in its integration and upgradability. *Integration* refers to the number of components that have been moved onto the chip. *Upgradability* means that the CPU can be taken off of the motherboard and replaced with a better (faster or feature-enhanced) chip. *Scalability* means that the entire system can be made larger to handle more capacity. For example, the AMD Opteron has an integrated memory controller, and can be scaled from two up to eight simultaneous processors.

Understand that the Wright brothers still hadn't invented the airplane, and people were still driving to work in ox carts. Computers cost many bags of gold, and although many people wanted one, not everyone could afford the price. That was back before there were any secondhand computers. This DX/SX marketing idea stuck around for the 80386 and 80486 families, and then went underground with the emerging Pentium "something-MHz" processors.

Budget-conscious buying is essentially what led to an entire line of derivative chips—the SX chips. Later, with the same market forces at work, Intel and AMD continued the practice of releasing less expensive chips with reduced capabilities (for example, Intel Celeron and AMD Duron).

386-SL and Power Management

Aside from everyone wanting a computer, more and more people also wanted to carry their computer around with them. Laptop machines were fairly large at the time (about the size of a sewing machine), with many companies trying to get them smaller and lighter. People had bigger laps, in those days, but battery power consumption was a problem, and so were monitors. Alien technology had provided us with liquid crystals, but LCD panels were still under development. Intel, for their part, began producing different chips that used less power, and for awhile, they added "SL" to the name to differentiate so-called mobile computing processors. Nowadays, the entire concept of mobile computing comes together under the "Centrino" brand name, and Pentium "M" chips.

The 386-SL came out in 1990, as the first *low-voltage* processor. Since then, Intel has advanced the idea of reduced power consumption, and produced an entire line of extremely small chips used in highly sophisticated network file servers (server blades). The SL ran at 20MHz or 25MHz, and used the existing 1.0-micron process to yield 855,000 transistors. Like the SX, it was a 32-bit CPU, but with a shrunken 16-bit processor bus. However, it had the full-size 32-bit address bus of the DX, giving it 4GB of addressable memory. The other interesting feature was that it was a highly integrated chip, bringing together the L-1 cache of the 486, as well as the memory controller.

 Laptop computers came about partly with the development of liquid crystal display (LCD) panel technology, and they began driving the research into size reduction and lower power consumption. To meet those needs, the SL line introduced lower power consumption and something called System Management Interrupts (SMI), with power management features for battery conservation, including several sleep modes. Windows 9x introduced power management to desktop machines, coming out of the engineering developments for laptops.

80486-DX

We're a little out of chronological order, but only to keep a couple of letters together. The 80486 line of chips came out in April 1989, a year before the 386-SL (which is how the SL took on an integrated L-1 cache). This was the chip everyone was talking about, what with color SVGA monitors, Windows 3.1, networking, and all kinds of other cool stuff taking place. People could "see" a difference in speed between a 386 and a 486 processor, although most people had no idea why. All anyone knew was that 486 was bigger, faster, and better than 386, and that the letters DX meant better bragging rights than SX.

CPU Ratings

Actual speed and apparent speed are two different things. Regardless of benchmark ratings, we tend to use subjective time to "feel" how quickly or slowly an application loads, or a screen update takes place. We "guess" the system is faster if it simply feels faster. Performance and efficiency changes in modern processors often make a slower-rated machine seem faster than technical ratings would indicate.

Two well-known CPU rating methods are Intel's iCOMP Index 2.0, and the AMD and Cyrix PR numbers. (*PR* stands for *Processor Rating*, so it's redundant to say PR-rating.) These numbers were intended to evaluate only a CPU's performance, not the overall system. The ratings were supposed to make it easier for non-technical customers to objectively determine performance, using more than just the MHz ratings, and across brand technology. Each system compiles a weighted average of how well the processor performs in several types of situations, combining such things as running an application, multimedia, speed benchmarks, and so on. With so much money riding on the numbers, marketing departments have made the ratings even more confusing than simply making a guess.

By 1991, Intel had passed the one-micron barrier, and the 50MHz 486 used a 0.8 micron process to yield 1.2 million transistors. The 486 ran at three basic clock speeds (25MHz, 33MHz, and 50MHz), but introduced CPU clock multipliers for the first time. The 50MHz 486 ran at a 3X multiplier of the ISA bus. It was a full 32-bit chip with the same 4GB of addressable memory and 64TB of virtual memory access as the 386-DX. However, it was the first chip to put an integrated L-1 memory cache and math coprocessor right onto the die. Keep in mind that the back-and-forth migration of secondary memory caches has mostly to do with manufacturing costs, transistor budgets, and die sizes.

486-SX

You might wonder how a chip with a built-in coprocessor could be sold as an SX version. In fact, Intel simply disabled the coprocessor and sold the chip for a lower price. The 486 motherboards came with an add-on socket for a so-called 487 secondary chip, but that chip was simply another 486 with the coprocessor enabled. When the customer installed the "new" chip, it deactivated the first chip, and took over as the main CPU. In all other features, the 486-SX was the same as the DX, even out to the processor bus. (Later chips have sometimes used this same idea, being released with certain functions disabled, primarily to reach a targeted market price.)

Clock Multipliers Again

Although the 486 and 386 were both 32-bit chips, the faster clock speed meant that a 486 could execute one instruction in two clock cycles (not clock ticks). The 386 required 4.5 cycles, and so the Marketing Department was quick to promote the new chip as being "twice as fast as those older 386 models." This may be where processor ratings began to wander off into the strange world of marketing hype. ("Hype" is short for *hyperbole*—pronounced "hi-PURR-buhlie"—which means an extravagant statement or figure of speech, not intended to be taken literally.)

The AT motherboards were still using a 33MHz main bus, meaning that bytes were traveling around the motherboard at a different speed from the processor. We saw the 386 clock speed hit 33MHz, matching the system bus. However, the 50MHz 486 was the first processor with a clock speed faster than the 25MHz motherboard.

Processor Design Specifications

Although manufacturing a CPU may seem like a scientific process, the final results are quite variable. A "batch" of chips comes out of the "oven," and the manufacturer takes a number of sample chips to install on test machines. They run each chip under increasing frequencies until it short circuits and melts. That upper limit is the highest possible speed for the chip. Most reputable companies reduce the highest frequency by some percentage, building in a wide safety margin. Finally, the chip is given a design specification rating.

Later processors tend to be "locked" at a design specification speed. (Some people can play with motherboard voltages to get around locked chip speeds.) In some cases, unscrupulous third-party distributors will re-mark the speed setting on the chip, making it very difficult to correctly identify the optimum performance configuration.

Almost any CPU can be set to run faster than its design specification. This is called over-clocking. For example, a 75MHz Pentium could be set on the motherboard (using jumpers) to run at 133MHz. Because of conservative estimates on the part of the manufacturers, an over-clocked chip may continue to function quite well in the short term. However, as time passes, the chip may begin to perform unreliably.

The first indication that over-clocking might become an accepted industry standard was with the 486/33-DX2. Here, the processor ran at 66MHz while the rest of the system ran at 33MHz. This is a 2:1 multiplier, and became known as 2X. Manufacturer over-clocking has increased, over the years, making it difficult to clearly define processor speeds. Modern third-party chipsets often provide for FSB over-clocking, and are often very stable at speeds higher than design specifications.

80486-DX2

Intel introduced the 486/66-DX2 in 1992, still with the 32-bit external bus and all the other features of the 80486. The "2" indicated the doubled speed of the processor core. In other words, the DX2 (66MHz) ran at twice the speed of the processor bus and system bus (33MHz). By 1994, this same technology pushed the chip to a 486-DX4, where the core speed was quadrupled (133MHz), but in the previous year, Intel was already on the market with the first Pentium chip and the PCI specification. The Pentium was the "Cadillac" of high-speed processors, so the 486-DX4 was another way to buy a less expensive, "high-speed" PC.

The 80286 was the second generation of chips, evolving from the 8086 (and unsuccessful 80186). The 386 was the third, and the 486 was the fourth generation. The fifth generation became the Pentium family, although for awhile the chips were called 80586, or P5 chips. Pentium refers to "5," but the name continued into the P6 (Pentium III and first Pentium 4s) generations for brand-recognition purposes. The "Prescott" core seems to be the first of the seventh generation (P7) chips.

 80386 and 80486 processors typically ran at 100MHz, with a processor bus of 33MHz or 66MHz. Although processor speeds continued to increase, bus speeds mostly stayed the same. It wasn't until 1998, when Intel released the Pentium II and BX chipset, that bus speeds increased to 100MHz.

Summary—Original Processors

Before we get into Pentium processors, be sure you understand the concept of Real Mode and 16-bit processing. Protected Mode is a way to keep the CPU from overwriting data from completely different, Real Mode DOS (16-bit) sessions. Most of the work done on the x86 line of chips had to do with advances into whole new areas of design and manufacturing. The 286 and 386 had enough transistors and a small enough micron process to open the door into large areas of RAM. The 486 demonstrated clock-multiplied chips.

Remember that all CPUs begin in Real Mode until a 32-bit instruction switches them into 32-bit Protected Mode. (This may be one of the reasons why Windows XP/2000 always require a FAT32 partition at the start of the command-line Setup process, even if you choose to create an NTFS partition during the installation.)

Modern chips, primarily the Pentium 4 and Athlon lines, have taken the individual technologies of older chips and consolidated them, in one fashion or another. Each individual engineering design has been carried out to nearly its maximum potential. Wherever possible, external chips and ideas have been brought onto the chip itself. However, both Intel and AMD have a budget, in terms of how many transistors they can put on a CPU. If they go beyond a certain point, the final market price may be unacceptable to consumers. When you understand each major design change, you'll better see how it was integrated into successive lines of Pentium chips.

Intel has always been the strong market leader in chip manufacturing, but AMD has followed with a similar, compatible chip at lower prices, with more features. Much of the variation in chip families had to do with giving customers a pricing choice. Certain features in newer chips have been either disabled, or taken from previous-generation chips to make a less expensive computer. Understand how a newer chip can use a smaller address bus and processor bus to fit onto an older motherboard. Be sure you know how secondary cache memory works, and that CPUs work almost exclusively with memory addresses.

Fifth Generation: Pentium Processors

Today's computer capabilities have long-since surpassed the needs of any conceivable office desktop application other than video teleconferencing, computer-aided design (CAD), and large database queries. Early Pentiums and SVGA monitors easily took care of processing problems with desktop publishing and complex financial analysis, and yet processors have continued to get faster, addressing far more memory than anyone usually installs in the machine. One area where intense CPU work takes place is with the extremely large numbers associated with film-quality 3D graphics.

When the first technical benchmark tests were developed, they included such things as file loading times, transfer rates, number crunching (FLOPS), printing speeds, and so forth. However, anyone who really wanted to know how well a computer worked would install Microsoft's *Flight Simulator* and see how well it played. Beginning at about that time, performance measures began to split between those people interested in business enterprise capabilities and the rest of the world. In today's market, computer games and the "gaming" industry have become the leading edge of PC development. As such, most of the technical development has been designed to do the number crunching related to multimedia sound mixing and fast-moving graphics. Real-world benchmarking now tends to be based on how well various complex games play.

We'll discuss such things as Net Burst, Hyper-Threading Technology, Hyper Transport, and Symmetrical Multi-Processing (SMP) in the following sections. Understand that most of these terms aren't really new technologies, so much as marketing phrases designed to explain the many tweaks and fixes taking place inside the CPU. Corporate IT managers are primarily interested in wide area networks (WANs), security, and the loads placed on enterprise file servers. Gamers are primarily interested in over-clocking and the fastest speeds possible, along with efficient use of memory and hard drive transfers. Technical advancement is now essentially geared toward these two primary markets.

Technology Overview

We're all familiar with the many Pentium processors, so before we get into each chip, we're going to briefly discuss the main features Intel has added to the entire line. All the home-market desktop Pentiums (not mobile chips), from the first series through to the Pentium 4, use a 32-bit internal architecture and 64-bit processor bus. Vendors distinguish the home market from the business, or *enterprise*, market, with the logic that large corporations have more money to spend on sophisticated technology like the Xeon and Itanium than home users. Pentium II Xeon processors, designed for the enterprise market, developed a 64-bit address bus. The three address bus sizes found in consumer Pentium processors include

➤ *32-bit*—Allows for 4GB of addressable memory (4,294,967,296 bytes). Used in original Pentium 60–200MHz, and Pentium MMX.

➤ *36-bit*—Allows for 64GB of addressable memory (68,719,476,736 bytes). Used from the Pentium Pro forward: Xeon, Itanium, Pentium III (P6), and Pentium 4 (P7).

➤ *31-bit*—Allows for 2GB of addressable memory (2,147,483,648 bytes). Used in the Pentium M series and Mobile Pentium technology.

Server-level 64-bit chips, such as the PIII Xeon, Itanium 2, and Athlon 64, use a 40-bit address bus to address 1 terabyte of memory (a thousand gigabytes).

MMX—Multimedia

Multimedia is a modern concept word coming out of references to the communications media. Back when we had only radio and television to play with, people referred to paper, magazines, and what we now call "hardcopy" information as *print media*. Television and movies were *visual media*, and music was *audio media*. Computers introduced email, the Internet, personal digital assistants (PDAs), real-time video, music and graphics editing, and computer games. Joining audio and visual events into a single computer experience became known as multimedia, for "multiple media."

The first specialized multimedia instructions were the MMX instructions added onto the Pentium MMX chip. Windows XP is named for the "Windows eXPerience." MMX stands for Multi-Media eXtensions to the microcode. The original Intel MMX technology introduced 57 new microcode instructions for accelerating calculations typical of audio, two-dimensional (2D) and three-dimensional graphics, video, speech synthesis, and voice recognition.

Somewhat reminiscent of how video processing moved out of the main CPU to add-on graphics cards, audio-visual information processing became a separate set of add-on x86 microcode instructions. Applications developers could streamline a game, for example, to take advantage of more efficient instructions. Presumably, these programs would then run more efficiently and seem faster.

MMX technology is a set of general-purpose, integer instructions that can be applied to a wide variety of multimedia and communications applications. The technology is hardware specific, meaning that the instructions are built into the system. To take advantage of MMX, software must be written specifically for these enhancements.

With an increased movement toward multimedia applications, the FPU had to become more complex. Although Intel hasn't made any revolutionary changes to the old math coprocessors, the Pentium 4 does use larger registers and enhancements to the microcode to work with 128-bit floating-point integers (decimal numbers). These large numbers come into play with 3D gaming, bump maps, and Surround Sound real-time audio mixing. (The largest a 128-bit number can be is 2^{128} or approximately 340,282,366,920,938,463,463,374,607,431,768,211,456.)

SSE and SIMD

It turned out that MMX didn't really give much of an immediately noticeable performance improvement. As a result, not many games were written to take advantage of the technology. "Real" gaming, at the time, was coming from dedicated systems such as the Nintendo units. However, Intel was already working on a better way to take advantage of the multiple pipelines inside the Pentium chips.

 Microsoft has always wanted to "own" the computer-age home. The company sees interactive gaming as the way to take over the living room, and from there, the rest of the house. As a result, Microsoft is heavily involved with Intel in building the technology platform to support modern games. The X-Box, not enterprise file servers, may turn out to be the first real implementation of 64-bit processing. Windows XP Media Center is another version of Windows (not on the exam), which is optimized for corporate video conferencing, entertainment industry multimedia development, and gaming speeds.

SIMD is short for *Single Instruction Multiple Data*, and is another extension of the microcode that tells dual-pipeline Pentium chips how to process different instructions simultaneously. Remember that the CPU is taking words out of a *single instruction*, and then executing the words in *multiple data* pipelines. The early Pentium II used primitive pipelines, and so Intel introduced additional Streaming SIMD Extensions (SSE) for the Pentium III. SSE (version 1) dramatically improved 3D graphics, streaming audio, video conferencing, and speech recognition.

 "Streaming" audio or video uses various buffering and processing advantages so that a listener or viewer doesn't notice hesitations in music or TV information. The Internet 2 technology is heavily geared toward worldwide streaming video, which requires higher bandwidth than the current Internet.

3DNow!

AMD developed 3DNow! technology to compete with the Intel SSE instruction set. They kept the Intel instructions, and added 21 new instructions, designed to improve K-6 integer and floating-point calculations. Like MMX, the additional instructions were designed to enhance 3D graphics rendering, as well as other multimedia applications. 3DNow! is particularly helpful in processing SIMD instructions.

SSE-2

The Pentium 4 added 144 instructions to the original MMX technology, along with 128 enhancements to the original SIMD instruction set. Secondly, the chip includes wider 128-bit FPU registers to go along with the "enhanced" floating-point calculations necessary to run modern games. (These new registers are XMM registers, not to be confused with MMX technology.) With such a dramatic change in the SSE instruction set, Intel decided to name the second revision SSE-2.

3DNow! Professional

Both Intel and AMD are in a heated competition for market share. Intel designed SSE-2 instructions for the Pentium 4 line, and AMD countered with additional instructions to the 3DNow! technology. Although 3DNow! Professional still supports SSE, it does not support SSE-2. Future AMD chips are unlikely to support Intel's multimedia instructions, just as Intel will likely not support any of AMD's gaming advances.

The Pentium "Prescott" series will introduce yet another set of instructions geared toward two processors working together. These may be called PNI (Prescott New Instructions, or SSE-3). AMD's Athlon 64 and Opteron support SSE, but not SSE-2. Nor does AMD expect to support the Prescott additions.

Pentium: First Series

Fifth generation processors—the original Pentium—came in three series of chips. The first series came in two clock speeds (60MHz and 66MHz), and presumably was going to get rid of the speed-rating in the name. However, most people simply called later chips a "Pentium-something" (for example, Pentium 133, Pentium 200). The chips continued with the 0.8-micron process, but now with 3.1 million transistors. The Pentium introduced *superscalar architecture*, meaning that two virtual 32-bit processors (and pipelining) could use one 32-bit address bus and a 64-bit processor bus. The physical CPU could effectively address 4GB of RAM and 64TB of virtual memory, like the 486 family. (The 66MHz could run 112MIPS.)

NOTE
It wasn't until the Pentium Pro was released in 1995 that the address bus expanded to 36 bits, addressing 64GB of RAM. However, the Pentium Pro wasn't designed for home users.

The Pentiums began using a second, L-2 cache (typically 256KB), and 273 pins in a *pin grid array (PGA)* form factor, running at the then-typical 5 volts. Note that the processor ran at 66MHz, which was a 1:1 clock of the new PCI system bus. On the other hand, the dual-pipeline technology gave the chip a performance benchmark similar to a 486-DX5.

One of the more important problems with the L-2 cache was that Intel had to sub-contract for the memory chips. As a result, the memory cache was installed outside the chip housing, and ran at a slower speed than the main CPU. To get the cache speed and CPU more in line, Intel designed a small integrated circuit board (a cartridge) for the next series of Pentium processors. The IC board required a slot, instead of a socket, and brought about Slot technology, discussed in the second half of this chapter.

NOTE
The 66MHz Pentium required 16 watts (W) of power and drew 3.2 amps, making it a very "hot" processor. For the first time, designers had to come up with ways to cool the chip. This led to chip-cooling fans and heat sinks, and eventually helped change the overall design of motherboards (moving the CPU toward the back for better cooling near the main housing fan).

Pentium: Second Series

By late 1994, the second series Pentiums were running at 75MHz, 90MHz, and 100MHz. Speeds continued to increase in 1995, going from 120MHz to 200MHz. This second series of processors used a different manufacturing technique, allowing for a significantly smaller die and a lower-voltage 3.3V (running somewhat cooler than the 5V series). The chips used a 296 *staggered pin grid array (SPGA)* form factor, and were physically incompatible with the first series chips. One of the improvements to the second series Pentiums included the new programmable interrupt controller (PIC), as well as a dual-processor interface that allowed two processors to be installed on a single motherboard.

NOTE
Symmetrical multi-processing (SMP) means that more than a single physical CPU is handling processing activities. For the moment, only high-end servers have used the feature, and Intel is pushing the Itanium 2 line with its dual processor capability. AMD's hyper transport bus allows up to eight processors to run together, and may bring the price of 2-processor systems into the home desktop range. The big problem is having an operating system that can handle such dual or multiple processing. Windows XP/2000 supports dual processor systems.

Pentium: Third Series and MMX

You should understand that although the second series Pentiums eventually topped out at 200MHz, Intel had released a Pentium Pro line, also in 1995. The Pentium Pro was designed to be a high-end CPU for use on networking file servers, and used a 64-bit processor bus, keeping the two 32-bit pipelines. To make matters even more confusing, a lot of people were getting into multimedia. In 1997 Intel released the Pentium MMX chips, running at either 166MHz or 200MHz. Life was getting very complicated for the average computer buyer. (The Pentium MMX line eventually topped out at 233MHz.)

The Pentium Pro was designed to run at different speeds, depending on its underlying motherboard. On a 60MHz motherboard, the Pentium Pro ran at 150MHz or 180MHz. On a 66MHz motherboard, the Pentium Pro ran at 166MHz or 200MHz. Once again, we see that over-clocking had become a formally accepted practice. Note that the FSB was still using the 66MHz PCI Conventional timing.

First series Pentium processors ran at 60MHz and 66MHz, using a pin grid array (PGA). Second series Pentiums ran at 90MHz and 100MHz, using a staggered pin grid array (SPGA). The Pentium Pro was a high-end processor designed for file servers (running at 150MHz, 166MHz, 180MHz, and 200MHz). The Pentium MMX was a regular "home user" chip with multimedia extensions built into the microcode, running at 166MHz, 200MHz, and 233MHz.

Sixth Generation: P6 Pentiums

The Pentium Pro was really the first of the sixth-generation chips, and Intel stopped using chip speeds in CPU naming conventions. Even so, the "6" in P6 refers to the traditional x86 number, with 686 following 586. For awhile, AMD and other chip makers continued with the 80x86 numbers, and the K-6 family referred to 686 chips.

Members of the P6 family include Pentium Pro, Pentium II, Pentium III, the first bargain-priced Celerons, and early Pentium 4s. (AMD countered with the budget-priced Durons.) Pentium II processors moved away from the socket and chip design, and introduced Slot 1 and Slot 2 architecture. The L-2 cache was moved onto the chip cartridge, keeping it close to the CPU.

Slot technology only lasted until Intel could afford to build its own L-2 cache. With the Pentium 4 and later Celerons, Intel switched back to the socket technology. AMD has also returned to sockets, and so Slot technology seems to have faded away. The biggest reason for the slots seems to have been the expense of manufacturing L-2 cache memory and having to sub-contract for the chips. (We may see it temporarily return with add-on L-3 cache chips.)

Some of the earlier Pentium Pros had an L-2 cache built directly into the chip, using an integrated bus. However, the cost of manufacturing was so high that most Pentium Pros were later released with a separate L-2 cache that was accessed through the wide backside processor bus running at core speed.

Sixth-generation Pentiums ran at different voltages, mostly between 5V and 3.3V, with low-voltage chips mostly in laptops. However, instead of having the chipset assign that voltage with jumpers, DIP switches, or a voltage regulator module (VRM), the voltage could be set automatically by something called the *voltage identification (VID)* pins. These four special voltage identification pins are located directly on the processor cartridge itself.

For more information on a comparison between traditional motherboards and the Pentium 233MHz, see the "A Look at Motherboards and the Pentium 233 MHz" video by Scott Mueller on the accompanying CD.

Pentium III

The Pentium III was released in 1999, giving consumers a choice between two different types of packaging: *flipped-chip pin grid array (FC-PGA)* Socket 370, or *single edge contact (SEC)* Slot 1 packaging. Another important (and somewhat controversial) feature of the Pentium III was a self-reportable processor serial number. Although this was introduced originally for security, the serial number was also used to manage corporate computer inventories (asset tracking). However, some people felt the feature might be used as an invasion of privacy, if the serial number could be reported out (stolen by the site developers) during a visit to an Internet site.

The Pentium III had a locked clock multiplier, which was designed in such a way that it could not be reset. However, unscrupulous dealers were able to actually disassemble the chip itself, making the necessary modifications to over-clock the chip. They would then reassemble the chip with different markings. Be careful at flea markets and other places where the price seems "too good to be true," and remember Robert Heinlein's TANSTAAFL (*There ain't no such thing as a free lunch!*).

Most companies in the Information Technology industry were enjoying a strong market as they moved into the year 2000, but not Intel. The company had re-deployed many of its engineers to work on the Itanium, but the project was in serious trouble. The newly released AMD Athlon "Thunderbird" was running circles around the Pentium III, which had already reached its highest design speed. There was no quick fix, and it looked as if Intel was going to be playing catch-up with AMD. The PIII core speed went from 450MHz to 1.1GHz, but the chips were unstable, forcing Intel to recall them. When the company changed to a new 0.13 micron process, it was able to bring the PIII up to a stable 1.2GHz.

For more information on a comparison between Pentium II and Pentium III motherboards, see the "Comparison of Physical Boards: Pentium II/III and AMD Athlon" video by Scott Mueller on the accompanying CD.

Celeron

Intel developed the Celeron processor in much the same way that the old 386 and 486 chips came out in both the full DX version and the bargain SX versions. Although previous low-cost chips reduced prices by removing the FPU, the Celeron's core processor was actually either a Pentium II or a Pentium III, depending on its version.

Celerons became Intel's budget line of processors, and were typically hobbled in some way so they wouldn't compete with the company's high-end products. The first chip, introduced in 1998, was a Pentium II processor with the L-2 cache disabled, severely reducing performance. Intel then added a small L-2 cache to subsequent Celeron chips, but they ended up outperforming the more expensive Pentium IIs of the day, causing a minor fiasco. Modern Celerons support the same features as their more expensive siblings, but generally lag behind in core speed.

> Although Celeron chips now are well over the 1GHz level, Intel seems to be less inclined to provide them for testing. AMD no longer produces the Duron line, and with pure speed ratings being insufficient to compare chips, Intel may either adopt the PR numbers or eliminate the Celeron line in favor of earlier versions of the Pentium 4.

The Pentium 4

"Willamette" was Intel's design-team code name for the core CPU that was to eventually become the Pentium 4. Unlike the Pentium III, which was basically an enhanced version of the Pentium Pro, the Pentium 4 was a ground-up redesign. The 0.18 mu Pentium III had topped out at 1GHz, but a new 0.13 micron process would allow speeds starting at 1GHz, with a theoretical ceiling of 10GHz. Together with core design changes, Intel decided it was time to retire the Pentium III and introduce the Pentium 4. (Those Roman numerals were getting to be sticky.)

Even with the new manufacturing process, the chip would be huge, at over 217 square millimeters and twice the size of a PIII. However, the size allowed for over 40 million transistors—more than any other processor on the market. In October 2000, Intel hired the popular "Blue Man Group" to star in a massive marketing push. Finally, the long-awaited day in November arrived and the media campaign came to a head. A 1.5GHz P4 animation executed a perfect dive into a sea of what was to become obsolete CPUs. Sadly, the picture-perfect advertising dive turned into a real-world belly flop.

The P4 couldn't keep up with the Athlon, or even the lowly Duron. In fact, the new chip couldn't even match the venerable Pentium III it was supposed to replace. Intel quickly countered with the release of a slower 1.3GHz chip, claiming that over-clocking generated too much heat, and therefore, reduced performance.

The lackluster performance of the chip in standard benchmarks shouldn't have been either a surprise or a major problem. The chip delivered on all its promised capabilities, but widely accepted industry performance tests emphasized business applications, whereas the Pentium 4 emphasized gaming and multimedia applications. The P4 could easily run business applications, but earlier, less-specialized CPUs tended to do better in the existing benchmarks. A more serious problem turned out to be Intel's decision to tie the P4 directly to Rambus RDRAM. The memory chips were hard to obtain, and when they were available, could easily be twice the price of comparable SDRAM used by other CPUs.

Customers weren't very excited about paying a premium for memory with no visible performance advantage. The new Hyper-Threading technology was a good idea, but it was deactivated in the first release. Even that wasn't really a bad decision, given how few programs—if any—could actually utilize the capability. Still, it left customers scratching their heads, wondering why they should spend money for a deactivated capability that their application software couldn't utilize.

To add gasoline to the fire, the i850 chipset supporting the Pentium 4 hadn't come out of development by the release date. Without a supporting chipset and motherboard, the Willamette was just a big, poorly designed Pentium III. Ultimately, the entire product launch ended up being similar to someone building a foundation down to bedrock, pitching a tent over the foundation, and then wondering why nobody was renting office space in the new high-rise building.

Eventually the i850 chipset was released, but performance was disappointing. VIA was already selling a competing chipset and board for the P4 that could use DDR-SDRAM. With the RDRAM problems, Intel quickly replaced the i850 with the i875 chipset. Soon after, by the second half of 2001, Intel changed to the 0.13-micron process, and replaced the P4 core with the new "Northwood" core. The modifications brought the chip up to speeds exceeding 3.0Ghz, and the new i875 400MHz chipset, together with the new processor, produced system transfer speeds approaching 800MHz. Interestingly, the new CPU and chipset happened to also work with SDRAM, like everyone else's chips.

For more information on a comparison between Pentium 4 and standard form factors, see the "Comparison of Physical Boards: Pentium 4 and Standard Form Factors" video by Scott Mueller on the accompanying CD.

Net Burst Technology

Net Burst technology is a combination of various features. The name presumably brings to mind images of zooming around the Internet, surfing with the greatest of ease. However, Net Burst has nothing to do with the Internet. The feature set includes

➤ Hyper-Threading (HT) technology

➤ A 400MHz System Bus (PCI 100MHz and 4X multiplier)

➤ An Execution Trace Cache (derived from the L-1 cache principle)

➤ The Rapid Execution Engine (Intel's new marketing name for multiple Arithmetic Logic Units—the ALU)

We're not going to get into all the details, but Net Burst also includes some secondary features, such as Advanced Transfer Cache, Advanced Dynamic Execution, Enhanced Floating Point and Multimedia Unit, and Streaming SIMD Extensions 2 (SSE-2). You should be able to see that a 400MHz or 800MHz FSB will help move data around the North bridge a lot faster than previous buses.

Dual Arithmetic Logic Units are included on the Pentium 4 die, clocked at twice the processor speed, and the upgraded feature was named the Rapid Execution Engine (REE). This eliminates bottlenecks due to arithmetic calculations. The Pentium 4, for the most part, has come even closer to being two entirely distinct 32-bit processors inside the housing. Clearly, a single ALU with two 32-bit processors would never do. REE allows the chip to shift repetitive tasks into a specialized area of the processor, with a dedicated memory cache, and running at twice the speed of the processor.

The Advanced Transfer Cache (ATC) focuses on widening the L-2 cache bus width to 256 bits. Using this type of integration, Intel was able to speed up the L-2 cache to the core CPU speed. The ATC bus is a way to increase throughput from the L-2 cache to make up for a reduced L-1 cache size (20KB). Later Pentiums are expected to have the L-2 cache built onto the die.

The Pentium 4 is capable of handling up to 6 instructions per clock cycle, using Advanced Dynamic Execution. Advanced Dynamic Execution is mostly a way for the CPU to keep track of more instruction fragments. A modern processor breaks apart instructions into smaller units of micro-ops. The CPU keeps track of these free-floating pieces of instructions inside the core. Because of certain problems with 20-level pipelining, the Pentium 4 must keep track of more of these fragments than previous chips.

Hyper-Threading (HT) Technology

In a nutshell, *hyper threading* allows a single CPU to logically divide itself into multiple virtual processors. This is the formalization of earlier virtual processes, where the microcode has been updated to handle full, protected separation between VMs. Each virtual processor functions as a complete, parallel processor. When a lengthy calculation stops a single processor cold until the operation is complete, hyper threading allows another virtual processor to continue executing instructions. This finally opens the door to true multi-threaded multi-tasking, where the operating system can place individual calls to each processor separately.

Oddly enough, SpeedStep technology, used in mobile computers, allows a chip to shut down depending on demand. In other words, when an area of the processor isn't being used for some period of time, it stops using electricity. The feature not only conserves battery power, but also reduces heat buildup. Hyper threading is designed to maximize CPU usage, where one or the other of the virtual processors is processing instructions all the time. This means that, in theory, most areas inside the CPU will be running all the time. Current Pentiums are already hot, and the 3.4GHz "Prescott" is expected to be even hotter. SpeedStep is a fine advantage, but HT Technology seems to cancel out that same advantage.

Mobile "Centrino" Technology

In 2003, laptops and notebook computers started selling as many units as desktop machines for the first time. With the power and portability of modern laptops so attractive, and telecommuting becoming a way to put corporate road warriors on the battle front, so to speak, Intel has combined many of the most useful features of a desktop under the umbrella of the Centrino marketing brand name. Perhaps the growing market will lead to lowering prices. Together with BlueTooth wireless protocols, we may see the end of the desktop machine for anything other than office production work.

Centrino mobile technology is a Pentium M processor (features from the Pentium III and Pentium 4) on an i855 chipset, with built-in wireless (802.11b) networking capabilities, and enhanced power management capabilities. Power management is directly related to battery power, and depends to a great extent on the CPU voltage. Microsoft's Windows power management features can turn off the monitor and hard drive. Centrino technology can actually adjust how much power the CPU uses, based on its processing needs at any given time. SpeedStep technology starts the CPU in "sleep mode," and then awakens various areas of the chip as they're needed.

Much like the "Intel Inside" sticker helped consumers know that they were buying an authentic Intel processor, the "Centrino" sticker on a box lets the consumer know that certain standardized features are included "right out of the box."

The Core Naming Convention

Both AMD's and Intel's corporate marketing departments have continually tried to sell chips based on brand recognition. This is presumably why the Pentium and Athlon name have stayed around for so long. To know what they're buying, knowledgeable people have begun referring directly to the project code names of the various chip technologies. Table 5.1 is a list of the recent processor cores, along with their most pertinent distinguishing features.

We include some information about AMD in the section following the table, but as far as we can see, CompTIA will mostly use chips that came after the K-6 line. The main thing to remember about AMD is that it uses Processor Rating numbers, rather than megahertz numbers, to rate the performance of their chips. Check the "Need to Know More?" section at the end of this chapter for books and Web sites that can go far more into specifications and features than we have room for here.

Table 5.1 Processor Cores and Features

Family	Core	Released	Rated	Bus Clock	Micron	Transistors	Form	Distinguishing Features
Pentium III	Coppermine	c. 1999	500MHz–1.13GHz	100–133MHz	0.25 mu 0.18 mu	9.5 million 25 million	Slot 1 FC-PGA	125–106mm die, SIMD, SSE, 512KB L-2, 32KB L-1
Pentium 4	Willamette 423	Nov. 2000	1.4–1.8GHz	400MHz (4X) 64-bit bus	0.18 mu	42 million	Socket 423	144 SSE-2 instructions, RDRAM, i850 chipset, aluminum interconnects, 20-stage pipeline, 256KB L-2, 217mm die, 20KB L-1
Pentium 4	Willamette 478	Aug. 2001	1.9–2.0GHz	400MHz (4X)	0.18 mu	42 million	Socket 478	"Prescott" 478 socket
Pentium 4	Northwood "A"	Jan. 2002	2.0–2.4GHz	400MHz (4X)	0.13 mu	55 million	Socket 478	146–131mm die, 512KB L-2, 20KB L-1
Pentium 4	Northwood "B"	Aug. 2002	2.5–2.6GHz	400MHz (PCI 100–4X)	0.13 mu	55 million	Socket 478	131mm die, 512KB L-2, i875 chipset, DDR memory

(continued)

Table 5.1	Processor Cores and Features *(continued)*							
Family	Core	Released	Rated	Bus Clock	Micron	Transistors	Form	Distinguishing Features
Pentium 4	Northwood "B"	May 2002	2.6–2.8GHz	533MHz (PCI 133—4X)	0.13 mu	55 million	Socket 478	Faster FSB
Pentium 4	Northwood	Nov. 2002	3.06GHz	533MHz (PCI 133—4X)	0.13 mu	55 million	Socket 478	Hyper-Threading Technology (HT)
Pentium 4	Northwood "C"	May 2003	2.4–3.4+GHz	800MHz (PCI 200—4X)	0.13 mu	55 million	Socket 478	Faster FSB
Pentium M		Apr. 2002	1.4–2.6GHz	400MHz (PCI 100—4X)	0.13 mu	55 million		SpeedStep Technology, 1.3/1.2V, 512KB L-2, 20KB L-1
Pentium M	Banias	Mar. 2003	900MHz– 1.7+GHZ	400MHz (PCI 100—4X)	0.13 mu 0.09 mu (late 2003)	77 million		1MB L-2, "Centrino," i855 chipset, SSE-2, 802.11b wireless, Low-voltage (1.18V, 0.98V), Ultra-Low voltage (1.0V, 0.84V), 100mm die

(continued)

Table 5.1 Processor Cores and Features *(continued)*

Family	Core	Released	Rated	Bus Clock	Micron	Transistors	Form	Distinguishing Features
Pentium 4	Prescott	Q4: 2003	3.2–4+GHz	800MHz (PCI 200–4X)	0.09 mu	100 million		13 "Prescott New Instructions" (PNI, [possibly SSE-3]), 1MB L-2 (on die), 28KB L-2, 81mm die
Pentium 4	Tejas	2005		1200MHz? (PCI Express)	0.09–0.045?			DDR-II memory, 32/64-bit chip, PCI Express graphics, possibly water cooled?
Pentium 5	Nehalem	2005?	6+GHz?					Probable SMP, possible build on Xeon "Nocona?"
Athlon K-7	Classic (Version C and A)	Jun. 1999	500MHz–1.0GHz	200MHz (PCI 100–2X)	0.25 mu 0.18 mu	22 million	Slot A	19 new 3DNow! instructions, SMP support, 10–15 stage pipeline, 512KB L-2, 128KB L-1

(continued)

Table 5.1 Processor Cores and Features *(continued)*

Family	Core	Released	Rated	Bus Clock	Micron	Transistors	Form	Distinguishing Features
Athlon (v. PIII)	Thunderbird (v. Coppermine)	Jun. 2000	650MHz–1.4GHz	200–266MHz (PCI 100, 133)	0.18 mu	37 million (15m L-2 cache)	Socket A	128KB L-1, 256KB L-2 (on die), 117mm die
Athlon XP (v. P4)	Palomino	Oct. 2001	1.3–1.7GHz 1500+ to 2100+	266MHz (PCI 133–2X)	0.18 mu	37.5 million	Socket A	129mm die, 128KB L-1, 256KB L-2 (on die), SSE support (not SSE-2)
Athlon 4 Mobile	Palomino	May 2001	850MHz–1.4GHz 1500+ to 1600+	200MHz (PCI 100–2X)	0.18 mu	37.5 million	Socket A	3DNow! Professional (52 new instructions), 128KB L-1, 256KB L-2, PowerNow! (v. SpeedStep), 1.4V
Athlon XP	Thoroughbred "A"	Jun. 2002	1.4–1.8GHz 1700+ to 2200+	266MHz (PCI 133–2X)	0.13 mu	37.2 million	Socket A	smaller, less power, 8-layer, 128KB L-1, 256KB L-2
Athlon XP	Thoroughbred "B"	Q1: 2003	1.4–2.25GHz 1600+ to 2800+	266–333MHz (PCI 133, 166)	0.13 mu	37.6 million	Socket A	400K transistors to reduce EMI, 9-layer, 1.6V

(continued)

Table 5.1 Processor Cores and Features *(continued)*

Family	Core	Released	Rated	Bus Clock	Micron	Transistors	Form	Distinguishing Features
Athlon XP	Barton	Feb. 2003	1.8–2.2+GHz 2500+ to 3200+	333–400MHz (PCI 166, 200)	0.13 mu	53.9 million	Socket A	115mm die, 128KB L-1, 512 KB L-2
Athlon DP	ClawHammer	2003	1.6–2.0+GHz 3000+ to 3400+	333MHz (PCI 333–1X)	0.13 mu	67 million	754-pin	Desktop, 2-way SMP, Hyper-Transport, 512K–1MB L-2, on-die memory controller, 104mm die
Athlon Opteron x86–64	Sledgehammer	Apr. 2003	1.4–1.8+GHz	333MHz 2-channel	0.13 mu	105.9 million	940-pin 939-pin	Enterprise, Hyper-Transport bus, 2-, 4-, then 8-way SMP, 128KB L-1 (on die), 1MB L-2 (on die), 1.5V, 193 mm die, expected SOI wafers

(continued)

Table 5.1   Processor Cores and Features *(continued)*

Family	Core	Released	Rated	Bus Clock	Micron	Transistors	Form	Distinguishing Features
Intel Xeon	Prestonia	Feb. 2002	1.8–3.06+GHz	400–533MHz (PCI 100, 133)	0.13 mu		Socket 603	20KB L-1, 512KB L-2 (on die), 2-way SMP, SSE-2
Intel Itanium-2 IA-64	McKinley	Jul. 2002?	1.0GHz	400MHz	128-bit bus (like 800MHz PCI)	0.18 mu	221 million	32KB L-1, 256KB L-2, 3MB L-3 (on die), 421mm die, eventual dual-core CPU

Source: www.geek.com "ChipGeek"

AMD

Fairchild Semiconductors may not have the same name recognition as IBM, but in the 1960s the company was at the forefront of what was to become the PC industry. In 1958, Jack Kilby of Texas Instruments developed an integrated circuit on a piece of germanium. The same year, Robert Noyce, a leading scientist at Fairchild, independently developed a separate integrated circuit. Then in 1959, Noyce used aluminum signal traces on a silicon-oxide layer over silicon to produce an even better IC. Gordon Moore, one of Fairchild's co-founders, was suitably impressed.

Noyce became Senior Manager at Fairchild, and developed a strong relationship with Jerry Sanders, one of the company's best sales people. Fairchild was partly in competition with Texas Instruments, but seriously competing with Motorola. And they were falling behind! By the mid-1960s, many of Fairchild's employees had had enough, and were leaving to form their own companies. More than a hundred businesses came out of that original group, and their area of California became known as Silicon Valley.

Among the first to leave Fairchild were Noyce and Moore, forming Intel Corporation. One of their first employees was Andy Grove, a brilliant scientist working at Fairchild. It happens that Grove was a refugee from Hungary, and had a reputation for being a brilliant man with a serious temper problem. (They didn't have "anger management classes" in those days.)

In May 1969, Jerry Sanders and seven other employees left to start their own company, Advanced Micro Devices—AMD. Initially headquartered in one of the co-founders' living rooms, the company managed to raise enough money by September to move to the back of a rug-cutting building in Santa Clara. Their mission was to build a successful semiconductor business, providing the building blocks of the "computation," communications, and "instrumentation" market. Back then, "computer" referred to an IBM mainframe, for the most part.

Right from the beginning, Intel was the "superstar headliner" of the business and technological community, with AMD being more the "opening band." Soon, Intel was jumping off with the 4004 microprocessor, and microprocessor technology was taking off. When Jerry Sanders came to his old friend Noyce and proposed a contract as a second-source manufacturing company, Noyce agreed.

Intel wasn't originally focused on building microprocessors, and AMD was busy developing a manufacturing line for non-volatile flash memory. Back then, nobody was too concerned about either market, but nowadays the largest application for this type of memory is in digital cameras, cell phones, and every other kind of consumer electronics imaginable. Of course, the microprocessor is the foundation of the PC market. But 1974 brought a business recession, and both companies nearly went out of business.

In 1975, a company by the name of MITS launched their Altair computer, and people took notice of this new microprocessor gizmo. Bill Gates and Paul Allen were investigating a programming language on a time-share mainframe, and thought they could rework it as a programming language for the Altair. So they took the code and announced they had a product to sell. Meanwhile, Intel and AMD both survived, and by 1976, microprocessors were becoming one of the fastest-growing products in history. Intel couldn't keep up with the demand, and when Sanders asked Noyce for second-source rights to Intel's microcode, Noyce agreed.

By 1979, Intel had emerged as the leading chip maker, and took the IBM contract for the first PC. The Intel 8088 and x86 architecture went on to make history, and AMD had a contract with Intel not only to make the chips, but also to use the microcode. With AMD being such a small company, compared to Intel, nobody paid much attention when they renewed their agreement in 1982. Noyce and Moore were pulling out of managing Intel, and it was Andy Grove who took over the reins.

NOTE IBM needed an operating system, and Gates and Allen approached them with QDOS (Quick and Dirty Operating System). Unfortunately, neither Gates nor Allen knew much about programming, so IBM had to fix QDOS so it would work. However, for some reason, IBM had signed an agreement that only the new Microsoft company would "own" the PC operating system license. A later court case led the way to MS-DOS and PC-DOS.

In 1983, Phoenix technologies reverse-engineered the IBM BIOS, and Lotus Corporation released its "1-2-3" spreadsheet. Steve Wozniak and Steve Jobs had just finished work on the first Apple computer, and over the next few years, other companies were trying to release "clones" of the IBM machine. The PC industry was on fire! At the same time, AMD was losing business and was in serious trouble. Andy Grove, over at Intel, was going after anyone who tried to clone chips, and IBM was trying to destroy anyone who tried to clone a PC.

Then Grove decided to cancel the contract with AMD, and that was the last straw. Jerry Sanders demanded arbitration, as part of the contract, and won a judgment against Intel. With that, AMD was able to begin cloning the 80286 and 80386 chip. AMD was back in business. Over the next ten years, lawsuits volleyed back and forth across California, becoming even more furious when Robert Noyce died. Current estimates are of legal fees topping $200 million. Both Sanders and Grove have retired, and new people now run both companies. However, the feud continues. When AMD announced the Opteron, Intel responded by slashing prices on its Pentium 4 chips. The winners? We—the people.

Microsoft has been pushed into developing two different versions of their upcoming 64-bit operating system. "Longhorn" is designed for Intel processors, and "Anvil" is apparently designed for AMD chips. Throw in the PCI Express bus, and who knows where desktop computing will be in the next few years? AMD has always been about performance, and for every Intel chip produced since the 386, AMD has countered with a less expensive chip, better performance, and more features. As we've seen, perhaps the real fork in the road to the future rests on two fundamental differences:

➤ Intel's incompatible IA-64 microcode versus AMD's x86-64 backward-compatible 64-bit code.

➤ Intel's Hyper-Threading technology versus AMD's new Hyper-Transport chip-to-chip bus. The Intel Itanium seems limited to two symmetrical processors, whereas AMD's Opteron can join eight processors together with the new bus.

Summary—Modern Processors

Frankly, we suspect that CompTIA will ask about only the broadest aspects of processors. Previous exams had questions about specific processor speeds, bus speeds, and the limited feature sets of chips up until about the Pentium II series. We've listed most of the important points in Table 5.1, but the things to remember about Pentiums (aside from their names) are

➤ MMX and what the acronym stands for. Understand that it was the basic set of specialized multimedia instructions.

➤ SIMD, SSE, SSE-2 as extensions to the original multimedia instructions. 3D Now! supports only Intel's SSE, and not later versions.

➤ The 32-bit internal architecture and 36-bit address bus working with a 64-bit processor bus. Note that the mobile chips use a 31-bit address bus.

➤ Net Burst, as a compilation of several ways to tweak performance at speeds over 2GHz.

➤ Hyper-Threading technology as a way to use two 32-bit processes in a single chip to create two fully separated virtual processors. All Pentiums can create virtual machines, but the machines had to share transistors.

HT technology uses separate transistors to allow real, simultaneous multi-threaded multi-tasking.

➤ The PCI version specifications in terms of the FSB clocks: 100, 133, 166, 200, 400, and 800MHz.

AMD processors are usually larger and often hotter than comparable Pentiums. However, late-model Pentiums with HT technology seem to be reaching new levels of heat, whereas the Opteron promises to be much cooler. Secondly, AMD and IBM are working together on silicon-on-insulator (SOI) technology, with IBM having just built a new fabrication plant (fab) for AMD in New York. Much like Linux seems to be a response to Microsoft's dominating the OS field, perhaps the chip industry is moving toward the underdog. If this is true, then perhaps the AMD Hyper-Transport bus will overtake parts of Intel's PCI Express proposed specification and become an industry standard.

Chipsets, Slots, and Sockets

The CPU may be the heart of a computer, but without a motherboard it isn't going to do much of anything. The motherboard is the underlying foundation for the computer, and it's built around a number of chips that support the computer's features and capabilities. IBM's original XT boards used six discrete chips to provide feature support, and AT boards used nine. Then, in 1986, a company called *Chips and Technologies* released an integrated chip that combined most of the functions of the AT support chips. They used other chips to act as buffers and minor controllers, and made an entire AT motherboard with only five chips.

These integrated supporting chips make up the chipset, and provide a way for us to use such things as USB, AGP, IDE controllers, ATA and UDMA transfers, PCI cards, memory, and almost everything else you can think of. It wasn't long before Intel stepped in and began making its own motherboards and chipsets to go along with its processors. Nowadays, there are many companies making motherboards and chipsets, but they license various technologies from Intel (PCI and socket technologies, for instance). Some of the third-party companies include VIA, NVidia (with their investment in high-speed graphics processors), SiS (Silicon Integrated Systems), ALi (formerly Acer Laboratories, Inc.), and Serverworks, to name a few.

VIA (headquartered in Taiwan) has emerged as the third-largest manufacturer in the industry. The company originally bought Cyrix, in an attempt to become a single-source provider of CPUs, chipsets, and motherboards. Recently the company sold the Cyrix division off to Cisco, but VIA continues to develop their own chipsets.

Sockets

Way back when PCs were a new invention, the CPU was soldered right onto the motherboard. Nobody thought about upgrading a processor, and so there was no particular need for an *interface connection*. When a new CPU entered the market, people either replaced the entire motherboard or bought a new computer. It wasn't until the days of the 486 chips that motherboards began using sockets as that connection point. Most microprocessors (the ones we're interested in) are flat. As a result, they have some number of connecting pins on one side, which slide into holes in a socket.

Because of the extremely small nature of the pins, they can be bent very easily. Early CPUs could be pulled out of their sockets with a chip wrench, designed to lift the chip out of its socket in a nearly perpendicular line, reducing bent pins. It wasn't long before Zero-Insertion Force (ZIF) sockets resolved the other half of the equation, providing a way to insert the chip without bending any pins. The ZIF lever is exactly that: a lever that raises or lowers the chip into a socket with zero manual force coming from your arm.

 A ZIF socket is a plastic socket with a small lever used to lift out or insert a CPU. The lever allows for zero insertion force, and prevents bent or broken pins.

When you look at a square piece of anything, it's often difficult to know which edge is the top or bottom. Just so, CPUs look like a gray square, and the underlying socket looks like another square with a bunch of holes. To help with the correct orientation, Intel began using a small indexing "dot," as you can see in Figure 5.1. The chip housing had a single missing pin, and the reverse side had a small marker, indicating the correct way to insert the chip.

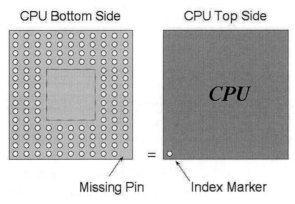

Figure 5.1 CPU indexing.

Slot Technology

We've already mentioned that Intel began using a different type of interface connection with the introduction of L-2 memory caches. Keep in mind that manufacturing a chip is both a technical marvel and a business enterprise. Every transistor, capacitor, and interconnect costs some amount of money. Not only that, but there's only so much room on a given silicon wafer, and so Intel, AMD, IBM, and any other chip manufacturer must make decisions regarding how many components will go onto a wafer.

Level 1 cache memory has usually been 128KB or less, with Pentium 4s reducing it even further, to around 20KB. Even so, L-1 memory went on-die, beginning with the 486, and continued the socket form factor. Nowadays, CPUs always include L-1 memory cells as part of the chip's transistors. AMD already includes L-2 memory on the chip die, and Intel is following suit (no pun intended). One of the benefits of 130 nm technology is that transistors are small enough to allow for 512KB–1MB worth of Level 2 memory on the die. However, that wasn't always the case.

Originally, Intel chose to have outside vendors manufacture Level 2 memory chips for the Pentiums, but the memory still had to function at speeds higher than system RAM. After all, why bother using a memory cache if data transfers are at the same speed as the memory controller? To provide that speed, L-2 chips use a wider bus than the processor bus, and also tend to be clocked at a higher speed than the memory bus. Today's L-2 chips, when they're not on the die, are clocked at the same speed as the CPU.

L-2 cache memory connects to the CPU through the backside bus. Intel's Advanced Transfer Cache (ATC) uses a 256-bit bus.

To link the L-2 cache to the CPU with both the wide backside bus and higher clock speed, Intel built a small IC cartridge that would hold the CPU, the cache memory, and a few additional components. The cartridge looked like a small network card, as shown in Figure 5.2, and fit into a slot. This wasn't an expansion slot, but simply the way the CPU joined the motherboard. The CPU was soldered directly onto the cartridge, but upgrading the processor merely involved replacing the cartridge.

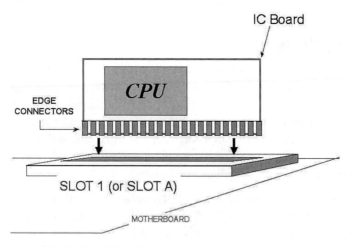

Figure 5.2 Pentium CPU cartridge and slot.

Slot technology stayed around only for as long as it took chip manufacturers to reduce their costs. When they no longer had to outsource the L-2 cache, Intel and AMD went back to the socket interface. One thing to note, though, is that Level 3 cache memory is making its appearance with multi-processor systems. High-speed chips generate a lot of heat, requiring a heat sink, or some type of liquid cooling. The large IC cartridges provided a commensurately large radiating surface, as well as room for a substantial chip-cooling fan. We may see the return of slot technology, for a short while, with the increased use of L-3 caches.

AMD and Socket A

Mounting a chip on a motherboard demands more than using glue or pins. Each chip must have a specific electrical connection. Aside from the voltage moving through the CPU, individual pins provide connections to specific areas inside the chip. As with other designs, Intel charged a licensing fee for their slot technology. When AMD first began producing their own processors, the chips used the same electrical interface as Intel. Not long afterward, AMD was unable to license Intel's technology, and so the company turned to Digital Equipment Corporation (DEC) and licensed their EV-6 bus technology.

 AMD's Slot A uses the same 242 pins and SC242 interface as Intel's Slot 1, but the two slots are electrically incompatible.

One of the interesting consequences of AMD having to turn to the EV-6 bus was their moving away from the PCI specification and front-side bus technology, also licensed through Intel. The DEC bus operated at 100MHz, but also provided for transfers on the half-tick (DDR memory). We've seen that Intel's decision to go with Rambus memory wasn't as successful as they'd hoped, but DDR RAM might not have come about had it not been for the long-standing feud between the two companies.

Table 5.2 is a brief listing of the various slots and sockets, along with a note as to the chips they support. Once again, space limitations don't allow for a comprehensive list of all CPUs and their form factors, and so we encourage you to have a more substantial preparation guide. That being said, this list should remind you of the socket and slot names you'll encounter on the exam.

 For the most part, the letter "A" in the interface indicates an AMD package.

Table 5.2 Sockets and Slots		
Name	**Pins**	**Chips**
Socket 7	321	Pentium 75–133, MMX, AMD K5, K6, Cyrix M1 Pentium Overdrive
Super 7 (100MHz bus)	321	AMD K6-2, K6-3, Cyrix M2 (not used by Intel)
Socket 8	387	Pentium Pro, Pentium III Overdrive

(continued)

Table 5.2 Sockets and Slots *(continued)*		
Name	**Pins**	**Chips**
Slot 1 (SC242)	242	Pentium II, Pentium III SEC, Celeron SEP (Intel only, no licensing)
Slot A (SC242)	242	Athlon SEC (replaced Super Socket 7)
Slot 2 (SC330)	330	(Xeon only—SECC2 form factor) Pentium II Xeon, Pentium III Xeon
Socket 370 (PGA 370)	370	Celeron, Celeron II, Pentium III, Cyrix III (three versions: PGA, SPGA, and FC-PGA; same chipset as Slot 1)
Socket A (Socket 462)	462	Duron, Athlon "Thunderbird" PGA (on-die L-2 cache)
Socket 423	423	Pentium 4 "Willamette," Xeon
Socket 478	478	Pentium 4 "Northwood," Xeon MP, Celeron
Socket 603		Pentium 4
Socket 754 Socket 940		AMD Hammer (x86-64)

Chipsets

With processors moving into 64-bit configurations, designed to work with more than a single CPU on the motherboard, AMD and Intel are moving toward integrated chipsets. Much the way Microsoft is having to develop versions of Windows for both AMD and Intel, third-party chipset manufacturers will provide motherboards specifically designed for a particular chip. IBM continues to be a strong presence in the chip-manufacturing business, with the PowerPC technology on the leading edge of technology. IBM and AMD seem to be working together lately, but the A+ exam will focus on Intel chipsets.

Table 5.3 lists the family groups of the Intel chipsets. You won't have to know everything about each board, but you should have an idea of the main differences in terms of feature support. Try not to get too exercised about remembering everything about every combination of systems, but have a general idea of important developmental changes. Note the evolving USB support, PCI specification, and the ATA support for IDE hard drives. Only the later chipsets support HT technology, but notice the increasing speed of the FSB, and the maximum amount of memory. Finally, note that RDRAM is supported with only a few chipsets.

An interesting feature of the i440BX was that over-clocking affected only the CPU and not the PCI bus. When the FSB was set to 133MHz, the PCI slots remained at 100MHz. This may be the first time that increasing the system speed didn't necessarily increase the speed of every other device associated with the FSB. Although the CPU and AGB can be increased, many hardware devices won't work with a PCI bus clocked beyond the specified speed.

Table 5.3	Intel Chipsets	
Chipset	**Processor Supported**	**Feature Support**
420	80486	
430 Socket 7	P5 Pentium	66MHz, 512KB L-2, 64–128MB SDRAM, USB support (PCI 2.0), no AGP support, ATA 16-33 (IDE drives)
440 Slot 1	P6 (Pentium Pro, Pentium II, Pentium III) (i440BX became a classic)	66–100MHz FSB, 512KB L-2, AGP X2, UDMA/33, USB, 256MB-1GB SDRAM, no AGP support
450 Socket 8	P6-Server (Pro, II, III) and Xeon in multiprocessor format	1–4GB SDRAM, 66MHz, no AGP, ATA-16 (IDE), no USB support
450 Slot 2	P6-Server (Pro, II, III) and Xeon in multiprocessor format	66–100MHz, 256MB–8GB SDRAM, AGP X2, USB, 512KB–2MB L-2, ATA-33, multiprocessor support
815 Socket 370	Celeron, Pentium III (value PCs)	133/100/66MHz, 512MB SDRAM, AGP X4, Intel 3D integrated graphics, PCI-X 2.2, ATA-100, USB 1.1
845 Socket 478	Celeron, Pentium 4 (mainstream PCs) (the i845PE was also a popular board)	400MHz, 3GB DDR-SDRAM, ATA-100, USB 2.0
850 Socket 423	Entry-level Pentium 4, Celeron	400MHz, 2GB RDRAM, ATA-100 (IDE), USB 1.1, AGP X4
850 Socket 478	Entry-level Pentium 4, Celeron	533MHz, 2GB RDRAM, ATA-100, AGP X4, USB 2.0, Net Burst
850 Socket 603	Entry-level Pentium 4, Celeron	400MHz, 4GB RDRAM (Colusa), 16GB DDR200 (E7500), AGP X4, ATA-100, USB 2, HT Technology, PCI-X

(continued)

Table 5.3 Intel Chipsets *(continued)*		
Chipset	**Processor Supported**	**Feature Support**
865	Pentium 4 (performance-level PC) (i845PE "Springdale" replaces i845PE)	800/533/400MHz, 4GB DDR-SDRAM, AGP X8, PCI-X 2.3, Ultra ATA 100, Serial ATA 150 (SATA), HT Technology, integrated graphics
875	Pentium 4	800/533MHz, 4GB DDR-SDRAM, AGP X8, no graphics, PCI-X 2.3, Ultra ATA 100, Serial ATA 150 (SATA), HT Technology, integrated graphics

Source: Geek.com and Intel.com

Hub Architecture

The 800 series chipset was released in 1999. The main difference was that it didn't use the North Bridge and South Bridge architecture. Instead, it used a hub architecture. *Hub architecture* is composed of three basic components: the Graphics and Memory Controller Hub (GMCH), the I/O Controller Hub (IOCH), and the Firmware Hub (FH). Keep in mind that North Bridge–South Bridge technology was introduced with the PCI 1.x specification, and the chipsets prior to the 800 series.

Hub architecture seems to be an attempt to assign three controllers, one to each of the main areas of work. It hasn't caught on, and now, in the 850-series chipset, the three hubs have been replaced with the Memory Controller Hub (MCH), and the I/O Controller Hub 2 (ICH2). Presumably, this is the second version of the I/O controller. Look at Figure 5.3, and notice the striking similarity between the "new" hub architecture and the previous North-South Bridge architecture. The only major differences seem to be the lack of ISA expansion slots and the potential switch to DDR-SDRAM.

Although the ISA slots may not be on the motherboard, the ISA bus is still supported by modern chipsets. For the moment, legacy I/O devices such as keyboards and mice expect the 8.3MHz transfer ISA rates. The 66MHz PCI clock can provide the ISA speed with a 1/8 divider, but the wiring for data transfers across the motherboard is still the ISA 16-bit architecture.

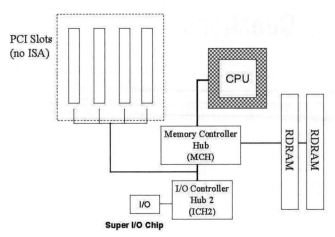

Figure 5.3   The 800-series chipset with hub.

Exam Prep Questions

Question 1

> The floating-point unit or coprocessor was internally integrated into which Intel microprocessor?
>
> ○ A. Intel 8088
> ○ B. Intel 8086
> ○ C. Intel 80286
> ○ D. Intel 80386
> ○ E. Intel 80486

Answer E is correct. The floating-point unit (FPU) or coprocessor was first integrated into the Intel 80486. The unit was disabled in the Intel 80486-SX for marketing reasons, but was still present.

Question 2

> Which was the first Intel microprocessor to be able to address more than one 1MB of memory?
>
> ○ A. Intel 8086
> ○ B. Intel 80286
> ○ C. Intel 80486
> ○ D. Intel 80386

Answer B is correct. The Intel 80286 could address 16MB of memory and was the first Intel microprocessor to break the 1MB limit.

Question 3

> Desktop Pentium processors contain a _____-bit address bus and a _____-bit internal bus.
>
> ○ A. 32, 64
> ○ B. 36, 64
> ○ C. 32, 36
> ○ D. 36, 32

Answer D is correct. This question is a pure rote-memory problem, based on your understanding of the difference between an address bus and the CPU's main, internal data path. Note that your only options are 32, 36, and 64. Remember that Pentiums typically have a 36-bit address bus. The internal bus is almost always smaller than the address bus. Answers A and C are incorrect because they indicate a 32-bit address bus. Answer B is incorrect because the internal bus is larger than the address bus. By process of elimination, answer D is the only response left.

Question 4

Flat CPUs use _____, whereas vertical CPUs work with _____ technology. (Choose all that apply)

❏ A. ZIF, Slot

❏ B. Socket 7, Slot A

❏ C. Socket 8, Slot 1

❏ D. Slot B, Socket 7

Answers A, B, and C are correct. Socket 7 and Socket 8 are both referred to as flat technologies, and the sockets mostly are zero-insertion force (ZIF) sockets. Vertical processors can use Slot 1 or Slot A, depending on whether they are Intel or AMD chips. Answer D is backward in the use of "slot" and "socket," and there's no such thing as Slot B.

Question 5

MMX enhancements refer to _____.

○ A. Video accelerator cards

○ B. L-1 and L-2 cache improvements

○ C. Memory management extensions

○ D. Multimedia extensions

Answer D is correct. MMX, or multimedia extensions, is a set of instructions on a CPU that helps speed up such things as video, audio, and speech recognition. Answer A is wrong because modern PCs have an accelerated graphics port (AGP) that uses a video card, but the card uses the MMX functions built into the CPU. There's no such thing as "memory management extensions," so answer C is wrong, and neither the Level 1 nor Level 2 cache have any sort of multimedia enhancements, so answer B is wrong.

Question 6

> Which of the following features are supported features on a modern chipset and motherboard? (Choose all that apply)
>
> ❑ A. UDMA/100
>
> ❑ B. 64MB RAM
>
> ❑ C. 100/400/733MHz FSB
>
> ❑ D. PIC-X

Answers A and B are correct. Ultra DMA is an IDE controller protocol and is supported by the underlying chipset. Almost any motherboard nowadays supports at least 64MB of memory, but all amounts of memory support are part of the chipset. Answer C is incorrect, and rests on your ability to use your eyes. Although PCI-X supports a 533MHz front side bus speed, it does not specify a 733MHz FSB, but rather, an 800MHz setting. Answer D is also incorrect, and a trick to fool the unsuspecting impatient person. PIC is a programmable interrupt controller, and is supported by the chipset. However, PCI-X is a specification. There is no PIC-X IRQ controller.

Question 7

> Which of the following are not used to connect a CPU to a motherboard? (Choose the two best answers)
>
> ❑ A. Socket 8
>
> ❑ B. Socket B
>
> ❑ C. Slot A
>
> ❑ D. Slot 4

Answers B and D are correct. Note that this is a tricky question because it asks you to choose what does *not* do something. If you aren't paying attention, you can easily choose the wrong answers based on what you know *will* work. Neither Socket B nor Slot 4 is associated with microprocessors and their packaging, making answers A and D incorrect choices for this question. Socket 8 (answer A) is a flat design used to install a CPU on the motherboard. Slot 1 is a vertical design, using a small circuit board with a single edge connector and a special processor slot on the motherboard.

Question 8

Which of the following offers a way for the CPU to execute simultaneous instructions?

○ A. Net Burst technology

○ B. Hyper-Threading technology

○ C. Hyper-Transport technology

○ D. Net Zero technology

Answer B is correct. Be careful and read the question! Note that it says "the" CPU, so you know this isn't a multi-processor system. Answer D is wrong, and you should see it immediately. Net Zero is an online service provider and has nothing to do with microcode or instructions. The real confusion lies between answers B and C, given they seem almost the same in their use of "hyper." Try to remember that Intel's "Net Burst" technology is a constellation of many features designed to optimize CPU capabilities. It (answer A) is the wrong answer, but remember the term. Answer C is wrong because the technology is specific to AMD's chips, designed for multiple AMD processors. Hyper-Threading technology carries a nice hint in the "threading." The formal name for true multi-tasking is "multi-threaded multi-tasking."

Question 9

You buy a laptop computer at a flea market and there seem to be some random errors showing up in strange places. Before you reformat the hard drive, you download a diagnostics program that will run on a single bootable floppy disk. When you try to run the .EXE program from the Explorer, an error message tells you that you must run it from a DOS command line. You restart the machine in MS-DOS mode, but the program still won't run. Why?

○ A. The CPU must be in Protected Mode.

○ B. The CPU must be in Real Mode.

○ C. The CPU must be 386 Enhance Mode.

○ D. Restart is causing a Windows problem.

○ E. The CPU is in Annoying Mode.

Answer B is correct. Okay, so answer E is only to lighten things up. We go to a lot of effort to show you scenario questions, regardless of whether you see them on the actual exam. These types of questions are well designed to demonstrate the kind of distraction you'll encounter in many types of questions. As always, first read the question through one time. Then, glance at the responses to get a sense of what you're being asked. Then go back and read the question again, very slowly! What exactly are you being told? The laptop and random errors are irrelevant. The real question is why a diagnostics program on a bootable floppy won't run in MS-DOS mode.

The responses indicate that the essence of the question rests on the CPU mode. Answers A and C are both incorrect because the restarted MS-DOS mode still is under the control of Windows, and isn't "real" DOS. Remember that all CPUs start in Real Mode until the operating system (Windows) can switch them over. Windows makes that switch, and doesn't switch back during a Restart. Answer D is wrong because the laptop obviously has problems, but if you can use the Explorer, Windows must be starting in some fashion. Answer B is correct because the diagnostics program requires Real Mode to run low-level checks on the system. Only in a pure DOS environment can the operating system on the bootable diagnostics disk set the CPU back to Real Mode. Observe that the question specifically indicates a bootable floppy, but that "you" tried to run the .EXE program. There's a reason diagnostics disks are bootable: to load a simple DOS operating system environment.

Question 10

Which Intel processors offered a full capability version and a reduced capability version? (Choose all that apply)

- ❏ A. 286
- ❏ B. 386
- ❏ C. Pentium
- ❏ D. 486

The correct answer is B, C, and D. The Intel 386 and 486 were released in both a full version (DX) and a budget version (SX). The Intel Celeron was a reduced function Pentium, again geared for the budget market. The Intel 286, answer A, never had a reduced function or budget version.

Need to Know More?

 Ace's Hardware

http://www.aceshardware.com/

"Technical information for the masters and the novices," Brian Neal, Publisher, Webmaster; Johan De Gelas, Senior Editor

A central site for technical news, hardware analysis, CPU architecture, and technology.

 Geek.com LLC

http://www.geek.com

Joel Evans, Chief Geek; Rob Hughes, Chief Technologist and ChipGeek; Sam Evans, Chief Editor

An excellent source of all-things-computer, including news, forums, PDAs, and everything involving being a "geek."

 Tom's Hardware Guide

http://www.tomshardware.com

Dr. Thomas Pabst. Since 1996, a premier source of hardware analysis, technology news, and reviews.

 The Advanced Micro Design (AMD) home site

http://www.amd.com

 The Intel Corporation home site

http://www.intel.com

 AnandTech, Inc.

http://www.Anandtech.com

Anand Lal Shimpi, Founder and CEO

An industry leader in technology, news, hardware analysis, and user forums.

 Overclockers.com

http://www.overclockers.com

Joe Citarella, Skip MacWilliam, and Ed Stroligo

A good source of information about CPUs, over-clocking, and motherboards; includes user forums and many related links to additional sites.

Mueller, Scott. *Upgrading and Repairing PCs, Academic Edition, 14th Edition.* Indianapolis, IN: Que Publishing, 2003. ISBN: 078972927X. This is one of the most comprehensive guides to everything inside a computer we've found, with easily understood examples and graphics.

Brooks, Charles. *A+ Training Guide, 5th Edition.* Indianapolis, IN: Que Publishing, 2003. ISBN: 0789730448.

Basic Electronics

Terms you'll need to understand:

- ✓ Alternating and direct current (AC/DC)
- ✓ Amps, volts, watts
- ✓ Resistor, ohms, potentiometer (POT)
- ✓ Capacitor, dielectric
- ✓ Multimeter
- ✓ Electrostatic discharge (ESD), electromagnetic interference (EMI)

Concepts you'll need to master:

- ✓ Analog and digital incremental steps
- ✓ Electrical flow, current, and circuits
- ✓ Potential and voltage
- ✓ Conductivity, insulation, and dielectrics
- ✓ Power supplies and conversion to DC
- ✓ ESD kits

Your A+ certification demonstrates that you have a certain level of competency in terms of troubleshooting, repairing, and maintaining PCs. We can split the entire field of computers into three very broad categories: hardware, software, and connectivity. CompTIA wants to know whether you have a solid grasp of the principles involved in all three of these categories. Obviously, the foundation rests on principles of electronics, electricity, mathematics, and even basic physics. This chapter is a sort of catch-all, designed to address the engineering questions you'll likely to encounter on the exam.

If you already understand electronics and basic electrical engineering, go ahead and skim the main topic headings to make sure you're ready for the types of questions you'll encounter. Although this isn't a preparation guide, one of our intended purposes for this book is to make our sample tests as close to the actual exams as we can. We could, simply, include a number of electronics questions in our tests, or we could do what we've chosen to do with this chapter. Each topic is a fast review of the necessary concepts, so if you end up getting lost, we'd suggest that you either do some further research, or postpone taking the exam until you've mastered the principles we're about to discuss.

Analog Versus Digital

In the fields of electronics and electrical engineering, analog and digital refer to the number of steps used to form a curve. A wave is a curve, and it can have either an infinite number of steps, or a set of numbered (incremental) steps. Each step can be represented by a bit of information, and can take on a value. The more steps to account for, the more bits that will be involved. Analog information has a potentially limitless number of values (settings) for varying states and conditions. Digital information has a limit in terms of how many bits a computer can work with at any given moment. Digital values are either on or off—one or zero, yes or no, exist or not exist. Remember that a "state" is basically the way something is at a specific time. In the analog world, everything changes all the time. In the digital world, there are only encoded "snapshots" of a thing.

Relative to the human mind, analog refers to the perceptions of the world around us. Our minds store mental images and we interpret those images as information. Computers operate in a digital environment, and are not (yet) capable of interpreting anything. To "interpret" something means to make sense of that thing—to understand it, grasp it, conceptualize it, or provide an explanation. For example, you interpret the words of this book and form a visual concept of the meaning of the word "computer." A machine works only with the encoded characters and their positions in a grid. You might say, "Ah-hah, I see…I get it!" A computer can only be programmed to output a series of shapes (the letters and punctuation) following a specified condition.

Analog information is abstract (not associated with any specific thing); digital information is concrete (factual). A computer can assign a value of two when it's told to, but it can't hold the infinite values of all possible sets of two. For example, the human mind understands the abstract concept of two, or "two-ness," and can apply it to any set of two specific apples, people, fingers, and so forth. The digital computer understands only a specific two, in a specific situation, at a specific time, in a specific context, and in a specific state.

The digital process can approximate an analog event. It can assign digital values to pieces of an event, representing changing moments over time. For example, the analog concept of "up" can mean many things, with infinite increments of direction and distance relative to gravity. Human beings perceive gravity directly as a feeling of weight, and we know that "up" is "up there." A computer doesn't feel gravity and would ask, "What is up? Starting when, and from where? Which direction, and for how long? What's the definition of direction?"

Consider a stairway, and the metric distance between 0 and 1. We could say the ground is zero, and one step in a stairway is 1. Does your foot go from the floor to the stair instantly? No, of course not. You move your foot one millimeter at a time, through all the values between 0 and 1. If we digitally examined one of your foot movements, we could take five snapshots, and assign five values: 0, 0.25, 0.5, 0.75, 1.0. Five values require a larger binary number than only two values. And even with five values, we would see a very "jerky" movement of your foot going through space.

Because analog information essentially has no boundaries, it includes the presence of noise (random information from random sources). Digital information never varies, has no noise, and always has an exact starting and ending state. Analog recording captures music in a series of waves with infinite steps. Digital recording breaks each wave into a series of snapshots, and then assigns values to each moment. The smaller we can make our snapshots, the more smoothly we can present the music to our analog ears. However, smaller increments mean more bit values—numbers.

An analog brain interprets a pattern of dots on a page of newspaper and sees a picture that means something. The mind sees shapes, patterns, and shades of gray and says, "Ah, that's Betty and her mom!" The digital processor sees the underlying digital format of the image, composed of black dots on a white field, and says, "There are 15,263 dots within a rectangle." The separation values of the dots, along with their sizes and even their existence, are exact values. There are no shades of gray. Each dot is only black or white. Only by the analog process of interpretation can we turn the dots into a shaded picture, and then link the picture with stored memories to form meaningful information.

Basic Electricity

Electricity: Nobody really knows what it is. We can observe and predict its effects, and we can formulate theories of what may be happening, but even today, we don't really know the exact nature of electricity. Although we'll use common electricity-as-water examples in this chapter, water doesn't usually flow backwards and forwards. On the other hand, you might just as easily think of electricity as money. Money is energy (stored as a symbol), and goes into and out of your pocket. You expend energy to do work, and someone hands you paper and metal symbols in return. When you go to the store, you exchange your paper and metal money for a candy bar. Your energy goes through a circuit between you, your boss, the money, your pocket, and the store.

In this example, money represents electrons. We could say that *voltage* is your *desire* to spend money. Suppose you desire a candy bar that you see behind a counter. The candy bar has no money—it's missing money, so to speak. You have a surplus of money (electrons) in your pocket, and so the candy bar attracts your cash. In other words, the lack of money in the candy bar is causing an attraction between it and the money in your pocket—a voltage potential. We could say that you have a surplus of desire to spend money. Voltage is the lack of electrons in one thing, attracting the surplus of electrons in something else: It's the attraction, or potential for movement.

Voltage is a potential flow of electricity, but *current* is the actual flowing movement of electricity. The closer you come to the candy bar, the more your desire increases. The more you eye that candy bar, and the shorter the distance between it and you, the higher the probability becomes that you'll discharge your money. When your desire reaches a certain point, your money begins to flow out of your pocket. The sales clerk is like a wire, or a pathway. When conditions are right, you come in contact with the clerk and the discharge takes place. You discharge money into the clerk, and the clerk charges you for the candy bar—taking your money. An equalization takes place.

This is only another way of looking at a complete circuit—a closed circuit. During the process, your desire joins with the candy bar, and it becomes part of you. (It reminds us of the Zen master who asked for a hot dog, and told the vendor to make him one with everything. *Badah-bump!*)

Current

Electrical current is a moving flow of electrons, moving in waves and cycles. When electrons flow in one direction, we refer to Direct Current (DC). When the flow changes directions, moving back and forth, we call it Alternating Current (AC). Both types of flow have unique benefits. On the other hand, an electrical *charge* means either some surplus amount of stored electrons (negative charge), or a shortage (lack) of electrons (positive charge). Understand that when something has a charge, electrons continue to move around, but they don't flow anywhere in a unified direction. To flow, current must have some type of conductor in a circuit.

Alternating current goes first in one direction, and then reverses to the other direction, then reverses back again in a regular *cyclical* process. In the United States, common AC runs at 60 cycles per second and 110 volts. The computer power supply converts 110V AC to Direct Current. Although certain components use very low levels of alternating current for timing events, this isn't the same as normal "house current."

We're going to use a common analogy for electricity, where water moves through various hoses, plumbing equipment, and objects. The analogy begins to break down with the idea of AC, given that water usually flows only in one direction. That being said, we'll propose some amount of electricity coming from a power source, and go on from there.

Negative to Positive Movement

Atoms contain an equal number of negatively charged *electrons* and positively charged *protons*. Protons are inside the nucleus of an atom and don't move around very much. Electrons travel around the outside of the nucleus, moving all the time—it's in their nature. An atom has a neutral charge because of the equal number of electrons and protons. The electrons and protons balance each other. When they're out of balance, the atom develops a charge.

Current thinking is that electrons are actually a wave function, and protons aren't fully responsible for positive charges, but we'll leave it up to you to research the particle physics.

Electricity flows from a negative charge to a positive charge—not the other way around. Back in the 1700s, when Benjamin Franklin was out flying his kite in that famous thunderstorm—where he had the metal key attached to the string—he was developing two things. The thing he became famous for was his original theory of electricity. The second—a footnote in history—was that he was trying to think up a clever comeback for his wife who'd told him to go fly a kite.

Franklin theorized that electricity was composed of two charges, positive and negative, and then promptly got it wrong by assigning active movement to the positive charges. For the next 250 years, children would be taught that electricity flows from the positive to the negative. This isn't how electricity works, and neither are electrons little planet-like balls orbiting around a sun-like nucleus. We knew that electrons were wave functions all the way back in 1910; it's just that nobody told our teachers.

Think of it this way: Electrons are used to moving around—it's in their nature. When a bunch (technical term) of electrons take a hike, they leave behind their positive counterparts. A surplus of protons is a positive charge. Something doesn't actually *build* a positive charge so much as it *loses* negative electrons.

Now suppose that something else comes wandering by with a surplus of electrons. In the first place, electrons are all charged the same way (negative), and so they repel each other. In the second place, opposite charges attract each other, just like in love. Finally, it's a natural law that charges will tend to equalize, moving toward a neutral balance of the same number of electrons and protons.

The thing containing the extra electrons is trying to get rid of the freeloaders, in an attempt to get back to a neutral state. Meanwhile, the thing with the surplus of protons is looking to fall in love with some electrons and hook up for awhile. When the two things reach a critical distance, the extra electrons on the first thing jump to the second thing. The process is called a discharge, and if the jump takes place over a gap, we might see a spark. In a moment, we'll refine the story and call the two "things" plates in a capacitor.

Amps and Volts

We measure the amount of current—flowing electrons—in *amps* (amperage). We measure the build-up of pressure behind the electrons in *volts* (V). Voltage is often called potential. In the United States, most personal computers connect to a wall socket providing 110 volts. *Watts* (W) are often called a "measure of work," and are the result of multiplying volts by amps (volts×amps = watts, watts/volts = amps). Using this formula, you can divide 110V by a 75W light bulb to determine that the bulb likely uses 1.5 amps.

In other words, you can multiply an amount of water by its water pressure to figure out if you have enough power (watts) to turn a particular water wheel or light a light bulb. Too little wattage and a bulb won't work well: Too much, and the filament will burn out. Remember that current refers to the amount of flowing electrons.

Amperage is like releasing the water pressure and pushing a flow of water through a hose. A light push of water hitting you from a garden hose may make you wet, but it won't do much more than that. On the other hand, a powerful push, sending water careening out of a water cannon, can knock you halfway down the block. In fact, even if the water pressure in the water cannon is fairly low, the sheer volume of water coming out of it can do a lot of damage.

 Low voltage (and current movement) with high amperage (released pressure) can cause significant injury. Capacitors store up electrical pressure, and can quickly release a lot of electrons in a large flow. The larger the capacitor, the higher the current—regardless of the voltage.

Circuits

Most of us learned that for electricity to flow, we have to build a complete circuit. In other words, electricity has to come out of one terminal, cross through a number of wires and stuff (technical term, again), and then flow back into a second terminal, using a *closed circuit*. When you plug a wire into a wall socket, electricity actually flows out into the wire, giving the wire a potential (a possible future) of some kind. The wire carries the same potential as the socket.

 Electricity does not flow out of a bare-ended wire, all over the floor, creating a mess. Electricity flows into the wire, but most of it stays within the wire. However, if you are exceptionally allergic to electrons, you may notice one or two of them in the surrounding carpet.

At some point, we've all had to walk from our home to school, and then back home again. A circuit is simply a starting point, and a pathway that eventually returns to the starting point. Most of us also discovered we could "cut through" an alley or someone's back yard to shorten our walk. A short circuit is only an alternate path between two points of a circuit. In addition to always wanting to party with protons, electrons invariably take the path of least resistance, which is usually the shortest path. (That's why it is called a *short*.)

NOTE   A short circuit isn't always shorter than the original path. When you touch a test lead to one point of a circuit, and place another lead some distance along in the circuit, you also create a "short" circuit between the two leads. If a component between the two leads has a high resistance, the electrons will flow through a path with less, or lower resistance. The flow will go through the test leads and meter, even though the distance is longer than the original path.

Electronic Components

There are hundreds of basic electrical components, but two important ones to know (for the exam) are *resistors* and *capacitors*. Keep in mind that when you connect a number of electrical components together and move electrical current through them, you have a circuit. When you break the line of a circuit with a conductor that can alternately close the circuit or keep the break open, you have a *switch*. A switch may react to heat, in which case it acts like a *fuse*. Transistors are also switches, but they respond to lesser amounts of current than that flowing through the main circuit.

Resistors and Ohms

Resistors "resist" (hold back) the flow of electricity. You may have encountered a sentence such as, "The pilgrim's progress was impeded by the dense vegetation and many rivers he encountered along the way." Impedance means that forward movement is blocked, slowed down, opposed, and resisted. Resistors restrict current flow. The physical structure of wire also restricts current flow, in which case we say the wire has some level of resistance. The more the resistance, the more the flow is held back, and the less the current flows. We measure resistance in *ohms*.

Everything in a circuit has some amount of resistance, just as it has some *capacity* (a capability) to capture and store a few electrons. When we calculate all the varying amounts of resistance and *capacitance* in a circuit, the overall result is the *impedance* (also measured in ohms). Using the earlier example, the forest might resist the pilgrim's progress. At some point, he might pause to rest, leaning against a tree. The tree would "contain" his movement for awhile. The tree's capability to resist movement makes it like a resistor. The same tree's capability to hold up progress also makes it behave a little bit like a capacitor: It has a degree of capacitance.

Capacitance—literally a capacitor's capacity—is the number of electrons a plate in a capacitor can hold under a given electrical pressure (voltage). We measure capacitance in farads (not on the exam). The more charge a device can hold, the greater its capacitance.

Joining two devices together, each with a different impedance in its circuitry, can cause distortions in the final output. Co-ax cable, terminators, and connectors all form a device with some amount of impedance (known as the characteristic impedance). Many times a cable modem connection fails because of improperly matched impedance. The modem is also a device, composed of smaller components, all of which determine the modem's impedance, which is then calculated as part of the overall circuit impedance.

Some resistors, called *potentiometers* (or "pots"), can change the amount of resistance. A good example of a potentiometer is the volume control on a radio. When you turn the volume control, you vary the resistance. This directly affects the current flowing to the speakers, and as such, controls the volume.

Multimeters

At one time, individual meters were used to measure different electrical values: Voltmeters measured electrical potential, ohmmeters measured resistance, and so on. Often one instrument was used for direct current and a different one for alternating current. Today, most of these instruments have been combined into one instrument called a *multimeter*. Most multimeters are small and portable, and a single device can measure ohms, volts, and amps for both DC and AC. They are simply the most versatile test instruments you can have.

When you use a multimeter to check a circuit, remember that a short circuit (a "short") has little if any resistance. However, keep in mind that a complete circuit does have *some* measure of ohms. You may be specifically testing a cable for *continuity*. Continuity simply means that the path of a circuit "continues" unbroken from a starting point. In this case, the continuity tester sends current out from one lead, through the device to be tested (the wire), and then back to the other lead. This is called *continuity checking*.

You should understand that you can't accurately measure the value of any specific component in a circuit. Even though you can put the test leads from the multimeter on each side of a component (like a resistor) that component is still interacting with other components in the circuit.

Capacitors and Dielectrics

The amount of resistance in a wired circuit usually depends on three things: the length of a wire, the thickness of a wire, and the type of metal in the wire. However, not all circuits require wire. A *dielectric* is a material that does a poor job of conducting (directing movement) electricity to one degree or another. When a material is a poor conductor, we call it an insulator, and it has a high *dielectric constant*. The material may still pass electrons (conduct them) to some degree, but not very efficiently. The insulation around a wire is a type of dielectric, as is air and the metal alloy used in a heat sink.

 You will not be tested on dielectrics, but you should know that air has a dielectric constant of 1.0. The higher the constant, the less conductive is the material, and the more it acts like an insulator. Rubber, with a high dielectric constant, is a good insulator. Water and gold, with low dielectric constants, are good conductors. The lower the dielectric constant, the better the conductor.

Capacitors and Direct Current

A capacitor has two plates, separated by a gap. It isn't a closed circuit, yet electricity flows into one plate, somewhat like the way it flows into a plain wire plugged into a wall socket. The gap prevents the continued flow of current, and so the plate begins to build up a charge. (Remember that electrical properties vary according to length, size, thickness, atomic structure, and various other factors.) A wire is a thin piece of metal, but a capacitor plate is much larger and wider than the wire. The plate is capable of holding many more electrons than the wire itself. You can imagine a sort of funnel, or bottleneck effect, where the narrow wire joins the wide capacitor plate.

Technically, a capacitor is two conductive plates separated by a dielectric—the insulating material we just mentioned. (Capacitors were once known as condensers—same thing.) DC is typically low-voltage current, and moves electrons along in a sort of "trickle of water." We can keep the trickle going, sending more and more electrons into a capacitor, all traveling in one direction. They'll crowd onto one plate until there just isn't room for any more. They can't get out again because the direct current keeps pushing more of them in through the "door." A very strong charge (surplus of electrons) begins to build inside the capacitor. The plate takes on a negative charge, while constant pressure prevents the electrons from sneaking back out along the wire.

At some point we can reverse the polarity of the current, changing it so as to flow in the opposite direction. With no more pressure at the door, the many bazillion (technical number) electrons that were smashed onto the plate come flying out in a serious rush to go somewhere else. Although this isn't how a well-educated electronics engineer might write it in a technical journal, the net result is that we have a charge that's much higher than the relative charge of the original direct current in the wire.

We have to be careful that we don't force so many electrons onto one plate of a capacitor that they get mashed (a different technical term) through the dielectric. In that case, we burn out the capacitor and possibly send shards of metal flying off to poke out your eye. Capacitors are rated with the capability to store some level of charge, based on the current. Try not to exceed that rating, or you'll poke someone's eye out!

Storage Capacity

Let's look at capacitors in a different way. Suppose your friend holds a small barrel, where the top "plate" and the bottom "plate" are separated by the air in the barrel. You've connected one end of a small hose (wire, or lead) to the bottom of the barrel. The other end of the hose is connected to a faucet (power supply). When you turn on the faucet, water (electrons) flows through the thin hose (current) and up into the barrel. When you turn the faucet off, gravity pushes the water in the barrel back down into the hose until the pressure is equalized.

There isn't much time for water to flow out of the barrel, because very quickly, you turn the faucet back on again. In a small barrel (capacitor), most of the water leaks out fairly quickly. In a large barrel, it takes time for the water to leak out through the connection to the thin hose. Using this bottleneck principle and a sort of pumping process, capacitors can be made to build a stored charge. Alternating current is like turning the faucet on, then turning it off, then turning it on, and then turning it off: over and over again, in cycles.

Now suppose you decide to play a trick on your friend, and connect the barrel to a fire hydrant. The next time you turn on the water, the pressure drives so much water into the barrel that it blows off the top. Imagine the fun—not to mention the shock on your friend's face! This is what happens when direct current is applied to a capacitor beyond its design rating.

Capacitors and Alternating Current

Let's wire a circuit containing a light bulb, a capacitor, and an AC power supply, in series. We know that current has to flow through the bulb's filament, going in one terminal and out the other. The resistance in the filament causes a traffic jam for the electrons, and they heat up to cause the glow of light. But here's something to keep in mind: The current doesn't care which terminal it goes into or comes out of at any given time.

Remember that alternating current reverses direction, and that a capacitor has two plates (not only one). We turn on the power and send it flying off in one direction, right into the capacitor. Electrons build up on the first plate until they can't go anywhere. The light bulb stays unlit.

At the same time, that plate in the capacitor is building up a strong negative charge. The electrons use a sort of field effect to reach through the dielectric and start pushing electrons away from the other plate. (This field effect, by the way, is similar to a principle of quantum physics used in flash memory cards.) Those electrons start moving away from the other end of the capacitor, heading down the wire to pass through the filament. But before the last electron has passed through the filament, the direction of current reverses.

The "pushing" current in one direction was keeping electrons stuffed onto our first plate. Suddenly the current "runs off in the opposite direction." A large amount of electricity, with a powerful negative charge, comes flying out of the capacitor and zooms back up the wire. It leaves behind a sort of vacuum of electrons on the first plate. (Remember that a positive charge is only an absence of electrons.) The two plates exchange functions, with the first plate now becoming positively charged. All the electrons we sent down the wire through the filament get "sucked" back up the wire, passing through the filament again. The process is so fast that we don't notice a flicker in the bulb.

Delicate electrical components may require alternating current at a very specific level. Current coming into the system may not always be at exactly the required level. We can use a capacitor to "condition" the power. In other words, we can design the amount and time of storage in such a way that only a specific charge leaves the plates when the current cycles back and forth. Any "extra" current will be trapped in the capacitor until a cycle of lower voltage comes along, at which time it can come out across the circuit and raise the power to the required level.

HAZMAT and MSD Sheets

Keep in mind that power supplies and integrated circuit (IC) boards can be classified as *Hazardous Material (HAZMAT)*, which may require special disposal considerations. Whenever hazardous materials are present in the workplace, U.S. law requires that a readily accessible Material Support Data (MSD) sheet be on-site and in a known location. These sheets, usually in a looseleaf binder, provide the details of that material and how to handle it properly. MSD sheets can almost always be downloaded or printed from the Internet.

Disposing of power supplies, laptop batteries, a battery backup Uninterruptible Power Supply (UPS), integrated circuit (IC) boards, and printed circuit boards (PCBs) may be subject to federal laws and/or local ordinances.

The Power Supply

The power supply converts alternating current to direct current at the voltages required by the system components. Internal system components generally use 24V, 12V, 5V, and 3V. Exact voltages vary, depending on specific parts. In the United States, a wall outlet typically provides 110VAC (Volts in AC form). Although the power supply is technically not a component of the motherboard, it is physically attached to the computer case, and connects to the motherboard through either a single, keyed connector, or a set of two connectors. The key connector was developed to eliminate the possibility of destroying a motherboard by reversing the connections.

Keying a connector means designing the plug and the socket with matching notches. If the notches don't line up, the plug can't fit into the socket. Note that connectors are keyed, but chips are indexed.

The motherboard distributes power to all its system components, except for high-current components that connect directly to the power supply, such as the main cooling fan or disk drives. Today's power supplies may be rated at anywhere from 300 to 600 watts or more, and are capable of powering almost any configuration of system components. Older computers, such as the early XTs, had power supplies rated at less than 100W and often failed to meet the demand of additional components.

The power supply is a swap-out, or exchange component, rather than a repair item. Voltage and current levels within a power supply can be lethal. Furthermore, computer-grade capacitors can hold a charge even after the supply is unplugged. Always treat a power supply with respect and replace it if it's defective. Do not repair it!

Capacitors store a charge for a period of time. Small capacitors, like the ones in memory cells, quickly leak away their charge. Large capacitors, such as those used in power supplies, can store a huge charge, and are capable of delivering a nasty shock even when the power cord has been disconnected. We've seen the tip of a screwdriver vaporized by someone accidentally shorting the terminals of a capacitor! Replace the word "screwdriver" with "finger," and you can see why power supplies are given a great deal of respect.

Power supplies contain capacitors that can store very high charges. Batteries and power supplies must be disposed of according to local government ordinances. Improper handling of a power supply can result in electrocution and other depressing problems.

The dielectric inside a capacitor degrades (breaks down) over a period of time, until it finally fails, allowing current to flow from one plate to the other. The resulting short circuit usually burns out the capacitor, leaving an acrid smell. The connected device usually stops working at this point, which is a pretty good indicator that something is wrong. Believe it or not, ancient technicians could actually open up an electrical device and find the fault by smelling the circuit board. (But then the wheel was invented and everything changed) .

Electromagnetic Interference (EMI)

You've probably seen magnetic fields when you put a magnet under a piece of paper holding some iron filings. When something has an electrical charge, it produces a field. All electrical circuits produce fields and have an influence, to some degree or another, on the atomic structure of their surrounding environment. When electricity modifies a surrounding area, we call it (simplistically) an *electromagnetic field*. When an electromagnetic field modifies the surrounding environment, we call that a *field effect*. Modifications generated by strong electrical currents and their fields are called *electromagnetic interference (EMI)*.

By way of example, a device called a *ballast* generates a powerful spark to fire the gases contained in a fluorescent lighting tube. That spark generates a strong electromagnetic wave across the radio spectrum, and nearby wires can pick up that wave the same way an antenna works with a radio. If those wires happen to be your network cables, you will have an excellent opportunity to experience EMI firsthand.

Early radio transmitters were called spark gap transmitters because they used this EMI effect to communicate all over the world. Florescent lights hadn't been invented yet, so operators would use the coil from a Model T Ford to supply the spark.

Electricity flowing through a conductor generates a field moving roughly in the same direction as the flow of current. The process is called *induction*, but you won't need to know that for the exam. Small currents, such as those in a parallel or video cable, have a lesser impact than large currents. Even so, when you bundle many cables next to each other—where the current is moving in similar directions—each cable enhances the field effect, and can increase the cables' combined EMI.

Another example (that actually happened to us at a client site) would be the counterweight used in an elevator system. These weights are huge blocks of metal, and over time, can build up a strong magnetic charge as they move up and down in the elevator shaft. A monitor against a wall next to the elevator shaft might show strange, intermittent distortions every time the elevator counterweight passes up or down the shaft behind it. Because the movement of the elevator is variable, the distortions would also appear random.

Electro-Static Discharge (ESD)

Your body routinely builds up static electricity that discharges to the ground when you touch something conductive. When this takes place, we call it an *Electro-Static Discharge (ESD)*. You should understand how static electricity can easily destroy the tiny components and circuits inside a computer. Computers are excellent conductors and easily become involved in ESD incidents.

 | EMI means *Electro-Magnetic Interference*. ESD means *Electro-Static Discharge*. When many electrical wires are placed near or next to each other, you can have EMI. Fluorescent lights (with their ballast) can also cause EMI. However, rubbing a cat's fur the wrong way or walking on a carpet when you work on a computer can generate ESD.

Microprocessors are manufactured on extremely small bits of silicon, with well over 12 or 100,000 components packed into wafers much thinner than a human hair. In this kind of crowd, an amazingly small electrical discharge can wreak havoc. Keep in mind that most processors run at about 3 volts or less. Many people think that an ESD incident either will totally destroy an IC board or cause no damage at all. In other words, if you've worked on a computer and it functions when you've finished, then apparently there was no problem with static electricity. This isn't true.

Human beings have an "awareness threshold" of approximately 3,000 volts, meaning that we probably won't feel a spark discharge below this level (assuming a very low amperage). On the other hand, walking across a carpet can produce anywhere between 1,500 to 35,000 volts of static electricity, depending upon the humidity of the surrounding air. Picking up a plastic bag can charge your body with between 1,200 and 20,000 volts. As long as the charge is contained within your body, you probably won't even notice it (until your hair begins standing on end).

ESD problems fall into three categories, with catastrophic failure—the component is killed—being only one of them. *Latent failures* are where a component has been damaged, but it continues to function. Over time, these weakened components begin to fail, losing data integrity or capabilities, until they eventually fail completely. An *upset failure* is where the discharge current is just enough to produce intermittent failures (gateway leaks). In many instances, an IC board with an upset failure will pass every quality control test and enter the field. However, like a damaged memory cell, the machine may develop a history of software losses, data corruption, and other hard-to-find problems.

The Hindenburg and ESD

Most of us have heard of the catastrophic destruction of the German zeppelin, the Hindenburg, which happened over sixty years ago. In 1937, the 800-foot Hindenburg was coming in for a landing, between thunderstorms, when it caught fire and burned to the ground in 37 seconds. Thirty-six people perished, and the U.S. Congress called in the FBI to investigate the disaster. At the time, nobody could explain what happened, and the historical finding was that leaking hydrogen gas caught fire, probably due to an errant lightening strike or static discharge. Sixty years later, modern forensic science sheds some light on the probable cause.

Addison Bains, a retired NASA hydrogen fuel expert, seems to have proven his theory that the disaster was an interaction between the outer skin of the ship and the way it was grounded to the internal skeleton. The chemical components used in the skin's paint were different from previous zeppelins, none of which had crashed, and included powdered aluminum and iron oxide. These chemicals form the basis for the rocket fuel used in today's space shuttles. At the time, engineers were more interested in the heat-reflective properties of aluminum, and didn't test for flammability.

Anything flying through the air picks up a static charge, related to the properties of the air. Understanding this, engineers planned for a discharge through the tie-down ropes, which dropped to the ground from the bow of the ship just prior to landing. Static electricity building on the ship's skin would be conducted into the main skeleton through small fiber connectors (string), and then move through the skeleton to the bow and down to the ground. Bains proposes that poor conductivity in many of the connectors isolated patches of the skin from the skeleton, leaving them with a high static potential that couldn't discharge.

When an isolated patch of the outer skin reached a high enough potential, a spark jumped to a nearby area that had already been discharged to the ground. Any one of those sparks was demonstrably hot enough to ignite the aluminum powder in the paint. Basically, the entire outer hull of the zeppelin was a giant rocket engine, and exploded into flames. Although the hydrogen gas used to lift the ship was part of the fuel, it probably had nothing to do with the cause of the accident. Although you won't necessarily burn your house to the ground if you don't manage ESD correctly, you could easily destroy a motherboard and any connected devices.

ESD Kits

Before you touch anything inside a computer, you should at least ground yourself by touching a metal part of the chassis (such as the power supply casing or the metal frame of the chassis). The problem with this solution is that although the computer and your body have equalized, the charge is still contained within the combined system. It hasn't been completely removed (discharged). A better way to ground yourself is to use an ESD kit.

An ESD kit consists of a wrist strap, with a built-in resistor connected to a ground wire. The kit also includes a special floor mat that discharges a current into the ground, bypassing the computer. An ESD kit with a floor mat is the only way to move the charge to the ground, thereby fully removing the charge.

 Remember that an ESD kit uses a wrist strap (with a resistor), and the strap is connected to a ground wire. The kit should also include a grounded floor mat, but the exam may not include the mat in a choice of responses.

By the way: Someone may have suggested that you place circuit boards, system boards, and loose chips on a piece of aluminum foil. This is not a good idea. Placing these pieces on aluminum foil can result in a small explosion, because many motherboards, expansion cards, and other boards have built-in lithium or nickel-cadmium (nicad, or NiCd) batteries. These batteries can overheat if they're short circuited, and react violently: exploding and throwing off pieces of their metal casings. This is another way to poke someone's eye out!

 Never place a circuit board of any kind onto a conductive surface such as metal foil. A possible static discharge might destroy the circuit board. Remember that ESD is electro*static* discharge. On the other hand, EMI is electro*magnetic* interference (when several wires are placed in close proximity) .

Supplemental Information

The telegraph system, invented back around 1830, begins with a switch and an electromagnet. When we close the switch, we activate an electromagnet at the other end of a wire. It pulls a piece of metal to its surface and makes a click. Samuel Morse developed an alphanumeric code based on the time between clicks. Short intervals were a "dot," and longer intervals were a "dash." These pulses of on/off electrical current, together with time intervals, continue to work in today's computers. Nowadays, though, we use high-frequency wave cycles and micro-oscillators.

Morse initially used a single wire to transmit data, with the Earth (dirt and rocks) being the "ground wire." Although this worked for short distances, problems cropped up over longer distances. Understand that with no communication taking place, a line potential is at zero. An electrical pulse, the start of a communication, sends a wave of electrons across the line. In order to flow, those electrons have to have a place to go. The wire takes on more and more electrons, and the ground has lots of room for them to go live with all their friends.

Suppose you send a 5V pulse 20 miles. The weather, standing water, and other variables at the other end might easily bring the ground potential up to that same 5V or more. If both the transmit line and the ground have an equal potential, there's no place for your electrons to go and the electromagnet won't turn on. This is the same as the wire having a zero potential. The electromagnet thinks nothing is trying to communicate. To get around this, engineers decided to use two wires.

Data and Reference Line

Data signals can be any type of organized electrical pulse. Early telegraphers used voltage alone, but today's computers work with differences between peaks and troughs in high-frequency waves. Sophisticated processes use phase differentials, voltage variance (NRZI), and reversed polarities to allow for bi-directional communications, duplexing and multiplexing, as well as things like clock-doubling and 4× clocking.

Somehow, a receiving device must be able to make a distinction between two electrical potentials. One way is to send a *reference* voltage along with the data pulse voltage. An example would be someone trying to talk to you in a night-club. If his voice is the same volume as the background room noise, you won't know he's talking unless you see his mouth move. The background noise is the reference signal, and it must be lower than the data signal.

Telegraphy went in this direction, taking the rocks and dirt out of the loop. A transmit line and a reference line became the basis for electrical communications, and carried forward into the voice telephone. For example, the data line might send a 5V pulse, and the reference line would send a 1V signal. Now the electromagnet on the other end finds a difference in line voltages and understands something is trying to communicate. Two wires provide a difference in volume, so to speak, and would be fine if all we ever did was talk and never had to listen. We use four wires in 10Base-T twisted-pair cable to provide two wires to transmit and two wires to receive data.

Suppose a reference line is designed to send a 1V differential, four volts less than the signal line. Now imagine the wires running next to a fluorescent light or co-ax bundle. The reference line might easily pick up an additional 4V (by induction) as it passes by the secondary power source. By the time the signal reaches the receiver, both the data line and reference line have the same voltage, and the electromagnet thinks nothing is happening. This would be like your friend talking to you in the back of the nightclub, and then both of you moving up closer to the band.

Exam Prep Questions

Question 1

A wrist strap for an ESD kit is made from three components, including a strap to attach to the operator's wrist and a wire to connect the wrist strap to the grounding pad. What is the third component?

- ○ A.   A break-away snap
- ○ B.   A wetting sponge
- ○ C.   A resistor
- ○ D.   A capacitor

Answer C is correct. All grounding straps include a resistor to limit current flow in the event of a short to protect the technician. Answer A is incorrect because although many wrist straps include a snap for attachment to the ground pad, it is not required. Answer B is incorrect because wetting sponges are neither needed or used. Answer D is incorrect because a capacitor will block direct current and not allow the balancing of potential between technician and ground pad.

Question 2

Voltage is the measure of

- ○ A.   Electrical current
- ○ B.   Electrical potential
- ○ C.   Power and work
- ○ D.   Storage potential

Answer B is correct. Electrical current is a flow of electrons. The amount of presssure in the flow is measured in amps, but the build-up of presssure is measured in volts. Voltage is often referred to as potential. Answer A is incorrect because electrical current is measured in amps. Answer C is incorrect because power and work are measured in watts. Answer D is incorrect because although capacitors and batteries store charges in amperage ratings, we rarely speak of the storage potential of a component, and storage isn't the same as potential (voltage).

Question 3

The power supply performs what function?

○ A. Provides consistent 110VAC to the system board

○ B. Converts AC to DC at the voltage required by the system board and system components

○ C. Protects the system components from power outages

○ D. Boosts power coming from the power utility to acceptable AC voltages for system components

Answer B is correct. Answer A is wrong because although a power supply provides consistent power, this isn't the primary function. System boards require direct current (DC) at several voltages, including 3.3V+, 5V+, 5V-, 12V+, and 12V-. Standard wall outlets in the United States provide 110VAC (volts in alternating current). The power supply's main purpose is to convert that AC to DC at the voltages required by the computer. Answer C is wrong because an uninterruptable power supply (UPS) with a battery and surge protector helps protect system boards. Because internal components require much less power than that available from the wall, answer D is actually the reverse condition.

Question 4

What basic electrical component can store a charge for a short period of time?

○ A. Resistor

○ B. Transistor

○ C. Capacitor

○ D. Diode

Answer C is correct. Capacitors store a quantity of electrons for a short period of time. Large capacitors can store a huge charge and are capable of delivering a shock even after the power cord has been disconnected. Answer A is wrong because resistors impede the movement of electrical current, and are measured in ohms. Answer D is wrong because a diode does not store current, and answer B is wrong because a transistor is a small switching device.

Question 5

A short circuit might show a reading of how many ohms? (Choose all that apply)
- ❏ A. 0
- ❏ B. 1
- ❏ C. 10
- ❏ D. 100

Answers A and B are correct. When electricity flows smoothly through a circuit, there is little, if any, resistance. A reading of from 0 to 2 or 3 ohms would usually indicate a short circuit. Any device used to block or impede that flow will show some amount of resistance.

Question 6

You are checking a faulty circuit board with your multimeter and have placed the probes on either side of a suspect resistor. The reading is nowhere near the value specified for the resistor. What should you do?
- ○ A. Replace the resistor with one having the correct value.
- ○ B. Solder another resistor in parallel to provide the correct resistance.
- ○ C. Nothing.
- ○ D. Solder another resistor in series to provide the proper resistance.

Answer C is correct. This is a trick question. Remember that you can't accurately measure an individual component while it is part of a circuit. To get an accurate reading, you would have to remove the resistor from the board and then measure it. Options A, B, and D are possible ways of changing resistance in a circuit. However, the question focuses on a specific, incorrect process.

Question 7

As a favor, you help a friend assemble a new computer on the kitchen table. After a week of trouble-free operation, the display starts acting up. You borrow a different monitor, and it also performs erratically. What is the likely problem?

○ A. Monitors usually become erratic just prior to a complete failure, and this one should be replaced.

○ B. You installed the wrong drivers. Re-boot in Safe Mode to bypass the video drivers, and run a complete Level-2 diagnostic.

○ C. An accidental static discharge caused a latent IC board failure, although neither of you saw or felt a spark.

○ D. The video cache buffer was set to an insufficient level, causing problems during graphic image editing.

Answer C is correct. In some cases a static discharge only weakens a component and that component then becomes erratic and fails at a later date. The question makes no mention of using an ESD kit during the assembly. Answer A is incorrect because a known-good monitor had the same problem. Answer B is incorrect because the monitor worked perfectly for a week with the installed drivers. Answer D is incorrect because there's no such thing as a "video cache buffer" with configurable settings.

Question 8

Four standard AA batteries wired in parallel will produce how much voltage?

○ A. 6 volts

○ B. 4 volts

○ C. 1.5 volts

○ D. 0 volts

Answer C is correct. Standard AA batteries each generate 1.5 volts of direct current. When they are wired in series, the voltages add. Four batteries wired in series would generate 6 volts (answer A). However, the batteries in this question are wired in parallel. When batteries are wired in parallel, the current available increases, but the voltage remains at the same level as the battery (1.5 volts).

Question 9

> You set your multimeter to measure ohms, touch the leads together, and get an off-the-scale reading. What would this indicate?
>
> ○ A. The multimeter is operating correctly.
> ○ B. The multimeter is not operating correctly.
> ○ C. Nothing. The leads of a multimeter should not be touched together.
> ○ D. The multimeter battery needs replacing.

Answer B is correct. A high ohm reading could be indicative of a broken lead or some other malfunction with the multimeter. Touching the two leads together should provide an almost perfect current path with 0 ohms, so answer A is not correct. Answer C is incorrect because touching the leads is a commonly used way to check and/or calibrate a multimeter. Answer D could be correct, if all other parts of the multimeter are working. As you do not know this, B becomes the better answer.

Question 10

> What device would best protect a PC against erratic power and blackouts?
>
> ○ A. A line conditioner
> ○ B. A surge protector
> ○ C. A UPS
> ○ D. An ATA

Answer C is correct. An uninterruptible power supply (UPS) contains a battery backup to provide power to the PC during power interruptions and blackouts. The UPS also provides line conditioning, meaning that erratic power events are stabilized before reaching the computer. Answer A is incorrect because line conditioning is a feature of the UPS, not a separate device. Answer B is incorrect because a surge protector provides no protection from a blackout. The ATA referenced in answer D is the AT Attachment bus specification associated with an IDE controller, and has nothing to do with power supply.

Need to Know More?

 Freedman, Alan. *Computer Desktop Encyclopedia, 2nd Edition*. New York, NY: AMACOM, 1999. ISBN: 0-814-479-855. Great for a fast look-up or refresher.

 Wolfgang, Larry D. *Understanding Basic Electronics, 1st Edition*. Newington, CT: The American Radio Relay League, Inc., 1992–2002. ISBN: 0-87259-398-3. This is a great book for beginners. Written in an easy-to-understand style with loads of illustrations, the book starts off with math skills, progressing into DC and AC electronics principles. It concludes with clear, simple explanations of how such components as diodes, transistors, and integrated circuits work.

 Amdahl, Kenn. *There Are No Electrons*. Broomfield, CO: Clearwater Publishing Company, Inc., 1991. ISBN: 0-9627815-9-2. Although widely criticized by engineering organizations everywhere, this book is an excellent, albeit controversial learning tool for understanding basic principles of electricity and electronics. Amdahl uses imaginary "Greenies" along with swords and sorcery to create highly entertaining stories of the fundamental concepts, rarely confusing the reader with technical jargon and formulas.

Peripherals: Input Devices

Terms you'll need to understand:

✓ Switches, capacitive

✓ Roller encoder

✓ Pixels, charge-coupled device (CCD), and dots per inch (dpi)

✓ Horizontal and vertical resolution

✓ Pixel (picture unit) and dpi (dots per inch)

Concepts you'll need to master:

✓ X-Y coordinates and grids

✓ Mechanical versus non-mechanical keyboard technology

✓ Image resolution versus optical resolution

Human beings understand information through written and spoken language. Computers, on the other hand, process information using binary machine language. Machine language—*digital* information—must be turned into something that people can understand—*analog* information. Standing between the human mind and the mechanical PC is some kind of interface. The three hardware aspects of that interface are input devices (such as keyboards), output devices (monitors and printers), and storage media devices (disks and tape, for example).

Whenever we connect something to a motherboard for the purpose of input, storage, or output, we refer to that thing as a *device*. We generally call something a *peripheral* device when it isn't directly connected to the motherboard. Sometimes peripheral devices are outside the box, but other times, they're added features. "Peripheral" means on the edge or outside of an area. The area we're talking about is the main board and chipset. For example, an expansion bus is directly connected to the motherboard. However, a scanner connects through a card that connects to the bus. That one- or two-step distancing from the motherboard generally defines a peripheral device.

We human beings need a way to talk with a machine, and the various tools we use to accomplish this are called *input devices*. On the other hand, the machine has to talk back to us and that requires *output devices*. We discuss the main output devices (monitors and printers) in Chapter 9, "Peripherals: Output Devices." Finally, there must be some way to keep the applications (programs), and the work we create with applications, from disappearing at the end of a session. This requires the *storage devices*, discussed in Chapter 8, "Peripherals: Storage Devices."

Keyboards

Arguably, the most important peripheral component is the keyboard. A keyboard has a set of key caps with language symbols for a human operator. The key caps are connected to a switch of some kind. When you press a key, it generates an electrical signal, and a microprocessor in the keyboard changes the signal to a digital code—a *scan code*. It then sends the scan code to the computer. Most PCs check to see whether a keyboard is attached during the Power-On, Self-Test (POST) process, and generate a keyboard error message if a keyboard can't be found. We discuss the POST at length in Chapter 13, "Booting, Startup Files, and Memory."

Switch Technology: Mechanical

Depending on how an electronic signal is generated by the key, there are two basic types of keyboards: mechanical (switches) and capacitive (non-mechanical). Switch technology tries to solve two problems: how to produce an electrical contact, and how to get the keycap back up after it's been pressed. The four basic switches are

➤ *Pure mechanical*—Metal contacts and a spring, providing audible feedback with a "click," along with resistance feedback for touch typists. They are durable and usually self-cleaning, and they last around 20 million keystrokes.

➤ *Foam element*—Like a plunger, but using foam, metal foil, and a spring. Compressible foam attaches to a stem, with a foil contact attached under the foam. Circuit board contacts are closed when the foil bridges them. The spring pushes the key back up after it's pressed. Foil gets dirty with corrosion, leading to intermittent key strikes. The foam reduces bounce, but at the same time, it gives the keyboard a "mushy" feel. Because the lack of audible feedback tends to hinder touch typists, the system sometimes resorts to sending a clicking sound to the PC speaker to provide audible feedback.

➤ *Rubber dome*—A rubber dome, similar to half of a handball with a carbon button contact on the underside of the dome. The carbon resists corrosion better than the foil of the foam switch. On a key press, the dome begins to collapse and then "snaps through" like the handball, which makes for good tactile feedback. The rubber re-forms after the key is released, pushing the key cap back up. The electrical contacts are sealed (but not the keyboard mechanics), protecting the contacts from dust and dirt. The system has few moving parts, making it reliable and inexpensive. However, it doesn't provide enough tactile feedback for the touch typist.

➤ *Membrane sheet*—A simplified version of the rubber dome, placing all keys together on what looks like a single-sheet rubber dome. This limits key travel, making membrane switches impractical for touch typists. The entire system, keys and membrane, is sealed, making the keyboard practically spill- and dustproof. This type of keyboard is often used in commercial and industrial environments for simple data entry (for example, in cash registers).

Debouncing

In mechanical and dome-type switches, most keys bounce somewhat when you press them, leading to several high-speed contacts. Keyboards also generate some amount of electrical noise whenever you press a key, which the CPU could interpret as something you meant to do. To clean up the noise, and to help the keyboard processor determine real key presses from noise, the processor constantly scans the keyboard, looking at the state (condition and status) of every key. This constant scanning is why you should never plug in or unplug a keyboard while the power is on.

Typically, *debouncing* waits for two scans before deciding that a key is legitimately depressed. Usually, key bounce is far faster than a human being can press a key twice.

Capacitive Technology: Non-mechanical

Capacitive switches are used in more expensive keyboards. They last longer, resist dust and dirt even better than rubber dome keyboards, and are the primary type of *non-mechanical* keyboards currently in use. Additionally, they offer a higher level of tactile feedback than a switch. The three main processes involved in a capacitive switch are as follows:

1. A capacitive switch puts the two conductive plates of a capacitor inside a housing. The upper plate connects to the key plunger (stem), and the bottom plate connects to a voltage sensor on the IC board inside the keyboard. Every key on the keyboard has its own voltage sensor.

2. A tiny amount of voltage continually charges the bottom plate of the key. When a key is up (normal state), the voltage and charge remain constant, and the current flow is static (unchanging). Electrons gather on the bottom plate until it can hold no more and the system reaches a balance point. However, when the key is pressed downward, the positive plate on the plunger begins to approach the bottom plate, narrowing the gap between the two plates.

3. As the plates move closer together, electrons are drawn onto the bottom plate by the positive charge on the plunger, causing a small current to flow. With moving current, the voltage in the wire drops slightly, and the voltage sensor wakes up. The sensor is responsible for one character, say the # symbol. As soon as it detects a change (drop) in its line voltage, it signals the microprocessor on the circuit board. That signal generates a scan code, the digital number the system uses to output a # sign (the ASCII 0035).

If two voltage sensors make a notification to the microprocessor that their keys have been activated, the microprocessor makes a value calculation, and outputs a key-combination character scan code. This is what happens when you press the Shift key plus the lowercase *m* key (0109) and see a resulting capital *M* (0077). The Shift, Control, and Alt keys are "extended" keys, and use programming to determine the final output calculation. Also note that on many keyboards the left and right extended keys each have different scan code values.

Usually, a mechanism provides tactile feedback. There is a strong click when the upper plate crosses a center point, making these keyboards exceptionally well suited for touch typists. Because of the enclosed housing and the lack of metal contacts, the capacitive switch is essentially corrosion free and immune to dust and dirt. The switch is highly resistant to bounce because the strike is not produced by a closed contact. Therefore, physical movement doesn't generate accidental, multiple contact connections. These keyboards are expensive, but they're also the most durable, rated at around 25 million or more keystrokes.

Emerging Keyboards

Keyboard technology hasn't really changed in the past 100 years. The position of the keys has changed, with two well-known systems being the QWERTY and DVORAK layouts. But the underlying technology is mostly an electronic copy of the old typewriters. So-called ergonomic keyboards are bent, or split in the middle, and are supposedly helpful in reducing repetitive stress injuries and carpal tunnel syndrome. However, these attempts have had limited success in the open market.

An interesting new technology is coming out of virtual reality sensing devices and military technology (the field of biometrics). Infrared light can be used to define a boundary in space, and certain electronic circuitry can then respond to changes, or breaks in the light pattern. Using this concept, the image of a keyboard can be projected onto a surface, such as a table in a surgical suite, with an infrared field layered just above the surface visual pattern. When someone touches a "key," they break the infrared beam at a location, and the internal electronics determine which real key would have been pressed.

Another technology involves scanning a person's eye with a miniature camera. As the person looks at a letter on a projected keyboard, the camera tracks the movement and links the visual position to the keyboard position. The internal electronics process the information as a keystroke. Another use for this type of technology is to use image-scanning systems to measure the patterns and speed a person uses with a keyboard. The combination is sufficiently unusual that it can act as a second-level password confirmation, in conjunction with the actual password characters being typed.

Docking Stations

You may find that CompTIA includes a notebook docking station as an input peripheral. There's no mystery here; only a simple way to use a notebook computer with a full-size monitor and keyboard. Simply put, a docking station is a box designed to join cable ends (and AC power) to the back panel of a notebook. Docking stations are usually designed to work with specific computer models, because of the exact connector locations on each back panel.

Notebook computers have become so powerful that many people use them as a primary system. A docking station provides a fast, simple connection between the notebook and larger peripherals that remain at a home or office location. One thing to keep in mind is that Windows NT offers different hardware configurations at start-up, but Windows 2000/XP try to rely on Plug and Play to sense hardware changes. Users might have a problem starting Windows on the basis of a Last Known Good configuration setting used with the docking station. When they try to start their machines as standalone notebooks, Windows might hesitate.

Mice and Trackballs (Pointing Devices)

Although people might think that Apple Computer invented the mouse, it was actually invented in 1964 by scientists at Stanford University. Xerox applied it to an experimental computer system called the Alto. The story of how Xerox pretty much gave away most of its technology, including the original laser-printer technology, is legendary. At the time, Xerox didn't think much money could be made from a so-called X-Y position indicator, but Steve Jobs and Steven Wozniak did. In 1979, Apple Computer bought the mouse technology and lured away most of the innovative scientists from the now-famous Palo Alto Research Center (PARC).

Mechanical Mouse

Two thin rollers are set at a right angle to each other inside a mouse or trackball. Each roller is attached to notched wheel mechanisms called *encoders*. Each roller also touches the rubberized ball. As the ball moves, friction turns the rollers, which in turn move the encoders attached to each roller.

Encoder wheels have very small notches on their edges, with fine contact points where they touch the wall of the mouse. By calculating the number of times a contact is made from both encoders, the system can calculate where to put the pointer (or cursor) on the screen. This is the X-Y matrix.

Mice come in many shapes and sizes, but a mouse is essentially a case with a rolling rubber ball underneath it. Turning the mouse upside down and putting a plastic ball on top makes it into a *trackball*. For convenience we use the term *mouse*, but the following discussion applies to trackballs as well. With the mouse, the case moves the ball against a mouse pad. With the trackball, the case stays in one place and your fingers move the ball.

Generally, a mouse requires some sort of software program (a device driver) to tell either the operating system or an application how to link the physical movements of the ball to an onscreen pointer. Either the device driver is loaded (installed) with special software, or it's built into an operating system. Windows typically installs generic software for most brand-name mice, and special driver software is necessary only for those with special features (such as a 5-button mouse).

Types of Mice

The different way that a mouse tracks the ball's movement distinguishes the type of mouse. A basic, inexpensive mouse is mechanical because the encoder wheel and contacts are metal and make physical movements.

Optical Mouse

An *optical* mouse has no moving parts, and works in conjunction with a reflective surface. Although optical mice work on almost any flat surface, they work best with a reflective mouse pad. As the mouse moves, a beam of light bounces from inside the casing to the reflective surface (a desk top or special pad), and then back onto a sensor inside the mouse. The sensor calculates the changes in the light beam to define the X-Y coordinates of the screen cursor.

Some mice are called *opto-mechanical* devices. These are hybrids of mechanical and optical mice. They use a rubber ball, but they replace the encoder contacts with a *photo-interrupter* disk. The device calculates the X-Y coordinates by counting interruptions to a beam of light, rather than by counting contacts with a mechanical wire.

Wireless Infrared

Although the method a mouse uses to calculate X-Y information is almost always the same, the resulting information (output) transfers to the computer in different ways. Most mice connect to the motherboard with a cable, but they can just as easily use wireless infrared technology or radio signals. Infrared technology uses a specific frequency of infrared light, much like the remote control of a television or VCR. The Blue Tooth wireless radio protocol works in a similar fashion, using radio transmissions rather than infrared light. We discuss wireless networking in Chapter 10, "Basic Networking."

Supplementary Information

Most of today's operating systems rely on some kind of GUI and a pointer. Over the years, many technologies have appeared and disappeared as engineers figured out different ways to move a pointer on a screen. One of the driving factors in the market has been the limited space available for notebook computers in many work environments. As such, many companies are trying to develop an integrated pointing device, such as the Philips/IBM TrackPoint, or some type of touch pad. PDAs use a stylus to either touch a letter on a screen, or to work with symbol recognition software such as Palm Inc.'s Graffiti language. Microsoft's Tablet PC uses actual handwriting recognition.

The TrackPoint is mostly a small joystick that uses micro-controller circuitry and specialized microcode. IBM developed the microcode, and Philips Semiconductors developed the controller. Essentially, the bottom end of the "stick" is connected to one end of an electrical circuit, and additional contacts surround the center of the stick. In its neutral position, the stick forms a broken circuit. As the stick moves in a given direction, it pushes down on one of the surrounding contacts to make a closed circuit. The electronics then determine which circuit was closed and translates that information into X-Y movements. More sophisticated joysticks include microcode for diagonal movements, as well as linear movements.

A touch pad is similar to a drawing tablet, where the circuitry lies beneath a thin conductive sheath, somewhat like a membrane keyboard. When the user moves a stylus, or even a fingertip, pressure closes a circuit somewhere along the matrix. The internal electronics then translate the X-Y position of the closed circuit into a pointer location. Interestingly enough, IBM is working with various companies to shrink the TrackPoint device down to a size that will fit on a ring. The device is supposed to work in conjunction with wireless throughput (or the conductive surface of your skin) to control a computer with a screen the size of a common wristwatch. Other technology is designed to work with wearable computers, or MP3 players integrated into a pair of sunglasses.

Modems

It isn't easy to decide whether a modem is an input device, used for *downloading* information to the local machine, or an output device, used for *uploading* information to another computer. For that reason, we'll include the basics of dial-up modems here, before we go any further, as the exam may ask you about a few of the basic modem commands. In Chapter 10, we examine other types of online connectivity.

> Modems come in many types and varieties, including dial-up modems, cable modems, digital subscriber line (DSL) modems, and wireless modems, to name just a few. Pay attention to the question and responses, and make sure you know which type of modem is involved. In most instances a dial-up connection refers to a dial-up modem. "High-speed connection" or "TCP/IP connection" typically refers to either a cable modem or a DSL line.

The word "modem" is really an acronym for *MODulator DEModulator*, which is the way analog signals are converted to digital signals and then back again. Computers work with digital information, whereas phone lines work mainly in analog mode. That being said, most telephone systems are being converted to all-digital signaling technology.

UART Chips

Modems can be either internal or external. An internal modem is usually installed as an expansion card, and uses an IRQ, configured by the operating system and/or a setup program. An external modem is easier to install because it connects to one of the COM (serial) ports, which the computer already understands. In other words, internal modems can—and often do—generate hard-to-diagnose problems because they're assigned to an IRQ and can cause IRQ conflicts. External modems rarely cause problems because the COM ports take a universally known pair of IRQs, and other devices stay away from those IRQs. (See Chapter 4, "Processor Mechanics, IRQs, and DMA," for a listing of standard IRQs.)

> You'll often find connectivity problems associated with internal modems not working. In many cases, either Windows has no driver for the modem, or the driver software isn't loaded. Before you do a complete reinstall of a system, be sure to check that you have the modem's model information and its associated drivers. External modems rarely have any problem, other than a physical failure in their circuitry (as with a power surge, for example).

Computers work with bytes, but the serial port transfers information in bits. Serial transfers take place one bit at a time in *series*, so we need a device to break apart each byte into its component bits. That device must then remember how to fit the bits back together again, into their original bytes. The device is the Universal Asynchronous Receiver Transmitter (UART) chip.

Three Types of UARTs

Most of today's PCs have a 16550A UART chip installed. The difference among the three types of UARTs is primarily how fast they can transfer information. The UARTs are as follows:

➤ *8250*—The original chip in XTs and PC-AT, with a 1-byte buffer.

➤ *16450*—Introduced with the AT, with a 2-byte buffer.

➤ *16550A*—Introduced in 486 and original Pentium computers; adds 16-byte *first-in, first-out (FIFO)* buffering to eliminate data overrun when a port receives data faster than it can process that data (needed for speeds faster than 15.5 kilobytes per second [KB/s]). Comes in two types: 16550AN and 16550AFN.

16550AN Versus 16550AFN

The original 16550AN had some problems limiting the buffer. This was fixed by the 16550AFN replacement chip.

The 8250 and 16450 UARTs send one interrupt to the CPU after each character is received. Adding a 16-byte buffer to the 16550A provided a way to accumulate more characters without losing some of them because of a buffer overflow. Another feature of the 16550A is that it uses only one interrupt to handle all the characters in the buffer. The buffer stores characters, waits for the CPU to be available, and interrupts only once at that time. This is a significant improvement in reliability with high-speed communication rates.

Basic Modem Commands

You'll almost never have to remember simple modem commands; however, you may find some questions on the exam relating to them. Some simple terminal emulators are still buried in among the many accessories that come with most operating systems. The Hayes corporation was one of the original companies to develop low-cost modems for PCs. As a result, many of today's commands originate from those first modems, leading to what is often referred to as a "Hayes-compatible" modem.

Table 7.1 lists the typical commands for manually controlling a modem, using their generic syntax (command-line format). Usually, the operating system or online service's installation routine performs this drudgework. These commands may not work on all modems, so consult the particular modem's reference manual for the exact commands. Most commands begin with an **AT** statement, with the exception of the few that begin with a **+++** statement (three plus signs).

Table 7.1	Basic Modem Commands
Command	**Translation**
+++	Escape (for configuration or hang-up)
A/	Repeat
ATA	Answer incoming call
ATD [*string*]	Dial, or attention; [*string*] might be a phone number
P	Pulse dialing, as in **ATDP**
T	Tone dialing, as in **ATDT**
, (comma)	Pause 2 seconds, as in **ATDT 9, 123-4567** for an outside line
!	Flash (depress the hook and then release)
W	Wait for dial tone, as in **ATDT 9 W 123-4567**
H	Hang up, as in **AT H**
O	Online (often used after working in +++ mode), as in **ATO**
Z*n*	Reset the modem to defaults, where *n* is usually 0 or 1, as in **AT Z0**
ATE	Echo to host (show command information on screen)
ATF*n*	Select transmission mode or speed, where *n* is a number
ATZ	Reset the modem (for example, AOL uses **ATZH0^M** for fast disconnect)
AT&F*n*	Return to factory defaults (if any)
ATI	Show product identification (for example, diagnostics and who made the modem)
ATL*n*	Speaker volume, where *n* is number 0, 1, 2, or 3
ATM*n*	Turn off the modem sound, as in **AT M0** (n = 0, 1, 2, or 3)
AT&C	Carrier detect
XON or XOF	Software flow control

Scanners

By now, you should be thinking of input as anything that sends or helps you send information to the CPU. Output, in our breakdown, is anything that receives information from the CPU. We sometimes think of input devices as being only mice or keyboards, but suppose you want to send a picture to the hard drive? To do this, information must be sent to the CPU through an adapter interface. The DMA controllers will probably perform some of the details of transferring data to the disk.

Simply stated, a scanner is a device that *converts* an analog image—a pattern—into digital information. On the other hand, a photocopier or a camera *transfers* an analog image to paper or to film, keeping it in analog form. An image can be a graphic, an alpha character, a bar code, a fingerprint, a retina, or any other pattern stored on a solid material. Naturally, a digital camera is like a scanner, only it converts real-life analog patterns to digital information.

Scanners "see" an image optically by using a light source and capturing the reflection. Some scanners, such as Magnetic Ink Character Recognition (MICR) systems, capture a magnetic pattern. Other specialized scanners capture transparencies by using a direct light source rather than reflected light. A slide-transparency scanner or adapter works this way.

A scanner is a peripheral input device, primarily because it isn't directly connected to the motherboard, but uses an interface. The interface is typically an expansion card, a SCSI interface, an existing parallel port, or a USB port. Different port connections produce different scanning speeds. Typically a SCSI connection is fastest, followed by FireWire, USB, and finally, a parallel port connection.

Charge-Coupled Devices (CCDs) and Resolution

A typical scanner or digital camera uses a series of photosensitive cells called Charge-Coupled Devices (CCDs), mounted in fixed rows. Each CCD registers the presence or absence of light. The point (or spot) of light being registered by one CCD is roughly equivalent to a dot on a piece of paper. The smaller the physical size of the CCD, the more *dots per inch (dpi)* of image it can acquire. For more information on dots and resolution, see Chapter 9.

Scanner resolution is usually measured in terms of *optical* dpi. This means the actual number of dots the scanner can discern, based on how many CCDs are built into it. Any image or pattern can be broken down into a number of discrete areas, or *pixels* (picture units). The smaller the area, the more pixels that area contains, and the finer the resolution. A CCD is often said to roughly correspond to one picture unit (pixel); however, this isn't technically accurate.

> A CCD is composed of many small diodes, and a decision process defines how many diodes will generate a pixel. Today's digital cameras use fewer diodes on a CCD to capture a "unit of picture." This allows other diodes to capture other pieces of the picture, generating many more pixels—the so-called *megapixel* resolutions.

The *optical resolution* of a scanner is the 1:1 ratio between a physical CCD and a single dot. Software enhancement (*interpolation*) is a way to add pixels beyond a scanner's capability to scan a picture area. When software is used to change the image clarity, we refer to that difference as *software resolution*, interpolated resolution, or enhanced resolution. Resolution is usually divided into the two following categories:

➤ Horizontal resolution depends on how close together the CCDs are placed in a single row. The smaller the CCDs and the closer they can fit together, the higher the number of pixels in a row. Larger horizontal resolution numbers refer to more CCDs per row.

➤ Vertical resolution depends on how slowly the light source and mirror mechanism move from the top to the bottom of the image. A slower speed means smaller incremental steps. The smaller the increments, the finer the resolution the scanner can produce.

When you see a 300×600 optical dpi rating, the first number applies to horizontal placement and size of the sensors—in this case, 300 CCDs in a row. The second number (600) refers to vertical movement. Today, most scanners have an optical resolution of 300×600, 600×600, or 1,200×1,200 dpi. However, the amount of memory and storage space required by a 1,200 dpi image is more than a typical person is willing to work with. In addition, no matter how high a resolution an image has, the resolution of the output device limits the resolution that can be displayed. Monitors generally have a 96 dpi resolution, with many printers being easily capable of resolutions of 750 dpi or more.

We cover dots per inch again in Chapter 9, but you should know that dpi is very different from dot pitch. Dots per inch are a measurement of how many "spots" can fit into a given area of paper, for the most part. Dot pitch, on the other hand, is a measurement of the distance between the centers of phosphor triads in a CRT monitor. Unfortunately, video monitors sometimes include dpi measurements as part of their specifications. This isn't accurate, and demonstrates that you can't always trust the manufacturer to give you accurate information.

A megapixel image produces a high-resolution printed photograph, but also results in a very large file. If you intend to use a digital camera to capture images for display on a monitor (for example, on a Web site), remember that monitors are low-resolution devices. Large files also use a lot of bandwidth during transfers, leading to viewing delays when someone tries to access a Web site.

As an example of scan resolutions in the real world, consider that the typical photographs you see in a magazine are scanned at about 200 dpi. Once again, there's an important relationship between the resolution possible from a scanner (for example, 1,200 dpi) or digital camera, and the final output of the scanned image. A good rule of thumb is to scan an image at approximately one-third of the final print resolution. Following that rule, a 720 dpi photo-inkjet printer would do very well with an image scanned at 240 dpi, using photo-quality paper. For plain old regular paper, a better scan resolution would be 120 dpi, so as to print at 360 dpi.

Scanner Connections

The primary difference between the parallel port and a SCSI adapter card is the *data transfer rate*. A parallel port moves eight bits of information at a time, whereas an internal interface card transfers data at bus speeds. Therefore, parallel ports are slower than internal card adapters. USB connections offer a reasonable compromise between an add-on SCSI adapter and the slow parallel port.

Some sheet-fed scanners are built into a keyboard, connected to the motherboard through the internal circuit board in the casing. The scanner borrows the slow keyboard cable to transfer data. Handheld scanners, not built into the keyboard, are very small and portable, often connecting through their own interface cable. The connecting cable usually provides power to this type of scanner.

This concept of borrowing a cable for power became a problem when many devices began using a single cable. USB technology (discussed in Chapter 10) had to deal with the problem, and introduced powered hubs.

Nowadays, many (if not most) scanners connect to the core system with a USB connection. USB and FireWire provide fast serial transfers and avoid the expense and configuration issues of SCSI controllers. USB and FireWire are discussed in Chapter 10.

Supplementary Information

When we speak about monitors in Chapter 9, we'll get into pixel units, dot pitch, and color triads, but for the moment, we'll say that a 24-bit scanner is capable of recognizing 256 levels of colors. 8 bits times 3 colors—Red, Green, Blue—is a 24-bit number. (Remember that 0–255 is two hundred and fifty-six numbers.) Taken together, these 256 levels are capable of generating the 16 million colors we see in monitor resolutions.

Working the math, 24 bits provides for 16.77 million addresses at 256 levels of intensity (or color depth). Working the numbers a bit more, we find out that 16-bit color addressing allows for 65,000 levels of intensity. These numbers should be familiar to you, if you've ever played with your monitor resolutions. Video resolution and color depth is dependent upon the amount of RAM available to the video subsystem, and the resolutions built into the monitor's driver software.

 Windows 98SE Plug and Play doesn't support AGP, although most monitor manufacturers provide the necessary support software on an installation CDROM. Windows 2000 and XP do support AGP. Many monitors require their own driver software to generate 800×600 or 1,024×768 resolutions. Be sure you have the proper video drivers prior to formatting a hard drive for a reinstall.

You've probably seen older digital images of a rainbow. In the images, you could easily see division points between the various colors. These bands of color are a result of how many incremental steps the computer can handle. Our eyes can perceive many colors between light red and regular red. If we make light red 1 and regular red 2, the computer knows only 1 and 2. Therefore it can't represent any of the additional colors we're accustomed to seeing with our analog eyes. However, we can make the incremental steps smaller, using 1.0, 1.25, 1.5, 1.75, and 2.0 to represent additional shades of red. Now the extra steps enable the computer to represent light red, not-so-light red, medium red, darker-than-medium red, pretty-close-to-regular red, and regular red.

Essentially, video technology and the capability of the human eye to perceive variations in color mean that we probably won't be seeing any increase in the overall number of color levels. 16-million colors are an awful lot of colors, after all. The real limitation is the size of the binary numbers the CPU can manipulate. The more incremental steps that a digital process can work with, the closer the output representation will come to the analog world. Think about 8-bit addressing and 24-bit resolution. In this instance, with the three RGB colors, each separate color takes 8 bits of information. If we move up to a 30-bit scanner, we have an extra 2 bits available per color (30–24 = 6, and 6/3 colors = 2). A 36-bit scanner provides an extra 4 bits per color.

Each increase in the number of incremental steps requires additional addressing space (for the underlying binary numbers). This is why a line drawing can be captured in 2 bits, but a black and white photo with shades of gray might use 8 or even 16 bits of information. Because the resolution levels are basically capped at 24 bits, any further information we can capture is assigned to the extra bits we find in 30-bit, 36-bit, or 48-bit scanning addresses. These extra bits might include information on reflections, sharpness, contrast, and so forth. The bottom line is that although scanning an image with a 48-bit scanner set at 1,200 dpi optical resolution enables you to have a great deal of control over shadows and shading, the resulting file may easily be larger than 64MB. That's *megabytes*!

Troubleshooting Input Devices

Most keyboards and mice are so inexpensive that we can simply replace them if they go bad. Likewise, keyboards and mice tend to have mechanical failures, where they simply stop working. However, there are a few situations where you should know how to diagnose a possible problem. The simplest cause of erratic behavior in a mouse is "gunk" on the internal roller bars, or oil build-up on the ball. To clean the mouse, turn it upside down and unscrew the retainer washer. Remove the ball and wipe it with a solvent (alcohol works well).

Cleaning the roller bars is somewhat problematic, but you can use your fingernail to scrape away wrapped threads or fibers. (See? That's why your mother told you not to bite your fingernails.) These fibers usually come from inexpensive mouse pads that tend to be made of fabric. The constant movement of the ball picks up tiny pieces of lint, which then wrap around the roller bars. A better solution would be to use an all-plastic pad (with microgrooves), specifically designed for mice.

Substitute First

We've encountered situations where a mouse pointer could travel only in a vertical axis, with no sideways movement at all. Trying various solutions didn't resolve the problem. The technician eventually reinstalled Windows, only to discover that the mouse still didn't work. A careful discussion with the computer owner revealed that the machine had been running during an electrical storm. Swapping out the mouse for a known-good replacement immediately corrected the problem. Always remember the following troubleshooting points:

> ➤ Not all problems are software related. As the preceding example demonstrates, one of the first diagnostics procedures for inexpensive devices is to simply swap them out and try a new or working replacement. After ruling out mechanical breakdown, you may be willing to invest the time to explore corrupted drivers or reinstall the operating system.

> ➤ Testing by replacement also works for more expensive devices, although the solution is also more expensive. Before trying to repair a Registry, or reinstalling a machine with a bad printer or monitor, first make sure that a known-good device replicates the same problem. Not everyone has an extra monitor lying around, but it's easier to try and borrow a friend's monitor than it is to reinstall the entire machine, only to discover that the monitor still doesn't work.

Test a Solution

Many systems are moving toward all-USB device connections. The main problem with this is that most BIOS chips don't offer native support for USB. Although this is changing, USB is still primarily part of the operating system, which means that Windows must be loaded before any USB devices will work. Before embarking upon low-level diagnosis and repair, make sure the keyboard will work during the boot process. A simple way to test this is to attempt to access the CMOS settings during the startup phase. If you can't use the keyboard to get into the CMOS, then make sure you have a PS/2 or a standard keyboard handy before you make any changes.

The most common problems with keyboards include broken key caps, sticky keys, or keys that don't work at all. In many instances, dirt and dust have accumulated inside the keyboard housing. Turn the keyboard upside down and shake it, tap it, or blow compressed air up between the keys. (Be sure to avert your eyes or wear safety goggles, as you'd be amazed what can come out of a keyboard!) Once again, replacing the entire keyboard is often less expensive than wasting too much time on repairs.

Faulty Connections and Corrupted Drivers

Loose connections or bent connector pins are common problems with docking stations and scanners. A typical problem with a docking station might be where the user can't print. Check to see that the notebook computer is pressed firmly (and correctly) into the docking station. Another problem is that a mouse or keyboard isn't working. If the connection to the notebook is solid, then the station's driver software may be at fault. Of course, it also may have a bad mouse or keyboard.

Scanners also can develop faulty connections, regardless of the type of cable they're using. However, the more common cause of scanner problems is the software driver. In many instances, a user had a previous scanner attached to the system, and never uninstalled the previous drivers after buying a new scanner. Check the Device Manager to see whether or not there's a listing for more than a single driver. Unfortunately, deleting the driver reference from the Device Manager won't always solve the problem. When the system reboots, Windows will find a scanner attached to the system, and then attempt to reinstall any good driver software it finds, anywhere on the drive.

Clearing out an obsolete scanner driver may often mean an investigative journey into the depths of the Registry. You can use the Find feature in the Registry Editor (REGEDIT.EXE) to search for the scanner's brand name or some other descriptive text. If you find an entry, check the path to the driver file or .DLL files. Create a temporary folder (\HOLD or something) and move the suspect file (or files) to that folder. If this solves the problem, delete the files in the temporary folder. If the system develops strange errors, return the files to their original location.

Summary—Input Devices

All things considered, the preceding discussion wasn't all that complicated. As far as keyboards, mice, and scanners are concerned, here are the main ideas to remember:

> ➤ The various switch technologies used in keyboards: mechanical, foam element, rubber dome, sheet membrane, and capacitive (non-mechanical).

> ➤ Mice use a pair of rollers and X-Y coordinates. Know how to clean a mouse ball and rollers, just in case you see a related question, and understand how an optical mouse uses reflected light.

➤ External modems use COM ports (know the addresses!) and you may find a question or two on the most basic modem commands, particularly: answer, attention, and disconnect. Know how to explain a UART chip.

➤ We'll cover dpi and pixels in Chapter 9, but you should understand a CCD, the concept of optical resolution, and the difference between horizontal and vertical resolutions.

Exam Prep Questions

Question 1

> Modems that interface with analog telephone lines require parallel transmission
> paths, and because of this, are almost always connected to the parallel port of
> the computer.
>
> ○ A. True
> ○ B. False

Answer B, false, is correct. Modems transmit data 1 bit at a time and, as such,
are serial devices. The parallel port transfers 8 bits at a time.

Question 2

> What kind of keyboard is considered mechanical? (Choose all that apply)
>
> ❑ A. Foam element
> ❑ B. Capacitive
> ❑ C. Membrane
> ❑ D. Rubber dome

Answers A, C, and D are correct. Foam element, membrane, and rubber
dome keyboards are considered mechanical. Answer B is incorrect because
the capacitive switch doesn't rely on metal contacts, but instead puts two
plastic plates inside a switch housing designed to sense changes in capacitance of a circuit.

Question 3

> Why is an optical mouse different from other types of mice?
>
> ○ A. Optical mice do not require a cable connecting them to the PC.
> ○ B. Optical mice have no moving parts.
> ○ C. Optical mice do not require the use of a mouse pad.
> ○ D. The friction ball in an optical mouse rarely requires cleaning.

Answer B is correct. An optical mouse has no moving parts and works in conjunction with a reflective mouse pad. As the mouse moves, a beam of light

reflects onto a sensor inside the mouse. The sensor calculates the changes in the light beam and defines the X-Y coordinates of the screen cursor. Answer A is incorrect because a wireless may be either mechanical or optical. Answer C is incorrect because any type of mouse will often work without a mouse pad, although a mouse pad usually provides more consistent control. Answer D is incorrect because an optical mouse doesn't use a roller (friction) ball.

Question 4

Most optical scanners use photosensitive devices called _____ to convert the scanned image into a machine-readable format.

○ A. Quartz tube emitters

○ B. Light-emitting diodes

○ C. Electro-optical couplers

○ D. Charge-coupled devices

Answer D is correct. Charge-coupled devices (CCDs) are photosensitive cells mounted in a fixed row. Each CCD registers whether there is light or no light—on or off. The point or spot of light being registered by one CCD is equivalent to a dot on a piece of paper. Answer B is incorrect because a light-emitting diode (LED) is used as a light transmitter, not a light sensor. Answers A and C are incorrect because there's no such thing as a "quartz tube emitter," nor is there an "electro-optical coupler."

Question 5

A dial-up modem uses the following command to connect to the Internet:

○ A. **ATD**

○ B. **ATA**

○ C. **ATX**

○ D. **AOL**

Answer A is correct. A dial-up modem uses the ATD (AT(tention) Dial) command to connect to the Internet. Answer B is incorrect because the ATA command answers an incoming call. Answer C refers to the ATX form factor for a motherboard. Answer D is the acronym for America OnLine.

Question 6

When a key is pressed on a capacitive keyboard, which of the following events take place?

○ A. Current does not flow in a capacitive keypad.

○ B. When the plates are moved together, electrons flow through the dielectric to the positive plate.

○ C. As the plates are moved together, more electrons are drawn onto the negative plate.

○ D. A piezoelectric effect within the pad generates an electrical current.

Answer C is correct. As the key moves the plates together, more electrons are drawn to the negative plate, causing a measurable current. Therefore, answer A is incorrect. Answer B is incorrect because electrons moving through the dielectric of a capacitor indicate the capacitor has failed. Answer D is incorrect because although the piezoelectric effect is used in many devices, including the motherboard clock and the igniter of a gas stove, it has yet to be used in a keyboard.

Need to Know More?

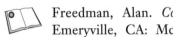

Freedman, Alan. *Computer Desktop Encyclopedia, 9th Edition*, Emeryville, CA: McGraw-Hill Osborne Media, 2001. ISBN: 0-0721-9306-9. Great for a fast look-up or refresher.

Messmer, Hans-Peter. *The Indispensable PC Hardware Book, 4th Edition*. Reading, MA: Addison-Wesley Publishing Company, 2001. ISBN: 0-201-596-164. This is a comprehensive, up-to-date reference book that covers far more than you will need to know for the exam.

Minasi, Mark. *The Complete PC Upgrade and Maintenance Guide, 12th Edition*. San Francisco, CA: Sybex Network Press, 2002. ISBN: 0-782-140-750. This is considered one of the best reference books available. In fact, Minasi's book was instrumental in the formulation of the first A+ exam.

Mueller, Scott. *Upgrading and Repairing PCs, 14th Edition*. Indianapolis, IN: Que Publishing, 2002. ISBN: 0-7897-2745-5. This is one of our favorites! If you are only going to have one reference book, give this one serious consideration.

Rosch, Winn. *Hardware Bible, 6th Edition*. Indianapolis, IN: Sams Publishing, 2003. ISBN: 0-7897-2859-1. This is a well-organized reference book that covers software issues as well as hardware.

Peripherals: Storage Devices

. . . .

Terms you'll need to understand:

✓ Interface, specification, integrated
✓ Disk, volume, format, partition
✓ Physical, logical, virtual
✓ Disk geometry, spindle, platter, head, slider, actuator

✓ Cylinder, track, sector, cluster, address
✓ IDE, EIDE, SCSI
✓ DMA, UDMA, ATA/ATAPI
✓ Host (main system), device
✓ Hot-swapping

Concepts you'll need to master:

✓ Stepper motor versus voice coil actuator
✓ Firmware, controller, and motherboard bus connection
✓ Logical formatting versus physical (low-level) formatting
✓ LBA (Large Block Addressing), areal density
✓ Disk buffer (cache)

✓ Sectors versus clusters; cylinders versus tracks
✓ DMA, PIO modes, UDMA modes
✓ ATA and Ultra ATA
✓ IDE specification versus SCSI bus
✓ Host adapter and device ID number (LUN [logical unit number])
✓ CLV (constant linear velocity), CAV (constant angular velocity)

Any cheesy science fiction movie worthy of the name usually has a couple of computers with spinning reels of magnetic tape and many panels of blinking lights. We're not quite sure about the blinking lights, but they're probably either output or decorative devices. CompTIA won't test you on decorative devices, although certain blinking lights, such as drive and network-card-activity LEDs, do have their uses. This chapter focuses on the storage devices you're most likely to encounter on the exam, and we cover output devices in the next chapter.

You must know the basic principles of hard drives, controllers, and transfer protocols, as well as the interface between a controller and the motherboard. The IDE and SCSI bus are the two main hardware interfaces. ATA and SCSI each specify how those connections will work. SCSI is the more confusing of the two because the same name applies both to the hardware and the (software) specification. On the other hand, IDE applies to hardware, whereas ATA applies to specifications.

 We discuss FDISK, partitioning, and FORMAT in the second half of this book. However, we make references to partitioning in this chapter. If you're not familiar with disk partitioning, then consider postponing your exam until after you've completed a more thorough preparation course.

Historic Drives

IBM introduced the first Random Access Method of Accounting and Control device back in 1956. The 305 RAMAC could store nearly 5MB of 7-bit characters, using 50 24-inch platters. It produced 8.8 bytes per second transfer rates, and held 2,000 bits per square inch, as opposed to the billions of bits-per-square-inch on a single modern-day platter. In those days, IBM leased out its equipment, and the RAMAC cost about $150 per megabit of storage, each month. Nowadays, hard drives cost about a dollar per megabyte.

Alan Shugart, only a few years out of college, was assigned to the Advanced Disk File project, to make the RAMAC more efficient. By 1968, the ADF had become much more compact, with an overall diameter of only two feet, and used slider bearings to allow for a separate read-write head for each platter surface. The platters were lubricated to provide better head movement. Then, a year later, Memorex hired Shugart to take over their disk drive development operations. In 1971, Shugart invented the first 8-inch drive system, capable of storing 100KB of data on a bendable, "floppy" disk. Because of intellectual property rights, IBM retained ownership of much of the drive technology, and released it in the IBM Displaywriter, a dedicated word processing machine.

Shugart left Memorex in 1973 to form Shugart Associates. A year later, perhaps because of the lack of marketable products, Shugart either quit or was removed from the company. However, in 1976, using Shugart's ideas, Memorex released the first 5.25-inch floppy drive. Meanwhile, Shugart teamed up with Finis Conner, another legend in the storage business, and the two of them founded Shugart Technology in 1980. A few years later, in 1986, Conner left to form Conner Peripherals, which went on to become the primary drive supplier for Compaq Computers.

Xerox bought out Shugart Associates, and (similar to other famous Xerox ventures) within three years, the company was out of business. But the legacy was the original floppy drive. To avoid confusion over Xerox's Shugart Associates name, Shugart Technology changed its name to Seagate Technology, which went on to become a $9-billion business. Ironically, Seagate Technologies and Conner Peripherals merged in 1996.

Shugart Drive Interface

The reason Shugart is so important is that he invented not only the original floppy drive, but also the original system for connecting the drive to a motherboard. The Shugart Associates System Interface (SASI) was the foundation for both today's ATA/ATAPI interface and the SCSI bus and interface. Shugart developed the first floppy disk, hard disk, SCSI drive, and controller interface. In fact, the Seagate ST-506 was the first 5MB drive designed for small computers. However, IBM chose the larger 10MB ST-412 for the XT.

IBM computers standardized the controller system on PC motherboards, but Apple Computer users also wanted a way to use disk drives. As a result, the Shugart interface became a platform-independent interface and bus connection. In 1982, ANSI approved the interface as the *Small Computer Systems Interface (SCSI)*. The name was changed because a standard isn't supposed to have a proprietary name. This same problem later applied to the IDE and AT Attachment standards. The original SCSI standard had only a few simple commands, a standardized cable and connector, and support for 1.5MB/s transfers.

NOTE

Serial transfers have always been slower than parallel transfers, and so, from the beginning, drive transfers were designed to be parallel. USB technology rests partly on a fundamental change in the way serial transfers take place, making the process much faster than parallel transfers. Some of those ideas crossed over to drive throughput, and the emerging Serial ATA specification will likely replace the original Parallel ATA.

The important point is that IBM computers and their clones went on to take approximately 90% of the PC market. Because so many computers used the soon-to-be-standard drive, controller, bus, and cabling, IDE drives became very inexpensive. The SCSI interface never developed built-in support, although a PC could use an add-on host controller and expansion card to connect with SCSI devices. The SCSI interface began the trend of putting controller boards right onto the device, as well as giving the device management and control over the motherboard bus to varying degrees. "Integrated" electronics—the basis for Integrated Drive Electronics (IDE)—is partly a result of non-SCSI systems competing with SCSI's faster throughput and device-oriented commands and control structure.

 In 1983, a company called Rodime introduced a 3.5-inch hard drive, and the form factor went on to become an industry standard. By 1986, Conner Peripherals had developed a voice coil actuator for 3.5-inch drives, then introduced a new, 1-inch high, "low profile" drive. A year earlier, Quantum had released a 10MB hard drive mounted on an ISA card. This provided hard drive storage for older PCs that didn't have a built-in disk. PrairieTek released a 2.5-inch drive in 1988, which became the standard form factor for portable and laptop computers. Then in 1991, Integrated Peripherals introduced a 1.8-inch drive, used as a PC Card hard drive for notebook computers. Hewlett-Packard followed up with a 1.3-inch micro drive, in 1992.

Terminology

We often refer to hard disks, fixed disks, and hard drives interchangeably. Familiar language joins the platters, drive mechanisms, drive controller, and cable/interface sub-system together as the hard drive, or simply "the drive." Technically speaking, a drive is a mechanical piece of hardware designed around a storage device. On the other hand, a *logical* drive is an area on a disk, set aside by an operating system for storing files. Many disks are partitioned with a single, Primary, Active Partition. Because it's a single logical drive, it takes the letter C. As a result, many people also refer to the hard drive as the C: drive, even though this leads to a great deal of confusion when it comes to understanding logical drives (volumes) as opposed to physical disks.

Logical drives require a drive letter and colon. As such, a Wintel computer can manage a maximum of 26 logical drives. In any IBM-compatible personal computer, the A: and B: drives are always assigned (by default) to floppy drives, regardless of whether the machine is a desktop, notebook, or network station. Be very careful that you don't confuse a physical disk with a logical drive.

Although many people call a fixed disk the hard drive, physical disks can contain from 1 to 24 logical drives. A system can have more than one physical disk, where each disk can have many logical drives. Regardless of how many physical disks, there can still be only 26 logical drives in the overall system. Tricky exam questions can trip you up by asking whether a fixed disk can contain 23 or 24 drives. (The answer is 24. See Chapter 12, "DOS," for more information on FDISK and partitions.)

Windows XP/2000 use the term "mounted" to mean that Windows has discovered a connected drive (mechanism) and can recognize the file system used on disks in that drive. A formatted disk is a volume, and so Windows indicates whether a volume is mounted, indicating that it can or can't access a disk in a drive.

A disk is a round storage area. Fixed disks tend to stay inside a computer, and removable disks tend to refer to portable disks that function similarly to a hard disk. A floppy disk is one thing; an optical disk is something else; and a removable disk (these days) usually refers to an Iomega disk.

To differentiate a hard drive (or other peripheral) from the rest of the system, we refer to the main system as the "host." You'll often see references to a host adapter, or commands coming from the host and returning to the host. Simply put, the host is the motherboard. Technically, a host is a control system that uses a peripheral device. SCSI systems require a host adapter, meaning that the adapter acts like a separate controller between the motherboard (the host) and whatever SCSI devices will be attached to the expansion card (the adapter). The SCSI bus has never been an integral part of IBM-compatible machines, and so host adapters are usually built onto expansion cards.

Disks Transfer Concept Overview

Suppose you have a 20MB music file stored as an MP3 on the hard disk. When you want to play that file, you send a request through the operating system to load the file into memory and play it, using an application. The drive controller positions the drive heads and begins reading the file into what? Most disks, nowadays, have an SRAM cache buffer built onto the logic board. The buffer is usually around 1–2MB, and it quickly fills up either with data waiting to be transferred to main memory, or with sector addresses most likely to be needed next.

Memory built onto a drive's logic board acts as both a small buffer and a cache. Be careful that you don't confuse this drive buffer with disk caching, used to store memory overflow.

The controller moves file information across "something," to the motherboard. That "something" is a bus and a cable of some sort. We'll review the IDE and SCSI bus in this chapter, and discuss cables and connectors in Chapter 11. The music data then crosses other motherboard buses before arriving in system RAM (the micro bus is discussed in Chapter 4, "Processor Mechanics, IRQs, and DMA"). The big problem is that the system memory chips, and the drive's ability to read information from its own platters, are both faster than the data transfers. The difference in speed creates a bottleneck between the drive and memory. Much of the changing ATA/ATAPI specification has to do with fixing that bottleneck.

Firmware

We also spoke about the programming instructions built into a CPU, in Chapter 4, calling it *microcode*. Many controllers (microcontrollers) include programming instructions stored in ROM chips located on their own logic board. Hard drives use this type of programming to dictate data transfers. To distinguish built-in controller programming from the microcode in a processor, we call it *firmware* (like software, only firmly established in the device). BIOS is a special case, and almost always refers to built-in instructions on a motherboard chipset. So we have BIOS instructions, microcode, firmware, and software. Each word indicates program instructions of some kind, but applies to a type of device.

Standards Organizations

There are two important standards organizations responsible for the specifications we so often hear about in technical discussions. The one is the InterNational Committee for Information Technology Standards (INCITS), sponsored by the Information Technology Industry Council (ITIC). The other is the American National Standards Institute (ANSI). Both organizations use similar rules.

The INCITS is subdivided into various technical committees. The T10 committee manages the SCSI interface, and the T13 committee (www.t13.org) manages the ATA specification. (The T11 committee develops Fibre Channel standards.) Each technical committee works on a particular type of device, but all the committees share information. The SCSI-3 standard, for instance, borrows from various other standards in this fashion.

Some of the SCSI standards also come out of IEEE specifications. The Institute of Electrical and Electronics Engineers (IEEE, pronounced "eye-triple-E") is a non-profit group made up of members from 150 countries, and is responsible for electrical engineering and communication standards. For example, the FireWire specification is IEEE-1394, and wireless networking is IEEE-802.11.

More often than not, manufacturers propose an idea for a standard, and then the committees determine whether it has merit as a sanctioned standard. After the committee approves it, the recommended standard moves up to INCITS and ANSI for full approval. In some instances, the widespread use of a particular technology creates a *de facto* standard, meaning that although it hasn't been formally approved by a standards organization, "everyone" uses it anyway. The technology becomes an "in fact" standard.

Table of Acronyms

This chapter, more than any other, involves so many acronyms that it's easy to get lost in the letters. We've listed most of the useful abbreviations and their meaning in Table 8.1, to give you a single reference point during your review.

Table 8.1 Storage Device Acronyms		
Abbreviation	Spell-out	Explanation
IDE	Integrated Drive Electronics	A 16-head hard drive with a built-in controller and logic board
EIDE	Enhanced IDE	A 256-head hard drive developed by Western Digital
ESDI	Enhanced Small Device Interface	An early de facto and later ANSI standard for the interface between the motherboard and a disk drive based on Seagate's ST-506 interface
SCSI	Small Computer Systems Interface	A combination bus, specification, and set of commands used to connect many types of peripheral devices to a PC (not limited to disks)
ATA	AT Attachment	Named after the AT form factor to specify the connection between an IDE drive and the motherboard

(continued)

Table 8.1	Storage Device Acronyms *(continued)*	
Abbreviation	**Spell-out**	**Explanation**
ATAPI	ATA Packet Interface	An extension to the ATA drive specification supporting devices such as CDROM, DVD, removable drives, and tape storage
PIO	Programmed Input/Output	A way of moving data between devices and memory, where data passes through the processor
DMA	Direct Memory Access	A way of moving data into system RAM without passing through the processor
UDMA	Ultra DMA (also known as Ultra ATA)	A modification to the original DMA channels and controllers to better handle bit information
CHS	Cylinder/Head/Sector	An addressing scheme used by the BIOS to find physical cylinder, head, and sector addresses
XCHS	eXtended CHS	An updated BIOS addressing scheme used to translate Logical CHS addresses to Physical addresses
LBA	Logical Block Addressing	A system developed to translate Logical CHS to Physical CHS addresses directly, bypassing BIOS translation tables

Disk Geometry

Technically, "geometry" has to do with lines and angles. "Topography" has to do with structures and surfaces. That being said, technical people speak about drive engineering principles in terms of geometry. Hard disks spin at thousands of revolutions per minute (rpm), with IDE drives typically rated at 5,400; 7,200; and 10,000rpm. More expensive SCSI disks are now up to 15,000rpm. These speeds make hard disks dramatically faster than 300rpm floppy disks.

Although we speak of a disk, you can see in Figure 8.1 that a hard disk is actually a stack of disks called *platters*. This picture depicts an older drive to more easily show the individual platters. Modern drives typically use fewer than four high-density platters.

The motherboard BIOS may show an IDE disk configured with 16 platters. This is a function of the IDE/ATA specification, regardless of how many platters are actually inside the housing.

Figure 8.1 A typical hard drive, the platters, and spindle.

Magnetism and Field Effects

If you've ever played with two magnets, you know that you can feel the push or pull effect without actually bringing the two magnets into contact with each other. In the same way, drive heads don't have to actually come into contact with a disk platter. Anything magnetic generates a magnetic field, flowing in a particular direction. The field can be stronger or weaker. The point where you feel the effect is a mathematical relationship between the strength of the field and the distance between the two fields.

Disk technology is a constant back-and-forth compromise between field strength and distance. A strong "spot" of magnetism on a platter means the drive heads can be quite some distance from the platter's surface. However, strong fields might interfere with and change neighboring bits of data. A weaker point of magnetism allows for thinner tracks and for storing data bits closer together. The trade-off is that the heads must come closer to the surface of the platter. Too close, and the heads begin to scrape along the surface of the platter, leading to wear and tear.

MFM and RLL Magnetic Encoding

Magnetism, like electricity, has a direction of flow. Depending on the direction, a read head can determine a 1 or a 0. For instance, if we say that "left" (L) is a one, and "right" (R) is a zero, we can store the number 11001 to mean LLRRL. As the head passes over a magnetic area on a disk, it interprets the direction for the field, and then uses the drive's firmware (programming) to convert the directions back to numbers. The write head uses the same tactic, relying on the tiny electromagnets in the heads to magnetize an area with one or the other field direction.

MFM stands for *modified frequency modulation*, and you won't have to know that for the exam. All that matters is that it's the encoding scheme used on floppy disks and older hard drives. RLL stands for *run length limited*, which you likewise don't need to remember (but at least familiarize yourself with the acronym letters). The primary advantage of both types of encoding is that they use fewer electrical pulses to store information than a system with no field encoding at all. The RLL system provides about twice as much data storage as MFM.

Any disk can use either MFM or RLL magnetic encoding (or some other system). The drive's disk controller and built-in logic determine the encoding scheme. Most PC drives use RLL encoding.

Drive Construction

A typical hard drive is made up of several different components. We won't go into the many details of each individual component, but we've listed a number of reference books and Web sites offering expanded details of hard drive technology in the "Need to Know More?" section at the end of this chapter. We summarize the various component names and their function in Table 8.2, and provide a summary overview following the table.

Table 8.2 Hard Drive Components	
Part Name	**Function and Explanation**
Platter	A circular, very thin structure coated on both sides with electromagnetic material; formatted by disk manufacturers into tracks and sectors with a "low level" or "physical" format process.
Spindle	Platters have a hole in the center and are mounted in a stack on a rotating center—the spindle.
Spindle motor	Controls the high-speed rotation of the spindle and attached platters.
Read-Write heads (head)	An electromagnetic device used to either sense or create magnetic fields. The combination of the read-write heads, the slider, and the head arm is also called a "head."
Slider (head slider)	A rugged mounting for the read-write heads that "slides" over the surface of a platter on a microscopic cushion of air. Also called "head slider."
Head arm	A long arm reaching from the head slider to the actuator motor. Each platter has an arm and slider on each side. The head arm is attached to the actuator (or head actuator).

(continued)

Table 8.2 Hard Drive Components *(continued)*	
Part Name	**Function and Explanation**
Actuator	All head arms are attached to the actuator, which positions the arms simultaneously over tracks on the platters. The actuator "motor" and the spindle movement are the only two mechanical events. Switching between read and write operations is an electronic event.
Logic board (controller)	An integrated circuit board containing spindle motor speed controls, head braking, interface commands and control, read-write circuitry, magnetic encoding instructions, address translation tables, and power management instructions.

Platters, Spindle, and Spindle Motor

A hard disk uses flat, round disks (the platters) coated on both sides with a special electromagnetic material. The platters all have a hole in the center and are stacked vertically onto a spindle. The spindle rotates at high speed, driven by a special spindle motor connected to the spindle. All the platters rotate together at the same speed and in one direction at a time. Read-write heads move back and forth across the platters, waiting for a particular sector to arrive below them. When the sector arrives, the head either reads information or writes information.

Read-Write Heads

The read head and the write head are small electromagnets designed to convert electricity to magnetism, or vice versa. The controller spins the platters until a sector arrives under the read-write heads. If that sector is "empty," the write head receives a pulse of electricity from the drive controller, which turns on a tiny electromagnet. The head then generates a magnetic field, flowing in a particular direction, which magnetizes a spot on the platter across a small gap of air. A read event works in the opposite direction, converting magnetism on the platter to electrical binary numbers. Remember that gap of air.

NOTE

If a hard drive is manufactured to have read-write heads on both the top and bottom sides of each platter, then head 0 would be the bottom read-write heads of platter 0. Head 1 would be the top read-write heads on platter 0. Head 2 would be the bottom read-write heads on platter 1, and head 3 would be the top read-write head for platter 1. Don't worry about it. Just remember that track 0 is on the outer edge, and contains the boot sector.

Head Sliders

Head sliders (or just "sliders") are the mechanisms at the ends of head arms that support the actual read-write heads. They're larger than the heads, making them easier to position over a platter. The head sliders take their name from their shape, looking somewhat like small sleds with runners (or rails). The shape of the runners provides the "lift," like an airplane wing, which gives us the term *flying height*. The read-write heads lie between the two main runners, often on their own runner. When the sliders lift away from the platter, they leave a gap of air.

Flying Height

The first disks used a read-write mechanism that actually came into contact with the surface of the disk. Modern disks use air currents, generated by the high-speed rotation of the platters, to raise the heads up on a cushion of air. It's somewhat like the principle of a hydrofoil boat. This space is variously called the floating height, the flying height, an air bearing, or the head gap.

A "micro-inch" is one-millionth of an inch, which works out to 39.37 microns. In 1962, the IBM 1301 Advanced Disk File Device introduced the idea of read-write heads that floated above the surface of the disk on a layer of air: an air bearing. That original floating distance was 250 micro-inches (9,842.5 microns, or 9,842,500 nanometers). Then, in 1973, IBM developed the 3340 disk, generally called a "Winchester" type drive, and reduced the flying height to a mere 17 micro-inches (669.3 microns, or 669,290 nm). You might recall that a human hair is about 150 microns thick. Modern disks have a flying height of approximately 5–20 nanometers (0.005–0.02 microns).

Given the extremely small distances between the heads and the platter surface, hard drives (like microchips) are put together in dust-free rooms called clean rooms. Even a particle of dust is so large compared to the flying height that it would look like a fishing boat dropped into a football field, compared to the players. However, the heads do require air in order to develop the flying height, and so hard drives are not sealed in a vacuum. Hard drives have a very fine filter to allow air into the housing. At very high altitudes, the air may be too thin for head-flying, in which case the heads "crash" onto the surface of the platter (causing a head crash).

Head Arms

You can see part of a head arm to the far left of Figure 8.1. Each read-write head and head slider has its own arm, made from thin, triangular pieces of metal. The arm supports the slider, making the mechanical bridge between the read-write heads and the actuator motor. Just as all platters move at the same time, so too, do all the head arms. The head arms move in and out, from center to edge. The platters move around and around. Again, all the platters move at the same time. All the head arms also move at the same time.

The controller determines which head on which slider at the end of which arm to turn on. When a read or write head is turned on, it becomes active, making that head the *active* head. We also say that the head is reading from or writing to the active *side*. When the format process lists head numbers, it's actually listing side numbers. (Nowadays, the format process typically lists only a percentage of completion.)

 Some confusion arises out of jargon terms, where people speak of a head being the same as a platter or track. For example, a disk may have 16 heads and 300 cylinders. Given two head arms (heads) for each platter, sixteen divided by two means the disk must have 8 platters. Each platter has 300 tracks, spaced at the same distances from the center. Each set of tracks on a circumference is a cylinder. Therefore, this disk has 300 tracks, times 2 sides, times 8 platters, equaling 4,800 separate tracks.

Head arms use a type of spring steel to press the sliders against the platters when the disk isn't moving. Older hard drives used a "parking" mechanism to ensure that arm assemblies weren't damaged while a computer was being moved. Modern drives use this spring-loaded idea to maintain an exact maximum distance during "flying" time. In other words, with such tiny distances in terms of head gap and magnetic fields, the arm is engineered to be pushed away from the surface only so far. A side benefit is that when the computer is turned off, the heads automatically "park" themselves on the surface of the platters.

One of the reasons why platters have become denser (using smaller points of magnetism) is that the weight of many head arms makes it difficult to accurately position them. Modern drives use head arms made from metal frames (a structural design) rather than solid pieces of metal. Less metal means less weight. The reduced weight means that the heads can be positioned closer to the surface of a platter. Closer positioning allows for smaller magnetic points. Newer hard drives might use as few as two platters, with an extremely high data density.

Areal Density

A given surface has only so much room: its area. Depending on how much "stuff" we pack into a given area, we can say that stuff is in a certain density. It's like the trees in a forest, where more trees per acre mean a higher tree density. We speak of how closely tracks are placed on a platter as the number of tracks per inch (TPI). We measure the bit-density in a given sector in bits per square inch (BPSI). Taken together, the track and bit density make up the *areal density* on the surface area of the platter.

Head Actuator Motor

The read-write heads are at the ends of head arms. Each arm is attached to a complicated device called a head actuator (or simply "actuator"), designed to extend and retract the arms to a precise distance from the center of the platters. Think of what your arm does when you use a broom handle to fish a winning lottery ticket out of a pond. Your brain is like the disk controller, sending pulses of electricity along the nerves in your body. The nerves control the muscles of your arm, which must not only balance the weight of the broom handle, but also move the tip of the pole in very precise movements. Now suppose you had to use four broom handles at the same time, but only one of them was necessary to get to the lottery ticket.

Stepper Motors and Voice Coils

Head actuators use either a stepper motor or a voice coil to move the head arms. A stepper motor rotates and stops at predefined points—steps—as it spins. As the motor spins, clockwise or counter-clockwise, it "reels in" or pushes out the head arm. (Remember that the platters spin in only one direction. It's the actuator motor that's moving in both directions.) For example, the actuator might move all the heads to the center of the platter, and then push them onward, one step at a time, until the heads are centered above one specific cylinder. The size of each step limits the width of a track. The controller then activates only one head to perform an action at a specific track location.

Stepper motors are often used to move both the actuator and the spindle. By linking the two movements, the controller can use a sort of grid logic to bring a particular sector into position at the same time as it moves the heads to the correct cylinder (the distance from the spindle motor). The problem is that mechanical steps are limited as to how small they can be. Mechanical motion always is much larger than electrical movement, and also is at least a thousand times slower. Think about a mechanical pendulum in a clock, as opposed to the vibrational oscillations of a crystal.

To get around this, voice coil motors use an electromagnet to attract or repel the end of a head arm in faster and smaller increments. Each head arm has a small area at the actuator end, wrapped in a coil of wire. When the controller sends an electrical current into the coil, it generates a magnetic field flowing in a particular direction. The field then interacts with the field of a permanent magnet, causing push or pull movements. Those movements then move the entire arm some distance. The controller can generate extremely precise distance movements through the amount of current in this coil of wire. It's like using a magnet to push a ball bearing back and forth across the surface of a table.

Relative Versus Absolute Positioning

Stepper motors work with built-in distances, based on each stepping point. For example, the actuator can move only in absolute steps of 10 inward, or 5 outward, or some other exact number. If changes in temperature change the location of a track on a platter, the stepper motor doesn't know anything about it. Like a robot, it will continue to position the heads over an absolute location in space. The result is that the heads fail to find data because the track and sector have moved out of position.

Voice coil motors use a combination of distance movement and feedback instructions to determine the position of a read-write head relative to the actual location of a track. In other words, the controller sends an instruction to "begin here, then move X distance inward." When the heads are positioned according to where the track "used to be," they send track information back to the controller. If the track has moved, because of thermal expansion or shrinking, the controller makes fine adjustments to the head position until the heads are centered over the track.

This problem of tracks moving in or out according to temperatures led to older hard disks requiring an occasional low-level reformat. Nowadays, floppy disks most often use stepper motors, and hard drives use voice coil actuators. The feedback system in a voice coil actuator uses certain codes placed on each track (servo codes), which the read-write heads pick up and send back to the controller for positioning feedback.

Logic Boards (Controllers)

We've seen that a drive controller must handle quite a variety of tasks in order to properly position a read-write head over a bit of data. The various circuits and chips making up this control structure are part of a logic board (integrated circuit board). The logic board can be in one of three places: built onto a motherboard; attached to a drive mechanism; or in an expansion slot on a bus.

 When you see a motherboard diagram with two IDE controllers, be sure to understand that these are technically the connecting points between the drive's own controller and the motherboard. IDE controllers use IRQ 14 or 15 to communicate with the CPU.

You might think of a controller as a traffic cop working at a busy intersection (a bus). Programming instructions are like traffic laws, defining the way data flows through the intersection. At certain times, traffic (processing) is heavy enough that having a "cop" at the intersection can speed things. The controller can override the standard bus rules by making individual decisions. For example, controllers often take over the PCI bus for short bursts of activity, to help speed up overall system performance. A DMA controller does the same thing, making its own decisions regarding whether or not to "bother" the CPU about data going to main memory.

The logic board is a very sensitive area, protected by shock mounts to prevent jostling and banging. Improper packaging and transportation can easily cause damage to not only the circuitry, but also the extremely delicate head arms and slider mechanisms. Additionally, a small amount of ESD can easily destroy the circuitry of a hard drive. Hard drives are so inexpensive nowadays that you may want to think twice before buying an even less expensive, used hard drive at an online auction site. Unless the seller packages and ships the drive professionally, you'll likely end up with a strange-looking paperweight.

Tracks, Cylinders, Sectors, and Clusters

The drive manufacturer magnetizes each platter with magnetic tracks and cylinders. This process is called the physical, or low-level formatting. Once again, a *track* is a thin band of magnetic material circling a disk some distance from the center. All tracks—the same distance from the center of each platter—make up a *cylinder*. If you were to take an apple corer and smash it down on a hard drive (not recommended), it would cut through one cylinder. The edge of the corer would be like the width of one track.

 OEM stands for Original Equipment Manufacturer. You'll often see references to how a disk is pre-formatted by the OEM. Pre-formatting should mean low-level formatting, but many out-of-the-box PCs are also logically formatted, and are then installed with OEM versions of Windows and some number of applications. The manufacturer, not the original software company, supports OEM versions of software (for example, Windows, Microsoft Office, and so on). A number of legal issues are beginning to crop up over the responsibilities assigned to a pre-installed PC vendor as opposed to the underlying component OEMs. These issues involve warranties, service and repair, and tech support, to name a few.

After the platters have been magnetized into tracks and sectors, the *logical* formatting process (defined by the operating system) then further subdivides the entire disk into *clusters*. Clusters must always fill an entire disk. FDISK (DOS and Windows 9x) or DISKPART (Windows XP/2000) partition the disk. FORMAT then performs the logical formatting. Tracks and cylinders are characterized as follows:

> *Tracks*—Concentric, circular paths placed on both sides of a platter. Each track is identified with a number, starting on the outer edge with Track 0.

> *Cylinder*—A set of tracks, one on each side of every platter, located the same distance away from the center.

 The boot sector explicitly points to head 0, cylinder 0, track 0, and sector 0 of the first platter (side 0). In common usage, "cylinder 0" may be dropped, making for head 0, track 0, sector 0. The boot sector is not the same as the Master Boot Record (MBR).

Over time, the magnetic coating of the platters begins to deteriorate, preventing it from holding a magnetic pattern. When this happens, the heads can't read or write data to a sector. Reformatting the disk, or using certain software programs such as SCANDISK or Norton Disk Doctor, causes the sector to be labeled as a *bad sector*. A bad sector is not the same thing as a cross-linked file. Even with modern engineering, most brand-new disks have some number of bad sectors. The manufacturer marks these as unusable during the physical formatting process.

Defragmenting a disk has nothing to do with making a bad sector inaccessible. DOS and Windows 9x use ScanDisk to examine each sector of every platter for bad sectors. Windows NT/2000/XP uses CheckDisk for the same purposes. Norton's Disk Doctor is usually faster and more user-friendly than Microsoft's built-in utilities. Something else to remember is that ScanDisk lets you cancel the program at any time. CheckDisk, on the other hand, can't be canceled. You have to wait until the program has gone through every sector on every track of the entire hard drive.

In Figure 8.2, we've taken the top platter of a stylized hard drive and outlined the tracks, a cylinder, two sectors, and one cluster. Note that the black ring is a single cylinder. On the top platter, the ring is also the top track of the cylinder. Below this platter is another platter, and if you could see the black ring going down into the graphic, every track in the cylinder would be the same distance from the spindle motor. In this example, 1 cluster happens to be made up of 4 sectors (2,048 bytes).

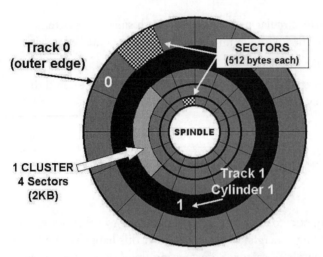

Figure 8.2 The basic division of a hard drive into tracks, sectors, and clusters.

Track 0

In Figure 8.2, the spindle motor is in the center of the platter. Track 0 is located on the outer edge of the platter. Each track moving inward from 0 takes the next incremental number. The illustration also shows cylinder 1 (including track 1) as the set of tracks located one step in from the outer edge. Remember that technical counting begins with zero. All the tracks in a cylinder are formatted at the same time.

 Some people think that track 0 is at the center of the disk. We've done the research, and, in fact, track 0 is on the outer edge.

Sectors

Each track is subdivided into sectors. Each Sector stores a fixed amount of data. Sectors never change size, and almost always store only 512 bytes of data (half a kilobyte). Magnetic encoding systems produce the binary data stored in the sectors. The physical sector actually takes up a little more space than 512 bytes. Some of that extra space is used by synchronization bytes (used for minor rotational adjustments to the spindle motor). Other extra bytes include an ID field (with the cylinder, head, and sector number), servo codes (for head positioning feedback), and a few error-correction code bytes (ECC bytes).

Perhaps a way to remember the word "sector" is it sounds like seating *sections*. A section in a sports stadium never changes size; it's only a section. During or after a game, people gather around in clusters, discussing the event. Depending on how exciting the game may have been, these clusters of people can be large, small, or medium sized; they change size.

Density: Bits Per Square Inch

The original XT hard drives used about 300 tracks per inch. When Conner Peripherals introduced the first voice coil actuator in 1986, the track density rose to about 1,000 TPI. Perhaps you can imagine how difficult it would've been to engineer a stepper motor with 1,000 steps in a single inch. Floppy disks are slower, simpler, and are standardized at 135 tracks per inch. On the other hand, modern disk drives have well over 30,000 TPI.

Zone Bit Recording

Take another look at the drawing in Figure 8.2. Notice that as a sector moves inward from Track 0 it becomes smaller. Therefore, data bits in the tracks closer to the center are packed more closely together than bits in outer-track sectors. Understand, too, that a track is a certain length, just like a racetrack. That length is the circumference of the circle on the platter. Therefore, the *linear density* is the number of bits that can be packed into a track. When a track's linear density increases, the bit density in each of its sectors also increases (magnetic bits have less space between them).

Older drives used the same number of sectors in every track, regardless of where the tracks were located. Now, with platter real estate at such a premium, we can't afford to waste space in low-density sectors. As a result, modern disks put a different number of sectors on different groups of tracks. The number of sectors is based on the lengths of the tracks. In a nutshell, outer tracks are longer and inner tracks are shorter. Therefore, outer tracks have more sectors than inner tracks.

To say this another way, platters are divided into zones of tracks. Each zone is defined by a certain number of sectors. In other words, the controller knows that all the tracks in a certain zone will have the same number of sectors. Like memory pages shrink an address for a known number of cells, zone addresses help speed things up by using a single size number for all the sectors in a particular area of the platter. The controller doesn't have to keep a table of individual addresses for every single sector on the platter.

Logical Formatting: Clusters

The operating system provides software to logically format a disk after it's been magnetized (again, the physical formatting). Partitioning sets aside how much space will be used for logical formatting. Hard disks may have one or more partitions (volumes). The second step in the process is to use FORMAT.COM to create a File Allocation Table (FAT) and divide each partition into clusters. The FAT is a group of sectors that have been reserved and set aside to keep track of file addresses.

The format process defines the minimum number of sectors contained in a cluster. Because FORMAT.COM is written specifically for the operating system, we can see that the operating system therefore determines both the type of FAT and the cluster size. DOS started with a 16-bit FAT. FAT32 and NTFS use a different scheme for both the file allocation table and the size of clusters. Every volume must be completely filled with clusters. (We'll discuss FAT32 and NTFS again in Chapter 14.)

Clusters consist of some number of sectors. Clusters must fill an entire volume. Each cluster takes more sectors, as the *volume* grows larger. "Volume" is the formal name for a logical drive.

The formatting process determines how many sectors will be inside each cluster. That determination takes place when you decide how large to make a partition. Clusters contain no data at the time you format the partition. As a result, the number of clusters and their size is reported at the end of the format process as the number and size of file allocation units.

Sector sizes are part of the low-level formatting process. A hard drive sector size is almost always fixed at 512 bytes. Bit density in each sector may vary, based on where the sector is located on the disk. The density changes, but not the size of the sector. On the other hand, cluster size is always defined by the operating system. FAT 16 uses fixed-size clusters. FAT32 and NTFS provide variable-size clusters, depending on the amount of information being stored in each cluster.

Supplementary Information

The following section is an overview of disk addressing, and how various disk sizes have certain limits. If you understand Large Block Addressing (LBA), you can skip to "Summary—Hard Disks" at this time.

When you save your letter to Mom, the system must be able to tell the disk to start magnetizing sectors somewhere on a track in a particular cylinder. When you then go to retrieve that letter, the operating system must also be able to request a known address from the drive controller. The original drive controllers (XT and AT boards) used real numbers associated with 1,024 actual cylinders, 16 heads, and 63 sectors (each 512 bytes) per track. Multiplying the numbers creates the maximum limit for a physical disk

(528MB or 528,482,304 bytes, at that time). These numbers are the physical *parameters* (limits and boundaries) of a hard disk.

Int 13h

Imagine a huge hotel with many rooms, and you arrive at the front desk asking for your room key. Your room is the start of the file, and the key is the specific address on the hard drive. The desk clerk is a special interrupt (Int 13h) used by the BIOS to figure out your room number. On an older hard drive, every room (address) had a key-hook (physical number) behind the desk clerk. In other words, BIOS could see every address to a real cylinder, head (track), and sector. But as disks (hotels) got larger and larger, there wasn't enough room to hang every key behind the desk.

 FDISK.EXE (and DISKPART.EXE) uses BIOS Interrupt 13h to determine disk size and partition information. The partition information is stored in the partition record, which is similar to the Master Boot Record. DOS (and Windows) use the partition record, bootstrap loader, and interrupt 13h to start the system and boot to a disk. Microsoft calls the partition where this information is stored the System partition. If Windows XP/2000 is located on another partition (for example, when both are installed on a single hard drive), Microsoft calls that partition where the Windows system files are located the Boot partition.

Suddenly there were way too many keys for the pegboard (addressing system). In other words, there were too many addresses for the BIOS to manage directly. So the "clerk" needed a way to move all the keys for the first few floors into a box, and replace them with all the keys for the next few levels. Without getting technical, this process is called *bit-shifting*. In a way, the BIOS began using virtual addresses much the way the 80286 processor used virtual memory.

CHS (Cylinder/Head/Sector)

The first hard drives, including the first IDE drives, used physical addresses. The combined Cylinder/Head/Sector address is known as the CHS table. IDE drives began with 16 heads, and the first AT Attachment rules determined how those systems would look for sector addresses. We could say this was ATA-1—the first de facto specification and set of rules. With standardization, everyone knew how to program the motherboard BIOS to work with an IDE drive controller, a physical CHS, standard cables, and specific connections to the motherboard. CHS introduced a volume address limit of 528MB.

Soon after ATA became a standard, Western Digital produced a hard drive with 256 heads. These became Extended IDE, or EIDE drives. Additionally, people wanted to connect tape drives and other devices, using the new ATA-IDE connection, and so the specification became ATA-2. The changes specified how to handle not only the additional drive heads, but also other types of devices. These devices, which eventually led to CDROM drives, sent "packets" of information through the controller, and so the name of the specification changed to the ATA Packet Interface (ATAPI), for devices other than hard drives. (ATA/ATAPI means a specification for ATA-type hard drives and ATAPI-type storage devices.)

XCHS (Extended CHS)

The Physical CHS (P-CHS) system worked for the first hard drives, but there weren't enough number combinations available for the additional heads and addresses in an EIDE drive. Remember that binary numbers ordinarily grow larger (wider) and use more transistors to store larger numbers. Unfortunately, Int 13h was a fixed-width 28-bit number. This is like our hotel's fixed-size pegboard not having enough room for additional room keys. To fix the problem, EIDE drives developed a logical table of addresses (like a table of contents in a book), and stored that table in the controller's firmware. But something would have to convert the logical addresses back to real numbers so that the BIOS could understand them—a translation system.

In a way, it would be like putting a separate "assistant clerk" on every few floors of our hotel. Each of them would report back to the main guy down in the lobby (BIOS). Using this system, the main clerk could read part of the room number (the floor number) and call up to the floor clerk (the logical address table). That clerk would then run downstairs and "shift" all the keys on the pegboard to the ones for the floors in his area (block). The main clerk could then re-examine the changed pegboard to find a particular key. It's a lot of work, and it reminds us of the theater example we used in Chapter 4.

As drive addressing became more complex, the ATA specification standardized the translations between the BIOS address tables and those tables that were right on the drive itself. These Logical CHS (L-CHS) tables acted as the sort of go-between, translating logical block addresses to physical addresses. The L-CHS translations were stored in the CMOS. Nowadays, configuring a hard drive means setting the address information and translation tables. Changing any of these parameters after the drive is installed makes the drive unreadable.

Modern CMOS can work with the drive controller and sector information on the physical disk to "auto-configure" most hard drives. This auto-configuration process stores the drive parameters in the CMOS.

Logical drive addresses (being "extended" from physical CHS addresses) became known as XCHS addresses. Note how "extended" is often abbreviated in an acronym with the letter "X." This works for MMX, ATX, XT, LPX, and so forth. The ATA specification provided a way for the BIOS Int 13h to handle a translation between logical and physical addresses. XCHS introduced an 8GB limit to volume addressing.

All BIOS chips support the XCHS concept, although XCHS isn't a standardized acronym. As such, manufacturers use different names for the addressing feature: Large disk access, LBA mode, Large BIOS, Translating BIOS, Enhanced (EIDE) BIOS, translation CHS, large CHS, or just plain XCHS. The one name you won't see is "What-a-pain-in-the-head CHS."

Large Block Addressing (LBA)

Up until this point, the BIOS interrupt was working with the hard drive controller, operating system, and application to "shift" address numbers through the fixed-length, 28-bit binary number. Everything was going through that desk clerk, so to speak, but the hotel was adding more and more floors (tracks) and plenty more rooms (sectors). There were more and more keys (sector addresses) to deal with and the management system was reaching a limit.

Integrated controllers (originally on SCSI drives and later on EIDE drives) were programmed to convert (translate) cylinder numbers into something the BIOS could understand. In other words, the controller translated physical numbers into logical parameters, which were then stored in the CMOS. BIOS could read the translated addresses as if they were real addresses. Just as memory engineers realized they could use "blocks" of addresses, disk manufacturers realized they could use logical parameters and addresses in a similar fashion. Translation tables began using blocks of disk addresses, sort of like memory pages.

Logical block addressing (LBA) is a way to handle the translation between logical addresses and the 28-bit physical numbers without having to bother the BIOS routines. In other words, LBA allows the device itself to handle address translations. However, because of the largest size 28-bit number (even with bit-shifting), IDE drives had a limit of approximately 136GB. (For technical reasons, it works out to around 137GB.)

ESDI and SCSI drives introduced logical addressing with disks using 1024 cylinders and 256 tracks. The additional (extended) tracks, together with L-CHS translation tables, allowed for disk sizes up to 8GB. Large Block Addressing (LBA) allows for EIDE disk partitions (and disks) to max out at 137GB.

A SCSI host adapter can convert L-CHS directly to LBA addresses. These conversions are included in the SCSI read/write commands. (The direct conversion is one of the reasons SCSI drives seem faster than IDE drives.) However, a SCSI volume is still limited to 8GB when using Int 13h BIOS-level CHS addressing. L-CHS is not the same as LBA.

For the moment, ATA/IDE drives larger than 137GB require Windows 2000/XP, an Ultra ATA/133 PCI controller card, and a supporting chipset. Without the underlying support platform, formatting a drive beyond its specifications will result in lost data. It isn't much different than when people tried to format a low-density floppy disk to a high-density format.

The 137GB Limit

The upgraded ATA specification helped standardize support for LBA. Many people thought the 137GB limit was unbreakable, being founded on the fundamental bit-size capability of Interrupt 13h. As with many limits, drive engineers have come up with various ways to play with the operating system, virtual interrupts, and other crafty schemes to get around that limit. That being so, the committees in charge of these things have been working on fundamentally changing all BIOS specifications to increase the size of Int 13h.

Maxtor, Compaq, Microsoft, and other industry leaders have worked with the ANSI T13 committee to release the ATA-6 specification, adopting a 48-bit addressing scheme to extend the maximum capacity of the ATA interface to 144 petabytes (PB, or 1 million terabytes). This will require a completely new interface, chipset, and updated firmware, as well as an operating system capable of handling 48-bit sector addresses and drive parameters. BIOS vendors will need to make sure that their firmware recognizes the new, bigger drives. Microsoft, Intel, Via, and every hard drive manufacturer have agreed.

Windows XP uses 32-bit code, although "Longhorn" and "Anvil" are being designed to use 64-bit code. Understand that operating system instructions often include storage addresses. A 32-bit operating system limits the volume size to 2.1 terabytes (TB, or 1 million gigabytes), even though the underlying hardware addressing can work with a larger disk. The SCSI interface is also based on 32-bit addressing, although the T10 SCSI standards committee expects to adopt a 64-bit addressing system with a maximum limit to 9.4 zettabytes (ZB). Serial ATA, part of the ATA/ATAPI-7 specification, will include the new 48-bit Int 13h addressing standard. The SATA addressing system is supposed to be backward compatible with the existing 28-bit addressing standard.

On a side note, a company called Nexsan Technologies has created an ATAboy2 specification as part of its trademarked InfiniSAN RAID storage systems. ATAboy2 provides options for connecting 2GB Fibre Channel systems to Storage Area Network (SAN) servers running ATA drives. This allows for multi-terabyte storage and up to 400MB/s throughput (peak). These kinds of storage needs are found in the broadcasting industry and graphics industry (for example, movie special effects). 1.68TB is enough storage for over 100 hours of digital video.

Like a regular SCSI interface, ATAboy2 supports 8 logical unit numbers (LUNs) per host controller. The ATAboy2 can also use a proposed Ultra ATA 160/230 SCSI specification, with transfer rates of 160MB/s. The ATAboy2 is designed to use ATA disks in heavy network storage situations, and brings the ATA specification into competition with SCSI drives. However, ATA disks tend to run at 10,000rpm, as opposed to high-end SCSI drives running at 15,000rpm.

IBM is shipping hard drive products that use a new coating material that should allow four times greater areal densities. The company calls the material called AntiFerromagnetically Coupled (AFC) media, and projects 100GB/square inch drives by sometime in 2004. AFC uses a 3-atom-thick layer of ruthenium (a precious metal similar to platinum) placed between two magnetic layers. The discovery was so astounding that IBM scientists started calling the ruthenium layer "pixie dust," as if it had magical properties. The "Travelstar" notebook drives were the first AFC drives, and store about 25.7GB/square inch.

IBM proposes that AFC media will allow for 400GB drives in desktop machines, and 200GB notebook computer drives. For comparison, 400GB is about equivalent to 400,000 books. 200GB is approximately the information on 42 DVDs, or 300 CDs. 6GB, on IBM's microdrives, is approximately 13 hours of MPEG-4 compressed digital video (about eight complete movies), and could easily be used in handheld devices.

Summary—Hard Disks

Let's do a final review of the differences between tracks, sectors, and clusters. Clusters are groups of sectors, and sectors are half-kilobyte pieces of tracks. Keep in mind the following points:

> ➤ Tracks are divided into sectors of 512 bytes. (You won't have to remember zones and areal density.)

> ➤ Sectors are combined into clusters, starting at 2KB (2,048 bytes, or 4 sectors).

> ➤ Clusters must fill the entire volume (a logical drive) from beginning to end.

> ➤ The size of the volume dictates the size of the clusters. Clusters will grow larger in order to fill the entire volume.

> ➤ A volume is the technical term for a logically formatted partition, as opposed to a low-level-formatted disk.

> ➤ The maximum number of FAT16 (DOS) clusters is 65,525.

> ➤ The largest cluster 16-bit DOS can make is 32KB. This limits FAT16 to 2GB as the largest logical drive that DOS can address.

> ➤ Logical Block Addressing (LBA) allows for access to 8GB hard drives.

> ➤ FAT32 and NTFS allow for larger logical drives, because they define cluster sizes differently than DOS. (Until recently, the maximum was 137GB.)

 Sectors are the basic storage unit on tracks; they are not clusters. Sectors can hold 512 bytes (not kilobytes) of information. Tracks are divided into sectors, but volumes are divided into clusters.

You should easily remember that hard disks are made up of platters, and that counting starts with 0. However, remember that a new drive installs into a system as either a master or a slave. IRQ 14 is for the main IDE drive, with a secondary drive typically being a CDROM, DVD drive, or some other drive that's slower than the primary drive. A secondary drive can be chained to a master drive on IRQ 14. However, IRQ 15 is set aside as an entirely separate, secondary connection, which can also have two drives. The IDE-ATA specification provides support for four drives, using two connectors on the motherboard.

Floppy Disks

Many years ago, very inexpensive notebooks appeared on the market that used a stylus-based operating system. The system used handwriting recognition and was available in various sizes, storing data in both text and graphic formats. These devices also offered many color styles, and cost about $1 at the local stationery supply store. The stylus cost about $.29. The main thing about these spiral-bound notebooks (or SBNs, as they were called) was that the data they stored was easily transportable. You ripped out a sheet of paper and jammed it into your pocket.

Portability and storage have always been issues for computer customers, which is why 3½-inch floppies lasted so long. If you needed to mail a file to someone, or drop off a copy of a file at a service bureau, you had to use floppy disks. Email changed all that, of course, but who wants to email a 100MB attachment? DSL and cable modems are changing that, however, and people also send files on CD-RWs.

The original floppy disks were made of bendable Mylar plastic, and were 8 inches round, with a soft plastic jacket. In 1974, PCs switched to a 5.25-inch disk called a mini-floppy. Not long afterwards, the protective jacket became rigid plastic and the disk shrank to the 3½-inch diameter we're all familiar with.

Floppy Disk Types

The original floppy disks used eight tracks, then changed to nine tracks. When a disk uses only one side for data storage, it's referred to as single-sided, single density. Density, in this case, refers to areal density: two sides, two areas, therefore, two sets of densities. Floppy disks use both sides for data storage, making them *double-sided, double density* disks. The idea of using both sides of the disk carried over into DVDs, but not CDROMs. "Double-sided" is abbreviated DS. "Low density" is abbreviated LD, and "high density" becomes HD. The four main floppy disk sizes and densities are named as follows:

➤ *DS, DD*—360K 5¼-inch double-sided, dual density

➤ *DS, HD*—1.2MB 5¼-inch double-sided, high density

➤ *DS, DD*—720K 3½-inch double-sided, double density

➤ *DS, HD*—1.44MB 3½-inch double-sided, high density

IBM developed a 2.9MB floppy disk for OS/2 distribution, referred to as "extra" density. Microsoft also had a proprietary disk-formatting process for storing 1.7MB on a typical floppy. Microsoft disks were referred to as Distributed Media Format (DMF). Windows 9x and above can read all normal sizes, along with the extra sizes, but neither the 2.8MB nor 1.7MB formats are supported by DOS.

Magnetic read-write heads must be small enough to distinguish an individual point of magnetism. Formatting a disk beyond its specified density may make these spots too small to be distinguished by the heads. Additionally, principles of physics teach us that magnetic areas too close to each other may cause interference and loss of magnetism.

Media Sensor Jumper

If you've ever seen a punch card, you know they are made out of a piece of heavy paper with patterns of small holes perforating the surface. A punch card reader beams light at one side of a card, and if a sensor on the other side picks up the light, it reads a "1." No light meant a "0." We see this same technique in floppy disk media sensors.

The back (or bottom) of a floppy disk is the side with a circular metal plate in the middle of the casing. Looking at the back, you'll notice a small hole in the upper-*right* corner of a 3½-inch disk. That hole is for the *media sensor*. If a beam of light (the media sensor light) can pass through the hole and make contact with a photo sensor, the system knows that a high-capacity 1.44MB disk is in the drive.

Extended-capacity 2.8MB disks had a different hole on the disk jacket, so a multicapacity floppy drive actually had two media sensors: one for 1.44MB and one for 2.8MB disks. (A 1.7MB DMF disk uses 21 sectors per track, rather than 18, and doesn't require a special media sensor.)

Low-density 720KB disks have no such hole in the media sensor position, so the media sensor light fails to make contact with the photo sensor. This led to an interesting scheme in which a special hole-punch tool was marketed for converting cheaper 720KB disks to 1.44MB disks. The reformatted disk eventually became unstable because of the magnetic structure of low-density disks. Putting too many tracks on the disk led to a rapid degradation of the format, with a catastrophic loss of data. (On the other hand, placing a piece of tape over the media sensor hole on a 1.44MB disk fools the drive into thinking that it contains a 720KB disk that can be formatted with no data loss.)

Write Protect

There's also a hole in the upper-*left* corner of the back of the disk, with a sliding piece of plastic. When this hole is covered, it locks the disk and prevents any writing to it, making it write-protected. *Write protection* makes it physically impossible to write data to the disk. This is a way to guarantee that a virus program can't be placed on the disk. There's no way to write-protect RAM, but a virus in memory can't transfer to a write-protected disk.

The hole in the upper-*left* corner, looking at the back of a floppy, is the write-protect tab. The hole in the upper-right corner is the media sensor. Write protection prevents any changes to the state of the floppy disk. The disk cannot be formatted or written to in any way; data can only be read from the disk.

Drive Select Jumper

One difference between floppy and hard drives is that the operating system designates floppies as either Drive A: or Drive B:. (Hard drives use their own jumpers to designate the drive as either a master or slave.) The *drive select jumper* defines the unique drive number, and in the overall scheme of drives and controllers, every drive must have its own drive number. The drive select jumper defines a floppy drive as either drive 0 or drive 1. Drive 0 does not necessarily correspond to Drive A:, just as Drive 1 does not necessarily correspond to Drive B:.

One of the fundamental things you must remember for the exam is that IBM (and all clone makers) designed Drive A: and Drive B: into every system. This will affect your understanding of partitioning, because all PCs continue to set aside two drives (A: and B:) for the basic floppy drives, regardless of whether a physical drive exists. Drive A: is the default, with Drive B: always present. The C: drive is always the third drive. Any additional drives take on the next consecutive letters of the alphabet.

If you'd like to test this, place a floppy disk in the "A: drive" and go to a DOS command line. Run the DIR command on the drive by typing **DIR A:**. After the directory listing, type **DIR B:**. On some systems, you'll get an amazing warning screen demanding that you insert a disk in the B: drive. Simply press OK, and you'll see the same directory listing. (Remember to type **EXIT** to get out of a DOS window that takes over the entire screen.) Interestingly enough, when you switch back to the Explorer, it will show the mounted drive as being the A: drive. However, when you click on the drive's icon, you may get the same warning message that you must insert a disk in the A: drive.

Diskette Change Line

AT boards use pin 34 to carry a signal called the *diskette change line*. This signal tells the system whether a disk in the drive is still the same disk since the last time a disk access was requested. The control signal is a pulse sent to the controller (to a status register) that changes one time on insertion, and one time on ejection.

When the drive responds with information that the heads have moved, the system knows whether a disk has been inserted. If a change signal isn't received between accesses, the controller assumes that the same disk is in the drive. This allows information that is stored in RAM to be used again without necessarily rereading the disk.

Troubleshooting Floppy Drives

When a floppy drive goes bad, you'll usually get an error message during a read-write operation. Typically, the message states that the system cannot write to the disk in Drive A:. Before you tear apart the system and replace the drive, try reseating the floppy disk in the drive. If you listen closely, you should hear a solid "thunk" (technical term) as the disk settles onto the spindle motor and pushes out the eject button on the front of the drive.

The sliding panel in the protective cover used to be called the "baffle." Now it's called the "shutter." When the system tries to access the disk, you should also hear the sound of the shutter being pulled back. If you don't, try ejecting and re-inserting the disk. More often than not, with floppy disks being used so infrequently, you might also try blowing out accumulated dust with a can of compressed air.

In some cases, a drive that worked well under Windows 95 develops a problem under Windows 98. Right-click for the Context menu on the "My Computer" icon, then get into the Properties menu. Select the "Performance" tab, then click on "File System." Click on "Floppy Disk" and remove a check mark next to "Search for New Floppy Drives Each Time Your Computer Starts." Secondly, click on the "Removable Disk" option and uncheck "Write-back caching" to disable it. This may also help with problems involving Iomega removable drives, tape backups, and external optical drives.

Examine all error messages closely. In some instances, the actual magnetic tracks on a floppy disk go bad. If this is the case, you'll often get an "Unable to write to boot sector" message during a Format operation. Try replacing the disk with a different one and run Format again. Other error messages indicate that the disk is simply write-protected, in which case, slide down the write-protect tab. (Note that Windows Me changed the way FORMAT.COM worked, and the inability to format the disk may be a consequence of the operating system, not a problem with the disk or drive.)

The ATA Specification

Let's go over two fundamental concepts one more time. On the one hand we have a drive controller (hardware logic board) and its built-in chips. On the other hand, we have information (data and software instructions) we want to transfer between disks and system memory. Controllers have one set of names, and transfer protocols have a whole other set of names. We're interested in IDE and SCSI hardware (drives), and the ATA and SCSI specifications (transfer protocols).

ATA specifies how data will be combined, managed, controlled, and validated as it moves from a magnetic spot on a disk through to system memory. People refer to each specification as having various "modes," which creates even more confusion. Because data transfers happen so often, hard drives work closely with DMA controllers, using *direct memory access* to offload work from the CPU. *Ultra* DMA is simply an evolution of DMA and became part of the ATA specification.

The IDE and ATA Acronyms

IDE originally stood for either IBM Disc Electronics or for Integrated Disc Electronics, depending on who was using the acronym. Back in those days, "disc" looked classier than "disk." (Nowadays, "fibre" looks more sophisticated than "fiber.") In any event, the IBM reference was too specific, but the other name was too generalized. Engineers were working with the IBM AT form factor, and everyone was calling it the "PC AT Interface." They were concerned about trademark problems, so when the technology finally went to the ANSI committee for standards approval, the reference name was changed to the generic "AT Attachment," or ATA.

Strictly speaking, IDE refers to *any* drive that has a built-in controller. The actual bus on the motherboard uses the ATA specification. The original controller used the 16-bit ISA connection. Later computers dropped the ISA bus in favor of the PCI bus. One of the advantages of an integrated controller (direct chipset support) is that the drive manufacturer doesn't need to worry about compatibility issues. SCSI drives require a SCSI controller, installed on the expansion bus, along with driver software and device ID numbers.

The original ATA IDE combination called a 40-pin keyed connector with a 5.25-inch form factor. The keyed connector allowed the drives to be plugged in only one way. Plugging in a drive backward can damage both the drive and its related circuits. Some connectors don't use a physical notch for keying, in which case the ribbon cables have matching colored stripes to indicate the correct orientation. The maximum length of the cables was specified as 18 inches.

Timing Signals and Buffers

Hard drive controllers have a small, built-in memory buffer. The reason for the buffer has to do with the difference between how fast the drive heads can move information, and how fast the timing strobe, cables, and DMA channels can transfer information to memory. At the drive itself, reading or writing is done in small groups—blocks—of data. For longer, more sustained file operations, such as during the boot process, while loading a very large application, or with games, data transfers take place in a continuous sequence. The *sequential transfer rate* for earlier ATA controllers would often fall to just above 10MB/s as the buffer filled up.

Consider a 20MB music file. It breaks down to, say, 512KB packets. Each packet hits the drive's buffer, and then has to wait while the system sends a transfer command. One of the reasons the buffer fills up is that the controller has to have a timing signal for each command transfer. The signal is somewhat like a motherboard clock tick, but uses a timing *strobe* with an "up" (positive) and a "down" (negative) transition cycle. With coordinated timing, these packets are then transferred in bursts—the *burst transfer rate*. (The "Packet Interface," in ATAPI, refers to managing packets.)

Command Turnaround

Fast ATA calls for the drive to wait for the strobe coming from the host (main system). This wait is known as *propagation delay* (not on the exam). After the signal arrives, the drive can respond by putting data into the buffer. The response time leads to *data turnaround delay*. The timing signal is a two-way (bi-directional) event between the computer and the drive. Fast ATA used only the positive cycle—the uptick—to send data.

Ultra ATA doubled the data transfer rate by making the drive, not the host, the source for both the timing strobe and the data transfer. In other words, the drive no longer had to wait for the main system to send a timing signal. Instead, it controlled all timing. Both the strobe signal and data signal traveled simultaneously down the cable in the same direction, eliminating the propagation delay. Now the drive didn't have to wait for signals coming from the opposite direction (sort of like Rambus memory going in only one direction). Ultra ATA also used both the positive and negative transition of the timing signal to double the frequency of data transfers, so data could be sent twice as fast without doubling the speed of the timing strobe (like using half ticks in DDR memory) .

Hard drive speed is partly related to the controller interface, but is mostly related to average seek time. Hard drives typically move data into a command buffer at about 10MB/s on a sustained basis. With a transfer rate of

16.7MB/s, you would think that Fast ATA would be capable of keeping the buffer from becoming full. The reason it can't has to do with the turnaround time between the commands coming from the PC and the execution of those commands by the drive. This command turnaround time causes an overall performance bottleneck.

How Command Turnaround Works

Command turnaround time delays come from the number of commands a PC makes to a drive, depending upon the size of the command requests. The requests are typically 4KB in size and are equivalent to the page size supported by the operating system. When a 4KB command comes from the host machine to save a file, it takes approximately 400 microseconds (4 milliseconds) for the drive controller to read the command data into its buffer.

Fast ATA, with a burst transfer rate of 16.7MB/s, had a sustained sequential data rate of 10.2MB/s. The buffer emptied 4KB in about 250 microseconds, leaving 150 microseconds of *overhead* between commands, to keep the filling and the emptying of the buffer in balance. A typical desktop PC has a command turnaround time of around 275 microseconds, and takes approximately 525 microseconds to empty the buffer. This reduced the effective transfer rate of Fast ATA to approximately 7.8MB/s (4,096 bytes divided by 525). Keep in mind that the drive had a burst transfer rate of 16.7MB/s.

7.8MB/s works out to 75% of the drive's 10.2MB/s sequential data rate. This means that for every 3 bytes being sent to the host, 1 byte accumulates in the buffer. A typical buffer holds 64KB worth of data, and 1 buffer's worth of data is accumulated for every 3 buffers of data being sent to the host. At that point, the drive "slips a rev," (*rev* is short for revolution) meaning that before the host can drain the buffer, the system has to wait until a requested sector rotates past the head a second time. The buffer typically holds 64KB, which means 1 slipped rev occurs for every 256KB of data being transferred.

The *effective* data transfer rate of the bus equals the burst transfer rate, minus the command turnaround time. By doubling the rate at which the buffer is emptied, Ultra ATA compensated for command turnaround overhead. Ultra ATA's 33MB/s burst transfer rate allowed a 4KB data block to transfer in 125 microseconds (half the time of Fast ATA), leaving 275 microseconds for overhead. 125 plus 275 equals 400 microseconds (the buffer fill rate), and as a result, the buffer doesn't accumulate data and can avoid slipped revs.

Table of Transfer Rates

Although we haven't discussed each of the various transfer modes, we'll put Table 8.3 here as a consolidated reference point. The listing shows the various transfer rates, not only for ATA, but also for SCSI and other types of interfaces. Following this table, we have a short review of each of the specifications, along with a review of the SCSI interface.

Table 8.3 Transfer Rates and Specifications	
I/O Interface	Maximum Speed (MB/s)
IDE/EIDE PIO Mode 0	3.30MB/s
IDE/EIDE PIO Mode 1	5.20MB/s
IDE/EIDE PIO Mode 2	8.30MB/s
IDE/EIDE PIO Mode 3	11.10MB/s
IDE/EIDE PIO Mode 4	16.70MB/s
UDMA/33	33.00MB/s
UDMA/66	66.00MB/s
ATA 100	100.00MB/s
ATA 133	133.00MB/s
Serial ATA	150.00MB/s
Serial ATA II	300.00MB/s
Serial ATA III	600.00MB/s
SCSI 1	5.00MB/s
SCSI 2	10.00MB/s
SCSI 2 Wide	20.00MB/s
Ultra SCSI	20.00MB/s
Ultra Wide SCSI	40.00MB/s
Ultra 2 SCSI	80.00MB/s
Ultra 160 SCSI	160.00MB/s
Ultra 320 SCSI	320.00MB/s
Serial Storage Architecture (SSA)	20.00–40.00MB/s
10MB Ethernet	1.28MB/s
100MB Ethernet	12.80MB/s
1GB Ethernet	131.00MB/s
Standard Parallel	0.15MB/s
Enhanced Parallel (ECP and EPP)	3.00MB/s
USB	1.50MB/s
IEEE-1394 (FireWire)	51.20MB/s
Fiber Channel (FC-AL)	100.00–200.00MB/s

Source: CompuClues Forum, **www.bitzenbytes.com**

ATA Modes

ATA first became a formal specification in 1981. Shortly thereafter, the ATA-2 modification added support for EIDE drives. Aside from logical addressing, the specification added Programmed Input/Output (PIO) modes, along with DMA transfer support. The first three PIO modes (0, 1, and 2) were assigned to the ATA-1 specification. ATA-2 added PIO modes 3 and 4. PIO modes use DMA transfers to bypass the CPU when transferring data to system memory.

The IDE port on the motherboard had to be on either a VESA local bus or a PCI bus if it was to run in modes 3 and 4. Most motherboards have two IDE controllers, but on older systems, only the first was connected to the then-emerging PCI bus. The second controller was connected to a legacy ISA bus and limited to PIO mode 2.

NOTE

Mixing fast and slow devices (such as hard disks and CDROM drives) on the primary controller can cause slower data transfer for the hard disk. Typically, all transfers travel at the speed of the slower device. Connect only similar types of disks to the primary controller, and make the faster of two disks the master.

ATA-2 (released in 1994) linked data transfers to the DMA controller. DMA-2 stayed in effect until the fourth specification, which introduced Ultra DMA. Some people talked about having a PIO Mode 5, but by the time it came up for standardization, the market was calling the fast transfer system UDMA. Earlier PIO modes went from 4–16.6MB/s. Ultra DMA immediately doubled the rate to 33.3MB/s, and people thought the entire mishmash should have a new name.

ATA-3: Fast ATA

ATA-2 provided support for drives larger than 504MB, and PIO modes 3 and 4. The updated PIO modes were referred to as ATA-3, or *Fast ATA*, and required upgraded device drivers, along with an enhanced BIOS. Fast ATA used burst transfers to develop 16.7MB/s throughput, along with Secure Mode, where a user could lock the hard drive with its own password (prior to loading the operating system).

The 32-bit PCI bus was becoming standard; however, ATA was designed to work with 16-bit transfers (for ISA bus compatibility). Understand that ATA applies not only to instruction commands and data packets, but also to the number of physical transfer wires in a conforming cable. Windows, Plug and Play, and IDE controllers began to provide an option to use 32-bit data transfers, the so-called 32-bit Access setting (found under the Device Manager). With proper BIOS support, the feature allowed the PCI bus to combine two 16-bit data packets coming from the drive, and then send the 32-bit packets to the CPU and system RAM.

ATA-4: Ultra ATA/33

In 1997, Quantum and Seagate introduced Ultra DMA/33, a process for doubling data transfers from IDE hard disks. The modification led to an updated ATA/ATAPI-4 specification, which became known as Ultra ATA. Intel backed the technology and included support for the process in their chipsets. The rest of the industry and disk manufacturers followed suit, and Ultra ATA became the standard.

 Ultra ATA is sometimes known as Advanced ATA and ATA/ATAPI-4, but most often known as Ultra ATA/33, referring to the 33MB/s burst transfer rate.

Ultra DMA (UDMA-2, UDMA/33)

Ultra ATA essentially brought together the relative speed of the CPU, system memory, and the actuator arm inside the disk. The CPU can use data very quickly, but moving the data between the disk and RAM is a bottleneck problem. DMA channels had to be upgraded to synchronize the new process of reducing the bottleneck between read-write heads and the transfers into and out of memory. (The way it was done was by using multi-word bits in the DMA controllers.)

 The SCSI Ultra 2 protocol also uses a bus-mastering DMA protocol sometimes referred to as Ultra DMA.

Remember that data transfers are essentially electrical pulses. Electricity moving at high speeds begins to change the surrounding environment because of physics and principles of electronics. The faster the speed, the more interference, and so engineers have to figure out how to compensate for that interference. CRC was one way to do it, and adding secondary reference lines to the transfer cable was another way.

UDMA Modes

Much as the earlier ATA specification used PIO modes, ATA-4 introduced UDMA modes. Modes 0–2 were part of ATA-4, with transfer rates of 16.7, 25.0, and 33.3MB/s, respectively. ATA-5 introduced Mode 3 (44.4MB/s) and Mode 4 (66.7MB/s). Ultra ATA/133, announced in 2001, is part of the ATA/ATAPI-6 specification. The change calls for Mode 5 (100MB/s) and Mode 6 (133MB/s). However, Serial ATA may supplant the latter mode, much the way UDMA supplanted the proposed PIO Mode "5."

Cyclical Redundancy Checking (CRC)

When transfer rates doubled to 33MB/s, the high-speed transfers began to introduce data errors. Cyclical Redundancy Check (CRC) is a way to verify data. The CRC (somewhat like parity checking codes) is calculated for each burst of data by both the host and the drive. The result is stored in CRC registers both on the host and the drive. After each burst, the host sends the contents of its CRC register back to the drive, which compares it against its own register's contents. Matching CRCs indicate the data sent was the same as the data received. This provided better data integrity, making an Ultra ATA drive more accurate as well as faster. (CRC checking is also used to store file sizes in rudimentary virus protection.)

ATA-5: Ultra ATA/66

Ultra ATA/66 doubled the Ultra ATA burst transfer rate by reducing setup times and increasing the strobe rate. The faster strobe rate caused even more EMI, which meant the standard 40-pin cable used by ATA and Ultra ATA had to be changed. A new, 40-pin, 80-conductor cable was developed, with 40 additional grounds lines between each of the original ground and signal lines. The additional 40 lines not only helped shield the signal from EMI, but provided reference lines for the original data, much like reference lines in networking cables.

Although the new CRC-enabled ATA cable used 80 wires, the header on the motherboard was still a 40-pin connector. This ensured backward compatibility between faster drives and existing chipsets. Serial ATA uses an entirely different cable and connector, and requires an adapter to work with older motherboards. The Ultra ATA/100 (and ATA/133) specification calls for the system to "step down" to older Ultra ATA/33-66 UDMA modes. Once again, we see the device taking over more control of the transfer system, and working with whatever hardware it finds on the system.

ATA-6: Ultra ATA/100

The biggest problem today is still the bottleneck between how fast the drive can read data and how fast it can transfer that data to main memory (RAM). Gaming and multimedia rely on sustained, sequential reads far more than previous office applications. To that extent, the transfer bus becomes more and more important. Bus mastering and packet bursts have pretty much reached the end of the road, in terms of speed, but the ATA specification standardizes IDE systems at 100MB/s and 133MB/s.

Current systems rarely reach even the 100MB/s transfer ceiling, mostly because of the parallel, 16-bit historical foundation of the ATA interface. In a way, it's like the change to a 48-bit hard drive addressing scheme. The hardware industry might agree to the standard, but the software industry will then have to develop entirely new operating systems. Another example is the PCI Express specification, which fundamentally redefines the way the motherboard (hardware) bus deals with peripherals.

Without a complementary operating system, all the hardware in the world means nothing. Hardware devices and buses won't do us any good unless we can use something like Windows (or the Mac OS, or Linux) to run them. Even then, what good is an operating system without applications? Our spreadsheets, word processors, databases, and multimedia applications will either have to be backward compatible, or they'll all have to be re-written for the new hardware. (Not that there's a problem, or anything.)

ATA-7: Ultra ATA/133

The T13 Committee began work on the ATA/ATAPI-7 in October 2001. The standard includes Ultra DMA mode 6, also known as Ultra DMA/133. Although the whole specification may give way to Serial ATA (SATA), for the moment it also includes a few new commands for use by digital video recorders, and the T13 version of Serial ATA. The ATA/ATAPI-7 document has been split into three volumes: one for the hard disk commands, one for the traditional parallel ATA (PATA) interface, and one for the SATA-1 interface.

Supplemental Information

Intel, along with Maxtor, IBM, Seagate, Dell, and APT Technologies, has been working to formalize a standard method of using serial transfers over the ATA bus. Remember that the original interface was designed around parallel transfers. Serial ATA combines data into packets at the device end and then transfers those packets along a high-speed cable with only 4 lines. The principle is the same as USB, and should set the introductory transfer rate to about 150MB/s.

The thinner, more flexible cable should also help in terms of smaller cases, reducing the hair ball of ribbon cables inside a desktop machine. Additionally, the new specification allows for something called "Hot Plug," which is pretty much the same as USB's hot-swapping capability. Parallel ATA requires not only the 40 data lines, but the additional reference lines to reduce EMI coming from high-speed transfers. SATA manages the data transfers by combining bits, rather than speeding them up. As a result, there's almost no EMI, and that's how we can have such thin cables and maintain data integrity. (SATA uses advances in data transfers developed for Ethernet, USB, FireWire, and AMD's Hyper Transport bus.)

PCI Express

PCI Express supports the older PCI bus method of using A, B, C, or D virtual interrupts. It also uses a newer system called Message Signaled Interrupt (MSI). MSI is optional in PCI 2.2 and 2.3 devices, but is the default for PCI Express devices. The MSI scheme is the preferred system for handling data packets over a serial link. The system is more effective in multi-processor systems because any device can issue interrupts to different hosts directly, without having to necessarily pass through the interrupt controllers.

Onboard disk caches (buffers) help with sequential and random access drive reads, but all that data still ends up slamming into the PCI bus, where it has to wait for turnaround times. Serial ATA works in conjunction with the PCI Express specification, and should fix this bottleneck. Although Intel tried to generate market support for their "HubLink" architecture, it seems SATA will probably connect to the South Bridge until the PCI Express bus becomes widely recognized. At that time, the hard drive should be able to use Serial ATA transfers, along with the new bus, to send packets of sequential data directly in and out of system memory, bypassing most of the host system.

The SCSI Specification

The SCSI interface was originally developed so that Apple Computer users could take advantage of some of the emerging drive technology being developed for IBM PCs. The interface is still commonly used, and supports a mixture of drives and devices within the same system (for example, disk drives, RAID arrays, tape backups, and scanners). A principle advantage of the SCSI interface is that it was developed from the ground up to be a fully integrated transfer system. Parallel ATA has always been more of a workaround between developing drive technology and changing motherboards. Although Serial ATA is more integrated, it too is still a bit of a back-end solution.

> The SCSI bus also allows computers that aren't IBM compatible to use hard drives that were developed specifically for IBM-type PCs. An important thing to remember about the SCSI interface is that the bus allows not only hard drives, but other devices to be connected to an external cable (outside the box).
>
> IDE and EIDE controllers also work with drives and other devices, but only allow two devices in a chain and do not support external devices.

Many manufacturers sell the same drive in both IDE and SCSI models, and put an extra chip on the SCSI circuit board. In that case, the extra chip is a SCSI (device) *adapter*. Because the extra chip requires data to go through an extra step, the IDE model performs slightly better. One of the extra steps is the command buffering, whereby the SCSI adapter can rearrange up to 256 commands.

SCSI devices can communicate independently of the CPU and can operate at the same time. IDE devices have individual controllers that can operate only one at a time. SCSI devices run a bypass around the CPU, similarly to DMA, for simple device-related tasks. This bypass keeps the CPU from bogging down. Another advantage of the SCSI interface is that if bad sectors develop on the disk, a SCSI system can mark the sector as bad and avoid crashing on a disk read. IDE systems require either reformatting the disk or running a disk repair utility. This is one reason why network mirrored drives tend to be SCSI drives.

Host Adapter: 8 ID Numbers

SCSI is different from IDE in the sense that it isn't restricted to disk drives. SCSI is a complete and separate bus. The bus connects to the motherboard through a *host adapter*. You'll often see references to a PCI SCSI adapter, where the host adapter fits into a PCI slot on the motherboard bus. In the old days, the same reference would have applied to an ISA SCSI adapter.

A single SCSI bus can hold up to eight devices, each with a unique identification (ID) number. The ID number can be from 0 to 7 and is called the *Logical Unit Number (LUN)*. For instance, LUN 0 might be assigned to a SCSI hard drive and LUN 4 might be a CDROM. LUN 7 might be the host adapter.

The main thing to remember about configuring a SCSI device is that the host adapter and every device must have a SCSI ID number. Device ID numbers are almost always between 0 and 6 (seven choices), with the host adapter usually set to 7 at the factory. ID 7 is the highest priority, and the adapter is critical. If the adapter ID is 7, that means it's the eighth device—leaving room for seven more devices.

A trick question on the exam might focus on the number of devices, but will ask you how many unique SCSI ID numbers are possible. Don't be confused by the 8 ID numbers and 7 devices on the overall SCSI bus.

Remember that the host adapter automatically takes up one ID number. The remaining seven hardware devices take up the remaining seven identification numbers. Be sure to remember that hexadecimal counting begins at zero. The host adapter takes up one of the ID numbers, leaving seven IDs for the other hardware devices.

Wide SCSI buses support 16 devices, rather than the 8 devices specified in regular SCSI. You'll probably see questions referring only to regular SCSI, but make a note of the difference.

The ID is set in much the same way that master/slave jumpers are set on an IDE hard drive. For no reason at all, and instead of making it simple, SCSI manufacturers use binary numbers represented by three jumpers. One SCSI manufacturer might have binary 000 as SCSI ID 0 (LUN 0) and binary 100 as SCSI ID 4. Just to be diabolical, another SCSI manufacturer might reverse the jumper settings for ID 4, making it 001.

SCSI-1—Only Hard Drives

The first set of standards, SCSI-1, was finalized in 1986 and included 18 commands, but the interface could send only one command at a time. Sometimes called Narrow SCSI, the 8-bit bus required a host adapter and used a unique SCSI ID number for each drive. It introduced the seven-device limit to a daisy chain—setting aside the host adapter—where the remaining devices could *only* be different types of hard drives.

A SCSI cable must be terminated at both ends, just like a network bus. A terminator is essentially a way to absorb signals and prevent bounce-back interference. Because the host adapter is usually at one end, it typically has a built-in terminator. (We discuss cable termination again in Chapter 10, "Basic Networking," and Chapter 11, "Cables and Connectors.") However, if you put the host adapter in the middle of the chain, you need to remember to remove the terminator mounted on the controller and install terminators at both ends of the cable. The original 132-ohm terminator didn't work well with high-speed transfer rates, sometimes causing data errors when more than one device was on a chain. Another problem with SCSI-1 was that the cable length was limited to 6 meters, which is approximately 19 feet.

SCSI-2—Additional Peripheral Devices

Release 2 of the specification lowered the terminator resistance, and called for an active (voltage-regulated) terminator. The lower impedance helped improve reliability. SCSI-2 included the original 18 commands (rewriting some of them) and added new commands, including specific support for drives *other than hard drives* (for example, CDROM, DAT, floptical, removable disk, standard QIC tape, magneto-optical, WORM drives, and scanners). Some drives still required third-party software drivers, but the seven-device limit stayed.

SCSI-2 also introduced bus-mastering controller support (onboard CPU/DMA controller) and support for multitasking environments. Up to 256 commands could be sent at one time to a device, which stored them in a buffer and reordered them for better efficiency. However, increased throughput and speed led to problems requiring a reduced cable length, with a maximum of 3 meters.

Although we list SCSI cable lengths and connectors here, Chapter 11 is where we focus on the many other types of connectors used in a PC system. The principle connector to know for SCSI is the 50-contact Centronix, and the 50-pin ribbon cable for drives. Be aware of the fact that SCSI cables use different connectors according to each specification. The questions we saw on the exam mostly had to do with SCSI-1, or regular SCSI. Fast Wide SCSI uses a 68-pin connector.

Understand that SCSI-2 is not the same as Ultra2 SCSI, which is a higher-performance feature set. SCSI-2 is a basic upgrade to the specification. The different names within that specification all apply to SCSI-2. The biggest problem with the entire SCSI interface is understanding which names apply to what aspects of the specification. (Who knows, but that might be a reason why ATA and IDE drives are the overwhelmingly dominant market force.)

The SCSI-2 specification brought about a change in the width of the bus. As the bus made the changeover from 8 bits to 16 bits, many minor variations led to the many names of SCSI, as follows:

➤ *Fast SCSI, or Fast-10 (8-bit)*—Capable of 10MB/s transfers, with a maximum cable length of 3 meters, used a 50-pin connector for internal drives, and a 50-pin connector (DB50) for external host and peripheral drives.

➤ *Ultra SCSI, or Fast-20 (8-bit)*—Capable of 20MB/s transfers, with a maximum cable length of 1.5 meters, used the same connectors as Fast-10.

➤ *Ultra2 SCSI (8-bit)*—Capable of 40MB/s transfers, with a maximum cable length of 12 meters (39 feet), also used the same connectors as Fast-10.

➤ *Fast Wide SCSI, Fast-10 (16-bit)*—Capable of 20MB/s transfers, with a maximum cable length of 1.5 meters (4.9 feet), used a new 68-pin internal and external connector (half-pitch DB68) for newer hard drives.

➤ *Ultra Wide SCSI, Fast-20 (16-bit)*—Capable of 40MB/s transfers, with the same cables and connectors as Fast-10.

SCSI-3 (Ultra SCSI)

Ultra SCSI is really a collection of many different standards, not all coming from the T10 Committee. As a result, SCSI-3 is seriously confusing. Aside from intertwined standards, manufacturers introduce their own feature names. We also see this with Intel's Net Burst and Hyper Threading Technology, as well as with Ultra ATA and Ultra DMA.

SCSI-3 uses the 16-bit bus carried over from SCSI-2. Originally, higher speeds meant shorter cables. Part of the changing specification was aimed at increasing cable length while keeping the speed improvements. There are a number of subsets to SCSI-3, referred to as the SCSI Parallel Interface (SPI). In fact, we no longer refer to SCSI-1, 2, or 3, but rather refer to the specific subsets as follows:

➤ *Ultra2 Wide (U2W) SCSI, or Ultra2 LVD SCSI, or Fast-40 (16-bit)*—Capable of 80MB/s transfers, with a maximum cable length of 12 meters, uses low-voltage differential (LVD) DB68 cables for some drives, or very high density (VHD) Centronix 68-pin connectors for RAID controllers and file servers.

➤ *Ultra3 SCSI, or Ultra160/m (16-bit)*—Capable of 160MB/ps transfers, with a maximum cable length of 12 meters, uses the same DB68 and Centronix 68-pin connectors as Fast-40, but also an 80-pin Single Connector Attachment (SCA) connector for RAID controllers and SCA drives. SCA drives can be connected to DB68 connectors with an adaptor.

SCA and Hot-Swapping

The SCA (Single Connector Attachment) specification (or sub-specification) introduced hot-swapping. Hot-swapping means that instead of having to shut down a file server and network whenever a drive went bad, the drive could be exchanged (swapped) while the system was still running. Networks have many disks in a *redundant array of inexpensive disks (RAID)*, designed to protect valuable data at all times. Bringing down a RAID array to swap out a faulty disk is contrary to the basic concept of real-time backups, and SCA drives avoid those shutdowns. This idea of hot-swapping peripherals was an important aspect of the developing USB specification.

Storage Area Networks (SANs) and iSCSI

Although people sometimes think that computers are expensive, valuable pieces of equipment, the data stored on computers is far more valuable. If you run a business and someone steals your computers, you can replace the hardware and software applications. It may be expensive, but at least they can be replaced. The data, on the other hand, is irreplaceable unless it has been backed up. Data backups and the need for accessibility from anywhere on the planet has led to the development of wide area networks devoted almost entirely to data storage.

Multinational corporations and research universities can have storage needs up into the thousands of gigabytes or more. Backing up such a database requires high-speed transfers, very large disks, and other evolving equipment. The Storage Networking Industry Association (SNIA) has launched the Storage Management Initiative (SMI) to develop a storage management standard for these types of storage networks. (SAN may also stand for Server Area Network, connecting many file servers, or System Area Network.)

On a regular LAN or WAN, most of the data transfers taking place are file access events, meaning that someone opens or saves a file, or accesses an application such as Word. Storage networks usually process block transfers, where large blocks of information are moved from one place to another over fiber optics or fibre channel networks. The Fibre Channel Protocol (FCP) is a serial SCSI command protocol used on these networks.

Storage area networks take advantage of the Internet to move large blocks of data across many different types of file servers. The Internet Small Computer Systems Interface (iSCSI) protocol defines the rules for transmitting block storage applications over TCP/IP networks. This leads to yet another set of acronyms, Fibre Channel over TCP/IP (FCIP), and the Internet Fibre Channel Protocol (iFCP). iSCSI interfaces can be directly connected to standard Gigabit Ethernet switches and/or IP routers, and provide for SCSI-3 commands to be encapsulated in TCP/IP packets and reliably delivered over IP networks.

Tape Backup Systems

When the CPU requests data from the disk, platters rotate and the heads move back and forth over them. The back-and-forth movement allows for *random access* of the data, rather than the sequential data reads of a tape cassette. *Sequential* access means that if you have a file stored somewhere on a tape, the machine must spin through a length of tape before it gets to the beginning of a file. A hard drive, on the other hand, skips over whole platters and tracks, going directly to the first cluster of a file.

 Although hard drives use random access to "seek" out a data address, data transfers take place either in short bursts or long sequential transfers.

Sequential reading takes place in a typical VCR or cassette tape unit. To get to a particular recording, we have to fast-forward or rewind to a location on a tape. The tape must first have enough room to store the complete file from beginning to end. Before we can add a file to a tape, we have to wait while the machine spins the tape all the way to the end of any used space, and the software determines whether there's enough room remaining for the whole file. If there isn't, we have to use a new tape.

Tape Formats

The basic tape cartridge used in most home-market tape machines was the *quarter-inch cartridge (QIC)* analog tape format. QIC was replaced by *digital audio tape (DAT)* storage, which was a competitive technology to CDROMs and DVDs. Although optical disks terminated all competition for the home backup market, the technology continues today on high-end tape systems that use digital linear tape (DLT).

DLT

DLT (digital linear tape) is a form of magnetic tape and drive system used for computer data storage and archiving. A special compression algorithm, known as Digital Lempel Ziv 1 (DLZ1), facilitates storage and retrieval of data at high speeds and in large quantities. In the DLT drive, data is written on the tape in dozens of straight-line (linear) tracks. Some cartridges can hold 70GB of data, using data compression. A variant of DLT technology, called SuperDLT, makes it possible to store upwards of 100GB on a single cartridge. Current systems generate between 30–32MB/s transfer rates, and can store between 200–300GB per tape. (It should be interesting to see what will happen to the tape market with IBM's new 400GB disks.)

DLT is one of several technologies developed in recent years to increase the data transfer rates and storage capacity of computer tape drives. Some examples of competing devices include the linear tape open (LTO) drive, the advanced intelligent tape (AIT) drive, and the Mammoth drive. Tape still provides the largest, least expensive format for storing data.

The LTO Specification

Linear Tape-Open (LTO) is an open standard for a backup tape system, providing formats for both fast data access and high storage capacity, developed jointly by Hewlett-Packard, IBM, and Seagate. IBM released the first LTO products in August, 2000. Standardization means that tapes will work on drives from different manufacturers. LTO uses a linear multi-channel bi-directional format, along with a device that automates a process of error correction, hardware data compression, enhanced track layouts, and efficient error correction code.

LTO was developed in two different formats, one for fast data access and another for greater storage capacity. The Accelis format uses 8mm-wide tape on a two-reel cartridge that loads at the mid-point of the tape to provide fast data access in read-intensive applications. The Ultrium format uses a single reel of half-inch-wide tape to maximize storage capacity, specifically for write-intensive applications, such as archival and backup functions.

Optical Disks

Since the introduction of the compact disk (CD), both the music industry and the computer industry have been coming together in the way they use optical storage technology. At the moment, writeable DVD standards are in a format competition between DVD-RW and DVD-RW+. However, we can review the main concepts relative to CDs, which also apply to *digital versatile disks (DVDs)*, for the most part. CDs come in three basic forms:

➤ *CDROM (DVD-ROM)*—Information is written by a manufacturer and becomes *Read-Only Memory*.

➤ *CD-R (DVD-R)*—Information can be written only once by a consumer, making these disks *Recordable*. CD-R disks are technically called Write Once, Read Many (WORM).

➤ *CD-RW (DVD-RW)*—Information can be written to and erased from 1 to approximately 25 times, making these disks *ReWriteable*. These are more expensive than other CD-Rs, and do have a limit as to the number of rewrites.

CDs start out as a layer of highly reflective aluminum foil sandwiched between layers of transparent plastic. A writing laser beam etches microscopic marks, or *pits* in the foil. A reading laser beam then bounced the reflections from non-pitted (flat) areas of the foil, back to a *photo sensor*. The combination of the pits and the flat areas (*lands*) results in the binary 1s and

0s of digital information. A standard CD can hold up to 1GB of information, but tradition has made 640MB (approximately 74 minutes of music) the size you'll see on almost every disk.

 The traditional 640MB size is mostly because CDROMs first became popular as music disks, and were used to convert vinyl records to the digital format. Vinyl recordings converted to somewhat less than 640MB of file space, but recording companies would add an extra song as a way to promote the new technology. This isn't all that different from the "extras" featured on DVDs. Assuming standard marketing practices, after DVDs become commonplace, many of those extras will probably go away.

Optical disks, unlike hard disks, return to the old, vinyl record method of writing in a long, single track. The track spirals from the inner edge of the disk to the outer edge. *Tracking* is where the laser maintains a specified optical path to read correct information. The reading laser tracks along the spiral, reading a 1 for reflective surfaces, or a 0 for non-reflective surfaces.

CLV and CAV

A problem with audio CDs is that the surface at the outer edge moves faster than the surface near the center, making music sound slower and slower as the laser reads data closer and closer to the spindle motor. To overcome this, audio CDs use a process called *Constant Linear Velocity (CLV)*. As the reading laser moves inward, the revolutions per minute of the spindle motor increase. A mechanical feedback system works to sustain an exact velocity (speed) as the reading laser moves closer or farther from the center. Unfortunately, this is an expensive manufacturing process.

Data disks, distinguished as CDROMs, developed a different method of handling velocity. *Constant Angular Velocity (CAV)* uses a small buffer to vary the data stream through a microprocessor. In other words, it doesn't matter how slow or fast data enters the buffer (from variable surface velocity) because the data coming out of the buffer is adjusted for speed.

A feature of the CAV process is that information regarding the mechanical environment is included with the data being stored. This means that the CDROM is constantly correcting itself for speed and signal strength, resulting in extremely reliable data reads. With the CLV CD, the spindle motor uses a mechanical process to adjust the head mechanism as it moves closer to or farther from the center, keeping speed constant.

The two methods used with CDs for handling variable surface velocity are CLV, where the speed of the spindle motor is controlled, and CAV, where processing adjusts the data stream.

The distinguishing feature of a data CD is that it reads information in segments that can be located anywhere on the disk, much like random access to a hard drive. Audio CDs are more like the sequential reads of a tape backup unit. The *seek*, or *access* time, is how fast the reading laser can be repositioned at the start of a requested segment of data. Repositioning doesn't matter on an audio CD, but on a typical data CD, the average access time is approximately 95ms (milliseconds) on a 24x drive. A typical hard drive has an average seek time of 4–10ms.

CD-R

The original CDROM worked with actual pits that were "burned" into the surface of a piece of foil by the manufacturer. To give consumers the ability to write CDs without putting someone's eye out, CD-Rs use a type of organic dye (not to be confused with a chip die, or engraving stamp). The dye is layered into the plastic of the disk, and heat from the laser changes the reflective properties of the dye as it passes by.

After the dye particle changes, it stays that way. Once again, reflection equates to 1 and less reflection equates to 0. Different colors of dye have different properties. Gold-green has a rated life of 10 years. Silver-blue has a rated life of 100 years. Reading a disk is a simple sweep over a disk, but to write a disk, the laser has to generate a certain temperature to change the dye, which takes time. Original 1x CD-Rs could take up to 90 minutes to write an entire disk. Current disks are much faster.

Transfer Ratios

Original specifications are usually referred to as a 1:1 ratio, written as 1x. In other words, the first AGP specification was 1x (sometimes X1), and the first CD players operated at 1x speeds (that is, one-to-one). Each stage of the technology evolves to increase performance ratios with a multiplier. When we say a CD "burner" is rated at 24x, we mean that the writing process takes place 24 times faster than the original technology. Generally speaking, 1x is roughly equal to a transfer rate of 150KB/s, or about 9MB per minute.

Increasing the spin velocity and size of the buffer in a CAV CD drive multiplies the throughput from the original buffer speed. Various multiples led to the designation of 2x, 4x, 16x, and so on. Audio CDs slow down the buffer for music, but data CDs favor faster throughput. A so-called 100× CD actually copies data to the hard drive before reading it.

 If the stream of data to be written to a CD-R isn't uniform, any interruption in the data flow destroys the CD. Writing or "burning" software uses either a series of buffers to ensure data continuity, or creates an image of the data as it will appear on the disk. It then reads out the image in a steady, continuous stream.

Performance specifications are commonly listed as a speed ratio of CD-R (write once), CD-RW (write many times), and CDROM (play only). Using the "X" numbers as multipliers of the original technology speeds, a 16×10×40× CD drive has three different speeds, according to the feature being used. This example demonstrates a 16:1 multiplier in writing to a CD-R disk, a 10:1 ratio in writing to an RW disk, and that the drive can play a CDROM at a 40:1 ratio, or forty times the speed of the original CD drives.

Troubleshooting

In some cases, a CD-RW drive doesn't write a disk at the rated speed. Before replacing the drive, consider that writing speed is also a function of the disk itself. Note that CD-Rs are rated according to how quickly the dye can be heated and cooled. For example, if the drive is rated at a 16× write speed, but the disk is only an 8× disk, the writing process is limited to 8×, regardless of the drive capability. This can sometimes happen when a drive has been upgraded but the user still has older disks left over.

Secondly, the writing process is linked to the writing software program. Various "burning" programs have settings for speeds and buffering. If the drive doesn't automatically detect the correct speed, then the user has to set the writing speed manually. Many drives have built-in circuitry to maintain a correct speed. As the drive becomes older and parts begin to wear out, the circuitry attempts to keep the drive at its original speed. When the circuitry can no longer compensate, the drive simply stops.

Although dust is the main problem in optical drives, a can of compressed air can usually keep them clean. However, because optical disks use transparent plastic around a data layer, a smudge, scratch, or anything that impairs the optical transparency generates read errors. A good nonabrasive plastic polish, such as those found in automotive stores, can sometimes buff out minor scratches. There are also small machines (such as Disk Doctor) that work well for minor repairs. In a major emergency, you can also use peanut butter (the oil film fills in the scratches and is highly transparent).

DVDs

DVDs were initially developed for the movie industry, and so people sometimes think the "V" stands for "video." However, because the disks are so versatile, they're more properly called *digital versatile disks*. Like CDs, we have DVDs for movies and music, and DVD-ROMs for computer information. Much the way music CD players can't read the data tracks of a CDROM, a music/video DVD is designed to work only with an audio/video (A/V) player. Likewise, a computer can read both data and music tracks on a CDROM, and so too can a computer's DVD drive.

MPEG Formats

The Motion Picture Experts Group (MPEG) is another bunch of people who set standards. MPEG files, .MOV files, and .AVI files are all specifications for storage and/or compression. MPEG-1 was designed mostly for small images (352×240) transferring at 1.5MB/s. MPEG-1 works well with animated .GIF images on Web sites.

MPEG-2 (the second version) incorporated support for High-Definition TV (HDTV) and resolutions up to 1,920×1,152. This release allowed for 135 minutes of video, with 3 channels of digital audio and 4 channels of subtitles. By only using 1 audio channel, a DVD can store more than 160 minutes of video. MPEG-2 is the current standard format for digital video and DVDs. MPEG-3 is not the same as an .MP3 audio file. MPEG-3 is specifically for HDTV and is incorporated into MPEG-2.

MPEG-4 is the next version of MPEG-2. With video-conferencing and 3D graphics taking up more bandwidth on the Internet, two things are happening: The first is that streaming applications are pushing for higher compression rates; the second is the development of Internet2 (mentioned in Chapter 10). MPEG-4 will use a higher compression factor, and include intelligent audio-video controls for conferencing. At the moment, the two leading streaming media companies are RealNetworks and Microsoft. Following closely behind them is Apple Computer, using its QuickTime format. Version 6 may increase the market share for QuickTime, given that it supports the MPEG-4 format.

All DVDs require bus mastering, and connect to a PCI bus, not an ISA bus. If the drive is used to play video, it also requires an MPEG decoder. The decoder, usually a hardware device, would normally require a slot in the bus. To conserve slots, many decoders are integrated onto video cards.

The photo sensor connects to a digital-to-analog converter (DAC) for music and video. For computer data and digital monitors, the information continues straight through in digital format. Computer DVD drives use the ATA/ATAPI interface, with a dual-connector 40-pin cable, and they require configuration as either a master or slave (primary or secondary) drive.

A DVD can hold approximately 17GB of data, which is pretty impressive compared to a 700MB CDROM or a 1.44MB floppy disk. A single disk can easily store 133 minutes of high-definition video, the accompanying Dolby

5.1 soundtrack in eight different languages, and subtitles for 32 additional languages. How does a DVD hold so much data? Actually, three factors are involved: more efficient error detection and compression, higher precision manufacturing, and multiple recording layers.

CDs and DVDs both start out as polycarbonate disks 12 centimeters in diameter, and approximately 1.2 millimeters thick. Each type of disk stores data on a long track, radiating out from the center of the disk to its edge. Both use light reflected from pits or bumps (or dye, on writeable disks) on the track to read data. However, at that point, the similarities begin to diverge.

One CD track is approximately 1,600 nanometers wide. A DVD track is 740 nanometers wide. Remember that a human hair is about 15,000 nanometers wide. If we were to cut a hair lengthwise into 10 separate strips, each length would be about the width of a single data track on a CD. Now take each of those pieces and cut them in half, lengthwise, again. The resulting strips of hair would be about the width of a single track on a DVD. That's small! In fact, it's so small that only certain types of light can read the data. Visible red light has a wavelength of 850 nm, which makes it wider than a DVD track. The next step, in terms of shorter frequencies, puts us into the infrared zone and that is where we have to be to read DVDs.

Okay, so a DVD track is narrow, but how long is it? If we were to straighten one out, it would be over 7 miles long. Now consider this: Not only can we record on both sides of a DVD, but we can also record multiple layers on each side. A single-layer DVD has what's called the primary layer. We can put a primary layer on both sides of a disk. Dual-layer DVDs have a second semi-transparent layer on top of each primary layer. Typically, the track on the second layer spirals in the opposite direction as the primary layer, moving from the outer rim to the center of the disk. The reading assembly shifts the focal point of the light beam so as to read each layer. In other words, the light reads the primary layer spiraling one way, then shifts the focal length and reads the other layer, spiraling back the other way. Laying out all the tracks on all the layers of a dual-layer DVD would make a line 30 miles long!

Much like CDROM drives, DVD drives also require speed compensation. It's like being on a merry-go-round. At the center, you aren't moving very fast. As you move toward the outer edge you go faster. To read the data accurately, the drive must pass the head (laser/receiver assembly) over each track at a constant velocity. As the laser moves outward from the center of a disk, the drive speeds up.

A communications satellite in a descending orbit works on the opposite principle of centrifugal force. Far out in space, the orbit is at one speed, much like twirling a set of keys at the end of a long chain. As the chain wraps around your finger, or the satellite comes closer to Earth, both the keys and the satellite speed up.

A DVD drive uses a spindle motor similar to the motors used in hard drives. However, the motor controls not only the speed of the head assembly moving in or out across the disk, it also controls the speed at which the disk spins.

Although the spindle motor is precise, the motor controlling the laser/receiver assembly is even more precise. The laser assembly changes focal points in microseconds, so as to read data from different layers. It must be able to move in sub-micron increments so that the head can follow the track as it spirals around. Add to all of this the capability to read CDs, which require a completely different type of drive, and we can really appreciate the capabilities of a common DVD drive.

Troubleshooting—Optical Disks and Drives

Given the engineering complexities, you might be wondering how to troubleshoot a DVD drive. After all, your Series-1, revision 2.2 eyeball and a #10 screwdriver probably aren't going to do the trick. Actually, troubleshooting DVDs is relatively simple, because there isn't much you can really do. Basically, if the disk is severely scratched or warped, it's a write-off. If you suspect the drive is the problem, try using a disk that you know is good.

Fortunately, DVD drives are pretty much bulletproof and you won't run across many problems. If you do, your repair options will be exhausted in about five minutes, and then it's time to toss and replace. Check the cables and connections. Blow out any dust with a can of compressed air, and clean the reading lens with a cleaning disk (not a cloth!). As with any peripheral drive, you might also try reinstalling the software drivers. If the drive still doesn't work, toss it in the circular file and replace it with a shiny new one.

Flash Memory

We know that RAM is made up of transistors and capacitors that require electrical current to maintain the status of a switch. We also know that a magnetic disk uses read-write heads to store a small magnetic field. Flash memory uses battery power to perform a read-write function, but stores information in transistors without power. How?

Quantum physics was first proposed in the early 1920s, as a theory for how the universe operates at extremely small levels. Einstein and Bohr, along with other famous scientists, worked out some of the original principles. Like electricity, we can now work with repeatable phenomena even though we still don't quite understand why they take place. As strange as it may seem, flash memory works with something called the Fowler-Nordheim tunneling effect. In a nutshell, electrons can influence other electrons across a barrier.

We briefly discussed transistors in Chapter 4, explaining that a control lead (gate) applies an increased charge of a certain polarity to a middle area between two oppositely charge sections. Memory cards are essentially two layers of electronics. Something like a transistor makes up one layer, with each transistor's control gate making up the other layer. There's a semi-conductive barrier between the two layers. When a charge is applied to the top layer, the tunneling effect causes electrons to pass through the barrier, changing the charge in the underlying transistor. The electrons can't get out because of the barrier. Certain electronics monitor how much charge exists. If that charge is less than one amount, it represents a 0; if there's more charge, it represents a 1.

The difference between ROM, PROM, EPROM, EEPROM, and Flash memory lies in two things. The first has to do with whether we change all the transistors at once, only a line (block) of transistors, or each individual transistor. The second has to do with the electrical method we use to make those changes. PROMs use a jolt of electricity. EEPROMs use ultraviolet light as the electrical source. Flash memory cards use regular DC current to change individual transistors.

The four most popular types of flash memory at the moment are CompactFlash, SmartMedia, Sony's MemoryStick, and ATA Data Flash. Table 8.4 shows the way that these memory cards interface with a device, as well as their varying amounts of storage memory.

The most popular types of flash memory cards for use in digital cameras are CompactFlash (CF), SmartMedia (SM), Memory Stick (MS), MultiMediaCard (MMC), Secure Digital (SD), and xD-Picture Card (xD) .

Table 8.4 Flash Memory Types and Storage

Card Name	Interface	Storage
ATA DataFlash (microdrive)	PC card, Type II (Hitachi)	350MB–4GB
CompactFlash	Proprietary Type 1, Type II	8MB–2GB (FAT16) 4GB (FAT32)
Smart Media	Fujifilm and Olympus	2–128MB (replaced by xD Picture Card)
xD Picture Card	Proprietary	16–512MB
Sony Memory Stick Memory Stick Pro	Proprietary (not compatible with MS)	4–128MB 256MB–1GB
Secure Digital (SD) MultiMedia Card (MMC)	Same form factor but different internals	4MB–1GB
Mini SD	Proprietary	16–256MB

Memory capacities continue to increase. Capacities are as of 2003.

Logic Gates

Have you ever wondered how a microprocessor actually thinks? How does it know something is true or false? How does it distinguish between AND and OR, TRUE and FALSE? Microprocessors have an area on their die that's taken up by *logic gates*. These gates are extremely small electronic components somewhat like transistors. The fundamental unit of a digital circuit, most logic gates have 2 input terminals and 1 output terminal, along with a single evaluation instruction for the comparative voltage levels at the input terminals. If the voltage is the same, the output sends a signal. If the voltage is different, the output sends a different signal. The output signals can represent a 1 or a 0.

There are seven basic logic gates: AND, OR, XOR, NOT, NAND, NOR, and XNOR. SmartMedia cards use NAND gates, but other EEPROM chips can be NOR-type chips. NAND technology has a write-erase advantage in storage processes, making it ideal for non-volatile storage. NOR-type chips have a read advantage in terms of random byte access but are slower when storing information. SmartMedia and NOR technology seems to have reached a maximum storage limit. NAND technology has taken the market lead in cell phones, digital cameras, and other consumer electronic devices. Toshiba is working to produce Mobile "DiskOnChip" and multilayer chip (MLC) technology to continually push the envelope of flash memory capabilities.

Exam Prep Questions

Question 1

> Which of the following statements is true?
>
> ○ A. An ATA drive uses an IDE controller.
>
> ○ B. An IDE controller uses an ATA bus.
>
> ○ C. An IDE drive uses an ATA controller.
>
> ○ D. An ATA bus uses an IDE controller.

Answer B is correct. An IDE controller uses an ATA bus. Any drive with a built-in controller is technically called an IDE drive when it uses the ATA specification. However, the question makes a distinction between a drive, a controller, and a bus. ATA is a specification for an interface bus. ATA is never a controller or a drive. Answers B and C have the correct use of IDE, but answer C includes an ATA controller.

Question 2

> How many external drives can you attach to the motherboard using the ATA specification?
>
> ○ A. 2
>
> ○ B. 4
>
> ○ C. 0
>
> ○ D. 7

Answer C is correct. This is a question that hopes you'll read the question so quickly you won't notice the "external" reference. The ATA ordinarily doesn't allow external devices to connect with the motherboard. Technically, there's always a workaround and certain adapters provide a way to install IDE drives externally. However, you shouldn't over-analyze any of the questions. Answers A and B—both wrong—might spark your memory of the 2 IDE controllers and 4 IDE drives. The question indicates the ATA specification; therefore it refers to IDE drives. Question D is incorrect, but hopes to fool you into remembering the 7 SCSI devices (with the eighth usually being the host adapter.)

Question 3

> On a typical IDE or EIDE controller, Drive 0 is called the _____ drive, with a default IRQ of _____.
>
> ○ A. Slave, 15
> ○ B. Slave, 14
> ○ C. Master, 15
> ○ D. Master, 14

Answer D is correct. When two drives are connected, one must be configured as the primary, or master (drive 0). The second must be configured as the secondary or slave (drive 1). IRQ 14 is set aside as the default for a primary (or master) hard drive controller.

Question 4

> The organization of a platter in a hard drive is described using which of the following pairs of terms? (Choose all that apply)
>
> ❑ A. Cylinders and tracks
> ❑ B. Sections and FAT
> ❑ C. Segments and clusters
> ❑ D. Sectors and clusters

Answers A and D are correct. Tracks are concentric, circular paths placed on both sides of the platter. They are identified by numbers, starting with track 0. Tracks in the same position on multiple platters are called cylinders. Tracks are divided into sectors during formatting, and the operating system stores data in clusters. A hard drive does not use sections or segments, so B and C are incorrect. In addition, the File Allocation Table (FAT) in answer B is used by the operating system to locate files.

Question 5

An IDE hard drive controller connection on a motherboard can operate up to how many disk drives?

○ A. One

○ B. Two

○ C. Four

○ D. Seven

Answer B is correct. Notice this time that the question specifies IDE drives (not the ATA specification). Here's an example of how one question might help you correctly answer another question where you had a problem. Because we're tricky devils, we chose the same numbers for all the responses as Question 2, excepting answer A (which is still wrong). Many motherboards have two IDE controllers, each of which can run 2 drives. The drives are not limited to only IDE hard drives. The system can run a total of four drives, using both controllers; however, the question asks about a single controller.

Question 6

A customer brings in a PC and complains that the DVD drive will not read her favorite DVD. What should you do first?

○ A. Check the alignment of the head with a calibrated test disk.

○ B. Try the drive with a DVD you know is good.

○ C. Remove the drive and try it with another PC.

○ D. Check the speed variation of the spindle motor with an oscilloscope.

Answer B is correct. It is a quick and easy way to either confirm or eliminate the owner's favorite DVD as the problem. Answers A and D are incorrect because the precision of the drive precludes field repair. Answer C is possible, but it would take a lot of time and would not necessarily identify the problem.

Question 7

> A DVD can hold much more data than a CD. Why? (Choose all that apply)
>
> ❑ A. The DVD uses more efficient error checking and compression.
>
> ❑ B. The DVD is manufactured to more precise standards.
>
> ❑ C. The DVD can have multiple tracks.
>
> ❑ D. The DVD is slightly larger in diameter.

Answers A, B, and C are correct. Answer D is incorrect because DVDs and CDs are the same size. This question doesn't test you on any of the low-level mechanics of optical disks, but in the anxiety of the exam room, you might find yourself breaking out in a cold sweat because you didn't study every single thing about every possible number, acronym, setting, specification, and so on. Always remember that if you have the conceptual background for the technology, you'll often be able to sit back, take a breath, and figure out the question. There are specific places where rote memory is all you can use, and we've tried to really drill those facts into your brain.

Question 8

> You arrive at a client site and discover that they're having a problem with a Windows 95 machine. In the course of solving the problem you have to install a new hard drive, but the client wants to keep the machine looking the way it always looked, for simplicity's sake. The new drive is an 80GB drive and you partition it with two partitions. Which of the following will allow you to make both partitions 40GB in size?
>
> ○ A. RGB
>
> ○ B. LBA
>
> ○ C. LBJ
>
> ○ D. RPG

Answer B is correct. These types of questions can make you nuts! However, the first step is to understand that scenario questions almost invariably include a whole lot of useless garbage designed purely to be a distraction. Every time you see a scenario question, glance at the responses to see what's important. In this instance, Windows 95 and the size of the hard drive is mostly irrelevant. All that matters is that there's a reasonably large drive and something is going to have to address that drive. Although you may not remember the details of Logical Block Addressing (LBA), you should remember the acronym as being important. Answer A is incorrect, and you should also be very familiar with the Red, Green, Blue acronym for a standard color monitor. Answer C is bogus, referring to Lyndon Baines Johnson, a past U.S. President. Answer D is likewise bogus, referring to a rocket-propelled grenade.

Question 9

Which of the following provides the most accurate data retrieval in a hard drive?

○ A. The voice actuator coil

○ B. The actuator stepper motor

○ C. Flying head gap

○ D. The biofeedback servo code instructions

Answer A is correct. Try the process of elimination on this one. Nothing in today's computers is built out of biological material (nerves, cells, blood, bone). You can eliminate answer D right off the bat as referring to a system for controlling brain waves. Answer C is interesting, but refers to the way read-write heads "float" over the hard drive. That likely isn't going to make for accurate data retrieval because it's too generic a term. Your problem is to choose between answers A and B. Even if you don't remember many of the details, the clue that answer C is wrong is in the "stepper" motor. Remember that mechanical steps aren't very accurate. That leaves the "whatchamacallit" in answer A—that voice actuator coil that works on principles of electronics and magnetism to generate extremely small movements.

Question 10

How many clusters are there in each sector on an NTFS volume set up as a 100GB partition?

○ A. 512

○ B. 4

○ C. A variable number

○ D. None

Answer D is correct. Although this might not look like a scenario question, it really is. All that matters is that the question asks about sectors and clusters and expects you to be dyslexic. Note that you're *not* being asked how many sectors are in a cluster, but rather how many clusters are in a sector. It's a reversal problem. Answer A is wrong, but keys in on the possible memory that a sector is typically 512KB. Answer B is wrong, but might get you thinking about 4KB clusters and VFAT. Answer C might get you thinking about how clusters always fill up the entire volume, but it's the wrong answer. The fact is that sectors go into clusters. There are never any clusters that go into sectors.

Need to Know More?

 Maxtor Inc., hard drive manufacturer—http://www.maxtor.com.

 Quantum, tape backup units and technology—http://www.quantum.com.

 Seagate Technologies, Inc.—http://www.seagate.com.

 Western Digital Corporation—http://www.wdc.com.

 Charles M. Kozierok. *The PC Guide, Site Version: 2.2.0.* Version Date: April 17, 2001. http://www.pcguide.com. This site is always in the process of being updated, but it has become one of the Web's leading sources for information on all things having to do with PCs. The articles are written for anyone from a newbie to a technician, and explain not only the "how," but the "why" of almost every aspect of computers.

 CompuClues@bitzenbytes.com—http://www.bitzenbytes.com. CompuClues is a loose collection of computer discussion groups segmented by topic. Bitzenbytes is the Web site that complements the CompuClues forums.

 Bigelow, Stephen. *Troubleshooting, Maintaining, and Repairing Personal Computers, 5th Edition.* New York, NY: McGraw-Hill Osborne Media, 2001. ISBN: 0-0721-3272-8. Detailed information from a break-fix standpoint can be found on the following pages: hard drives (pages 341–358), CDROM drives (pages 207–220), floppy drives (pages 310–325), and tape drives (pages 792–803).

 Karney, James. *Upgrade and Maintain Your PC, 3rd Edition.* Indianapolis, IN: Hungry Minds, 1998. ISBN: 1-55828-585-7. Hard drives are covered on pages 303–340.

 Messmer, Hans-Peter. *The Indispensable PC Hardware Book, 4th Edition.* Boston, MA: Addison-Wesley Publishing Company, 2001. ISBN: 0-201-596-164. This is a comprehensive, up-to-date reference book that covers far more than you will need to know for the exam.

 Minasi, Mark. *The Complete PC Upgrade and Maintenance Guide, 12th Edition.* San Francisco, CA: Sybex Network Press, 2002. ISBN: 0-782-140-750. This is considered one of the best reference books available. In fact, Minasi's book was instrumental in the formulation of the first A+ exam.

Rosch, Winn. *Hardware Bible, 6th Edition.* Indianapolis, IN: Sams Publishing, 2003. ISBN: 0-7897-2859-1. This is a well-organized reference book that covers software issues as well as hardware.

 Brooks, Charles J. *A+ Training Guide, 5th Edition.* Indianapolis, IN: Que Certification, 2003. ISBN: 0-7897-3044-8. This book is a valuable resource for reference material on Windows security and policies.

Peripherals: Output Devices

Terms you'll need to understand:

- ✓ Video display terminal (VDT), cathode ray tube (CRT), liquid crystal display (LCD)
- ✓ Red, green, and blue (RGB); cyan, magenta, and yellow (CMY)
- ✓ Pixel, dots per inch (dpi)
- ✓ Triad (triangular color units)
- ✓ Dot matrix, ink jet, and laser printers

Concepts you'll need to master:

- ✓ Display resolutions
- ✓ Interlaced versus non-interlaced screen refresh
- ✓ Resolution versus dpi
- ✓ Electrophotographic (EP) drum and relative negative electrostatic charge
- ✓ Laser printing process steps

Chapters 7 and 8 looked at getting data into the system and storing that data. In between, we get output from the system that tells us about errors, or shows us the cursor location and changing letters as we type. Output also includes the files we mail to someone, or store on external disks, as well as the printed hardcopy and photographs we generate. Whenever someone or something receives information from a computer, that computer is using an output device. If everything goes well, the information coming out of the computer makes sense to a human being. On the other hand, output can just as easily be meaningless garbage or noise.

Transient Versus Final Output

Output relates to time, in the sense that the output information may last a short or long time. The names we assign to each are *transient* output and *final* output, respectively. *Transient output* is the stream of data being sent somewhere for fleeting observation or temporary storage. *Final output* is data that moves away from the system completely and stays fixed in time. "Transient" is a fancy way of saying "just passing through."

An example of transient output is when you press a key on the keyboard and input a scan code to the system. The code exists only long enough to be picked up by the CPU. Additionally, you have no way to verify which code you sent because you have no way to directly see a translation of that code. The CPU accepts the code, and then sends it on to the video subsystem. The video subsystem is in charge of outputting a representation of the scan code to the screen, where it becomes a character. Then the screen displays the output only long enough for you to act on it.

Final output is just that: final. After you've completed inputting and the system has finished its calculating, the result (you hope) is something useful (a report, spreadsheet, or database, for instance). When you save a file and copy it to a disk, you're creating output both from an application (the file), and from the overall system (the copy on the disk).

When a sound card produces sounds from a speaker, we have two forms of output. The sound you're hearing with your ears is final output, and you store the results in your brain. On the other hand, the music information moving through RAM and the CPU is transient output. Finally, the underlying .WAV file, stored to disk, is stored information.

The video monitor is the standard output device for working with a computer. The printer is the most common peripheral for final output going to somewhere outside the computer. Characters on a screen are transient and change from moment to moment. A *screen capture* of a particular set of characters at a particular moment in time can be sent to the printer. The paper with the image of what was on the screen is final output. Final output can be stored and retrieved, for use at a later time.

Video Displays

Monitors have been called Cathode Ray Tubes (CRTs); Video Display Terminals (VDTs); CONsole (CON), which is the DOS device name; or simply "the screen." In this section, we refer to display monitors generically as monitors. The two main categories of computer monitors are cathode tube and Liquid Crystal Display (LCD).

A CRT (monitor) is a vacuum tube with an electron gun at one end of the tube (the narrow end), and a large piece of glass at the other end (the wider end). The inside surface of the viewing pane is coated with a layer of dots made up of three different kinds of phosphor (a chemical). The electron gun is made up of three different electron beams. Each beam shoots a stream of electrons at the phosphors, with each beam making one type of phosphor glow. When we look at the glass face of the monitor, we're actually seeing through the glass to the backside of the phosphor layer. In monochrome monitors, there is only one layer of phosphors, either green or amber, and a single electron beam.

Colors: RGB and CMY

Color monitors work with each of the three primary colors to form a picture unit, or *pixel*. We can create every color of *light* by using three primary colors: red (R), green (G), and blue (B), making the so-called RGB colors. RGB colors are used when we're working with direct light. If we're working with *reflected light* (for example, light bouncing off of paper to our eyes), we use three different colors. Reflected color is composed of cyan (bluish [C]), magenta (pinkish red [M]), and yellow (Y). Color printers work with solid colors (ink) and reflected light (paper), and so they use a CMY process. RGB monitors create their own light.

NOTE | CMY is also used in LCD panels. Solid materials reflect light and react differently than glowing light does when they're blended together.

When three different phosphors are arranged in a triangle of dots, they become a *triad* (discussed in a moment). The video card can manipulate the electrons to change how each dot glows. By combining red, blue, and green glowing light, we can fool the eye into thinking that it sees all sorts of colors in between. One triad, in an RGB monitor, makes up one pixel.

Pixels and Triads

A pixel is a fancy name for a dot. Each phosphor dot on the inside of a monitor is a single pixel. A pixel is loosely defined as a "picture unit," which is a term invented by Microsoft. We can use three pixel dots to create all the colors of the rainbow. Combining three colors into an RGB "dot" is called a pixel *triad* (from "trio," meaning three). The *resolution* measurement is a result of how closely pixels can be bunched together in an inch.

 The word "resolution," in the context of computer video, should technically be replaced with "pixel addressability." We're really discussing how many pixels can be addressed in something called the video frame buffer, but you won't need to worry about a frame buffer for the exam.

Triads are very small, so the inside of the CRT has a lot of them next to each other in horizontal and vertical lines. Lines of triads, across and down the inside face of the tube, form a large matrix. Lighting up the lines, and the way it's done, has to do with interlacing (discussed in a moment). Take a look at the lower-right corner of Figure 9.1, where you can see how a pixel is made up of three-dot triads. Also note the resolution and "sharpness" has to do with the size of each pixel and triad.

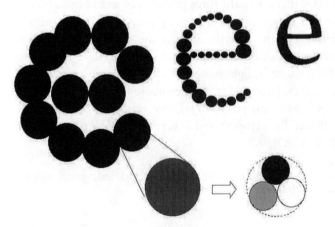

Figure 9.1 Smaller pixels mean sharper resolution.

Dots Per Inch (dpi)

If you've ever used a graphics program that allows you to zoom in on an image, imagine the gleam in a person's eye in a photograph. At low resolution, zooming in to a certain pixel level shows that all the pixels are square. You'll discover that only seven or eight squares were used to form the "gleam of light," making the pupil look like a mix between a rectangle and a cross.

If you scan that same photograph again with, say, a 1,200 dpi optical scanner, and then zoom in to the same pixel level, you'll discover a difference. First, you'll have to click the zoom button a few additional times to get down to the pixel squares. Second, the gleam in the eye is now made up of perhaps 25 or more pixels. The pixel squares are much smaller than those in the first image.

Smaller dots mean sharper image resolutions. This principle applies exactly the same way as with printing dots. Under a microscope, the dots in printer resolution are actually round. The phosphorus spots on the back face of a CRT are generally also round. Pixels in a graphic image are square.

Remember that printed images resolve with dots per inch (dpi), but displayed images resolve with picture units (pixels).

Resolution

True resolution should refer to the smallest object capable of being displayed on the screen, and therefore would be more related to *dot pitch*. A neurotically correct definition of resolution is "the degree of detail visible on a monitor, and therefore is related to the size of the electron beams, the degree of focus in their alignment, the arrangement of the pixel triads, and video bandwidth." But who's neurotic?

Common terminology defines resolution as the smallest piece of light or darkness that a screen can physically display. A standard VGA monitor has 640 pixels in a horizontal axis (line), and 480 pixels in vertical lines. We use the "×," in this case, to mean the word "by," so the measurement is commonly written as 640×480. (To remember that the horizontal measurement comes first, just remember that "H" is before "V" in the alphabet.)

An RGB monitor uses lighted dots, each of which is one pixel. LCD panels use molecular crystals to form pixels. Gas-plasma screens use a pinpoint flash of heated gas to describe a pixel. A typical 640×480 pixel screen contains 640 dots on each of the 480 lines. This equals approximately 300,000 pixels.

Scanners and monitors define *optical resolution* by the number of pixels per inch. The only difference is that a scanner pixel is equal to one charge-coupled device (CCD), and the optical resolution is limited by the physical size of each CCD. The point—or spot of light—being registered by one CCD, then, is the "pixel" equivalent of a dot of ink on a piece of paper. Printers use spots of ink, and the smallest amount of ink that can be produced is equal to a printer "dot." The more *dots per inch (dpi)*, the higher the image resolution.

 CCDs are arranged in a matrix and the information from each device is read in a serial process. CMOS imaging takes advantage of a different structure, and allows data to be read from the entire grid (matrix) at once. For the moment, CCD imaging has a greater market share than CMOS imaging. A scanner acquires an image and, during the process, limits each dot of the image to the size of the CCD. A printer outputs an image already in memory. Regardless of the resolution of the already-acquired image, the printer limits the dots of the image to the size of ink spots.

 Both printers and scanners measure output resolution in dots per inch (dpi). Monitors measure resolution in pixels. However, remember that scanners measure *optical* resolution in pixels, because the CCDs are reading (input) points of light.

Optical resolution is an input resolution. "Dots per inch" is an output resolution. Optical resolution takes place while the scanner is reading in data. When the scanner stores the resulting file (output), the optical resolution becomes the horizontal dpi measurement.

Color Resolution

Different graphics modes also can display varying numbers of colors. We use a third number to refer to the number of colors associated with pixel resolution. A monitor resolution of 640×480×256 means that the monitor uses 640 pixels horizontally by 480 pixels vertically, and can display 256 colors. The Super Video Graphics Array (SVGA) standard is typically 1,280 by 1,024 pixels (1,280×1,024) or 1,600 by 1,200 (1,600×1,200).

CRT monitors are capable of displaying a range of resolutions and scaling them to fit the screen. Most LCD panels have a fixed number of crystals, leading to a typical resolution of 1,024×768. Generally, LCD monitors can display only one resolution at full-screen size, using one cell per pixel. (Actually, LCD panels can be set to display at lower resolutions, and in some cases higher resolutions, but the resulting image quality may become unstable.)

The usual way to achieve lower resolutions is to use only a portion of the screen, and then use software to re-scale the images to fill the screen. This can lead to jagged edges (aliasing) in text, lines, and fine details, making the process more suited to photographs. (Removing the jagged edges is called *anti-aliasing*.)

We saw an interesting question that had to do with the image size on the screen. Ordinarily, if a true black border appears around the image, then either the monitor is failing or the image controls need to be adjusted. In terms of resolution, changing from a lower to a higher resolution on a CRT monitor typically shrinks all the various parts of the image on the screen, but doesn't produce a black band around the outside of the entire image.

On the other hand, changing the image resolution on an LCD panel can potentially cause a black band to appear around the edge of the panel. The display is designed to match the number of pixels in an image, and so the LCD process turns crystals on and off, based on usage. If the resolution is set too low for the panel, the entire image can become too small to go all the way to the edges of the panel. (This rarely happens anymore, but be aware of the possible question.)

Dot Pitch

Dots-per-inch is not the same thing as *dot pitch*. Technically, dot pitch is the diagonal measurement between the centers of two neighboring triads. Because the triangles are all arranged in the same way, this works out to be the same measurement as from the center of any two dots of the same color. Dot pitch is measured in millimeters. Generally, a smaller dot pitch means sharper images. However, a very small dot pitch can result in a loss of brightness and contrast. Typically, a good dot pitch ranges from .28mm to .25mm.

Screen Size

After resolution, the next most popular way of differentiating monitors is by screen size. CRT monitors borrow from the television industry, and measure screen size diagonally. The box that holds the cathode tube has a physical diagonal measurement. The actual tube has a different measurement. Then, the actual size of the displayed image is even smaller than the physical edges of the tube against the edge of the casing. Monitors often provide both the physical dimensions, and the viewing area dimensions—how much of the tube you actually can see.

Because LCD panels use crystals, and don't rely on a widening beam of electrons, they have an explicit viewing area. The size of the screen is the same as the screen measurement, so a 17-inch LCD monitor provides a 17-inch viewing area. However, LCD panels continue to use the diagonal measurement that originated with the television industry.

Raster: Image Size

Technically, the area used to display the actual image is called the *raster*. The raster varies according to the resolution of the monitor and the internal physics of the screen. VGA at 640×480 on a 15-inch screen displays differently than SVGA at 1,024×768. Televisions (and many copy machines) usually *over-scan* the image, putting the actual edge out beyond the physical edge of the screen. However, because a computer image contains information right up to the edge and often beyond the raster edge, PC monitor images are designed to be smaller than the physical edges.

Many video cards have logic to automatically resize the raster, depending on the brand name and model of the monitor. On the outside of the monitor are a number of physical controls that can manually adjust the raster, along with the brightness, contrast, centering position, and so on.

Portrait Versus Landscape

Any monitor larger than 16 inches is called a full-page monitor because it can display a full page in a one-to-one (1:1) ratio. A monitor that is wider than it is tall is called a landscape monitor and can usually display two pages side by side. A monitor that is taller than it is wide is called a portrait monitor.

Silly as it may seem (and computer jargon is often downright goofy), the orientation of a page or monitor is called *portrait* or *landscape* because of the way painters turn their canvases one way or the other. A painter who was painting a person usually did the head, shoulders, and upper torso, which created a tall narrow painting—a portrait of that person.

On the other hand, to capture the expanse of an outdoor scene, a painter would turn the canvas sideways to achieve a wide view—a landscape view of the scene. To this day, when the paper is tall and narrow (such as for a letter), it is said to have a portrait orientation. When the paper is wide and short (such as for a spreadsheet), it is called landscape orientation.

Windows Resolution Controls

Be sure to understand how to change monitor resolution from within Windows. The maximum rated resolution is a combination of the smallest picture unit the monitor can display, and the capability of either the CPU or an add-on graphics card to address those picture units in memory. Monitor resolution takes into account a possible graphics card, video memory (for processing addresses), the system bus, the operating system, and software drivers.

Windows 9x and NT/XP all use the right-click Context menu to access the Display Properties dialog screen. The "Settings" tab provides access to supported resolutions for the installed system. Remember the "Advanced" button. This navigational path is one way to get into the configuration settings for the graphics card. Another way is through the Control Panel. Choose "Display" to generate the same Display Properties dialog box as shown from the desktop.

Choose "System" from the Control Panel to open up access to the Device Manager. In the Device Manager, the "Display Adapters" heading stores the actual graphics card information. The "Monitors" heading lists the brand and type of monitor (not the underlying graphics card). The best way to upgrade a graphics card is to install the hardware, and then go into the Device Manager and delete the previous listing. Restart the machine and let Windows "find" a new device. At that point, Windows will either recognize the card internally or ask you whether you have a disk containing device drivers.

Scan Cycle and Refresh Rate

Because an electron gun is a kind of mechanical device, it can only blast electrons into one triad at a time. But when you view a document on a monitor, it stays on the monitor: It doesn't appear for an instant, and then fade away. Phosphors only glow for a short time. The glow quickly fades away (kind of like a capacitor) and the image must be redrawn. A *redraw* is simply a technical term for blasting those phosphor triads with electrons a second time, to make them glow again. In other words, the electron beam must activate the chemicals again and again to refresh the level of light (like a memory refresh).

When an electron beam redraws a screen of information, it typically begins at the upper-left corner (as we face the monitor), and goes back and forth across the monitor, moving down one line at a time like a typewriter. Eventually, it reaches the bottom-right corner. The *scan cycle* is the time it takes for the beam to sweep from the top left to the bottom right of the screen. The entire time for one complete sweep—the cycle—is called the *refresh rate*. The faster the refresh rate, the less time the phosphors have to fade.

When the beam of electrons reaches the lowest set of dots, it starts over again at the top left. If the image hasn't changed at all, it does the whole thing over again, refreshing the image. If the image has changed, the new information is processed (in the frame buffer) before being sent to the electron gun and drawn to the screen. Understand that whether there's a new or old image, the electron beam is constantly moving back and forth across the inside layer of phosphors.

The video card tells the monitor how to time the scan cycle by sending a *scan frequency* to the monitor. Recall from our discussion of motherboards that frequency is measured in cycles per second: hertz (Hz) and megahertz (MHz). The electron beam must synchronize with the scan frequency to redraw the screen. A good scan frequency (or refresh rate) is between 75–90MHz, to reduce "flickering" images.

CRT monitors always have some degree of flickering because of the chemicals fading and the electron beams having to refresh their glow. LCD crystals have so little amount of fade that it's unnoticeable. As a result, LCD monitors appear to have no flickering at all. Your eyes (and optic nerve) notice the flickering in a CRT, even though your brain compensates and makes you think you're seeing a steady image. All that compensation can lead to headaches, depending on they way you're built, the room lighting, and how long you're staring at the monitor. LCD panels tend to reduce headaches, and that's another reason why many monitor companies are closing out their line of CRT monitors completely.

Non-interlaced (1) and Interlaced (2)

When the electron beam sweeps across the pixels from top to bottom and left to right, all in one pass, we call it *non-interlaced*. This involves sweeping past every pixel triad, one after the other, covering the entire screen once, and then beginning over again.

On the other hand, when the beam sweeps from top to bottom in *two* passes, we call it *interlaced*. First it refreshes the odd lines, and then the even lines—like weaving, or lacing a shoe half a side at a time. Figure 9.2 shows an interlaced monitor in the process of redrawing a screen. Every other row of pixels is glowing, and each row in between is black (the phosphors have lost their glow).

Be sure to understand that non-interlaced means a big wad (technical term) of glowing chemicals, while interlacing is lacing two things together. You can count on this being on the exam! Non-interlaced is a one-time pass by the electron gun. Interlaced is a two-time pass. You might even remember that "non" is very close to "one," which could stand for 1 pass over the screen. Sneakers use laces, and we interlace them by weaving in and out of two or more holes.

Both refresh modes take the same amount of time. However, interlaced mode provides a more stable image (less flicker). The problem is that CRT manufacturers sometimes slow the refresh rate in interlaced monitors. The slower rate allows for cheaper manufacturing and, therefore, cheaper monitors. The ideal would be to have an interlaced monitor with the *same* refresh rate as a non-interlaced monitor. LCD crystals provide far better image stability, with no discernable flicker. As a result, CRT monitors are quickly being retired in favor of LCD panels. (Reduced power consumption, less heat, smaller footprint, and much less weight, also has a lot to do with the change.)

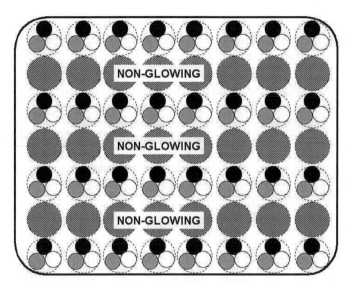

Figure 9.2 An interlaced monitor during a screen redraw.

Flicker

If you've ever watched a movie shown on an old projector, you know that the flicker comes from the spaces between each frame as it passes the projector's beam of light. The refresh rate includes a momentary pause during which the upper lines of triads are starting to fade and the electron gun is swinging into action to light them up again. We see this as a flicker (technically called…a flicker).

You can see the actual interlacing process if you stand in front and a bit off to the side of a CRT monitor in a typical office environment. Florescent lights flicker as the ballast triggers the explosive gases inside the lighting tubes. The rate of flicker in the light is different than the refresh rate of the monitor, causing a so-called *beat wave* every half second or so. Another way to see interlacing is to videotape a television set or monitor. The frame rate in the video camera is different from the refresh rate, and when you play back the video you'll see the same beat wave.

VGA

IBM's first color monitors used a Color Graphics Adapter (CGA). Following CGA mode, the company released an Enhanced Graphics Adapter (EGA). In 1987, IBM introduced a new Video Graphics Array (VGA) system. Actually a superset of EGA, VGA was designed to provide higher pixel resolution and graphics capabilities.

The VGA sub-system didn't really support any processing on its own, so the CPU had to manage all the new calculations and logic. This made VGA very dependent on processor speed and linked it directly to the computer's processor in terms of speed comparisons. Installing the same model VGA monitor on a 386 system or a 486 system gave the appearance of making the monitor on the 486 seem faster, cleaner, and sharper. This was one of the first examples of apparent speed, as opposed to actual speed generated by technical specifications.

 Safe Mode, in Windows, is when the monitor resolution goes to 640×480×16 (colors) as the original and default VGA standard. Windows sets the monitor to standard VGA mode, regardless of what resolution was last set during normal operation. Safe Mode is used to troubleshoot hardware and software devices, and therefore also ignores an installed graphics card.

XGA

VGA was followed by eXtended Graphics Array (XGA), growing out of technology developed for the 8514/A monitor. The first release supported 1,024×768 resolutions at 256 colors. XGA-2 provided 800×600 resolution at 16 million colors, and 1,024×768 resolutions at 65,536 colors. When Windows can't find a display adapter, it defaults to the Default Monitor device. XGA is included as a possible driver for a higher-resolution monitor. However, it rarely works with modern LCD panels and other monitors. Be sure that you don't lose any software drivers and disks associated with a monitor and graphics card.

SVGA

Super VGA (SVGA) and Ultimate VGA (UVGA) aren't standards, and they mean different things to different manufacturers. "Ultimate," in particular, seems a bit optimistic, given statements from IBM like "10MB of hard disk is all anyone will ever need." The common ground for standardization seems to be the Video Electronics Standards Association VGA BIOS extensions, sometimes (improperly) called VESA SVGA. These extensions at least allow programmers to try and provide a common software interface. VESA is also an active leader in developing standard digital connections for LCD panels.

SVGA can produce millions of colors at a number of different resolutions, depending on the card and the manufacturer. The VESA resolution standards range from 640×400 to 1,280×1,024, with 256 colors.

 Remember 15-pin video and 9-pin COM port connectors. Most analog monitors use a 15-pin connector, where the back panel of the PC has a *female* connector and the cable has a male connector (also 15-pin). Serial (COM) connectors are usually 9-pin connectors. (See Chapter 11, "Cables and Connectors.")

A newer specification includes the Super Extended Graphics Array (SXGA), and the Ultra Extended Graphics Array (UXGA). An SXGA system references 1,280×1,024 resolutions, and UXGA indicates 1,600×1,200 resolution. The number of colors any given resolution can generate is usually dependent on the amount of graphics memory. Modern graphics cards almost always provide enough memory for the highest resolutions and colors. However, not all computers come with graphics cards. Many chipsets include "onboard" graphics, but have insufficient memory for very high resolutions. ("Onboard" graphics has nothing to do with either an add-on video card or the AGP.)

Accelerated Graphics Port (AGP)

Displaying data involves a number of sub-systems, all of which work together. The basic display sub-systems are a monitor, a video adapter (controller), and a possible graphics card. A typical motherboard has a video interface connector as part of the system board. Earlier motherboards typically used a specialized ISA or PCI slot for a graphics accelerator card. In the real world, so many people were adding processing power to their video system that by 1997, motherboards evolved to include a new, Accelerated Graphics Port (AGP) specification.

Although a motherboard may come equipped with an AGP, this doesn't mean that an add-on video accelerator card isn't required. The AGP is only a bus, and, on its own, doesn't add video capability. Modern systems often advertise "onboard graphics" as a feature. This doesn't necessarily mean they come with sophisticated graphics processing.

Remember that the AGP is a type of bus, dedicated to accelerated graphics processing. The *P* stands for "port," not processing. CompTIA may call the AGP a "common" expansion bus. Technically, this isn't true. AGP (like PCI and SCSI) is a specification that happens to include a slot for a specialized video "expansion" card. If you see a question that asks you to pick various common expansion buses and AGP is among the responses, you might have to accept the terminology, just to pass the exam.

PC gaming, business presentations, multimedia, video, and the overall demands of the GUI environment are all driving the development of higher processing speeds and better quality images (particularly 3D and movement). When a computer is sold with so-called onboard graphics, the motherboard has some amount of built-in memory and processing dedicated to graphics processing. For basic, everyday use, this integrated graphics capacity is fine. It's only when the PC is used for more complex graphics that an accelerator card begins to make sense. (Nowadays, graphics cards are so inexpensive that even the onboard graphics really apply only to the most basic, inexpensive systems.)

The accelerated graphics port itself differs from previous motherboard expansion slots, in that it is a specialized bus dedicated to fast graphics processing. The AGP slot is usually located near the memory slots, but is shorter than DIMM slots and closer to the CPU. (The maximum AGP bus length is 9 inches, because of timing requirements.) The data interface may be 8, 16, 24, 32, or 64 bits wide. AGP slots are almost always brown. Certain graphical processing (texture maps) may still be done in system memory, bypassing the local memory found on add-on graphics accelerator cards.

Windows versions up through Windows 98 don't include built-in support for an AGP bus. However, modern graphics cards include software drivers for not only the card, but also Windows drivers for the AGP. Windows 2000 and XP provide built-in support, as well as support for many add-on cards.

The AGP was designed to deliver increased bandwidth and graphics processing speed. Based on the PCI 2.1 standard, the AGP doubles the 33MHz PCI bus clock (with its 133MB/s transfer rate). The AGP expects to see a 66MHz clock, and thereby provides 266MB/s transfer rates. In ×2 mode, the port uses—what ought to be familiar to you by now—both the rising and the falling edge of the clock. This doubles the transfer rate yet again, producing 532MB/s throughput. The bus also uses additional signal wires for pipelining and queuing. In other words, it isn't just the timing that allows for enhanced graphics processing, but the overall combination of several features. Pentium chips use a wider bus (64 bits), clocked at 66MHz. The AGP uses a narrower bus with a clock multiplier.

Textures (often used in computer games) are large data transfers, often larger than 128KB/s. With transfer rates close to main memory speeds, the port can bypass the local memory on a video card, moving the textures directly in and out of main memory. In a way, the AGP is capable of acting like direct memory access channels for the specialized processor on a video card. Intel happened to notice this one afternoon, and invented the term DIrect Memory Execute (DIME) to distinguish ordinary DMA from the capability of the AGP to directly "execute" texture instructions in main memory.

AGP provides an overall system performance increase for several reasons. Aside from high transfer rates, video cards no longer have to share the PCI bus controller with other devices. AGP is a dedicated bus connected directly to the PCI bus. With large texture information executing directly in system memory, AGP is able to bypass the previous video buffers and signal routing methods (unified memory architecture, or UMA).

Finally, AGP uses its own chip, with AGP RAM. (Some of this memory becomes "onboard" graphics memory when a video card isn't installed in the slot.) This isn't so different from the way add-on accelerator cards include specialized processors, but AGP is designed to be built into the motherboard and integrated with the CPU. Instead of using main memory, the CPU can send graphics data directly to the integrated AGP memory. This is much faster than trying to transfer data through the PCI bus controller. Better integration provides for a sort of teamwork between the AGP and CPU, with both the central processor and the AGP chip being able to access main memory at the same time.

AGP ×4 provides for 1GB/s throughput. Understand that these high speeds are designed to move information in and out of main memory to the graphics accelerator. To reach the gigabyte transfer rates, the front-side bus speed had to be increased. The introduction of a 100MHz bus and an 800MB/s transfer rate, along with the movement to SDRAM and DDR SDRAM, was just what AGP needed. The following is a listing of the various AGP modes, their clock speeds, and their transfer rates:

➤ *AGP ×1*—66MHz clock, 266MB/s throughput

➤ *AGP ×2*—66MHz clock, 533MB/s throughput

➤ *AGP ×4*—66MHz clock, 1,066MB/s throughput

➤ *AGP ×8*—66MHz clock, approximately 2.1GB/s throughput

Modern VRAM and WRAM cards, not to mention Rambus RAM cards, offer video memory with transfer rates of up to 1.6GB/s. This is more than AGP ×4 mode, and the graphics cards use their own local memory for texture. AGP RAM isn't as fast as these memory chips, but although these cards use a PCI slot, they take advantage of the higher data transfer speed of AGP. Dropping prices and inexpensive RAM may make these cards a preferred installation over AGP. However, the likelihood is that AGP will be installed on all motherboards anyway.

Intel has announced that the PCI Express specification will be the end of AGP, topping out at ×8.

Graphics Accelerator Cards

Not long ago, video cards boasted 8MB of VRAM and people who had such a card considered their machines to be very powerful. Of course, not too long before that, anyone with a 10-megabyte hard drive was considered to be a power user. Time passes and everything changes. For the moment, graphics accelerator cards commonly have anywhere from 32–128MB of DDR SDRAM. The cards use their own graphics processing unit (GPU), designed to convert digital information into pixels, and new releases of video card chipsets appear on the market every six months to a year.

To give you an idea of how much processing power goes into graphics processing, a screen resolution of 1,024×768 requires a system to calculate and produce the exact color and data for 786,432 pixels for every screen refresh. The screen is then redrawn anywhere from 30–90 times per second. Before the screen can display the pixels, they must be converted from digital information back to analog, in a RAMDAC. This RAM *digital-to-analog converter* works with most of today's monitors to break down the pixel information into colors. A refresh rate, whether it's a CRT or an LCD panel, is directly dependent upon how quickly the RAMDAC can process data. Digital LCD monitors are designed to directly accept digital information, reducing the need for the middleman, so to speak.

An important aspect of add-on graphics cards is that they typically include specialized connectors for evolving display technologies, such as S-Video (S-VHS), DVD, and the Digital Visual Interface (DVI) used by digital monitors. Popular trends today include using multiple monitors or watching movies via the PC. Integrated graphics and AGP don't always provide the connectivity that an add-on card has to offer.

Modern graphics cards support resolutions of up to 2,048×1,536 pixels, in True Color. The number of colors a monitor can display depends upon whether the colors are using 16- or 32-bit addressing. A graphics card must fill each line of the screen with some number of pixels, and the speed by which this is done is called a *fill rate*. High-end cards have a fill rate of nearly one billion pixels (gigapixels) per second. A faster fill rate also affects the refresh rate. For the human eye to see fluid motion, the refresh rate must be at least 30 times per second. Video cards also handle the special 3D processing need for lighting changes (direction, reflections, and so on) and anti-aliasing.

Microsoft has released the specifications for Pixel Shader 1.4, part of the DirectX 8.1 multimedia standard. Leading video card manufacturers (such as ATI, 3dfx, NVidia) can use these specifications to render textures. Textures (shaded polygons) are used in games for such things as walls, hair, water, wood, or other object surfaces. The 1.4 specification provides for single-pass rendering of up to six textures, as opposed to four in the previous version

(1.3). The AGP is designed to help with texture processing, but the bulk of the work is done on the graphics card.

Less expensive video cards continue to use VRAM, but the trend is moving toward DDR SDRAM. In some cases (commodity machines), both the CPU and video card may share the additional 4–8MB of video RAM, reducing the overall cost of the PC.

Liquid Crystal Displays (LCDs)

A fascinating property of liquid crystals is that they exist in either a solid or a near-liquid state, depending on electrical conditions. In their near-liquid state, the crystals can pass light. Another interesting feature is that the crystals have a tendency to be straight (like rods) in their natural state, but they twist into a right angle under electrical stimulation. This capability of passsing light when they're straight or turning at right angles and blocking light gave rise to the LCD panel. (It wasn't really alien technology, no matter what anyone tells you.)

The electron gun in a CRT produces light by fluorescing a layer of chemical phosphors. Liquid crystals rely on a background source of light to pass through each crystal. If light can pass through the crystal, our eyes can see it. When the crystal is turned off, it won't let light pass and we see an area of black. Each crystal can be either on or off, much like binary computer numbers can be either 0 (off) or 1 (on).

Because a CRT uses a vacuum tube to contain the beam of electrons, physics mandates that the tube be a certain depth. LCD technology allows for a much thinner screen than the bulky CRT, which gives rise to the name *flat-panel display* or LCD panel. Flat-panel technology is most often thought of as an LCD monitor, but other displays can be categorized as flat panel: for example, LCD panels, gas plasma panels—also called plasma display panels (PDPs)—and electro-luminescent display (ELD) monitors.

A flat technology monitor (FTM) is not the same as a flat-panel display. Flat technology monitors technically describe a CRT that uses a flat screen to reduce glare. Flat panel displays are LCD monitors of some type. FTMs are still tubes, featured in today's monitors as having "Very Flat Screen" features.

Until recently, LCD panels were almost always found on laptop or notebook computers. As color technology and the use of *active matrix* advanced, full-size LCD monitors reached the consumer market. Flat-panel technology also brought new television screens and high-definition television (HDTV) to the home market. The ability to control the size of the crystals (and therefore the size of the pixels) allows for ways to produce very high resolutions. LCD technology has replaced cathode ray technology in the computer monitor industry, and will probably do the same in the television industry.

Flat-panel displays work with the computer through either an analog or a digital connection. Although analog LCD monitors are fairly standardized, requiring no additional hardware, digital LCD monitors usually require a digital video card. At the moment, there isn't a strong industry standard for these digital video cards. The two market leaders are the Digital Display Working Group's Digital Video Interface (DVI) and the Digital Flat Panel (DFP) from the Video Electronics Standards Association (VESA).

LCD Panel Construction

An LCD panel is made of two polarized planes of glass placed at right angles to each other. Sandwiched between the panes of glass is a layer of liquid crystals (with that weird bending quality). Behind the back panel is a fluorescent light source that tries to get through the two misaligned panels of glass. In the default state, the light is blocked, and the panel appears black.

Polarization

Have you ever used polarized sunglasses? The science used in making these glasses works on the principle that most light tends to be polarized (lined up) according to its wavelength. It's somewhat like iron molecules facing the same direction around a magnet. The molecules in lenses of polarized glasses are constructed so they line up in rows leaning over at an angle. The molecules of regular glass don't line up this way. Because polarized sunglasses have this alignment property, the lenses allow only light waves traveling at the correct angle to pass, which is only a fraction of the entire spectrum of sunlight.

If you hold a polarized lens in front of another polarized lens and rotate the first lens, all the light will gradually be blocked and the background will turn black. When the polar alignment of one lens is 90° (at right angles) against the other, no light passes.

Each liquid crystal is in a matrix, with very thin wires leading to a set of switches along the top and side edges of the glass panels. When electrical current is sent to a specific X-Y location on the grid, the crystal at that point goes into its act, bending 90° and turning almost transparent.

What's so cool about this process is this: Let's say the light coming in from the back is vertically aligned (straight up and down). The crystal is also up and down, but the front pane of glass is horizontally aligned (left and right). When the liquid crystal becomes transparent and twists over on its side, it carries the light over sideways and passes it through the front pane. Let there be light! We can envision all these little liquid crystals doing the Macarena dance, and when they bend down in a group, they form images.

In any event, forming an image pattern always involves making a series of dots. If you can create a dot of light against a background of black, you've met the basic criterion for making an image. Depending on how often a crystal is turned on in relation to the crystals next to it, the human eye can be fooled into thinking that it sees about 16 shades of gray.

Passive and Active Matrix

The basic difference between passive and active matrix is the number of switches. Passive matrix has only one switch per column. Active matrix gives every liquid crystal its own switch address. Separate addresses increase the speed of pinpointing a specific X-Y coordinate, allowing each crystal to be turned on and off more quickly. Active matrix also provides better control over how long a crystal stays on in relation to its neighboring crystals (response time).

Active matrix LCD panels are essentially huge integrated circuits, much like microprocessors. The number of components in an active matrix LCD is at least three times the number in a passive matrix panel. Active matrix panels have much better contrast ratios and response times than the older passive matrix models.

You can choose to slow down your monitor's response time by going to the Control Panel, selecting the Mouse option, and then checking the "Show Pointer Trails" box on the "Motion" tab. The result is much like what used to be called "an annoyance" in early passive matrix laptop monitors. "Trails" is a leftover term from the hallucinogenic days of the '60s. (Don't ask!)

Color and Light Revisited

Eventually, liquid crystals were developed that could cut out all colors of light except one. The number of crystals in the matrix was tripled and sets of crystals were put together in triads. Each triad was made up of a cyan, magenta, and yellow crystal (the CMY colors), and the triads acted the same as in a CRT monitor. However, instead of an electron beam striking phosphors, every crystal in every triad in the matrix was assigned its own on/off switch.

Because the crystals act like very tiny camera shutters, they can't produce light on their own. On the other hand, a fluorescent light doesn't need the space of an electron gun and beam. LCD panels can have very thin light sources behind them, making the entire panel far thinner than a CRT, which is perfect for notebook and laptop computers.

Twisted Nematic

LCD panels have a limited angle of viewing because of the physics of polarization and light transmission. Therefore, the types of crystals have been modified to allow light to branch off to the sides. Without getting into scientific jargon, we can see three modifications to the crystals:

➤ Super-twisted nematic (also known as super-twisted nematic display, or STND)

➤ Double super-twisted nematic

➤ Triple super-twisted nematic

The first two modifications allow a wider viewing angle and a brighter contrast in the panels. The third kind, triple super-twisted nematic, allows for the color subtraction method of CMY along with added brightness and side viewing.

Contrast Ratio

Contrast is essentially the difference between the black text of letters on a page and the white background of the piece of paper. The ratio between the black and white is the *contrast ratio*. Contrast ratio is, for the most part, what we tend to use when we judge the quality of a picture. If a picture has a high contrast ratio, we think of it as being sharper than a picture with a lower contrast ratio—even if the lower contrast picture has a much higher screen resolution.

Higher contrast provides both a sharper image, and a more pure-looking white. Older passive matrix LCD panels had a typical contrast ratio of 15:1, showing washed-out colors and a lack of detail. Normal room lighting could easily make the image impossible to see. Active matrix LCD panels, used in today's flat-panel displays, offer contrast ratios of more than 400:1. (Lower-quality LCD panels may provide a contrast ratio of 200:1.) Slide film has a typical contrast ratio of over 500:1. Some (expensive) flat-panel displays offer contrast ratios as high as 850:1.

NOTE Samsung is working to produce even brighter contrasts by including a fourth crystal into the pixel mix. (Would that make it a "quadroid?" A quartet?) This extra crystal is set to a pure, bright white. The idea is almost reminiscent of how pairs of communication wires use a reference signal. Each pixel in this type of monitor would have a white contrast "reference" right next to it. Motorola, on the other hand, is working with bioluminescence (the stuff fireflies use) to remove the background light source. If the technology works, it would mean each individual pixel would produce its own light, making for extremely sharp images.

Scan Rates and Response Time

As we just mentioned, LCD panels have a matrix of wires. Remember too, that VGA resolution is 640×480 pixels in a matrix. Therefore, a VGA liquid crystal display panel requires 640 transistor switches along the sides, and 480 along the top and bottom to produce 640×480 dots of light in a single color. As in a CRT, the rows are activated sequentially, moving from top to bottom. This means that LCD monitors also have a refresh rate, as groups of crystals are switched on and off similarly to CRT monitors.

Some LCD panels divide the screen into a top half and a bottom half, allowing a *simultaneous* refresh of two rows, one in each half, which is similar to interlacing (but not the same thing). This dual-scanning process decreases the contrast, making the screen less bright. On the other hand, it consumes less power than panels that use a single refresh rate.

Either way, the response time of LCD is an important factor for gaming, with its animated graphics. Earlier monitors took from 40–200ms to move a crystal through its twist-and-relax cycle. This explains the shadowy trail when the cursor moved, and why the starting position of the cursor seemed to take a moment to catch up with the actual location.

Current monitors are at about 17–20ms response times, making them fast enough for many games. Once again, the gaming industry and video conferencing (across the Internet) are driving technology. A 30ms response time is amply sufficient for non-animated graphics, such as the typical office applications, basic games, and simple online communications.

Plasma Display Panels (PDPs)

A Plasma Display Panel (PDP) is a type of flat-panel display. Instead of sandwiched liquid crystals, an ionized gas is placed between the panels. One panel has circuit lines going across in rows, and the other panel has circuits going up and down in columns. Each plasma "cell" has a control address. The controller sends a charge through the gas, making it glow as a dot of light. The type of gas determines the color of the glow. Color plasma displays use three different gases to generate the typical red-green-blue primary colors.

Plasma displays can be scaled to very large sizes and provide excellent brightness and contrast, making them an attractive technology for large-screen televisions. The technology is still expensive, but with modern engineering techniques constantly improving, there seems to be a strong competitive race shaping up between LCD and plasma technology.

Troubleshooting Monitors

Whatever you do, don't open up a monitor and try to fix it from the inside! The most common problems are that there's no image at all, or that the monitor fails to display a set resolution. Secondary problems involve the image itself. As ridiculous as it sounds, among the most common solutions for a "dead" monitor are checking the power to see whether it's plugged in, and checking the brightness control to see whether it's been turned down too far.

Display resolution problems are almost always the result of a bad or missing video driver. The first place to look is in the Device Manager under the Display Adapter listing. If there's an exclamation point or red "X" next to the display, delete it and restart Windows. Windows should automatically reinstall the driver. If the driver is corrupted, then try using the System File Checker (SFC) option. Otherwise, you may have to reinstall the driver from original installation disks.

CRT monitors can develop alignment problems with the electron gun. In these situations, the image appears warped, bent, a strange greenish color, or otherwise messed up (technical term). Ordinarily, there's not a lot you can do, but before you scrap the monitor, check the various image controls to see whether it's merely a changed setting. Another problem with electron beams is that they're susceptible to external electromagnetic interference. Magnetic fields are measured in "gauss," and many monitors offer a "degaussing" tool to remove EMI. With CRT technology on its way out, it may be best to resolve a severe image problem by buying a new monitor.

LCD panels are fairly delicate, and can develop dead pixels. There's nothing you can do about this problem, other than be very careful when you clean the display panel. Never use a strong solvent, and check the recommended cleaning method for the vendor's particular panel. In all cases, use a soft cloth such as terrycloth or lint-free cotton. Never use paper towels, as they can scratch the panel surface. For many LCD panels you'll find that the recommended cleaning solution is a non-ammonia Windex or pH-balanced soap. Don't use dish soap because it's designed to remove grease and has a high solvent content. Another option is denatured alcohol. Always put the liquid on the cloth, never directly on the monitor.

Summary—Monitors

Think of the preceding discussion on monitors as if you were in the process of buying a new monitor for your own system. What would you want to know, and how would you go about analyzing the various types of monitors on the market? We've tried to use each heading as a reflection of the categories you would see on a spec sheet for a monitor. The exam is going to test your knowledge of monitors in terms of how they develop problems. If you understand the specifications, you'll have no problem understanding exam questions. Focus your attention on the following points:

➤ Monitors fall into two basic categories: CRT and LCD. CRTs use the RGB colors (direct light) and LCD panels and printers use CMY colors (reflected light).

➤ All monitors use pixels and work at some level of resolution. You should understand dot pitch and how monitor resolutions are defined. The VGA standard is part of the most basic video configuration used in Windows Safe Mode (all versions of Windows from Windows 95 through XP).

➤ Resolution relates to screen size, in that if you have a large screen and a low resolution, you'll see a lot of jagged edges (aliasing) on diagonal lines. Monitors work with video drivers to produce varying screen resolutions. The size of the screen image (the raster) is not the same as the image resolution, and you should understand the two concepts.

➤ Be sure you understand scan cycles and refresh rates. You'll definitely run into a question on interlacing versus non-interlaced monitors. If you're not clear on the definitions, skim the chapter again.

You should understand the concepts and principles of AGP, which is closely related to the PCI bus. The PCI bus evolved in an effort to overcome the 16-bit limitations of the ISA bus. The AGP evolved in a similar fashion, to offload high-speed graphics processing from the PCI bus. If you're comfortable with the function of a graphics card, you should have no problem with AGP.

Printers

Printer output is by far the most common way to share information among people. The driving forces in printer technology tend to be speed and resolution. Printer resolution is measured in dots per inch (dpi). Think of a newspaper picture composed of black and white dots. The more dots in a given area, the darker the area. Everything is black and white; the shades of gray are only less dense areas of dots. The smaller the dots, the sharper the edges of the area. The basic types of printers are

➤ *Impact printers*—Includes the daisy wheel and dot matrix

➤ *Direct thermal printers*—Includes some fax machines and inexpensive and high-portability printers

➤ *Thermal ink/color printers*—Includes inkjet and bubble jet

➤ *Laser printers*

For the exam, remember that the most common printer cable is a 25-pin male DB25 connector on one end, and a 36-pin male Centronics connector on the other. Serial interfaces (ports) use a male 9-pin connector on the back panel of the PC's chassis.

Typically, printers connect to the CPU by either a serial interface or a parallel interface. You must remember the difference between a 9-pin serial cable and a 25-pin parallel cable. The confusing part is the 25-pin *serial* printer cable. (See Chapter 11 for more detailed information.)

Form Feed

Printers almost always require a piece of paper—a *form*. The paper must be moved into the printer, where it waits for printing, and then moved out of the printer. The old printing press used human labor as a paper-feed mechanism. A human being inserted paper into the press and used a letterpress to lay down a series of aligned letters on the paper. The letterpress was then raised, and the human laborer reached in and lifted off the sheet of paper. Very few people use human labor for printing anymore, and the process has become nearly obsolete. However, we still see it in the $1.95 laptop notebook systems being sold on the market these days, where the printer is integrated into the system. In these instances, the integrated printer is your hand.

Feeding a form—a *form feed*—involves pulling a piece of paper into a printer, aligning it in front of a printing mechanism, and moving it back out of the printer. If only one piece of paper (a single form) is moved through the printer at a time, the printer is commonly called a *sheet feed printer*. If the pieces of paper are connected into one long perforated sheet and move through the printer continuously, the printer is called a *continuous feed printer*.

Impact Printers

The term *impact* applies to dot matrix printers because a mechanical device is driven forward in space until it rams into the surface of the ink ribbon with great impact. Think about the process of impact printing with a pin-based dot matrix printer. A rod of metal—the pin—must be held in a ready position within the print head. This is done with an electromagnet that pulls the base of the pin back against a coiled spring. A control signal from the CPU turns off the power to the magnet, and the spring gathers momentum to push the pin forward. Gradually, the pin gathers speed until it smashes into the ribbon, driving the ribbon backward into the paper and stopping suddenly.

Ink is forcibly thrown from the back of the ribbon, splattering all over the paper. The paper ends up crushed between the pin, the ribbon, and the roller platen behind the paper. The ribbon and the pin exchange phone numbers and insurance information, and then the CPU calls the electromagnet to turn on the magnetism again. The pin is hauled away by the magnetic tow truck and returned to its housing in the print head. The paper is left to recover in the hospital. The piece of ribbon moves away from the scene with only a few scratches.

All this happens very quickly from a human perspective, but at a microcosmic level, it takes a lot of time. No matter how strong the spring is, it must be very small. It has to overcome inertia in the pin; then the electromagnet has to overcome the resistance when it pulls the pin back into the head. In addition, the pins themselves must be able to withstand the carnage and "pinslaughter" of being pounded into the paper again and again, at least a few million times. Let's take a moment of silence to remember those heroic pins that have paved the way to the modern day inkjet and laser printer.

Print Head

A dot matrix printer uses a *print head*, housing a number of very small pins. The print head moves back and forth along a *guide rail*. As each line prints, the paper moves up one line. The pins in the print head are pushed toward the ribbon and paper in various combinations to form characters. The number of pins defines the quality of the character, just as the number of dots defines printer resolution.

With only nine pins, there's a limit to how many pins can form the curve at the top of, for example, the number 9. However, with twenty-four pins, the pins are much smaller, so more of them can be used to form the curve at the top of the number 9, resulting in a sharper-looking character.

Make a note that dot matrix printers are distinguished by how many pins the print head uses. Common varieties are 9-pin, 18-pin, and 24-pin print heads.

Home Position

Dot matrix and many inkjet printers require that the print head start in an exact location—the *home* position. Some printers use a system of counting a series of pulses sent by the printer's motor. When the correct number of pulses has been counted, the print head is in the home position. Other printers use an optical sensing device to locate the print head in the home position. (This should remind you of the stepper motor versus the voice coil actuator and servo code feedback system in a hard drive.)

Typically, when power is supplied to a printer at startup, part of the initialization procedure is to set the print head to its home location. When the print head is aligned, many printers will sound two beeps to let you know the printer is ready to accept print jobs. If the printer fails to run the initialization routine, the built-in ROM chip may be bad, or the AC power supply could have failed.

Paper Movement

Dot matrix printers use either a tractor-feed or pressure roller (friction) method of pulling paper through the printer. A pressure roller presses down on a piece of paper, holding it tight against the *platen* (the big roller behind the paper and ribbon). When the print head slams the pins into the ribbon and paper, the platen takes the pounding. After the line of characters has been printed, the platen turns, as do the tractor gears on the sides of the platen. As the gears turn, they pull the paper forward one line.

The platen has no real effect on moving the paper, so it doesn't need to be cleaned. However, the tractor gears don't always turn at the same speed, so if the paper isn't lined up exactly, and the tractor wheels don't turn at the same speed, the paper begins to develop a slant as it moves through the printer and eventually will jam.

Cleaning a dot-matrix printer is usually a preventative maintenance measure. Naturally, vacuuming out dust and debris periodically, or using a can of compressed air to blow out dust, is a simple process. The internal tractor belts and the rubber parts of the pressure rollers can often be cleaned with a proper chemical rubber-cleaning compound. Keeping torn pieces of paper out of the internal drive mechanism is another periodic cleaning task. In some cases, failures in the motors or mechanics can lead to wrinkled or torn paper, in which case the printer requires factory maintenance.

Continuous/Tractor Fed

Continuous-form paper is a very long, single sheet of paper with a perforated divider line every 11 (U.S. letter size) or 14 (legal size) inches and with a series of holes along both sides. The perforations allow individual sheets to be separated after the print job. The holes along the sides fit over a pair of *form tractors* or a *sprocket* that rotates and then pulls the paper forward (or backward) into the printer. Most continuous-form paper is several sheets thick (for such things as carbon-copy invoices) and can be preprinted, containing blanks to be filled in with variable data.

The difference between a form tractor and a sprocket is that a form tractor is a belt that has knobs protruding from the outer surface (like a tractor belt encircling the wheels of a military tank). A *sprocket-feed* (also called a *pin-feed*) printer uses a less expensive plastic wheel with molded pins protruding around the edge of the wheel. Again, the pins align with the holes on the edge of the paper. Because a tractor belt has more knobs per inch than a sprocket, tractor-feed printers can work with smaller increments of movement, so line spacing can be smaller. However, the tractor belt has a tendency to slip with usage, whereas the sprocket wheel is usually glued onto a kind of axle.

Friction Feed

One of the original single-sheet, friction-feed printers was a *typewriter*. This device used a biochemical software application called The Human Typist to produce output. It pulled a single sheet of paper through the printer with friction and rollers. Friction-feed devices rely on the friction of a *pinch roller* to catch the leading edge of a piece of paper and then draw it forward into the printer. The leading edge is the first edge (though not always the top edge) that goes into the printer. A roller mechanism then presses down on the surface of the paper, rolling it along a *paper path*. These rollers continue to turn, moving the paper along the paper path until there's no more paper to work against—usually when the paper has reached the *output tray* and the print job is complete.

 Remember the pinch roller. Laser printers use a similar process, with a pickup roller, paper path, and output tray.

Paper Jams

A likely cause of paper jams in printers is either the wrong type of paper (inkjet) or too many sheets of paper trying to get into the printer (laser). A laser printer uses a paper pickup roller and registration rollers to grab a piece of paper from the paper bin. A *rubber separation pad* prevents more than one sheet of paper from entering the printer at a time.

 Remember that laser printers tend to develop paper jams if the separation pad fails to prevent more than one sheet of paper at a time from being pulled into the printer. This can sometimes happen if there's a grease or oil buildup on the pad. Clean it with denatured alcohol.

Cleaning

Although oil is beneficial in places where constant mechanical movement can wear down a part, it becomes a detriment where friction is required. Common areas of a printer that depend on friction are pinch rollers, platens, tractor belts and sprockets, and paper separation wheels. Print rollers are designed to rub against a piece of paper and pull it through a printer. Print rollers need friction to work, so they're often made of rubber. Rubber against paper tends to produce a lot of friction. Grease on rubber is like wax on a ski. The more grease buildup, the less friction the rubber has.

 We saw some questions on the exam that had to do with lubricating parts of a printer. Aside from possibly using some light oil on a bi-directional print-head rail, most printers don't provide for this type of general maintenance.

When oil or grease begins to build up on surfaces that require a lot of friction, the most common way to clean them is with rubbing alcohol. Alcohol is a liquid solvent that evaporates, leaving almost no residue of any kind. Rubber wheels used in various rollers, areas under tractor belts, and sometimes the platen roller behind the paper on a dot matrix printer can benefit from being cleaned with alcohol.

The solvent properties of rubbing alcohol break down oils, grease from fingers, and ink residues for removal. Rubbing alcohol is a grease solvent that evaporates into the air, leaving no residue. Use alcohol on parts that need to retain their friction. Electrical circuits should be as clean and dry as possible to avoid an accidental short circuit in the wrong place. Use alcohol on any parts that shouldn't have any liquid residue on them (electronic or electrical conducting parts).

Special cleaning kits are available that include a cleaning solvent, rubber restorers for cleaning roller wheels, and pressure dusters. A blast of compressed air can blow dust out of keyboards and printers as opposed to having pieces of a physical duster (like a feather duster) fall into a delicate mechanism. In addition, you should always check the instructions on rubber-cleaning chemicals. Some chemicals are destructive to various types of rubber. Check the printer's reference manual as well before using solvents.

 Always be sure that you've disconnected components from all electrical power sources before cleaning them with liquids. Liquids tend to conduct electricity and can lead to an annoying case of electrocution.

Electronic components made of plastic usually come with a reference manual of some kind. Somewhere in the beginning of these manuals is a short statement about cleaning the components with a damp cloth and mild detergent. Denatured alcohol is a good, delicate de-greaser. This instruction applies to computer parts and external printer parts as well.

Paint and lacquer thinners are designed to take paint and grease off metal or wood that you're about to paint. Electronic components are *delicate*, so use some common sense when answering questions dealing with how to clean devices such as printers. If the component is delicate, you don't use hydrochloric acid to clean it!

Ink Pixels and Resolution

Advances in inkjet technology allow for the controlled breakup of a single drop of ink into even smaller parts, guaranteeing the size and spread of pieces (droplets). These pieces of ink are how inkjet printers can provide better print resolutions than a laser printer. However, the slight amount of drying time it takes for the ink to be absorbed into the paper allows a microscopic amount of *capillary bleeding* (spreading out into paper threads), which reduces the original resolution. Use high-quality glossy paper, along with appropriate drying times, to reproduce photographic-quality resolutions with an inkjet printer.

Ink Bubbles

Print heads in an inkjet printer have extremely tiny nozzles (orifices) for spewing out the dots of ink. A hole can be engineered to be much smaller than the rods used by a dot matrix printer, because the hole doesn't require the structural strength to withstand being smashed into a ribbon hundreds of times per minute. Not only can the dot of ink be much finer than the diameter of a pin, but multiple cartridges can contain the four typical colors of ink (CMY plus black). Depending on the color required, any or all of the cartridges can be told to put a drop of ink on a specific spot on the paper.

Ink is held in a containing well in the print head until the CPU sends a control signal for that color of ink. The control signal generates a rapid heat increase in a *thermal resistor*, heating the ink and causing it to expand to form a bubble under the ink in the well. The bubble expands just enough to force a tiny drop of ink from the orifice and onto the paper.

Ink/Bubble Jet Versus Piezoelectric

The problem with ink bubbles is that the resulting dot is a single size when it leaves the orifice, and it has a tiny amount of splatter when it hits the paper—much like a raindrop hitting the ground. Another problem is that we can only guess at the size of the original bubble. Incremental differences from one bubble to the next are extremely small, but they do exist.

To solve these problems, the bubble-forming process changed from a thermal resistor to a *piezoelectric crystal*. These crystals have the unusual attribute of changing size when an electrical charge is sent through them. This change is exactly related to the amount of charge and the size of the crystal. If an exactly increasing charge is sent across a crystal, the crystal contracts and pulls an exact amount of ink down from the well above it. When the charge ends, the crystal returns to its original size, forcing the drop of ink out of the orifice.

We can also use electronic frequencies to "bend" a drop across a cutting edge as it emerges from the orifice. With a specific frequency and a drop of a specific size, we can cut exact sub-drops with a controlled "splatter pattern." This allows for resolutions of greater than 1,440 dpi (some printers currently have a resolution of 2,880×720 dpi).

Inkjet technology is faster than impact-pin printing because the jet of ink has only a single mechanical step: the movement of bubbling. Also, blowing liquid ink drops is a lot quieter than ramming a metal pin against a piece of paper and a roll bar (platen).

Thermal Paper and Thermal Printers

Thermal paper is a type of paper used mainly in small calculators, inexpensive fax machines, and some very small thermal printers designed for cash registers and laptop computers. This paper is chemically treated so that a print head can heat it in the typical dotted patterns. The print head is essentially the same as a dot matrix print head, but it uses heated pins to form a mark on the thermal paper rather than pressure on an ink ribbon.

Thermal paper is somewhat expensive, and it is very sensitive to ultraviolet (UV) light (i.e., sunlight), which can fade the images on the paper to the point of being illegible.

Troubleshooting Printers

The jets (orifices) in a printer cartridge are tiny, and there are many of them. If they aren't used regularly they can become blocked with dried ink. This often results in white streaks, or a cartridge that doesn't work at all. Prevent this by printing a test page or running the printer's cleaning cycle on a weekly basis. Cartridges should also be purged occasionally, using the printer's purge function. In this process, the jets are heated and cleaned. Check the printer's manual for more information on purging.

Laser printers should also be cleaned regularly. Cartridges drop small amounts of toner, and so every few months, clean the paper path with a vacuum cleaner and damp cloth.

Check the connections! Be sure that the power cord is well seated, and that the cables are correctly attached to the proper ports. With any device, including cables, printers, monitors, mice, keyboards, modems, or any other peripheral, try to swap out the device with one that you know is working. You'll save yourself a lot of time and effort by simply verifying whether the problem is with the device.

One way to test the printer is to run the self-tests program. This is internal to the printer, and not dependent upon the computer or operating system. Another way to test the printer port is to try a Print Screen from a DOS prompt. The PRN printer port is always available, and should produce output if it's working. Remember that you may have to generate a manual form feed to eject the paper with the screen shot (the "Print Screen" key). You can do this by typing ECHO ^L> PRN from a DOS prompt, and pressing Enter. This sends a form feed control signal to the printer. Another way is to open NotePad or WordPad and print a blank page. Windows will then eject a page with the screen shot.

In some instances, two different devices may have been using the same port. For example, a port may have been used for a scanner, and then returned to the printer. Re-boot the machine to reset the I/O configuration. Sometimes a new peripheral installation makes modifications to the CONFIG.SYS or AUTOEXEC.BAT files. It's rare, but it happens, and it's an overlooked diagnostic area.

Poor quality, faded, or smudged characters may indicate an old or damaged printer ribbon on an impact printer. Check the ribbon and replace it. Badly formed characters may indicate a damaged pin in the print head. This usually requires factory maintenance or replacement. Continuous lines of horizontal dots may also mean that some of the electronics in the print head are dead (particularly an output transistor).

Laser Printers

Around 1980, a new technology was being moved forward from the famous Xerox Palo Alto Research Center (PARC) labs. It was called ElectroPhotographic (EP) printing, better known as the laser printer. Dot matrix and inkjet printers put dots of ink on paper. A laser printer also puts dots on a piece of paper, but they're made up of tiny pieces of plastic toner, heated until they bond with the paper. Regardless of how small those pieces of plastic are, they're still solid matter and probably can't be made smaller than a liquid dot of ink. For this reason, current ink jet printers can attain resolutions of 1,400 dpi or higher, but current laser printers are limited to around 600 dpi.

 Laser printer toner is a near-microscopic combination of plastic resin and some organic compounds bonded to iron particles. Remember that toner powder is made up of plastic, metal (iron), and organic material. Because of the metal, toner cartridges and laser printers build up static electricity, attracting dust and dirt. Be sure to routinely clean the paper path and user-maintenance areas.

The Laser Printing Process

The A+ exam devotes a number of questions to the specific mechanics of printing with a laser printer. We suggest that you take the time to understand the step-by-step movement of a piece of paper through the printer. Although the technical science behind the electrostatic and electrophotographic (EP) process may seem obscure, we found that by knowing the process we could usually puzzle out a correct response to these questions.

 Remember that EP is short for "electrophotographic." The EP drum is where images are created. The developer roller, on the other hand, is inside the toner cartridge.

In a laser printer, a page of information is formed in RAM first, and then transferred as a whole unit to the paper (similar to how a photocopier works). The process requires a heating time to *fuse* (bond) the image on the paper permanently. A camera uses reflected light from an object to influence the molecular structure of a piece of film and to capture an image. A scanner also uses reflected light, but it's bounced onto a CCD and transferred to a file for storage. The printer is called a *laser* printer because it uses a laser beam to draw a sort of photographic image onto the photosensitive drum.

Ink: How Long Will It Last?

Remember that an inkjet printer puts ink on paper. The ink soaks into the fibers of the paper itself. A high-quality ink is designed to be resistant to ultraviolet light and won't fade or otherwise degrade. Because the ink is literally a part of the paper, it usually will last as long as the paper lasts.

Laser printing uses bits of plastic that effectively are melted onto the surface of the paper. Although the plastic is also impervious to UV light and its fading effects, the bond between the paper and the plastic is degradable. At the moment, laser-printed information hasn't been around long enough to really test its longevity against embedded ink. However, for historical and archival documents, it's worth keeping in mind that the fused bond between the paper and the plastic is an area of weakness.

The Printing Components

A laser printer is a complex grouping of subsystems, all of which interact exactly to move a blank piece of paper from the input side to the output side. In between, information is stored to the paper. Table 9.1 shows the main components of a laser printer. Figure 9.3, in the following section, shows how the various components interact with the EP drum and paper.

Table 9.1 Laser Printer Subsystems	
System Name	**Description and Purpose**
AC/DC power supply	The DC power supply converts AC from the main power supply to the voltages typically used on an integrated circuit board.
High-voltage power supply	Produces the 1,000 volts or more needed to create a static electricity charge, which pulls toner particles into position.
Main motor	Provides the mechanical energy needed by the many small motors that move various rollers, the drum, and mechanical processes.
EP drum	The large cylinder coated with electrophotographic material that stores an electrical image of a page to be printed.
Writing mechanism	An image in RAM must first be written on the drum as a latent (preliminary) electrical image. The writing mechanism moves the laser beam to write an electrical image.
Primary corona wire	Conditions the EP drum with an exact negative surface charge.
Scanner motor assembly	Made up of a mirror and motor, used to move a beam of reflected laser light across the photosensitive drum.
Toner cartridge	The cartridge includes a number of subassemblies for cleaning, developing, and moving toner particles. Toner is attracted to the EP drum.
Transfer corona wire	Charges the paper below the EP drum to draw toner particles away from the drum, onto the paper.
Fusing assembly	Provides the heat and pressure necessary to bond (fuse) plastic toner particles to paper. (Unit also has a thermal sensor to prevent overheating and fires.)

(continued)

Table 9.1 Laser Printer Subsystems *(continued)*	
System Name	**Description and Purpose**
Erase lamp assembly	After the image is developed and transferred to paper, the erase assembly removes the latent image, clears, and resets the EP drum. (It does not erase and clean toner particles.)
Cleaning unit and scraper blade	Removes leftover toner particles from the EP drum, after the image has been fused to paper.
Paper control assembly	This includes the entire process and all the mechanics of grabbing the leading edge of a piece of paper and moving it through the paper path to the output tray (see Figure 9.4).
Main logic assembly	Sometimes called the electronic control package (ECP), this includes all the circuitry for communicating with the CPU, the control panel, and the internal memory of the printer.
Control panel assembly	The user interface where the printer control codes can be entered for configuration or manual paper operations. Also displays error and problem codes.

The Printing Steps

The heart of the Image Formation System (IFS) is the photosensitive EP drum. This drum is an extruded aluminum cylinder coated with a nontoxic organic compound that reacts to light in an unusual way: It turns light into electricity, a process called *photoconductivity*. When light touches the compound, it generates a bit of electricity that is conducted through the compound.

Figure 9.3 is a stylized representation of the various parts involved in the printing process. (Note that the EP drum revolves in a clockwise, left-to-right direction.) We didn't see any questions on the exam asking you to identify parts by letters, but we feel it may help you to keep the steps in their right order if you can visualize them. A good starting point is with the EP drum. It begins with a neutral charge in its photoconductive surface. Creating an image requires setting up an electrical charge on the drum in a particular fashion.

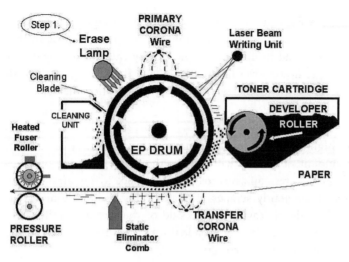

Figure 9.3 The main parts of a laser printing cycle.

Erasing—Step 1

When the laser beam touches a point on the drum, it changes that point to a "less negatively" charged spot (discussed in the "Writing" step). An electrical image is written on the drum this way, line by line, in a series of more-positive dots against a generally negative surface charge, until the entire image is captured on the drum. The stored image is the *latent* image. Each page of printed material begins with a latent image.

Latent images are like a memory of a picture. If a drum simply accumulated images and printed them, it wouldn't take very long before we'd have a piece of paper covered in black. All the remembered images would build up, one on top of the other. (Take 5 or 10 photographic slides, put them on top of each other, and then try to look through them.)

To remove the previously charged dots from the drum, a series of *erase lights* are set up near the drum's surface. The erase lights are filtered to provide a specific wavelength that bleeds away any electrical charge from the drum. After the drum has been erased, it has a *neutral charge*—that is, no electrical charge at all.

An area that can be confusing during the exam is the difference between "cleaning" old toner particles from the EP drum, and "erasing" an image from the drum. Think of it this way: You erase a picture. You don't clean a picture.

Understand that the EP drum continues to revolve throughout a printing cycle. The reason each of these sub-assemblies is a separate unit is so that each one can be activated in different sequences by the control logic. For example, the eraser lamp removes latent images, and the drum goes through a toner cleaning before the corona wire turns on to condition the drum.

Cleaning

No matter how high the quality of the drum and toner, one way or another, a microscopic amount of residue will stay on the drum from the previous latent image. After the erase unit returns the EP surface to a neutral charge, a rubber *cleaning blade* gently scrapes it clean of any residual toner. This residue drops into a debris cavity on the side of the cleaning unit, down below the blade. In some cartridges, residual toner can be returned to the main toner supply in the toner cartridge.

The EP drum must be clean of all toner particles to take on a new image. (This is one of the cases where, if you think about it logically, you can almost work out the details in your mind when you're facing a question.)

Conditioning

After it's been erased, the surface of the EP drum has no electrical charge. As a result, the neutral surface of the drum has no sensitivity to light and can't store any kind of image. The drum must be given a negative charge that's completely and evenly distributed across its entire surface. That electrical charging process is called *conditioning*.

An extremely powerful negative charge of electricity is swept across the surface of the drum. This voltage is at about –6,000 volts (negative charge) and is distributed by a very thin wire called the *corona wire*, which is located close to the drum. The drum and the corona wire share a "ground" with the high-voltage power supply, and their proximity generates the electrical field. After the negative charge has been applied to the drum, it once again becomes photoconductive.

Corona Ionization

Essentially, the high voltage being sent through the corona wire causes a short circuit between the wire and the image drum. The air around the wire breaks down, causing a corona (an envelope of energy) to form. The corona ionizes the molecules in the air surrounding the drum, and negative charges migrate to the drum surface.

Because a short circuit isn't healthy for high-voltage power supplies, a primary grid is put between the wire and the drum, allowing for a regulating process of controlled voltages—the regulating grid voltage, typically −600 to −1,000 volts. The charge on the drum is set to this regulating voltage.

Writing

When a beam of light touches the surface of the drum, it discharges a small amount of electricity, usually about −100 volts. Because the surrounding area of the drum is between −600 and −1,000 volts, this spot (or dot) is "more positively charged" than the surrounding area. In other words, the dot is less negatively charged and we say that it has a *relative positive charge*.

Because we've started with negative charges and the light from the laser beam siphons off about 100V, there is a higher (less negative) charge where the light touched. There's a more negative charge where the light missed. This creates a sort of electrical "hole" in the drum's surface. That "hole" is essentially positively charged, and attracts negatively charged toner particles as long as they're not quite as negatively charged as the main drum surface.

The image in memory is transferred to the *writing mechanism*. This is a sophisticated device that controls the way in which the laser beam moves over the surface of the drum. It also controls when the beam is lit or turned off. Remember that the beam produces an electrical spot on the drum each time it turns on.

Developing

At this point, an invisible pattern of electrostatic charge differentials is sitting on the surface of the drum. Overall, the charge is negative, but at each data point, there's a relatively positive dot standing out from the surrounding area. Somehow, we're going to have to move toner from the cartridge onto the drum. To do this, we use a long metal sleeve with a permanent magnet inside. This sleeve is called a *toner cylinder*, or sometimes the *developer roller*.

The toner cylinder is constantly turning in the middle of all the toner powder. Toner powder is held in the toner trough. As the cylinder turns, it attracts particles to its metal sleeve. The high-voltage power supply sends current, but this time through the toner cylinder, which charges the toner *particles* with a negative charge. The charge is somewhere between the charge on the drum and the places where the light touched the surface.

Think of the drum surface as a flat surface. It's clear colored. Wherever the laser beam touches, the surface sinks downward. This leaves a sort of hole, or "dip" in the surface. The dips are also clear. There isn't any toner in them.

Toner particles are attracted only to the dips, and they're pushed away from the main surface area. The developing process is sort of like shoveling toner particles into the holes until the surface is level with the rest of the drum. An image develops wherever the black toner particles fill in the electrostatic holes on the drum.

The toner on the toner cylinder is kept at a single microscopic layer by a *restricting blade*. The rotation of the cylinder moves charged toner on the cylinder always closer to the EP drum. Where there was no light, the higher negative charge now repels the less negatively charged toner particles. Where there was light, there's less of a charge than on the toner particles, so the toner particles are attracted to the surface of the drum in those places. (A fluctuation mechanism helps ensure that toner particles are more attracted to the drum than the cylinder.)

 Remember that you can't develop an image unless you first write it to the EP drum. The process is very much like taking a photograph. You can't develop an image unless you first "snap the picture" (write the image).

Transfer Corona Wire

The surface of the drum now has a layer of toner powder in an image pattern. The powder has to be laid down on a piece of paper in that precise pattern. It must be *transferred* to the paper. The problem is that although the toner was originally attracted to the drum by feelings of electromagnetic love, it now has to be pried away from the drum, kicking and screaming.

A different corona wire, this time called the *transfer corona wire*, charges the paper at this point, similar to the way the drum was charged. This time, the paper takes on a very high *positive* charge. If you've ever rubbed a comb against cloth and then held the comb over a piece of tissue paper, you saw how the comb attracted the tissue. This is a problem with laser printers: The paper must be charged enough to pull the toner particles off the drum, but not so much that the paper wraps itself around the drum.

The size and stiffness of the paper, along with the relatively small size of the drum, work to prevent the wrapping problem. Additionally, a static eliminator called an *eliminator comb* works to counteract the attraction between the paper and the drum. Just like in rock music, everything is attracted to the drum(mer).

Remember that the primary (main) corona wire works with strong levels of negatively charged energy. The laser beam produces less negative energy, but everything on the EP drum is still essentially negative. The transfer corona is responsible for getting the toner particles to transfer from the EP drum to the paper. The transfer corona wire generates a strong positive charge—the opposite of the EP drum's negative charge. Opposites attract, and that's how particles leave the EP drum. Remember: primary corona, negative; transfer corona, positive.

Fusing

After the toner particles get onto the paper, they're held there only by a combination of gravity and a residual electrostatic charge in both the paper and the toner. If you've ever had a printer jam and pulled a piece of paper out of a laser printer before it was fused, you've seen how easily the toner rubs off onto anything it comes in contact with. Toner must be "bonded" to the paper before the print process is complete. This bonding process is called *fusing*.

The *fusing assembly* is a quartz heating lamp inside a roller tube, positioned above a rubber *pressure roller*. This *heating roller* is made of a high-quality, nonstick material. As the paper is drawn between the heated upper roller and the rubber lower roller, the toner is subjected to enough heat to melt it (180° Celsius) and is then pressed into the paper by the bottom roller. The fusing assembly is the combination of the heating roller and pressure roller, but only the upper roller produces the heat.

The temperature of the heating lamp must be highly controlled to prevent fires and internal damage to the printer. Remember that the temperature sensor on the heated fuser roller is designed to shut down the system in the event that the temperatures get high enough inside the printer to cause a fire.

Also remember that when toner particles rub off a "printed" piece of paper, the problem is most likely a failed fusing assembly or heating roller.

End of Cycle

Finally, a fabric-cleaning pad, located on the opposite side of the heated upper roller, rubs off any residual melted toner. The paper, with its fused image, is rolled out of the printer and deposited in the output tray. During the final stages, the drum is in the process of being cleaned and erased, as you saw at the beginning of the cycle (Step 1).

Once again, an even distribution of light passes over the entire surface of the drum, bleeding off all electrostatic charges. The drum is then ready to be conditioned and the next page printed. This happens for every sheet passing through the laser printer.

Be sure to remember the difference between the primary corona and the secondary corona wires. The primary wire charges the EP drum so it can attract toner. The secondary wire charges the paper so it can pull toner away from the EP drum. First comes the drum. Then comes the paper. There's no logical sense to running the paper under a blank drum.

The Paper Feed Process

When you send a print command to the laser printer, the main motor begins to turn. This starts the EP drum, the fusing assembly, and the feed rollers that move the paper along. However, there are three mechanical rollers that aren't part of this process: the paper pickup roller, and a pair of registration rollers. They are controlled by a separate clutch mechanism, and stay stationary.

Figure 9.4 shows the outside of a typical laser printer. We've made the larger pickup roller and the two registration rollers black. After the printing cycle is under way, a clutch engages the pickup roller, dropping it down onto the surface of the top piece of paper in the paper tray. The pickup roller is "notched," and makes only one turn—just enough to push the edge of the paper forward until it catches between the registration rollers.

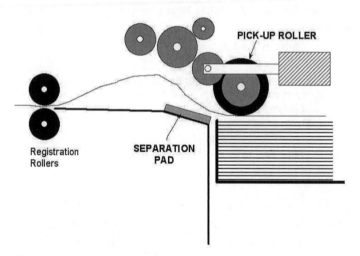

PICK-UP ROLLER

Registration Rollers

SEPARATION PAD

Figure 9.4 The laser printer's paper feed process.

Just as the paper leaves the paper tray, a small rubber *separation pad*, right below the pickup roller, tries to make sure that only one piece of paper is pulled into the printer. If everything works correctly, the registration rollers continue to turn until the entire sheet of paper has passed between them. One of the most common causes of paper jams in laser printers is when more than one piece of paper moves between the registration rollers and tries to go through the printer. This is also called a "misfeed" or "paper feed" error.

 When a paper jam (or feed error) occurs, the most common cause of the jam is either more than one page entering the system or the paper separation pad. Typically, if the wrong type of paper is being used, the pickup roller can't move the first page. If the pickup roller can move the paper, then the other most likely problem is that the separator pad can't separate two sheets.

Troubleshooting Laser Printers

The diagnostic process for a laser printer centers mostly around the error messages sent to the Control Panel. The printer's reference manual should have a section describing the error codes. As always, make sure the power cord is plugged in (at both the wall and the printer), and verify that the proper cable connections are correctly seated. The next step is to figure out whether the error is a network problem or local to the printer itself.

A bad cable or faulty internal circuit board can produce a "warming up" message that doesn't go away. "Paper out" messages may mean that the pickup roller can't grab the first piece of paper. Take the paper out and "fan" it, blowing lightly between the pages to make sure they'll move more easily. The "paper jam" message more often means poor-quality paper or a bent leading edge. You'll have to explore the various accessible parts of the paper path to clear the offending page. In some instances, a worn pickup assembly can cause repeated paper jams. In rare cases, a problem with the fusing assembly can cause paper jams.

If a page comes out of the printer completely black, the most likely culprit is a problem with the primary corona wire. The EP drum is capturing toner particles, but the laser beam can't write image "spots" to the surface. This may also be a failure in the internal electronics of the writing assembly. When the paper comes out with a smudged image, and toner rubs off, the problem is in the fusing assembly.

Low toner levels should generate a "Low toner" message. However, the symptom of a cartridge in need of replacement is either faded print or vertical streaks along the paper. If the streaks are white, it may mean that something is stuck to the EP drum and interfering with the toner particles. A black or dark streak would more likely mean that the EP surface isn't being correctly erased. Other problems associated with poor-quality output involve the transfer corona, cheap paper, or problems with the high-voltage power supply.

Replacing the toner cartridge is usually the first diagnostic step for any type of vertical streaking, distortion, or missing text problem. If that doesn't fix it, there's a more serious problem with one of the sub-assemblies. When the printed image is fused but distorted, it may simply be that the paper is going into the printer at a slight angle. Clean the pickup rollers and check the paper alignment in the paper supply tray.

Summary—Printers

Unfortunately, the exam is going to test you on the raw memorization of how a laser printer runs a print job. In our opinion, there are only a few areas on the test that require brute-force memory, with the rest of the topics being context related. In other words, if you understand computers and you've worked with Windows, then you can generally figure out the answers to a question based on experience and on visual images of how each area works. Exceptions are the port IRQs and addresses, the order in which certain files load at startup, and the steps involved in laser printing. Please read the test-taking strategies we discussed in Chapter 1, if you haven't already done so.

Examine the details in Figure 9.3, and commit them to memory in whatever fashion suits you. If you have the basic sense of how the EP drum works, and you understand the cleaning, erasing, and conditioning steps, you can generally make an educated guess at a correct response to a question by comparing the responses themselves. You should know that at the end of the process, after developing, the printer must somehow put an image on a piece of paper. Transferring comes before fusing, and if you can remember the first few steps and the last few steps, you should be able to figure out the middle steps.

As for troubleshooting printer problems, we've chosen the topics in the section to point you to the specific areas you'll encounter on the exam. Obviously there can be many other problems with printers, but you won't be tested on the entire realm of every printer problem in the world. Know how a dot matrix printer works, and how the print head goes back and forth over a rail. Be sure you understand paper feeding, and how both dot matrix and laser printers can develop problems with paper jams.

Fonts

The words *font* and *typeface* are used to describe two ways of looking at a letter. A font is the overall way a set of characters looks. A typeface refers to whether the font characters are bolded, italicized, or plain (regular). In the days of hot-metal type, three different character sets had to be created to produce the three changes in the typeface of a single font.

Raster Versus Bitmap Fonts

Imagine a blue square with black lines making up the outline of the square. You can draw that square in two different ways. One way is called a *vector drawing*. You send a mathematical point coordinate to the computer, which puts the point on the screen and virtually extends a line for a specified length in a specified direction. From the end of that line, the computer can extend the line in a different direction. Each time you click the mouse one time and move in a new direction, you tell the computer to remember the new length and direction.

When it comes time to print, the printer prints the line(s). Because the computer knows where every intersection for each part of the line is located, it can fill in any area enclosed by that line with some color. This fill color is a single color (in this example, blue) surrounded by the connecting line points. The computer remembers only numbers; it doesn't care what kind of shape you're drawing. When you use a coloring book to connect numbered dots and make a picture to color, the dots and their numbers are similar to the data the computer stores about a vector graphic.

Another way to draw the square is with dots (pixels). Starting at a certain point, the computer draws small dots at each point where you click the mouse. These types of images are called *bitmaps*, because the computer stores every single bit (dot) of the image. If you draw lines and then color them in, every dot used for every line and every part of the coloring is a separate piece of data to be stored.

The vector-drawing process mathematically creates *raster* images. Microsoft calls vector-based fonts *vector fonts*. You might also hear them called *raster fonts*. On the other hand, bitmap (.BMP) images are grids of pixels. A grid position either has a dot of some color or is blank (containing the background color). To change the size of a vector image, you simply tell the computer to change the image's stored numbers and recalculate the lengths of the virtual lines. To change the size of a bitmap image, the computer has to change the size of every one of the image's dots and recalculate the overall image.

TrueType Fonts (.TTF Files)

We've seen that dot matrix and thermal ink technology printers place dots of ink on paper. Because of this capability to reduce anything to a series of dots, an application can create a font in memory, break down each letter to a dot, and send it to the printer as a bitmap graphic image. It takes a lot of time to create a grid for every letter and to determine which squares in the grid will be dots.

Another problem with bitmaps involves the size of the dots. If you create a square using 16 dots, where each dot is one inch in diameter, you would have a nice four-inch square. But suppose you wanted to enlarge that square to 16 inches? The original dots are only one inch wide, so the bigger square would look fuzzy because of the spaces between the one-inch dots.

Adobe's Postscript font description language provides a way to tell a computer how to draw a letter from a mathematical description (vector drawing). The advantage of this is that regardless of how large or small the letter is, the computer sees it only as a series of mathematical points, only joined by line segments during the "rendering" stage. The virtual lines and the places where they change directions can be as long or as short as you choose, making for very little degradation at the edges and therefore a sharper-looking font. You can change the font's color on the fly by telling the computer which fill color to use.

Microsoft and Adobe had an argument over how much it would cost Microsoft to license the Adobe process. Eventually, Microsoft figured out a way to make its own raster fonts and named the process TrueType. The original invention wasn't perfect, so Microsoft worked on it and released a second version that fixed the problems in the first version.

TrueType and TrueType II fonts are vector-based raster fonts. TrueType fonts can be *scaled* (enlarged or shrunk), in increments of 1 point, by the computer, from the minimum display capabilities of a printer or monitor to as large as 999 points. A point is 1/72 of an inch, making a 72-point letter 1 inch tall.

NOTE Modern laser printers often allow a font to be scaled in increments of less than 1 point.

Windows 3.x includes three vector-based fonts stored in files that use a .FON extension, as well as a number of TrueType fonts. Each TrueType font uses both a TTF file and a companion FOT file for each typeface. When a laser printer contains the stored calculations for a vector font, those fonts are called internal fonts. Windows added a feature whereby it could work with printers to convert its TrueType fonts to graphics, and the printer would print what Windows was showing on the screen even if there were no matching internal fonts.

Exam Prep Questions

Question 1

> A black band around the screen image of an LCD panel can indicate what type of problem?
>
> ○ A. Resolution has been set lower than the panel maximum.
>
> ○ B. There is a device driver mismatch.
>
> ○ C. More colors have been selected than the panel can display.
>
> ○ D. The scan rate is too slow for the resolution.

Answer A is correct. On an LCD panel, changing the image resolution can potentially cause a black band to appear around the edge of the panel. Because the display is designed to match the number of pixels in an image, the LCD process turns on crystals based on usage. If the resolution is set too low for the panel, the image would be too small to go all the way to the edges of the panel. This is one of those rote-memory factoids you should just know. Answers B, C, and D are all distractions based on some type of seemingly related logic. You'll rarely see this type of problem with today's LCD monitors, but remember the problem, just in case.

Question 2

> What is the standard resolution for a VGA monitor?
>
> ○ A. 480 horizontal × 640 vertical
>
> ○ B. 800 horizontal × 600 vertical
>
> ○ C. 640 horizontal × 480 vertical
>
> ○ D. 600 horizontal × 400 vertical

Answer C is correct. A standard VGA monitor has a resolution of 640 pixels horizontally and 480 pixels vertically. We use the × to mean the word "by," so the measurement is commonly written as 640×480. The other answers are invalid VGA screen resolutions.

Question 3

> What is a pixel?
>
> ○ A. A dot of ink on a page
>
> ○ B. A 1-micron unit of image
>
> ○ C. A fairy-like creature
>
> ○ D. A single picture unit

Answer D is correct. Microsoft invented the term "pixel" to mean a single picture unit. Pixels are used mostly in image resolutions where some kind of light is involved. Answer A is incorrect because dots per inch (dpi) are used where some kind of ink is involved. Answer B is incorrect because a pixel really doesn't have a particular measurement. It's a descriptive word for a single point in an image, and almost always applies to electronic representations. Depending on resolution, the actual size can vary, so it isn't always 1 micron.

Question 4

> How many times does the electron beam sweep from top to bottom to fully refresh an interlaced monitor's screen?
>
> ○ A. Two
>
> ○ B. One
>
> ○ C. Four
>
> ○ D. None of the above

Answer A is correct. Interlaced mode means the electron beam sweeps from top to bottom, taking two passes to do so. First it refreshes the odd lines, and then the even lines. Non-interlaced mode is where the beam moves across the tube only one time.

Question 5

> What is the purpose of the erase lamp in a laser printer?
>
> ○ A. The erase lamp places spaces between dots.
>
> ○ B. The erase lamp removes toner from the drum.
>
> ○ C. The erase lamp allows printing of special fonts.
>
> ○ D. The erase lamp resets the photosensitive drum to clear.

Answer D is correct. The laser beam writes a preliminary, or latent, image to the drum before transferring the image to paper. To clear the latent image, an erase lamp resets the drum to clear. Remember that toner is removed by the cleaning blade, which makes answer B incorrect.

Question 6

The main motor in a laser printer turns which of the following subsystems? (Choose all that apply)

❏ A. EP drum

❏ B. Fusing rollers

❏ C. Paper pickup roller

❏ D. Feed rollers

❏ E. Registration rollers

Answers A, B, and D are correct. Anaswer C is incorrect because the paper pickup roller is used to move the top sheet of paper in a paper tray far enough that the registration rollers can grab it and pull it into the printer. It uses a motor separate from the main motor. The EP drum, fusing rollers, and feed rollers are all part of the main assembly being moved by the main motor. Answer E is wrong because the registration rollers work in conjunction with the paper pickup system to grab a piece of paper before it enters the main system.

Question 7

Print rollers should be cleaned with what type of solvent?

○ A. Alcohol

○ B. Mild soap and water

○ C. Thinner

○ D. Print rollers are brushed clean; solvents are not recommended

Answer A is correct. Print rollers need friction to work properly. Therefore, they must be cleaned with a solvent that will dissolve grease and leave no residue. Alcohol has these properties and is an excellent solvent for cleaning print rollers. Answer B is incorrect as soap will leave a sticky residue. Answer C is incorrect because thinner is a corrosive solvent. Answer D is incorrect because a brush will not remove the grease that causes a loss of friction.

Question 8

When a piece of paper comes out of a laser printer almost completely black, the primary corona wire has failed to properly charge which of the following things?

- ○ A. The separation pad
- ○ B. The heating roller
- ○ C. The EP drum
- ○ D. The paper

Answer C is correct. The primary corona wire is used to place a negative charge on the electrophotographic (EP) drum. This removes toner from those areas that will not produce an image. (The secondary corona wire places a charge on the paper to attract toner to the correct locations. If the drum fails to charge correctly, the entire drum will take on toner and transfer it to the whole piece of paper. Answer A is incorrect because the separation pad prevents more than one sheet of paper from entering the printer at any given time. Answer B is incorrect because the fusing assembly contains the heating roller and is used to fuse the image toner particles to the paper. Answer D is incorrect because if the paper is completely black, something failed to place a defined image on the paper. On the other hand, if the paper fails to charge, no toner sticks to the paper for fusing.

Question 9

The thermal fuse fails in a laser printer. What is the most probable cause?

- ○ A. The fuser overheated.
- ○ B. The corona wire shorted.
- ○ C. The drum overcharged.
- ○ D. The laser diode needs changing.

Answer A is correct. The fuser step of the printing process involves high amounts of heat to melt the toner and to fuse it to the paper. For safety, a thermal fuse is inserted in the fuser circuit to prevent possible fire hazards. Answer B is incorrect because a short circuit at the corona wire would shut down the printer or cause a fire. The corona wire does not have a *thermal* fuse. Answer C is incorrect because the EP drum does not use heat, and answer D is incorrect because the laser printer contains no such thing as a laser diode.

Question 10

What is a monitor called when it draws every other line on the screen, and then returns and draws skipped lines?

○ A. Interfaced

○ B. Non-interfaced

○ C. Interlaced

○ D. Non-interlaced

Answer C is correct. Monitors either are interlaced or non-interlaced. They're not inter*faced* or non-interfaced. Note that only one letter makes the difference! When the electron gun at the back of a CRT monitor draws every odd line, and then returns and draws every even line, it is interlaced (like lacing up shoes). If the electron gun draws every line in a single pass (no skipping lines), the monitor is a non-interlaced monitor.

Need to Know More?

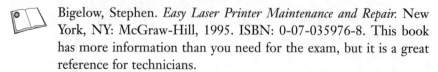

Bigelow, Stephen. *Easy Laser Printer Maintenance and Repair.* New York, NY: McGraw-Hill, 1995. ISBN: 0-07-035976-8. This book has more information than you need for the exam, but it is a great reference for technicians.

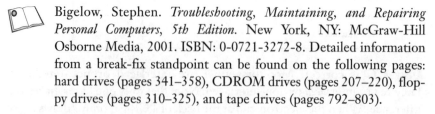

Bigelow, Stephen. *Troubleshooting, Maintaining, and Repairing Personal Computers, 5th Edition.* New York, NY: McGraw-Hill Osborne Media, 2001. ISBN: 0-0721-3272-8. Detailed information from a break-fix standpoint can be found on the following pages: hard drives (pages 341–358), CDROM drives (pages 207–220), floppy drives (pages 310–325), and tape drives (pages 792–803).

Messmer, Hans-Peter. *The Indispensable PC Hardware Book, 4th Edition.* Reading, MA: Addison-Wesley Publishing Company, 2001. ISBN: 0-201-596-164. This is a comprehensive, up-to-date reference book that covers far more than you will need to know for the exam.

Minasi, Mark. *The Complete PC Upgrade and Maintenance Guide, 12th Edition.* San Francisco, CA: Sybex Network Press, 2002. ISBN: 0-782-140-750. This is considered one of the best reference books available. In fact, Minasi's book was instrumental in the formulation of the first A+ exam.

Rosch, Winn. *Hardware Bible, 6th Edition.* Indianapolis, IN: Sams Publishing, 2003. ISBN: 0-7897-2859-1. This is a well-organized reference book that covers software issues as well as hardware.

Basic Networking

Terms you'll need to understand:

✓ Universal Serial Bus (USB), FireWire (IEEE-1394)
✓ Megabits per second (Mbps) and megabytes per second (MB/s)
✓ Network interface card (NIC)
✓ Ethernet and token ring architectures
✓ Packet collisions
✓ Backbone and backplane
✓ Hub, bridge, router

Concepts you'll need to master:

✓ Serial connectivity
✓ Client/server and peer-to-peer network
✓ Baseband versus Broadband
✓ Star, ring, and bus topologies
✓ Spread spectrum radio broadcasting
✓ Frequency bands and channels
✓ Network devices, device addresses, and network segments (sections)

Before you start stressing about the complexities of networking, remember that a computer is only a bunch of parts put together by human beings just like you. Someone wanted to do something with information, and was inspired to invent a particular way to do it. When it worked, lots of people started using it, and then complained that it was too slow and too expensive, or that it had some problems. Then, someone else came along and figured out a better way. Part by part, each area of computer technology grew out of previous problems.

A+ certification demonstrates that you have a certain level of skill and familiarity with the basic concepts and principles of PCs and Windows. Networking is far beyond the scope of a "cram" book, and we use this chapter mostly to highlight the concepts you'll need to remember for the exam. Of all the areas you can be tested on (according to CompTIA's listed objectives), networking is the most complex. Be sure to read at least one book that covers the basic principles of networking in detail. We've listed a few suggestions in the "Need to Know More?" section at the end of this chapter.

Let's start our network section by mentioning three technologies that are *not* networks—SCSI, USB, and FireWire. Why discuss them if they're not networks? Well, the reason is that these three buses are similar to networks, and by the time we finish, you'll have a much better understanding of the origins of networking. The SCSI bus interface (covered in Chapter 8, "Peripherals: Storage Devices") is a type of device management system. It was designed to attach peripheral devices to a PC's motherboard. As such, it isn't a true networking protocol. USB and Apple Computer's *FireWire* (the same as Sony's *i.Link*) are also bus interfaces, not networking protocols. *FireWire* is one of the marketing names for the IEEE-1394 specification.

A true networking protocol is designed to allow more than a single computer (not a single device) to connect to (and communicate with) other computers. Simplistically, networks connect computers. A bus connects a motherboard to some number of devices. In terms of the exam, the two important network *protocols* are Ethernet and Token Ring. The two important network types (*categories*) are Peer-to-Peer and Client/Server.

Plug 'n' Play (PnP)

PnP comes from the expression plug-and-play (spoken as plug 'n' play). It was first introduced in Windows 95, but the concept originates with the old EISA bus. "PnP" is shorthand for a process in which the operating system works with the underlying hardware in an attempt to automatically configure peripheral devices. Keep in mind that a truly workable auto-configuration process involves more than just the operating system. The DMI pool (see Chapter 2, "Motherboards,") is part of the PnP specification.

The PnP standard is an agreement among hardware, software, and operating systems developers regarding how to "plug" (install) something into the system and have it "play" (work) automatically. PnP is both a hardware and software solution. Not only do PnP devices have to be built according to the specification, but they also require a compatible operating system and compatible BIOS.

The three aspects described in the PnP industry specification are

➤ PnP-compatible hardware

➤ PnP BIOS

➤ PnP operating system

After a device has been configured, the PnP operating system assigns various system resources (such as memory and time slices) for as long as the computer is running. (See Chapter 13, "Booting, Startup Files, and Memory," for more on Windows system resources.) PnP technology allows a device to tell the operating system what resources it needs. The OS (Windows, for the most part) then gives the device those resources.

Generally, you'll have to manually configure an older (non-PnP) device and its expansion card. As far as the operating system is concerned, it doesn't "see" the device, and may end up assigning necessary resources to some other card—a PnP-compliant one. Windows doesn't include the older card in the memory resource pool, and the device probably won't work. Part of manually configuring a non-PnP device is that you can explicitly tell Windows to set aside (reserve) some amount of resource memory. This goes along with sometimes having to manually configure an IRQ setting.

A PnP operating system does not *require* PnP hardware. Older hardware won't be auto-configured by a PnP operating system, but this means only that it must be configured manually. Non-PnP hardware can still run on a PnP system.

Although the technical standard describes only the three major components, Microsoft also includes a fourth component. You may find a question on the exam concerning PnP-aware application software. "Software application awareness" refers to this so-called fourth specification.

Chaining Devices

When controllers began taking on more intelligence, it became possible for several devices to access a single controller (for example, PCI steering).

Peripheral devices, such as scanners and the newly emerging Iomega Zip drive, used the parallel port, not a motherboard controller. Rather than add more parallel ports and controllers to the motherboard, a "pass-through" connection was added to the device itself. This allows a *downstream* device (added afterward) to pass data that has nothing to do with the first device, through to the host (usually the PC).

In other words, the host can connect to one device, and then a second device can be connected to the first device in a process called daisy-chaining (from the way children used to make flower necklaces out of daisies). The original concept carried forward into FireWire technology, which was then copied with USB technology.

An IDE or EIDE disk must be mounted inside the computer. There is no standard provision for an IDE ribbon cable to run to external devices. For a while, kits were available on the market that allowed a connection to an external IDE drive through the parallel port, but the wide acceptance of Iomega's Jaz and Zip drives have relegated these kits to novelty status.

Using this type of chaining, a second device doesn't have to directly connect to the PC. It's similar to the way a single IDE controller provides for two hard drives: a master and a slave. For example, if an Iomega Zip drive connects to the PC through the parallel port controller, you can attach a printer to the pass-through connector on the back of the Zip drive. "The printer's connected to the Zip drive; the Zip drive's connected to the printer port. The printer port's connected to the motherboard, and they all go singin' along."

When devices are chained to a single controller, that controller handles the prioritization of the data stream going to and from the host. The primary controller sends appropriate information to individual device controllers. In the previous example, the I/O port controller is the host, and both the Zip drive and printer are chained devices. The problem with pass-through connectors is that only two devices can be connected to the host, much as an IDE controller can have only two connected drives.

Typical floppy drive controllers for IBM PCs and clones allow only two floppy drives to be connected with a single cable. On the exam, you'll likely be tested on how many devices can be attached to certain types of cable interfaces. For example, SCSI allows a total of up to 8 devices—one host adapter and seven peripherals. (SCSI-2 allows up to 16 devices, including the host adapter.) Always remember that a SCSI interface requires a host; therefore, only 7 additional devices can be connected to the interface. Floppy disk, IDE, EIDE controllers (and most pass-through connections) allow only two devices.

Universal Serial Bus (USB)

Although parallel transfers are faster than serial transfers are, parallel bits get out of sync when they have to travel too far. This is known as *signal skew* or *jitter*, and is why both parallel and typical SCSI interfaces require fairly short cables. Serial cables can be much longer than parallel cables, but the COM port is very slow, transferring data at only 115,000 bits per second (0.014MB/s). If we could boost the speed of serial transfers, we'd get the best of both—faster transfer and longer cables.

This problem of signal skew at high-speed parallel transfer rates shows up at the microscopic level in DDR memory modules. Rambus memory uses a serial configuration, leading to latency (waiting) problems. DDR uses a parallel system, but has problems with skew.

Another problem is that we have too many devices for the limited number of basic I/O ports on a typical PC motherboard. A modem takes one of the COM ports, regardless of whether it's internal or external. Although a typical back panel has two PS/2 connectors, a mouse still uses one of the serial controllers. Anyone who uses two printers is either on a network or using an A/B box, so the back panel eventually eliminated all but one LPT port.

Printer Switching Boxes

To use a different printer, you ordinarily have to shut down the system and detach the printer from the parallel port. You then attach a different printer and restart the machine, re-opening the application and sending the print job to the different printer. A switch box enables you to change printers without shutting down the system, almost like daisy-chaining two printers to the LPT port. Instead of chaining the devices, the switch box acts more like a railroad switch, changing the data stream to one of several internal connectors.

An A/B switch box is a device that enables you to use two printers on one PC, simply by changing a switch. Switch boxes are usually found in any store that sells peripheral devices, and typically provide connections for two, three, or four printers (A/B/C/D). Windows uses a different printer driver for each type of printer (for example, HP Laserjet, Epson Inkjet, Cannon Bubble Jet, and so on), and each printer is configured in the Printers dialog box.

To install a new printer driver, navigate the Start | Settings | Printers menus, or choose the Control Panel and double-click on the Printers icon (Printers and Faxes, in XP). (This may require a Windows installation CD.) Simply picking a different printer in Windows is not the same as actually changing the physical printer. An HP Laserjet won't print in color, no matter how the job is sent from Windows. Likewise, simply changing the switch on the A/B box won't tell Windows how to use the different printer. Both the switch box and the Windows-designated printer configuration must be changed.

Back in the old days, whenever you added an expansion card to an internal bus slot, you'd have to reconfigure the system to deal with IRQs and DMA lines. Plug and Play and the PCI bus went a long way toward making cards and devices more intelligent, but even today, internal modems can lead to mysterious screen freezes or disconnects because of the vagaries of configuration settings. To get around the limited I/O ports and the need to configure add-on device cards, the industry developed two new serial transfer architectures: IEEE-1394 and the Universal Serial Bus (USB).

From the start, Apple Computers had developed the Apple Desktop Bus (ADB) as a way of connecting several simple devices (for example, the keyboard and mouse) to a single serial bus. This same concept was carried forward to Macintosh and NeXT machines, and companies like Sun Microsystems and others included the idea in their machines. IBM-compatible PCs didn't have this capability. At the same time, Apple was developing a much faster serial bus for high-speed transfers involving more complex and more expensive devices. Apple FireWire was eventually certified as the IEEE-1394 standard, and was designed from the ground up to be used for video conferencing, multimedia productions, and other applications requiring large throughput.

Intel and Microsoft got together with Compaq, DEC, IBM, NEC, and Northern Telecom and decided to bring the concept of a multi-device serial bus to PCs. The result was the USB specification. Although USB is faster than Apple's ADB, and includes hot-swapping capabilities, most of the technology comes from the IEEE-1394 standard—Apple's FireWire. The USB port was supposed to take over from the Apple ADB.

Intel originally worked together with Apple, intending that USB would bring together PCs and Macs, or at least make them more complementary to each other. Given that FireWire was already designed for high-speed multimedia and video, Intel developed USB with slower, less expensive devices in mind. To boost the USB performance up to the level of FireWire would make it cost prohibitive, as well as less reliable. Back then, Intel often said that USB was going to be complementary to the IEEE-1394 standard, and was not intended to replace FireWire.

 NOTE Nowadays, USB is supposed to somehow replace FireWire. The two technologies are very different, but FireWire can be installed on most motherboards with an inexpensive add-on card. Some expansion cards include both USB and FireWire capabilities.

USB works primarily by putting a really cool magical symbol on a wire, as shown in Figure 10.1. The symbol then moves data into another dimension, which speeds up...no, we're kidding. The main advantage of USB is that it provides fast data transfers over a serial bus, sometimes called *fast serial transfers* (strangely enough). Another advantage of USB technology is that additional devices may be connected to a PC through the use of hubs (discussed in a moment).

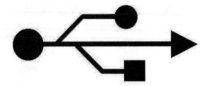

Figure 10.1 The USB mark on cables, connectors, hubs, and peripheral devices.

The special symbol marks a device, cable, or connector as being part of the USB family. Used in conjunction with Plug and Play, USB removes the need for dedicated cards and slots, and allows for hot-swapping peripherals. The operating system (Windows) understands USB peripherals as if they were installed in an expansion slot. This means (presumably) that configuration problems should vanish. USB has done a very good job of doing just that, and manual configurations are becoming a thing of the past (for the most part).

 Ordinarily, plugging in or unplugging a device requires that the machine be powered down (to avoid power surges). An important advantage of the Universal Serial Bus is that it allows hot-swapping. Hot-swapping means that USB and PnP allow you to change or add a device without powering down the PC.

Keep in mind that USB has certain practical limits, as a result of power consumption and bandwidth allocation. The practical limit to daisy-chaining is 127 devices, but there's no guarantee that every system will actually work with that many devices.

USB 1.0 and 1.1

Version 1.0 of the USB specification was released in January 1996, and provided for data transfers on both a low and a high "channel." The low-speed channel could transfer data at rates of 1.5 megabits per second (Mbps), or 0.1875 megabytes per second (MB/s), ten times faster than the COM port.

The high channel could transfer data at what was originally called a "high speed" rate of 12Mbps (1.5MB/s). When USB 2.0 entered the market, "high speed" had to be redefined to fit the new 480Mbps transfer mode. The original high speed was changed to "full" speed. Version 1.1 was released in September of 1998, with clarifications as to how USB ports would work, and solutions to problems that showed up in version 1.0.

You'll most likely be tested on values in terms of megabits per second, rather than megabytes. If you remember the three megabit speeds, all you'll have to do is divide by 8 to calculate the megabytes per second. For example, divide 1.5 megabits by 8 bits, and the result is 0.18 megabytes per second.

USB 1.0 and 1.1 provide for a transfer rate of 1.5Mbps (1,500,000 bits) using a low channel, or "slow" channel, and 12Mbps (12,000,000 bits) using the high channel.

The important things to remember about both USB versions 1.0 and 1.1 are that

➤ There are two channels: high and low.

➤ The high channel transfers at 12Mbps.

➤ The low sub-channel (for slow devices such as pointing devices and keyboards) transfers at 1.5Mbps.

Powered USB Hubs

Many peripheral devices are powered through the devices' cables. However, this can sometimes overload power circuits, particularly in portable laptops with limited battery life. To overcome this, USB hubs include a power supply, so that the hubs themselves can provide power to their devices. (Remember that USB hubs provide both connectivity and power.)

Windows 98, Windows Me, Windows 2000, and Windows XP all include support for USB. (Windows NT 4.x did not include USB support.) Version 1.0 provided a simple way for PCs to daisy-chain more than two peripheral devices by using a USB *hub*. We discuss network hubs later in this chapter, but for the moment, you should understand levels and tiers as part of the USB specification. (USB hubs aren't the same as a network hub.)

USB technology allows a maximum of 127 devices to be chained together to a single controller. The hub system uses a *tiered star* topology. "Star" means that all devices are linked to a central point, with the wires radiating outward like a star. "Tiered" means that within the star, devices can be plugged into additional hubs—one after another, in several levels (tiers). Figure 10.2 shows the way this is done. In the figure, the tiers are numbered 1 through 5. The rules for USB hubs are as follows:

➤ The topology is tiered star.

➤ 1 USB controller can sustain up to 127 devices.

➤ Hubs can be plugged into the cable, and multiple devices can then be plugged into each hub.

➤ A hub can also be plugged into another hub, leading to a new or lower level (tier) of devices.

➤ You can have as many as 5 tiers of hubs.

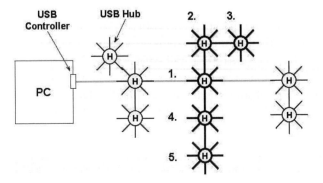

Figure 10.2 USB tiered-star topology.

(Note that angles and lines positions don't matter. This is only a stylized representation of the 5-tiered hub and star image to demonstrate the 5 "tiers.")

 Most PCs nowadays come with USB support, and at least two USB controllers. In theory, that means that at 127 devices per controller, the system could support 254 devices. In fact, that won't ever happen. First of all, every operating device in the chain sends electrical data up and down the cables. Those cables can support only so much activity, depending on the type of data. Secondly, the specification includes certain technical descriptions having to do with how USB allocates bandwidth. Taken together, the practical support is far less than the specified maximum. (Not to mention that we find it difficult to imagine a PC with 127 peripheral devices all attached at the same time!)

There is a small bus inside a USB hub, with terminators at both ends and wires leading to connectors on the outer casing of the hub. Devices connect to a hub, and the hub then connects to a cable. Other cables then connect the hub to the computer. When a hub can be connected to another hub, which in turn connects to a main USB cable, this is a *tiered-star topology*.

 You should be very careful in your understanding of USB technology, making sure that you don't confuse the serial bus with a network. USB is not a networking protocol. It is a serial interface that allows for chaining devices through the use of special USB hubs.

Hubs also provide a *bi-directional repeater*. A repeater receives a signal, rebuilds it, and sends it out again. This is important because a single USB cable has a limit of 5 meters (approximately 15 feet). If you want to go any farther than 5 meters, you need a repeater to rebuild (and re-time) the signal.

USB 2.0

USB 2.0 introduced a new high-speed mode, offering transfer rates of 480Mbps (60MB/s). Notice that the new mode is sixty megabytes per second, or 40 times faster than the version 1.1 high-speed mode. The revision kept the previous low and high channels, but there is a large difference between the two lower-level channels and the new mode. (Don't confuse high channel with high-speed mode.) Table 10.1 shows the different data rates of all three versions.

Table 10.1	USB Signal Transfer Rates	
Version	**Mbps**	**MB/s**
1.0 (low)	1.5	0.1875
1.1 (high)	12	1.5
2.0	480	60

Keep in mind that two data signals (packets) can't exist in the same space at the same time. This is true in all of reality, with anything, and so a problem arises in a USB cable when a very high-speed device sends information at the same time as a slow-speed device—a mouse, for instance. When a fast and a slow drive are both connected to the same IDE controller, the controller sets to the lowest speed. This is much like what happens in USB 2.0.

Version 1.1 hubs were fairly simple devices, designed to move only two channels of information at closely related speeds. Version 2.0 is designed for high transfer speeds, but comes with the price of delays and wasted bandwidth if slower devices take up that bandwidth. One solution is to provide more sophisticated (and more expensive) hubs, but that would mean consumers would have to buy more equipment, and nobody really wants that...do they?

USB 1.1 was often unable to transfer at 12Mbps. Keep in mind that USB 1.1 was primarily designed as a new interface for slow devices. When the technology caught on, vendors began making all kinds of USB-enabled devices, including many high-speed multimedia devices. Remember, too, that USB was quickly evolving toward a combination replacement for both the slow serial port and the high-speed capability of FireWire. The difference between 12 and 1.5 isn't all that much. On the other hand, the difference between 480 and 1.5 is huge! The transfer speed of the entire bus can be held back by data coming from a low-channel device.

USB 2.0 was designed to add the benefits of high-speed video and multimedia. (How the intent changed from the original is anyone's guess.) The problem is that when three devices are transmitting at the same time, then (simplistically) each channel takes a third of the bandwidth. 480 divided by three means that a so-called high-speed transfer would be taking place at an effective 160Mbps (actually less), with a 60% reduction in speed. With a lot of slower-speed devices and only one or two high-speed devices (for example, a video conferencing camera), the problem becomes even more severe. We don't notice speed difference in printing, but slowdowns and hesitations in music or video are readily apparent.

An Ethernet 10 networking card transfers all data at middle-channel speeds. If a mouse slows down just a tiny bit while an Ethernet card is sending information, it isn't all that important—we don't really notice.

USB would have to transfer data at better than 166MB/s to take advantage of advances in hard drive technology. The bus would have to also be able to handle UDMA /166, music jukeboxes, and Web cams. Although it was originally going to do all this, USB appears to be going toward simpler peripherals. The PCI Express and serial ATA (SATA) specifications will likely manage high-speed devices. On the other hand, USB hubs offer a lot of simple system expansion.

Consumers can opt to replace their simple and low-cost USB 1.1 hubs with complex, higher-cost and higher-speed USB 2.0 hubs, which can then step up the speed from the slower-speed, USB 1.1–compatible device. Understand that although data packets from an earlier USB device can be sped up, if a USB 1.1 hub is between the device and the computer, everything slows back down to the version 1.1 standard, including USB 2.0 hubs.

Like an IDE drive controller, if you mix 2.0 and 1.x hubs, any device downstream from the 1.x hub will be limited to the lower speed of the 1.x hub. We've mentioned (in Chapter 8) how CDROM drives use buffering to transfer information more quickly. USB 2.0 hubs use a similar process. USB version 2.0 brings about improvements in three areas:

➤ Speed

➤ Power

➤ Buffering

USB Troubleshooting

One of the most important things to understand about USB is that Windows manages the technology. Although USB support is built into most modern chipsets, people forget that legacy COM and LPT ports don't support hot-swapping. Laptop docking stations cause problems, in this respect, where someone starts up the system and tries to plug in a mouse after Windows loads. This would work with a USB mouse, but not a traditional PS/2 mouse.

Another problem is when someone tries to connect a USB 2.0 device to a USB 1.1 hub. The two are not interchangeable. In some instances, the 2.0 device won't even work. In other cases, the hub will limit the transfer speed to the 12.5Mbps high-channel maximum. When a USB device or hub doesn't appear to be working correctly, check the version rating. A version 1.1 device should work on a 2.0 hub.

Although not all USB 2.0 devices will work on every system, the specifications call for all 2.0-compliant computers (laptop, notebook, desktop, and so on) to be capable of supporting all three USB transfer rates. In other words, the computers are supposed to handle all the speeds, but that doesn't mean devices are required to handle all three speeds. If the overall system develops a problem after adding in a new USB device, chances are the problem is a device compatibility issue (unless it's just a bad device, out of the box).

When a device and hub match, try using a different USB port. Also try using a known-good device. When a problem persists, go into the Device Manager and check that Windows recognizes the USB ports. If there's an exclamation point next to the system device, delete the driver and restart the machine. Windows should reinstall the driver. If that doesn't work, try using small explosives. It won't solve the problem, but will often relieve your frustration.

Installing a new USB device may cause Windows to use an internal, generic device driver when the system restarts. If that driver isn't written for the device, you may end up spending a lot of time trying to figure out why the device isn't working. Before wasting too much time, check the driver in the Device Manager. If it doesn't seem to be the correct one, use the "Update Driver" option to install the correct driver from the device's installation disk. Delete the older, or generic Windows driver and restart the machine.

Supplementary Information

USB is the most popular serial technology on the market. Perhaps the fact that there are no royalty fees associated with the standard has something to do with it, but for whatever reason, the popularity and low cost of USB is leading to the elimination of the COM and LPT ports completely. USB support is built into the South bridge, and so-called legacy-free machines are moving the industry toward true plug-and-play simplicity. Any device you buy can simply be plugged into a USB port and off you go. In fact, a secondary specification to USB is "On-the-Go," or USB OTG. This will (theoretically) make it possible to connect handheld devices (such as PDAs and digital cameras) to other devices without a proprietary data-transfer cradle.

In Chapter 3, "Memory: Types and Forms," we mentioned that we can create faster throughput by using a change in *state* of the clock. You may recall that it wasn't the clock tick itself that was used for timing, but rather the change in voltage state as the clock went from a *pause* to a tick. The increasing voltage was one state, with the tick itself being a separate event. As the clock returns to its pre-tick condition, the reducing voltage is a second state. This allows for two instructions per clock tick, rather than only one instruction being linked to the tick.

The "pause" condition, where zero voltage is being applied to the clock, constitutes a *reference point*. When the voltage goes up to generate a tick, that event is distinct from when the voltage *returns to zero*. Up until USB, this was how many digital processes worked with voltage changes. The speed increases in the USB specification were developed through a process called *Non-Return-to-Zero-Inverted (NRZI)* encoding.

NRZI Encoding

NRZI encoding means that only *variations* in the voltage produce a change in state. A steady voltage represents a 1, and *any change at all* in voltage represents a 0. The change could be a drop in voltage or a return to zero voltage, but with NRZI, the return to zero is no longer required—no reference point is necessary. This works both ways. If the voltage changes a lot, it causes a string of 0s. If the voltage stays steady, it causes a string of 1s. On the other hand, a string of 1s or 0s can set the voltage to a steady state or a varying state, respectively. When NRZI is used to synchronize a sending and receiving clock through steady voltage, it uses a process called *bit stuffing* (not on the exam). The sending clock literally stuffs extra bits into the data stream, forcing a line of 1s, thereby signaling that a specific voltage is present.

 | NRZI is one of the ways that USB can generate much higher throughput than earlier serial transfer protocols.

IEEE-1394

We said earlier that FireWire and Sony's i.Link are both marketing names for the IEEE-1394 standard. FireWire was designed around video applications, particularly video cameras and video software. Motion video requires extremely high processing speed and bandwidth. Although the architecture is also designed for linking many devices together, we typically see an IEEE-1394 cable used to connect a camera or video-editing equipment to a PC.

The current standard calls for three signal rates of 100Mbps (12.5MB/s), 200Mbps (25MB/s), or 400Mbps (50MB/s). Although most cards support the 200Mbps rate, most of the devices on the market run at up to only 100Mbps. FireWire and i.Link, like SCSI and USB, allocate bandwidth to the speed of the designated device. To that end, not all the connected devices are required to run at 400Mbps.

NOTE

CompTIA will probably refer to these technologies in the more common "bits per second" at the highest speed. IEEE 1394 is designed to deliver speeds of up to 400Mbps. The new 1394b standard (already on the shelves of Apple resellers) delivers data at up to 800 megabits per second, whereas USB 2.0 is designed to exchange data at 480Mbps.

USB 2.0 is 40 times the speed of USB 1.0 and slightly faster (theoretically) than the existing FireWire 400Mbps specification. A file that took 80 seconds to transfer with USB 1.0 should take about 2 seconds with either USB 2.0 or FireWire. The new FireWire specification should make the transfer in about 1 second.

IEEE-1394 uses what's called a *daisy-chained and branched topology*, where each adapter card allows for up to 63 nodes, with 16 devices chained from each node. It's pretty much the same concept as USB tiered stars, but for some reason PC developers don't like to use Apple Computer terminology. The specification provides a performance improvement over ultra-wide SCSI, and costs significantly less. However, the devices all use power from the computer, unlike the powered hubs of USB. IEEE-1394 is fully PnP compatible, and supports hot-swapping capability.

We'll discuss cables and connectors in the next chapter, and mention FireWire connectors. Make a note (for the real world) that FireWire and i.Link connectors can be either 4-pin or 6-pin connectors, with either 4 or 6 leads in the actual cables. USB cables are 4-lead cables, and the difference has to do with the fact that the computer is sending power to the devices along the extra leads in the IEEE-1394 cables. Remember, USB powers the devices in a long chain through the hubs.

FireWire and i.Link transfer information from device to device. USB moves information through the computer. Aside from this detour through the computer, USB was designed to include very slow devices that can easily slow down any higher-speed devices on the cable system. One way to see the real-world implications of this is to run benchmark tests on a USB hard drive.

In an IEEE-1394 constellation, if a 200Mbps and a 100Mbps device are on the same cable, the difference is 2:1. On a USB system, a high-speed video camera running together with a 1.5Mbps device leads to a difference of around 320:1. Additionally, the farther from the computer a device is located in a USB chain, the higher the latency (delay) in signals reaching the CPU. Typically, a PC attaches many slow-speed devices (such as a mouse or keyboard) close to the computer, with higher-speed devices farther away.

Summary—Bus Transfers

You're going to encounter questions having to do with cable connectors (see Chapter 11), transfer rates, the USB and the SCSI acronyms, and serial versus parallel buses. One approach to choosing the correct responses is to memorize the raw numbers and facts. Another approach is to understand why all this stuff (technical term) was invented in the first place. If you can imagine yourself out in the field, using and resolving problems with USB devices and SCSI cables, answering one or two questions about how they work may not be as worrisome. The main points to remember in the preceding section are as follows:

➤ Daisy-chaining devices means connecting one after another in a chain. Know the names of the various ways hubs and devices can be strung together in a chain. Pay attention to tiered topology as it applies to the USB interface.

➤ Be sure to understand the three versions of the USB specification, and the three channels used for data transfers. Know the difference between a hub and a port, and use the question responses as an aid to remembering the transfer rates of each channel.

➤ You already know what PnP means, but you'll be tested on the formal definition of Plug and Play. Remember what is and isn't technically required for devices and a PnP operating system. You can use a non-PnP device on a Windows machine, as long as you manually configure it.

➤ One way or another, memorize the fact that IEEE-1394 is associated with FireWire and Sony's i.Link systems.

Networking Overview

Networks typically connect computers to other computers and peripherals. Again, USB and IEEE-1394 are designed to connect peripherals to a single computer—they're not network protocols. Networking is done to share resources, either for convenience or to save money. Connecting computers together in a network requires three things: a network interface card (NIC); a Network Operating System (NOS); and a medium for transmitting data from one computer to another (usually some type of wire). We'll focus most of our attention on wire (cable) transmission mediums.

The networking area is full of fuzzy and contradicting terminology. Before client servers, network software was called a *redirector*. With the advent of client servers, the name of the software on the server became the Network Operating System and the software on the nodes (computers and stuff) became the Client. The term "redirector" is no longer used and will not be referenced on the test. Today, Network Operating Systems run only on a server, Client software runs on client nodes, and Network Software runs on nodes in a peer-to-peer network.

Although dialing into a network doesn't require a network setup, the modem connects to a connection server, which then connects to a network or the Internet, using standard networking tools.

Categories and Types

Networks fall into two broad categories: *peer-to-peer* and *client/server*. We can also divide each category into two types: *Ethernet* and *token passing*. All computers are equal in a peer-to-peer network (think of a "jury of your peers," or "peer pressure"), and you can choose what data and resources you want to share. Client/server networks are configured in such a way that one or more computers act as *file servers* (or just *servers*), with the rest acting as *clients*. Servers, which control the overall network, are usually dedicated to storing data. A file server is like a lawyer, serving clients with filing, applications, and processing.

There are several different types of token passing networks. IBM's token ring is by far the most popular for local area networking.

Peer-to-peer networks (the focus included with Windows for Workgroups 3.11 and Windows 95/98) don't have dedicated servers and therefore are less expensive to set up. Instead, PCs share their own resources with the other PCs connected to the network. For example, you might access Sue's hard drive to retrieve a spreadsheet, and she might choose to print a document using a printer connected to your PC. Although security is provided to determine who can use what resources, peer-to-peer networks don't have the same level of security as client/server networks.

Peer-to-peer is where each computer is a peer (equal) to the other. Client/server is where a central file server provides services to many clients. All versions of Windows later than Windows 3.11 provide built-in peer-to-peer networking. Windows 95 and 98 primarily focused on peer-to-peer. Windows Me was targeted as Microsoft's decision to include more sophisticated networking and setup help in the home operating system. Windows NT/2000 and Windows XP (in their server versions) provide both peer-to-peer and client/server networking.

Windows Me went on to become Windows 2000, then XP, with the "Connection Wizard" as a way to dramatically simplify the network installation and configuration process.

Both peer-to-peer and client/server networks use software that performs the redirector function, but that software is called different things depending on the category. Beginning with Windows for Workgroups (WFW version 3.11), Microsoft provided a peer-to-peer redirector as part of the operating system. Therefore, we rarely talk about redirectors as being available in an OS, but refer to whether the feature is activated or not. Reference to a redirector usually means client/server networking.

Windows peer-to-peer networking was really designed for small workgroups of around 10 computers. Other network operating systems, such as Artisoft's LANtastic, were more sophisticated, but also were designed for fairly small installations. When a site expands to more than around ten machines, client/server networking is usually a better way to go. In this type of situation, domains and Windows domain management make a lot of sense. Peer-to-peer networking doesn't offer centralized management, meaning that someone has to run around to every PC and make configuration changes.

We'll examine networking security and User accounts in more depth in Chapter 15, "Windows NT, 2000, and XP." Peer-to-peer networking provides simple account management on each machine. Sue's machine, in our previous example, must be configured right on the machine to allow you access to whatever folder or drive in which she might store her spreadsheets. In other words, someone has to actually go to that machine to make the configuration change. Domain management is a way to make a one-time configuration setting, joining Sue, her User ID, and/or her machine to a client/server domain. From that point on, the network administrator can change Sue's permissions without having to be at her machine.

All shared data resides on a centralized file server, and the administrator can set remote permissions there, too. That means that instead of you being allowed into Sue's machine, both you and she are given access to a third machine: the file server. Sue would transfer a copy of a spreadsheet to the server, and then you would transfer that copy to your own machine. Windows XP Remote Desktop is a sort of hybrid mixture of peer-to-peer networking and remote management software. Remote Desktop allows you to enter into Sue's machine directly, given permissions, across a client/server network. (Remote Desktop is a Microsoft evolution from such programs as Symantec's PC Anywhere.)

P2P Networking

Internet P2P networking, referring to "point-to-point," is essentially peer-"2"-peer networking. Networking software such as Kazaa Media Desktop, Win MX, Soul Seek, or Lime Wire must still be installed on each machine. The transfer system uses the Internet as the main transmission media, with each machine on the P2P sub-network using a machine identifier. Although certain computers are designated as central points of origin, any machine on the P2P network can exchange resources with any other machine.

Napster is a memorable case history where P2P networking and sharing music without paying royalties led to problems. Many corporations, as well as various departments of the government, use P2P networking as a fast, inexpensive alternative to client/server networking. However, these sub-networks also use the Internet as their backplane, with all the subsequent lack of security issues and concerns.

Network Interface Card (NIC)

A network interface card plugs into the expansion bus of a motherboard and provides several necessary networking features. Initially, a NIC (pronounced "nick") provides a unique network address for the PC. This unique address, the Media Access Control (MAC) address, is assigned by the manufacturer and stored in ROM on the card. Secondly, the NIC provides a connection to the media (or cable) used for the network. Finally, it provides the processor and buffers used to send and receive packets of data over the network cable.

MAC Addresses

Every device or node attached to a network must have a unique *MAC address*. For the most part, each device's NIC contains the MAC address. The address is actually burned into a chip by the card manufacturer. The Media Access Control (MAC) sub-layer is a lower level in the OSI model. The MAC layer is extremely important because it defines the addressing used by all the network nodes. So how do the numerous network interface card manufactures know that the MAC address they're using is unique?

The MAC sub-layer specifies three groups of 24-bit binary addresses. A typical hexadecimal representation of a binary MAC address would be something like 00:D0:B7:2E:B3:24. This is a lot easier to read than 00000000:11010000:10110111, then the next four hex characters, and finally the last four.

The first 24 bits (00:D0) form a unique vendor code assigned to the manufacturer. The last 24 bits (B3:24) are a serial number, assigned by the manufacturer to the card. The middle group identifies the particular card and can be configured to some extent. As long as everybody plays by the rules, any complete MAC address will be unique.

The NIC provides the network address for the PC. If you change the NIC, you change the way the network sees the computer and its address. This can have interesting repercussions, depending on the network's configuration and security.

Network Software

Although we mostly refer to client software, a network operating system does include a redirector. The redirector monitors the CPU and determines whether data requests are *local* (inside the computer) or *remote* (outside, on the network). If the data is on a local hard drive, the request is routed to the drive. If the data isn't on the server's drives, the request is "redirected" to the NIC for transmission over the network.

Originally, the redirector sort of wrapped itself around the operating system, using a particular interrupt (int 21) to join to the machine's OS. Windows was written to build the redirector in as part of the main operating system. Even so, the concept continues, where Windows sort of "keeps an eye on things" to determine what operations are supposed to happen on the local machine, and what events are supposed to leave the machine for some other destination.

Media

All networks communicate over some kind of media. This can be as simple as a pair of twisted wires, or as exotic as fiber optics and radio transmission. For the purposes of this discussion, we'll refer to the central media cable as the *backplane*. This isn't technically correct, but we're using it to refer to the main network "highway" where signals move around to various terminals. Ethernet is one of the first network types and one of the most popular, so let's start there.

Ethernet (IEEE-802.3)

Xerox Corporation originally developed Ethernet as an experimental coaxial cable network back in the 1970s. Ethernet is a *baseband* network, meaning that only one signal can be on the network at a time and that the signal takes up the entire bandwidth. (Baseband is neither a category nor a protocol; it's a way to transmit signals.) Originally, Ethernet ran at 3Mbps over a thick coaxial cable. Xerox, together with Digital Equipment Corporation (DEC) and Intel Corporation, developed version 1.0 of the 10Mbps Ethernet specification, and in 1985, the specification was approved. The specification became ANSI/IEEE Std. 802.3, and the cable was named 10Base5. (The exact meaning of 10Base5 is discussed in Chapter 11.)

Since the original standard was approved, ongoing developments and faster transmission rates have continued. Fast Ethernet, using Category 5 wiring, runs at 100Mbps. The Gigabit Ethernet standard (1,000Mbps) includes two primary additions: 1000Base-T for UTP (see Chapter 11) copper cable, and 1000Base-X STP copper cable. Gigabit Ethernet also specifies standards for single and multi-mode fiber optic cable.

In an Ethernet network, the NIC "listens" to the cable, checking to see whether another PC is "talking." If no other PCs are transmitting at that moment, the card sends out a data transmission. As more terminals come online (join the network), each new card waits for a quiet moment (when no signal voltage is on the line) before transmitting data. If data signals moved instantaneously, each card would know when any other card was sending. But because data signals don't move instantaneously, there is a time delay over the length of wire, from one end of the network to the other.

When two network interface cards transmit at the same time, and the signals meet in the middle somewhere, we have what's known as a *collision*. A collision creates a spike, or bump, in the voltage. The transmitting NICs detect this spike and send out a *jam signal*, which is nothing more than a stream of 0s and 1s designed to fill up the network. This causes all the cards on the network to stop transmitting. A random number generator on each of the transmitting cards then picks a time to begin transmitting again, after an initial silence. This feature is why Ethernet is often called a carrier sense, multiple access, collision detection (CSMACD) network.

Terminators

Network transmission speeds take place with frequencies well into the radio range. *Shielded* coaxial wire prevents the cable from becoming an antenna, interfering with data transmissions. The cable uses a resister at each end (called a terminator). A terminator prevents signals traveling along the wire from reflecting back onto each other from the cable ends. Network devices attach to the cable with a *tap* (connector) and share the cable as the transmission media. (See Chapter 11 for illustrations of coaxial cable and terminators.)

Terminating resistors maintain error-free data travel along the transmission media, by absorbing any signal that reaches the end of the cable. This prevents the signal from "bouncing back" along the cable and crashing into other signals traveling along the bus (wire). In a long backplane, it isn't unusual for a PC to transmit from one end while a PC at the other end is still hearing silence and transmits at the same time.

Remember that electronic cables or media that carry data or signals are essentially a *bus*. To prevent errors caused by signals bouncing back along the bus from the ends of the cable, a terminating resistor must be at both ends. These are called *terminators*. Terminators absorb signals to keep them from reflecting back along the cable. The SCSI specification defines a bus, and so SCSI devices also use terminators. A SCSI bus must be terminated at both ends, with the host adapter (card) usually acting as the motherboard termination point. The last device in the SCSI chain must also be properly terminated.

Token Ring (IEEE-802.5)

Ethernet networks also are called *probabilistic*, meaning that moving data is a matter of "probably" avoiding a collision in the middle of all those packets contending (arguing) for attention. IBM wanted to develop a *deterministic* system of making sure data would avoid a collision. Token ring networking uses a different system of transmission. A token ring network connects PCs in a ring, called a *ring topology*, and then passes an empty data packet from one PC to another. This symbol of what could eventually become data is the token.

A *token* is a sort of placeholder for something that it represents, like a token of appreciation (instead of actual money for a job well done). When a terminal requires data from another terminal, it waits for the token to come around, and then places its request (along with the NIC address of the PC from which it wants information) in the token. The token then becomes an actual data *packet*, and it passes around the ring to the appropriate PC.

Token ring networking is like a group of people sitting around a dinner table. If someone wants mashed potatoes, they wait for a pause in the conversation, and then pass a note with their request around the table to the person nearest the potatoes. That person reads the note and hands the potatoes to whoever is nearest in the ring. Then everyone passes the mashed potatoes along. When the person who sent the request gets the bowl, he dishes out some potatoes onto his plate—the local hard drive. With every resource waiting for the token before it transmits, there are no longer any collisions.

Ethernet, on the other hand, is a little like an old telephone party line. Regardless of how many people are talking on the phone, each person can hear every other person. The trick is to listen for the specific voice of the caller who's addressing you and ignore all the rest. Networks are a little more sophisticated than that.

Bus and Star Topology

An Ethernet backplane is a single, long, heavy piece of coaxial cable that snakes its way through an office suite. This type of topology, using only one wire, is called a *bus topology*, or *linear bus topology*. (Note that the word "topology" defines the type of cable as being part of a network. A SCSI bus connection has 50 wires in the ribbon cable.) The cable can transport only one signal at a time, which means that only two devices can "talk" back and forth at any given time. All the PCs share the same cable, and any given PC can transmit when the bus isn't moving someone else's signal. All PCs on the bus can hear the transmission, but only the addressed PC copies the transmission into its buffer for processing. It's like saying, "John, pass me the potatoes." In the analogy, "John" is the MAC address.

A hub is a box containing a small internal bus. When you connect a twisted pair or USB cable to a hub, you are actually connecting it to a bus. The cables branching out from the hub look much like the legs of a starfish. Because of these hubs and branches, we call this type of installation a *star topology*. Figure 10.3 shows a linear bus topology (top), and a hub and star topology (bottom). Note the terminator resistors at each end of the linear bus.

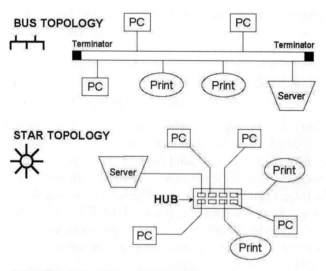

Figure 10.3 Outline of bus and star topologies.

Bridges and Routers

People wanted to add more computers to the network. As networks became larger and larger, they ran into various limits. One limit is that signal strength and quality decays over distance (requiring a repeater of some kind). A second problem is that more transmissions lead to more signals, which, in turn, increases the probability of jam signals and slowdowns. A *bridge* is a way to break down a large network running at full capacity into smaller groups of segments.

Bridges work with only the addresses of the network cards on a specific network. When a bridge is installed in the middle of a network, it logs all the NIC addresses on either side of it (in a routing table). It then passes traffic only if that traffic has a destination address on the other side of the bridge. The bridge allows for more PCs to be connected to the network without creating traffic bottlenecks.

 A *bridge* segments a network—divides it into smaller parts of the same network. It does not create two separate networks. This is a key point to remember. The bridge transmits data across to another segment only if the packet address refers to a network card on the other side of the bridge. The bridge is part of the overall, single network. A bridge is like a local phone book for a single area code.

However, even with bridges to ease the traffic congestion, there is a limit to how many addresses can be maintained and processed by a given device. It's similar to the way a single area code can have only so many phone numbers. *Routers* (rhymes with "shouters") were developed to operate at the network level (not at the individual resource level). Routers, to continue the analogy, store only area codes.

The Router

With the introduction of the bridge, networks became so huge that individual NICs began running into trouble trying to figure out how to address a specific machine. If you think about it, the phone system (network) had a similar problem. At first, only four digits were used (NIC address) because only a couple of thousand phones existed. Then, each town began having enough phones that three additional exchange numbers (segment address) had to be added, making up our familiar, seven-digit number.

As more people began using phones, and towns became more crowded, we began to run out of exchange numbers. The country had to be broken down into separate networks made up of several towns (and their internal exchange numbers), and then broken again into sections within a given city. Using the three-digit area code numbers is like routing addresses to each overall network making up a section of a city, or a different town.

If you're calling someone nearby, you generally don't need to use an area code, unless you happen to live on the border of a separate area code. However, once you travel outside your neighborhood, you do have to dial an area code (then the exchange number, and then the four-digit phone number).

Routers direct traffic to different, whole networks, using a single listing for each overall network's address. A routing number is somewhat like the area code. Understand that we're speaking of an entire network to which many local machines are connected, not a segment. A router is like a phone book that holds only area codes. A segment is a piece of a single network, joining some number of individual machines.

When a router is installed between two networks, it only passes packets having another network address. Routers don't care about each NIC address because they're only concerned with networks as a whole. This is how many networks can be connected together to form one big inter-network like the Internet.

TCP/IP Addresses

The Internet uses a protocol called Transmission Control Protocol/Internet Protocol (TCP/IP), which establishes the format for addressing networks and stations on the network. In this environment, every PC has two addresses: The NIC has its built-in address, and the card is assigned a second, TCP/IP address. Bridges use the built-in MAC address and routers use the TCP/IP address.

Under this format, every station is assigned a multi-digit network address that is broken into four blocks. This is the IP address. For example, a specific PC may have the address 192.168.001.115. Some of these digits represent the network address, and the others represent the PC itself. A *subnet mask* determines what the digits represent. A Domain Name Server (DNS), which cross-references numeric addresses with names, is usually somewhere on the network to make addresses easier to remember.

A firewall is like a router that can be programmed to accept or reject traffic based on IP addresses and content, such as packet contents. A firewall can also be set up to accept or reject certain protocols. Windows XP includes a somewhat simplistic firewall, and we'll discuss it in Chapter 16, "Troubleshooting." Some hardware routers have firewall features, but in most instances, the firewall is a software application. Most networks have both routers and a firewall.

The OSI Model

Networking eventually became so complicated that the Open System Interconnection (OSI) committee was formed to create the OSI model for networking—yet another set of standards. Figure 10.4 shows the seven layers that are defined in the OSI model. We won't go into extensive detail on each layer, but you should be able to recognize the layer names to pick them out of a lineup, and you should have at least a summary idea of their basic functions.

The OSI is traditionally presented from the highest (Layer 7) to the lowest, as shown in Figure 10.4. However, we'll discuss them in the opposite directions, starting with the hardware and ending with the application software. There's no particular reason for this, other than we're talking about NICs, bridges, routers, and other hardware, and it seems to keep the flow of the discussion more linear.

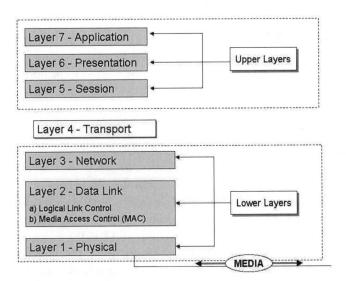

Figure 10.4 The OSI model.

Layer 1—Physical Layer

The Physical layer places data on the network media (the backplane) and ensures that the media is capable of carrying that data. Layer 1 specifies the type and gauge of wire, voltage levels, connectors, maximum distances, and other media details. The Physical layer is the lowest layer in the OSI model and, as such, is part of the OSI *lower layers*.

Layer 2—Data Link Layer

The Data Link layer is responsible for error-free communication between two network devices or nodes. The Data Link layer is a part of the lower layers, and is the only layer that is broken into sub-layers. Sub-layers don't use a number, and are always referred to by their name or initials.

The Logical Link Control (LLC) sub-layer rests on top of the MAC sub-layer and provides for connectionless and connection-oriented communication. Connection-oriented communication is much like a telephone circuit, created at the beginning of a conversation and maintained throughout the conversation. When the conversation ends, the connection terminates. Connectionless communication is done on a frame-by-frame basis. Because each frame is autonomous (on its own), no link is established or maintained. Connectionless communication is faster than connection-oriented, but not quite as reliable. The main function of the LLC sub-layer is to provide a way for upper-layer protocols to share transmission media.

Layer 3—Network Layer

Layer 3 is also considered a lower layer. This layer specifies path determination and packet switching between networks. Before any of this can be done, there has to be an existing structure for network addressing. Layer 2 (below Layer 3) already provides MAC addresses for every node on a network, so why do we need another addressing function at Layer 3?

MAC addressing is limited as to the number of available addresses. If we tried to use MAC addresses for communication across all networks, we would quickly run out of unique addresses, or the addresses would have to be so large that they'd be unusable. The Network layer uses a routable protocol to set up a higher-level addressing structure. Several routable protocols are available, including Internet Protocol (the IP portion of TCP/IP), Novell's Internet Packet Exchange (IPX), and Appletalk, from Apple Computers. Each protocol is capable of providing a network-addressing scheme and can use packets that have a field for network address.

Layer 4—Transport Layer

The Transport layer resides between the upper layers and the lower layers of the OSI model. It really isn't a part of either layer. This layer establishes end-to-end connections and divides upper-layer communications (like an email, for instance) into separate, independent segments (pieces). Layer 4 also ensures reliable data flow. It's at this layer that you would find protocols such as TCP or UDP.

Layer 5—Session Layer

The Session layer establishes, manages, and terminates communications by coordinating service requests and responses between two or more stations. Sun's Network File System (NFS) and IBM's Structured Query Language (SQL) are examples of protocols used at the Session layer.

 NOTE

The upper layers, including Session, Presentation, and Application, make the rules for how applications (software programs) communicate with the network and each other. The lower layers take care of getting data from one station to another.

Layer 6—Presentation Layer

The Presentation layer makes sure that information delivered to the Application layer is readable and properly formatted. Formatting includes such things as data encryption/decryption, data compression/decompression, and data representation. Examples of data formats used at the Presentation layer include ASCII, EBCDIC, MIDI, MPEG, JPEG, and GIF, to name only a few.

Layer 7—Application Layer

The Application layer is at the top of the OSI stack and closest to user applications (the stuff you're working with). For example, a word processor application, by itself, would not be part of the Application layer. However, if we were to use that word processor to generate email, it would use the Application layer. In other words, any application that reaches out over the network in some form of communication process is considered to be a Layer 7 application.

Summary—Network Overview

We were surprised to see networking added to the A+ exam, until we realized that simple networking is built into all the recent versions of Windows. What used to be a complex field of corporate PC management is now often found in residential homes and small businesses. You won't need to know the low-level details of the OSI model, but you should understand that an OSI model exists, and that it has seven layers. Some of the concepts to remember from this section include

➤ The difference between Ethernet and token ring, and the difference between peer-to-peer and client/server

➤ Terminators and packet collisions

➤ Network cards (NICs)

➤ Network software, network operating systems, and client software

➤ Bus and star topologies, and how to recognize a simple drawing of each

➤ The difference between a bridge and a router

➤ The names of the seven OSI model layers

In the following section, pay attention to the concept of the TCP/IP protocol, domain names, and an IP address. You should be able to recognize an IP address from your own Web-browsing experience, but you'll have to be able to identify the individual components making up an email address.

The Internet

Although you don't need to know the details of TCP for the exam, you should know that an IP address is typically about 12 digits long and difficult to remember. *Domain names* are a way to cross-reference the address number to an actual name. A DNS server (Domain Name System server) keeps track of these references, allowing people to use address names that are much easier to remember.

When you type a Universal Resource Locator (URL) into your Web browser, the DNS server translates it to an IP address and then passes the request along to the Internet (using the Transport layer). One of the subdivisions of the overall Internet is the World Wide Web (WWW). The HyperText Markup Language (HTML) was created to preserve nicely formatted documents, instead of the plain old text files that were all you could send over the original Internet. The HyperText Transfer Protocol (HTTP) was invented to transmit those HTML documents over the World Wide Web.

This is why a typical URL is written as http://www.symbolics.com. The symbolics is the domain name, and the "com" is the type of domain. The periods ("dots") are separators, as are the colon and two forward slashes. In 1985, symbolics.com was assigned as the first registered domain name. Until recently, only a limited number of domain types—for example, com (commercial), net (network), org (organization), edu (education), and gov (government)—were available.

HTTP and XML

Most of us have seen the http:// preface to an Internet URL. We've mentioned that the hypertext transfer protocol was designed to transfer hypertext markup language (HTML) documents to and from Web sites. HTML is a way of formatting text, and producing fonts, typefaces, lines, paragraphs, bullets, and all the other formatting we're used to seeing in modern word processors. HTML is a language that tells a Web browser how to show you a document.

XML is an extended markup language, designed to handle information formatting. In other words, HTML formats the characters and blank space of a document, but we also want a way to format the actual information in a document. If you want to put the characters "Bob Smith" on a Web page, HTML can make those characters bold or italic, large or small; put a bullet in front of them, or put them in a table.

Bob Smith is a name, and that name can be conveyed in different ways, depending on the associated information. For instance, Bob might be Jane Smith's husband, or Kelly Smith's father. Bob might be the CEO of a corporation or a boat owner. Bob might also be a male human being, or he could be the owner of an insurance policy. The information about Bob can be categorized in many ways, depending on context. XML is a way to design "tags" that tell the system how to use additional information.

In the URL http://www.jamesgjones.com, the James G. Jones domain is a *commercial* domain and therefore has a .com suffix. The URL http://www.comptia.org indicates that CompTIA is an *org*anization because it has the .org suffix. *Gov*ernment agencies typically use .gov as their suffix, and *edu*cational institutions use .edu.

With the explosive popularity of the Web, we started running out of addresses. The Internet Network Information Center (InterNIC), funded by the National Science Foundation, came together to coordinate a whole series of new extensions—for example, bus (business), co (country), tv (television), ws (Web site). We now have enough addresses to last until at least next week.

Email Addresses

An email address requires an additional username to go along with the domain name. The separator between the two is the @ sign. The username is to the left of the separator, and the domain name is to the right. A typical email address would be aplus@jamesgjones.com. In this case, the username "aplus" comes first, then the @ separator, then the "jamesgjones" domain name, then the dot separator, and finally the "com" to signify the type of domain.

An email address has a username and a domain name, with the username to the left of an @ sign, and the domain name to the right of the @ separator.

Online Connections

Many people, accessing the Internet, don't have their own routers, networks, or assigned IP addresses, so how do they get online? In most cases, dial-up connections use a telephone line and modem with an Internet Service Provider (ISP). The ISP connects your call, assigns a TCP/IP address to your PC for that session, and routes your data (using its router) to the Internet. Even with a 56.6Kbps modem, this is a slow task, so many people and small businesses are moving to faster broadband service, such as cable modems, ISDN, DSL, satellite wireless connections, or *multi-channel multi-point distribution services (MMDS)*.

Broadband connections are changing constantly. Theoretically, any kind of transmission system could be used to connect a PC to the Internet. You've probably already heard of fiber optic connections, but there are cellular towers, laser beams, microwaves, and even electrical power lines. Even broadband itself is pointing a way to *ultraband*, the next step in even faster connections.

Cable

Remember the first Ethernet networks and the coaxial cable? Your cable television service uses a big, thick cable to connect from the wall to your TV or VCR. There's no reason a digital signal can't be transmitted across the cable. Everyone's got cable (right?). The cable provides a bus network, much like Ethernet, and your PC connects to a special cable modem that becomes the tap.

The coaxial cable connects to a *node* (intersection point) in your neighborhood. From there, the cable changes to fiber optics. Information travels at very high speeds from the node to the cable company, and then out to the Internet. Cable modem connections are "always on" and tend to use a fixed IP address, making the PC vulnerable to possible security breaches.

Integrated Services Digital Network (ISDN)

ISDN is a set of standards that can provide up to 128Kbps of digital transmission over an ordinary phone line going into homes and small businesses. The service is provided over one of the pairs of wires already installed at your location. Unlike modems, which are affected by the vagaries of analog phone lines, ISDN uses a powered network termination device in place of the modem. This device must be installed at both your end and your provider's end of the transmission.

The throughput in an ISDN line is exactly as rated; however, in the case of ISDN, you need an inexpensive router or bridge at your location. This is often provided by the telephone company, and connects by using a NIC with a straightforward and easy installation. After the service is operational, you don't have to wait for dialing. You're continually connected directly to the Internet. Essentially, ISDN eliminates analog signaling and replaces it with a point-to-point digital link.

Digital Subscriber Line (DSL)

DSL is provided in many variations and speeds. Although the local telephone company provides the service, many individuals contract through an ISP for a total service. As with ISDN, you need a local router or bridge (often provided by the ISP). This special "modem" uses an existing pair of wires, if they're available at the location. However, unlike ISDN, if the extra pair of wires isn't available, the signal can be transposed over your active telephone line.

A DSL connection is always on, meaning that you're always connected to the Internet, and typically provides download speeds (reading a Web page) of 1.5Mbps and upload speeds (sending a file) of 128Kbps. To be eligible for a DSL connection, the PC must be within three miles of a central telephone office; otherwise, the signal begins to degrade beyond the value of the specialized connection. Unlike a cable connection and its neighborhood node, the phone line is a direct connection to the home or business, so speeds aren't subject to how many people are using the line at any given time.

Satellite Wireless

A broadband wireless connection to the Internet works like a satellite television account, using a small satellite dish to send and receive signals. The satellite relays signals through to a service provider with a connection to the Internet. Once again, a digital device handles the encoding and decoding of signals between your PC and the satellite, and the connection is always on. Typically, high-speed downloads from the provider use the satellite link while the subscriber uses a slower land-line link provided by a local service provider for uploads.

Current satellite wireless isn't as fast as other types of connections, with a typical transmission rate of around 395Kbps. Even so, this is about seven times faster than a dial-up modem. On the other hand, you have to have a clear view of the sky in the direction of the satellite and there's a small amount of delay time as signals pass through the satellite relay.

MMDS

One of the newer technologies appearing on the scene is based on a line-of-sight transmission from a digital transceiver at the PC location to a tall transmission tower. Signals from the tower are decoded through a wireless modem with speeds of up to 5.6Mbps. Although this is an exciting possibility, signals can't pass through or around solid objects. The transceiver must be within 35 miles of a tower, and because the system uses wireless transmission frequencies, speeds can be affected by how many people are using the connection at any one time.

 Although you may see a reference on the exam to MMDS, the technology has pretty much been replaced by 3G cellular technology.

Troubleshooting Networks

Obviously, troubleshooting a network is an entire professional category. An A+ technician should have a basic sense of what's going on in a typical network, and understand enough of the terminology to carry on a conversation with a Network Administrator. Two important programs used to test a network connection, including Internet connections, are the PING command and TRACEROUTE.

PING

PING uses the Internet Control Message Protocol (ICMP) to send data packets to another computer (a host). It then returns a message with the amount of time, in milliseconds, it took for the packet to return. You can execute PING from a DOS prompt, or by using the Start I Run option and typing CMD. Typically, the time involved is less than 1,000 milliseconds (1 second). If the ping time is longer than a second, there could be a problem. However, tracing that problem isn't always simple. The first place to check is on the host computer from which you're pinging. On a corporate network, there are additional tools available for tracking down a problem. Finally, a series of asterisks (*****) indicates that there was no response from the other host.

TRACEROUTE

As you know from reading any email header, the Internet uses many other networks and segments to transfer information. In particular, the Internet uses file servers all over the world to pass along information. Each time a data packet crosses to another section, we call it a "hop." TRACEROUTE is much like the PING command, in that it returns a message from another IP address. However, instead of giving only the time it took to reach that other host, the TRACEROUTE report includes the time it took for each hop.

Traceroute usually queries each host in a hop three times, and returns the time for each of those three probes. Once again, times under one second are usually an indication of no problem. Longer than 1,000 milliseconds, or a series of asterisks, indicates a problem. It isn't likely that the problem is with your own machine (the host issuing the Traceroute command). More often, the problem lies out on the network, or on the host machine's network.

PING and **TRACEROUTE** are command-line tools used to test the amount of time taken by a data packet to reach an IP address. If the time is less than 1,000 milliseconds (1 second), there's no real problem. A series of asterisks or times longer than one second usually indicate a problem. **PING** is for the total time from your machine to the destination host. **TRACEROUTE** is used to time the various hops—the route—a packet takes to reach the destination IP address.

Supplemental Information

The following information is not on the exam, but it's worth noting. Understanding information in context—where something came from and where it's going—can often help you to better retain the details of that information. By January 2002, approximately 30% of the Internet's total available address space was in use. Since 1995, the number of users and addresses was doubling on almost a monthly basis. Concerns began to grow as to when the Internet would run out of 32-bit IP addresses.

The Internet Protocol Next Generation (IPng) group is part of the Internet Engineering Task Force (IETF). These organizations began working toward a new set of protocols to replace the existing Internet Protocol version 4 (IPv.4). A draft of Internet Protocol version 6 (IPv.6) was put in place near the end of 1998. Although China and other parts of Asia are having some problems in terms of assigning new IP addresses, the growth of the Internet has slowed significantly. Europe is having a few connectivity problems because of the rapid increase in mobile phone technology, and the many areas where land service will probably never be installed. (Cell phones, mobile computing, and text messaging all use Internet addresses.) However, the fear of running out of IP addresses has abated.

Aside from a potential address crunch, the tremendous growth of the World Wide Web, along with its completely open architecture, produced an amazing flow of all kinds of information across the Internet. Originally developed for research and governmental purposes, such things as e-commerce and multimedia streaming are taking up more bandwidth. The existing Internet can't handle the extremely large file transfers (for example, an entire movie or a large university's research database).

Internet2 began in 1996 as a way to experiment with new technologies designed to make the best use of broadband and digital technology. The project was started by various corporations, universities, and non-profit organizations, and provides a sort of laboratory for companies and researchers. There are now over 200 organizations joined together in the Internet2 project, including Intel, IBM, Microsoft, Cisco, and other large technology companies. The project is designed to plan the future of the Internet.

Qwest originally ran the U.S. high-speed optical network (Abilene) that connects many of the member organizations. The Canadian counterpart is called the Canadian Network for the Advancement of Research, Industry, and Education (CANARIE). The Canadian system is working with a sort of virtual disk drive, built out of the entire network, with information being stored on parts of the network in much the same way a hard drive uses sectors and clusters. The "Wavelength," as it's called, is a virtual disk drive 5,000 miles in diameter.

In this case, the data transmission itself is used as a storage medium, with transfer rates of approximately 50ms, at 5,000Mbps (5MB/s). Because the CANARIE system is an optical network, the information is converted to photons, which travel around the network in a never-ending flow. Any information on the system is immediately accessible, as it continually flows around the "drive," sort of like a hard drive's random access capabilities.

A recent Internet2 conference attempted to bring the entire member audience together, from all over the world, in a real-time video conferencing environment. There were some problems, but the technology worked. This makes it likely that online education and real-time remote medical attention will arrive in the not-too-distant future. Instead of sending photographic images or .AVI files as email attachments, a high-speed broadband Internet would allow anyone (or everyone) to connect with a live video feed. The project has already been able to transmit HDTV over the network on a small scale. Instead of today's halting and pause-laden video and sound, the new technology has broadcast quality.

802.11 Wireless Networking

Ask any four people to describe wireless networking and you will get six different descriptions. We are going to restrict ourselves predominantly to wireless networking as described in the IEEE-802.11 standard. This is the largest and fastest-growing type of wireless network, and it is also the one you may be asked about on the test. However, before we get into wireless networking, let's cover some of the basics.

Radio

Electromagnetic energy moves in waves. Frequency is the number of waves passing a certain point every second. Electricity moving through a wire radiates electromagnetic energy into the surrounding space. Other wires, at a distance, can pick up that radiating energy. When we set this up on purpose, we've built a radio. When we didn't intend for the transfer to happen, we have EMI. The A+ exam considers wireless networking to be computing devices connected by infrared light or radio waves.

We use energy and frequencies to transmit information. Morse code, for example, is a pattern where a radio wave is either present or not. Voice, music, and video information is more sophisticated. A *carrier wave* is a radio wave at an exact frequency. Information is the result of the difference between the carrier wave and additional frequencies going along with that carrier wave. A "band" is the width of the combined carrier wave and information frequencies used to transmit some particular type of information. (Any set of frequencies within a stated boundary is a band, or a frequency spectrum.)

When a transmitter uses a particular band of frequencies, another transmitter with the same frequencies can either block (jam) the first transmission or interfere with it. As a result, the Federal Communications Commission (FCC) determines who can use particular ranges of radio frequencies in the United States, and how those frequencies may be used. The FCC coordinates with the International Telecommunications Union (ITCU), as do other countries, to keep frequency assignments consistent throughout the world.

The ISM Band

The FCC has assigned a particular set of frequencies to be used by less-regulated devices. That band is called the *Industrial/Scientific/Medical (ISM)* band. A "channel" is a block of frequencies within the frequency band (range). The channel number (or name) is an easy reference for the hard-to-remember frequency number. Channel numbers are like domain names, where the domain's underlying IP address would be difficult to remember.

The ISM band, unlike other communications bands, does not require someone to have a documented site survey, an inspection, equipment-type certification, an operator's license, and a valid station license. As a result, the band is popular for many consumer electronics, such as cordless telephones, microwave ovens, and hospital monitoring equipment. The recent popularity of mobile computing and wireless connectivity led the IEEE and FCC to develop the 802.11 specification for wireless networking.

IEEE-802.11 and Spread Spectrum Radio

The entire radio spectrum is extremely crowded. Therefore, most radio transmissions attempt to pack the maximum amount of information into as narrow a frequency range as possible. 802.11 wireless networks use spread spectrum transmissions, which do just the opposite. They spread a signal across a range of frequencies but use a type of frequency division multiplexing so other transmissions can use the same frequencies without interference.

Spread Spectrum

There are subdivisions of frequencies within the overall 2.4–2.4835GHz band. Each subdivision has a channel number (once again, for easy reference). 802.11b specifies fourteen channels, but in North America, the FCC allows only eleven channels. Each channel begins with the specific frequency of the carrier wave, and allows for a "spread" of additional frequencies during the transmission of information. This "fan" of peripheral (side) frequencies leads to the term *spread spectrum broadcasting*.

Narrow band transmissions use one specific carrier wave frequency and a limited set of secondary frequencies. For example, when you tune your FM radio to 101.3MHz, you receive a signal transmitted on that same 101.3MHz frequency. But if a nearby transmitter is also set to 101.3Mhz, it can block the signal you want to hear. (Narrow band transmission is like a rifle bullet moving through the air.)

Spread spectrum broadcasting uses two primary types of differing technologies. The one is Frequency Hopping Spread Spectrum (FHSS), and the other is Direct Sequence Spread Spectrum (DSSS). Imagine that you want to transmit the word "CAT." Each letter must be converted to electromagnetic information in a transmitter, and then converted back to letters in a receiver.

802.11 wireless signals generally have a range of about 1,000 feet in open areas, and between 250–400 feet in closed areas. The primary difference between the three sub-sets in the following list has to do with their frequency bands and transfer rates. Remember that 802.11 is the overall specification, using the ISM band. Each subset uses a letter of the alphabet to differentiate it from the overall 802.11 specification, as follows:

➤ *802.11a*—Uses the 5GHz ISM band and *orthogonal frequency division multiplexing (OFDM)* to reach transfer speeds of 54Mbps. OFDM divides the available channel into sub-channels and encodes a portion of the signal across each sub-channel in parallel.

➤ *802.11b ("Wi-Fi")*—Uses *frequency hopping spread spectrum (FHSS)* in the 2.4GHz ISM band to reach transfer speeds approaching 11Mbps. Again, the channel is broken into sub-channels, and the transmitter jumps from sub-channel to sub-channel (frequency hopping) in a mathematically determined pattern.

➤ *802.11g*—Also uses the 2.4GHz band. However, unlike 802.11b, 802.11g uses *direct sequence spread spectrum (DSSS)* and can reach 54Mbps speeds. DSSS essentially smears a signal across a wide band (channel) of frequencies. The receiver listens to the entire band and rebuilds the signal.

Technically speaking, 802.11 wireless transmissions generate faster or slower transfer rates, depending on a combination of variables such as distance, obstacles, and broadcast method. The aforementioned transfer rates are the specified maximums. Some equipment manufacturers use non-specified technology to increase transfer rates. However, without any standardization, one manufacturer's device may not work at non-specified rates when used with a different manufacturer's device.

Frequency Hopping

Frequency hopping specifies a range of frequencies within the larger set of assigned bandwidth. The transmitter generates a pattern whereby it will pick one of those frequencies, then another, then another, and so on. Each frequency is used for only a fraction of a second, to send very small packets of information. FHSS sends part of the letter *C* across each frequency in the pattern, then the letter *A*, and finally the *T*.

There are two advantages to this type of "hopping." The first is that it's extremely difficult to jam a particular frequency, because the transmitter is using any one of a number of frequencies in a pattern. The second is that other devices transmitting on the same set of frequencies have a hard time interfering with each other's transmissions. In the event that two transmitters happen to coincide on a specific frequency and block each other, the transmitter resends that fractional part of the packet again a microsecond later.

The disadvantages of frequency hopping are that it takes time to pick each "hop" frequency, and it's somewhat expensive. Because FHSS uses a pattern to transmit information, the receiver must also be set to exactly that same pattern before it can receive each packet. The SSID (discussed in a moment) defines the particular hopping pattern. When a transmitter uses a specific pattern, the receiver must be set to the same pattern, using the exact same SSID. (FHSS is like hopping from stone to stone while crossing a river.)

Direct Sequence Spread Spectrum

Direct sequence broadcasting requires less power and doesn't use frequency hopping. Instead, the band of frequencies is much wider than FHSS and the transmitter sends multiple copies of each packet. To use our CAT example, the transmitter breaks the word into each letter and sends, say, forty copies each of *C*, *A*, and *T*. Each packet has an identifier, which the receiver uses to "listen." No matter on which frequency the first *C* arrives, the receiver takes it and ignores all the other copies. Then it does the same with the *A* and the *T*. DSSS is less expensive to generate, and takes less time to transmit information. (DSSS is like a shotgun blast moving through the air.)

802.11b uses frequency hopping spread spectrum (FHSS) broadcasting, but because of the time necessary to generate the hopping pattern, it's limited to 11Mbps. 802.11g uses direct sequence spread spectrum (DSSS) broadcasting. Without the extra time involved, 802.11g can transfer 54Mbps. 802.11a also uses DSSS to generate 54Mpbs, but transmissions take place on the 5–6GHz band (channel).

802.11 Components and Structure

Most wireless networks are set up for mobile computing and laptops. Therefore, the most common piece of equipment is an 802.11 PC Card. Each card is a self-contained radio transmitter, with the network interface and firmware built onto the card. In fact, you can put together an entire network with nothing more than these interface cards.

 Many manufacturers are working toward a better standardization in device technology. The Wireless Ethernet Compatibility Alliance is a group of vendors working together with the IEEE committees. As such, you may hear people refer to wireless networks as WECA networks.

An *ad-hoc* network uses only interface cards, with no central point of contact. Computers can communicate directly with each other, using their wireless network cards. This is all well and good, but it doesn't take into account standalone printers, shared Internet connections, or any other type of network devices. Ad-hoc networks work well for a few stations, but they run into problems when more computers join the network. An *infrastructure network* is more appropriate for networks with five or more stations.

Infrastructure networks use one or more *access points* to provide a central point of connectivity. An access point is a box with an antenna, which plugs into a power source and acts the same as a hub in a wired network. Most access points include additional functionality, such as bridging to wired networks or routing to the Internet. Most access points also provide a way to hand off stations as users move from one access point to another. This "roaming" feature isn't at all standardized between manufacturers, so only buy equipment from the same vendor if you plan to allow hand-offs between access points.

802.11 wireless networks use a wireless network interface card, in the computer, and an access point to connect with standalone devices and other networks (wired or wireless). Access points are not required when two computers connect directly. Access points and NICs have their own, separate configuration setup programs.

A Wi-Fi Home Network

"Wi-Fi" is short for wireless fidelity, which means a wireless LAN. (Nobody knows how that happened, but interestingly enough, we've heard that another name for an Australian local area network is a LAN Down Under.) Let's suppose that your mom has been using a DSL router (provided by her ISP), which connected to her laptop through a 10Base-T crossover cable and a PCMCIA network card. She's wanted to surf the Net, chat with friends, and do her email while lying in bed. Hearing about wireless networking, she went to the store and came home with a brand-new wireless interface card for her laptop, and an access point.

Following the quick-start instructions, she unpacked the access point and plugged it into the wall. She then connected it to her router with the enclosed 10Base-T patch cable. Next, she loaded the software from the enclosed CD. When that was done, she shut down the laptop, replaced the 10Base-T NIC with the 802.11b card, and fired up the laptop again, just as instructed. Astonishingly, it all worked beautifully! It's that easy to set up. Wireless equipment is usually pre-configured so that when everything comes from the same manufacturer it all works, right out of the box.

A few days later, the neighbors down the street bought the same wireless equipment. They don't have a DSL line, and were surfing the Net on their dial-up system. Suddenly, they discovered a stranger on "their" system, using a different name. On top of that, their online connection became very fast. Things really got spooky when they unplugged their modem but stayed online. Meanwhile, your mom noticed her connection slowing down, and she began having problems with printing. It's up to you to come over and fix everything.

WLAN Configuration

Here's the problem: Everyone chose the default settings, so they're all on the same network. When the neighbors set up their system, your mom's router (access point) saw the new station, and assigned it an IP address, just as it did when she turned on her own laptop. She and the people at the end of the block became part of the same network, and everybody began accessing the Internet through your mom's DSL line and router. To untangle the mess, you'll have to manually configure your mom's network.

The good news is that most access points have an HTML interface, making the setup program pretty easy to navigate. The bad news is that each manufacturer provides commands that they think are appropriate. ("Inappropriate" means anything that could encourage a call to customer service.) The worse news is that there are very few explanations for any of the commands or their settings (parameters). Not all manufacturers agree on appropriate operating parameters, but every command or setting has an effect on every other setting.

SSID

Every 802.11b network has a configurable *service set identification (SSID)*. This is used as the name of the network, but it's also used to determine the spread spectrum transmission parameters. To communicate, each device must use the same SSID. Each manufacturer assigns a default setting to their devices (often the manufacturer's name), and neither your mom nor the neighbors changed the setting. As a result, each device within range becomes part of the same network. Remember, they all bought the same OEM equipment from the computer store.

The first step is to log in to your mom's access point and change the SSID to something unique. You'll be able to access the laptop's NIC setup program from the computer. And, because the laptop is networked with the access point, you'll also be able to run the setup program for the access point. However, if you use your mom's laptop to make the change, the moment the change takes effect, all communication stops. Why?

You changed the access point's SSID, making it different from the laptop's default ID. To re-establish communications, you'll have to access the laptop's setup program and change the SSID to match the one you just assigned to the access point. After the change, you'll have to restart the laptop. At that point, both the laptop and the access point are sending out a beacon on each frequency of the assigned channel.

Each device searches each frequency for a beacon with the correct SSID. When the laptop hops to a frequency and looks for a beacon from the access point, it may not find one. The access point may reach that frequency a moment later, but the laptop has already hopped to a different frequency. The search continues, taking time, until both devices happen to find each other during the search process. When they find each other, they link up and begin communicating.

NOTE You can log in to an access point over the network by launching an Internet browser and typing the IP address in the URL field. You can also use a crossover cable to connect the computer's NIC directly to the access point's LAN interface. Both methods require a username and password, which are provided in the reference documentation. Always change the default SSID and password setting on new wireless networking equipment.

Wireless Equivalency Privacy (WEP)

Although it's difficult to eavesdrop on FHSS signals as they hop from frequency to frequency, it can be done. Therefore, the 802.11 specification calls for Wireless Equivalency Privacy (WEP) as a second level of privacy and security. WEP allows a device to send encrypted data over a wireless link. The user chooses a secret key made up of a string of letters, numbers, or both. The device then uses this string, together with a complex algorithm, to encrypt each packet of data prior to transmission. The data can be unencrypted only by a device using the exact same key.

Each device's setup program includes a page for setting encryption. Typically, the device uses a 64-bit key or a 128-bit key. The longer key is more secure, but it takes longer to process. Mom isn't involved with military defense contracts, so we'll keep it simple and choose the 64-bit key. After the key length is set, we need to designate a string of characters as the actual encryption key. Different manufacturers require the key to be entered as either hex or decimal numbers, or a character phrase. Whichever method, be sure that the key is identical for every station on the network.

In addition to generating the encryption key, the system can be configured as either *open* or *closed*. In an open system, the access point sends out a beacon and only those stations with the correct encryption key can decipher the data in the beacon. On a closed system, the access point doesn't send a beacon. Each station sends an active probe, requesting a connection from the access point. The access point will respond only to active probes with the correct key, SSID, and channel number.

An active probe (on a closed system) takes longer to establish a link. However, the networks are more secure. Typically, you should start with an open system to see whether everything links up. Then, if you want to, you can change to a closed system.

Wireless Security

Despite all the stories to the contrary, 802.11 networks are both reliable and secure. However, they must be set up correctly! Running the equipment with default settings may be reliable, but it's far from secure. To figure out an SSID and a WEP code requires either a lot of time, or a computer on the order of a super-computer. When the first hackers broke into a wireless network, they didn't just happen to wander down the street in their car and connect to a secure network. They already knew some of the security keys. The story was picked up, and because so many people never make any configuration changes, other hackers were able to also break into wireless networks.

The important thing to remember about any WLAN is that there are several ways to make them secure. When nobody uses those configuration options, anyone knowing the default settings can access almost any network. Similarly, Windows has been designed as a standardized platform across "all" PCs. Without any configuration changes, security patches, or other attempts by computer users to change the default settings, any knowledgeable person can quickly access that Windows machine. Most of the scare stories about WLANs, as well as the rampant exchange of computer viruses, rest on this widespread reliance on default settings. Knowledge is power, and, in this case, ignorance is a cracked system.

Setting the Channel

Changing the SSID creates a new network. We could leave the channel set at the default, but we know there is at least one other network on this channel. Moving to a different channel is a better idea, and reduces even more the chance of accidentally connecting with the neighbors down the street. With the laptop and access point on the same SSID, it's a straightforward process to call up the access point's configuration page and change the channel field. Given that the neighbors are using the default, any other should be fine.

 Changing the channel also breaks the connection. However, the PC and access point will begin scanning the channels until they reconnect.

The FCC allows 11 channels (out of 14) for North American 802.11b networking. One of the problems with spread spectrum broadcasting is that there's only a 5MHz separation between each channel's carrier wave. On the other hand, a typical transmission uses a 30MHz frequency spread. The result is about a 15MHz plus or minus signal on either side of the channel's "central" frequency. That means a lot of overlap when two channels are close together. To avoid that overlap, 802.11b configurations work with channels 1, 6, and 11 (in the U.S.).

 Japan uses only channel 14, and Europe provides thirteen channels.

It happens that the default is channel 1, so we'll switch mom's network to channel 6. After that, we shut everything down, restart, and see whether everything communicates. Be patient. If nothing seems to be happening after a minute or so, try shutting down and restarting the laptop. If there's still a problem, turn off the power to the access point and restart it. If that doesn't work, log back in to the laptop and access point, and verify that each is using identical settings. Hopefully, sooner or later things will start communicating.

 You can make the network even more secure by enabling MAC filtering. The MAC stands for Media Access Control (Layer 2 of the OSI model), and refers to the programmed address for the network interface card itself (set by the OEM). If you feel additional security is warranted, you can list approved MAC addresses in the access point setup program. The access point will then respond only to NICs with listed MAC addresses.

Bluetooth

Any discussion of wireless networks will inevitably bring up Bluetooth. Ericsson Communications, a Scandinavian communications company, developed the technology. Bluetooth gets its name from Harald Bluetooth, the king of Denmark who, in the late 10th century, united the country. Presumably, Bluetooth technology will unite handheld and portable devices. Bluetooth technology is limited to short-range (5–10 meters) FHSS radio in the 2.4GHz ISM band. It was designed to eliminate the rat's nest of cables accompanying a computer; it was not designed to replace large-scale networking. Bluetooth enables printers, scanners, PDAs, and telephones to automatically interface with a Bluetooth-enabled computer and form a "piconet."

"Pico" means very small (one trillionth). "Net" refers to a network. As such, a piconet is an ad-hoc network made up of devices using Bluetooth technology. Piconets can support up to eight active devices, with one device acting as the master and the others being slaves. The network exists only for as long as there's a connection, and transfers at about 1Mbps. (A piconet is sometimes called a Personal Area Network, or PAN.) When multiple piconets, on different frequencies, communicate with each other, the combined network is called a "scatternet."

Infrared Wireless

Infrared (IR) wireless uses light frequencies, and works with a transmitter and receiver. A wireless mouse uses IR technology, as do common television remote controls. Many printers also have an infrared port. The transmitter and receiver are often built into modern motherboards and devices, and use a small plastic window to radiate the infrared light. The *Infrared Data Association (IrDA)* specifies that data can be transmitted from 0–3.3 yards. Speeds range from 0.9 to about 4Mpbs.

Fiber Optics

Fiber optic cable (or simply *fiber*) is a bundle of at least two fiber strands (one for send, and one for receive). The strands are made of glass and each strand is wrapped in a plastic shield. The entire bundle is then wrapped in an outer jacket. Fiber cable looks like wire, but conducts light rather than electricity. "Long-haul" fiber optic uses a laser beam as the light source, which has a very low skew factor and stays coherent (straight line) over longer distances than light-emitting diodes (LEDs). The two main types of fiber optic cable are

➤ *Single-mode*—Uses a laser source and can travel 22 kilometers (km) before requiring a repeater. The transmission path within the fiber is 5 microns wide.

➤ *Multimode*—Uses an LED source and can travel only 6km. Its transmission path is 62 microns wide.

Multimode and Single-mode

Imagine shooting pellets down the barrel of a BB gun. Each pellet has a diameter of 0.177 inches, and the barrel has a diameter just a little bit larger than 0.177 inch. All the BBs travel in a straight line covering the same distance. Now imagine shooting a bunch of BBs down a cannon barrel with a diameter of 24 inches. Some of the BBs go straight down the barrel, but others bounce off the walls, following a zigzag course down the barrel. Do all of the BBs travel the same distance down the barrel? No, the ones bouncing off the walls travel much farther (in the zigzag pattern). Even though all of the BBs started at the same speed, the ones bouncing around arrive at the end of the barrel much later than the ones that followed a straight path. Now apply this analogy to fiber optics.

When laser light moves down a 5-micron path in single-mode fiber, there's very little room to start bouncing off the "walls" of the cable. This is much like the BBs traveling down the barrel of a BB gun. The light has only one "mode" of travel, so the fiber is called *single-mode*. *Multimode* fiber is much like the cannon barrel. When light travels down multimode fiber, some of it immediately begins bouncing off the walls of the cable and traveling on different paths to the end of the fiber. This is like shooting BBs down that cannon barrel.

Because the light is going to bounce around anyway, multimode fiber uses a much less directional (and cheaper) LED in place of the laser. Single-mode fiber maintains the light signals in sequence, so we have to worry only about attenuation (loss of signal strength). On the other hand, light bouncing down a multimode fiber quickly gets out of sequence, which is why single-mode fiber can cover more distance between repeaters than multimode. See? Particle physics isn't really so difficult after all.

A Fibre Channel (same thing as fiber optics, but spelled differently for no apparent reason) requires two fibers. Light is unidirectional, meaning that one beam can send (transmit) information, but another beam must return (receive) information. The standardized speeds of a fiber optic channel are usually based on multiples of the base 51.84Mbps, which is called Optical Carrier One (OC-1). These standards go all the way up to OC-192, which is 9.6 Gigabits per second (Gbps). As is true of optical disks, dirt smudges and other interference can stop the transmissions. Although some people think a fiber cable cannot be repaired, this isn't true. A break can be fixed with a *fusion splicer* or mechanical splicer, and certain instruments can tell a technician how far away a break has occurred.

Connectors

Fiber optic connectors use bayonet (ST) connectors or snap-on (SC) connectors. The ST connector is much like the BNC connectors used in 10Base-2 connections (discussed in the next chapter). The snap-on SC connectors look much like a modular data connector or RJ-45 connector. Both single-mode fiber and multimode fiber use each type of connector. However, you cannot use connectors designed for single-mode fiber on multimode fiber and vice versa.

The connectors are configured for a single fiber (simplex) or for two fibers (duplex). Simplex connectors are rarely color coded or keyed, making it next to quite difficult to determine which fiber goes to transmit and which fiber goes to receive. Fortunately, there's a simple test. If they're connected the wrong way, the link goes down. High-capacity network backbones use fiber, so chances are that somebody will inform you of the mistake rather quickly.

Connect the Glowing Red Dots

Somebody will eventually tell you to look at the fibers and connect the one that glows red to the receive jack. If you cannot tell which is the receive jack, look at the jacks and the one that is not glowing red is the receive jack. For those of you who have done this, you know that it works. But you should still use your remaining eye to read the rest of this sidebar. (Just kidding.)

Fiber optic networks use infrared light. Human beings can't see infrared light. You can see the glowing red fiber or jack because the intensity of the light is completely overwhelming the receptors in your eye and they're all firing signals to your brain, which interprets the mess as red. You will not be blinded, but it is still a really bad idea to go around looking into active fiber cables and jacks. A more professional technique is to use a wooden stick, like a tong depressor, coated with a phosphorescent paint. The paint glows when it's exposed to infrared light (much like the inside of a CRT monitor). Hold the stick in front of a cable or jack to detect a signal.

Duplex ST connectors are snap-on, and so are duplex SC connectors. But each type of connector uses a different format, so they are incompatible with each other. On top of that, the guys working on FDDI (fiber distributed data interface) wanted something different, so they came up with a duplex FDDI connector, for no particular reason. That connector won't work with either ST or SC connectors. Fortunately, you'll have to recognize only the SC and ST connectors shown in Figures 10.5 and 10.6, as far as the CompTIA exam objectives are listed.

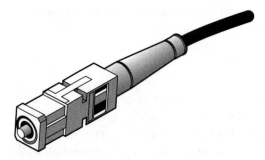

Figure 10.5   A typical SC-type fiber cable connector.

Figure 10.6 A typical ST-type fiber cable connector.

Exam Prep Questions

Question 1

> What are two major benefits of using a USB?
>
> ❑ A. Ability to use Plug and Play components external to the PC
>
> ❑ B. Speed of transmission
>
> ❑ C. Ability to connect many computers together with a single cable
>
> ❑ D. Ability to fully use parallel transmission

Answers A and B are correct. USB uses high-speed serial transmission to connect peripheral devices to a PC. USB does not use parallel transmission and is not designed for connecting multiple PCs, so answers C and D are incorrect.

Question 2

> Which of the following standards made home networking practical?
>
> ○ A. IEEE-1394
>
> ○ B. IEEE-802.11
>
> ○ C. USB
>
> ○ D. SCSI-2

Answer B is correct. The wireless networking standard is technically known as 802.11 (802.11b). Answer A is incorrect because IEEE-1394 technology, also called FireWire or i.Link, is used primarily to connect video equipment with PCs and to connect many devices to a single PC. Networking connects many PCs together. Answers C and D are incorrect because USB and SCSI likewise connect peripheral devices to a single computer. Think of "SCSI drives," and "USB keyboards," and you'll see that they're really not networking technologies.

Question 3

What are the two major types of network architecture?

❑ A. Broadband

❑ B. Peer-to-server

❑ C. Bus

❑ D. Token ring

Answers C and D are correct. Bus and token ring networking are two very general categories of networking, not to be confused with bus and star topologies. Answer A is incorrect because broadband is a description of transmission capacity. Answer B is incorrect because "peer-to-server" doesn't exist, although client/server networking uses a file server. Although both peer-to-peer and client/server could also be two major categories, the inclusion of the false peer-to-server as an option points to the C and D combination.

Question 4

How many simultaneous signals can travel on an Ethernet network without error?

○ A. One

○ B. Two, when early token release is implemented

○ C. 1,024

○ D. Up to 10, on a 10MHz network

Answer A is correct. An Ethernet bus (wire) allows only one signal at a time to use the network. More than one signal can easily create an error condition known as a collision. Ethernet and token ring are two different kinds of networks. In a token ring network, the token is the only thing that travels across the wire, managing signals from each PC so as to avoid collisions. That being said, when you see a reference to Ethernet networking, it will almost never refer to a token ring system.

Question 5

Which device is most typically used to assign IP addresses to sub-networks?

○ A. A router

○ B. A bridge

○ C. A NIC

○ D. A TCP/IP

Answer A is correct. A router is used to gather addresses for an entire network or various subnetworks (the "area codes"). Answer B is incorrect because a bridge is used to break a single network into segments, storing the addresses of only the resources in that one network (the "exchange numbers"). The network interface card is abbreviated as NIC, so answer C is incorrect. Answer D is incorrect because TCP/IP is a packet addressing protocol and uses various IP addresses to ensure that information packets arrive at their correct destination.

Question 6

802.11b uses which type of spread spectrum radio?

○ A. OFDM

○ B. FHSS

○ C. DSSS

○ D. None of the above

Answer B is correct. Frequency hopping spread spectrum (FHSS) produces transfer speeds of 11Mbps on the 2.4GHz band. Answer A is incorrect because OFDM is used by 802.11a on the 5GHz band for wireless networking. Answer C is incorrect because although 802.11g uses direct sequence spread spectrum (DSSS) on the 2.4GHz band, it can transfer data at up to 54Mbps.

Question 7

> Which OSI layer would be responsible for converting Outlook email to the format necessary for the Internet?
>
> ○ A. The Transport layer
> ○ B. The Application layer
> ○ C. The Presentation layer
> ○ D. The Media layer

Answer C is correct. This is another one of those "deer-in-the-headlights" questions, because the OSI layer is hard to remember. Before you take the exam, make up lots of small index cards, one for each layer, its number, name, and a short description. Tape the cards all over the house, on mirrors, cupboards, over your bed, or wherever else you think of. Remember these layers. Answer D is wrong, right off the bat, because the "media" is the network backplane. The Physical layer is the lowest level, and connects to the media. Answer A is tricky because the question is asking about "formatting," but the Transport layer carries the email across the Internet. Answer B is likewise tricky because the question asks about Outlook, an application. Answer C is the right one because it "presents" the email (from the Application layer) to the next layer, and formats it correctly for the network protocol.

Question 8

> A Windows XP domain was set up to manage a project for a financial company. Originally, there were 30 people working on the project, but the company quickly began to grow. What would be the best way to maintain an efficient throughput on the network?
>
> ○ A. Use a bridge
> ○ B. Use a router
> ○ C. Use a repeater
> ○ D. Use additional hubs
> ○ E. Fire some employees to reduce traffic

Answer A is correct. Remember, this is a scenario question, so read it once, and then glance at the list of responses to see what's important. Something about the size of the network matters. Domains, clients, employees, and finances are all distractions. A bridge splits a big network into smaller pieces, but the pieces are all still on the same network. Answer B is wrong because the router would connect more than a single network. The question states that there is only "the network," meaning one network only. Answer C is incorrect because a repeater only adds back in signal strength over long distances. Answer D is incorrect because hubs connect network devices to the network. The company is growing, so obviously it also is adding hubs all the time. Answer E is just there to lighten the mood.

Question 9

Which type of networking would provide remote management of a Windows 95 printer server and three printers?

- ○ A. Ethernet
- ○ B. Client/server
- ○ C. Token Ring
- ○ D. Peer-to-peer

Answer B is correct. You may easily find questions on the exam that don't necessarily use the formal descriptions or words we've discussed. Just because we say types (categories) are different from protocols, that doesn't mean the IT industry always uses the same words. The reference to Windows 95 and print servers is irrelevant, because you can see that the responses are asking for remote management to something on the network. Answers A and C are incorrect because they're too general. The real choice is between B and D. Remember that peer-to-peer networking means someone has to configure each PC every time permissions and access change, making answer D the wrong choice. Client/server, answer B, refers to a central file server and spread-out clients.

Question 10

USB version 1.1 was an upgrade to the original version 1.0, and provided which of the following transfer rates? (Choose all that apply)

- ❏ A. 1.0Mbps
- ❏ B. 1.1Mbps
- ❏ C. 1.4Mbps
- ❏ D. 1.5Mbps

Answer D is correct. This really is a trick question. First of all, the "Choose all that apply" will likely get you all fired up to pull out your memorized details of transfer rates, and you know that USB has three important numbers. Therefore you'll be trying to figure out at least two correct responses if you're not careful. In fact, there's only a single correct choice. Secondly, the numbers all look pretty much the same and two of them mirror the version numbers: answers A and B, both of which are wrong. Thirdly, USB 1.0 and 1.1 both support the original 1.5Mbps listed in answer D. Answers A, B, and C are all the wrong speeds, and are all incorrect choices.

Need to Know More?

 http://www.whatis.com—A technical Web site resource with short articles describing many aspects of information technology and networking.

 http://www.webopedia.com—An online encyclopedia devoted to technical terms, featuring additional links to other Web-based articles, research, and white papers.

 Harwood, Mike and Bird, Drew. *Network+ Training Guide.* Indianapolis, IN: Que, 2002. ISBN: 0789728303. One of many books that provide the basics of networking in much more depth than we have room for in a review book.

 Lowe, Doug. *Networking For Dummies.* Indianapolis, IN: Wiley, 2001. ISBN: 0764516779. The "For Dummies" books are another excellent way to get a more expanded explanation of the basic concepts and terms having to do with anything. This book is simpler to read than a certification training manual, but has more about networks than we have room for here.

 Groth, David and McBee Jim. *Cabling: The Complete Guide to Network Wiring.* Alameda, CA: Sybex, Inc., 2000. ISBN: 0-7821-2645-6. As far as we are concerned, this is the best book ever written on network wiring. If you are in the industry, you need your own copy.

 Derfler, Frank J. *Guide to Connectivity, 3rd Edition.* Indianapolis, IN: Ziff Davis Press, 1995. ISBN: 1-56276-274-5.

 Derfler, Frank J. and Lee Freed. *How Networks Work.* Indianapolis, IN: Ziff Davis Press, 1993. ISBN: 1-56276-129-3 (Basic).

 Freedman, Alan. *Computer Desktop Encyclopedia, 9th Edition.* McGraw-Hill Osborne Media, 2001. ISBN: 0-0721-9306-9. Great for a fast look-up or refresher.

 Ross, John. *The Book of WI-FI.* San Francisco, CA: No Starch Press, Inc., 2003. ISBN: 1-886411-45-x. This is a good, hands-on, "let's set it up" book for people with little, if any, networking experience.

 Gast, Matthew S. *802.11 Wireless Networks, The Definitive Guide.* Sebastopol, CA: O'Reilly & Associates. ISBN: 0-596-00183-5. A very good practical resource book for all aspects of 802.11 networking. This is not a beginner's book.

Cables and Connectors

Terms you'll need to understand:

✓ Interface and port
✓ Input/output (I/O) bus
✓ COMmunications (COM) port and Line Printer Terminal (LPT)
✓ Serial and parallel
✓ Device names
✓ DB25, DB9, Centronix, SCSI
✓ DIN, mini-DIN, PS/2, and USB
✓ Co-ax, twisted-pair
✓ RJ-11 and RJ-45 modular connector

Concepts you'll need to master:

✓ Plug (male) and socket (female), pins and contacts
✓ Connector, cable, back panel (of the PC)
✓ Serial and parallel data transfer
✓ Coaxial cable types and naming conventions
✓ Terminators and signal reflection
✓ Categories of twisted-pair wire
✓ Shielding and insulation

When you press a power switch to turn on a computer, lights blink, drives begin to whirl, and speakers beep. Eventually, some music plays and the system is ready to go (you hope!). From the AC connector plugging into a wall, to the phone cord that plugs into a modem, everything connected to the CPU uses a particular type of wiring scheme and connector. We also can say that the motherboard is connected to the CPU as a supporting chipset. Additional cables and connectors, then, link everything else to the motherboard.

We've all seen the spaghetti mess of cables around a computer. That mess can be separated into two main groups, each based on a type of wire and the plugs and sockets joined to that wire. A plug has pins sticking out of it, just like a toaster plug, and we refer to it as a *male* connector. A socket has holes in it, like a wall socket, and we refer to it as a *female* connector. Male and female, in this case, have nothing whatsoever to do with gender. They're merely technical terms. Cables cannot reproduce on their own, regardless of what they may seem to be doing at night, behind your desk.

A socket may sometimes be called a *jack*.

For the sake of our discussion, a *cable* is some kind of wire with a connector at each end. In a computer system, we also have an interface between every component. An *interface* is a meeting place: a sort of boundary between two information streams. The specific connection is called a *port*. For example, your desire to send a piece of mail puts you within the boundaries of the postal system. The post office would be your interface. The clerk behind a counter would be a software port. The actual counter would be a hardware port. Our focus will be on hardware connections.

A protocol is a set of rules that specify how two devices should communicate, or "interface." In the post office example, part of the protocol dictates that your communication should be enclosed in an envelope or box. Another part of the protocol demands that you purchase some amount of postage, based on the weight of your package, or "packet." Yet another part of the protocol determines when you may post your letter, and when the post office will deliver it.

A word of warning: Parallel and serial cables will mostly likely give you the most aggravation on the exam. Although the industry refers to wiring schemes as "pin-outs," making no distinction between actual pins and holes, we'll be as explicit as possible in our separation. A pin is a small post. A pin slides into a hole. Inside the connector, behind the pins or holes, wires attach to *contacts*. Plugs and sockets all have some number of contacts. The wiring scheme (or pin-out) specifies which wire attaches to what contact. All connectors, regardless of whether they use pins or holes, are described as having some number of "pins." This is actually the number of contact points.

Legacy I/O Interfaces

The XT motherboards used a basic set of data connections to move data in and out of the processor. Many of today's ports and interfaces are inherited from the original XT architecture, which, together with DOS, introduced the device names. Back in the beginning, the keyboard and mouse input devices connected through serial ports or through dedicated interface cards. The video *console* and printers (both output devices) used the video and parallel ports, respectively. Some printers used interface cards, as did tape backups and scanners. Older printers could use either a serial port or the more familiar parallel port.

 Because the original XT machines used a DB25 connector as a serial port, a 25-pin serial plug is sometimes called an XT connector. The AT form factor introduced a second, 9-pin serial port. A DB9 serial connector is sometimes referred to as an AT serial plug.

Although you may never see an LPT3 port, DOS-based operating systems (including Windows) still reserve the name. The device names used by PCs for basic hardware interfaces are

> *Serial ports*—COMmunications (COM)1, COM2, COM3, COM4

> *Generic serial port*—AUXiliary (AUX), rarely used for anything anymore

> *Parallel ports*—Line Printer Terminal, or Line PrinTer (LPT)1, LPT2, LPT3, LPT4

> *Generic printer port*—PRiNter (PRN)

> *Video monitor*—CONsole (CON)

> *System clock*—CLOCK$

There is also the NUL device (a sort of printer device), used as a sort of black hole in space. Any data sent to the NUL device simply vanishes, making this a place to send text messages that you don't want the end user to see. For example, the **PAUSE** command in a batch file outputs **Press any key...** to the screen. Using **Pause > NUL** will send all output from the command into oblivion, leaving only a paused blank screen with a blinking cursor. (An even more obscure trick is to use the **CTTY** terminal driver to hand input or output control over to something other than the screen. This turns off all screen output completely until another **CTTY** command is issued.)

Each I/O connection uses a specific plug or socket on the back panel of the computer. The connectors then work with a *controller interface* to the motherboard. In other words, the connector joins the device to the computer housing. The controller moves the data to and from the motherboard. The interface is where data pulses change to a different media. (Remember the OSI layers and the underlying media?) Early machines used separate controller boards, some of which occupied various bus slots. Modern devices often have a built-in controller on a logic board.

A motherboard may not have serial ports or a direct motherboard mouse port. In that case, you can install an expansion card with a mouse port. This type of mouse is generally referred to as a *bus mouse* (because of the expansion card's bus slot). When older software used both the physical COM1 and COM2 ports, people often had to install a separate bus mouse. It then had to be configured to use COM3 or COM4 (logical ports).

There are four COM ports: two physical connectors and two logical ports. COM1 and COM2 are actual DB9 connectors, but COM3 and COM4 borrow the connectors and assign two separate addresses. We list the IRQs and addresses in Chapter 4, "Processor Mechanics, IRQs, and DMA." Be sure you know them before you sit for the exam.

Nowadays, the basic ports are built into the motherboard and don't use a separate adapter slot. The controller interface for the primary and secondary IDE controllers, the floppy controller, two serial ports, and a parallel port have been consolidated into the Super I/O chip, mounted right on the motherboard. Some systems include additional peripherals, such as a SCSI host adapter, an AGP, integrated mouse ports, a possible network interface card (NIC), a sound card, and sometimes a modem.

We'll remind you here that the floppy drive controller, having been one of the very first devices installed on early PCs, is still assigned to IRQ 6 by default. (See Chapter 4 for a complete listing of the IRQs.)

Floppy and Hard Disk Controllers

Almost every disk drive has one connector for electrical power, and a separate connector for control/data signals. These connectors are fairly well standardized across the industry and across drives. Because these cables have so many wires running through them, they're designed to be flat and flexible to save space. They're usually called *ribbon cables* because of their similarity to ribbons.

Typically, the control connector uses either a large 34-pin edge connector, or a smaller, *pinhead* connector. Obsolete 5 ¼-inch drives used the edge connectors, whereas 3 ½-inch drives use the pinhead connector. When IDE and EIDE drives finally became standardized, the controllers were integrated onto the motherboard. Today, most IDE and EIDE (as well as some SCSI) controllers are included in the Super I/O chip.

Don't confuse smaller floppy drive ribbon cables with the typical 50-pin SCSI ribbon cable. Although we didn't see any questions about it on the exam, make a note that old, dual-floppy systems used three connectors. The middle wires of the two drive cables were visibly flipped (or crossed) between the connectors so that the controller could differentiate the two drives. Nowadays, with many systems eliminating the floppy drive completely, the two IDE controllers differentiate between the four possible IDE drives.

15-Pin VGA

Most PCs have a built-in 15-pin standard VGA connector, used to connect an analog monitor with the system board and onboard graphics. This isn't always the case, and custom-built machines often use a separate expansion card as the only video connector. Make a note that, for the moment, a VGA connector and onboard graphics do not support digital video signals.

We mentioned in Chapter 9, "Peripherals: Output Devices," that add-on graphics cards often provide specialized connectors to be used with digital and flat-panel LCD monitors. The DVI-A connector is used only for (A)nalog monitors. A DVI-D connector is used for (D)igital video monitors. As yet, there is no standard for flat-panel displays. A DFP connector is used to transmit signals to a *Digital Flat Panel* monitor.

The exam will present you with a standard VGA video connector on a stylized back panel (see Figure 11.5). You should be able to recognize the video port as the only one with 15 pins. Keep in mind that the VGA *socket on the computer is female.* The cable coming from the monitor uses a 15-pin male plug.

Parallel (LPT) Ports: 8 Bits Across

The majority of printers (except various network printers) use a 25-pin *parallel* interface to connect to a computer. Parallel ports use the LPT device name, and transfer information in a row, eight bits across. You can think of parallel transfer as an army of British soldiers in a gun battle. They would line up in rows of 8, and the first row would stand up to shoot at the opposition. When the bullets were transferred, the first row would kneel down and the row behind them would stand up and fire. The cycle continued until the back row had fired their rifles, after which, the first row was reloaded and ready to fire again.

Many devices are moving to include USB, FireWire, and wireless connections. This chapter focuses on traditional and legacy ports and cables. USB and FireWire are discussed in the previous chapter.

In the gun battle example, you can imagine that by increasing the numbers of soldiers in each row, more bullets could be fired across the battle field. The British learned this technique from the Romans, who used it with archers to shoot arrows. Computers use the same process to transfer data bits across a parallel bus. An 8-bit bus is like eight riflemen firing at the enemy. A 16-bit, 32-bit, 64-bit, or 128-bit bus increases the "front line," so to speak, and moves more data (arrows or bullets) across the line of fire.

Parallel wiring is where a circuit provides alternate conducting paths (more than one) for electric current. A string of lights wired in parallel is somewhat like a ladder, where each bulb and socket is a separate rung. If one bulb burns out, current still travels up the sides of the ladder through the terminals in the sockets, and the rest of the lights (on their own rungs) continue to glow.

Serial wiring (discussed in a moment) is where an electric circuit provides only one conducting path for electric current. A string of lights wired in series is like an old string of Christmas tree lights. If one bulb burned out, the entire chain went dark.

You might think that because a parallel cable transfers eight bits at a time, it would have eight pins and be wider than a serial cable. You might also think that a serial cable uses only one pin because it transfers one bit at a time. Neither of these suppositions is true. Parallel data transfers move *bytes* of information, and serial transfers move *bits*. Other than that, the width of the connectors and the number of wires bear no relation to the number of data bits being transferred.

Types of Parallel Ports

If we say that 8 bits equals 1 byte, we can see how parallel wiring puts a complete byte through the interface, row after row. Depending upon how fast those bytes move through the interface, the throughput goes up in terms of kilobytes, megabytes, or gigabytes per second. Parallel ports are available in the following types:

➤ *Unidirectional (original parallel port)*—Data flows out, but can't come back in. (Printers could not communicate with the CPU.)

➤ *Standard bidirectional*—Peripherals can send status messages back to the CPU for action.

➤ *Standard Parallel Port (SPP)*—This is a setting often found in laptops and notebooks.

➤ *Extended Capabilities Port (ECP)*—ECP ports are about 10 times faster than the standard bi-directional port.

➤ *Enhanced Parallel Port (EPP)*—Also called *fast mode parallel port*, EPP ports are also about 10 times faster than the standard bi-directional port.

A typical retail system will likely have a standard bi-directional parallel port. Some custom-built machines may not have an expected port, which may cause difficulties with installing and configuring parallel-interface devices such as an Iomega ZIP drive or scanner. Before you spend hours delving into Windows and the Device Manager, make sure the problem isn't simply an unsupported hardware port.

Finally, the maximum length of a serial cable is 50 feet. A parallel cable shouldn't be any longer than 25 feet. We didn't see questions about these particular cable lengths, but make a note, just in case. In the old days, cable lengths made a difference in terms of locating a printer in an office. Nowadays, most printers can be installed on a network, and distance isn't a problem.

Serial (COM) Ports: 1 Bit After Another

Serial ports transfer information in a line, one bit at a time, much like ants following one another. Because only one bit (not an eight-bit byte) moves through the interface, serial ports are typically slower than parallel ports. If a parallel port is like an army of soldiers marching eight abreast in columns, the serial port can be thought of as "the ants go marching one by one." Understand that at the micro level of memory modules, Rambus DRAM serial transfers are basically as fast as DDR SDRAM parallel transfers. For this segment, we're talking about legacy hardware interfaces.

Bits, Bytes, and Baud

Microprocessors work with bytes (for example, 8-bit units). Serial devices also work with bytes, but they assemble them one bit at a time. Bus connections are often involved in breaking apart bytes into bits, or assembling bits into bytes. Bits are binary digits (0s and 1s). In terms of data transfers to these older devices, eight bits make up one byte, which typically corresponds to one character (a letter, number, or symbol).

Today, data rates are measured in kilobytes per second (KB/s) and megabytes per second (MB/s). The term *baud rate* refers to the number of discrete signal events per second in a data transfer, not bits per second. The term *baud* has fallen out of use. In the early days of 110 and 300 baud modems, the baud rate equaled the bit rate. More sophisticated signaling allowed the bit rate to greatly exceed the baud rate, and today we generally refer to a modem by its theoretical maximum in kilobytes per second (KB/s) .

DB25

You may want to use a pencil and some paper to draw the following DB25 connectors as we discuss them. This is a good way to really remember which is which. An IEEE-1284 cable, commonly called a parallel printer cable—the cable, not the back panel socket—uses a male DB25 plug. The plug goes into a socket on the computer's back panel. At the other end—the one going into the printer—the cable uses a Centronics 36-pin (C36) male connector. Both the parallel and serial forms of the DB25 connector use 25 contacts, making life confusing. The female port, found on the back panel, is sometimes called a Type A connector.

 Although the correct name is either a DB25S or DB25P (*S* for socket, and *P* for plug), the exam will most assuredly drop the *S* and *P*, leaving you to figure out from a graphic whether a question refers to a printer or serial connection. You likely won't have to recognize the serial 25-pin connector, but be sure to know what it looks like anyway.

On the back panel of the computer, the interface point is a *female* DB25 socket, meaning that it has twenty-five little holes. As we've said, you may find a 25-pin *male* connector in an exam graphic, meaning it has twenty-five little posts. Not long ago, computers came with both a 25-pin female parallel port and a 25-pin male serial port. They also had a 9-pin male serial port. In other words, they had one parallel port and two serial ports.

Originally, the DB25 serial connector was used for serial printers and modems. Modern computers replaced the DB25 serial connector with a DB9 serial connector. Remember that you'll most likely find one LPT connector (with 25 holes) and two 9-pin COM ports. The back panel still has one parallel and two serial ports, but one of the serial connectors changed (from twenty-five pins to nine pins).

Nowadays, a typical serial cable connects an external modem. COM ports on the back panel are male plugs with pins. Therefore, the serial cable uses a female DB9 socket. At the other end, the cable uses a 25-pin plug to connect with the modem. Figure 11.1 shows each type of DB25 connector found on a back panel. The female parallel port is on top. The male serial port is on the bottom.

 You should remember that the printer *cable*—not the back panel—uses 25 pins. Perhaps a way to remember is that dot-matrix printers use pins to form characters, and the pins are like the pins on the cable. When we set up a system, one of the last steps is to "plug in the printer." Remembering that phrase also may help you to remember that the printer cable has a pin-plug that connects to a socket on the computer. This is one of those last-minute facts you'll want to write down on the scratch paper you'll be given when you enter the exam room. Another immediate list should be the LPT and COM port addresses.

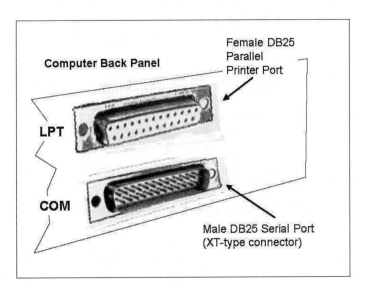

Figure 11.1 Two types of DB25 connectors.

You may be tempted to ignore the difference between the two DB25 connectors, thinking that twenty-five pin serial connections are obsolete. This isn't the case in many business environments. You'll often find terminals connecting to mainframes and minicomputers working with high-speed line printers and other serial peripherals. The software is often text only, on monochrome consoles. Because of upgrade costs, many of these systems are still in place and connect with 25-pin serial connectors.

 If nothing else, be sure to understand that you can't simply interchange the terms LPT, parallel, and 25-pin cable. Not every 25-pin cable is the same.

RS-232 and DB9

Serial connectors on PCs come in two flavors: a 9-pin DB9, or a 25-pin DB25. As we've seen, this makes life very confusing. Parallel and serial cables both can use a 25-pin DB25 connector. Back before computers, electronics and radio standards were set by certain organizations. The Electronic Industries Association (EIA) would eventually standardize the serial connectors on PCs, but before that happened there was a "Recommended Specification." The RS-232C was the (r)ecommended (s)pecification for PC serial connectors until a "D" version of the specification was released in 1987. In 1991, the EIA joined with the Telecommunications Industry Association (TIA) to release the EIA/TIA-232E standard (an "E" version). Most people refer to the serial connectors as RS-232C or just RS-232.

The EIA-232 standard provides for the two types of serial connectors we see in most computer systems today. The two COM ports on a typical back panel each use a 9-pin male DB9 connector. Older machines used a 25-pin male DB25 connector as the serial printer connector, which eventually disappeared. Apple Macintosh computers often used an RS-232C port.

 The RS-232 standards have been updated to RS-422 and RS-423, which support higher transfer rates and are less susceptible to EMI. Apple Macintosh computers use an RS-422 port, which is backward compatible with an RS-232C connector. RS-422 allows for multiple connections in a chain (like USB), whereas RS-423 supports only point-to-point connections.

We mentioned that we still see serial 25-pin connectors on modem cables, connecting at the modem end. One way to distinguish a serial cable is that the cable itself is thinner than a parallel cable. Figure 11.2 shows a standard parallel cable. The DB25 plug is on the left side, with a male RS-232 (or DB25P) serial connector below it. On the printer end, note the Centronix connector going to the printer.

Be very careful that you read a question correctly. A printer port is a female connector found on the back panel of a computer. A printer cable connector is a male, 25-pin plug used at the computer end of the cable. If you find a 25-pin male connector on the back panel of an older PC, it's almost always a serial connection.

External modem cables connect to the back panel with a female DB9 connector. The back panel uses a 9-pin male plug to slide into the female cable connector. You must remember that the parallel port on the back panel is always female.

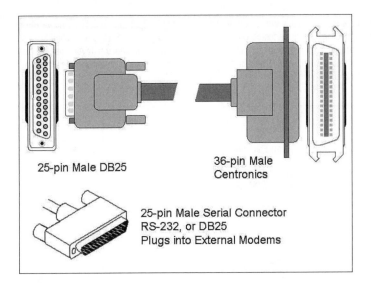

25-pin Male DB25

36-pin Male
Centronics

25-pin Male Serial Connector
RS-232, or DB25
Plugs into External Modems

Figure 11.2   A typical parallel cable connecting a PC to a printer.

36-Pin Centronics Connector

Centronics Corporation was one of the original printer companies. At the time, it created a parallel interface for its dot matrix printers that became the standard for later printer connections. A typical printer cable connects to the *printer* with a Centronics male connector that is 36 pins wide. A Centronics 36-pin connector (C36) is shown on the right side of the cable in Figure 11.2.

On the exam, Centronics is used only for printer connectors. Don't confuse a 36-pin Centronics connector and a 50-pin SCSI connector.

SCSI Connectors

SCSI devices can be connected to the computer either internally or externally. When a SCSI device is external, it can be mounted in an individual box. Several SCSI devices may be mounted together in larger, tower enclosures. Many devices use what is considered the preferred connector, according to the SCSI-2 standard: a smaller 50-pin SCSI connector with two rows of 25 pins. This connector is frequently referred to as a 50-pin mini D shell (MDS50) connector. Figure 11.3 shows a typical SCSI connector. Note that it looks somewhat similar to a Centronics plug, but with 50 pins.

 There isn't any easy way to remember the number of contact points in the various connectors. You'll be tested on the 9-pin serial, 15-pin video, 25-pin parallel, 36-pin Centronics connectors, and the 50-pin SCSI cable, so do whatever you can to remember them. You'll also be tested on RJ-45 modular connectors, discussed at the end of this chapter.

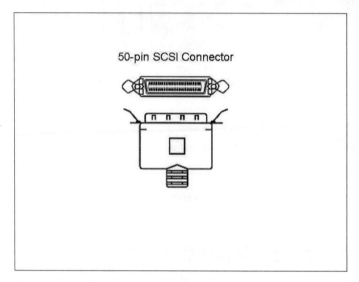

Figure 11.3 A standard 50-pin SCSI connector.

PS/2, USB, and FireWire Connectors

The original AT motherboards used two types of keyboard connectors: either a five-pin DIN (known as an AT connector), or a six-pin Mini-DIN (generally known as a PS/2 connector). The bigger 5-pin connector gave way to the smaller PS/2 connector used by IBM. Eventually, AT keyboards switched to the PS/2 style connector, and until recently, both keyboards and mice routinely used the smaller connector. Today's motherboards often come with two PS/2 connectors and at least two USB connectors. In Figure 11.4, you can see the relative size differences between the AT DIN connectors and PS/2 Mini-DIN connectors, along with the different shape of USB and FireWire cable ends.

5-pin DIN connectors may still be used for Musical Instrument Digital Interface (MIDI) connections to musical equipment. A PC back panel will probably never have an AT-style DIN connector (the MIDI connection requires an adapter), but you may find the cable out in the field.

Also, be aware that many chipsets do not have built-in support for a USB keyboard before an operating system is loaded. Before you make low-level system changes to CMOS or other system settings, make sure that using a boot floppy provides keyboard support and access to configuration settings.

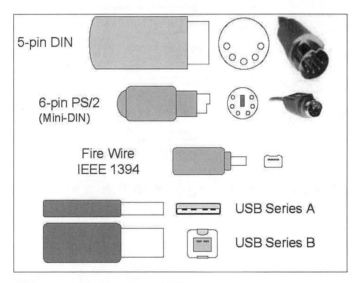

Figure 11.4   Keyboard, mouse, and USB connectors.

The difference in all these connectors is in both the number of pins and their shape. Keep in mind that the keyboard/mouse connection is often still configured as a COM port, even though it's installed as a PS/2 connector. (A USB mouse uses a separate I/O bus and does not take over a COM port.)

Also note that the USB specification includes both A and B type connectors. Type A is thin and flat. Type B is squarer and somewhat larger. FireWire cables can be either 4-pin or 6-pin, depending on their implementation. The connectors are somewhat square, but they're still thinner and smaller than USB type B connectors.

Back Panel Connectors

Newer PCs almost always have a dedicated PS/2 connector (6-pin Mini-DIN) for the mouse and keyboard, and two 9-pin serial male ports. The older back panel at the top of Figure 11.5 shows how closely the serial and parallel ports resemble each other. The DB25 connectors are either next to or above each other, and the only way to remember the printer port is that it has a female connector. The lower panel is more typical of today's PCs. Note that the parallel port is now the only 25-pin connector.

 Remember the relative sizes and shapes of the connectors. You may have to recognize them by their outlines.

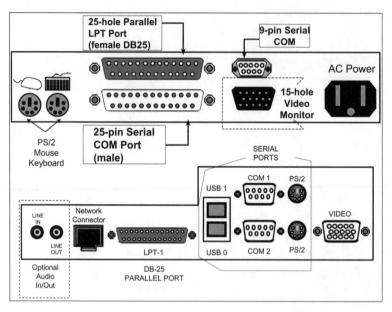

Figure 11.5 Typical back panels.

Summary—Standard Cables

The back panel of a computer box has various types of interface connectors, often called ports. Each of these ports uses either a male or female connector. The cable connecting to the port uses its opposite-gender connector. Even though we refer to plugs and sockets with pins and holes, we speak of a cable's pin-out to mean how each wire is used. For example, we never refer to a "9-hole" connector, nor do we speak of a "9-contact" connector. On modern computer back panels, you'll generally find

➤ 1 parallel port (LPT), using a female DB25 connector with 25 holes

➤ 2 serial ports (COM), using male DB9 connectors, each with 9 pins

➤ 2 Mini-DIN connectors, using female PS/2 style connectors, each with 6 holes

➤ 2 USB Type B ports

➤ 1 VGA connector, using a female 15-pin connector with 15 holes (the monitor cable has 15 pins)

You'll be tested on several common cable connectors. Although you won't need to know the exact pin-outs, you should remember the following cables. Remember that "male" or "female" determines pins or holes, respectively. "Pins" also refers to the number of wires and contacts, as follows:

➤ *Parallel printer cable*—Uses a male 25-pin DB25 connector at the computer end.

➤ *Centronics printer connector*—Is a male 36-pin (C36) connector developed by the Centronics corporation, and is at the printer end of a typical printer cable.

➤ *External modem cable*—Uses a 9-pin *female* DB9 connector at the computer end and a 25-pin *male* RS-232 (also called a male DB25, or DB25P) connector at the modem end.

➤ *SCSI cable*—The only SCSI cable we saw on the exam was a 50-pin ribbon cable, typically used to connect a device to an internal controller.

The original DOS device names for the various I/O ports were LPT (1, 2, 3, and 4), COM (1, 2, 3, and 4), CON (video console), AUX (auxiliary), PRN (printer), and NUL (a black-hole throwaway device). The printer typically uses an LPT port, but you can also send printer output to the PRN device.

Consistency has never been a strong point in the computer industry, so you can't just assume that a serial connector has nine pins. Neither can you assume that serial connectors are always used for modems. Serial connectors can be

➤ DB9 (nine-pin)

➤ DB25 (25-pin, male [RS-232])

➤ Keyboard or mouse (6-pin Mini-DIN, or PS/2)

➤ AT keyboard or MIDI connectors (5-pin DIN, or AT connector)

Although USB devices use a serial transfer process, we don't commonly call them serial devices in the original sense. Nor are they networking devices. USB devices are simply that—USB devices—and they use USB connectors, not "serial" connectors. Even so, the bus may be referred to as a fast serial bus.

We doubt that you'll be tested on sound card cables and connectors, and we haven't seen graphics of a PC front panel. Many computers offer additional sound and USB connectors on the front panel, for convenience. Joysticks sometimes use specialized connectors, as do microphones. The de facto standard for microphone and speaker jacks seems to be the 1/8-inch mini-phone plug (not at all associated with RJ-11 modular phone connectors).

Network Cables and Connectors

We said that the wires around a computer can be sorted by groups, depending on their connectors. Our second big group is network connections. Network cables can, themselves, be grouped. But in this case, the differences lie in the physical structure of the wire and/or the transmission rate for data. The two types of cables we discuss here are coaxial cable and twisted pair. If you're reading this book out of chapter order, we discussed fiber optics and wireless networking in Chapter 10, "Basic Networking."

Coaxial Cable

The first coaxial (abbreviated as *co-ax*) cable was quite thick and heavy, and became known as "Thicknet." It was initially standardized as *10Base5* Ethernet. Breaking this down, the name means that 10 megabits (not bytes) can travel across a baseband piece of cable to a maximum distance of 500 meters. Always remember that the *5* or *2* in the name refers to meters (not feet!) times one hundred. Five hundred meters is approximately 1,600 feet. (For a discussion of baseband and broadband, refer to Chapter 2, "Motherboards.")

 The co-ax naming convention continued forward, so remember that the name is megabits per second (Mbps) + "Base" + Distance (in hundreds of meters the signal can travel). 10Base5 means 10Mbps over 5(00) meters (not feet). 10Base2 is 10Mbps over 200 meters. 100Base-T is 100Mbps over twisted pair.

CompTIA will likely refer to 10Base2 as having a cable length limit of 200 meters. However, you may see a reference to 10Base2 as having a maximum length of 185 meters. If you don't see 200 as a response choice, but you do see 185, then go with the 185. The *2* in the name, though, refers to 200 meters.

Thicknet gave way to a thinner wire called 10Base2 (Thinnet). The reduced thickness was easier to handle, but meant a subsequent reduction in the maximum transmission distance. Although the wire could still move a single 10Mbps baseband signal, the maximum distance dropped to 200 meters (approximately 650 feet).

10Base5 Thicknet terminals originally connected to the cable with a *tap* (sometimes called a *vampire tap*). These connectors ($65 to $95 apiece) look like tiny jaws with a pair of long, sharp teeth. The teeth drive right through the insulation and into the core wire. Taps eventually gave way to *bayonet nut connectors (BNCs)*, and *T-connectors* ($1 to $3 apiece). Figure 11.6 shows the shielded core of co-ax cable. Figure 11.7 shows a standard T-connector and two terminators at the end of a short bus.

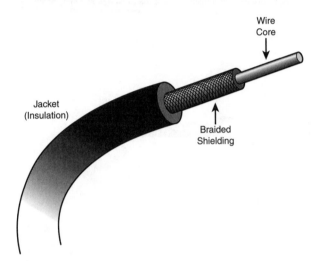

Figure 11.6   Coaxial cable with shielding and insulation.

Terminators

Both 10Base5 and 10Base2 require terminators at both ends of the cable, as you can see in Figure 11.7. (Remember that a SCSI chain also requires proper termination.) If the cable breaks or a terminator isn't installed, the entire network can perform erratically and fail. In a nutshell, signals traveling over a wire are pulses of electricity. You can't place your ear next to a co-ax cable and hear little voices, music, or words. Neither can you put on a pair of glasses and see numbers and letters in a wire. It's all about electrical voltages, frequency cycles, and other technical stuff.

Transmission accuracy is vaguely like the smooth action of a series of waves. When a wave crashes into a wall, the water bounces back and confuses the waves following behind. This type of interference leads to major transmission problems. Air is like a wall, and an open-ended wire "connects" to the air. A terminator is like a long, absorbent beach, allowing the energy of a wave to run its course until it has no more energy left to bounce backward.

Technically, a terminator is a small resistor that absorbs electricity at the end of a wire.

A regular SCSI bus allows up to seven device connections plus one host adapter. It does not require seven devices. (Later SCSI chains allow up to 15 devices plus the one host adaper.) Each device is supplied with a way of terminating the cable. Some devices use a resistor that physically plugs into a socket. Others include an embedded resistor that can be set through software configuration, or a jumper. (See Chapter 8, "Peripherals: Storage Devices," for a discussion of the SCSI bus and specification.)

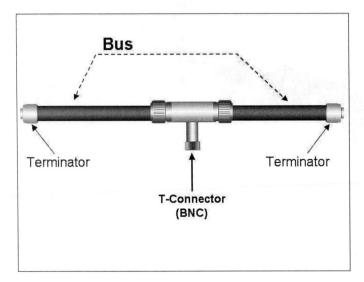

Figure 11.7 Co-ax with T-connector and terminators.

RG Coaxial Cable Types

Business networks, these days, are rarely wired with co-ax. Most of wiring has long since been replaced with 10Base-T, which we discuss following this segment. However, co-ax is still the medium of choice for broadband connectivity in residential and small business applications. Cable television providers offer cable modems with a connection between a computer and a neighborhood hub. The segment wire is often co-ax cable. The cable from the hub to the main provider network is more often fiber optic or even a wireless system.

After people buy cable modems, they usually end up having to buy a separate piece of co-ax for the hook up. So off they go to Radio Shack, and if they're lucky, they buy cables with pre-installed connectors. If they're *really* lucky, the cable might even have the same *characteristic impedance* as the cable company's wire. But what if customers have to install the connectors on their own? The likelihood is they'll use whatever tools are handy: perhaps a rusty Boy Scout knife and a 2-pound sledgehammer. The results aren't pretty, but at least everybody will later agree where the problem lies.

Characteristic Impedance

Unfortunately, there are thousands of types of co-ax cable, and sooner or later, you're going to have to tangle with a co-ax problem. Co-ax has many different characteristics, but perhaps the most important is the *characteristic impedance*. In Chapter 6, "Basic Electronics," we said that impedance is a function of both resistance and capacitance in a cable, and is measured in ohms. You should know that any change in impedance will reflect signals, (which is a problem). For example, if you connect a 50-ohm cable to a 100-ohm cable, some portion of the signals moving across the junction will be reflected. The greater the mismatch, the more signal is reflected. It's that "wall" again that we mentioned in the previous "Terminators" section.

 The worst of all mismatches is a severed cable, which is why terminating resistors are installed at the end of 10Base5 and 10Base2 cables. Think about it: A cable is a piece of wire, cut from a larger piece. Both ends are severed, leaving an open cable connecting to the air. Air has a much different impedance than wire.

A more complex problem is a mismatch in characteristic impedance. RG58 coax has a characteristic impedance of 50 ohms. RG59 coax has a characteristic impedance of 75 ohms. Both are commonly used, general-purpose cables that look identical. Suppose the cable company uses RG58, and the customer bought a piece of RG59 co-ax? When the customer attaches a 75-ohm cable to the cable company's 50-ohm socket, a significant amount of signal will be reflected. Will the cable modem work? Yes...probably, but its performance will be slow and often erratic. All the wiring looks okay, so you might think the modem is defective.

 CompTIA lists RG connectors as an objective for the A+ exam. You may actually see a question about these connectors, which is why we're discussing them in this book. We've never seen any such questions, but the only way you'll know the information is to use rote memory.

You'll often run across this type of problem in residential and small business applications. How can the problem be avoided in the first place? The first step is to find out what type of cable the provider company is using. Most cable types are marked on the outside insulation. If you can see the cable, you can probably read the type. If the actual cable isn't visible, a phone call to the cable company will usually get you an answer.

The next step is to determine the characteristic impedance of each type of cable. You can do this using a table, easily available on the Internet. We provide some of the more common types and their impedance in Table 11.1.

Table 11.1 Common Coaxial Cable Types and Impedance		
Type	Impedance (ohms)	Outside Dimensions (inches)
RG6	75	.332
RG8	52	.405
RG58	50	.195
RG59	75	.242
RG212 (replaces RG58)	50	.332
RG213 (replaces RG8)	50	.405

Finally, you'll have to make sure that the connecting cable has the same impedance as the modem, and whether or not the modem has a switch for different impedance settings. If it does, check to see that the switch is set to the correct position for the cable. Ah...but what if the modem doesn't have a switch, and it calls for a 75-ohm cable?

To solve this problem, you'll have to purchase a matching transformer (about $2) and insert it at the point where the impedance changes. Simple, right? Of course we haven't mentioned those other characteristics we talked about at the start of this segment. These are such things as velocity factor, physical dimensions, dielectric type, and cover, to name just a few. In a perfect world, all these characteristics would also match. However, taken together, they can't begin to account for the problems caused by connector installations and impedance mismatches.

 Sooner or later you are going to want to install co-ax and cable connectors yourself. Don't even think about it unless you first have a good crimper, wire stripper, and gauge, made especially for the cable you are using. Then be sure to test the cable before putting it in service or providing it to a customer.

Twisted Pair

Because of limits in cable length and the difficulty of installing stiff co-ax cable, most of today's Ethernet networks use the 10Base-T standard, which calls for different *categories* of wire, based on their quality (grade). The "T" in 10Base-T stands for *twisted-pair* wiring, which is exactly what it sounds like—pairs of wires twisted together. For example, Category 5 cables are made up of four pairs of wires (eight individual wires). Each individual pair is twisted around itself throughout the length of the cable. All the pairs are then twisted together. Although Category 5 network cable looks almost the same as the twisted-pair cable used for telephones, the wire must conform to a much higher-quality standard.

Categories

We use five categories to distinguish the quality differences between what look like the same wire. Category 1, 2, and 3 (C1, C2, and C3) are also referred to as CAT1, CAT2, and CAT3. These first three types were originally intended for voice-grade analog signals (telephony). However, some already-existing C3 cables were used for early network installations. Category 4 (C4) could be used for digital data signals, but it doesn't meet the standards called for in 10Base-T. The quality of the wire would severely limit transmission speeds and the length of cable runs. Category 5 (C5) and the newer Category 6 (C6) are both data-grade cable, and can be used for digital signaling up to, and including, 100Mbps Fast Ethernet.

 CAT5 wiring is sufficient for base-10 networking. The introduction of 100Base-T pushed the limits of existing Category 5 installations, and many felt an upgrade was needed. We list the various extensions to the 10Base-T standards in the "Summary" section, later in this chapter. CompTIA objectives refer to CAT5e and CAT6, so you should make a note of the names and basic throughput capabilities.

Category 5 (CAT5) Cable

Category 5 cable wire has either a solid core or a *stranded* core. Stranded-core wire is made up of many very thin strands of wire and is much more flexible than solid-core wire. Patch cables, and other short cables we regularly move around, are made with stranded-core cable for the flexibility. Solid-core wire is less flexible, but it has less signal loss (attenuation) per meter than flexible core. Solid-core wire is used for longer cable runs (up to 100 meters), and is usually permanently installed in walls or ceilings.

STP and UTP—Shielded and Unshielded Twisted Pair

The core wire in a cable, usually copper, carries electrical pulses in some frequency. In Chapter 6, we discussed electromagnetic interference (EMI) and electrostatic discharge (ESD). The first level of defense against these problems is the insulation wrapped around the wire's metal core. Insulation is a poor conductor and doesn't allow electrical energy to pass through it very well.

High-frequency electrical current is the basic concept behind radio broadcasting. Computer networks move data through cables at frequencies high enough that they begin acting like small radio antennas. When cables are close enough together, one wire can easily pick up information being broadcast by the other. This is another type of electromagnetic interference, and leads to complex problems of wiring, cabling, and pin configuration.

We can put a second line of defense between the outer insulation and the core, called *shielding*. Figure 11.6 (under the previous "Coaxial Cable" heading) shows co-ax cable shielding made up of braided metal or foil, wrapped around the inner wire core. The shielding keeps radio and electromagnetic energy contained. Shielding is often used with co-ax cable, but may also be used with *shielded twisted-pair (STP)* wire.

Category 5 and Category 6 cable are both considered Unshielded Twisted-Pair (UTP) cable. However, you'll occasionally come across shielded twisted-pair (STP) cable. Shielded 10Base-T cable is primarily used in IBM Token Ring networks, and is very different from C5 UTP cable. In fact, IBM has its own system for rating this type of cable: Type 1 through Type 6. Fortunately, you won't have to know the IBM Type ratings for the exam, but out in the field you'll probably find, and should know about, C5 STP.

A so-called drop ceiling (acoustical tile suspended on a frame) is called a *plenum-type* ceiling, and allows air to circulate. Co-ax, UTP, and STP cable can have regular insulation or Teflon insulation. Regular insulation gives off toxic fumes when it burns, so the U.S. Fire and Safety Code requires Teflon insulation for all plenum ceiling installations. Therefore, cable wire can be purchased in either plenum-type or non-plenum.

Summary—Network Cables

You'll be tested on a conceptual understanding of the basic principles of networking and the wiring used in networks. The common naming convention for co-ax network wire is to use the Mbps + "Base" + Distance (in hundreds of meters). That convention went away with 10Base-T. The "Base" in the name refers to baseband transmission. The main types of wiring you'll want to remember include the following:

➤ *Thicknet (10Base5)*—Ethernet coaxial cable capable of 10Mbps over a maximum distance of 500 meters.

➤ *Thinnet (10Base2)*—Ethernet coaxial cable capable of 10Mbps over a maximum distance of 200 meters (remember, CompTIA may say the maximum is 185 meters).

➤ *Twisted Pair (10Base-T)*—Ethernet four-pair wire with either a stranded or solid core; terminated with RJ-45 modular connectors.

 10Base2 coaxial cables use T-connectors (BNC) and terminators at the open end of a bus.

Twisted-pair wiring comes in several categories. Category 4 (CAT4) is usually insufficient to carry digital signals over any great length of wire. As far as the exam is concerned, most networks use CAT5 (Category 5) wiring. A true C5 installation must use devices, connectors, and cable that all carry a Category 5 (or higher) rating.

Twisted-Pair Categories

The two main types of twisted-pair wiring are Unshielded and Shielded. Unshielded twisted-pair wire is known as UTP wire. Shielded twisted-pair wire is known as STP wire. Twisted-pair wiring joins three concepts together, depending upon the transmission rate, how the data is being transmitted, and signal encoding. Although there are as many variations as there are manufactures, you will most often run into one of the following three twisted-pair configurations:

➤ *10Base-T*—10Mbps, baseband, over two twisted-pair cables

➤ *100Base-T2*—100Mbps, baseband, over two twisted-pair cables

➤ *100Base-T4*—100Mbps, baseband, over four-wire twisted-pair cables

There is still CAT3, CAT4, and CAT5 wiring, but as networks reach ever-higher transmission rates, the wiring specifications are being updated to handle the changes. The following is a list of the various specifications:

➤ *CAT3 Standard (1988)*—UTP cable and hardware must be able to maintain a transmission rate of 16MHz.

➤ *CAT4 Standard*—UTP cable and hardware must be able to maintain a transmission rate of 20MHz.

➤ *CAT5 Standard (1992)*—UTP cable and hardware must be able to maintain a transmission rate of 100MHz. The 10Base-T standard limits

CAT5 cable runs to a maximum length of 100m (328 feet). CAT5 performance is possible only when cable, connector modules, patch cords, and all electronics carry the same C5 rating.

➤ *CAT5e Standard (Enhanced Category 5)*—Cable and hardware must be able to maintain a transmission rate of 350–400MHz.

➤ *CAT6 and CAT7 Standard*—Categories 6, 6e, and 7 represent emerging capabilities of UTP cable and equipment. Cable and hardware must be able to maintain a transmission rate at or above 550MHz.

RJ-11, RJ-45, and Modular Connectors

Back in the 1960s, the Bell Telephone Company began transitioning commercial customers from 25-pair trunk lines to twisted-pair modular cable. Because the company owned the wire, it was also responsible for making any wiring changes in a building when a customer outgrew the existing technology. People wanted to easily move a phone from one place to another, but in those days, phones were wired directly to the cable inside the wall. The new system would allow customers to simply disconnect the phone and plug it into a *modular jack*, using a *modular connector*. Adding or changing the wiring scheme in an entire building can easily cost ten times more than the original work, so the company needed a standard that could handle evolving technology.

Telephone conversations rarely need more than two lines, and the RJ-11 connector was the then-current standard for the home market. RJ-11 can have 1, 2, or 3 pairs of wires. The RJ-45 specification adds an extra pair to make 4 pairs of wires. The current standard for residential voice installations is RJ-11, whereas business installations use RJ-45. All current voice installations use twisted-pair wire. Bell decided to add the additional pairs and twist the wire to avoid *crosstalk*. Crosstalk is vaguely similar to EMI, where two data streams moving in close proximity can "leak" bits from one stream into the other and produce garbled confusion.

The form factor (shape) of the connector stayed almost the same as the home system, but the RJ-45 connector was designed to be used with four-pair wire. It was a little wider than the RJ-11, providing room for the extra pair. Commercial installations began using four-pair wire for all telecommunications. (After all, what home user would ever want networking capabilities?)

Remember that RJ-45 connectors and Category 5 cable work with four pairs of wire: 8 wires. RJ-11 and twisted-pair wire (telephone) work with two pairs (4 wires) or three pairs (6 wires). Telephone conversations can be sent over data-grade wire, but data can rarely be sent over telephone wire without losing integrity.

Oxidation and Data Integrity

The original RJ-45 specification called for copper contacts. However, copper begins to oxidize (tarnish) after it's installed. Oxidation breaks down the physical structure of metals, and although this poses no particular problem for telecommunications, it becomes a major problem for data communications. Any slight oxidation can easily degrade an installation from Category 5 down to Category 3, and seriously compromise network performance.

Clearly the quality of the contacts had to improve, so a new specification for modular data connectors developed, requiring non-corroding gold contacts. *Your* problem is that there isn't a commonly accepted name for the "modular data connector."

Figure 11.8 shows a modular connector and a section of CAT5 wire. The only way to tell the two grades of RJ-45 connectors apart is through the manufacturer's labeling, if there is a one. That being said, another way is that the less expensive RJ-45 connectors tarnish over time. When they do, they cause an increasing number of errors, reduced throughput, and node failures. You can install a network with a few hundred computers, and then wait and see. If you experience connectivity problems half a year later, the connectors were probably the cheaper version. This isn't the preferred way of testing network integrity.

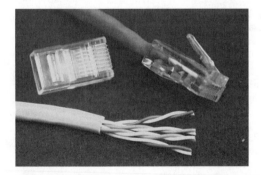

Figure 11.8 A typical RJ-45 connector with twisted-pair wire.

A computer patch cable uses two RJ-45 modular connectors (one at each end) and looks very much like a modular phone cord. Although it's difficult to see, stranded patch cable is always round. It can be flattened (with a hammer), but that would degrade the cable to Category 3 or less. Modular phone cord (silver satin) is always flat and untwisted. Pay attention to the wire's physical shape: The two types are easily recognizable.

Wiring Schemes: Pin-outs

You should have at least one reference source in your A+ preparation strategy that shows the specific pin configuration for various cables. That being said, consider four pairs of thin wires, each connecting to one of eight contacts in a plug. Each pair is color-coded, and each contact has a number. Starting from one side, the contacts are numbers 1–8. Modular connectors use only four wires (two pairs), and we'll mention those color-coded as orange, orange-white striped, blue, and blue-white striped.

Anyone can choose any four wires to make a patch cable, but two confusing standards are the Northern Telecommunication, Inc. 568-A standard and the American Telephone and Telegraph (AT&T) 568-B standard. One might wire orange to pin 1 and orange-white to pin 2. The other might wire orange-white to pin 1, with solid orange to pin 2. These two cables will most likely work together in a network, but there will be intermittent data problems because of that one small difference in polarity.

Most people call network connectors RJ-45 connectors, which is okay until a lowest-bidder contractor actually begins an installation. RJ-45 telephony connectors are much cheaper than modular data connectors, but that oxidation problem can degrade the installation. Understand that data still can run on the degraded cable, so long as the distances are well below specified maximums, and transmission speeds are held to 10Mbps. However, if a customer sets up a long cable run or upgrades to 100Base-T, things can get pretty ugly!

CompTIA uses the terms RJ-45 and "modular data connector" interchangeably, as do most people. The A+ exam doesn't differentiate between RJ-45 connectors, modular connectors, or data connectors. The majority of network problems can be traced to the Physical layer, and using the wrong connectors is the primary cause of those problems.

RJ-11 connectors use two- or three-pair wire, and are designed for home telephone conversations. Both RJ-45 connectors and modular data connectors use the same form factor. However, both are wider than RJ-11 telephone connectors. RJ-45 connectors use four pairs of wire, but can have either copper (low-grade) or gold (non-oxidizing) contacts. Gold RJ-45 data connectors are more expensive (55 to 80 cents) than copper RJ-45 phone connectors (8 to 10 cents).

Exam Prep Questions

Question 1

A DB25 _____ connector is used to connect the _____ port to a printer.

- ○ A. male, COM
- ○ B. female, COM
- ○ C. female, LPT
- ○ D. male, LPT

Answer D is correct. The "25" in DB25 refers to the number of pins on the cable connector or back panel connector. When the cable has 25 pins, it fits into an LPT socket with 25 holes and is called a DB25 parallel cable. This question is ambiguous because the connector can refer to the cable connector or the back panel connector. We believe CompTIA will always mean the cable connector.

Question 2

A modem connects to the serial COM2 port using a _____ connector.

- ○ A. DB15
- ○ B. DB9
- ○ C. Centronics
- ○ D. DB25

Answer B is correct. The COM port serial cables use a 9-pin DB9 connector. Video connectors are usually 15-pin connectors, and the Centronics connector is used to connect a 25-pin DB25 cable to a printer, at the printer end.

Question 3

Which of the following two designations do not apply to parallel interfaces? (Choose all that apply)

- ❑ A. ECP
- ❑ B. EPP
- ❑ C. ECC
- ❑ D. UTP

Answers C and D are correct. Answer A is incorrect because ECP is the Extend Capabilities Port. Answer B is incorrect because EPP is the Enhanced Parallel Port. Answer C is correct because ECC is a type of parity and does not apply to parallel interfaces. Answer D is correct because UTP is a type of twisted-pair wiring (unshielded) and does not apply to the parallel interface. Note that the question asks which do *not* apply.

Question 4

A Centronics printer cable uses a _____ pin connector, and a typical SCSI-2 cable uses a _____ pin connector.

○ A. 25, 36
○ B. 36, 50
○ C. 50, 25
○ D. 25, 9

Answer B is correct. A Centronics cable is a 36-pin connector. A SCSI cable is usually a 50-pin mini D-shell connector. Parallel cables are 25 pins, and serial cables are 9 pins. You'll have to remember these in whatever fashion suits you.

Question 5

10Base2 Ethernet coaxial cable is sometimes referred to as _____, and has a distance limit of _____ meters.

○ A. Thinnet, 200
○ B. Thinnet, 500
○ C. Thicknet, 500
○ D. Thicknet, 200

Answer A is correct. 10Base2 Ethernet coaxial cable, sometimes referred to as Thinnet, has a distance limit of 200 meters. 10Base5, the original coaxial cable, was thicker than 10Base2. Thicknet and Thinnet refer to the relative thickness of the cable wire. The 10 refers to the megabits per second transmission rate, and the last number is how many hundreds of meters the signal can travel. 10Base5 is 500 meters, whereas 10Base2 is 200 meters.

Question 6

Which connectors are you likely to find on a PC using an Intel 800–series chipset? (Choose all that apply)

❑ A. PS/2

❑ B. RJ-11

❑ C. RS-232

❑ D. RG-59

Answers A and B are correct. This is a nifty little trick question. First of all, you know that answer A is correct because most PCs continue to use the PS/2 mouse and keyboard connectors. However, you have three remaining options, and no particular clue as to how many are correct. (CompTIA will usually ask you to choose a specific number of responses, thereby giving you a clue.) You may not remember the RG co-ax connectors, but you should remember that "RG" refers to coaxial cable. The real problem is between the RJ-11 and RS-232. You'll likely think, "RJ-11 is for phones." However, consider that a dial-up modem must connect to a phone line, right? So answer B is correct, even if you think the PC would have only an RJ-45 connector. Finally, answer C is wrong because the RS-232 is the formal name for a 25-pin serial cable connector.

Question 7

Which of the two following cable systems does not require a terminator at both ends?

❑ A. Ethernet

❑ B. Centronics

❑ C. SCSI

❑ D. IDE

Answers B and D are correct. Always watch out for those negative-type questions, where something is "not" required. Ethernet cables (answer A) and SCSI buses (answer C) both require terminators. Answer B refers to the Centronics corporation's printer connector, which, because it's only a connector, does not require termination. It's the right answer because it doesn't need a terminator. Answer D is likewise a correct answer, because an IDE controller doesn't require a terminator. Note that "cabling system" is one of those ambiguous turns of phrase CompTIA is known for.

Question 8

A Windows 95 or Windows 98 machine running ScanDisk from a DOS command line requires that it does not have which one of the following physical ports?

○ A. COM2

○ B. LPT1

○ C. COM4

○ D. PS/2

Answer C is correct. We thought we'd try to drive you insane with a language question. First of all, as with all scenario questions, examine the responses, and then tear apart the question until you know only what you're being asked. Windows and DOS are irrelevant. When you break down the language, the question asks, "A machine does not have which physical port." Everything else is essentially a double or triple negative. Answer A refers to the actual, physical COM2 port, which exists. Answer B likewise refers to the physical parallel port, which exists. Answer D refers to a physical 6-pin PS/2 port and connector, which also exists. Therefore, all three responses exist, and make for incorrect responses. Answer C, COM4, refers to a logical port, not a physical port. The port is built in to the system, making it required, if you think about it, but it isn't a physical port. Therefore, answer C is the only non-physical port.

Question 9

Which of the following wiring categories would best ensure that a 10Base-T installation would accurately transmit data over a 200-meter cable run?

○ A. 10Base2

○ B. 10Base5

○ C. CAT3

○ D. CAT5

Answer D is correct. The question tries to trick you with the reference to 200 meters, and the 10Base2 co-ax cable. However, the question also gives you a clue that 10Base-T wiring comes in categories. Answers A and B are incorrect because they both refer to coaxial cable, not twisted pair. Answer C is incorrect because CAT3 wire was intended for voice transmission and introduces far too much signal degradation to handle a 200-meter cable run.

Question 10

Which of the following two types of wire use shielding?

- ❏ A. STP
- ❏ B. UTS
- ❏ C. UTP
- ❏ D. Thicknet

Answers A and D are correct. Both STP (shielded twisted pair) and coaxial Thicknet cable use shielding. Answers B and C are not only wrong, but the letters are so close together that you might easily get confused over the arrangement of the letters and forget that UTP (answer C) stands for *un*shielded twisted pair. UTS (answer B) is a bogus option.

Need to Know More?

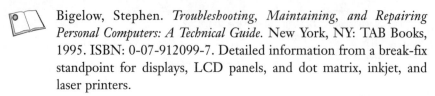

Bigelow, Stephen. *Troubleshooting, Maintaining, and Repairing Personal Computers: A Technical Guide*. New York, NY: TAB Books, 1995. ISBN: 0-07-912099-7. Detailed information from a break-fix standpoint for displays, LCD panels, and dot matrix, inkjet, and laser printers.

Messmer, Hans-Peter. *The Indispensable PC Hardware Book*. Reading, MA: Addison-Wesley, 1995. ISBN: 0-201-87697-3. This book contains much information, in great detail, about monitors and displays.

Minasi, Mark. *The Complete PC Upgrade and Maintenance Guide*. San Francisco, CA: Sybex Network Press, 1996. ISBN: 0-7821-1956-5. This resource is a great source of information on peripherals from a repair standpoint.

Rosch, Winn. *Hardware Bible*. Indianapolis, IN: Sams Publishing, 1994. ISBN: 0-672-30954-8. This book contains everything you'd want to know about computer hardware.

Tooly, Mike. *Data Communications Pocket Book*. Oxford, England: Newnes Press, 1997. ISBN: 0-7506-2884-7. If you can find it, this is a great reference you can throw in your pocket.

Groth, David and McBee, Jim. *Cabling, The Complete Guide to Network Wiring*. Alameda, CA: Sybex Publishing, 2000. ISBN: 0-7821-2645-6. This is the first book to buy when you go into networking. A must-have for anybody remotely involved with any phase of networking.

Hardware Practice Exam

It's time to take the exam! A countdown timer will go a long way toward putting some pressure into the mix. If you don't have one, we suggest you buy an inexpensive one. In Chapter 1 of this book, we covered many test-taking strategies. Although you'll be taking the exam on a computer, we've made the following test an accurate representation of the questions. Before taking this sample test, you should feel very comfortable about your knowledge. The next chapter holds the answer key and explanations. Remember, if you cheat, you're only hurting yourself!

Give yourself 90 minutes to complete this exam. Sit at a table or desk, and try to make the surface as empty and clean as you can. Lay down a piece of paper and a pencil and spend 5 minutes writing down the things you most want to have handy (from the Cram Sheet and your notes). Remember that you'll be allowed to have a blank sheet of paper and a pencil in the exam room. However, you won't be allowed to bring anything else in with you. You can use this paper for last-minute cram points you scribble down, or you can use it to break apart complex lists of possible responses to questions.

The Questions

You get only one chance to be surprised in a book like this. You might think you can go back and pretend you didn't see the questions, but it won't work. It's like reading the end of a novel first. You may be able to go back and experience some excitement by finding out how the story arrived at that ending, but it isn't the same thing. If you skim the answers to this test before you take it, you won't get an accurate assessment of your knowledge.

Keep in mind that we've already developed careers in the PC industry, and we aren't going in to take your exam for you. We're trying to prepare *you* for a career, and only you can create an accurate simulation of the test environment. Try to re-create the exam rooms you remember from school or other times in your life. The more accurate your simulation, the easier you'll feel when you're faced with the real thing.

Single-Choice and Multiple-Choice Responses

Every question on the current exam is supposed to be a multiple-choice question, with only a single correct response. Previous tests have had what are called "scenario" questions, where you're asked to fill in a sentence, or pick a likely set of options. These types of questions aren't supposed to be on the final exam, and we saw none on the final beta versions.

The current exam uses a very tricky way to get around the forbidden scenario questions. You'll be given a paragraph with a number of blanks. Each response has a list of words that can fill in the blanks in the order they appear. Be careful! It takes only one mistake to read a set out of order and produce an incorrect response.

If you haven't yet, you might want to read through Chapter 1, where we speak about the test environment and adaptive testing. If you already read Chapter 1, we'll remind you that we've chosen to continue the now-discontinued practice of allowing multiple answers. This is so that we can use a printed sample test to vary the complexity level and difficulty of the questions. As we said in the beginning, "If you can get through our test, you'll have no trouble with the real exam."

 You can assume there is only a single correct response for all questions excepting where noted. Multiple-choice responses explicitly ask you to choose all that apply, choose a specific number of responses, or to choose more than a single response.

Picking the Right Answer

Go back and refresh your memory with some of the strategies we discussed in Chapter 1. Think about some of the types of questions you're about to encounter. Keep in mind that the people creating these kinds of tests (ourselves included) take a sort of twisted pleasure in trying to screw you up! We've been where you are, and we made it through. So we think it's only fair that you should have to sweat a little.

Oh come on...lighten up! We're not trying to ruin your life. What we want you to do is to go into the test with your eyes wide open and all your senses on full alert. This is war! Look at each question as though it were a possible bomb. Keep your eyes peeled for the following:

➤ Words like "best," "required," "most appropriate." These are red flags telling you that there are multiple possibilities, based on how an *unstated* industry standard might apply.

➤ Long lists of commands. These can easily be read in the wrong order if you don't have your eyes focused. Write them down on your scratch paper, and put numbers next to them to ensure the proper order.

➤ Questions that try to draw images in your mind. Let the image come, and try to see it clearly. Add in sounds and action. These questions are often troubleshooting steps involving step-by-step menu choices.

Confusing Questions

By the time this test reached your hands, many people read it through, reviewed it, made suggestions, and researched every single word and punctuation mark. The test has been designed with psychology in mind, and with a full knowledge of many other tests. If there's confusion about a particular question, you can pretty much bet your next paycheck that the confusion was particularly built into that question!

That being said, we found a number of questions that really were confusing! To that end, we've tried to highlight those areas of knowledge throughout the book, and to give you our thoughts as to how we analyzed the questions. In our own version of the exam, we've tried to cause you some confusion as well, but in very specific ways.

Part of our preparation methodology is based on the idea that you've read the book and you're feeling fairly confident. You should also have a fair amount of intuition going for you, based on your hands-on experience with computers. Using those assumptions, we still want to throw a few curve balls at you so that you'll be somewhat familiar with the "Yikes!" feeling when it hits you in the real exam (and it will!).

Remember: Trust your instincts! If you get some of our most confusing questions right, you'll probably do extremely well on the CompTIA exam. If you get them wrong, don't feel bad. The questions are designed to be difficult. After you've checked the answers, you'll be more likely to remember where you tripped, and we'll have crammed that much more information into your head.

The Exam Framework

The questions you're about to see have not been organized in any specific order. We've made no attempt to follow the progression of this book, nor to follow any other sort of logical progression. This is a general test of your overall knowledge of microcomputer hardware. The Operating System sample test is at the end of the second half of this book.

The real world comes at you from every direction at once, and frequently you'll have to juggle many important problems at the same time. This test has also been designed with possible job interviews in mind, where you're taken into a repair or service environment and turned loose for an hour or so.

Many of the questions use jargon phrasing and shortened versions of terminology. Throughout the book we've tried to highlight the many different ways of saying the same thing. We've used different words to refer to various terms, and inter-mixed acronyms with the full spelling of the terms. Repeatedly, we've tried to prepare you for the varying ways that technical professionals refer to problems and tools of the trade.

The A+ exam was created by a committee of professionals, each of whom has a different way of talking about computers. We've tried to extract as many of those styles as possible, and to jumble them together in a similar way as to what we found on the exam. Life is rarely simple, and the exam (in our opinion) is actually quite difficult.

Beginning the Exam

From the time you complete your notes on the blank sheet of paper, you have 90 minutes to complete the test. Take your time. Imagine you're shipwrecked on a desert island, and have absolutely nothing else to do for the rest of your life. Read every word in the question carefully, with interest and even fascination. Don't read the responses right off the bat. Instead, read the whole question a second time before you look at the responses.

After you've read the question, contemplate what you think is the correct response. Only then should you read each response on its own. Don't try to fit it in with the question; just read it as an interesting set of words. When you've read each response as though it were a random fact, go back and read the question one more time. It sounds like a lot of time, but you'll be far less likely to misread anything if you follow this type of agenda.

A common flaw in the human mind is to immediately attempt to make sense out of incoming data. This flaw is often used against you on various exams. By reading the question on its own, and then reading each response without thinking about the question, you overload the "surprise circuit" and stand a better chance in overcoming this problem. After your mind stops trying to puzzle over the question, you're ready to actually read the question as it stands.

Start your timer, and begin the exam now.

Questions

Question 1

An expansion bus provides connectivity between which of the following?

- ○ A. System components
- ○ B. IDE controllers
- ○ C. Hardware devices
- ○ D. Slot risers

Question 2

How many devices can be attached to a SCSI chain?

- ○ A. 5
- ○ B. 6
- ○ C. 7
- ○ D. 8

Question 3

If you use IRQ 2 in an AT system, which IRQ cannot be manually configured?

- ○ A. IRQ 13
- ○ B. IRQ 5
- ○ C. IRQ 9
- ○ D. IRQ 8

Question 4

What is the correct acronym for Synchronous memory?

- ○ A. SRAM
- ○ B. DRAM
- ○ C. SDRAM
- ○ D. RDRAM

Question 5

Which of the following DMA channels is used for secondary PIC steering?

○ A. Channel 2

○ B. Channel 9

○ C. Channel 2 and 9

○ D. None of the above

Question 6

Pentium 4 processors use a 64-bit address bus and 64-bit processor bus.

○ A. True

○ B. False

Question 7

Which of the following would aid system cooling?

○ A. Removing the expansion covers in the back of the system case for increased airflow

○ B. Attaching covers to any open expansion slots on the back of the system unit

○ C. Placing the system unit against a cool inside wall

○ D. Opening windows to increase airflow in the room

Question 8

Which is the common default IRQ used for LPT2?

○ A. IRQ 5

○ B. IRQ 9

○ C. IRQ 7

○ D. IRQ 14

Question 9

When a piece of paper comes out of a laser printer almost completely black, the primary corona wire has failed to properly charge which of the following things?

○ A. The separation pad

○ B. The heating roller

○ C. The EP drum

○ D. The paper

Question 10

The keyboard sends a _____ to the CPU following a keypress.

○ A. Key code

○ B. Scan code

○ C. ASCII code

○ D. Translation code

Question 11

Which of the following statements is true?

○ A. An ATA drive uses an IDE controller.

○ B. An IDE controller uses an ATA bus.

○ C. An IDE drive uses an ATA controller.

○ D. An ATA controller uses an IDE bus.

Question 12

The thermal fuse fails in a laser printer. What is the most probable cause?

○ A. The fuser overheated.

○ B. The corona wire shorted.

○ C. The drum overcharged.

○ D. The laser diode needs changing.

Question 13

How would you deactivate the infrared port on a laptop computer running Windows XP?

O A. Go to My Computer I Control Panel I Add-Remove Hardware; select IrDA, and select Remove.

O B. Go to the Device Manager, expand the Infrared Devices node, select IrDA, and select Disable.

O C. The infrared port is a system board component and must be deactivated on the system board.

O D. Infrared ports are autosensing and do not need to be deactivated.

Question 14

The print from a dot matrix printer is erratic, with some characters only partially printed. What needs to be done?

O A. The ribbon needs to be replaced.

O B. The print head needs to be aligned.

O C. A lighter-weight paper needs to be used.

O D. The tractor feed needs adjusting.

Question 15

How do the data tracks of a DVD differ from those of a CD?

O A. The DVD has multiple tracks running in parallel. The CD has only one track.

O B. DVD data tracks are longer and wider than CD data tracks.

O C. CD data tracks are shorter and thicker than DVD tracks.

O D. There is no difference. The DVD holds more data because the pits are compressed.

Question 16

Windows 98 recognizes an internal modem as a standard modem and does not identify the type and manufacturer. Why?

- ○ A. Windows 98 does not have a driver for this modem.
- ○ B. The modem is not PnP.
- ○ C. The SYSTEM.DAT does not have a listing.
- ○ D. The modem is not seated correctly.

Question 17

Windows Safe Mode loads which of the following display drivers?

- ○ A. SVGA
- ○ B. VGA
- ○ C. EGA
- ○ D. CGA

Question 18

RGB monitors commonly use which type of connection to display information?

- ○ A. CMY
- ○ B. DVI
- ○ C. 9-pin analog
- ○ D. 15-pin analog

Question 19

Which of the following most closely resembles the technology used for the AGP?

- ○ A. DMA controller
- ○ B. IRQ controller
- ○ C. PCI controller
- ○ D. IDE controller

Question 20

A company has three buildings on campus, connected through a fiber optic cable with commercial hubs. Each building has been wired to Cat-5, and the business runs multiple TCP/IP networks. Which NIC interface would be the best choice when adding a notebook computer to the network?

- ○ A. 10Base-2
- ○ B. 10Base-5
- ○ C. 10Base-T
- ○ D. IEEE-8270 compliant

Question 21

Your clients have a local printer connected to the back panel parallel port, but when they try to print a document, nothing happens. One diagnostics test is to check the port assignment for the printer. Which set of steps would you use?

- ○ A. Settings, Printers, Properties, Details
- ○ B. Settings, Control Panel, Printers, Ports
- ○ C. My Computer, Properties, Device Manager, System Properties
- ○ D. Settings, Printers, View, Options

Question 22

PCI400 CMOS is clocked to 133MHz, and has a throughput of 8.33KB/s.

- ○ A. True
- ○ B. False

Question 23

What device would best protect a PC against erratic power and blackouts?

- ○ A. A line conditioner
- ○ B. A surge protector
- ○ C. A UPS
- ○ D. An ATA

Question 24

A Pentium 4 CPU uses a 4X multiplier of Intel's Pentium PC100 specification.

○ A. True

○ B. False

Question 25

What is the default interrupt and address for COM1?

○ A. IRQ 4 and 02FEh

○ B. IRQ 5 and 03F8h

○ C. IRQ 4 and 03F8h

○ D. IRQ 3 and 02E8h

Question 26

What does the small *h* following an address indicate?

○ A. The address should be read in hexadecimal.

○ B. The address uses a high-order bit.

○ C. The address is a default address.

○ D. The address uses hard coding.

Question 27

Which of the following resolutions apply to a standard VGA monitor? (Choose the two best answers)

❏ A. 640 pixels

❏ B. 480 pixels

❏ C. 600 pixels

❏ D. 800 pixels

Question 28

What is a monitor called when it draws every other line on the screen, then returns and draws skipped lines?

○ A. Interfaced

○ B. Non-interfaced

○ C. Interlaced

○ D. Non-interlaced

Question 29

A patch cable in a 10Base-T Ethernet network breaks. What is the most likely result?

○ A. The entire network crashes.

○ B. Only the PC attached to that cable loses connectivity.

○ C. The network operating system forces a system shutdown.

○ D. Nothing.

Question 30

What is the default networking protocol used on the Internet?

○ A. IPX/SPX

○ B. DNS

○ C. TCP/IP

○ D. MIME

Question 31

NRZI means that Non-Return-to-Zero-Inverted encoding is used for which of the following?

○ A. Divide-by-zero errors in a Pentium processor

○ B. To maintain a positive DC voltage

○ C. As a self-diagnostics system to maintain 0 ohm circuits

○ D. As a type of signaling throughput

Question 32

Which type of memory is licensed by Intel, and used to maximize performance in Microsoft Windows?

- ○ A. WRAM
- ○ B. VRAM
- ○ C. RDRAM
- ○ D. SDRAM

Question 33

Choose the correct navigational path to follow to discover an IRQ conflict.

- ○ A. Start | Programs | Accessories | Device Manager
- ○ B. Start | Settings | Control Panel | Device Manager
- ○ C. Start | Settings | Control Panel | System Devices
- ○ D. Start | Programs | Accessories | System Devices

Question 34

A network user wants to send an email message for a meeting using Outlook. Which OSI layer is primarily responsible for that transfer?

- ○ A. Application layer
- ○ B. IP Transfer layer
- ○ C. Link Transmission layer
- ○ D. Network Services layer

Question 35

The memory controller and the backside bus both derive their timing signals from the PCI bus.

- ○ A. True
- ○ B. False

Question 36

Desktop Pentium processors contain a _____-bit address bus, and a _____-bit internal bus.

- ○ A. 32, 64
- ○ B. 36, 64
- ○ C. 32, 36
- ○ D. 36, 32

Question 37

The best type of keyboard to use on the floor of a small-engine manufacturing plant would be

- ○ A. Mechanical
- ○ B. Foam element
- ○ C. Membrane sheet
- ○ D. Rubber dome

Question 38

How many DMA controllers and DMA channels are on an ATX system board?

- ○ A. 2 controllers and 8 DMA channels
- ○ B. 1 controller and 16 DMA channels
- ○ C. 1 controller and 4 DMA channels
- ○ D. 2 controllers and 16 DMA channels

Question 39

A customer complains that when he moves the mouse, the cursor sometimes fails to move along the screen. What would be the first thing to check?

- ○ A. Dirt on the encoder wheels
- ○ B. A bad photo-interrupter
- ○ C. Dirt on the roller bars
- ○ D. The Device Manager

Question 40

Which of the following determines how many CCDs are built into a flatbed scanner?

○ A. Vertical resolution

○ B. Optical resolution

○ C. Horizontal resolution

○ D. Interpolated resolution

Question 41

What is the standard resolution for a VGA monitor?

○ A. 480×640

○ B. 800×600

○ C. 640×480

○ D. 600×400

Question 42

A monitor shows a strange band of transparent green, fading from the left edge toward the center. Adjusting the panel controls does nothing to affect the problem. The most likely next consideration would be

○ A. External degaussing factors

○ B. ESD

○ C. Electron gun misalignment

○ D. EMI

Question 43

What is the best cleaning solution to use on a dirty system case?

○ A. Alcohol

○ B. Carbosol

○ C. Mild soap and water

○ D. Diluted muratic acid

Question 44

Which of the following are not used to connect a CPU to a motherboard? (Choose the two best answers)

- ❑ A. Socket 8
- ❑ B. Socket B
- ❑ C. Slot A
- ❑ D. Slot 4

Question 45

Which electrical component commonly found in computers can hold an electrical charge even when disconnected from power?

- ○ A. A resistor
- ○ B. A capacitor
- ○ C. A diode
- ○ D. A transistor

Question 46

A good fuse will give what kind of reading when tested with a standard multimeter?

- ○ A. High DC volts value
- ○ B. Low ohm value
- ○ C. High ohm value
- ○ D. High capacitance value

Question 47

To reduce possible ESD damage while repairing a PC, what is the most effective way to ground yourself?

- ○ A. With a copper strap attached to the workbench
- ○ B. With a copper strap attached to the PC
- ○ C. By touching the chassis while replacing components
- ○ D. None of the above

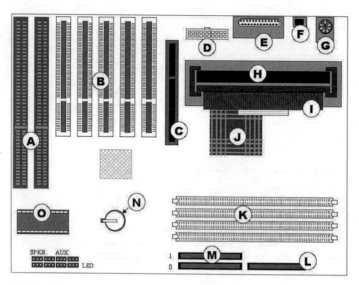

Exhibit 1   Use this motherboard diagram to answer questions 48 through 52.

Question 48

What are the two items that the letter *M* points to?

○ A. IDE controllers

○ B. ISA bus slots

○ C. USB controllers

○ D. Secondary cache chips

Question 49

What is the item that the letter *H* points to?

○ A. Modem

○ B. Battery

○ C. CPU

○ D. Parallel interface

Question 50

What are the two items the letter *A* points to?

○ A. PCI slots

○ B. 8-bit ISA slots

○ C. Memory banks

○ D. 16-bit ISA slots

Question 51

What is the letter *K* labeling?

○ A. PCI bus

○ B. SIMM slots

○ C. ZIF socket

○ D. BIOS chip

Question 52

What does the letter *D* point to?

○ A. AT keyboard connector

○ B. Orientation chip

○ C. Power connector

○ D. LPT connector

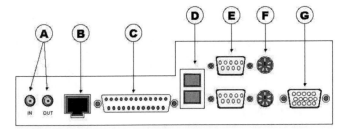

Exhibit 2   Use this chassis back panel diagram to answer questions 53 through 55.

Question 53

A parallel printer cable connects to which item (designated by a letter)?

○ A. C

○ B. D

○ C. E

○ D. F

Question 54

What items does the letter *E* point to?

○ A. Video interface connectors

○ B. USB interface connectors

○ C. Serial interface connectors

○ D. PS/2 interface connectors

Question 55

A USB port is shown in the diagram by which letter?

○ A. B

○ B. C

○ C. D

○ D. E

Question 56

Which is the best type of wireless network to use when connecting a desktop PC to a laptop?

○ A. Infrastructure

○ B. Ad hoc

○ C. Piconet

○ D. Bluetooth

Question 57

Which of the following two designations do not apply to parallel interfaces? (Choose all that apply)

- ❏ A. ECP
- ❏ B. EPP
- ❏ C. ECC
- ❏ D. UTP

Question 58

What is the best and simplest solution for resolving Ethernet congestion?

- ○ A. Add another hub to the network.
- ○ B. Segment the network with a router.
- ○ C. Segment the network with a bridge.
- ○ D. Set up a secondary IP network token.

Question 59

Most people use a USB DB9 connector on the back panel of the computer to connect a USB keyboard with a hub.

- ○ A. True
- ○ B. False

Question 60

What type of expansion buses are included on most system boards? (Choose all that apply)

- ❏ A. MCA
- ❏ B. ISA
- ❏ C. PCI
- ❏ D. EIDE
- ❏ E. VESA

Question 61

The PC100 standard was developed to ensure that

- ○ A. All motherboards ran at 100MHz.
- ○ B. Hardware devices would match the PCI standard.
- ○ C. All memory modules ran at 100MHz.
- ○ D. Some memory modules ran at 100MHz.

Question 62

Which of the following responses correctly identify a cable that uses the NTFS transfer protocol?

- ○ A. 10Base-T
- ○ B. CAT-5e
- ○ C. None
- ○ D. Both

Question 63

Which device can be connected to the computer and recognized while the computer is running?

- ○ A. A 101 keyboard
- ○ B. A CRT monitor
- ○ C. A serial joystick
- ○ D. A USB scanner

Question 64

Which type of connectors do the AMD Athlon and Duron processors use? (Choose the two best answers)

- ❏ A. Socket 370
- ❏ B. Slot A
- ❏ C. Socket 8
- ❏ D. Socket A

Question 65

IRQ 14 is the default IRQ assigned to which of the following?

○ A. Secondary disk controller

○ B. Primary disk controller

○ C. Master slave disk controller

○ D. CDROM drive controller

Question 66

A cable has a 25-pin male connector at one end and a Centronics 36-pin male connector at the other end. A common use for this cable is best described by which of the following choices?

○ A. A parallel printer connection

○ B. A modem connection

○ C. A serial printer connection

○ D. A SCSI device connection

Question 67

In what order does hierarchical memory priority take place?

○ A. L-2, RAM, L-1

○ B. RAM, L-1, L-2

○ C. L-1, L-2, RAM

○ D. RAM, L-1, disk

Question 68

The number 5 in the 10Base-5 standard refers to which of the following?

○ A. The maximum length of the cable in hundreds of meters

○ B. The width of the cable in centimeters

○ C. The width of the center conductor in millimeters

○ D. The maximum number of connections per meter

Question 69

Which layer is primarily responsible for making connections to the Internet and routing data packets?

○ A. Layer 1—Physical media

○ B. Layer 2—Data Link management

○ C. Layer 3—Network layer

○ D. Layer 4—Transfer layer

Question 70

Which of the following connectors are not used in a typical networking situation? (Choose all that apply)

❑ A. DB25

❑ B. RJ-11

❑ C. RJ-45

❑ D. DB15

Hardware Practice Exam Answer Key

1. C

2. C

3. C

4. C

5. D

6. B

7. B

8. A

9. C

10. B

11. B

12. A

13. B

14. A

15. C

16. A

17. B

18. D

19. A

20. C

21. A

22. B

23. C

24. B

25. C

26. A

27. A and B

28. C

29. B

30. C

31. D

32. C

33. C

34. A

35. B

36. D

37. C

38. A

39. C

40. B

41. C

42. D

43. C

44. B and D

45. B

46. B

47. D

48. A

49. C

50. D

51. B

52. C

53. A

54. C

55. C

56. A

57. C and D

58. C

59. B

60. B and C

61. D

62. C

63. D

64. B and D

65. B

66. A

67. C

68. A

69. C

70. B and D

Question 1

Answer C is correct. Note that the question refers only to expansion buses. Answer A is incorrect because system components often use the motherboard or main bus to connect, and do not require an expansion bus. Answer B is incorrect because IDE controllers are typically on the motherboard, not expansion cards. Answer D could be construed as possibly correct, but the question is testing you for your conceptual knowledge of an expansion bus. Slot risers might apply to "riser cards," but when you have to go through complex definition and word acrobatics, the chances are the answer is usually wrong.

Question 2

Answer C is correct. This is a tricky question because the question specifically uses the word "devices." The host adapter for a SCSI card automatically takes up one of eight possible ID numbers. That leaves room for up to seven devices to be daisy-chained to the SCSI controller, each with a unique ID number. Answers A and B are technically correct, but the implication of the question is that you're being tested on the limits of a SCSI chain. For that reason, answers A and B are incorrect in this *context*. Answer D is incorrect because the host adapter usually takes the eighth ID number (LUN, or logical unit number).

Question 3

Answer C is correct. Note that the question refers to "manual configuration." The AT BIOS cascades IRQ 9 to IRQ 2. If the system is using IRQ 2, then it must also be using IRQ 9. PCI steering also uses IRQ 9, so you shouldn't use it for manual device configuration. Answer A, IRQ 13, is a red herring. This IRQ is typically set aside for a math coprocessor. Answer B is incorrect because IRQ 5 is the default line assigned to LPT2. Answer D is incorrect because IRQ 8 is the default line set aside for the system clock.

Question 4

Answer C is correct. Be careful with these types of questions that seem to be a no-brainer. Synchronous memory is technically called Synchronous

DRAM, or SDRAM. However, the question has an "S" and the word "memory," so if you're not on your toes, you could easily choose answer A, SRAM, as an incorrect response. SRAM is Static RAM, or static memory. Answer B is incorrect because it refers to Dynamic RAM and isn't necessarily synchronous. Answer D is incorrect because it specifies Rambus DRAM, or Rambus memory.

Question 5

Answer D is correct. We can't emphasize enough that you must be very careful when you read each question. Answers A, B, and C are incorrect because they have nothing to do with Programmable Interrupt Controllers. Make sure that you have nothing on your mind, or any other appointments on the day of the exam!

First note that the question links DMA channels with some sort of steering. Note also that the question refers to "PIC steering," not PCI steering. Many people have a slight tendency towards dyslexic letter or symbol reversals, and this question plays on that tendency. Additionally, we expect to see something, so we see it. Be careful! The *PCI* specification allows for IRQ steering, and cascading between two interrupt controllers—*not* DMA channels. Although this question looks like it could be legitimate, go back and check each false reference and how they're combined to mess with your mind.

Question 6

Answer B is correct. Excepting historical chips, every CPU since the 8086 has a different size address bus and processor bus. The question indicates the same size between the buses. This question is testing you for your ability to differentiate the address bus from all other buses. Remember that the address bus is internal to the chip and assigns large address numbers to access memory. The processor bus connects the CPU to the motherboard.

Question 7

Answer B is correct. The expansion slot covers are part of the engineering design to allow for optimal airflow within the case of any PC that uses expansion slots and covers. Answer A is incorrect because removing unused slot covers often interferes with designed air circulation and generally increases the temperature around the CPU. Answers C and D might provide minimal aid in cooling the overall environment, but they are incorrect in the context of the "system cooling" referred to in the question.

Question 8

Answer A is correct. LPT2 uses IRQ 5, although we rarely see a second parallel printer port on a modern machine. CompTIA has no problem testing you on archaic or obsolete technology, because the default IRQs still exist in today's machines. Answer B is incorrect because IRQ 9 generally cascades to IRQ 2. Answer C is incorrect because LPT1 is assigned to IRQ 7 by default. Answer D is incorrect because IRQ 14 is normally assigned to the primary disk controller.

Question 9

Answer C is correct. The primary corona wire is used to place a negative charge on the electrophotographic (EP) drum. This removes toner from those areas that will not produce an image. (The secondary corona wire places a charge on the paper to attract toner to the correct locations. See Chapter 9.) If the drum fails to charge correctly, the entire drum will take on toner and transfer it to the whole piece of paper. Answer A is incorrect because the separation pad prevents more than one sheet of paper from entering the printer at any given time. Answer B is incorrect because the fusing assembly contains the heating roller and is used to fuse the image toner particles to the paper. Answer D is incorrect because if the paper is completely black, something failed to place a defined image on the paper. On the other hand, if the paper fails to charge, no toner sticks to the paper for fusing.

Question 10

Answer B is correct. Keyboard controllers and circuitry generate a scan code whenever a key is pressed (see Chapter 7). Answer A is incorrect because the term "key code" is bogus. Although the scan code refers to the ASCII table, answer C is incorrect because the question asks about something being sent by the keyboard, not what the CPU interprets. Answer D is also a bogus option.

Question 11

Answer B is correct. The responses all ask you to make a distinction between a drive, a controller, and a bus. An IDE drive refers to a drive with a built-in controller, and it uses a bus of some type. ATA is a specification for an interface bus. ATA is never a controller or a drive. Answer A is incorrect because it translates to "A bus specification uses a controller." Answer C is incorrect because ATA specifies how controllers work; it isn't a controller device. Answer D is incorrect because it reverses the concept of controller and bus specification.

Question 12

Answer A is correct. The fuser step of the printing process involves high amounts of heat to melt the toner and to fuse it to the paper. For safety, a thermal fuse is inserted in the fuser circuit to prevent possible fire hazards. Answer B is incorrect because a short circuit at the corona wire would shut down the printer or cause a fire. The corona wire does not have a *thermal* fuse. Answer C is incorrect because the EP drum does not use heat, and answer D is incorrect because the laser printer contains no such thing as a laser diode.

Question 13

Answer B is correct. Watch out for the reference to Windows XP. It isn't necessary to the question, and is there for confusion purposes. The main point of the question has to do with an infrared port. This is an I/O device, and should clue you to the fact that the response will involve the Device Manager. Answer A is incorrect because an I/O port is not a removable device. Answer C is incorrect because the Device Manager, not motherboard jumpers, ordinarily manages I/O ports. Answer D is a bogus option: Ports aren't referred to as "autosensing."

Question 14

Answer A is correct. The clue is that some characters are printing only partially. The immediate diagnostic test would be to replace the existing ink ribbon. Answer B is incorrect because print head alignment is not a common cause of partial character printing. Answer C is incorrect because the weight of the paper has little direct connection to the print quality. Answer D is incorrect because the tractor feed could cause misalignment of characters, but would be unlikely to cause partial printing.

Question 15

Answer C is correct. Answer A is incorrect because both DVDs and CDs use spiraling tracks (see Chapter 8). Although the DVD has multiple tracks, they're not concentric rings (as found on hard drives). Answer B is incorrect because DVD tracks are thinner than CD tracks, so as to put more data on the disk. Answer D is incorrect because there's a substantial difference in track geometry between DVDs and compact disks.

Question 16

Answer A is correct. If Windows 9x can access the device and understand that the device is a modem, it attempts to find an internal device driver for the specific modem. Windows uses PnP BIOS to read the manufacturer's name and the model of the modem, if available. However, whether or not the device is PnP, Windows understands it is a modem. If no specific internal device driver is found, Windows assigns a generic device driver and calls it a Standard Modem. After the name and settings are assigned, they are written to the SYSTEM.DAT file. Answer B is incorrect because although the modem is not PnP, Windows still recognizes it enough to assign resources and a device name. Answers C and D are incorrect because the device must be listed and correctly seated if it shows up in the Device Manager.

Question 17

Answer B is correct. The Windows Safe Mode installs a keyboard driver and a standard VGA display driver (SVGA stands for Super VGA). Safe Mode bypasses network connections without loading network drivers. Safe Mode is a diagnostic mode designed to reduce configuration problems to their absolute minimum. CGA and EGA graphics modes are obsolete standards, so answers C and D are incorrect. Answer A is incorrect because SVGA graphic modes have numerous configuration options, making it an inappropriate mode for troubleshooting possible display problems.

Question 18

Answer D is correct. Note that the question specifies an RGB monitor, which stands for Red-Green-Blue. The question also asks about a connector. Most RGB monitors are cathode ray (CRTs) and use 15-pin analog video connectors. Answer A is incorrect because it refers to Cyan-Magenta-Yellow color processing in LCD panels and printing. Answer B is incorrect because it refers to a Digital Video Interface connector, most often used for LCD panels. Answer C is incorrect because it refers to the 9-pin serial connector.

Question 19

Answer A is correct. This is a very complicated question, as it requires that you have an underlying understanding of the Accelerated Graphics Port and how it differs from the traditional video sub-system. AGP was designed to work directly with main memory and the video memory on graphics expansion cards. The AGP uses Intel's Direct Memory Execute (DIME) instructions. Answer B is incorrect because the AGP is not a controller for multiple devices. Answer C is incorrect because the PCI bus controls many devices, and AGP is a separate bus that connects to the PCI bus. Answer D is incorrect because IDE controllers are a drive technology, not video or graphics technology. (If you got this right, pat yourself on the back!)

Question 20

Answer C is correct. Once again, this question goes to some lengths to distract you with complicated references to fiber optics technology. Break down the question and figure out, "What's really going on here?" A network exists. A notebook computer is being added. It requires a NIC. The building uses category 5 wire, which specifically refers to 10Base-T twisted pair (see Chapter 11). Answers A and B are incorrect because they refer to coaxial cable, not twisted pair. Answer D is a bogus response, as network card interfaces aren't referred to by their IEEE specifications.

Question 21

Answer A is correct. You'll likely encounter a number of questions involving Windows menu pathways. For the most part, the incorrect responses usually go awry by the second- or third-level option. You should have a pretty good image of the Windows Start menu for Windows 98, Me, 2000, and XP. Even if you don't, logic should give you a pretty good tool to decode these types of questions. Answer B is incorrect because we don't configure printers through a global "Ports" option. Each individual printer has a tab for port configuration under its own Properties. Answer C is incorrect because we don't use the Device Manager to configure individual printers. Answer D is incorrect because "View Options" almost always refers to how folder information displays. Secondly, answer D is incorrect because the Start menu has a "Settings" option, which expands to "Control Panel." From there, you can choose Printers.

Question 22

Answer B is correct. Although this question looks complicated, referring to timing cycles and throughput, it isn't really. Note that the focus of the question is on the PCI specification. CMOS is a type of ROM used at the chipset level to store configurations. The PCI specification has to do with standardizing RAM modules (see Chapter 3). When PCI is followed by a number—anywhere from 100 to 3,200—it refers to some type of SIMM specification. There's no such thing as "PCI CMOS."

Question 23

Answer C is correct. An uninterruptible power supply (UPS) contains a battery backup to provide power to the PC during power interruptions and blackouts. The UPS also provides line conditioning, meaning that erratic power events are stabilized before reaching the computer. Answer A is incorrect because line conditioning is a feature of the UPS, not a separate device. Answer B is incorrect because a surge protector provides no protection from a blackout. The ATA referenced in answer D is the AT Attachment bus specification associated with an IDE controller, and has nothing to do with power supply.

Question 24

Answer B is correct. Once again, the PCI specification has to do with memory modules, and not microprocessors. This is another of those seeming no-brainer questions that you might easily get wrong if you're not thinking clearly. The "4" in the Pentium name refers to the generation of chips, not a particular specification or a multiplier. Clock multipliers derive from the front side bus, not a memory module.

Question 25

Answer C is correct. COM1 uses IRQ 4 and address 03F8h for the default installation. (COM1 is odd and uses even IRQs.) Answers A and B are not COM addresses. Answer D is the default address for COM4. COM ports 1 and 3 use IRQ 4, whereas COM ports 2 and 4 use IRQ 3. This is a rote-memory question, and you'll have to do your best to remember the addresses for just long enough to pass the exam. Then you can always look them up.

Question 26

Answer A is correct. A common indicator that a number or address is a hexadecimal unit is either a lowercase or an uppercase "h" before or after the unit. Answer B is incorrect because we don't reference any type of bit in an address listing. Answers C and D are bogus options.

Question 27

Answers A and B are correct. A standard VGA monitor has a resolution of 640×480. Answers C and D are incorrect because although an SVGA monitor can be configured to a 640×480 resolution, 600×800 is a more common configuration. Remember that *pixels* (picture units) designate graphic resolution in displayed images such as monitors or graphics. *Dots per inch (dpi)* designate printed or scanned resolutions.

Question 28

Answer C is correct. Monitors either are interlaced or non-interlaced. They're not inter*faced* or non-interfaced. Note that only one letter makes the difference! When the electron gun at the back of a CRT monitor draws every odd line, then returns and draws every even line, it is interlaced (like lacing up shoes). If the electron gun draws every line in a single pass (no skipping lines), the monitor is a non-interlaced monitor.

Question 29

Answer B is correct. 10Base-T is twisted-pair wiring. Twisted pair enables each PC to connect to a hub directly. If the wire breaks, only the specific PC connected by that wire is affected. Answer A is incorrect because the overall network connection is designed in such a way that each PC has its own connection. Wiring integrity is not dependent on a functional connection between every PC. Answer C is incorrect because the operating system hasn't crashed. There's only a bad cable. Answer D is incorrect because *something* will happen when a cable breaks.

Question 30

Answer C is correct. The Internet is a Unix-based network that uses Transmission Control Protocol/Internet Protocol (TCP/IP) networking protocols. Answer A is incorrect because Internet Packet Exchange/Sequenced Packet Exchange (IPX/SPX) is typically used in local area networks (LANs) running NetWare. Answer B is incorrect because DNS is a service that converts host names to IP addresses. The Multipurpose Internet Mail Extensions (MIME), in answer D, is an email protocol. Once again, use your real-world experience and rote memory to connect the Internet to TCP/IP.

Question 31

Answer D is correct. This is a type of obscure question CompTIA sometimes uses to make sure the exam gives at least everyone some amount of headache pain. The best strategy for these types of questions is usually a process of elimination. Answer A is incorrect because a divide-by-zero error is usually a math coprocessor or chip error. The question refers to "encoding." Answer B is incorrect because nothing can maintain a positive DC voltage. Answer C is incorrect because electrical circuitry is rarely self-diagnosing. The circuit either works or doesn't work. Answer D is the last response, when all others have been set aside. NRZI encoding is used in USB technology, and also in certain types of memory technology (see Chapters 3 and 10).

Question 32

Answer C is correct. Note that references to Windows and performance are red herrings, used to distract you from the real question. You should know that Intel and Rambus DRAM are linked. You should also know that answers A, B, and D are incorrect because they refer to the generic names for Windows RAM, Video RAM, and Synchronous DRAM, respectively. None of these are proprietary types of memory.

Question 33

Answer C is correct. Once again, a reference to an IRQ conflict almost always refers to the Device Manager, even though IRQ conflicts are extremely difficult to resolve on a modern machine. The question is also tricky because it doesn't refer to a specific operating system. Don't be fooled! Examine each response in terms of how you would look for the Device Manager. Answers A and D are incorrect because the Device Manager is part of either the System applet in the Control Panel or a Properties menu, never the Accessories menu, regardless of which OS is installed. Answer B is incorrect because Device Manager is a tab on the System Properties menu, within the Control Panel. The Device Manager is never (by default) a separate listing on its own in the Control Panel window.

Question 34

Answer A is correct. This is a psychological question, in that it appears to ask you to understand the entire breakdown of the OSI model. Before you panic with these types of questions, examine each response for "name recognition," and see whether you can eliminate bogus options. You'll have to use rote memory (possibly using index cards with each layer name, taped on the walls at home) to remember the layer names. Answers B, C, and D are all bogus names. You should have a general idea of the layer functions, but remember that A+ is not designed to make you a full-fledged network engineer.

Question 35

Answer B is correct. This is a good example of an ambivalent question. Although everything technically derives its time from a clock associated with the PCI specification, the PCI bus itself doesn't generate system timing. The front side bus is the base timing used for multipliers, but it isn't referenced in the question. Perhaps the most critical distinction between the backside bus and every other bus is that it's directly tied to the CPU. The backside bus is used for second-level memory caching, with either an L-2 or L-3 cache. Remember that system memory is fast, but not as fast as cache memory. The backside bus does, technically, use the front side bus for timing, but is usually referred to in relation to a fraction (or divider) of the CPU's clock speed.

Question 36

Answer D is correct. This question is a pure rote-memory problem, based on your understanding of the difference between an address bus and the CPU's main, internal data path. Note that your only options are 32, 36, and 64. Remember that Pentiums typically have a 36-bit address bus. The internal bus is almost always smaller than the address bus. Answers A and C are incorrect because they indicate a 32-bit address bus. Answer B is incorrect because the internal bus is larger than the address bus. By process of elimination, answer D is the only response left. (See Chapters 4 and 5.)

Question 37

Answer C is correct. The "manufacturing plant" reference should be your main clue. Why include the reference in a keyboard question unless it has something to do with dust, dirt, and keyboard problems? Answers A, B, and D are all subject to problems with water and dust interfering with the key stem and the underlying electrical circuitry. Answer C indicates a completely enclosed type of keyboard particularly designed to practically eliminate external dirt and moisture.

Question 38

Answer A is correct. XT motherboards contained one DMA controller with four channels. The AT system board added a second controller and four more channels, making a total of two DMA controllers with eight channels (four channels per controller). The ATX (as well as the LPX and NLX) form factor is an outgrowth of the AT motherboard, continuing the use of two controllers and eight channels. Answer B is incorrect because it's the IRQ sub-system that has 16 channels. Remember that IRQ = 16 and DMA = 8 (channels).

Question 39

Answer C is correct. Once again, parse the question! "What's really going on here?" The question includes a mouse and jerky movement. Everything else is distraction. The simplest things to check are the roller bars. Always remember your real-world experience. Would you immediately go into the Device Manager with a bad mouse? No, so answer D is incorrect. Answers A and B are incorrect because, again, when was the last time you tore apart a mouse to examine the electronics inside?

Question 40

Answer B is correct. This is a seriously tricky question, demanding that you have a complete understanding of various types of device resolutions. (See Chapters 7 and 9 for a complete explanation of CCDs.) You can eliminate answer A because vertical scanner resolution is based on steps, not CCDs. Likewise, you can eliminate answer D because it refers to software manipulation. Always remember the CCDs and "optics" are directly linked. The optical resolution is specifically related to the number of light sensors in the scanner. Answer C is incorrect because it relates to how close together are "some number" of CCDs.

Question 41

Answer C is correct. A standard VGA monitor has a resolution of 640 pixels horizontally and 480 pixels vertically. You should know this setting automatically from your real-world experience with Safe Mode. Therefore, you can eliminate answers B and D as being related to SVGA. The real trick, here, is the reversal between answers A and C. Yet again, be very careful that you take your time and read the responses clearly. Answer A is incorrect because it's backwards.

Question 42

Answer D is correct. This is another seriously tricky question! Everything in the question is designed to get you thinking about degaussing. If you're impatient, you'll find the word in the first response. However, the real question has to do with the *cause* of the problem, not the solution to the problem! Answer A is incorrect because it is not a consideration in terms of what's causing the problem. Answer B is incorrect because electrostatic discharge doesn't usually cause image distortion. Answer C is incorrect because the problem refers to a strange color, and doesn't reference the image at all. Another clue is the use of "degaussing" in the first response, which refers to magnetic interference. EMI is electro...magnetic...interference.

Question 43

Answer C is correct. Mild soapy water is non-corrosive and provides the best cleaning solution for plastic, vinyl, or metal cases. Answer A is incorrect because alcohol is used mainly where no residue should be left, such as certain internal metal or electrical parts. Answer B is incorrect because "carbosol" is a fictional term. Answer D is incorrect because muratic acid (diluted or otherwise) is a form of hydrochloric acid used to clean concrete.

Question 44

Answers B and D are correct. Note that this is a tricky question because it asks you to choose what does *not* do something. If you aren't paying attention, you can easily choose the wrong answers based on what you know *will* work. Neither Socket B nor Slot 4 is associated with microprocessors and their packaging. Answers A and D are incorrect choices for this question because they actually do exist. Socket 8 (answer A) is a flat design used to install a CPU on the motherboard. Slot A (answer C) is AMD's vertical design, using a small circuit board with a single edge connector and a special processor slot on the motherboard.

Question 45

Answer B is correct. Tricky question warning! Answers B, C, and D are incorrect. Resistors, diodes, and transistors are other electronic components often found on a motherboard, but all three of these components require a flow of electricity to function. Although RAM modules often use capacitors, and require constant electrical current to maintain their settings, RAM isn't the only place where capacitors are used. The other main use is in power supplies. Large capacitors often store electricity, even when they've been disconnected from everything.

Question 46

Answer B is correct. A fuse is a breakable part of a circuit line. Ohms are used to measure resistance. If the circuit enters a condition beyond a specified tolerance, the fuse breaks, and the circuit line is interrupted. If the fuse is unbroken, it appears as a normal part of the circuit line and has no more resistance than any other part of the circuit line. Answer C is incorrect because a high ohm value would mean there is a great deal of resistance in the circuit coming from somewhere else on the circuit. A low ohm reading at the fuse would indicate that current is flowing through the fuse with no interruption and the fuse is good. Answer A is incorrect because we don't use DC voltages to test a circuit for a fuse. Answer D is incorrect because capacitance is an electrical property, not a testable condition with a standard multimeter (see Chapter 6).

Question 47

Answer D is correct. This is another tricky question, based on what's technically correct. Proper ESD control involves a ground strap, which must have a resistor placed in the line so the technician isn't electrocuted in the event of a short. All the responses (other than "none") offer ways to ground the technician, but none of the options offer protection against an electrostatic discharge. The question asks for the *most effective* way to reduce ESD damage, and none of the listed options interferes with an electrostatic discharge.

Question 48

Answer A is correct. A good approach to this question is to first eliminate what you know to be incorrect answers. Answer B is incorrect because ISA bus slots are usually long and divided, and are typically located near the edge of a motherboard. Answer C is incorrect because the USB controllers are typically in a single housing, also at the back of the board, near the chip and cooling system. Answer D is incorrect because secondary cache (L-2) chips are single SRAM chips, directly in the CPU or on the die. We've added the "1 0" clue to indicate two controllers. Note that interpreting a flat graphic isn't at all easy, so think carefully about the location of motherboard connections.

Question 49

Answer C is correct. Typically, the CPU is the largest chip on a motherboard. This diagram shows a heat sink close to a large object. Again, elimination is a better strategy for this question. Answer B is incorrect because batteries are much smaller, and usually round. Answer A is incorrect because a modem would be taking up a bus slot, and this diagram has all slots empty. Answer D is incorrect because legacy I/O ports and controllers, such as a parallel interface, are usually small and near the back of the board.

Question 50

Answer D is correct. Although the diagram does not show 16 connector points, the general shape of an expansion slot is fairly accurate. 16-bit slots are longer than PCI slots, and there would be only a few ISA slots (if they exist). Answer B is incorrect because no computers use 8-bit ISA slots anymore, at all. Letter B (response A) indicates the four or five white PCI slots. Memory banks (response C) are usually distant from the bus slots, and don't have the "bridge" separation of a typical slot. If you know the common shapes, you should be able to separate out an old technology such as ISA slots.

Question 51

Answer B is correct. The SIMM (or DIMM) memory banks are usually closer to the outer edge of the motherboard, narrow, and visually thinner than PCI slots. The letter B points to a PCI bus. Answer C is incorrect because a zero-insertion-force (ZIF) socket will have some kind of handle (like a paper cutter) connected to the socket. Letter K clearly indicates a slot of some kind. Answer D is incorrect because the BIOS chip, pointed to by O, is usually pre-installed on a motherboard and is smaller than the CPU socket. This motherboard uses slot technology, as opposed to socket technology, to mount the CPU. Lastly, answer A is incorrect because it points to ISA connectors. The tip off is the inclusion of PCI slots indicated by the answer B. ISA and PCI connectors look similar in diagrams, but PCI expansion slots are smaller.

Question 52

Answer C is correct. The main power supply almost always connects to the computer near the edge of the motherboard with a thick, short pin-connector. Answer A is incorrect because modern computers don't use AT connectors. They use PS/2 or USB connectors. Answer B is incorrect because there's no such thing as an "orientation chip." Finally, letters E, F, and G, are very close to the edge, and grouped together. Answer D is incorrect because an LPT connector is a 25-pin D-connector mounted to the back panel. Most of the small device I/O controllers should show as directly next to the edge of the board. The Power connector is typically a slight ways in from the edge.

Question 53

Answer A is correct. Be very careful that you don't "remember" the letter identifier, and then choose that letter as the correct response letter! Most modern PCs have only one printer port and that connector is a DB25 female connector. When there are two serial ports, one is almost always a 9-pin connector and the other a DB25 male connector. This panel shows only one 25-pin connector, so letter C is pointing to the parallel port in response A. Letter D points to the USB connectors, E points to a pair of 9-pin serial ports, and F points to a pair of 6-pin PS/2 connectors.

Question 54

Answer C is correct. The video connector (answer A) is a 15-pin connector, and you can count on the fact that there will be only one video connector on an exam exhibit. If you remember that PS/2 connectors are round, answers A and D can be eliminated. USB connectors (answer B) are square and about the size of a PS/2 connector, as indicated by two USB ports in letter D. An RJ-45 connector (letter B) is somewhat square, but try to remember how the shape differs from a USB connector. Usually there will be only one parallel port, and it's much wider than the two, typical, 9-pin serial connectors.

Question 55

Answer C is correct. USB ports are square and typically come as a vertical pair, as pointed to by letter D. Network connectors (if they're built in) are almost always RJ-45 connectors with the recognizable clip-slot at the bottom (like a modular phone jack). Although the question asks about only a single USB port, it doesn't exclude more than one.

Question 56

Answer A is correct. Here's another very tricky question that requires you to remember that an access point acts somewhat like a network hub. "Wireless" points you toward 802.11b, one of the CompTIA objectives on the exam (see Chapter 10). There's a reason the question includes both a desktop PC and a laptop machine in a wireless network. Answer D can be eliminated because even though the network could technically use Bluetooth technology, there's a distance limitation of about 10 meters. Answer C is incorrect because it refers to a small network of Bluetooth devices that exists for only as long as there's a connection. Therefore you're left with a choice between answers A and B. Answer B is incorrect because we usually refer to an "ad hoc" network as being a couple of wireless laptops communicating directly with each other. In this situation, we know there's also a desktop machine.

Question 57

Answers C and D are correct. Danger, danger, Will Robinson! Once again you're being asked to choose what does *not* apply, not what *will* apply. You should know that parallel ports include answer A, the ECP protocol, and answer B, the EPP protocol. Therefore they're the wrong answers for this question. As a result, only answers C and D apply. Secondly, ECC is a type of error correction and doesn't apply to a parallel port. Finally, UTP is a type of twisted pair (unshielded) wire that has to do with networks.

Question 58

Answer C is correct. In Chapter 10 we indicate that a bridge is specifically designed to reduce network traffic congestion by segmenting an existing network. Answer B is incorrect because routers move traffic between networks. Answer A is incorrect because hubs provide a way to add additional devices to a network (increasing possible congestion). Answer D, "Set up a secondary IP network token," is purely fictitious. A token, in a token ring network, uses an Internet Protocol (IP) address to correctly transfer data packets. Note that the question asks about the best and simplest solutions, not some more sophisticated solution.

Question 59

Answer B is correct. There's no such thing as a USB DB9 connector. Most people would connect any USB device with a USB connector, either on the back panel, or on the front of the case.

Question 60

Answers B and C are correct. This is another example of an ambivalent question. What does "most system boards" mean? The best strategy is to eliminate what you know are obsolete technologies. Answer D is incorrect because it doesn't refer to a bus at all, but refers to a type of hard drive. Answer A, IBM's Micro Channel Architecture (MCA) and answer E, the VESA Local bus, haven't been around for years. The VESA Local bus was entirely replaced (in PCs) by the PCI bus. That leaves the PCI (answer C) and ISA buses (answer B). Although you won't likely see many ISA bus slots in a modern system, the underlying ISA bus architecture still exists to support legacy I/O ports and devices such as parallel and COM ports.

Question 61

Answer D is correct. This question relies on tricky semantics, this time, instead of misdirection. Answer B is incorrect because the PCI100 standard has to do with memory modules, and not all hardware devices. Of the remaining three options, your choice is between "all" and "some." Answer A is incorrect because the standard has to do with memory, not motherboards. Answer C is semantically incorrect. The PCI100 standard has been supplanted by many later versions, including PCI800, PCI1600, and so forth. Secondly, there were many memory modules on motherboards prior to the PCI100 implementation. The technically correct answer is that *some* memory modules were affected by the standard. However, "technically" refers to the use of language in this case, not the underlying technology and engineering.

Question 62

Answer C is correct. By now you should have a good sense of how multiple-choice questions can completely mess you up in the event you're not thinking clearly. You should know for a fact that there's no such thing as the "NTFS transfer protocol." Therefore, answers A and B can't be correct. Answer D proposes they're both correct, which makes little logical sense. NTFS stands for the Windows NT File System, and relates more to things like FAT16 and FAT32. As such, only answer C indicates that none of the responses matters at all.

Question 63

Answer D is correct. The reference to a "running computer" should clue you in to the concept of hot-swapping. Hot-swapping should lead you to think about USB and FireWire. Only answer D contains "USB" as part of the response. Answer B is incorrect because we almost never change out a monitor while anything is running. Answers A and C are debatable. Both keyboards and joysticks come in USB types, but neither response includes USB in the same way as answer D. Therefore, it's possible that a 101 keyboard could be a PS/2 keyboard. Finally, answer C refers to a serial joystick, which would mean a serial DB9 connector.

Question 64

Answers B and D are correct. This question relies on rote memory. You must know that AMD had to change its underlying processor mounting when it moved away from Intel. In both the slot and socket technologies, the letter A links with the company name (AMD). Even if you're not sure which socket or slot goes with each chip, you should be able to recognize the A in answers B and D, and eliminate answers A and C. (See Chapter 5 for details on chipsets, slots, and sockets.)

Question 65

Answer B is correct. IRQ 14 is assigned to the primary disk controller. Answer A is incorrect because IRQ 15 is assigned to the secondary disk controller. Answer C is incorrect because there's no such thing as a "master slave disk controller." Answer D is incorrect because we don't set an optical drive as a primary drive. The CDROM drive could be the slave drive on IRQ 14, but it would probably significantly impair the hard drive's performance.

Question 66

Answer A is correct. The clues here are both the 25-pin male connector and the Centronics connector. Serial cables can have DB25 female connectors, but the Centronics connector indicates that the question is referring to a parallel printer cable. Most parallel cables have a DB25 and Centronics connector. Serial cables tend to have two DB25 connectors and no Centronics connector. Answer B is incorrect because a modem cable would have a DB25 female connector on one end and a 9-pin serial connector at the other. Answer C is incorrect because the 36-pin male Centronics specifies that this is not a serial printer connection. Answer D is incorrect because the DB25 connector specifies that it is not a SCSI cable. SCSI cables often use 50-pin ribbon cables.

Question 67

Answer C is correct. Hierarchical memory is discussed in Chapters 3 and 4, and refers to the order in which the CPU looks at various types of memory for instructions. Answer A is incorrect because it places a Level 2 cache ahead of an L-1 cache. Answer B is technically a correct order, but the CPU always looks first in very fast L-1 memory, then in gradually slower memory types. So although it's a legitimate order, it isn't the correct answer in terms of priorities. Answer C is correct because L-1 is very fast, L-2 is slower, and RAM is the slowest type of memory in the hierarchy. So, L-1 takes first priority. Answer D is wrong because it skips the L-2 cache and goes directly to disk storage and virtual memory.

Question 68

Answer A is correct. Originally, the last digit in network wiring referred to the maximum length of a cable in hundreds of meters. 10Base-5 refers to a cable with a 500-meter maximum length. 10Base-2 is a thinner cable, with a maximum length of 200 meters. When 10Base-T wiring was introduced, the

"T" indicated twisted pair. Nothing in the cable designation refers to centimeters or millimeters, so answers B and C are incorrect. Be sure to remember that the name refers to distance, not the number of connections, as in the incorrect answer D.

Question 69

Answer C is correct. Once again you'll have to rely on rote memory and sight recognition of the OSI layers. You should have a basic understanding of what each layer represents, as discussed in Chapter 10. The question asks about a connection to the Internet, but it could just as easily refer to any network. Answers A, B, and D all use incorrect layer names. Additionally, the Physical layer refers to all wiring, and isn't exclusive to network routing. The Transfer layer, or Layer 4, has a bogus name but might indicate data transfers, not routing capabilities.

Question 70

Answers B and D are correct. Yet again, be very careful to note that this is a negative-correct question where you must select what is *not* used. Also note that this is a "typical" network "situation." Most networks use printers, but not all of them, and so a network would probably have a DB25 connector somewhere in the system, as indicated in answer A. Another way to look at it is that printers often can have installed NICs, whereas monitors (DB15 connector) never use a network card. So answer A (DB25) *is* used! Most networks also use RJ-45 connectors with Cat-5 cable, as indicated in answer C. Once again, something that *is* used.

Parsing the remaining choices, we would guess that a DB15 video connector is present, but not part of the networking concept. Video connectors always apply to standalone systems, and don't involve NICs. Likewise, an RJ-11 phone connector might be used to connect a modem, but not in a typical networking situation, using a shared modem. This is a good example of the type of ambiguity we found on the exam, where CompTIA makes certain assumptions. Technically, all networks use monitors, so you'll have to use some psychology to figure out what the question means by "typical network."

PART 2
Operating System Exam

DOS

Terms you'll need to understand:

✓ Command interpreter, command line, switch
✓ Hidden and system file attributes (ATTRIB.EXE)
✓ Environment memory
✓ Search path, parent and child directories
✓ File allocation table (FAT)
✓ File fragmentation (DEFRAG.EXE)
✓ Wildcards, variables
✓ Shells

Concepts you'll need to master:

✓ Command interpreters and operating system kernels
✓ Partitions and logical drives versus physical disks (FDISK.EXE)
✓ Directories (folders) and sub-directories (subfolders)
✓ File systems, file management, filenames
✓ Tracks, sectors, and clusters (SCANDISK.EXE)
✓ File searches (DIR)
✓ Operating systems versus shells

Although you may not think you'll ever encounter DOS, you should know that it's the underlying operating system for the entire Windows 9x family. Even Windows NT, Windows 2000, and Windows XP include troubleshooting utilities based on DOS commands. There's no doubt that if you want to understand Windows, you must know something about DOS—the *Disk Operating System*. In this half of the book we separate out 16-bit and 32-bit Windows. "Windows 9x" includes Windows 95, 98, and Me.

Why Read This Chapter?

We'll be tracking the gradual elimination of DOS and the evolution of Windows into a true operating system by keeping tabs on what happened to the system files and the use of an operating system *kernel*. Windows XP still installs a file called COMMAND.COM on the hard drive, in the System32 folder. Running CMD.EXE opens a DOS-like window. Finally, the Recovery Console application looks much like the old DOS command environment, and in many instances, works the same way.

In the world of PCs, everything started with DOS, and every time you use the Find tool in the Windows Explorer, you're dealing with DOS (*.* wildcards, file extensions, associations, and file types). Aside from the historical context, four additional reasons for knowing about DOS come to mind:

➤ Preparing a disk for an operating system—any PC operating system—requires partitioning software (FDISK or DISKPART) and logical drive software (FORMAT.COM). These programs are command-line programs and are discussed in this chapter, together with the concepts of file space allocation and file naming.

➤ Windows 9x and Me both start by loading the files IO.SYS and MSDOS.SYS, which are DOS files.

➤ Key troubleshooting utilities you use for network and PC diagnostics are based on DOS, including the Windows 2000 and Windows XP Recovery Console.

➤ Disk-level decisions involving FAT32 versus NTFS, why and how to partition a disk, and the concept of disk volumes all use the original concepts coming out of DOS.

Locked Files and Windows

Here's an interesting problem you might easily encounter in modern-day Windows, and the only way to fix it seems to be through the use of DOS and the ATTRIB command. Microsoft Word creates a number of temporary files when it opens a document. Choose the folder that holds the open document, then use the File | Open menu to see these files with their .TMP extensions.

If the system crashes, Windows doesn't have a chance to remove those temporary files. What makes this interesting is that Word tracks the temporary files in its own application software. When a document is open, Word sends a notification to Windows to lock the document. "Locked" means that if you try to open the file a second time, Word informs you that the document is in use, and asks whether you want to open a copy. This is to protect original data on a network, where two people may try to open the same file at the same time.

The temporary files are hidden, but you can see them with the Explorer's View | Folder Options | View tab and "Show All Files" option enabled. Following the crash, if you try to delete the orphaned .TMP files, Windows informs you that they're locked and doesn't allow you to remove them. On the other hand, when you try to open the Word file you were in when the system crashed, you get a message that the document is locked. Word asks you whether you want to open a copy. If you do, and then try to save the copy with the original file name, Word tells you that you cannot overwrite an open file.

One option would be to restart Windows in MS-DOS Command mode (or run CMD.EXE), and then delete the document. Here is where you can see the difference between a clean version of DOS and Command mode. When you try to delete one of these orphaned Word files from (what you think is) DOS, you get the same Windows error message, informing you that the document is in use, and that you may not remove it. In other words, Windows is still controlling the file management, even when you think you're in DOS.

NOTE

Another way to see that Command mode isn't really DOS is to type **EXIT** and press Enter. You'll return to Windows. The executable command for Windows is **WIN.COM**, not "exit." However, "exit" is the standard command to leave what's called a "shell" environment.

The only way to successfully remove the orphaned file(s) is to start the machine in a clean DOS environment and use the ATTRIB command. The following chapter describes what a clean (or pure) DOS environment means. We also examine commands such as ATTRIB.EXE and DIR.

NOTE You can use either the **DIR /A:H /S** command or the **ATTRIB *.* /S** command to find the files, always remembering that they have their Hidden attribute turned on. When you get a directory listing, you can navigate to the proper folder by using **CD** commands. After you've arrived at the folder, you'll have to use the **ATTRIB -H *.TMP** switch to unhide the files so you can delete them. The **DEL** command cannot find hidden files.

In the previous scenario, you'll also have the experience of seeing the underlying DOS filenames, without their convenient Long File Names. If you have one folder named C:\Program Files\Microsoft Office\Microsoft Word and another folder named C:\Program Files\Microsoft Office\Microsoft Excel, you'll have to figure out which *micros~1* folder you want to get into. You'll also have to know how to use the CD command to change to the Program Files directory listed as *progra~1*.

You should be seeing that solving this single problem involves a good working knowledge of DOS commands. This is only one example of everyday problems that can crop up in Windows, and where using a command line or DOS is the solution. Setting aside the fact that you'll be required to correctly answer a number of DOS-related exam questions, there is little doubt in our minds that you'll encounter DOS on a regular basis, even if you think you're "only" running Windows. This is true for Windows Server 2003 and many enterprise networking environments as well, even if you won't be tested on them in the A+ exam.

Operating Systems

A software *program* is a set of instructions put together in an organized way that tells a microprocessor what to do. We write a program in English so that a human being can understand it. A *programming language* is a special way to use human language so that the instructions can be turned into *machine language*—that is, compiled. COBOL, Visual Basic, C++, Java, C#, and Assembler are examples of programming languages.

Compilers and Machine Language

What are compilers? Programs must spell out, in excruciating detail, every single instruction to the microprocessor. No matter how short a speech-based language might be, it still takes far too much space to write even a simple program. Therefore, computer languages use shorthand words to cram as much information as possible into the smallest amount of space. Move becomes **MOV**, Jump To becomes **JMP**, Delete or erase becomes **DEL**, Remove Directory becomes **RD**, directory of files becomes **DIR**, and so on.

After a program has been written so that a human being can understand it, the result can be reduced even further into something that a machine can understand—*machine language*. Machine language is composed entirely of 1s and 0s. The process of final reduction is called *compiling the program*. After the program has been compiled (using a separate application called a *compiler*), the instructions are run as fast as possible. Compiled (binary) programs in DOS have either one of two extensions: .COM (command program) or .EXE (executable program).

Batch programs, with .BAT extensions, are not compiled and are entered as plain-English lists of commands. AUTOEXEC.BAT is a batch file, and the name is a reserved name used from within COMMAND.COM.

Applications

We usually divide software programs into two categories: *operating systems* and *applications*. Applications are groups of program files that make up a tool of some kind. We use applications to create user data (files). Human beings use applications to produce documents, spreadsheets, databases, mailing lists, new airplane designs, virtual realities, and test scenarios (simulations), to name a few. America Online is an application, as are the component applications that make up Microsoft Office. Microsoft Word is part of the Microsoft Office suite (a group of related applications), and is made up of many different program files.

Here's an example of how an application borrows part of an operating system. When you choose the Edit I Copy command from an application's main menu, you're using the graphical interface to access the **COPY** command from the underlying operating system.

In many cases, smaller programs help out larger, primary programs. These smaller programs are referred to as software tools, *utilities*, or simply "tools." ScanDisk, Defrag, SYSEDIT, and MSINFO are examples of utilities.

Utility programs were originally created as standalone software designed to do a single thing. Over time, and with the necessity of using many of these utilities on a regular basis, we began to see smaller programs joined together under a common interface. Most of the diagnostics utilities found under Windows 2000 and XP are these types of utility suites. Two good examples are the Administrative Tools and the selective startup MSCONFIG.EXE program.

Commands and Programs

Certain programs stand on their own, and are called executable files. Windows considers files with the following extensions to be executable: .COM, .EXE, .BAT, and in some instances, .PIF (Program Information File). An executable file is the same as a command that you run from a "command line." FORMAT.COM and FDISK.EXE are examples of command programs.

Microsoft now refers to utility groups as Consoles, using Snap-ins as ever-smaller divisions of programming code. The Administrative Tools and Control Panel are good examples of console programs. For that reason, Windows XP now considers the .MSC extension to be executable from within Windows, although it isn't really a compiled, executable program in the traditional sense of the concept.

Although it's an editor, REGEDIT.EXE is more of a utility program, designed for the specific purpose of editing a Windows Registry (sometimes called the system registration). WP.EXE is an application program that runs a word processor and borrows part of the operating system whenever it copies a paragraph or file from one place to another.

When you issue a command, you're using one of the operating system program files to gather computer-related instructions and *apply* them. (That's where the word "application" comes from.) A command is somewhat different than a program, in that a user types a command name on a command line. A program, on the other hand, is the set of instructions the computer actually uses to execute a sequence of events. Developers compile a program; users type a command.

A command is usually a word followed by several additional switches (for example, FORMAT A: /U). A program is contained within a file (for example, FORMAT.COM). The command interpreter must have the programming instructions to be able to keep all the letters in the word "FORMAT" together, and separate out the A: and /U as separate command modifiers.

A personal computer can only do *exactly* what it's told to do. A human being creates every single detail of what a computer knows how to do. The human being using a computer is either a programmer or an operator (user). An operator relies on what the programmer told the computer to do, by using special instructions built into a program. Those special instructions are the commands.

Loading and Running a Program

One of the fundamental (and often confusing) principles of using a computer is the idea that a program "loads" into memory in order to "run." We've talked about how RAM loses data when the power is turned off. We've also mentioned that disks store data without requiring a constant power supply. Running a program is when the system executes the instructions contained in a file stored on a disk. In other words, the command interpreter "runs" through a list of instructions.

Windows NT uses the word *initialize* to distinguish between loading a device driver and running it at a later time. This concept was carried forward into Windows 2000 and Windows XP (for example, services).

A program is *executed* (run) either when we type something on a command line (and press Enter), or when another program *calls* (programming word) the first program. The computer must load a file before it can be run. Upon execution, the instructions that the computer needs at any given moment are *copied* (not moved) into memory from the program file. This is what we mean by *loading a file*. The original file remains stored on the disk, untouched and unchanged unless certain instructions make a change to the stored file.

Viruses often copy themselves into RAM and use programming instructions to change the original file on the disk. Understand that the file itself doesn't go into memory, but that a copy of the programmed instructions goes into memory.

DOS History

A long time ago, in a place far away, a young girl suggested to her father that a new toy for electronics hobbyists should be called the Altair, after a star system named in a *Star Trek* episode. The Altair, released in 1970, was based on the Intel 8080 chip and was the first computer a person could take home. It had 256 bytes of memory, could hold about four lines of text instructions, and was operated by flipping switches on and off. Even though it had no keyboard, Bill Gates and Paul Allen were fascinated with it and spent long nights organizing a version of Beginner's All-purpose Symbolic Instruction Code (BASIC) for the machine. They called it Altair Basic.

When a switch was flipped to either on or off, the computer circuitry could use that information in some way. A series of switches taken together could form a binary number. The computer was designed to work with groups of switches, and those groups were called *registers*. Registers have now become very small transistors on a microprocessor, and they continue to store binary numbers.

Gates decided that Altair Basic should have some sort of file management and disk storage capability, so he upgraded the original system. This was the first conceptual hint of the File Manager, which went on to become the Windows Explorer. Gates's and Allen's interest in operating languages and their belief that microprocessors would change the world led them to incorporate Microsoft in 1975 (to market a traffic-counting machine). At the time, software was stored on cards by punching holes in them.

CP/M

The Intel 8080 processor found its way into another computer called the Imsai 8080, which came with a floppy drive and was targeted at small businesses. The floppy drive circuitry was controlled by an operating system called Control Program for Microcomputers (CP/M), designed by Gary Kildall.

Kildall was working for a company called Intergalactic Digital Research and wanted a scaled-down language that would work with microprocessors rather than mainframe computers. Perhaps because of a government cover-up or something else, the company eventually dropped "Intergalactic," leaving only the name Digital Research. Intel didn't think there was much use for CP/M, so it granted Kildall full rights to it. Features of CP/M included the following:

➤ Used only 4KB of memory space.

➤ Introduced a 64KB command file and used a dot (period) plus three-letter (.COM) extension to signify the type of file. (COM files, short for COMmand files, still have a maximum size of 64KB.)

➤ Used a command interpreter, or command processor program, called CCP (short for console command processor).

➤ Used two fundamental files called Basic DOS (BDOS) and BIOS to handle files and I/O processing.

Apple

Back in 1974, the most popular microprocessors were the Intel 8080 and the Motorola 6800. One of the 6800's inventors, Chuck Peddle, quit Motorola in 1975 and started a new company called MOS Technologies. MOS began manufacturing the 6501 microprocessor, which resembled Motorola's 6800. In 1976, Steve Wozniak and Steve Jobs took some MOS 6502 chips and built the first Apple computers—the Apple I.

At the time, Charles Tandy, who had been unsuccessful in buying Imsai computers, created his own Tandy TRS-80 product line based on another chip—the Zilog Z-80. Both the TRS-80 and the Apple I computers came fully assembled and, to help keep costs down, used only uppercase letters in their operating system. Neither Radio Shack nor Apple Corporation could keep the computers in stock. An immediate problem between the Apple and the CP/M systems was that

➤ Operating systems don't necessarily work on all microchips.

➤ The Apple MOS-6502 was an 8-bit processor and couldn't run CP/M.

The Apple II model upgrade added an optional floppy drive and ran a program called VisiCalc—the first real spreadsheet application—created by Dan Bricklin, Dan Fylstra, and Bob Frankston. Businesses could use small PCs to create spreadsheets, and suddenly the PC market came alive. Meanwhile, Gates and Allen were updating BASIC and introducing other programming languages that would work on Intel and Zilog chips. Eventually, Apple turned away from the MOS chips and went to Motorola chips.

CP/M was a hot programming language, and some very exciting software applications based on the language were arriving on the market. However, these programs ran only on Intel and Zilog chips. Rather than spend the long hours necessary to translate BASIC into a form that would work with the Apple computers, Gates and Allen chose to license CP/M from Kildall. They began selling CP/M with an add-on board that held a Zilog chip. Apple customers could put the Microsoft card into their computers and run CP/M-based programs.

86-DOS

Meanwhile, in Seattle, Tim Patterson was making motherboards for a company called Seattle Computer Products (SCP). Intel had just produced its first 16-bit 8086 chip, and Patterson needed a 16-bit operating system to go with the 8086. Kildall was saying that he would soon be finished with the CP/M-86 (the first vaporware). Patterson decided he couldn't wait, so he wrote his own operating system.

In 1980, Patterson created a Quick and Dirty Operating System (QDOS). QDOS soon became 86-DOS (for the 8086 processor), then SCP-DOS (after the Seattle company), and then simply the *disk operating system (DOS)*. In polite company, though, we refer to the "D" in DOS as standing for disk.

To simplify matters for the growing number of programmers writing for the CP/M operating system, Patterson kept the basic CP/M file management structure—the way CP/M looked, and the way it loaded itself and programs into memory. This compatibility is often referred to as the "look and feel" of an operating system. Along the way, he added something called a *file allocation table (FAT)*, which he found in Gates's Altair Basic.

Keep an eye on the FAT, because it carried all the way into Windows 9x. FAT16, FAT32, and all the other file management systems started here.

PC-DOS

At about the same time, in 1980, IBM approached Microsoft about a possible 8-bit PC (microcomputer). IBM was making mainframes for the most part, and looked to young Microsoft as one of the leading (if not only) businesses creating computer languages for microcomputers. IBM thought that PCs were mainly a passing hobby, but Gates and Allen were convinced that the microprocessor and the so-called *personal* computer would change the world. They convinced IBM to change its design to a 16-bit processor, and when IBM asked who had a 16-bit operating system, Gates is said to have replied "Gary Kildall." At that point, history gets a bit fuzzy, but somehow Kildall didn't sell IBM the rights to CP/M.

Gates and Allen purchased Patterson's 86-DOS for around $50,000 and suggested to IBM that Microsoft become the vendor for BASIC, FORTRAN, Pascal, COBOL, and the 8086 Assembly language. They also proposed that Microsoft would license 86-DOS to IBM as the operating system for the new PC. IBM agreed (another historical blunder), and in 1981, released the first personal computer with Microsoft's DOS 1.0, which IBM called PC-DOS. (Patterson became successful in his own right and eventually went to work for Microsoft.) It wasn't until the release of DOS 5.0 that Microsoft finally started selling its own generic version of MS-DOS on the open market.

PCs using IBM's PC-DOS continued to use COMMAND.COM (the command interpreter), along with IBMDOS.COM and IBMBIO.COM. PCs using Microsoft's MS-DOS went on to use the COMMAND.COM interpreter, and changed the two other system files to IO.SYS and MSDOS.SYS.

Keep an eye on MSDOS.SYS, because it carried through all the way into Windows 98 and Windows Me.

CP/M into DOS

Without applications, few people would be interested in computers. At the time, the most popular applications were dBase II and WordStar, both of which ran on CP/M. Because IBM didn't have much in the way of interesting software, it pushed very strongly to make DOS similar enough to CP/M that it could run those other applications. Among the changes that DOS brought about were the following:

➤ Variable record lengths

➤ Large EXEcutable (.EXE) format files, along with smaller 64KB CP/M-style .COM files

➤ Terminate-and-stay-resident (TSR) programs that could end (terminate), but stay (reside) in memory and snap back onto the screen without reloading

➤ A FAT, short for File Allocation Table, which could keep track of all the pieces of files on a disk

➤ The capability to use device names to perform I/O operations on peripheral devices (screens and printers) the same way that it worked with files

 Even today, we can use the **COPY** command to copy a file to the screen (the CONsole) and show the results on the monitor (**COPY CON filename.txt**). Likewise, we can copy a file to a printer and have the hardware device produce a printed output (**COPY filename.txt PRN**).

DOS kept the CP/M-style eight-character filenames, followed by a period, then a three-character extension. DOS also kept the C> prompt format at the command line. Compatibility also meant keeping the CP/M-style file control blocks (FCBs), program segment prefixes (PSPs), and the way in which CP/M used memory addresses for loading.

 Although Windows apparently bears little resemblance to DOS, the continued use of the C:\ annotation for the root directory (folder) of Drive C: traces all the way back to CP/M. File associations wouldn't work at all without file extensions, which also date all the way back to CP/M. File associations are part of the Explorer's "Open With" menu option.

DOS also kept the CP/M representation of a directory as a *dot* and the parent directory (the directory one step above) as two dots, or *dot-dot*. We discuss the two dots in more detail later in this chapter when we look at directories and sub-directories, which are the same as folders and subfolders. DOS also introduced the capability to use a reserved extension for files containing plain-English scripts. These *batch files*, with the .BAT extension, use rudimentary reserved words and need not be compiled into machine language.

Batch files are plain ASCII text files containing DOS commands on separate lines. Batch files must have a .BAT extension, and are considered executable program files. COMMAND.COM contains a number of internal commands that can be used by batch files. Some of the internal commands include the **ECHO**, **@**, **ERRORLEVEL**, **PAUSE**, **FOR**, **CHOICE**, and **IF** commands.

The exam sometimes refers to COMMAND.COM as a "batch command processor," although the proper name is "command interpreter."

MS-DOS and PC-DOS

Beginning with the release of DOS 5.0, two versions of DOS were sold in the consumer market: the IBM version and the Microsoft version—PC-DOS and MS-DOS, respectively. Any DOS questions on the exam will use the MS-DOS version.

 The **VER** command (internal) is used to discover which version of DOS is running on a PC. At the command prompt, type **VER** and press Enter. The screen returns the version number and tells you whether the computer is using PC-DOS or MS-DOS (or some other variation). This command continues into all versions of Windows, although you must go to a command prompt to run it.

A fundamental difference between the IBM and the Microsoft versions of DOS is that they use two system files with different names. MS-DOS uses IO.SYS and MSDOS.SYS, and PC-DOS uses IBMBIO.COM and IBMDOS.COM.

 IO.SYS and MSDOS.SYS are the two hidden system files that combine with COMMAND.COM (not hidden) to form the fundamental DOS operating system.

From DOS to Windows 9x

Windows 3.0, 3.1, 3.11, and Windows for Workgroups (3.11) are *not* operating systems. Windows is a GUI using a *shell*, which, theoretically, makes the daily operation of an IBM-compatible computer somewhat easier than using the DOS command line. However, Windows 3.x and Windows 9x still require DOS to run.

The release of Windows 95 included DOS 7.0, which made a real break from all prior DOS versions. Windows 95 isn't a true operating system either, but more of a hybrid between DOS and NT. Nevertheless, many people have accepted Microsoft's claim that Windows 9x is an operating system. Windows 98 was a minor release of Windows, and included DOS 7.1 as the underlying OS. (Windows Me used DOS 8.0.) Windows 2000 narrowed the gap between DOS and Windows NT, and Windows XP was the final integration of a 32-bit network operating system with the home computer and consumer market.

The Command Interpreter

An operating system includes many component programs, each of which tell a computer how to work in various ways. Therefore, either an operating system (OS) or an OS kernel makes all the computer hardware work. The point where human beings meet the operating system is the *user interface*. DOS is a *text-based* interface, in that you type words and letters. Windows is a *graphical* user interface, in that you use representational graphics and a pointer.

CompTIA proposes that an operating system (software) is made up of two things: a *command interpreter* that works with program and system files, and a *user interface* that allows a human being to instruct the command interpreter what to do. In our opinion, an operating system requires a file system and several other critical components, but we'll focus your attention on what CompTIA calls an operating system.

For the exam, remember that an operating system may be referred to as three components: *system files*, a *command interpreter*, and a *user interface*.

With so many separate files making up an operating system, there must be an oversight manager of some kind to distinguish between a letter you're typing to your mother and a *string* (line or group) of characters you're typing to instruct the computer to do something. COMMAND.COM is the DOS *command interpreter*, which is also used by Windows 9x to control the computer. We issue commands at the *command line* (discussed in a moment).

In Windows 2000 and XP, COMMAND.COM continues to open a so-called DOS window. You can do so by selecting the Start I Run option and typing **COMMAND**. However, a command line is now run from a program file called CMD.EXE and generates a command-line window. Note that depending on which of these options you choose, you get different results. (When you are in DOS, remember to type **EXIT** and press Enter to return to Windows.)

The Command Line

Being text based, DOS uses a series of letters, entered in a row, as commands. These character strings contain *reserved words*, which are the starting points for a set of instructions that "command" the computer to do something. An example of a reserved word is "copy." An example of a reserved character is the colon (:). The colon is used by DOS to mean the word "drive."

The text that you enter is called a command line—a line of typing. The A> or the C> next to a blinking cursor is called the *prompt*, or *DOS prompt*. The *command prompt* is the blinking cursor that shows you where the next character will appear on the monitor screen. After you've typed out a character string and pressed the Enter key, the command interpreter looks at the string and decides what to do about it—it "parses" the line.

The command interpreter literally interprets keyboard or mouse input and makes decisions as to whether to change the computer or pass the input on to an application program.

The DOS prompt is the combination of symbols at the left-most column of a plain screen, together with the blinking cursor, or *insertion point* of the command prompt. The default prompt is the A> or the C> symbol, but you can change the way the prompt looks (with the PROMPT command). Beginning with Windows 95, the default prompt became A:\ or C:\, meaning the root directory of either the A: drive or the C: drive.

The blinking bar in Windows is called the insertion point, descended from the old command prompt. Windows installs a simple AUTOEXEC.BAT file, which runs during the startup process and executes a prompt command. **PROMPT=pg** changes the DOS prompt from C> to an indication of the drive and path (discussed later in this chapter), making the familiar C:\ prompt.

Parsing

When you enter a command, DOS breaks up the letters, symbols, and numbers into units that match internal patterns of characters. Breaking apart a line of characters into a pattern of meaningful pieces is called *parsing* the line. The patterns of characters are commands, and the commands are part of either the DOS system files or a program file. When news analysts would break apart former President Clinton's sentences so as to understand what he actually meant, they would be parsing his sentences.

Syntax

The dictionary defines *syntax* to be the way words are put together to form sentences, clauses, or phrases. A DOS command line is an instruction to DOS to do something, and DOS reads it much like we read a sentence.

The conventional standard for listing the syntax of a command is to begin with the command, followed by square brackets ([ ]) that enclose each and every possible *switch*. Italicized words that come after the command usually refer to some additional characters that you're supposed to enter to replace the word. For example, DIR [d:] [path] [filename [.ext]] [/P] [/W] [/S] means that the DIR command can (but need not) be followed by any of the items listed in square brackets.

Switches

A command line uses variable words, numbers, and symbols to produce different results. The words represent program files that DOS can find along the search path (discussed later in this chapter). The important things to remember about switches include the following:

➤ Switches almost always start with a single forward slash (/) and are immediately followed by a letter or a character.

➤ Some programmers use the dash (-) as a switch indicator. This is not the same as using a plus or minus (+/-) to turn an attribute on or off.

➤ A space separates the command word from the switch.

DIR Switch Examples

When you use the DIRectory (DIR) command to list a large directory, you see the entire directory go flying up the screen, shooting out of the top of the monitor, and making a mess all over the floor. To prevent this from happening, use one of the following switches:

DIR /p—Tells DOS to stop the list every 23 lines, which make up a screen page. ("P" is short for "by the page.")

DIR /w—Tells DOS to show the files in a "wide" format (that is, across the screen).

DIR /s—Tells DOS to show not only the current directory's files but also all the files in every sub-directory (now called a sub-folder) below the current one.

Switches can often be combined to provide combined variations of any command that supports multiple switches. In the case of DIR /s /p, you're asking DOS to show you all the files in this directory and any sub-directories, and also to stop the display every 23 lines until you press any key.

The /? Switch

DOS versions 5 and later, as well as most command-line programs, include a rudimentary built-in Help feature that acts as a quick reminder of how a command can be used. As far back as version 3, MS-DOS provided a complete help file with an expanded Help feature on how to use commands. This Help utility is still available on some Windows installation CDs (Browse, Tools, OldMSDos, and HELP.COM). PC-DOS didn't include the expanded Help feature until later versions.

At a DOS prompt (including the Recovery Console), you can almost always enter [*command*] */?* to obtain a cheat sheet on how to use that command. For example, **DIR** */?* or **ATTRIB** */?* shows all the switches and a brief explanation of what each does.

File Mask (Specification)

Switches modify a command's action and results. The *file mask*, or file specification, defines the grouping of files that will be affected by the command. In other words, most commands are used to either list file information or modify file information. The DIR command with no switches and no file mask lists every file. The DIR command with no file mask and the /P switch still lists every file, but pauses the listing. The DIR command with the *.TXT file mask shows only files with a .TXT extension.

When you issue a command with a file specification, the command will only operate on the specific files matching that specification. If you specify a file that doesn't exist, you'll get a "File not found" error message. The file specification may include the full pathname for a file, allowing a command to operate on files found in a different location from the default (logged) directory.

An example of a full path file specification would be where you want to list the .SYS (driver) files in the Windows I/O Sub-system folder. Suppose you're logged onto the root directory of the D: drive and you issue a DIR command. The result will be a listing of all the files in D:\. To use a file mask for the system files, you would type **DIR C:\WINDOWS\SYSTEM\IOSUBSYS*.SYS** and press Enter.

Error Messages

People sometimes forget that a computer doesn't have a conceptual mind, and that it can't actually harbor a grudge or get angry—at least not yet. Everything that happens on a computer is created by a human being. When something goes wrong and a message of some kind shows up on the screen, that message—called an error message—isn't simply a casual expletive that the computer thought up on the spur of the moment!

The actual text of the error messages must not only be written into a program, but it also ought to have some kind of connection to an underlying event. Within a program, connecting an error message to an event is sometimes called *trapping* an error. The programmer uses what's called an IF...THEN logic statement to display an error message on the screen. (A proposed error message we've seen recently as a candidate to be written into the

Windows interface is "Closing current Windows session. Would you like to begin another game?")

For instance, the following statement might be used to trap for a missing file error: IF *filename* X on the command line doesn't match *filename* X in the directory allocation table (DAT), THEN type the message `File not found` to the screen. "Invalid media type" is a much more frightening error message, and can appear when the boot-up routine can't read anything at all from an installed hard drive.

 A message referring to invalid media means that something is seriously wrong with the disk in either the hard drive or the floppy drive. In some cases, a virus has wiped out the entire disk, including partition tables and everything else. In other cases, a hardware component has failed or the CMOS settings have told the machine that no hard disk is installed.

The "Any Key" (PAUSE)

The most common way to allow time for a user to read an error message is to temporarily *pause* the screen until the user provides further input. Remember that the keyboard processor is constantly scanning the keyboard for status changes and key-press activity. When the error message reads, "Press any key to continue," it literally means that you can press any key on the keyboard. The most common keys to press are the spacebar, the Enter key, or the ESCape (ESC) key. In DOS, one of the internal batch file commands is **PAUSE**.

COMMAND.COM

DOS is really a package of many programs and utilities that take up a lot of space in a default directory called C:\DOS (C:\WINDOWS\COMMAND in Windows 9x). When we talk about DOS, we're referring to the whole package and all the various subprograms. However, the essence of the operating system is the command interpreter (COMMAND.COM) and the two hidden *system files* that handle basic I/O.

COMMAND.COM usually loads into memory when a computer boots up. Some of its routines stay in system memory during the entire session (the time during which the computer is turned on). They can be accessed faster if they stay in fast RAM, rather than requiring slow disk access over and over again. The parts of the interpreter that stay in memory are called the *resident* parts. The parts of COMMAND.COM that move back and forth between the disk and memory are called the *transient* parts.

When a computer is running, we call that a *session*. Windows opens up a DOS session as a virtual machine. Keep an eye on how a real machine works, because you'll have an easier time understanding what Windows is doing when it creates the Virtual Machine (VM), or you run a 16-bit application under Windows XP/2000.

The Recovery Console is an administrative tool found in Windows 2000 and XP, which essentially provides a way to bring up a non-transient DOS environment. CMD.EXE is transient, meaning that after the program or command terminates, the command window disappears and you're returned to the desktop. Resident means something "lives in" memory. Transient means it's "just passing through."

Internal and External Commands

COMMAND.COM includes a number of internal commands and instructions on how to use batch files. Batch files are simple programs using plain-text language to execute a series of events. Some examples of internal commands are COPY, DEL, DIR, and ECHO. They're called internal commands in order to differentiate them from *external commands*. External commands are the many other program files included in the overall operating system. Examples of external commands in DOS include ATTRIB, FDISK, FORMAT, SCANDISK, or DEFRAG.

Keep in mind that in an open operating system, the command interpreter is directly associated with a number of low-level system files. DOS uses two critical system files and keeps them hidden from the casual user. A specific attribute is assigned to system (S) files, and SYS.COM is a utility command written to specifically operate on those system files. (We'll discuss SYS.COM and ATTRIB.EXE later in this chapter.)

Windows XP no longer provides a way to change the System attribute from within Windows. You should know that you'll have to go to a command line or use the Recovery Console to remove the S attribute from files such as BOOT.INI.

The Environment

The environment is an area of memory that DOS keeps aside to store operating system settings. (Remember that CMOS is a chip that stores hardware configuration settings.) Because the information being stored changes, we call the places where that information is stored *environment variables*. PROMPT, PATH, and COMSPEC act as both environment commands and environment variables. The common way to set the environment variables is with the AUTOEXEC.BAT file. This batch file is discussed in its own section later in this chapter. To list the environment to the screen, type **SET** and press Enter.

Variables

A mathematical or computer variable is an interesting device, and one that you already know how to use—you just don't know that you know it. As is often the case, confusion can arise when someone uses a formal word to describe a common event.

Variables are *placeholders* that are written down somewhere, and that act as stand-ins for something real that will happen later. You probably took algebra in high school and used the symbol x in equations as a variable. The x stands for "whatever I'm supposed to find to get the right answer on the test, later." The opposite of a variable is a *constant*, sometimes referred to as a *literal*. Constants never vary, which, oddly enough, is why they're called constants.

A classroom containing a number of desks is a constant situation. Suppose that 15 desks are in the room. Each semester, those 15 desks sit in the same place (the classroom). If you were asked what those were, you would say, "Those are desks." However, each semester, 15 different students enroll in the class and sit at the desks. The desks are the *variables,* and the students are the *data being held by the variable.*

Depending on which semester it was, if you were asked whose desks those were, you would say, "That's Bill's desk" or "That's Sharon's desk." Bill and Sharon are the data being assigned to the variables (desks) at a particular moment in time. The next semester you would point to the same desks and say, "That's Donna's desk" or "That's Phillip's desk."

If you number each desk 1 through 15, you're *naming* the variables. Therefore, a computer programmer could say "Go get the data in '12.' **IF '12'** is empty, **THEN 'ANSWER'** = 0. **IF '12'** is not empty, **THEN 'STUDENT'** = '**12**.'" The number 12 is a variable representing desk number 12, which is either empty or contains a student. **ANSWER** and **STUDENT** are additional variables that also hold information that can change.

By providing the computer with a list of student names and their desk numbers each semester, the computer can tell you whether the desk is empty, whether the student is present, and what the student's name is.

The DOS environment is a small, 256-byte area of memory set aside to store configuration settings for the operating system to use. One way to use up the 256 bytes is to have a *path* containing that many characters. Another way is to run several instances of COMMAND.COM at the same time.

16-bit Windows created its own little area of environment memory called *resources.* Windows resources can run out of room just as the DOS environment could run out of room. The evolution of Windows into 9x and 2000 was directly linked to how Windows took over memory management and the environment. Windows XP features adjustable resource allocation, and finally ends the problem of running out of resources.

SET [variable]

The important variables to note are COMSPEC=, PATH=, PROMPT=, and TMP=. These are all set manually, except for COMSPEC=, which tells DOS where COMMAND.COM is located. When we say *manually*, we mean either that the user enters a SET command at the command line, or that the SET commands can be listed in the AUTOEXEC.BAT batch file. For instance, SET Temp=c:\dumb assigns temporary files to the "dumb" sub-directory in the root of Drive C:. Applications look for a TEMP variable in the environment to find the locations for their temporary files.

When you install an application on your machine, Windows and the operating system use an environment variable to keep track of the many files that are opened and then closed during the process. These are temporary files in that they aren't part of the application you find listed on the Start | Programs menu option, and are deleted (you hope) at the end of the installation routine. The files are stored in a temporary folder (usually \Windows\Temp), and the name of that folder is stored in the **TMP=** environment variable.

You can set an environment variable manually by typing SET [variable name]=[value setting] at the command line. To change the PROMPT variable at any time, type SET PROMPT=Hello World at the command line and press Enter. This means that instead of the DOS command line starting with C:\WINDOWS>_, it would start with Hello World_. Typing PROMPT=$p Hello World$g and pressing Enter would cause the command line to start with C:\WINDOWS Hello World>_.

The **COMSPEC=** environment variable is automatically set by COMMAND.COM during the boot process. The default value for this variable setting will always be the drive containing the boot disk and the name of the command interpreter file (almost always COMMAND.COM).

Warning! COMSPEC can be changed, but you should know exactly what you're doing before you change it. In the past days of dual-floppy machines, power users would create a virtual disk in system memory using RAMDRIVE.SYS. COMMAND.COM could then be copied to the RAM disk and COMSPEC set to point to that virtual disk as the location of the command interpreter. RAMDRIVE.SYS is still available in Windows 9x.

The SET command itself is usually required only for variables other than common DOS variables. Otherwise, entering only the variable's name and a DOS character separator is sufficient. However, it's good practice to always use the SET command when changing environment variables. Another example at the command line would be to type SET PATH=C:\;d:\Utils;E:\ windows\ComMaND. Note again that in the PATH variable, the case of the letters is ignored.

The semicolon is the formal separator used to separate out multiple "requests" (as in requesting different directories in a search path). The equal sign or a space is the formal character separator following a command (in this case, the variable name).

Typing the **SET** command and pressing Enter at a DOS command prompt produces a report of the current settings. For example, a typical environment SET report shows the following:

```
TMP=C:\WINDOWS\TEMP
winbootdir=C:\WINDOWS
COMSPEC=C:\COMMAND.COM
WINPMT=$P$G
PROMPT=Type EXIT to$_Return to Windows$_$p$g
PATH=C:\WINDOWS;C:\WINDOWS\COMMAND;C:\;C:\DOS;D:\UTILS;D:\BATCH;
     D:\WINUTILS
```

An interesting property of the DOS environment is that the names of the environment variables are automatically converted to uppercase in all instances. After you've passed the certification exam, you might be interested in researching how the winbootdir= and windir= variables can show up as lowercase.

PROMPT=

PROMPT is a reserved word for an internal DOS command, and is an environment command that affects the way DOS looks on the screen when you're not doing anything. The prompt to the left of the blinking cursor simply exists, prompting you to do something. The prompt command does not require the use of SET, even in an AUTOEXEC.BAT file.

PROMPT uses special symbols called *metastrings* in conjunction with the word "prompt." When you type **PROMPT** followed by a dollar sign ($) and a metastring, DOS sends the information you entered to ANSI.SYS (an auxiliary system file that comes with DOS) and changes the environment. The PROMPT command and switches are not case sensitive, meaning that you can enter them in uppercase, lowercase, or any combination of the two.

DOS uses the .SYS extension in both system files and device driver files. Check the possible responses to any question asking you about these files or the extension.

The command PROMPT=PG (not case sensitive) makes the prompt show the default drive, directory, and the > character (C:\DOS>_). The command

```
PROMPT=Type  "EXIT"  to$_return  to  Windows$_$p$g
```
(without spaces in Windows$_$p$g) produces a three-line prompt at a DOS screen as follows:

```
Type "EXIT" to
return to Windows
C:\DOS>_
```

The equal character (=) is used by DOS to signify a space. Therefore, you need not enter it, but it's good practice to use it so that you don't accidentally omit a space. The command PROMPT=pg works the same as the command prompt Pg because these commands are not case sensitive. However, it is *not* the same as PROMPT= $p $ g.

SET TEMP=

Both Windows and DOS applications use a temporary directory to store overflow files, swap files, and other temporary files. DOS and Windows know where to put those files by looking at the TMP= (DOS) or the TEMP= (Windows) setting.

The temporary directories are not required to be called \TMP or \TEMP. They can be called anything you like and can be located anywhere on any accessible drive. The important thing is that the SET TEMP= line of the AUTOEXEC.BAT file places the TEMP *variable* in the environment and names the variable's setting—in this case, a sub-folder.

If you have enough RAM, you can locate a temporary directory on a RAM drive (a virtual drive created with the RAMDRIVE.SYS program). This is sometimes useful for storing temporary Internet files. The RAM drive vanishes when the computer is shut down, automatically removing everything stored to that virtual drive.

The Path

The path is a common cause of trouble at the software level. PATH= is an internal environment command. The path is also the true name of a file. When we tell someone about a file name, we imply the rest: the drive and the sub-directory chain. When you talk to DOS about a file, you must write out the entire filename, or you can make a specific sub-directory the default location. This is still true when you work with a command line in any version of Windows.

Directories can contain sub-directories, each of which can contain more sub-directories, each of which can contain more sub-directories, and so on down until the entire name of a sub-directory and file reaches a limit. DOS created this limit, setting it to 256 characters. The full name for a file, including its drive and sub-folder, is called the *pathname*. When it doesn't include the directory information, the file uses a *filename*.

Suppose you want to rename every file in a folder with a .DOC extension to the same name, but with a .OLD extension. Unless you have a third-party utility, you'll have to go to an MS-DOS Window and use the REName command (REN). In this case, you would enter REN *.DOC *.OLD. Note that the *.doc and *.old are the mask, or file specification, or "file spec."

> A keyboard buffer and command-line character limitation set Windows Long File Name limits. The default command line is 127 characters. Batch files and environment variables support up to 244 characters. If no other characters are necessary in a variable name or command-line statement, a long filename can be up to 255 characters.

Keep in mind that the maximum number of characters in the full name of all the directory levels and the filename is 256. (This is a different 256 than the default environment size.) If you have a file named `C:\level2\level3\4thlevel\level5\onemore\yikes\holycow\MYFILE.DOC`, there are 65 characters in the entire pathname. This example contains eight directories—one root directory and seven sub-directories. MYFILE.DOC is a data file in the directory at the eighth level.

Each directory is symbolized by the backslash at the right end of its name. The *root* directory—the highest, or topmost folder on the drive—is represented by a plain backslash (\ ) to the right of a drive letter. The backslash in C:\ represents the root of Drive C:. In the previous example, "level2\" has a backslash at the end of its name, showing that level2 is a directory name. This continues all the way to MYFILE.DOC, which has no backslash, signifying that this is a data file.

> Unix uses the forward slash (/) to represent the division in directories. Because the people who actually invented the Internet (not Al Gore) were familiar with Unix, Web addresses show the directory level on the computers hosting the Web site with these symbols. For instance, in **http://www.ibm.com/support/all_download/drivers.html**, you can see that "support" is a sub-directory of the main data directory for the overall site. The "all_download" folder is a sub-directory of the "support" folder. Finally, the data file containing the Web page for the various software drivers is called "drivers.html."

Search Path

When you enter a word in a command line, COMMAND.COM parses the line and looks for a program file matching that word. If the command word is not found internally, COMMAND.COM looks elsewhere for a file with a .COM, an .EXE, or a .BAT extension—in that order. But where does DOS look? It looks in any directory listed in the *search path*. A typical search path might look like PATH=C:\;C:\Windows\Command;D:\dosutils.

Suppose that we've made the D:\JUNK directory the default directory by typing **D:** and then pressing Enter, and then typing **CD\JUNK** and pressing Enter once again. Our current location, then, is D:\JUNK. We're "logged in to" the D:\JUNK folder. Now suppose we type **FOURMAT A:** and then press Enter. What will happen? (*Pay attention, and check the spelling!*)

COMMAND.COM parses the line, finds A: to be a valid drive location, and expects FOURMAT to be a program file or internal command. DOS attempts to execute the command through COMMAND.COM in the following order:

1. It first looks inside itself for the character string FOURMAT (which it won't find) and then in the current directory for a program file that begins with FOURMAT. Here, it looks first for FOURMAT.COM, then for FOURMAT.EXE, and finally for FOURMAT.BAT.

> If FOURMAT.COM and FOURMAT.EXE both exist in the same directory, COMMAND.COM executes the .COM file first and never knows that the .EXE file exists alongside it. .COM files come first, then .EXE files, and finally .BAT files.

2. If FOURMAT.COM/EXE/BAT does not exist in the current directory, COMMAND.COM turns to the DOS environment and looks for an environment variable named PATH.

3. If PATH= exists, COMMAND.COM starts with the first directory listed and repeats step 1.

4. If FOURMAT is still not found, COMMAND.COM starts with each directory after each semicolon and repeats step 1.

5. If FOURMAT is not found in any of these places, DOS writes an error message to the screen that reads "File(s) not found". In this instance, the odds are that DOS wouldn't find FOURMAT.COM because the actual filename is FORMAT.COM and that command is located in the DOS sub-directory.

> A search path is a list of directories that DOS can search to find a program name entered on the command line. The advantage of a path is that you can enter the command without being logged in to the specific directory containing the program file. Likewise, a search path allows you to type only the filename, without the full pathname.

DOS Commands

The main thing to remember about DOS is that COMMAND.COM is the command processor (or command interpreter) and that it uses MSDOS.SYS and IO.SYS to make up the trio of the DOS operating system. DOS comes with many other programs in addition to the main trio. As we've said, anything that comes with DOS but that isn't inside COMMAND.COM is an external command. If it can be entered on the DOS command line (MS-DOS prompt) or used in a batch or an AUTOEXEC.BAT file, it's a command.

Device drivers (.SYS files) could be called commands, but they're more accurately called "driver files." 16-bit device drivers are almost always loaded in a CONFIG.SYS file, or referenced in SYSTEM.INI.

Chapter 11 mentioned the internal DOS device names. These can be used to instruct the basic devices that come with any PC. If you remember, some of these devices are PRN (printer), CON (video console), COM (communications), and LPT (line printer). When you type COPY FILENAME.TXT PRN and press Enter, you tell DOS to copy a file called filename.txt to the printer. The file is then printed.

The right angle bracket (>) is also called a *redirector*. Issuing the **ECHO ^L >PRN** command redirects a carriage return and line feed to the printer, causing a laser printer to eject a sheet of paper. Another example is where you enter **TYPE AUTOEXEC.BAT > [*somefile*].TXT** command and DOS types out the contents of the batch file but redirects the output into a new file ([*somefile*].txt). If that new file exists, the contents overwrite whatever was in it. If it doesn't exist, DOS creates it. Using the **TYPE AUTOEXEC.BAT >> [*somefile*].TXT** command tells DOS to append (add) the contents to the redirected file. In other words, the two angle brackets (>>) mean "add the output to the destination."

ATTRIB.EXE

Files contain additional information that can be used by the operating and file management systems. For example, a file's header information generally contains identification data that other programs can read. This is how file-viewing applications such as Quick View can identify the correct viewer used to show the file.

Regardless of the extension a file uses, the header information remains the same. You might rename THISFILE.DOC to THISFILE.BMP, but the header information maintains the fact that the file is a document file, not a Windows Bitmap image. The Explorer will become confused and ask you what program you'd like to use to open the file (based on file association), but Quick View will correctly identify the file and present a document.

Every file has another important piece of attached data: its *attribute bit*. The DOS and Windows basic file attributes come in four flavors: R (read-only), A (archive), S (system), and H (hidden). Additionally, folders have a D (directory) attribute, which can be seen with the DIR /V (for Verbose) switch in DOS 7.x and later. (ATTRIB does not show the directory attribute.) Attributes show under the Properties listing for any file, and you can change them by checking or un-checking a box.

Network operating systems include several additional attributes for the purposes of rights and permissions.

Each standard attribute can be turned on or off by using the plus (+) or minus (–) sign associated with the external ATTRIB command. If an attribute is turned on, it shows in the results of issuing the command with no switches. The syntax for ATTRIB.EXE is

```
ATTRIB [+R | -R] [+A | -A] [+S | -S] [+H | -H] [[drive:]
    [path]filename] [/S]
    +    Sets an attribute.
    -    Clears an attribute.
    R    Read-only file attribute.
    A    Archive file attribute.
    S    System file attribute.
    H    Hidden file attribute.
    /S   Processes files in all directories in the specified path.
```

The results of using the ATTRIB command show the current attribute of a given file or set of files specified in the file mask. DOS 6.x added several switches to the DIR command, where specific files could be shown on the basis of their attribute. For example, DIR /A:H shows a listing of all hidden files in a directory. Another switch added to DIR is the /S for sub-directories. Prior to these changes in DIR, the only way to see every file in every sub-directory was to use ATTRIB, CHKDSK, or TREE.

DOS 7.x modified the /v (for verbose) switch to include all attributes, including (D)irectories (also known as folders). To see this, open an MS-DOS window or command line and type DIR /A:H /V /P. The resulting report shows you how the /v switch provides an Attributes column where you can see the Directory attribute. The /v switch also displays the Long File Names version of the files and folders. The /A:H (for attributes:hidden) switch selects only hidden files for display. Finally, the /P (for page) switch pauses the screen every 23 lines until you press a key. Type DIR /A /V /P to see the entire listing, with the attributes for all the files. Type DIR /A /P (without the /V switch), and the attributes are no longer presented.

The ATTRIB command is used primarily to change file attributes. One example of this is when a computer can't start in Safe Mode and you want to manually back up the Registry. Typing ATTRIB -H -R C:\Windows\SYSTEM.DAT unhides the file and removes the Read-Only attribute. Without this step, the COPY command will not find the file. (Note that you should only do this if you know what you're doing.) Look at the following example of the ATTRIB command:

```
   SHR      IO.DOS          C:\IO.DOS
   SHR      MSDOS.DOS       C:\MSDOS.DOS
A   H       BOOTLOG.PRV     C:\BOOTLOG.PRV
    R        COMMAND.DOS     C:\COMMAND.DOS
    R        WINA20.386      C:\WINA20.386
A           CONFIG.DOS      C:\CONFIG.DOS
A           AUTOEXEC.DOS    C:\AUTOEXEC.DOS
    HR       SUHDLOG.DAT     C:\SUHDLOG.DAT
    H        MSDOS.--        C:\MSDOS.--
    H        SETUPLOG.TXT    C:\SETUPLOG.TXT
A           COMMAND.COM     C:\COMMAND.COM
```

In this case, IO.DOS is a system, hidden, read-only file. The DIR /A:[option] command lists only those files with the specific attributes you state. In both the DIR and the ATTRIB command, the /S "sub-directories" switch is used to show files you've specified in both the default folder and any of its subfolders.

You can use the ATTRIB *.* /S >PRN command to get a full printout of every file on the disk. The > redirector sends the results of the command to the printer. Another method is to type DIR *.* /S >PRN, which sends the entire directory listing to the printer.

If you want the listing saved to a text file, type DIR *.* /S >[filename].TXT (where [filename] can be any allowable filename). The screen will pause while DOS redirects the listing to the file, and then present you with a prompt. A new text file, with whatever name you assigned to it, will now be available in the folder you named (or the current default folder if you did not include a path). You can open this text file in any word processor and use it like a standard document.

The **TREE** command in versions prior to DOS 7.0 could be used to produce a full listing of files or a graphical report of all directories on a logical drive. Microsoft removed the **TREE** command in DOS 7.0, leaving shareware utilities as the only way to meet this need. Strangely enough, the **TREE** command also reappears in the Windows XP Recovery Console and the XP command line (CMD.EXE). (PC Magazine has a Tree replacement utility for Windows 9x that installs on the Properties menu.)

Hidden Files

Certain files on a drive are so important that if they don't exist, the system will fail to boot. On the other hand, the DEL (delete) command makes it very easy to delete the files. One of the more dangerous aspects of the Windows Explorer is that files can be easily deleted, regardless of whether they are hidden or otherwise protected.

The R (Read-Only) attribute means that a file can be opened and read, but not changed. Read-Only does *not* protect the file from being deleted. The hidden and system attributes make the file undeletable by a normal DEL command. If you type **DEL IO.SYS** and press Enter, the result will be "File(s) not found." IO.SYS is hidden, and you can't delete a file in a DOS screen, or session, unless DOS can see it.

Remember that a hidden file is only more difficult, but not impossible, to delete. Using Windows Explorer or changing the attribute to -H makes the file visible to DOS, after which it can be easily deleted.

The **DIR** Command: File Searches

One of the commands used almost routinely in DOS and Windows is the DIR command, which shows a directory listing. You may think that Windows doesn't use this command, but every time you call up the Explorer, Windows is using the DIR command to get a listing of the files you're seeing.

If you try to find a file by using the Search or Find options in Windows, you're presented with a field in the dialog boxes where you enter some parts of a filename, and a file mask (specification). If you've ever used the "Save As" or "Open" menu option in any application, your options for the *type* of file include the DOS names. For example, Figure 12.1 shows the default in Microsoft Word is to save a new file as a Word document (*.doc), and the drop-down list box shows how Windows continues to use DOS wildcards.

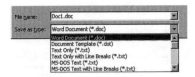

Figure 12.1   The file Save As "*" wildcard and extensions.

Wildcards

You probably know that in certain poker games the dealer can make a card "wild." The wildcard can represent any other card. In fact, the wildcard becomes a variable just like the blank tile in a Scrabble game, or one of our previously mentioned student's desks. You can use the card, and it can represent whatever you'd like it to. The card stays the same, but what it represents changes according to the dealer's rule.

DOS has two reserved symbols that represent this sort of variable: the asterisk (*) and the question mark (?). You can use the wildcards in the Explorer's Find: All Files | "Named:" dialog box, exactly the way they've always worked in DOS. The asterisk and question mark each have a slightly different way of working, though, which works out in the following manner:

➤ The asterisk symbol represents one or more characters to the right of the point where the asterisk is used. You can limit its results to the first eight characters in a filename by placing a single dot (period) after the asterisk (that is, *.).

➤ The question mark symbol represents only a single character. If more than one character is needed, more than one question mark must be used. When the question mark is used, it means one character must be available for every question mark typed.

There will most likely be at least one question on the exam involving wildcards. Be sure you understand that a question mark (?) represents a single character and that the asterisk (*) represents multiple characters.

Perhaps the easiest way to demonstrate wildcards is to show various ways they would be used with the DIR command. Let's suppose we have a number of files with a .WKS extension in a directory and another set of files that have a .XLS extension. The main part of the filename can be anywhere from one to eight characters; however, a number of the files start with REP for report, followed by a date (for example, REP1999, REP00, REP01, REP02, REP2003).

Let's further suppose that this directory has a number of files with many different extensions. There might be a SPREADS.XLS, THISONE.TXT, THATONE.MIS, NEWFILE.DLL, OLD.BAK, REAL.DOC, RUSS.DOC, and MY.WRK. The DIR command would look as follows:

```
DIR
Volume Serial Number is 2F34-10F5
Directory of X:\Example

.                   <DIR>
..                  <DIR>
REP1999   XLS
REP00     XLS
REP01     XLS
REP02     XLS
REP2003   XLS
SPREADS   XLS
THISONE   TXT
THATONE   MIS
NEWFILE   DLL
OLD       BAK
REAL      DOC
RUSS      DOC
MY        WRK
         13 file(s)
          2 dir(s)
```

If we were to try and find every file that was an Excel spreadsheet (.XLS extension), we would have to use the DIR *.XLS command. Note that the default in Explorer is to search for all sub-directories. This can be limited to a single directory by un-checking the "Include subfolders" check box. (The DOS command to search subdirectories would be DIR *.XLS /S, where the /S means (S)ub-directory or (S)ub-folder.) The results would look as follows:

```
DIR *.XLS

REP1999   XLS
REP00     XLS
REP01     XLS
REP02     XLS
REP2003   XLS
SPREADS   XLS
          6 file(s)      15 bytes
```

If you were to use DIR ???????.XLS under the assumption that you would find anything in the main name, it wouldn't work. The reason is that the question mark doesn't just represent any single character. It means that some character *must* exist as well. In this instance, you would be telling DOS to look for a file that absolutely must have seven characters, a period, and the .XLS extension. Although there may be a few files with both a seven-letter name and an .XLS extension, there are also files with some other number of characters to the left of the dot. The results would show as

```
DIR ???????.xls

REP1999  XLS
REP2003  XLS
        2 file(s)       6 bytes
```

The DIR ?.* command would search for any file with only one character in the name, along with an extension. There might be 200 files in a directory, but if none of them had only one character and an extension, DOS would return the "0 file(s)" message, as follows:

```
DIR ?.*

..              <DIR>      08-05-03  1
        0 file(s)          0 bytes
```

If you wanted to find every file that was a report file, you would use DIR REP*.* because all these files begin with the letters REP, and the company's naming standards require that all reports begin with the letters REP, as follows:

```
DIR rep*.*

REP1999  XLS
REP00    XLS
REP01    XLS
REP02    XLS
REP2003  XLS
        5 file(s)    15 bytes
```

 Developing a consistent way to name your files allows you to use the DOS wildcards to search for those files in a logical manner.

To find all the temp files on Drive C:, you would have to know that almost all Windows temp files end with .TMP. Another form of temporary file has the ~ (tilde, pronounced "till-deh") as the first character. You can't use the command-line DIR to find two different types of files. For instance, you can't use DIR ~*.* ; *.TMP on a command line. The semicolon isn't allowed. However, you *can* type *.TMP; ~*.* in Explorer, using the semicolon as a separator.

Using DOS in the situation just described, you would have to issue two DIR sequences. The first would be DIR C:\~*.* /S to find any file that began with a tilde, starting from the root directory of Drive C: and looking in every sub-directory on the drive. The second would be to use DIR C:*.TMP /S to find any file in any sub-directory on Drive C: with a .TMP extension.

Saving Search Results

Here's another use for the > symbol. Whenever you issue a command, that command performs an action. Many times the command also *outputs* some type of result. The result can be in the form of messages or, in the case of the DIR command, the listing of your directory.

If you use the > redirector, you can send the output results from DIR to either a printer or another file. Using DIR C:*.TMP /S > PRN would redirect the results of searching for every .TMP file on the entire Drive C: to the print-er, where you could go over the list at your leisure. Another way would be to use DIR C:*.TMP /S > C:\SOMEFILE.TXT, which would create a file called SOMEFILE.TXT in the root directory of Drive C: that would contain all the files listed in the search result. Later, you can open C:\SOMEFILE.TXT with Microsoft Word, Notepad, EDIT, or any other application that can read a plain ASCII text file.

A more sophisticated use of the > redirector would be to first run the DIR C:*.TMP /S > C:\SOMEFILE.TXT to generate a listing of all temp files in the "somefile.txt" file. Then issue the command DIR C:\~*.* /S >> C:\ SOMEFILE.TXT (using the >> double redirector). As we said earlier, this will append the results of the second command to the report because "some-file.txt" already exists.

NOTE

What's sad about Windows is that it's extremely difficult to save the search *parame-ters* (filenames and types) as an icon on your desktop. Windows says it will save the search, but it won't save the *.TMP or A*.EXE parameters in the shortcut.

Web browsers routinely cache Internet site information such as graphics, cookies, and pages. However, "cleaning out the cache" is a manual process in most cases, unless you use a third-party utility. If the cache isn't emptied, it can grow to thousands and thousands of files. Additionally, temporary files aren't always deleted as an application cleans up after itself. This, too, can lead to thousands of files, thereby slowing down the system.

To clean out a cache is a fairly simple thing. Find the cache directory (folder) assigned in the Preferences of your Web browser. Click on the folder in Explorer, which is the same as having the operating system do a search of that folder for *.* files (every file with any name). Select them all with either Ctrl+A (Select All) or "Shift Select." To use the Shift key to select every file between one file and another, highlight the first file, hold down the Shift key, scroll to the last (or other) file, and click to highlight it while still holding down the Shift key. Then press the DEL key.

> Windows 2000 and Windows XP provide the Disk Cleanup utility tool to help clean out some of these types of files. Windows 9x users can have a similar option with third-party commercial software such as the Norton Utilities (Symantec, Inc.).

Finding temporary files is where knowing wildcards comes in handy. From the Search dialog box, you can enter ~*.* ; *.TMP to find all files that begin with the tilde, and all files that end with .TMP. When they've been found, you can delete them all.

Summary—DOS

Understanding DOS is an important part of understanding computers, whether you're looking at a folder listing in the Explorer or using an MS-DOS Window to run a game. Before you take the exam you should have a clear understanding of the following:

➤ The command interpreter and underlying system files (COMMAND.COM, MSDOS.SYS, and IO.SYS)

➤ Wildcards and searching for files with the DIR command

➤ The Path and search path, and how DOS uses environment variables to keep track of file locations

➤ The difference between internal and external commands, and what it means to load a program into memory

➤ File attributes and the ATTRIB.EXE program, used to locate files that have been modified or to hide files from a directory listing

Keep in mind that although DOS was disconnected from Windows NT, Windows 2000, and Windows XP, the Recovery Console operates in a traditional DOS-like environment. One way or another, you're going to encounter the command line, and you should know what it is and how it works before you go for an A+ certification.

Logical Formatting and Partitions: FDISK

Before we get into this topic, let's make sure we all understand that a physical disk is a bunch of machinery with platters that store magnetic information. Up until now, we've used the word "drive" interchangeably with "disk," but in this segment, it's critical that you understand the difference. A disk is not a logical drive.

In Chapter 8, we said that many people refer to the disk in a mechanical housing as a drive. In this discussion, you must understand that a drive is a logical designation created by an operating system! For instance, a floppy disk is a physical item that you insert into a floppy disk mechanism. For the operating system to recognize the disk, that mechanism must be given a symbolic name. DOS and Windows designate a mechanical disk sub-system by the letters A through Z. (We'll discuss volumes in a moment.)

Partitions

A *partition* is an area on a disk: just that—an area. If that area has been *formatted* by an operating system, it becomes a *logical drive*. Logical drives are assigned both a drive letter and a *volume* name. *Low-level formatting* is where a manufacturer actually magnetizes the tracks on a disk. *Logical formatting* is where an operating system installs its file management system.

Regardless of how many fixed disks are installed in the system, each one must be partitioned with FDISK (for FAT32) or by DISKPART (Windows NT/2000/XP), and then formatted. The default in FDISK is to use the entire disk as a single partition. In other words, you must partition a secondary disk or other disk. It must then be formatted. Otherwise, you won't see the disk in the Explorer.

Volumes

Logical formatting means that some amount of space is set aside on a physical disk (hard drive) as a discrete area in which to store data and program files. These areas are the partitions, but they are routinely referred to as *volumes* and must be given a volume name during the partitioning process. (You see this name next to the drive symbol in the Explorer.) Each partition must have a volume name, and after a volume is formatted, it becomes a logical *drive*. Effectively, and for the sake of clarity, partition and volume mean the same thing in this section.

Mounting Volumes

The volume name is used to explicitly designate a partition, and is assigned during the **FDISK** "Create a Partition" procedure. (32-bit Windows provides the Disk Management console as another way to partition drives in a limited fashion.) As a safety measure, to avoid accidentally deleting a partition and wiping out any information on that area of the disk, you must enter the volume name of the partition before you delete it. The **FORMAT** command enables you to create a volume name on a floppy disk. Windows Explorer uses the **FORMAT** command when you right-click on the floppy drive icon and select Format.

The Windows 9x Explorer does not let you format a hard drive containing files. To partition and format a hard drive, you must use a DOS command line. Format is also one of the commands available in the Windows Recovery Console. After a disk has been partitioned and formatted into logical drives, Windows NT/2000/XP makes a further, subtle differentiation regarding *mounting* a volume.

Mounting a volume means making a formatted disk available to the Explorer. For example, a CDROM drive will show itself as existing on the system. However, placing an actual CDROM in the drive "mounts" that volume, and the Explorer then looks in the drive and on the disk for file information. The entire concept derives from networking terminology, but you should be aware of the term.

A physical disk can contain a number of partitions that DOS recognizes as logical drives. Almost all PCs have a physical hard drive (disk) and at least one logical drive (on a partition). An exception would be a diskless network terminal, from which the hard disk is removed and from which the terminal is booted up with a floppy disk. Microsoft created certain names for the various conceptual areas of a fixed disk as follows:

➤ *Fixed disk drive*—The actual set of platters attached to a drive controller. Disk drives are listed with numbers.

➤ *Partition or logical drive*—An area set aside on a disk for storage. Logical drives are assigned the letters A through Z by the operating system. (Fixed disks are assigned letters C through Z. Floppy disk drives always take the letters A and B.)

> *Volume label*—The actual 11-character name of a logical drive.

> *Primary partition*—A bootable area of a fixed disk, assigned a drive letter (C:, D:, and so on). Primary partitions may not be subdivided. The maximum number of primary partitions in Windows 9x is three.

> *Extended partition*—A non-bootable area of a disk. Extended partitions are not assigned a drive letter. Extended partitions may be subdivided into logical drives, which are then assigned a drive letter. (There can only be one extended partition on each fixed disk, but it may be further partitioned into multiple logical drives.)

> *Status*—The letter used to show which partition is active (A). The Active partition defines which Primary partition is being used to boot the system.

> *Type*—The term used to list either a Primary (PRI), Extended (EXT), or non-DOS partition.

> *System*—The term used to list the type of file system being used. DOS partitions are FAT16 and FAT32. Other types include HPFS and NTFS.

Number of Volumes

The absolute and technical maximum number of logical drives is 26 (A through Z). However, the A: and B: drive designators are built into DOS, and are always considered floppy disk drives. The letter *C* is always the first letter assigned to a hard disk, so Drive C: is considered the first bootable logical drive (Active Primary partition) on a hard disk. That makes three letters being used in almost every situation. A printout of an FDISK information report shows how each word is used.

```
                    Display Partition Information

Current fixed disk drive: 1

Partition  Status   Type    Volume Label  Mbytes   System   Usage
    1        A     Non-DOS                   2                %
    2              Non-DOS                  250              24%
  C: 3             PRI DOS   W95_5-8-97     300     FAT16    29%
    4              EXT DOS                  478              46%
Total disk space is  1030 Mbytes (1 Mbyte = 1048576 bytes)

The Extended DOS Partition contains Logical DOS Drives.
Do you want to display the logical drive information (Y/N)..?[Y]
------------------------------------------------------------
                 Display Logical DOS Drive Information
```

```
Drv Volume Label  Mbytes  System  Usage
D:  ALL-DATA         300   FAT16    63%
E:  DATA             178   FAT16    37%

    Total Extended DOS Partition size is    478 Mbytes
       (1 MByte = 1048576 bytes)
```

In Windows 2000, XP, and Windows NT, the FDISK.EXE program became part of the Computer Management or Disk Administration utility. This provides a graphic, interactive way of partitioning a disk, much as the Powerquest Partition Magic utility program does. However, Powerquest does such a superior job of working with partitions that we strongly encourage you to work with Partition Magic if you expect to do a lot of partitioning.

Primary and Extended Partitions

Partitions are categorized as either *primary* or *extended*. Now here's where it gets tricky. If you have a PC with a fixed disk (hard drive), that means it *must* have a set of platters for storing information. One way or another, a useable computer boots up from either Drive A: or Drive C: (or a bootable CDROM). That means three letters are taken, because A and B are built into COMMAND.COM, and C is automatically assigned to the fixed disk.

When you lay this all out, it means that a hard drive can technically have a maximum of 24 logical drives. To make things even more confusing, a logical drive (in the real world) refers to either the Primary or Extended partitions. If you have a Primary partition (required to boot a machine) *and* an Extended partition, the Extended partition can have a maximum of 23 logical drives. The floppy disk drive takes up 2 drive letters, and the Primary partition takes up 1 drive letter (A:/B: floppy; C: Primary), leaving 23 letters in the alphabet.

Formatting a disk (technically called *logical formatting*) means that the DOS file system is used to create the FAT, the DAT (directory allocation table), and the root directory. Formatting also defines the number and size of clusters on the volume.

Be sure to remember that COMMAND.COM can recognize 24 drives beyond drives A: and B:, but that an extended DOS partition can contain a maximum of only 23 logical drives. Drive C: is almost always a Primary partition.

Because the volume (logical drive) might be smaller than the physical disk, the names "volume" and "drive" are not interchangeable with "disk."

You can partition a disk into logical drives or volumes, but you cannot partition a drive into logical disks.

The external DOS program used to partition a physical disk is FDISK.EXE. The external DOS program used to format a logical drive is FORMAT.COM. Partitioning a disk completely destroys not only all the data on a disk, but any logical formatting on that disk as well.

An extended partition is different from a primary partition in that it isn't bootable. Some operating systems can boot from an extended partition. The extended partition usually takes up all remaining space following any primary partitions. Extended partitions must then be divided up into logical drives.

We highly recommend that you play around with FDISK on a system where there is no important data. This is a great way to use an old 486 machine you may have lying around. The exam assumes that you're thoroughly familiar with partitioning and formatting. The best way to find all the "gotchas" is to run through every option in FDISK.

Windows XP/2000 both provide access to a different partitioning program from within their Setup programs. Additionally, you can work with this DISKPART.EXE program at the Recovery Console command line, although it isn't as simple as FDISK. Finally, be aware that all versions of Windows begin with a FAT32 partition. During the installation process, Windows XP/2000 pauses to run a conversion routine if you've chosen the NTFS system, but only after first setting up the FAT32 system.

LASTDRIVE=

Certain DOS settings are automatically set to a default value. As mentioned previously, this is done in the environment with an environment variable. (Remember, the DOS environment shell is 256 bytes by default, and the prompt is C:\ or A:\.) LASTDRIVE, set in a CONFIG.SYS file, is the environment variable that contains the last letter of the alphabet DOS can use to assign recognition to a logical drive.

Until Windows 98, the default number of logical drives was set to five. Drives A: and B: are automatically set as floppy drives, and the first non-removable disk (drive 0) is set to C:. LASTDRIVE=K increases the number of logical drives that DOS can "see" to 11, with Drive K: being the last.

The default setting of 5 drives for **LASTDRIVE** leaves D: and E: open as additional, available logical drives following drives A:, B:, and C:, which are found on a system with a hard disk.

LASTDRIVE is set in the CONFIG.SYS file in a DOS and Windows 3.x machine. The directive still exists in MSDOS.SYS on a Windows 9x machine. **LASTDRIVE** can be increased by creating an optional CONFIG.SYS file in the root directory of the boot partition. (Note that Windows XP/2000 set the default last drive to Z.)

We said there was a limit to how many logical drives a fixed disk could contain. There's also a limit to the number of logical drives LASTDRIVE will recognize. Remember that the reason for the limit of 24 logical drives is that drives A: and B: always exist in the system, even if they don't physically exist on the PC. There are 26 letters in the alphabet, so 26 minus 2 (A: and B:) leaves 24.

An interesting fact to keep in mind is that Novell uses the default drive F: to search for the LOGIN.EXE command. However, during the installation of the client software, Novell requires that the LASTDRIVE be set to Z:. Note that whereas to access drives you always use the drive letter and a colon, the LASTDRIVE= statement doesn't require a colon, as in LASTDRIVE=K.

LASTDRIVE is an important (though not required) CONFIG.SYS file directive for networks and is important when many partitions exist on a big hard drive. If no line for **LASTDRIVE** exists, DOS assumes that only five logical drives exist on the system. Later versions of Windows set the default to **LASTDRIVE=Z**. If you can't access a drive on an older machine, check to see whether there's a CONFIG.SYS file, and whether it has the directive.

FORMAT.COM

Partitioning a disk tells the operating system only how the disk is divided into potential drive space. No matter which operating system (for example, DOS, OS/2, NT, or XP) you choose to install on any given partition, you need to set up the partition as a logical drive with some kind of file system. The FORMAT command prepares the drive's file system in the following manner:

➤ Creates a boot sector, two copies of the FAT, and the root directory

➤ Performs a low-level check for bad sectors, marking any that it finds as unusable

➤ Provides an optional single-step system files transfer to make a disk bootable (FORMAT /S)

➤ Enables the user to label a disk with a volume name at the end of the FORMAT process

During a *quick format* (FORMAT [d:] /Q), the program changes only the FAT on the disk and tells DOS that every sector on the drive is now available for data. Data still resides on the disk, but DOS has been told that it can write over anything and put a new entry into the FAT. Unconditional formatting (/U) erases data from the entire disk. "Safe" formatting places a hidden file on a floppy disk, reducing the entire storage area of the disk.

To completely format a disk and have FORMAT.COM examine the entire disk, use the **FORMAT [d:] /U** switch. **/U** is for Unconditional, and **[d:]** is the drive being formatted.

LABEL.EXE

Oddly enough, a DIR listing (since the time of DOS 1.0) includes a line that states "Volume in Drive [X:]" and possibly a label of up to 11 characters. However, there was no way to label a disk other than running a format on it and putting the label on at the end. DOS 3.0 introduced the LABEL command, which allowed a volume label to be put on a disk without it being formatted. Windows Explorer enables you to rename the volume by simply highlighting the drive letter and pressing F2 to edit the name.

SYS.COM

SYS.COM is a special DOS program that has one purpose only: to copy the system files to another bootable disk. The destination disk must first have been formatted and be empty of all files, or formatted as a bootable disk. (That being said, the Windows 98 version requires only that the disk be formatted.) SYS.COM replaces corrupted system files on a hard drive or floppy drive by copying clean versions of the system files from a working (hopefully virus-free), bootable floppy.

When a working hard drive suddenly produces an error at boot-up that reads "Non-system disk or disk error. Replace and press any key when ready," it may mean that the system files have become corrupted. It could also mean that someone forgot to take a data floppy out of Drive A: when he or she shut down the system the last time. SYS.COM is the first step to try to fix the problem (after you check to see whether there's a floppy in the drive).

The boot sector includes the Master Boot Record (MBR). You can't just copy the DOS system files with the COPY command because of the specific location of both the files and a special bootstrap loader (discussed in Chapter 13). Additionally, both IO.SYS and MSDOS.SYS are hidden files, and COPY won't see them.

SYS.COM is indicated when a hard drive stops (following the POST) and the message "Bad or missing command interpreter" appears. The command to copy the system files from Drive A: (bootable disk) to drive C: (with corrupted files) is **SYS C:** or **SYS A: C:**.

An even more frightening message following the POST is "Non-system disk or disk error" when you're booting from a hard drive. Boot from your emergency boot disk and see whether you can log on to Drive C:. If you can, try SYS.COM. (Note that you can also try the Repair option from the Windows XP/2000 start menu, or the **fixmbr** command in the Recovery Console.)

A bootable floppy starts the operating system and provides a way to test for access to the hard drive. If the system boots and you type **c:** and press Enter, you should log on to Drive C: regardless of whether that drive is bootable. If you can't log on to Drive C:, a more serious problem exists.

File Systems

Many people think of day-to-day file management as saving, copying, deleting, moving, and modifying files. For clarity, we'll use the term *maintenance* to mean what a user does with files. We'll use the term *management* to mean fundamental operating system processes.

An operating system must include a file system to make sense of the bits of magnetized coating on a disk. The file system keeps track of where all the parts of files are located, the directories and filenames, and the used and unused space on a disk—allocated space and free space, respectively. The file system continually updates the cluster locations of all the parts of a file. When we speak of DOS, we'll use the term "directory." When we speak of Windows, we'll use the term "folder." Both terms mean the same thing, but understanding a directory will show you why a command line uses the Change Directory (**cd**) command.

 The Windows 9x Long File Names feature uses the DOS file system to actually store the data on the physical disk. However, Windows controls how the FAT is used.

DOS was set up to work with 16 bits worth of addresses, allowing for 65,525 clusters. Back then, no one ever imagined that PCs would be important or useful enough to need more than 10MB of space. The original 16-bit FAT continues to this day. The FAT32 system is an actual change to the basic 16-bit file allocation table, and uses 32-bit addressing along with adjustable cluster sizes.

Directories (Folders)

A DOS *directory* is a special type of file. Directories and their sub-directories are used to keep together files having a common purpose—to organize a disk. For example, C:\DOS usually contains all the DOS operating system files, and C:\MSOFFICE contains the files that pertain to Microsoft Office. Today, we speak of folders and sub-folders, but many of the routine operations involving running a computer are still linked to the concept of directories.

All files have names. All files also contain data. All directories are files. We use a *directory name* to contain filenames. These are fundamental principles of files. DOS uses the file allocation table to keep track of data, and the directory allocation table to keep track of the filenames.

Directory Tree

A directory and all its sub-directories are an example of a hierarchy. The original designers thought it looked like a tree, and the first part of a tree is the root. If you suppose that a *directory tree* looks somewhat like a root system, then smaller and smaller roots *branch* off of a larger root. The left pane of the Explorer shows the directory tree ("tree view"), while the right pane shows both the files and the sub-directories contained within a highlighted directory ("file view").

The FAT uses the root directory as the starting point for all the files on a given volume. The root directory can contain only a limited number of files, including both data and program files and sub-directory names.

The root directory, with its representative backslash, is at the top of the tree (level 1). The root directory is still a file, containing both data files and directory files. When a sub-directory contains files, it becomes a lower level in the hierarchy. Level 2 is represented by an indented line coming down from the root, and there are smaller horizontal lines "branching" to the right. This stepladder design of lines and branches unfolds when you click on the little + or – sign to the left of a directory name in Explorer.

Every volume must have its own root directory on the first track and sector of the partition. The maximum number of directory entries in a FAT16 root directory is 512. To have more than 512 file and directory names, you must use at least one sub-directory. Sub-directories can have as many directory entries as there is room on the disk.

An interesting problem on some hard drives occurred when DOS prevented the user from creating a new file. Users would get an error message referring to insufficient disk space, but they had a 500MB partition available. This happened when users put all their files into the root directory. With no sub-directories, the directory table ran out of room for a new filename and DOS issued the out-of-space error.

Directory Management

To create a directory, DOS uses the command MD (Make Directory). To create a directory called "example" branching from the root directory, the command is MD\EXAMPLE (note the backslash). To create a directory one level below whichever is the current (default) directory, the command is MD EXAMPLE (note the space). In the first example, the backslash explicitly names the root directory as the directory that will contain the new "example" sub-directory.

To delete a directory, the original command was RD (Remove Directory). If there were files in the directory, the files had to be removed first (DEL *.*). Only then could the directory be removed (RD c:\EXAMPLE). DOS 6.0 introduced the DELTREE command, which could take out a whole directory and all its sub-directories in one step. (Explorer happily removes a directory and all its sub-directories if you simply press the Delete key.)

To change from one directory to another, DOS uses the CD (Change Directory) command. Used with an absolute name, CD takes you to that exact directory. Used with a space before another directory name, the command takes you down to the next sub-directory from the current location.

Relative and Absolute Locations

If we all are facing the same direction to begin with and someone yells, "Turn left!" we'll all end up facing the same way. On the other hand, if we're all facing different directions and someone yells the same thing, we'll end up facing different directions. No matter how many of us are facing in different directions, if someone yells, "Turn north!" then we'll all end up facing one way (assuming everyone has a compass and understands basic geography).

North, south, east, and west are absolute directions on the planet Earth. No matter which direction you're facing, north is always in a specific direction. Left and right, on the other hand, are relative directions. When people say "left" or "right," you need to know which way they're facing to determine what absolute direction they're talking about.

If you issue the command CD\WINDOWS\SYSTEM, you'll be taken to the root directory (the first backslash) and then moved down through WINDOWS to SYSTEM. However, if you issue the command CD SYSTEM (using a space after the CD), DOS starts from wherever you are and tries to go down one level to a sub-directory called "System." If you happen to be in the Windows directory, this command works. If you happen to be in some other directory and there isn't a SYSTEM subfolder in that folder, you get a "File(s) not found" error.

NOTE

A space after the **CD** command is a relative "down" designation. Before issuing such a command, be sure there is a location to go down to; if there isn't, DOS returns an error message. The **CD ..** command always moves up toward the root, one step at a time. Even at the root, DOS will *not* return an error message.

Dot, Dot-Dot, and Dot-Dot-Dot

The CD command (also known as CHDIR) is used to change the *default directory* to another directory. The default directory is the directory where COMMAND.COM first looks for any referenced program entered on a command line. If you type CD and press Enter, DOS returns the name of the default directory.

TIP

If you type **TRUENAME**, an undocumented DOS command, DOS also returns the actual drive and path of the current location. This can be used on networks, and also where long folder names have been "mapped" to a substitute drive letter (if you use the **SUBST** command). Note that this trick was removed from Windows XP.

If you are logged onto the C:\WINDOWS\SYSTEM directory, you've made that directory the default directory. If you then type CD.. (two dots in a row), DOS changes the default to the directory immediately above the existing one—the parent directory. Beginning with Windows 98, you can type CD... (three dots in a row) to move up the directory tree two steps at a time.

When you type the full pathname to a file, you're giving DOS an absolute name. If you say "Change directories (CD) to the C:\WINDOWS\COMMAND directory," DOS knows exactly where that is. On the other hand, you can use what's called the "dot-dot" (. .) to tell DOS "CD to the next directory up from here." The dot and the dot-dot are still there from CP/M.

From the C:\WINDOWS\SYSTEM directory, you could type the absolute location by issuing the command CD c:\WINDOWS (note the space after "CD"). This would change the default location to one step above where you are, but it means typing a lot more characters.

ALERT

Typing two dots after the **CD** command moves you up one level from where you are, to the parent directory. Typing three dots after the command moves you up two levels from the current folder. The dot commands do not work from outside the cursor location. To change a directory on a different drive you must use the **CD** command and name the new location.

The single dot represents "here" to DOS. You can use it as a shortcut with a program command such as XCOPY when you want to copy all the files in a single directory of Drive A: (floppy disk) to the current directory. Instead of typing out the whole location, you can enter XCOPY A: . with the single dot after the A: to tell DOS that you want the files to arrive "here." This is handy if you're copying a lot of files from Drive A: to a network location like J:\pdj16\US\station5\2004\edu-work\process\managers\march. In this instance, you can log in to the network location and use the single dot rather than retyping the entire path.

You can also use dot commands to go up and then down. For example, from the C:\Windows folder you can go to the C:\Junk folder (assuming it exists) by typing **CD** **..\Junk**.

Directory Name or Filename?

In the name C:\WINDOWS\SYSTEM, "SYSTEM" can be either a filename or a sub-directory name. The last name in a path, or complete file and directory listing, is somewhat ambiguous. You can see this uncertainty when using the **XCOPY** command to copy a series of files to a different sub-directory. **XCOPY** asks you whether you want the destination to be a file or a directory.

Even though sub-directories can have an extension, convention has it that filenames use from one- to three-character extensions, whereas sub-directories stay with just the eight main characters of typical filenames. This helps keep sub-directories and files separate. Additionally, because sub-directories are files (albeit of a special type), DOS provides angle brackets (< and >) and the **DIR** abbreviation (<DIR>) to indicate that something is a sub-directory.

Because sub-directories are files, they can also have one- to three-character extensions. However, many application programmers forget to consider this, and those applications can't show the 8.3 type of sub-directory names in their File I Open dialog boxes. In some instances, this will even crash an application or an installation routine.

File Management

We've said that, technically, an operating system includes a file management system and a command processor. File management involves controlling filenames and keeping track of the files on a hard disk. The file management system must have a way to write to, read from, and locate tracks, sectors, and clusters. DOS and Windows use some version of a FAT, along with a root directory, as part of their file management systems.

File Allocation Table (FAT)

The formatting process creates a *root* directory (folder) that must be at a specific physical location on a logical drive. The FAT is designed for a maximum number of *entries* (filenames) in that root directory, which limits the maximum number of clusters (not sectors) in the root directory. The directory allocation table (DAT), along with the FAT, keeps track of the *directory structure*. DOS uses a particular format for making directories on a disk.

> The file allocation table is literally a table with bits of information about files. The first piece of data is the name (address) of the cluster that holds the beginning 2KB of a file—about one page of typing.

The FAT is absolutely critical to the maintenance of all the data on a given disk. Without an allocation table, there's no way to know where anything is on that disk. For this reason, DOS maintains two copies of the FAT in case one of the copies becomes corrupted. Some third-party software tools can recover a disk through the use of the second copy of the FAT. However, this assumes that the second copy isn't corrupted, which usually is not the case.

FAT32 Clusters

Clusters are fixed at a minimum of 2KB (four 512-byte sectors), meaning that even a 3-byte file would take up 2,048 bytes worth of space on a small logical drive. As the size of the volume grows larger, the formatting process increases the size of the clusters. FAT16 fills up a volume with clusters, meaning that on a 2GB disk, each cluster will have expanded to 32KB in size. That same 3-byte file would now take up 32,768 bytes of storage space.

> When a small file on a large disk uses up a whole cluster, the unused portion is called *slack space*. It isn't at all unusual for a large volume with many small files to have many megabytes of slack space.

FAT32 uses a different cluster size adjustment, and can work with volumes up to 2TB (terabytes) in size. The same 32KB cluster created by FAT16 uses only 4KB of space on a 2GB volume formatted with FAT32. FAT32 makes more efficient use of a disk by cutting down on slack space. Additionally, the smaller cluster size on large hard drives shortens the amount of time needed by the read/write heads (seek time) to find a file.

SCANDISK and CHKDSK (Check Disk)

From the beginning (DOS 1.0), there had to be a way to reconcile the FAT with what was actually on the disk. One of the external programs that came with DOS was the program CHKDSK.EXE (Check Disk) that checked the disk for discrepancies between the allocation table and file clusters.

CHKDSK looked at the FAT for a beginning and ending cluster address for a file. Then DOS went to that address on the disk (the cylinder, track, and sector) and checked to see whether any readable information was in the cluster. DOS didn't read the file for news about how Granny was doing in Oshkosh; rather, it used the drive's read-write heads to copy the information into RAM and write it back again. It then checked the directory listing and name against the records in the FAT. If all went well, CHKDSK went on to the next entry in the FAT and did it all over again. CHKDSK has been completely replaced by SCANDISK (SCANDISK.EXE).

 CHKDSK is an obsolete program and can wreak total havoc on a Windows 9x computer. Never run this program! Always use **SCANDISK** or a proven third-party utility.

Having said this, Check Disk (a revised version) makes its reappearance under the Windows 2000 and Windows XP Recovery Console, and as part of routine disk maintenance processes. Only in XP/2000 does Check Disk replace ScanDisk. Be sure that you know which version of Windows is running, and, again, don't use **CHKDSK** in Windows 9x or Me.

If a cluster address in the FAT does not match the data on the disk, SCANDISK returns a message to the user that there are lost clusters or cross-linked files. *Lost clusters* are areas of the disk that have been allocated to a specific file when the file itself wasn't closed correctly (maybe because of a crash or a lockup). Cross-linked files are more scary. Cross-linking means that, according to the FAT, two files occupy the same space somewhere in a group of clusters. Possibly, either the FAT or the DAT has been corrupted. This can sometimes happen when the power goes out or is turned off while the computer is running an application.

CHKDSK was the only way (without third-party utilities) to validate the FAT and the DAT prior to DOS 6.0, when ScanDisk was introduced. One of the first utilities provided by Symantec's Norton Utilities was Disk Doctor, which gave a user the capability of checking a disk for sectors that were either bad or becoming bad. If bad sectors were found, Disk Doctor would attempt to move any data within them and mark the sectors as bad. CHKDSK does not check for bad sectors in which the physical disk is damaged or unusable.

ScanDisk finally allowed a way for DOS owners to attempt to fix cross-linking, lost clusters, and bad sectors. You don't have to reformat a hard drive just to set aside bad sectors anymore. ScanDisk can't be used on a network drive, but it can be used under Windows.

ScanDisk is a way to scan a disk for problems and then work toward repairing some of those problems. **DEFRAG** is a way to speed up disk access by combining parts of files from all over a disk into organized, continuous *blocks* of clusters.

DEFRAG.EXE

If you write a two-page letter and save it as NAME1.DOC, the file system notes the name of the file and puts the two pages onto the hard drive in a set of clusters. Suppose that you then write another two-page letter and save it as NAME2.DOC. Again, the file system keeps track of the name and the clusters containing the second file. How does the file system know which clusters have which data in them?

Keep the picture of your two letters in mind. Suppose that you decide to make some additions to the first letter. You open your application (say, a word processor) and load NAME1.DOC into memory. You add another two pages of text and then re-save the letter. It still has the same name, but now you have two additional pages of data.

If the file system tries to store the added two new pages next to the original two pages, there isn't any room. Your second file, NAME2.DOC, has taken the neighboring set of clusters. Therefore, the file system skips the two pages of NAME2.DOC and puts the additional pages of NAME1.DOC after the end of NAME2.DOC. If you look at Figure 12.2, you can see how your files can eventually end up in pieces, scattered all over the hard drive. When many files are scattered over a drive, we say the drive is fragmented and is in need of defragmenting, or "defragging."

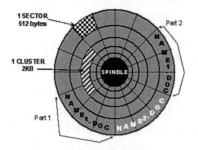

Figure 12.2 Stylized disk showing a file splitting up another file.

DEFRAG.EXE was added to DOS 6.0 as a way to put all the parts of files into one continuous group of clusters. This is a typical maintenance chore and should be done on a regular basis. Prior to DOS 6.x, the only way to defragment a file was to use a third-party software utility tool. Because DOS originally included almost no utilities, an entire industry of utility companies sprang up around this void. The Norton utility was called Speed Disk.

The nice thing about third-party utilities is that they're not tied to the operating system's command interpreter. DEFRAG.EXE could run only if it was the correct version, based on a matching version of COMMAND.COM. Even copying DEFRAG.EXE from Windows 95 OS/R-A to OS/R-B wouldn't work. Norton Utilities' SPEEDISK could be run on any system, regardless of what version of COMMAND.COM was installed.

Another important consideration is that the Windows XP/2000 version of DeFrag does not move files together into a contiguous area of the partition. Only a third-party utility can do this, which has important consequences in terms of a fragmented virtual memory swap file. Microsoft's **DEFRAG** cannot defragment swap files at all.

The DOS version of DEFRAG.EXE is run from the command line. DOS 7.0 (Windows 95) includes DEFRAG.EXE in the C:\WINDOWS subdirectory, but could also run it from within a window. Following Windows 95, DEFRAG became a graphics-only application, meaning it could be run only in a window, not from the command line. In each ensuing discussion of specific operating systems, we'll focus on the different maintenance utilities that were added to help troubleshoot a problem.

Filenames

Certain filenaming conventions were developed in the DOS world, and computer people are often judged on the elegance of their procedures. You *can* create an archive file with something like WinZip or PKZip and call it ARCHIVE.698 (instead of ARCHIVE.ZIP). However, if another technician needs to conduct research into which type of file it is, you'll probably be considered ignorant (at best).

This system has carried forward to the extent that many applications routinely assign a specific extension to their data files. You can override the process if you know how, but most people haven't learned how. Even in the Explorer, the default installation is to hide the "type" extensions, and you must choose View | Folder Options | View tab: "Files and Folders," and check the "Show All Files" check box to unhide file types (extensions). In Windows XP this is even more complicated, requiring the additional steps of selecting "Show hidden files and folders" and unchecking the "Hide extensions for known file types."

Some filenames are absolute—for instance, AUTOEXEC.BAT, CONFIG.SYS, SYSTEM.DAT, and USER.DAT. If you spell these in any way other than the required way, they won't work in the expected manner. The best policy is to learn the common extensions and stick with the program. Computers are hard enough to deal with, and you don't need to spend extra time decoding someone else's surreal filenaming ideas.

Non-displayed Periods

One confusing aspect of DOS is that when a DIR listing of files in a directory is printed or sent to the screen, no periods appear. It looks like the filenames are split into one to eight characters, a big empty space, and then one to three characters or the <DIR> notation. You can see the periods in Windows Explorer, if a folder has an extension, but not in an MS-DOS window.

Although the screen or printer doesn't print the periods in the filenames, DOS needs those periods. If you try to find a file without using the period, you will receive a "File not found" response.

Characters Allowed in DOS Filenames

We've spoken about the 8.3 filename format. Which characters, then, can you use for filenames? These characters are found in the ASCII character set. The original set was 128 characters until IBM added another 128 characters (high-bit) for the extended ASCII character set. DOS allows any character between ASCII decimal number 33 and 255.

Windows 95 (borrowing a Macintosh and networking idea) wanted to overcome the limits of DOS characters, particularly the space character. Long File Names can be seen in any 32-bit version of Windows, but DOS (7.x) keeps track of the files through the use of a tilde (~) and consecutive numbers to truncate the long filename into its first eight characters (that is, prior to the extension). The allowed characters in DOS are

➤ The letters A through Z

➤ The numbers 0 through 9

➤ ', ~, ", !, @, #, $, %, ^, &, (,), -, _, {, }

➤ High-bit characters from 127 through 255

The lower the scan code number of a character, the higher the filename will be on a directory listing sorted by name. This is confusing to some people who expect a list sorted by name to have all names beginning with "A" at the top and all names beginning with "Z" at the bottom. Because 1 is a lower number than 2, all files beginning with 1 will move to the top of a directory listing. For example, 11NOV98.DOC will appear directly below 1JAN98.DOC, and 2FEB98.DOC will be third.

To force a filename to the top of a directory listing, begin the name with something like !, @, or # because these have very low scan codes.

By convention, temporary files often start with a tilde (~), an underscore (_), a percent sign (%), a dollar sign ($), or an ampersand (&). Table 12.1 shows common filename extensions in DOS.

The use of the tilde (~) is a configuration option in the Windows 9x setup, and can also be changed if you modify the Registry.

Table 12.1	Common DOS Filename Extensions
Extension	**Type of File**
.COM	64KB compiled command file
.EXE	Large compiled executable file
.BAT	ASCII plain-text batch file
.MSC	Microsoft Console file
.MSI	Windows Installer file
.SYS	System driver software/instruction file
.GRP	Windows program group file
.BAK, .OLD	Backup file
.TMP	Temporary file (usually deletable)
.INI	Initialization file (DOS and Windows)
.DLL	Windows Dynamic Link Library
.INF	Windows 9x autoscript setup program
.VXD	Windows and DOS 7.x virtual device driver file
.DRV	Driver software file
.TXT	Plain ASCII file created by text editor
.HLP	Windows HELP hypertext file
.GID	Expanded help file, after first use

(continued)

Table 12.1	Common DOS Filename Extensions *(continued)*
Extension	**Type of File**
.DOC	Document file (full character sets, formatting)
.WRI	Windows 3.x MS Write file
.BMP	Windows bitmap graphics file
.GIF	Proprietary graphic information file
.PNG	"PNG's Not GIF," an open standard graphics file to replace .GIF format
.WMF	Windows metafile graphics file
.PCX	MS Paint raster image
.ICO	Windows icon file
.LNK	Windows shortcut file
.TTF	TrueType font file
.OVL	Program overlay file
.SCR	Script file or screensaver file
.DAT	Data file
.ZIP	Archive file
.EX_, .CO_	Microsoft expand/extract archive
.DIZ	Internet shareware description text
.WAV	Waveform sound file
.MID	MIDI sound file
.CB, .CAB	Windows 9x cabinet file

For a complete listing of all file extensions, visit **http://filext.com/index.php**.

Summary—Disk Management

This segment has covered a variety of complex topics. Formatting a drive and assigning it a logical drive letter is different from partitioning a disk and assigning it a volume name. Be sure that you understand the following concepts before moving on to the next chapters:

➤ Partitions and drives, with a particular emphasis on the difference between primary and extended partitions.

➤ The number of logical drives that may be assigned to any system of disks. A computer may have more than one physical hard drive, and multiple operating systems. Each operating system can only understand a maximum number of drive letters—26.

➤ The difference between FDISK (partitioning) and FORMAT (logical drive letter assignment).

➤ SYS.COM, the specialized utility used to replace system files on a damaged boot disk.

➤ File systems and the FAT, including the difference between FAT16 and FAT32 (discussed further in Chapter 13) and file allocation units.

➤ Naming conventions used in DOS, even with Windows 2000 and XP, and how DOS filenames—as opposed to Long File Names—allow only certain characters.

➤ Common file extensions and the way extensions are used as file associations in Windows Explorer.

➤ Directories and sub-directories, folders and sub-folders, and navigating the search path.

➤ Fragmented disks, and how to use DEFRAG to bring files into contiguous clusters; Scan Disk and repairing a hard drive.

Operating Systems Versus Shells

For many years, people were marketing *menu* programs and *shells* for the text-based DOS, hoping to make *using* computers one thing (user interface), and *configuring* them another. A computer menu is a list of options (choices) written to the screen. The user selects one of the options and presses keys or clicks a mouse button to pick one of the options. Menu choices are essentially the same as *program items* in 16-bit Windows and *shortcuts* in 32-bit Windows.

 Even today, when you run CMD.EXE or choose Start | Run and enter **COMMAND.COM**, you are creating a DOS shell. It appears to you as a DOS or text-based window, but it is, in fact, a small shell.

In time, menu programs became more sophisticated. Some companies included security features in their menu programs where a user could access the command processor only through the menu. By controlling how the menu program passed commands to the command processor (the file's properties), menu programs began to become more and more like shells.

File Properties

These days, the defining characteristics of a menu choice are often included in what we call *properties*. Borland's Quattro Pro spreadsheet introduced the idea of using the mouse's right button to call up a menu for changing the properties of whatever the mouse was pointing to. The idea quickly caught on, and now most Windows-based applications access a properties menu from the right mouse button.

 NOTE You can also use Shift-F10 in Explorer to call up the Properties menu for any highlighted file.

On the main Program Manager menu in 16-bit Windows, File | Properties lists the essential properties of a program. 32-bit Windows incorporates the right-click of the mouse (alternative mouse click) to create a context-sensitive properties menu, meaning that the properties change depending upon the context of what the mouse is pointing to.

Shells

A *shell* is where the command processor loads another instance of itself, resulting in two or more separate command processors being "resident" in RAM. Both Windows File Manager and the Windows 9x Explorer are programs that pass a user's intentions to the underlying DOS command processor. They place a *layer* between the user's actions and the underlying operating system. This layer is what we mean by the term *shell*.

 NOTE In Windows NT, 2000, and XP, the Explorer is completely integrated into the operating system. The Windows Explorer isn't quite the same thing as the Microsoft Internet Explorer browser.

In a DOS session, the resident part of COMMAND.COM sitting in conventional memory intercepts keystrokes from the keyboard and then passes them on to the CPU. Strictly speaking, COMMAND.COM is creating a shell around the operating environment where any instruction that enters the environment is tracked before the instruction can move out of the environment.

Another way to think of a shell is that it acts like an executive secretary screening calls to the boss. Anyone (that is, the program instruction) who wants to contact the executive must first go through the secretary. The secretary has a list of high-priority people who get passed through immediately. Other people are directed to someone else, depending on their business. Network operating systems often use a shell that works alongside the COMMAND.COM interpreter. Both shells look at incoming program instructions to see which operating system should take the call.

A CONFIG.SYS file uses an optional *directive* (statement) called SHELL= to tell COMMAND.COM to increase the size of the environment space in memory. SHELL=C:\COMMAND.COM /E:1024 /P increases the environment to 1,024 bytes and keeps it permanent (the P). The SHELL= directive also sets an environment variable that tells the operating system where to find its command processor. In this case, DOS always knows that COMMAND.COM is in the root directory of Drive C:.

NOTE | The memory environment is still a configuration option for 16-bit DOS sessions under Windows 9x. To see this, locate the DOSPRMPT.PIF shortcut to COMMAND.COM and examine the properties (right-click). On the Memory tab, each type of memory can be configured, along with the environment size.

To create a *transparent* (unnoticed) interface with the computer, Microsoft introduced a Windows applet called File Manager (WINFILE.EXE) as a replacement for the DIR, COPY, MOVE, RENAME (REN), DELETE (DEL), MD, CD, and RD commands. An *applet* is a self-contained program application that works from within an overseeing parent application. For instance, in the overall "application" of your kitchen, a can opener would be analogous to an applet. In time, the distinction between an application and an applet has become blurred.

The Windows 3.x File Manager is an applet under the Program Manager (PROGMAN.EXE) domain, its companion interface program. PROGMAN.EXE runs first and then offers the opportunity to run the File Manager interface from within it.

Windows Explorer (EXPLORER.EXE) creates the Windows 9x Desktop interface (folder) and runs constantly during a Windows session. On the other hand, File Manager must be explicitly run and closed from within PROGMAN.EXE. To see this, press Ctrl+Alt+Delete in a Windows session from a plain desktop. Task Manager (TASKMAN.EXE) runs, and Windows Explorer is one of the tasks. Both 16-bit and 32-bit Windows have the Task Manager utility program.

SYSTEM.INI and **SHELL=**

The SHELL= line in the SYSTEM.INI file defines the interface program that Windows presents to the user at startup. In Windows 3.x, the two shells are Program Manager and File Manager. By default, the line reads **SHELL=PROGMAN.EXE**, which loads Program Manager as the user interface for Windows 3.x.

By editing the SYSTEM.INI file and changing the line to **SHELL=WINFILE.EXE**, Windows 3.x starts with File Manager as the primary interface. However, File Manager doesn't include a desktop area for creating program groups and icons. The Microsoft Web site still offers MSDOS.EXE (the old MS-DOS Executive from Windows 2.x) for use as a shell interface.

Windows 95 first extended the File Manager's capabilities to include the desktop, icons, and program groups (folders). File Manager became EXPLORER.EXE.

Batch Files

A batch file is a file containing a list of commands, one on each line of the file. Naming the file with the .BAT extension tells DOS (and Windows) that this file is an executable program file. DOS then reads each line of the file as though a user was entering that line. When the user turns on the computer, the last command in the AUTOEXEC.BAT file might call, for example, MENU.BAT, which draws a menu on the screen. More often, the last command is C:\Windows\WIN to start Windows.

For the exam, remember that when statements are put into a text file that can be interpreted by COMMAND.COM (a command processor), we refer to that file as a *batch file*. AUTOEXEC.BAT is a batch file. CONFIG.SYS is a configuration file. Both files can also be called *startup command files*.

Batch files are often used to automate the process of running a program by storing complex configuration switches. Some programs require configuration switches to be entered at a command line. Batch files enable the computer to literally type commands to itself in exactly the same way a human being uses the command interface. Other programs can be configured only from within a CONFIG.SYS file.

AUTOEXEC.BAT

If you ever look inside COMMAND.COM, you'll find a reference to a file with a specific name: AUTOEXEC.BAT. This is a batch file and is just like any other batch file that can be created using a text editor. If the file has this name, spelled this way, and it resides in the root directory, DOS processes any instructions in this file as the final step in the boot process. Like CONFIG.SYS, AUTOEXEC.BAT is not required to boot the computer. If AUTOEXEC.BAT does exist, COMMAND.COM processes it as the last step in the boot process.

 Observe the way a programming sequence in the command processor looks for a specific file in a specific location. This example of "hard coding" a set of events will show up again during the boot process, and later with Windows NT and Windows XP/2000.

AUTOEXEC.BAT files may still be necessary on a Windows 9x or even an NT machine. They're particularly useful in configuring 16-bit device drivers that require a CONFIG.SYS file. These configuration switches might be for non-PnP-compliant 16-bit devices, such as CDROM drives and sound cards. The character strings following a command name can be exceptionally complicated and arcane. A batch file is a good way to store this kind of complexity within a file that acts as a simple one-word command.

After the last command line in the AUTOEXEC.BAT file has been processed, control returns to COMMAND.COM, and the computer is ready to begin a working session. If an application's startup program file is the last command, the last thing AUTOEXEC.BAT does is start the application, placing the user at whatever startup location that application normally provides.

A Sample Batch File

A batch file is a plain-text file composed of command lines and saved with the .BAT extension. Using the DOS Editor (EDIT.COM) or the Windows Notepad, you can create a new file with the following lines:

```
@ECHO OFF
DIR C:\ /P
ECHO This is a test line
PAUSE
REM I don't want this line to show
DIR C:\ /W
```

When you finish entering these lines, pressing Enter at the end of each line, save your work as some filename with the .BAT extension—for example, C:\TRYTHIS.BAT. Remember that it *must* be plain ASCII text. Open a DOS window by choosing Start | Run and typing COMMAND as the program you want to run.

When you type TRYTHIS at the command line and press Enter, this batch file gives a directory listing of the root directory on Drive C:, pausing every 23 lines for a keypress (DIR C:\ /p). When the DIR is finished, it displays the onscreen message "This is a test line".

> The **ECHO** command is a batch file command that tells DOS to type to the screen whatever follows **ECHO** and a space. The **@ECHO OFF** line tells DOS to not show on the screen any line of the batch file unless it begins with the word **ECHO**.

The PAUSE command (internal to COMMAND.COM) pauses the process and places the generic message "Press any key to continue..." at the next line below the test-line row. When you press a key, the batch file skips the following line:

```
REM I don't want this line to show.
```

> **REM** (short for *remark*) is an internal DOS batch file command that must begin in the first column of a new line. **REM**, followed by a space, causes COMMAND.COM to bypass the line and move processing to the next line.
>
> **REM** is often used to *remark out* a line in the AUTOEXEC.BAT or CONFIG.SYS file in a test situation where you might want to keep the commands in the line, but bypass them for a number of sessions until you've figured out some particular problem. Then you can delete the REM from each line, one at a time. Those lines will once again act as commands.
>
> Windows allows this type of "commenting out" in the WIN.INI and SYSTEM.INI files through the use of a semicolon (;) followed by a space in the first column of the line. **REM** doesn't work in a Windows INI file, and a semicolon doesn't work in a DOS batch file.

Because the line following the PAUSE command has been "commented out" and isn't processed, you don't see "I don't want this line to show" on the screen. The next thing you *do* see is another DIR listing of the root directory, but this time in wide format and without the pause (DIR C:\ /w). When the DIR is finished listing, the batch file turns control back over to COMMAND.COM and returns the DOS prompt.

This is exactly how the AUTOEXEC.BAT file works, and you can edit the file with DOS's Edit, the Windows Notepad, WordPad, or any other word processor that creates .TXT files. Be sure that you save the file in plain ASCII, because it's not unusual for someone to edit the CONFIG.SYS file or AUTOEXEC.BAT file with Microsoft Word and then save it as a .DOC file, which contains all kinds of extended, non-ASCII characters. When this happens, the computer either throws up and dies when it hits the non-ASCII file, or bypasses the file completely. If the AUTOEXEC.BAT file contains network login commands, the user can end up mystified as to why he or she can't log on to the network.

Always make a backup copy of the latest working CONFIG.SYS and AUTOEXEC.BAT files before editing them so that you have a current, uncorrupted version in case of emergencies.

Practice Exam Questions

Question 1

Files with which of the following extensions can be executed from the DOS command prompt? (Check all that apply)

❏ A. .TXT

❏ B. .EXE

❏ C. .COM

❏ D. .BAT

Answers B, C, and D are correct. Executable (.EXE), command (.COM), and batch (.BAT) files can be executed from the command prompt. Answer A is incorrect because text (.TXT) files contain text data and must be accessed by another program application.

Question 2

Which of the following **DIR** commands would find all files that begin with "A" and are device drivers?

○ A. **DIR *A.SYS**

○ B. **DIR A?????.SYS**

○ C. **DIR A.***

○ D. **DIR A*.SYS**

Answer D is correct. The asterisk (*) wildcard overrides anything to the right of the symbol in either the main filename or the extension. Answer A is incorrect because it would find all files with a .SYS extension, regardless of what letter they started with. Answer B is incorrect because it would find only files that begin with A and contain six characters in their main filenames. There may be some files with fewer or more characters than six. Answer C is incorrect because it would find any file beginning with "A" regardless of what extension it had (such as .EXE or .DOC).

Question 3

DEFRAG.EXE is used to scan a disk for bad sectors, mark them as unusable, and bring all files into contiguous sequence.

○ A. True

○ B. False

Answer B, false, is correct. Defragmenting a disk brings files into contiguous blocks, thereby improving the system's efficiency. SCANDISK.EXE is used to check for disk-level problems, such as bad sectors, cross-linked files, or corrupted FAT listings.

Question 4

A hard drive can have up to _____ logical drives, and an extended partition can have up to _____ logical drives.

○ A. 24, 23

○ B. 26, 24

○ C. 1, 26

○ D. 23, 1

Answer A is correct. Note the reference to a hard drive, meaning a fixed disk not including a floppy drive. A: and B: are reserved drive names for floppy disk mechanisms. A single fixed disk can take all the remaining letters of the alphabet (24). An Extended partition can be created only after a Primary partition has been created, and the Primary partition takes up one letter. If the Primary partition uses the C: designation, that leaves 23 letters in the alphabet remaining. Answer B is incorrect because the floppy disks take two letters. Answer C is incorrect because it's possible for a fixed disk to have many more than just one logical drive. Answer D is incorrect because in addition to any logical drives contained within an Extended partition, a Primary partition is considered a logical drive.

Question 5

> DOS system files must be located in the _____ partition, and that partition
> must be set to _____ for the computer to start DOS.
>
> ○ A. first, Primary
> ○ B. Primary, Active
> ○ C. current, initialize
> ○ D. Extended, DOS

Answer B is correct. The DOS system files must reside in a Primary partition, and that partition must be made Active. Answer A is incorrect because
the Primary partition does not have to be the first partition on the disk.
Answer C is incorrect because until the system boots up, there is no "current" or default partition or drive. Answer D is incorrect because DOS cannot be booted from an Extended partition.

Question 6

> Which of the following programs would be the best solution in a situation where
> the computer fails to boot and produces an "Invalid media type" error message?
>
> ○ A. Repair.com
> ○ B. FIX /MBR
> ○ C. SYS A: C:
> ○ D. FDISK /MBR

Answer C is correct. Although the sys command won't guarantee that the
problem will be solved, there is a strong possibility that the system files have
become corrupted or otherwise damaged on the bootable disk. Answer A is
incorrect because although Repair is an option on the Windows 2000/XP
startup menu and might repair an installation, there's no such program as
REPAIR.COM. Answer B is incorrect because there's no FIX program,
regardless of the switches. Answer D is incorrect, even though the FDISK
program can use the /MBR switch to sometimes recover a master boot record.
However, it isn't the "best solution" by any means.

Question 7

When you choose Start I Run and type **AOL**, and then click on OK, you receive the following message: "Cannot find the file 'aol' (or one of its components." What does the error mean?

- ○ A. AOL.EXE cannot be run from the command line.
- ○ B. The pathname is incorrect.
- ○ C. Windows requires AOL.EXE to be in the C:\Program Files folder.
- ○ D. The filename is incorrect.

Answer B is correct. This is a tricky question because you have to decide whether AOL.EXE exists on the computer at all. Given that every response seems to indicate the assumption that the program exists, there must be something else wrong. Try a process of elimination. Answer C is incorrect because although the Program Files folder is a default installation location, it isn't a required location. Answer A is incorrect because almost any executable file can be run from a command line, and that doesn't seem to be where the question is leading you. Answers B and D seem to be related. Given the assumption that the file exists, the likelihood is that it's spelled correctly, otherwise it wouldn't be in the question. Answer B is the remaining correct option because the error message indicates that Windows simply can't find the file without more information. That additional information is the entire name of the file, including its folder location. The entire name is known as the pathname.

Question 8

To bypass the execution of a line in a configuration file, which two of the following choices are used?

- ❑ A. **REM**
- ❑ B. :
- ❑ C. ;
- ❑ D. //

Answers A and C are correct. REM (an abbreviation of remark) is used in DOS to bypass (comment out or remark out) a line in batch files and configuration files such as CONFIG.SYS and AUTOEXEC.BAT. Windows uses the semicolon (;) to bypass lines in .INI files, which are also configuration files. Answer B is incorrect because the colon is used to signify drive letters.

Answer D is incorrect because paired forward slashes are commonly used as a directory statement in networking operating systems and the Internet.

Question 9

Which command would you use to create a bootable floppy disk from the Command Mode?

- ○ A. **Format a: /u /s**
- ○ B. **Format a: /u**
- ○ C. **Format a: /boot**
- ○ D. **Format a:**

Answer A is correct. Once again, you must be familiar with command-line options and events. It won't matter if you're in DOS or the Recovery Console, you're going to have to deal with these problems. If all you've ever done is used the Explorer to format a disk, you would be well advised to either postpone your exam or do some hurry-up work with basic text commands. Answer B is incorrect because it would only format the disk (unconditionally) and fail to transfer the system files. The disk would not boot the system. Answer C is incorrect because there is no /boot switch for FORMAT.COM. Answer D is much like answer B, in that it would simply format the disk and not transfer the system files. It would also most likely format the disk by using the default "quick format" program option.

Question 10

Which of the following files are executable? (Choose the three best answers)

- ❏ A. .EXE
- ❏ B. .BAT
- ❏ C. .INI
- ❏ D. .COM

Answers A, B, and D are correct. Files with .BAT, .EXE, and .COM extensions are all considered executable. Although Windows considers .PIF files to be executable, files ending in .INI (answer C) are Windows configuration files and can't be executed from a command line. However, you can run an .INI file by double-clicking on it within the Explorer. Be careful that you don't confuse "run" with "executable." An executable file is a program file.

Running a file from the Explorer is very different from entering the filename in the Start | Run dialog box, or trying to execute it from the MS-DOS environment. Windows is actually using the File Associations feature to run NOTEPAD.EXE first when you double-click the filename. Notepad then opens the .INI file.

Need to Know More?

DOS books are getting harder to find, and they all cover this operating system in far more depth than required by the A+ exam. However, if you really want to get into it, here are three in particular that we like:

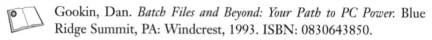 Gookin, Dan. *Batch Files and Beyond: Your Path to PC Power.* Blue Ridge Summit, PA: Windcrest, 1993. ISBN: 0830643850.

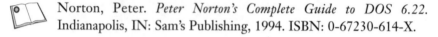 Minasi, Mark. *DOS 6.2.* San Francisco, CA: Sybex Network Press. ISBN: 1-56205-289-6.

Norton, Peter. *Peter Norton's Complete Guide to DOS 6.22.* Indianapolis, IN: Sam's Publishing, 1994. ISBN: 0-67230-614-X.

Booting, Startup Files, and Memory

Terms you'll need to understand:

✓ Bootable disk
✓ Virtual, emulate, and simulate
✓ WIN.COM
✓ SYSTEM.INI and WIN.INI
✓ Conventional memory and extended memory
✓ Swap files
✓ HIMEM.SYS and EMM386.EXE
✓ System resources

Concepts you'll need to master:

✓ Booting and system files
✓ CONFIG.SYS
✓ Virtual Real Mode and the virtual machine (VM)
✓ Initialization (.INI) files
✓ Virtual memory
✓ Virtual device drivers (VxD)
✓ Windows memory and system resources

Chapter 12, "DOS," spoke about how DOS was the underlying Windows operating system up until Windows versions 2000 and XP. DOS and the Windows 3.x shell were parts of a migration path toward a 32-bit operating system. Everything Microsoft has been doing over the past decade can be linked to the problems of backward compatibility with DOS. We also understand that some readers may be encountering both DOS and 16-bit Windows for the first time, in their exam preparation, and so this chapter highlights the important things to keep in mind.

Windows 95 brought a more subtle change to the computer industry than a new interface and 32-bit applications. For the first time, computers began to take on individually specific configurations. It became much more difficult for support personnel to speak with an end user, knowing most of the settings on that user's machine. Tech support began to fall back on reformatting or reinstalling a machine, rather than being able to fix a problem. In a similar fashion, it's almost impossible to describe a universal boot sequence for modern-day computers. For this reason, we're going to take the time to discuss the original boot-up process in detail, in the hopes that you'll better be able to see how to diagnose Windows startup problems—an important part of the A+ exam.

We'll be using DOS and Windows 9x, for the most part, throughout the explanation of booting and memory. Windows NT, 2000, and XP are completely different operating systems, and are covered in the next chapters. Where a process has remained the same through every operating system, we'll make a reference to XP and 2000. All references to loading system files, memory, and file management specify DOS and Windows 9x, unless otherwise stated.

Booting and System Files

Everything about starting a PC revolves around the *Master Boot Record (MBR)* and the process of joining the motherboard BIOS to the operating system. COMMAND.COM works IO.SYS and an optional CONFIG.SYS file, before passing control to MSDOS.SYS, the third of the three critical system files. We've tried to focus your attention on important points by using Exam Alerts, but you should also work with a computer and pay attention to everything taking place when you turn on the power.

When you turn on the PC's power switch, the POST routine in the ROM BIOS chip *initializes* the system and runs a test of all the system components. Prior to Plug and Play, you had to physically turn off the computer before plugging in a new peripheral. Even now, you'll often still be required to shut down and restart Windows while it updates Registry settings. *Hot-swapping* means that you can add or remove a device while the machine is running.

However, installing a device for the first time still requires an explanation of that device to the operating system.

The Three-Fingered Salute

When an irreversible error occurs in memory, the CPU freezes up and the computer won't accept input. Sometimes, the mouse pointer moves around, but clicking won't do anything. Other times, the system won't even recognize keystrokes. In either case, if this happens to you, you're experiencing a computer crash. We've heard that in the business world, problems are considered opportunities. If you keep reminding yourself that a computer crash is really an opportunity, perhaps you'll feel better about it.

From a DOS environment, Ctrl+Alt+Del generates a warm reboot. In Windows 9x, the same keystrokes bring up the Task Manager. All running programs are listed in the Task Manager, and any one of them can (you hope) be shut down. Highlight a frozen program and click End Task (sometimes it requires more than one try). (The Task Manager becomes available in Windows XP if you right-click on the taskbar.)

The POST is run only when power to the CPU is turned off and then turned on again. A *system reset* (accomplished with the Reset button) or a *warm boot* (accomplished with Ctrl+Alt+Del) does not always include the POST. That being said, many modern machines now generate a POST during any kind of system reset.

If the computer is so locked up that even the keyboard can't access the system, the only way to restart the computer is either to turn the power off and then back on, or to use the Reset button on the face of the casing. This type of lockup is called a *hard crash*, and it requires a *cold boot* to restart the computer. Until recently, pressing a Reset button would not call a POST routine, even though a cold boot includes the routine. However, modern systems usually do call the POST from the Reset buttons, making no distinction between a system reset and a cold boot.

There are a few ways of telling whether the machine has just entered a cold boot or is going through a warm reboot. One way is to watch the monitor during the startup process. A cold boot almost always runs a simple memory diagnostics routine (parity checking), and you'll often see a count of the available memory on the screen. Another way is to see a momentary CMOS settings display, or the notification of which key to press to access those settings. Finally, a POST operation always accesses the built-in speaker, generating one of the beep codes discussed later in this chapter.

Booting Overview

There's an old saying that relates to pulling yourself up by your own boot-straps. The reference is to bettering your position in life by relying completely on your own talents and capabilities, not waiting for someone else to lend a hand. Because DOS loads itself (sort of by its own bootstraps), the startup process has come to be known as the *boot* process, or *booting up* the computer. It does not have anything to do with the number of people who put their foot through the screen, back when PCs were just entering the market.

Following the hardware test, the POST looks to the ROM BIOS on the motherboard and begins a simple parity-checking program to test the main memory chips. The parity program writes information to each chip and then reads the information and compares it. Sometimes you can see this parity-checking process take place by the rapidly incrementing numbers at the top of a black startup screen. Parity is discussed in Chapter 3, "Memory: Types and Forms."

Each succeeding version of DOS and the BIOS contains fixes (or *patches*) for problems. The system moves some of these patches to lower memory, so they won't have to be constantly read from the ROM chip. This is the reserved motherboard BIOS area of memory (how DOS uses memory is discussed in the "Memory" section, later in this chapter). Patches routinely overwrite instructions in the ROM chip.

Finally, the BIOS looks in the first sector (track 0, sector 0) of a floppy disk in Drive A: for a *bootstrap loader* built into the operating system. If it finds the bootstrap loader there, it transfers control to the bootstrap loader to load the operating system. Otherwise, depending on the CMOS settings, BIOS looks at the first sector on Drive C:, a SCSI disk, or even a CDROM for the boot-strap loader.

Some operating systems allow booting from an extended partition. Iomega provides a utility that enables the system to boot from a removable hard drive. Whatever the case, the boot process searches for a bootstrap loader.

Windows 9x looks in the boot sector, where it finds IO.SYS. Windows NT and OS/2 can be booted from a *boot track*, making it possible to load the rest of the operating system from a different partition than the Primary, Active one. The NT Loader, however, must still be linked with the Master Boot Record.

ROM BIOS Looks at the Boot Sector

Formatting divides the disk into two specific areas: a *system* area for DOS system files and a *files* area for data and programs. The system area is the boot sector. Formatting also sets up two copies of the FAT and creates the root directory. If the disk will start DOS, COMMAND.COM and the two system files must be in the root directory of that disk. The boot sector is

➤ Always the first sector (sector 0) of the first track (track 0) of the first cylinder (cylinder 0) of the disk

➤ 512 bytes long, just like any other sector

➤ Contained on all disks, regardless of whether they are bootable

In a moment, we'll discuss the partition loader. The Master Boot Record is the first available track of a bootable partition. The boot *sector* is the first sector on the disk. The boot record is contained within the boot sector.

The FAT (and directory table) comes directly after the boot sector, and takes up different amounts of room, depending on how large the drive is. The reason for two copies of the FAT is to offer some slight protection against one being corrupted. A *boot-sector virus* is where the boot sector of the disk has become corrupted (infected). We discuss viruses in the "Viruses" section of Chapter 16, "Troubleshooting."

The root directory comes after the FAT. In FAT16 systems, the size of the root directory is 16 kilobytes. The 16KB limit on a FAT16 file system format is what makes the 512-name limit in the root directory. The general file storage area follows the root directory. Make a note that Virtual FAT (VFAT) uses the FAT as a *vector* table. Vectors are discussed in the "Memory" section of this chapter. Note also that FAT32 uses a 32-bit File Allocation Table, allowing for more files in the root directory.

BASIC Bootstrap Loader

The boot sector also contains a very small program written in BASIC. This program calls a small part of IO.SYS called the *bootstrap loader*, which either loads the so-called DOS *kernel* (system files) into memory at startup, or writes the message "Non-system disk or disk error. Replace and press any key when ready," to the screen. The DOS kernel manages system-level functions, such as file management and memory management. For the computer to understand itself and for the kernel to be loaded, the DOS system files must be present in the boot disk's root directory.

The bootstrap loader works in conjunction with the system files and must be in the boot sector. Simply copying COMMAND.COM and the two hidden system files to a floppy disk won't extract the bootstrap loader. The only way to install the bootstrap loader into the boot sector is with FORMAT.COM (**FORMAT [drive:] /S**) or SYS.COM.

The bootstrap loader contains a *BIOS parameter block (BPB)*, which contains information about the physical structure of the disk. If it's a hard disk, the BPB is read only once because the disk won't be removed. If it's a floppy disk, every time the disk is accessed, DOS works with the change-line process (see the "Change-Line Jumper" section of Chapter 8, "Peripherals: Storage Devices") to read the BPB.

Partition Loader

If the boot disk is a fixed disk, the boot sector also has a small *partition loader* program with 16 bytes of information per partition, identifying the operating system, the starting and ending sector of the partition, and which partition is bootable. The partition loader points the boot process toward the Active, Primary partition for that fixed disk. The Active partition (set with FDISK) is what makes the hard disk bootable.

The BPB and partition loader—taken together—are properly called the Master Boot Record. An undocumented switch for FDISK can sometimes re-create the MBR. In some cases, this may be a way to eliminate a boot-sector virus when a virus protection program isn't available. To use the switch, type **FDISK /MBR** from a DOS screen (not from a DOS window running within the Windows shell or Explorer). You should be extremely careful about using the /MBR switch with a suspected virus because certain viral infections can cause the total loss of an entire partition and all its data.

The boot sector, sometimes improperly called the Master Boot Record (MBR), is found on cylinder 0, head 0, track 0, sector 0. The boot sector is the absolute first sector on a disk. Whether a disk is bootable or not, all disks have a boot sector. The boot sector contains the partition loader.

Technically, the Master Boot Record is the BPB and partition loader. On the exam, though, the Master Boot Record probably refers to the entire boot sector. DOS and Windows 9x use a bootstrap loader. Windows NT/2000/XP use the NT Loader (NTLDR) file.

Bootstrap Loads IO.SYS

ROM BIOS runs the bootstrap loader, which loads the I/O device management system, IO.SYS and MSDOS.SYS. IO.SYS lists the original DOS devices, such as COM, LPT, and PRN ports. The two DOS system files have their attributes set to Hidden, Read-Only, System. ATTRIB.EXE is the DOS program used to change file attributes: Archive (A), Hidden (H), Read-Only (R), and System (S). In DOS 7.x, Windows 9x uses MSDOS.SYS and IO.SYS differently.

NOTE

Windows 9x continues to use both MSDOS.SYS and IO.SYS. The files have been modified to perform slightly different operations, but IO.SYS is still the low-level input-output manager.

IO.SYS Checks for CONFIG.SYS

Following the bootstrap loader, IO.SYS loads first. Once again, IO.SYS contains generic device drivers for the basic peripherals expected to be used on the computer, such as the monitor, disk drives, keyboard, communications, and printer I/O ports. It also contains a module called SYSINIT, which runs through a startup procedure and device driver initialization. SYSINIT (inside IO.SYS) calls the CONFIG.SYS file (if it exists) to initialize 16-bit devices. If the CONFIG.SYS file does not exist, the boot process continues onward.

ALERT

IO.SYS always loads first, *no matter what.* Whether it's DOS, Windows 3.x, Windows 9x, or Windows Me, IO.SYS is always the first program file that loads following the POST and bootstrap routines. In Windows 9x and Me, IO.SYS contains a hard-coded device driver loading instruction for HIMEM.SYS.

SYSINIT

After IO.SYS is loaded into memory, the computer begins to wake up a bit and discover what it is. Up until this point, the motherboard and ROM BIOS have been mostly controlling the startup process. This is like when you first realize you're starting to wake up in the morning, but haven't opened your eyes yet. All you know is that you're alive—you're not sure yet who you are (depending on what kind of night you had).

Part of the SYSINIT module is a set of instructions that looks for a file named \CONFIG.SYS (with the backslash). This name, which is explicitly written into the program, is spelled exactly that way and contains a specific reference to the root directory (\) of the boot disk. The following are true of CONFIG.SYS:

➤ It is *not* a required file for booting up.

➤ It contains references to the location and configuration of software programs. These programs contain additional instructions on how to run hardware devices (software *device driver files*, or *drivers*).

➤ It must be a plain ASCII text file created by the user or sometimes by an installation routine.

➤ It uses reserved command words called *directives* to configure various system options.

The CONFIG.SYS File and Directives

If CONFIG.SYS exists, IO.SYS reads the file line by line. DOS specifies the way in which each line of the CONFIG.SYS file is written. The file is much like a batch file, in that DOS examines each line of text as a line of instructions. Because this is a .SYS file and not a program, we use the term *directives* rather than *commands* to refer to the reserved words.

Windows 95 joined a generic CONFIG.SYS file to the IO.SYS. Most of the directives were moved into the updated file, and CONFIG.SYS (theoretically) went away. However, compatibility issues with legacy systems (older systems) forced knowledgeable users to create a configuration file on their own, and to often create a subsequent AUTOEXEC.BAT file.

 IO.SYS only began loading device drivers with Windows 95. The initial programming for HIMEM.SYS and other directives can be seen in IO.SYS all the way back in DOS 6.x, but it wasn't activated until Windows 95.

CONFIG.SYS may still be necessary, even with Windows Plug and Play. It isn't required by 32-bit Windows; however, the implication for people learning about operating systems is that CONFIG.SYS was required by earlier versions of DOS and 16-bit Windows. This is not true.

 Although WIN.INI is a necessary file in the Windows startup process, it does not have to exist prior to starting Windows. If the file does not exist, Windows creates a generic version. CONFIG.SYS, AUTOEXEC.BAT, and WIN.INI are unusual in that they're not absolutely essential.

A computer can be started without a CONFIG.SYS and an AUTOEXEC.BAT file. If there are CDROM drivers or sound card drivers in the file, those devices won't operate unless ROM BIOS recognizes a bootable CDROM. However, the basic computer will start and run. Read any questions about CONFIG.SYS very carefully.

 The only files absolutely required to boot a computer into DOS and Windows 9x are IO.SYS, MSDOS.SYS, and COMMAND.COM. The CONFIG.SYS file is optional.

CONFIG.SYS and MSDOS.SYS

The DOS system files attempt to find each device driver listed in CONFIG.SYS (in the order in which they're found) and to execute the instructions in each file. PnP specifications generally allow for new devices to be folded into the operating system through Internet downloads. However, prior to PnP (and in some cases, even with PnP), device drivers may be required for 16-bit devices.

NOTE

CONFIG.SYS is examined before the full operating system has loaded. There has been no opportunity to issue a **PATH** statement, so each device must be listed by its full pathname.

After all the device drivers have worked out their differences, found one another, and settled down into RAM, control passes to MSDOS.SYS, which loads into a lower area of DOS memory. MSDOS.SYS contains all the support functions necessary to run programs and to allow program development. Prior to Windows 9x, the interrupt listing was held in this file, along with various patches, fixes, and updates to DOS.

When DOS runs through the lines in the CONFIG.SYS file, the files referred to are either found or not found. Assuming that all the device drivers are found and loaded into memory, the CONFIG.SYS file eventually ends, and returns control to IO.SYS.

IO.SYS Runs Twice

Let's take a moment to mention HIMEM.SYS here. HIMEM.SYS is technically a software driver designed to allow access to any memory beyond the first 1MB. It originally loaded from a CONFIG.SYS file, back when all device drivers were being installed from this file. When the market reached a point where nearly every machine had more than 1MB of memory, HIMEM.SYS became a critical file. DOS 7.0 (Windows 95/98) folded the loading directive into IO.SYS, to make sure HIMEM.SYS would always be installed, and to eliminate the possibility of accidentally failing to load it from an optional CONFIG.SYS file.

DOS 7.0 also changed the basic system files, using the hidden IO.SYS to read configuration information from either the MSDOS.SYS hidden file, a CONFIG.SYS file, or *both*. However, IO.SYS must still be in the root directory of the bootable partition, and MSDOS.SYS (also hidden) must also be in the root directory. In Windows 9x, the "Starting Windows 9x..." message, displayed on the screen following the initial POST and parity check, is written into IO.SYS.

IO.SYS runs *once* to determine whether a CONFIG.SYS file should be read. If the file exists, then IO.SYS drops out to allow the CONFIG.SYS file to load any existing Real Mode device drivers. After the CONFIG.SYS file has completed, IO.SYS then returns *again*, to read MSDOS.SYS for the rest of the startup process.

This quick pass into CONFIG.SYS can lead to some confusion on the exam. Our information comes from the Microsoft technical description of the Windows startup process, although it was difficult to find. In our opinion, the exam makes an assumption that this first look at CONFIG.SYS doesn't take place.

Technically speaking, IO.SYS reads CONFIG.SYS, then MSDOS.SYS, then passes control to MSDOS.SYS. After MSDOS.SYS, control passes to COMMAND.COM, which reads CONFIG.SYS *again* before passing control to AUTOEXEC.BAT.

Although, technically, CONFIG.SYS is read twice, we believe the exam expects CONFIG.SYS (if it exists) to process following COMMAND.COM. This is one of those ambiguous, imprecise questions where Microsoft says what happens, but the proper response isn't listed on the exam.

IO.SYS and 16-bit Device Drivers

IO.SYS does the same thing in Windows 9x and Me as it does with DOS. It sets up *segment addressing* (discussed later in this chapter) in conventional memory, and loads low-level Real Mode device drivers into low memory. IO.SYS then reads MSDOS.SYS or an existing CONFIG.SYS file. If a CONFIG.SYS file, an AUTOEXEC.BAT file, or both are supposed to run, IO.SYS loads COMMAND.COM to run the two files. Depending on which lines are found in these files, COMMAND.COM runs various Real Mode commands and programs.

Remember that whatever is loaded into the DOS environment at this point descends to any DOS sessions run from within Windows. The Properties option for COMMAND.COM enables you to configure the DOS session environment (Widows 9x only).

Before loading hardware device drivers from a CONFIG.SYS and an AUTOEXEC.BAT file, try commenting them out to see whether the Windows 9x auto-detection capabilities can run those devices with VxDs. (VxDs are discussed in the "Virtual Device Drivers" section of this chapter.)

MSDOS.SYS

Whether or not CONFIG.SYS, AUTOEXEC.BAT, or both exist, IO.SYS reads the MSDOS.SYS file first, then reads it again for VxDs (virtual device drivers) and other configuration settings. MSDOS.SYS is a plain ASCII text file that can be edited by DOS's EDIT.COM, the Windows Notepad (NOTEPAD.EXE), or Microsoft's WordPad (save as .TXT file type, but keep the .SYS extension). The important point is that all attributes are set on the file, making it hidden, system, and read-only. Before you can edit MSDOS.SYS, you're expected to know what you're doing and how to change the file attributes.

The MSDOS.SYS file tells Windows 9x about multiple booting options, Startup menus, which mode to start in, and whether the Windows GUI is supposed to start at all following boot-up.

 If you press and hold the Shift key, instead of the F8 key, before the Windows splash screen, MSDOS.SYS is bypassed and is not read at all. MSDOS.SYS can also be edited so as to force Windows 9x to start in plain DOS. Starting Windows from the command prompt then requires typing **WIN** and pressing Enter.

MSDOS.SYS Passes to COMMAND.COM

If IO.SYS doesn't find a CONFIG.SYS file, it hands off control to MSDOS.SYS, which looks for COMMAND.COM in the root directory of the boot disk. COMMAND.COM must be from the same version of DOS as the system files are, or the process comes to a screeching halt with the message "Incorrect DOS version."

Beginning with DOS 5.0, COMMAND.COM could be loaded into conventional memory or upper memory. However, regardless of the area of memory, COMMAND.COM runs and installs itself into some part of the first 1MB of RAM (conventional memory).

COMMAND.COM moves its resident portion into RAM and checks to see if an AUTOEXEC.BAT file exists (spelled exactly that way) in the root directory. If AUTOEXEC.BAT exists, COMMAND.COM runs the batch commands in that file.

When the last command has been run, COMMAND.COM returns a prompt on the screen, and the machine is ready to work. If the last command of the AUTOEXE.BAT file is WIN, the process continues and loads Windows.

Summary—The Boot Process

The boot process is how a box full of plastic, silicon, wire and metal links up with a bunch of letters and characters (the OS) to become a useful computer. Yes it's complicated! That's why it took a couple of weeks to invent computers in the first place. The main things to remember are the following:

➤ The motherboard ROM BIOS chip contains a tiny routine, written in BASIC, which reaches out to look for certain files on the hard drive.

➤ The two system files, IO.SYS and MSDOS.SYS, work to load very low-level instructions into memory (for example, the interrupt vector tables), which the operating system uses to access hardware devices, memory, and the CPU.

➤ COMMAND.COM contains program code with references to the AUTOEXEC.BAT file and a listing of startup error messages.

➤ IO.SYS contains coded language that explains to the operating system how to handle certain device operations. The file also calls an optional CONFIG.SYS file.

➤ If a CONFIG.SYS file exists, each line in the file loads device and control instructions into memory. In many cases, additional configuration settings are added using "SET" in an AUTOEXEC.BAT file.

➤ The order in which each file loads and runs is critical.

Keep in mind that neither the CONFIG.SYS nor AUTOEXEC.BAT are required, but if they exist, they run at the points in the preceding list. Windows 9x still uses the same steps, although most of what used to be in the CONFIG.SYS file has now been coded into IO.SYS.

The preceding section is one of the most complex in this book. If you're not sure of the order in which each file runs, go back and scan the subheadings we've used. Go back and read the text where you aren't sure of what's going on. All this happens quickly, but it takes a lot of words to explain. Try to extract the essential points, and list them in whatever way is most comfortable for you.

Don't feel bad if you don't immediately understand everything we've talked about. Watch your computer the next time you switch it on, and see whether you can follow some of the on-screen cues to what's taking place. Shut down the machine and restart in MS-DOS Mode. This isn't a completely clean DOS session, but it will give you the opportunity to examine your hard drive for IO.SYS and MSDOS.SYS. Avoid using the Explorer, but try to find the files with DOS commands (DIR /A:H).

Beep Codes

We've seen that the POST routine resides in ROM BIOS and executes when power is supplied to the motherboard at startup. During the time the POST runs and completes, no operating system is loaded, and no device drivers have been put into memory. Therefore, the PC has no way of working with a disk, a monitor, floppy drives, or any other device that requires a driver, including a keyboard. There's only one way for the POST to communicate with you—the system speaker.

The POST produces a pattern of sounds, depending on the exit condition it finds on completion of the program. These sounds access the motherboard's speaker and produce a *beep*. Most programs use *error codes* (also known as *exit codes*) to provide a way to tell the world what happened when the program finished. The batch file ERRORLEVEL command also can use these error codes. An error code may include a code for successful completion with no errors.

The **CHOICE** command, used in batch files, uses **ERRORLEVEL**, the **GOTO** command, and Labels to provide interactive options. If you create a simple batch file using the **CHOICE** command to write one of three messages to the screen, you'll get a strong understanding of how batch files work. (The messages can be anything: Hi, I'm number 1, This is hard, I hate computers, and so on.)

Table 13.1 lists some of the main beep codes associated with a POST exit. The PC's speaker beep is a DOS bell control signal (decimal .007, or ^G). *Bell* refers to the old teletype machine bells.

Table 13.1	Typical BIOS Beep Codes
Number of Beeps	**Meaning**
None	There must always be at least one beep. If you don't hear a beep when the POST has completed, then the PC speaker may be bad. Otherwise, the motherboard has failed, or the power supply is bad.
1	Successful. The POST has completed successfully. If you can see everything on the monitor, then the system started okay. The most common problem for a successful POST, but no monitor, is lack of power to the monitor. Check the monitor's fuse and power supply. If the monitor still has no picture following a 1-beep successful POST, then the video card may have a bad memory chip.

(continued)

Table 13.1	Typical BIOS Beep Codes *(continued)*
Number of Beeps	**Meaning**
	To check the video memory, try reseating the SIMMs and rebooting the machine. If the SIMMs are in tightly and there's still no image, then you'll probably need to buy a new video card, because the SIMMs are usually soldered onto the IC board.
2, 3, or 4	Memory. The POST checks the first 64KB of main memory. If you hear 2, 3, or 4 beeps, then either video or main memory has a problem. If the video is working, then there was a parity error in the first 64KB of system memory (low memory). Try switching SIMMs between memory banks. If a reboot generates 1 beep, then you have a bad memory module in the switched bank.
4	Clock. 4 beeps can also mean a bad timer oscillator.

If you hear more than four beeps at startup, you might have a precarious situation. The motherboard could be smoking, or the CMOS could have lost its mind. However, a repeating series of beeps usually indicates that a network configuration file or user's logon script is failing to find various devices and drivers. Another possible cause, not related to the POST, is that following a successful startup, something (maybe your arm) is resting on the keyboard and the keyboard buffer is sounding an alert.

The Bootable Disk

Back when every PC used DOS, making a bootable disk was a simple process. You would insert a diskette into Drive A: and format it with system files (FORMAT A: /S). You would copy over a few useful DOS utilities, and from that point on, you could access just about any machine that could spin the floppy drive. Today, bootable disks have different purposes, and they're created in different ways, depending on the operating system and the user interface.

 You're sure to encounter questions on the exam having to do with how to create a boot disk, an emergency startup disk, or an emergency repair disk (ERD). We examine the ERD in upcoming chapters.

DOS Bootable Disk

Making a disk bootable means that the three system files (IO.SYS, MSDOS.SYS, and COMMAND.COM) are copied to the disk. Along with the system files, the bootstrap loader is also placed in the boot sector. If the disk can start the operating system, the disk is bootable. Follow these steps to make a bootable DOS disk:

1. On a working PC, insert a 1.44MB standard floppy disk into Drive A:. Exit all applications, or otherwise set the system to a DOS prompt (command line).

2. Type FORMAT A: /S /U and press Enter to format Drive A: and transfer the system files, formatting the diskette unconditionally. Allow the process to complete.

3. Leave the new diskette in Drive A: and restart the machine. If the machine successfully boots up, you'll be asked for the date (press Enter) and the time (press Enter), and you'll then arrive at an A> prompt (or the A:\> prompt in DOS 7.0 or later).

Making a DOS-Bootable Disk from Windows Explorer

To make a bootable DOS disk from Windows Explorer

1. Insert a disk into Drive A:. Start the Explorer or select Start | Run and enter **explorer.exe** in the dialog box. Windows 9x doesn't allow you to format a hard drive, and the Format Disk option does not appear unless you have a disk in Drive A:.

2. Right-click on the Drive A: icon. Select Format from the context menu. Make sure that you click on the Copy System Files radio button.

 Remember that you can create an emergency startup disk in Windows 9x by selecting Start | Settings | Control Panel | Add Remove Programs and by clicking on the Startup Disk tab.

 The technical term for *right-clicking* (on the exam) is *alternative-click*. Don't confuse this with Alt+click or the Alt key. Another way of calling up the context menu is to highlight an object and press Shift+F10.

We spoke about clusters and sectors in Chapter 8, "Peripherals: Storage Devices." If you check the report box in the Explorer's format dialog box, you'll find that a formatted disk has some number of "allocation units," and that each allocation unit is a certain size. An allocation unit is simply a cluster that contains no data. When file information stores to the disk, those used allocation units become clusters. In other words, you can find out how large your clusters are from the format report. Unfortunately, you won't get a nice pretty report like this if you format the hard drive from DOS.

Bootable Disk Utility Files

You can assume that the only time you'll need a bootable disk is in an emergency. In that case you'll need to do some detective work, and probably some repair work as well. The repair work could simply be editing a CONFIG.SYS file, or it could be as drastic as performing an FDISK re-partitioning of the hard drive.

A Windows 9x emergency startup disk isn't quite the same as a DOS bootable disk. The emergency disk boots the system using IO.SYS, MSDOS.SYS, and COMMAND.COM. However, it includes a number of utility programs that the process automatically copies to the emergency disk. If Windows 9x is workable and the problem involves accessing the hard drive, the emergency startup disk boots the system and tries to load Windows.

FDISK is used only to view the existing partition setup of a hard disk, or to completely destroy all information on the hard disk; there is no in-between. If you can think of *any* other option for solving a problem, you should attempt that before using FDISK to completely reinstall the disk.

In Windows 2000 and XP, disk operations take place under the Computer Management console (Programs | Administrative Tools in Windows XP, and Settings | Control Panel | Administrative Tools in Windows 2000). Windows NT/2000/XP don't include FDISK, but you can use the program from a Windows 98SE startup disk.

If Windows 9x can't load, IO.SYS still produces a "Starting Windows..." message, but the start sequence ends at a plain DOS prompt. In this case, no text-based Startup menu appears, and you'll need to know DOS commands to continue solving the problem. The message is hard-coded into IO.SYS, and is not Windows talking with you in a self-conscious fashion.

A Windows 98 emergency boot disk does some interesting things with a RAM drive, and includes all the utility files you'll need. However, some of the utility files that should be copied to a plain DOS bootable diskette include FORMAT.COM, FDISK.EXE, EDIT.COM (for editing ASCII startup files), SYS.COM, SCANDISK.EXE (the DOS version), and ATTRIB.EXE.

If you use EDIT.COM on any system prior to Windows 95, you *must* include QBASIC.EXE as the support file for the editor (or it won't run). EDIT.COM can be found on the installation CDROM if it isn't in the \Windows\Command folder.

A Note About RAMDRIVE.SYS

A so-called RAM drive is a virtual disk drive set up in main memory. The disk exists for only as long as the system has power. The Windows 98 emergency boot disk creates a RAM drive, then uses EXPAND.EXE to extract a number of utilities from a .CAB file to the virtual disk. Oddly enough, although FDISK is on the floppy disk, FORMAT.COM is put on the virtual disk. Microsoft includes an interesting little program to set some environment variables and let the system know the RAM drive's letter. This may seem like a lot of work to generate a boot disk, but it was the only way to create an archive file with more files than could be stored on a common 1.44MB floppy, then guarantee that those files would be available to the system.

Take a close look at the CONFIG.SYS file and AUTOEXEC.BAT files on this startup disk. They include some interesting ways of doing things. One of the more interesting features is a start-up menu that uses certain features in the CONFIG.SYS file. Another is a simple DOS Help system for many DOS commands. You'll see references to running a "help" program, with no drive letter. You also won't find that Help file on the floppy. It's one of the files extracted from the .CAB file onto the RAM drive.

Bootable Disk Configuration Files

Every PC should have its own dedicated bootable disk. That disk should include up-to-date copies of critical startup files. Check to see whether the machine has a CONFIG.SYS and AUTOEXEC.BAT file. If it has a CDROM drive, but no BIOS support, a device driver must load in the CONFIG.SYS file. References to the device driver might exist in the AUTOEXEC.BAT file as well (for example, MSCDEX.EXE).

Place the PC's emergency boot disk in that PC's *system binder*, along with a current printout of a "System Information" (MSINFO32.EXE) report. Put any backup driver files in the system binder as well.

A *system binder* is a three-ring binder containing configuration printouts, unusual instructions relating to a PC, and a number of vinyl disk-sized pocket pages. These vinyl pages hold critical installation disks for drivers, the operating system, and other important devices. The system binder is a good place to keep current backup copies of the SYSTEM.DAT and USER.DAT Registry files, along with CDROMs.

Make sure that you have copies of any device drivers that reside on the hard drive (if you can access the drive). If you can't find original installation disks for SCSI devices, a sound card, a mouse, or other devices, back up copies of any sub-directories with driver files to disk.

There's no point in making a backup copy of the Registry because the entire disk will have to be reinstalled in the event of a major crash. A third-party "disk image" program is very useful in situations like this because it creates a bit-by-bit exact copy of an entire disk or partition.

16-Bit Windows

DOS programs often included a separate installation *routine* (program) to make sure that every step of the installation was followed correctly. You can usually tell whether you're looking at a DOS or Windows application by the name of its installation program. DOS programs continue to use INSTALL.EXE as the first file to run in setting up the program. Windows programs use SETUP.EXE.

Windows itself uses a Setup program, which goes farther than the DOS installation routines. SETUP.EXE (or winnt.exe in Windows XP/2000) not only copies (and expands) files to various locations on the disk, but also examines the hardware and software in the system. The theory behind this examination is that users shouldn't need to know how their computers run. Following the Microsoft lead, most modern installation programs attempt to identify the existing system before installing their applications.

 Windows XP typically uses a graphical setup program. It either runs from within a previous version of Windows or generates a GUI from a bootable CDROM. However, you can run the text-based setup program from a command line. The file is **winnt.exe**, located in the **\I386** folder on the CDROM. Assuming the setup disk is the D: drive, type **d:\i386\winnt.exe** and press Enter. If it's an upgrade version, replace the XP disk with a previous CD for Windows 95, 98, or Me in the drive when XP asks for a valid End User License Agreement (EULA).

Most installation and setup programs make a number of assumptions about the destination computer—the default setup—and offer the computer owner a way to take only limited control over the installation. Typically, the installation routine offers a somewhat misleading Express and Custom pair of setup options.

You should always choose either the "Custom" or "Advanced" option, if the setup routine offers one. In every case we've seen, there are default settings for any steps in the program that offer a choice. In situations where you don't know what you're doing, you can choose the default. However, in places where you do know what you're looking at, you may often disagree with what some faraway programmer has decided to do to your system.

The key Windows 9x setup file is SETUP.INF (information file). SETUP.INF contains entries that determine which files will be copied during the installation. Note that Windows and other applications still use .INF setup files. SETUP.EXE also uses EXPAND.EXE to decompress the files on the Windows installation disks. Because the files are stored in a compressed format, the DOS COPY command isn't enough to fully install Windows from original disks.

You can usually tell that Microsoft has compressed a file by looking at the last character in the file's extension. Microsoft's proprietary archive process usually makes this last character an underscore (PROGRAM.EX_). Microsoft uses a different format to create the .CAB files (from "storage cabinet") you see on an installation CDROM. Cabinet files are a different form of .ZIP files (created with PKZip or WinZip), although most of today's third-party archive programs can read .CAB files.

All the way back in DOS 5.0, Microsoft began installing a program in the root directory of the Primary, Active drive that tells Windows that the computer (processor) could support 386 Enhanced Mode. You may still find WINA20.386, located in the C:\ root directory (read-only). After SETUP.EXE determines that Windows can be installed on the computer and determines whether there's enough room on the disk, it copies the core files and many of the required files to the hard drive.

SETUP.EXE creates a \WINDOWS sub-directory (typically on Drive C: at the root directory). It also creates a \WINDOWS\SYSTEM (or SYSTEM32) directory that Windows searches regardless of which other sub-directories are listed in the DOS PATH= environment variable. (Note that Windows 2000 creates a WINNT directory on the C: drive, by default.)

WIN.COM

MS-DOS 4.0 introduced something Microsoft called the DOS Shell, which was really a rudimentary graphic file maintenance and menu program. This complicated menu system was run from DOSSHELL.BAT, which used a very small stub program loader (SHELLB) to push the main program (SHELLC) into memory. SHELLB was about 3.5KB, whereas SHELLC was 150KB. This began the custom of using a loader program. WIN.COM is the next iteration of that loader stub. It calls into memory USER.EXE, GDI.EXE, and KERNEL.EXE—the core Windows (3.x) files.

During the setup process, SETUP.EXE combines VGALOGO.LGO and VGALOGO.RLE (the Microsoft logo screen) with WIN.CNF and creates WIN.COM, which loads the Windows program into memory and continues forward in graphical mode. Depending on whether an automatic or custom installation was chosen, the routine pauses at various points to offer further choices in terms of which applets will be installed.

 VGALOGO.* are the two files Windows 9x uses on systems with VGA graphics capabilities. Where the system used a CGA or EGA monitor, Windows had two files each for CGALOGO.* and EGALOGO.*, which it could compile into WIN.COM.

Typing **WIN** at the command prompt, or having the AUTOEXEC.BAT file enter it for you, runs WIN.COM, which does some preliminary checking before it begins to search for the necessary core files for the Windows program. WIN.COM checks to see what type of computer, CPU, and memory are installed. The memory might be real, extended, or expanded.

Next, WIN.COM checks to see which device drivers have been loaded—especially virtual memory devices (HIMEM.SYS)—and then makes a decision regarding the mode in which Windows should start. WIN.COM allows switches on its command line. These switches force Windows to load by using certain *modes of operation*. Depending on the amount of memory, the type of processor, and whether an extended memory device driver is present, the 16-bit Windows WIN.COM switches were

➤ /R—Real Mode

➤ /S or /2—Standard Mode

➤ /3—Enhanced Mode

➤ /B—To keep a boot log text file of any problems encountered during startup

Windows 9x Switches

You can almost always get simple help by using the /? switch after a command. As you can see in the following results, 32-bit WIN.COM offers some useful switches and a fast way to start Safe Mode. On a bad machine, you can use either the Explorer or the DOS rename command (REN) to rename

WIN.COM to WEN.COM. Then use the /D:M switch to force a possible Safe Mode. (Be sure to rename WEN.COM back to WIN.COM after you've fixed the problem.)

```
C:\WINDOWS>win /?
Starts Windows.
WIN [/D:[F][M][S][V][X]]

/D    Used for troubleshooting when Windows does not start correctly.
 :F   Turns off 32-bit disk access.
      Equivalent to SYSTEM.INI file setting: 32BitDiskAccess=FALSE.
 :M   Enables Safe mode.
      This is automatically enabled during Safe start (function key F5).
 :N   Enables Safe mode with networking.
      This is automatically enabled during Safe start (function key F6).
 :S   Specifies that Windows should not use ROM address space between
      F000:0000 and 1 MB for a break point.
      Equivalent to SYSTEM.INI file setting: SystemROMBreakPoint=FALSE.
 :V   Specifies that the ROM routine will handle interrupts from the hard
      disk controller.
      Equivalent to SYSTEM.INI file setting: VirtualHDIRQ=FALSE.
 :X   Excludes all of the adapter area from the range of memory that
      Windows scans to find unused space.
      Equivalent to SYSTEM.INI file setting: EMMExclude=A000-FFFF.
```

Initialization (.INI) Files

The so-called Windows 9x operating system environment includes a number of support files, just as DOS does. Windows was designed to succeed DOS and become the main (and only) interface between the computer and the user. As a result, Microsoft tried to gather as many device drivers as possible and pull them together under a single umbrella. Additionally, as program files became larger, some of their supporting code was moved outside the .EXE or the .COM files to additional files. These files are required to run the application because the main executable file contains internal references to those files. Generally, these support files are located in a specific directory called a *working directory*.

 A working directory is the same thing as the Start in: folder (and path) listed under any shortcut's Properties menu. The program looks in the working directory for related files, and also for data files. Hard-coded references to support files rarely contain path information (which varies according to system setups), so the application reference manual refers to how certain files must be in a particular folder.

For various reasons, PC users often found it useful to locate the main program files in one place and some of the auxiliary files somewhere else. Not only that, but an application's data files are often placed on completely different drives (as in networks). To make some sense out of all this, certain types of configuration files were created to hold information regarding how the main executable file was supposed to run. These particular configuration files are called *initialization files*, and almost always have a .INI extension (read "eye-enn-eye").

In a menu or shell, properties describe important information about the location of the main executable file and how to run it. Initialization files, on the other hand, describe to an executable file important information about how that program should run and where to find external support files. In other words, menu properties point to executable files. Initialization files configure applications.

The two .INI files used by Windows are the WIN.INI file and the SYSTEM.INI file. Both files are plain ASCII text files located by default in the \WINDOWS directory. New sections can be added to .INI files either by other programs or by the user. Sections are enclosed in square brackets (for example, **[restrictions]**) with a unique name.

SYSEDIT.EXE

SYSEDIT.EXE, located in the \WINDOWS\SYSTEM directory, is a small editing utility applet that opens and cascades the primary configuration files (for all versions of Windows). In 16-bit Windows, the main files are CONFIG.SYS and AUTOEXEC.BAT for DOS, and SYSTEM.INI and WIN.INI for Windows. All four files are opened and arranged (cascade style) and can be viewed and edited. Windows 3.x and Windows 9x also include PROTOCOL.INI for Real Mode networking protocols and configuration settings.

Choose Start | Run and type **SYSEDIT** to run the program. Otherwise, you can set it up by dragging the SYSEDIT.EXE program onto the Start button to put it into your Programs menu.

MSINFO32.EXE

Microsoft's System Information is one of the more interesting diagnostics programs available in Windows 98, Me, 2000, and XP. Oddly enough, MSINFO32.EXE isn't available in Windows 95 or Windows NT. However, if you've installed MS Office (97 or later), you can find MSINFO32 as one of the optional utilities. Windows 2000 and XP use WINMSD.EXE (from the old Microsoft Diagnostics MSD program) to call MSINFO32.EXE. However, you can also choose Start | Run and type `msinfo32`.

The nice thing about this program is that it not only gives you a comprehensive report of the system and environment, but also includes a Tools menu. The dropdown list provides a quick way to get to Microsoft's System Configuration Utility (MSCONFIG.EXE). The Tools option also provides quick access to Dr. Watson, the System File Checker (SFC), the Registry Checker, ScanDisk, and a Version Control utility, to name a few tools.

We'll discuss MSCONFIG.EXE in the "Troubleshooting" chapter, but it, too, offers a quick examination of the SYSTEM.INI and WIN.INI files. Depending on which version of Windows, the System Configuration Utility shows the CONFIG.SYS and AUTOEXEC.BAT files, along with other programs used in the Startup process.

SYSTEM.INI

The SYSTEM.INI file is the initialization file that Windows looks at when all the necessary and core system files have been installed. It contains the controls for the interface between Windows and DOS, and is where various Windows VxDs are loaded into memory. The SYSTEM.INI file is a plain ASCII text file that can be edited by WORDPAD.EXE, NOTEPAD.EXE (Windows applets), the DOS Editor (EDIT.COM), SYSEDIT.EXE, or any word processor that saves files in plain ASCII low-bit format.

NOTE
WordPad is capable of saving to file types other than .TXT (plain text). Be sure you choose the text format, or SYSTEM.INI becomes unreadable to Windows. Although the file "type" is .TXT, make sure to keep the .INI extension in the actual filename. It doesn't matter what the extension is; the underlying file will be in plain ASCII text format.

SYSTEM.INI is divided into *sections*, each of which has a heading enclosed in square brackets ([ ]). The most common areas of user interest are the [386Enh] section for 16-bit device drivers and the [boot] section, where the SHELL= line points to the shell file that runs at startup. This shell statement was moved into MSDOS.SYS for Windows 9x and calls the Windows Desktop. The old Windows 3.1 Program Manager (PROGMAN.EXE) still runs just fine under Windows 9x, as does the old File Manager (WINFILE.EXE). (File Manager finally disappears from Windows XP, but you can still load the Program Manager for some odd reason.)

NOTE
The File Manager offers a fast way to accomplish certain directory and file management tools. It's also a way to move around using the underlying DOS filenames, instead of Long File Names. For example, you might use File Manager to see the directory names you'll have to use if you're in a DOS window, rather than trying to puzzle them out at the command line. Choose Start | Run | and enter **winfile.exe** to get to the applet.

The thing to remember about the SYSTEM.INI and WIN.INI files (or any other Windows .INI file) is that you can't use REM (Remark) to comment out a line in the file. Instead, use a semicolon (;) in the first column of the specific line, followed by at least one space. REM is used for DOS batch files.

SYSTEM.INI runs alongside the Windows 9x Registry (SYSTEM.DAT and USER.DAT). Chapter 14, "Windows 9x," discusses the differences between the three files. Until there are no more 16-bit legacy devices, there may still be a need for this particular file.

Remember that SYSTEM.INI installs device drivers and VxDs. Windows 9x continues to use the SYSTEM.INI file to load certain types of 16-bit device drivers, so even Window 9x and XP machines often have a SYSTEM.INI file.

WIN.INI

The second basic initialization file that Windows looks through at startup is WIN.INI. The file isn't required, but if it doesn't exist, Windows creates a default version. The WIN.INI file is where information about the overall user environment for Windows is stored. Whereas SYSTEM.INI is similar to the CONFIG.SYS file in the DOS startup process, WIN.INI is similar to the AUTOEXEC.BAT file at the end of the booting process. To some extent, WIN.INI is also similar to USER.DAT, the Registry file that holds individual end-user configuration settings, or the CURRENT_USER Registry key.

WIN.INI contains the [windows] section, where programs can be set to run automatically without putting them in the Startup group window. LOAD= tells a program to run minimized on Windows startup, and RUN= tells a program to run normally at Windows startup.

When you can't find a reference to some program that seems to run from the Startup program group, you might find it referenced in either the LOAD= or RUN= line at the top of the WIN.INI file. Screensavers and antivirus programs used to use this line, as did mouse configurations. You'll also have to do a manual search through the Registry for certain startup files that don't show in the Windows\Start Menu folder.

The WIN.INI file contains a listing of the fonts installed into Windows, along with associated extensions for programs—file associations. For example, the [extensions] section of the WIN.INI file might have the line

```
bmp=C:\windows\ mspaint.exe ^.bmp
```

which tells Windows that any time it sees a DOS file with a .BMP extension, it can make an assumption that the program MSPAINT.EXE will be used to open that file.

There may be some peculiar scenarios on the A+ exam, and one of the more unusual is a situation in which either the SYSTEM.INI or WIN.INI file is missing. If the SYSTEM.INI file is missing, Windows simply won't start at all, and it produces an error message to that effect. If the WIN.INI file is missing, Windows starts in default VGA Mode (assuming Enhanced Mode is possible). This is the precursor to the Windows 9x Safe Mode, where Windows starts with a basic configuration. When Windows can't find a WIN.INI file, it creates one when it starts. Any environmental customization (for example, colors, icon spacing, or mouse configurations) will be missing, but you will at least be in Windows.

File Associations

Have you ever used the F2 key or the Properties menu to rename an executable file (application type) in the Windows Explorer? If you change the extension (assuming it's even visible) you'll get an "Alert!" message telling you that you may be unable to run the program and that the filenaming police have been dispatched to arrest you immediately. Why is there an alert message at all?

Originally, files were *associated* in the [extensions] section of the WIN.INI file by selecting File | Associate in File Manager. This used to be a simple process in Windows 3.x and has (predictably enough) become far more complex under later versions of Windows. Associating a program means that you can double-click on a filename in either File Manager or Windows Explorer, and Windows runs a program that can work with the file. But how does Windows know which program to run?

Here's where you really need to know all about file extensions: those three letters to the right of the period in a filename that we talked about in Chapter 12. A common association is that any file ending with a .DOC extension automatically opens Microsoft Word. Windows installs with certain pre-defined associations. Typically, .INI files, .BAT files, and .TXT files are associated with the Notepad or WordPad text editors. Many shareware programs (try before you buy) include a .DIZ description file. If you download a lot of shareware, you can easily associate the .DIZ extension with Notepad, thereby making it easy to double-click on the description and read it.

A default installation typically hides the extensions in Windows Explorer. Whether or not you unhide the extensions, the associations are what produce the icon and description in the Explorer window. The Windows 3.x File Manager shows all file extensions by default, and choosing File | Associate immediately calls up a dialog box. Today's Windows, on the other hand, requires that you either do some detective work to find out what program is already associated with an extension, or fill out a nearly incomprehensible description form.

To set, change, or delete the file associations in Windows 9x, open the Explorer. Choose View | Folder Options | File Types tab. This is where all current file extensions are listed. Click on any particular extension and choose Edit to see the program's name and what should happen when you double-click on the application's filename in the Explorer. Note that many programs can "hijack" the file associations, changing them to their own applications. Certain third-party applications can prevent this sort of hidden reconfiguration of your system.

Memory

An operating system is software and, as such, loads into memory. It's important to understand the memory environment and how DOS, Windows, and any other software lives in that environment. In this context, the three main types of memory are

➤ Conventional memory

➤ Expanded memory (EMS)

➤ Extended memory (XMS)

The BIOS contains tables of interrupts, copyright information, testing routines, error messages, and some instructions to put characters on the screen in color. The ROM chips also hold a scaled-down version of BASIC that the chip can use to execute instructions on how to move all the stored information into lower memory. Because DOS doesn't start running until after start-up, this code in the ROM chips controls the lights and beeps and initializes the printer and the keyboard.

You can think of memory as divided into two basic worlds: the world of what used to come with 8088/8086 PCs and the world of everything that was invented later. Remember that computers still face day-to-day limitations, based on the way in which the first XT worked. These limitations have been forced on the manufacturers by the entire concept of backward compatibility. Windows 2000 was the first break from that backward compatibility and the subsequent limitations.

The Costs of Doing Business

Technical people sometimes forget that a computer is a tool that often is used in business to earn profits. A fundamental principle of business is that everything must pay for itself and that whatever remains is profit. Imagine a company using 30,000 computers with Windows 95 as the operating system.

Say that the price of a single copy of Windows 2000 is $50 (taking into consideration volume discounts, upgrade discounts, and so on), and then multiply $50 by the 30,000 computers. Simply purchasing the software would cost $1.5 million, which doesn't include shipping, taxes, and other incidental charges.

This company has an entire information systems (IS) staff and can assign five full-time employees the task of installing the upgrade on every computer. The rest of the staff must handle day-to-day problems and questions. Suppose that these five employees each make a salary of $16 per hour.

If it took only 30 minutes per computer to back up the original machine and install the upgrade, each computer would cost $8 in labor for one IS employee and possibly an additional half-hour of the person whose desk had the computer. Considering only the IS staff, 30,000 machines at $8 each would cost $240,000 in time and labor. With no problems, no errors, and a perfect first-time installation, it's already costing the company $1.74 million. We haven't even looked at the downtime of every salaried employee whose computer is unusable during the upgrade, from the $8-per-hour clerk to the $175,000-per-year executive (assuming $84 per hour with a loss of $42 of computer time). Nor have we looked at the time costs that the mailroom uses to process all those incoming copies of Windows 2000.

Those 30-minute-per-machine upgrades mean 15,000 work hours divided by the 5 IS employees, or 3,000 hours per IS employee. Assuming an 8-hour workday, it would take each IS employee 375 days to accomplish the upgrade. Naturally, with time off for weekends and sleep, you can see that it would take more than a year simply to change the company from Windows 95 to 2000. Then, think of what this would mean if the main spreadsheet program didn't work on the upgrade—if Windows 2000 wasn't backward compatible.

Conventional Memory

The CPU's address bus assigns particular memory addresses to bits of data. The memory controller keeps track of specific locations in memory. These addresses and bits of data are constantly being shuttled across buses and through the system. If the CPU can move 16 bits of information around in its own registers (internal bus), it stands to reason that it should be able to pass 16 bits of information to everything around it (external). Reason, however, has never been a strong point in the computer world.

The 8088 could keep track of a bit more (no pun intended) than a million separate addresses in memory, or 1MB (1,048,576 bits). As you know, every bit of data takes on an address as it moves around to various devices. This is like mailing a picture of your new car to a friend. The post office has no interest in the picture (the data bit), only the address on the envelope. Imagine that you were a single mail carrier and had a million addresses to work with every day.

Segments

To make it easier to keep track of the first megabyte of memory, the 8088/86 CPU used 16 "regional ZIP Codes," so to speak, called *segments*. Each segment of memory is 64KB long. Because the 8088/86 could address only 1MB of memory, this was fine. Newer chips have the capability to address far more than 1MB of memory and to do so more directly.

Memory segments are numbered, and the smaller numbers are said to be lower than the larger, higher numbers. For this reason, data stored in the first segments of RAM is said to be in *low memory*.

 The original addressing scheme of the 8088/86 chips, using 16 segments of 64KB of memory, is the foundation of all later memory organization. This 1MB of RAM, divided into segments, is referred to as *conventional memory*. Memory addresses are expressed in hexadecimal numbers.

If you use binary math to calculate the number of addresses available to a 16-bit processor, you'll see that the number is less than the actual number available. Binary math alone doesn't go the whole distance (it would take 20 bits) because of the two-part address involving the segment and the offset. Without going into the details, you should know that memory error messages are reported using both parts of the address.

The *segment address* is one of the 16 regional segments of the 1MB. The *offset address* is the specific address within the 64KB length of the segment. The combination of segment and offset addresses is what enables a 16-bit processor to address 20 bits of addresses, or 1MB. (See Chapter 3, "Memory: Types and Forms," for a discussion on memory pages, which is another way of talking about a memory segment.)

Although you might not be tested on this low level of detail, if you plan to work on computers, you should at least know what a segment address and an offset address look like. A typical example presented on the screen would be *SEGMENT:OFFSET* and appear as 30F9:0102. You'll often see these types of numbers in Windows error messages.

80286 and Vectors

The 8088/86 chips used single addresses for each segment:offset location in memory. The registers in the chip held the actual address number as it directly related to a *real address* in 1MB of memory. This direct, real, one-to-one relationship is known today as Real Mode. The need for compatibility has kept Real Mode, along with the original 1MB of directly addressable memory, alive to this day (in 16-bit virtual machine windows). Windows XP finally ended all support for Real Mode.

The 286 chip changed from segment:offset addressing to something called *selector:offset addressing*. Instead of using a real segment, the registers held a pointer, or *vector*, to some other segment. Because the selector pointer is a smaller number than the full segment address, more selectors can fit into the same number of registers. This concept of using one address to refer to another address describe a process called *mapping* or *aliasing*. (Note that "anti-aliasing" is also used with font technology to mean something completely different.)

Aliasing and Mapping

When you rent a box at the post office, you're telling the post office that instead of putting an address on your big house, you want to put your address on a small box that will *refer* mail to your house. Instead of having to walk all the way to your house, the postal service can immediately move an envelope into your box, and *you* can then come pick it up. The box is vastly smaller than your house, and the distance from the incoming mail dock far shorter.

A cooperative venture between the post office (the CPU), which *could* deliver all the way to your house, and you (the hardware), who walks to the post office, results in faster processing. The side benefit is access to a larger storage area—the whole post office. In a nutshell, this is how expanded memory works.

The external DOS subst command (for *substitute*) is a way to shrink a long path of many sub-directories (with many characters) into the two characters of a drive letter and colon. You can substitute C:\WINDOWS\ SYSTEM\VBRUNS\100 with the letter "G." Then, instead of entering the full path, you can refer to it by using the aliased drive letter, G:. This is called *drive mapping*.

A substituted drive appears in the Windows Explorer just like any other drive letter. Opening that drive shows all the files in the particular sub-folder of the aliased drive. This can become even more sophisticated with drive shortcuts and mirrored drives in Windows XP.

The 286 chip used some of its registers to provide an indicator to a real segment in additional sets of 1MB of memory. In other words, instead of a real address in a single megabyte of real memory, the register held a sort of P.O. box number that referred to a whole new megabyte of memory. When the address was called, the CPU was pointed to this new megabyte to get the segment:offset address. Using this scheme, the 286 could address up to 16MB of memory.

Aliasing and mapping are used in expanded memory, interrupt vector tables, and most importantly, in the pseudo-32-bit FAT of the Windows 9x Installable File System (IFS) and VFAT. The concept is also used in networking, where very long pathnames (which include volumes and drives) are mapped to single drive letters. Mapping is commonly used to create network drive letters out of specific sub-directories. Aliases are commonly used in Windows shortcuts (.LNK files), which are iconic representations of pointers to executable files somewhere on the drive. Most people refer to drive mapping and shortcuts, and not so much to aliasing.

When air-traffic control assigns a vector to an airplane, the controller is essentially pointing the pilot in a certain direction. The interrupt vector tables tell DOS where to look to find a particular set of interrupts. The undocumented TRUENAME (gone from XP) command returns the formal name of a sub-directory, regardless of how it may masquerade as a mapped or substituted drive letter.

Low Memory (Segment 1)

When DOS begins to load, even before the system files are hauled up by their bootstraps, BIOS installs its main I/O tools, tables, and instructions in the area of conventional memory that IBM originally reserved for them. The DOS "kernel" is also put into low memory. Low memory is the first segment of the conventional 1MB of RAM (0000h to 9000h). Remember, this first megabyte is *conventional memory* and is addressed in the old, 8088/86 *real* way—Real Mode.

DOS uses low-memory to map out the first megabyte of memory and stores this map in a location within the first segment of RAM. The first segment can easily be very crowded, containing device drivers, parts of COMMAND.COM, pieces of TSRs, disk buffers, and environment and file controls. The first segment of memory commonly contains

➤ The interrupt vector table and DOS BIOS low-memory control

➤ IO.SYS and MSDOS.SYS

➤ Device drivers, such as MOUSE.SYS and ANSI.SYS

➤ Disk buffers

➤ Stacks (the way the CPU prioritizes and keeps track of tasks that were interrupted by more important tasks)

➤ The environment and file control blocks (FCBs)

➤ The resident part of COMMAND.COM, which is always in memory and produces the message "Abort, Retry, Ignore, Fail?"

➤ Pieces of the transient part of COMMAND.COM, which periodically drops out of memory to disk and then returns when it's needed

➤ The stack and data parts of programs (for example, the MODE or PRINT commands), which are running but lurking in the background waiting to be called on

When an event needs to interrupt the CPU, whatever generated the interrupt first checks the *interrupt vector table* for directions on where to look for the actual interrupt instructions. This table is in the first segment (low memory) from 0000h to 1000h. BIOS, DOS, the interrupt controller chip, the main CPU, and any software programs that are running, all use the interrupt vector table.

COMMAND.COM is a fairly large file, and for efficiency's sake, it doesn't load completely into RAM and remain there using up space. Some parts of COMMAND.COM are used only rarely, whereas other parts must be available constantly. For example, the part that watches for a missing disk must be in memory all the time because the event causing the missing disk can happen at any time. This part of COMMAND.COM is *resident* because it's always living (residing) in memory.

The resident part of COMMAND.COM is like a sentry. It keeps an eye out for a commanding officer while the rest of the command is taking a break. When you exit an application and go to a DOS command line, the resident part calls the *transient* part of COMMAND.COM, which hurries back from the disk and jumps into memory just in time to produce the C:\> prompt and begin parsing the command line.

Upper Memory (Segments 10–16)

Passing over the 640KB of applications memory, the very top segment of memory, from F000h to FFFFh, is also taken at the beginning of the startup process. The BIOS is installed to this segment and runs the self-tests generated at the POST. This is also where the ROM-level BIOS instructions are stored for drive controllers, keyboard polling, the system clock, and I/O ports (serial and LPT). Finally, the upper memory area also holds a map of all the available memory addresses.

IBM originally left a small 64KB gap directly above the area set aside for running programs. This area occurs at segment A000h and was quickly grabbed by enterprising memory management software utilities or was sometimes configurable by DIP switches. Instead of 640KB of user memory, this allowed for an additional 64KB, making 704KB available. Because this extra segment has always been there and has always been unclaimed, 32-bit operating systems routinely provide 704KB of usable memory for a virtual PC running in a DOS window.

Video RAM (B000)

The 64KB block after A000h was intended for EGA and VGA video extensions. IBM's common monochrome adapter (CMA)—also known as monochrome display adapter (MDA)—also laid claim to this area. However, as soon as CGA and color monitors arrived on the market, B000h to B800h became available to be stolen. Early memory managers could grab the 32KB between B000h and B800h for extra RAM on top of the previous 64KB.

Working with a CGA monitor was like looking through a screen door through silk underwear at a pine tree blowing in a sandstorm, without your glasses on. Not that it was a badly crafted monitor—it just turned the user's eyes into coffee cups. Aside from resolution problems, the adapter card didn't have enough memory, and any scrolling would cause the screen to go black before it redrew itself. CGA vanished as soon as it could, leaving its IBM-reserved memory area free for memory management software.

The most commonly used DOS command with a CGA monitor was the **CLS** (**CL**ear **S**creen) command. This command not only clears all text from the screen but also usually converts any residual color back to black and white. **CLS** is an internal DOS command, written into COMMAND.COM.

Shortly after the failed CGA attempt, IBM introduced EGA, VGA, and the 8514/A color monitors. EGA and VGA demanded a lot of memory and went back to the A000h block to start high-resolution memory processing.

The 640K Barrier

Understand that DOS functions take up the first 64KB segment of the basic 1MB of conventional memory. ROM BIOS, the motherboard,

COMMAND.COM, and other parts of DOS take additional 64KB segments at the top of the conventional memory. Below these upper functions, video adapters, network cards, and certain drive controllers take up even more space. Because the top and the bottom of the 640KB user area is locked in by these other memory tenants, with most of the space taken at the top, people refer to the 640KB limit as the "640K barrier" or as hitting the "640K wall."

The *base memory* is whatever memory from the 640KB of user memory is left, after everything has loaded and all drivers and TSRs (Terminate and Stay Resident programs) are in place. DOS 6.2 included a memory optimization software utility (MEMMAKER.EXE) that could provide close to 600KB of base memory. This optimization process took advantage of every unused piece of memory in the 1MB of conventional memory.

Virtual Memory

When Windows runs an application, that application looks at what it *thinks* is DOS and works with various memory addresses. In fact, Windows intercepts every addressing call from the program and hands the program an address based on Windows' own memory decisions. If a lot of memory has been used, Windows starts using disk space as additional, virtual memory.

When Windows puts an application's memory addresses on the disk, it uses chunks, and it doesn't tell the program that the apparent memory is somewhere on a disk. The application thinks it's addressing a continuous set of addresses in a RAM segment. When the application calls for memory addresses that aren't in actual RAM, it generates a *page fault request*, telling Windows to go to the disk and find those addresses. Windows then *pages* (loads) those addresses back into RAM and hands them to the application as if everything was completely normal.

Swap Files

Windows has two ways to set aside space on a hard drive to handle page overflow: *temporary* and *permanent* swap files. Windows 3.x could manage a maximum of only 16MB of installed RAM, but it could use far more virtual memory by saving 4KB pages (chunks) of memory to the disk as a swap file.

The difference between a permanent and temporary swap file is mostly speed of access, leading to system performance issues. If Windows is going to swap out memory to the disk, it has two options: It can create a file somewhere on the disk and put memory there, or it can go to an already existing file. If it has to create the file at the moment, then it's a temporary swap file. Windows 9x, NT, 2000, and XP adjust the size of the temporary swap file according to necessity. However, you still can create a permanent swap file out of contiguous sectors and save some time by not making Windows have to create the file when it needs it.

Controlling Swap Files

Windows recommends a file size for the virtual memory swap file, and this recommendation can be changed. Windows 9x decided to drop the "swap file" name in favor of the more sophisticated-sounding "virtual memory." Either way, the file calculates all *available space* on the Windows installation drive, together with the largest block of contiguous, unfragmented space, to recommend a file 2.4 times the size of the *physical memory* installed on the computer.

The default location of the Windows swap file is the \Windows folder or the root directory. However, you can change this by choosing the My Computer properties and going to the Performance tab. Swap files are the same thing as Virtual Memory. When you "allow Windows to manage virtual memory," the system creates a temporary file. If you choose to set memory limits and manage the swap file yourself, you create a permanent file. (You can also tell Windows to use a different drive or partition for virtual memory.)

NOTE

Because Windows would like to take total control of the user's system, the alert message following a reconfiguration to permanent swap file status is terrifying. It speaks of the end of the world and total collapse of civilization as we know it. Instead of a button labeled OK, the button actually says, "A pox on you and yours!" Disabling virtual memory on this tab window merely disallows Windows from creating temporary swap files and adjusting their size on the fly.

You should know that each version of Windows may have a slightly different navigational pathway to the virtual memory settings. However, the concept to understand is that virtual memory refers to an area of storage on a disk, not actual RAM.

A permanent swap file is a bit faster than a temporary swap file. A temporary swap file must be created and saved before Windows can transfer memory blocks to the disk. It's better to defragment (DEFRAG.EXE) the disk before loading Windows and changing virtual memory to make the swap file permanent.

The Windows XP swap file is PAGEFILE.SYS, but the Windows 9x swap file is named 386SPART.PAR. Typically, the files change names in different versions of Windows, and we don't have the room to go into each file and its properties in depth. You should take some time to work with the Virtual Memory settings and the Performance tab in Windows 9x and Windows XP or 2000 to better understand how these settings can affect system perform-ance. Change the settings, and then use Explorer to find the resulting swap file. It'll usually be a very large, hidden file on the Windows installation volume.

HIMEM.SYS and EMM386.EXE

Properly speaking, any memory beyond the first 1MB of conventional mem-ory is extended memory. However, because there was no way to use this memory until the Lotus/Intel/Microsoft (LIM) specifications and hardware cards arrived on the market, the residue of expanded memory still exists. Even under Windows 9x, extended memory can be configured so that a part of it is used as expanded memory.

For any kind of memory beyond the conventional 1MB to be accessible by DOS, a memory manager device driver must be loaded from the CONFIG.SYS file. Originally, the device was only an expanded memory manager. With DOS 5.0, Microsoft began selling DOS directly to the cus-tomer. This generic DOS used HIMEM.SYS as a doorway manager to extended memory. Part of HIMEM.SYS is its capability to access unused parts of the conventional 1MB, which it calls *upper memory blocks (UMBs)*.

HIMEM.SYS does not provide expanded memory configuration. EMM386.EXE is the expanded memory device drive but it can't run unless HIMEM.SYS has been loaded first. In DOS and 16-bit Windows, all this was done in the CONFIG.SYS (Configure the System) file. Windows 95 began incorporating the loading of HIMEM.SYS into the IO.SYS system file. If an old legacy program requires expanded memory, then EMM386.EXE still loads from a CONFIG.SYS file, and one will have to be created.

Do whatever you need to do to separate the correct names and characteristics for *expanded* (EMS) and *extended* (XMS) memory from conventional memory. The exam will contain questions about how each type of memory works, and the correct names. You might use the *386* in EMM386.EXE to think of the old days, back when the 80386 processor was a hot item. Today, practically nothing uses expanded mem-ory, so perhaps you can associate *expanded* with *old* and *386*. Another way might be that the "X" in XMS is the Roman numeral "TEN" and X-TEN sounds a lot like extended.

Upper Memory Blocks (UMBs)

DOS and Windows 3.x machines wanted to have as much base memory (640KB application memory) as possible for running DOS applications.

DOS 5.0 introduced a change to COMMAND.COM that allowed it to use high memory and upper memory blocks (UMBs) to store parts of itself.

Upper memory blocks are managed by EMM386.EXE, which can run only after HIMEM.SYS has opened the door to extended memory. Therefore, the only way the DOS=UMB directive can be used is if the HIMEM.SYS driver is loaded first. Windows 95 REMs out any reference to EMM386 in the CONFIG.SYS file, leaving the user to configure the DOSPRMPT.PIF file for legacy expanded memory. Windows XP now provides Compatibility Mode for this sort of thing.

After HIMEM.SYS opens access to all memory above the 1MB of conventional memory, COMMAND.COM can be loaded into the *High Memory Area (HMA)*. DOS=HIGH places most of the command processor into the HMA (above A000h). To use even more extra memory, the UMBs can be made accessible only through the expanded memory driver (EMM386.EXE).

The important thing to remember is that DOS used lots of confusing names, files, types of memory, and so on. You should be aware of these names, as much of today's command-line work is descended from DOS. Understand that EMM386.EXE allows high memory and UMBs to be used for applications and drivers, and not only expanded memory. High memory can hold programs by using DEVICEHIGH= (in CONFIG.SYS) and LOADHIGH= (in AUTOEXEC.BAT).

Translation Buffers

Windows still requires DOS to handle certain functions, such as reading or writing a file to disk. To do this, Windows switches the CPU back to Real Mode so that DOS can run in Real Mode and read the conventional memory for instructions. To communicate with DOS, Windows places *translation buffers* in the upper memory 384KB area. (Windows NT/2000/XP are legitimate operating systems and handle disk I/O directly.)

Translation buffers act as a kind of vector table for Windows to hand addresses to DOS. Windows also uses translation buffers to make Real Mode networking calls to a network operating system. Windows allocates two 4KB translation buffers (8KB) for each virtual PC. Running a DOS application creates a virtual PC. Therefore, each running 16-bit application (showing on the taskbar) uses 8KB of real memory in the form of translation buffers.

Networked physical computers use six 4KB translation buffers per virtual PC, which is 24KB per application.

The Windows Environment: Global Heap

The names used for memory in a DOS session change after Windows is running. All memory becomes the global heap, or simply "the heap." The *global* heap is the entire amount of memory available at startup. Windows reads the existing environment from HIMEM.SYS. It then examines any programs DOS has installed, and takes whatever memory is left.

The global heap is all the available memory Windows can see at Startup. The global heap is divided into three main areas:

➤ *Conventional memory*—This is the same as base memory in DOS real sessions, (that is, segments above low memory and below A000h).

➤ *High memory*—If DOS has set aside areas above the A000h segment for use by applications, Windows takes control of that area and adds it to the global heap of memory.

➤ *Extended memory*—After Windows starts, the virtual memory driver (HIMEM.SYS) passes on information about how much additional memory exists in the system. Windows then takes away control of that memory from DOS.

After Windows has taken over the management of RAM, it makes no difference whether the memory is extended or conventional. Windows sees all memory as part of the global heap. Windows loads program code into the heap by putting it first into lower segments and then into increasingly higher segments. The global heap is divided into two areas: USER.EXE and GDI.EXE. Each smaller area also has a *local* heap of memory.

System Resources

All *free memory* (not conventional memory) available from the first DOS prompt is referred to as *base* memory (640KB), the high-memory area (HMA) above A000h, and *extended* memory (beyond 1MB). After Windows (all versions) is up and running, it takes control of memory on the system and loads device drivers, program code, and data files into free memory. DOS is out of the loop except for file management at the disk level and hardware management at the interrupt level.

 For the exam, remember that although there is a formal distinction between base memory and conventional memory, questions will usually apply the term "conventional" memory to the 640KB used for applications, and will refer to high memory by name.

System Resources is actually a report of the local heap. Some of the local heap is always in use, and some of it is freed up as code moves in and out of memory. The following system resources are special areas set aside by Windows:

➤ The USER and GDI local heaps together make up the Free System Resources percentage seen under the Help | About | (System) menu option from any main menu in a Windows-compliant application.

➤ Everything in the Windows environment (both 16-bit and 32-bit) uses a percentage of the system resources, including icons, windows, programs, applications, data, menus, program tools, and screensavers.

➤ System resources are reported as a percentage available. Typically, between 50%–85% of the resources should be available at any given time (taking into account all programs running in that session).

NOTE

So-called memory doubler software does not double the amount of installed RAM; rather, it doubles the amount of system resources available from the two local heaps.

Programs are supposed to be written in such a way that memory is taken from the free system resources and given up again when the code for that program terminates. Unfortunately, not all programmers follow the rules, and not all programs work the way they were intended to work.

If something takes up resources, but fails to release them back to the heaps at conclusion, those resources never return to the Windows resources memory. This problem is sometimes referred to as a *resource leak*. Windows must be exited and restarted to re-create a new heap and start again with maximum free resources. This problem has been fixed, for the most part, in Windows XP. Instead of a fixed amount of resource memory, XP can allocate any amount main memory to system resources.

An "Out of memory" error in earlier versions of Windows referred to the lack of enough free system resources, not to the amount of total free memory on the computer. Windows XP uses an entirely different system kernel and memory management technique. As a result, it has almost no problems with leaking resources, locked programs, stolen memory segments, and misbehaving applications.

Task Switching

Task switching means that the loaded parts of a program and its data files are taken out of RAM and stored to the disk as a kind of photographic snapshot.

All the program code for a word processor is saved out of RAM onto a special area of the hard drive called a *swap file*. The data or documents being worked on at the moment of the switch are also stored to the swap file.

Sometimes the CPU is in the middle of doing something when an IRQ comes along with an interruption. Depending upon how important that interruption is, the CPU has to put down whatever it was doing and pick up whatever the IRQ needs. The "place" in memory where the CPU keeps track of what processing it puts down is called a *stack*. If there are too many interruptions, the CPU can generate a *stack overflow error*. Task switching uses a process similar to that of the stacks used by the CPU.

Because it takes a certain amount of time to spin the disk, move the read-write heads, and store the information on disk, task switching is relatively slow. Not only must the contents of memory be stored, but a new program must be loaded into RAM and prepared for the user. Each new task being loaded into RAM requires a new snapshot of RAM: a *window*.

A way was needed to keep every program in memory and go beyond the 640K barrier of conventional memory so that the slowness of disk swapping RAM could be overcome. Then the *page frame* and expanded memory arrived. Now a program could be saved into expanded or extended memory just as easily as it could be saved to disk, and the 286 Protected Mode would (theoretically) keep everything nice and separate.

Page Frame Memory and Page Swapping

The 286 chip's Protected Mode and a LIM expanded memory card gave users access to 16MB of memory for programs and data to use. The idea was that if something could keep track of those snapshots of conventional RAM and shift them up into expanded memory, several programs could be run at once in the same base memory area. The 80286's protection features would make sure (in theory) that each program in memory had its own specially protected area and that, if something went wrong, the program could be shut down in only that area while everything else continued to run.

If you think of expanded memory as a sort of warehouse on the second floor of a building, then you can imagine a loading dock on the first floor. When a program is running, it's like a truck being loaded from the dock. If another truck (program) has to be loaded (run), then in the imaginary warehouse, all the boxes (program code) from the first truck have to be sent back up to the warehouse (expanded memory) on an elevator. New boxes have to be sent down the elevator, and the second truck has to change places with the first. The elevator is like the page frame. (We discussed memory pages in Chapter 3.)

Task switching is like a Lazy Susan on a dining room table. Someone who wants an item spins the rotating platter until the choice comes around. However, instead of the other choices becoming available to the other side of the table, the other programs are spun through the page frame doorway into expanded memory or are saved to the disk.

Task switching to expanded memory was a nice idea, but it didn't work out quite as planned. DOS had a hard time keeping the various balls it was juggling in the air and tracking which parts of memory were supposed to be used for what. Aside from that, the 64KB page frame area was becoming a bottleneck because users had to move a 550KB process through it during a switch and another 612KB process back up into EMS memory.

The 286 had some internal problems as well. For example, when a program crashed in a so-called protected area, it usually brought the entire system tumbling down with it, regardless of how well the program area was protected. This led to a reboot, which would cancel whatever had been going on with any other programs. The swap file would be erased during the reboot, and any data that hadn't been saved would be lost.

Virtual Device Drivers (VxDs)

The lowest area of the global heap (memory) is set aside for Windows to load Windows-based device drivers that handle the interface between Windows, DOS, and hardware devices. Remember that the CONFIG.SYS file in DOS installs device drivers in the first segment of conventional memory before it loads Windows. The Windows device drivers are loaded into the lowest segment of the global heap, which is usually just above the low-memory area set aside by DOS.

Windows has its own device drivers that handle the keyboard, mouse, printers, video monitors, sound cards, scanners, and anything else that connects to the motherboard. All these device drivers are listed in the SYSTEM.INI file with any additional information they might need during startup.

 For the exam, remember that a virtual device driver (VxD) is a 32-bit Protected Mode .DLL file that manages a system resource (that is, a hardware device or installed software) such that more than one application can use the resource at the same time. The 32-bit Protected Mode comes from the 32-bit 80386 chip architecture and therefore is available for only a 386 or faster CPU.

The VxD abbreviation is used to refer to any (V)irtual *device* (D)river, where *x* is used as a stand-in variable. The specific device driver replaces the *x* with a character or characters referring to the specific type of driver. For example, a VDD is a virtual *display* driver, where *D* represents *display*.

VxDs work together with DOS to support multitasking in that more than one application can access the device at the same time in an arbitrated (managed) way. The VxDs work together with Windows to process interrupts and to carry out I/O processes for specific applications. Each process doesn't interfere with another application's use of the same device. All the hardware devices on a typical computer have a VxD, including the program interrupt controller (PIC), the timer oscillator, DMA channels, disk controller(s), serial and parallel ports, keyboard and input devices, math coprocessor, and monitor display.

A virtual device driver is generally written to hold code for specific operations of a device that might not be included in the basic Windows installation. Any device that can retain configuration information from an application, or that might mess up a request from an application, requires a VxD. Virtual drivers can also be written for any driver software that was installed by DOS during the CONFIG.SYS process.

When a VxD is a software driver, it usually surrounds the existing device and provides a specialized environment coming from Windows. This fools the existing device into thinking that only one computer, running one application, is present. The system thinks that only that application will be using the hardware device controlled by the real driver. VxDs act like a liaison between the Windows control management system and the individual device looking for a secure set of memory addresses.

 For the exam, remember that VxDs are installed from the SYSTEM.INI file, usually in the **[386Enh]** section of the file, and begin with DEVICE=, the same as they do in the CONFIG.SYS file. Windows 95 extended this process and tries to substitute a VxD for any device listed in a CONFIG.SYS file.

Summary—Windows Memory

Once again, we want to reassure you that this stuff (technical term) is complicated! Programs and computers use memory all the time, and the ways that memory is accessed and configured are pretty important concepts to remember. Go over the following list to make sure you have a good understanding of each point:

➤ The three basic types of main memory are conventional, expanded, and extended memory.

➤ Memory addressing is done with segments, and real memory uses 16 64KB segments. Depending upon the address number of a segment, it can be low or high memory.

➤ When we use one thing to point to something else, we're redirecting traffic. Web sites often use one URL to redirect the browser to another address. DOS uses vector tables to send instructions to other memory addresses. Network drive mapping and the DOS SUBST (substitute) command redirect requests to a drive letter to a different path name.

➤ Conventional memory has a 640KB "barrier." This was the main reason extended memory was developed. Windows uses HIMEM.SYS as an extended memory manager, and you should know the difference between expanded (EMS) and extended (XMS) memory.

➤ One of the most inelegant features of 32-bit Windows is in its use of swap files and virtual memory. You should understand how a swap file is a way for Windows to pretend it has more memory than installed memory modules.

➤ You don't need to remember all the technical details of how translation buffers work, and so on, but you must remember that HIMEM.SYS manages memory and system resources.

➤ Be sure you have a reasonable understanding of the Windows memory heap.

➤ Learn the basics of Virtual Device Drivers (VxDs) because you'll not only see more discussion in the following chapters, but you'll have lots of encounters with device problems and the Windows Device Manager when you troubleshoot a problem machine.

An Example CONFIG.SYS File

The following CONFIG.SYS file was processed by MEMMAKER, a DOS memory-optimization utility. Let's again discuss the fundamental directives and what they do using a real-world example.

Be sure that you don't get caught saying that MEMMAKER speeds up the overall system performance. MEMMAKER only increases the amount of conventional memory available to DOS applications by moving whatever it can into high memory and UMBs (if they're available). Technically, this can speed up some applications, but for the exam, MEMMAKER affects space, not performance.

```
DEVICE=C:\DOS\SETVER.EXE
DEVICE=C:\WINDOWS\HIMEM.SYS /TESTMEM:OFF
DEVICE=C:\WINDOWS\EMM386.EXE RAM I=B000-B7FF WIN=CD00-CFFF
BUFFERS=40,0
FILES=70
DOS=UMB
LASTDRIVE=K
FCBS=16,0
DOS=HIGH
STACKS=9,256
SHELL=C:\COMMAND.COM /P /E:1024
DEVICE=C:\BUSLOGIC\BTDOSM.SYS /D
DEVICEHIGH /L:3,19344 =C:\BUSLOGIC\BTCDROM.SYS /D:MSCD0001
DEVICEHIGH /L:1,22576 =D:\IOMEGA\ASPIPPM1.SYS FILE=SMC.
ILM SPEED=10
DEVICE=D:\IOMEGA\SCSICFG.EXE /V
DEVICE=D:\IOMEGA\SCSIDRVR.SYS
DEVICEHIGH /L:1,5888 =C:\DOS\RAMDRIVE.SYS 2048 /E
DEVICE=C:\WINDOWS\IFSHLP.SYS
```

A quick (but subtle) way to see that this PC is not running Windows 9x is to notice the fact that EMM386 has no REM (remark) in front of it, and the existence of the line DOS=UMB. In Windows 9x, SETUP.EXE automatically removes any expanded memory drivers from an existing CONFIG.SYS file during the installation process.

Remember that Windows 9x requires HIMEM.SYS to access extended memory for virtual memory management. HIMEM.SYS has been hard-coded into the IO.SYS file, which took over configuration from CONFIG.SYS. Windows 9x also uses REM to cancel any reference to SMARTDRV or EMM386.EXE.

Points of Interest

Notice that the DEVICEHIGH= directive has been put in by MEMMAKER. The /L:# value is automatically configured when MEMMAKER optimizes the specific addresses. The BusLogic SCSI adapter driver controlling the CDROM has been moved to high memory, as has an Iomega driver.

EMM386.EXE (expanded memory) has been told that Windows 3.x is present and to include (the /I= line to "I"nclude) a range of memory addresses for use by devices. This is the I=B000-B7FF switch on the EMM386 line.

The following line has installed a RAM drive:

```
DEVICEHIGH /L:1,5888 =C:\ DOS\RAMDRIVE.SYS 2048 /E
```

The /L:1,5888 was added by MEMMAKER to put the device driver in high memory. RAMDRIVE.SYS loads the RAM drive device driver and creates a 2MB RAM drive in extended (/E) memory. A companion line in the AUTOEXEC.BAT file could then be used (SET TEMP=G:\) to tell DOS to use the RAM drive for temporary files.

 RAMDRIVE.SYS comes with both DOS 6.x and Windows 9x and can create a virtual disk drive out of RAM. Because a RAM drive moves at the speed of memory, it can sometimes be useful for temporary files. However, the drive vanishes when the system is powered off.

Finally, HIMEM.SYS is used with an unusual /TESTMEM:OFF switch. During boot-up, when HIMEM loads, it tests the memory in almost the same way that the parity check is done during the POST. This second memory integrity check can take a long enough time that you can turn it off if you'd like. /TESTMEM:ON¦OFF is the settings switch to either turn off the memory checking or force it to take place (useful with nonparity memory).

 Windows 3.x could address a maximum of only 64MB of memory. Even though DOS could recognize more than that, 16-bit Windows would show "3% Remaining Resources" and fail almost as soon as it loaded. An undocumented way around this was to borrow the HIMEM.SYS file from Windows 95 OS/R-B and install it in place of the version that came with DOS 6.x. This would fool Windows 3.11 into believing it could use more than 64MB of RAM.

DEVICE= and DEVICEHIGH=

The DEVICE= directive indicates that a device is attached to the system. In this case, the device driver (usually files with a .SYS extension) can be found on Drive D: in the \IOMEGA sub-directory. The specific name of the device driver file is ASPIPPM1.SYS. With a little experience, we might guess that this refers to an Iomega Zip, Jaz, or Ditto (tape) drive. A typical statement in the preceding CONFIG.SYS file appears as follows:

```
DEVICE=D:\IOMEGA\ASPIPPM1.SYS FILE=SMC.ILM SPEED=10
```

 Remember that the CONFIG.SYS file is executed prior to the AUTOEXEC.BAT file during the boot process. The PATH environment variable can be set only after the system is under the control of the operating system. The **PATH** command can be run only in a batch file or at the DOS command line. PATH= is always found in the first few lines of the AUTOEXEC.BAT file.

Because no search path has been set when the CONFIG.SYS runs, every device must have its full pathname and filename in the directive. Because no path has been set, DOS can look for the driver file only in the root directory of the bootable disk in the boot drive. This is the directory that DOS is logged in to as the current directory at boot-up.

If enough memory was available in high memory (above conventional memory, according to the exam), the DEVICEHIGH= directive (DOS 5.0 and later) would attempt to load the Iomega (device) driver above the 640KB of base memory. In this case, the DEVICE= directive means that the driver is intended to load into conventional (base) memory.

MEMMAKER automatically runs hundreds of configuration settings to see which programs can make the most efficient use of high memory, UMBs, or both. In this case, it determined that the Iomega driver should stay in conventional base memory.

 DOS marks an intentional space between characters with an equal sign (=), a semicolon (;), or a space (spacebar or ASCII decimal .0032 scan code). An equal sign or a semicolon is used most often to ensure that a space is marked and to leave no room for misinterpretation. You can enter **.0032** if you hold down the Alt key at the same time as you enter the digits on the numeric keypad of the keyboard.

Again, the line we're examining is

```
DEVICE=D:\IOMEGA\ASPIPPM1.SYS FILE=SMC.ILM SPEED=10
```

A space and more information follow the device driver. `FILE=SMC.ILM` probably refers to a data file in which either further configuration settings are stored through customer configuration or the device reads factory-configured values.

During SETUP.EXE (all Windows versions) or INSTALL.EXE (DOS) for a new device, a typical detection program uses simple tests to check for the existence of certain hardware and software. This is not the same as the POST looking at CMOS settings.

Depending on whether Yes or No returns from a setup test, the new device's installation routine often chooses one of several files containing factory-configured values. These files are usually taken from the installation disk that comes with the device. Some knowledgeable guesswork would indicate that SMC.ILM is one of these factory configuration files relating to some device made by Iomega.

The exam might ask you to explain why Windows 9x notices a particular device attached to the system but can't provide the manufacturer's information and settings. Windows 9x has a large internal database of many devices made by today's hardware manufacturers.

If Windows 9x can read settings information from a BIOS chip on a PnP-compatible device, it configures the device with its correct settings. If Windows 9x can recognize that a generic type of device is attached to an I/O port, it tries to use generic settings, which might work.

If Windows 9x notices only that a device exists at an I/O port, but can't even tell which general class (Registry) the device falls into, it tries to prompt the user for specific configuration settings by using the Have Disk option dialog box during installation.

If neither PnP processing nor generic device awareness takes place, the device is ignored in a full PnP-enabled configuration. If PnP is not enabled, Windows 9x resource management stops short of managing device resources.

MSDET.INF

Windows 9x uses detection modules called by MSDET.INF during setup. These .DLL modules contain general settings information about classes (general categories) of devices. MSDET.INF calls specific .DLL files that try to read information from a device through PnP BIOS chips on the device. If PnP doesn't work, the .DLL generates common settings for that class of device. The settings are stored in the Registry following completion of the setup routine. This so-called auto-detection became available starting with Windows 95.

The data resulting from the checking process is stored in the DETLOG.TXT file (detection log text file), and the device has either a manufacturer's name and settings stored in the Registry or a generic class name. To distinguish between true PnP compatibility and the best-guess capabilities built into Windows 9x, we use the term *auto-detect* here, although it is not the formal name of a feature in Windows 9x.

At the end of the SMC.ILM filename is yet another space and the SPEED=10 setting value. Note that no internal way exists of knowing what this refers to beyond some sort of speed setting with 10 being the value. The speed setting is explained only in the device's technical reference documentation.

A classic way to troubleshoot a PC is to bypass every reference to any device from all configuration files. Inexperienced technicians tend to use the Delete key to delete the entire file or to delete a line in a configuration file. In this situation, if it should turn out that the device was a critical system driver (such as a SCSI controller), the technician is left with only his or her memory to replace the line.

Regardless of whether CONFIG.SYS supports the **REM** statement, typing **REM** followed by a space at the beginning of any line in CONFIG.SYS or AUTOEXEC.BAT causes DOS to bypass the line without executing any instructions. In Windows .INI files, use the semicolon (;) followed by a space to accomplish the same bypass.

If it should turn out that a configuration line is necessary, it can be reactivated by deleting the **REM** or the semicolon, removing the necessity of trying to remember what you've deleted at a later date.

Exam Prep Questions

Question 1

When a PC is first powered up, COMMAND.COM, AUTOEXEC.BAT, and CONFIG.SYS files load in which order?

○ A. AUTOEXEC.BAT, CONFIG.SYS, COMMAND.COM

○ B. COMMAND.COM, CONFIG.SYS, AUTOEXEC.BAT

○ C. CONFIG.SYS, COMMAND.COM, AUTOEXEC.BAT

○ D. COMMAND.COM, AUTOEXEC.BAT, CONFIG.SYS

Answer C is correct. CONFIG.SYS initializes 16-bit Real Mode devices and sets the environment, and then the command interpreter, COMMAND.COM, loads. After the interpreter is loaded, commands contained in the AUTOEXEC.BAT batch file are processed.

Question 2

A Windows Me machine no longer uses either a POST or a command interpreter because the Registry controls the entire process for the machine.

○ A. True

○ B. False

Answer B, false, is correct. All computers use a boot process involving a power-on self test (POST), regardless of what operating system is installed. The Windows Registry manages system configuration for Windows 9x machines running a Microsoft operating system and can begin to operate only after the system files have taken charge of the system.

Question 3

Windows 9x uses SYSTEM.DAT and USER.DAT to run driver software. Which initialization file is used in the case of a 16-bit legacy device?

○ A. WIN.INI

○ B. SYSTEM.INI

○ C. WIN.COM

○ D. PROGMAN.INI

Answer B is correct. SYSTEM.INI must be present for certain 16-bit hardware devices to be recognized by any version of Windows 95, 98, or Me. Answer A is incorrect because WIN.INI stores user configurations in a 16-bit Windows (3.x) environment. Answer C is incorrect because WIN.COM is the loader program for Windows and doesn't store any settings. Answer D, PROGMAN.INI, refers to the Windows 3.x Program Manager desktop shell and was sometimes used for rudimentary security.

Question 4

Windows 95, 98, and Me all load the _____ memory manager from the _____ system file.

○ A. EMM386.EXE, MSDOS.SYS

○ B. EMM386.EXE, CONFIG.SYS

○ C. HIMEM.SYS, IO.SYS

○ D. HIMEM.SYS, MSDOS.SYS

Answer C is correct. Beginning with Windows 95, HIMEM.SYS was loaded from within the IO.SYS system file. In DOS and Windows 3.x, extended memory was accessed through the DEVICE= line in the CONFIG.SYS file. Answers A and B are incorrect because EMM386.EXE is an expanded memory manager, not extended memory. HIMEM.SYS accesses XMS memory. Answer D is incorrect because MSDOS.SYS is concerned with how Windows starts up, not basic system access.

Question 5

Virtual Real Mode creates a _____ based on an _____ chip.

○ A. Virtual XT, 80286

○ B. Command session, 80386

○ C. Real machine, 80286

○ D. Virtual machine, 8088/86

Answer D is correct. The Virtual Machine (VM) is a software-generated copy of the first XT machine that was based on the 8088/86 CPU. It addresses memory in a "real" way. Answer A is incorrect because although a VM is a virtual XT, the chip emulation is not a 286. Answer B is incorrect because of the 386 chip and the improper term "command session." Answer C is incorrect because of the 286 chip and the improper term "real machine."

Question 6

IO.SYS is loaded into the _____ memory area of _____ memory.

- ⚪ A. low, conventional
- ⚪ B. high, low
- ⚪ C. base, conventional
- ⚪ D. conventional, low

Answer A is correct. IO.SYS contains basic functions and tables required by the BIOS and motherboard. It loads into the low area of the first 1MB of conventional memory. Answer B is incorrect because the high and low areas of memory are contained within what's called conventional or (incorrectly) base memory. Technically, base memory is whatever memory is left to the user for applications. Answer C is incorrect because base and conventional memory refer to the overall first megabyte of memory. Answer D is incorrect because the terms are in reverse order of proper usage.

Question 7

Windows 98 creates a permanent swap file when you choose to specify virtual memory settings in the system's performance dialog box.

- ⚪ A. True
- ⚪ B. False

Answer A, true, is correct. The performance tab of the System properties dialog box under the Control Panel allows user configuration of temporary or permanent swap files. When Windows manages virtual memory, it usually uses a temporary swap file that can grow to take over all empty (contiguous) space on a hard drive. Specifying the virtual memory settings creates a permanent swap file, both limiting the amount of drive space Windows will take over and saving the time it takes to create the temporary swap file during each session.

Question 8

> What three system files are critical to successfully booting DOS?
>
> ○ A. MSDOS.SYS
> ○ B. CONFIG.SYS
> ○ C. IO.SYS
> ○ D. COMMAND.COM

Answers A, C, and D are correct. Answer B is incorrect because the CONFIG.SYS file is an optional file, and not required to successfully boot DOS.

Question 9

> Which one of the following is not a type of memory used by Windows?
>
> ○ A. Expanded Memory
> ○ B. Random Access Memory
> ○ C. Extended Memory
> ○ D. Conventional Memory

Answer B is correct. This is a tricky question, but it is also representative of some you will see on the test. Notice that it's phrased in the negative, "Which is not...". Most people are conditioned to expect questions asking what does exist, as opposed to what does not exist. If you're not paying attention, your natural inclination will be to transpose the question into the positive and promptly get it wrong. Second, there is no correct answer. Windows uses all four types of memory listed. However, you are asked to select one. Three of the answers technically refer to how memory is used. Only one (RAM) is a physical type of memory. You can't argue the correctness of a question on the test, so the only way to correctly answer the question is to answer it incorrectly.

Question 10

A user brings you a computer complaining of erratic performance. When you boot the computer there is no beep code whatsoever. Why would there be no beep code on startup?

- ○ A. There is a parity error in the first 640K of main memory.
- ○ B. One or more of the memory modules are defective or installed incorrectly.
- ○ C. The battery backup for the CMOS has expired and needs to be replaced.
- ○ D. The speaker is unplugged, defective, or missing.

Answer D is correct. A PC always produces a beep code at startup. No audible beep indicates the speaker is missing, defective, or unplugged. Before you can do additional troubleshooting, you need to replace or reattach the speaker. Answer A is incorrect because failed parity rarely produces any message at all, and has no beep code associated with it. Answer B is incorrect because the POST is not designed to return error testing results for bad memory chips. Answer C is incorrect because the POST doesn't test the CMOS battery condition at all.

Need to Know More?

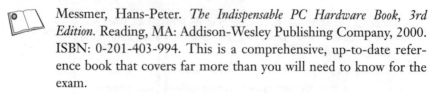

Messmer, Hans-Peter. *The Indispensable PC Hardware Book, 3rd Edition.* Reading, MA: Addison-Wesley Publishing Company, 2000. ISBN: 0-201-403-994. This is a comprehensive, up-to-date reference book that covers far more than you will need to know for the exam.

Minasi, Mark. *The Complete PC Upgrade and Maintenance Guide, 11th Edition.* San Francisco, CA: Sybex Network Press, 2000. ISBN: 0-782-128-009. This is considered one of the best reference books available. In fact, Minasi's book was instrumental in the formulation of the first A+ exam.

Rosch, Winn. *Hardware Bible, 5th Edition.* Indianapolis, IN: Sams Publishing, 1999. ISBN: 0-789-717-433. This is a well-organized reference book that covers software issues as well as hardware.

Mueller, Scott. *Upgrading and Repairing PCs, 14th Edition.* Indianapolis, IN: Que, 2000. ISBN: 0-7897-2745-5. This is one of our favorites. If you are going to have only one reference book, give this one serious consideration.

Freedman, Alan. *Computer Desktop Encyclopedia, 2nd Edition.* AMACOM, 1999. ISBN: 0-814-479-855. This is great for a fast lookup or refresher.

Microsoft Windows 95 Resource Kit. Redmond, WA: Microsoft Press, ISBN: 1-55615-678-2. This is the definitive resource for all Windows 95 questions. It assumes that you have a good working knowledge of Windows 95.

Windows 9x

Terms you'll need to understand:

✓ Version release number

✓ FAT32, FAT16, 32-bit, 16-bit, Virtual FAT (VFAT), NTFS

✓ File attributes (Hidden, System, Read-only)

✓ .INI files and log files (BOOTLOG.TXT and LOGVIEW.EXE)

✓ Safe Mode, Real Mode, Virtual Machine (VM) and VMM32, DOS command mode

✓ History log and version control

Concepts you'll need to master:

✓ Vectors (pointers) and aliasing (mapping), truncated filenames

✓ The Registry (SYSTEM.DAT and USER.DAT)

✓ Configuration settings, CONFIG.SYS and AUTOTEXEC.BAT

✓ HKey handles and keys

✓ The installation and startup process for Windows

✓ Static and dynamic Virtual device Drivers (VxDs)

✓ Long File Names (LFNs) and Installable File System (IFS)

✓ How Windows evolved from a 16-bit core to the 32-bit Windows NT core

When Windows 95 was released (to much fanfare and rock-and-roll music), the world stood back to wonder at the final integration of DOS and Windows NT in a fully backward-compatible, 32-bit operating system. We were there! At last, we had the final version of Windows. So why do we still have Windows NT? And how come there's Windows 98SE, Windows Me, Windows 2000, and Windows XP?

In this chapter we'll continue to refer to Windows 95, Windows 98, Windows 98SE, and Windows Me as *Windows 9x*. Where we use only the word "Windows," we mean 95/98/SE and Me. Otherwise, we'll refer to the version names we're differentiating. We'll refer to Windows NT, Windows 2000, and Windows XP by their specific names, or with a shorthanded Windows NT/2000/XP. In situations where we refer to Windows XP alone, you can include Windows NT and Windows 2000 in the reference. We'll use parentheses or notes to specify when a feature is specifically limited to a particular Windows version.

The Windows 9x Registry

Before we go any further, we want to be absolutely sure that you understand the fact that the Windows 9x Registry is very different from the Windows XP Registry. The Windows Registry is made up of many underlying files. Windows 9x primarily uses SYSTEM.DAT and USER.DAT (for the purposes of the exam). Windows XP/2000/NT have many more files, in various locations, and Microsoft calls those files *hives*. We could make a reasonable backup of the Windows 9x Registry without too much of a problem. That's no longer the case with Windows XP.

 You'll find various tips, notes, and references throughout this chapter that explain ways to do something in Windows. Many of the tools and tips won't work at all in Windows 2000/XP. We'll include an indication that something works in *all* versions of Windows, where it's appropriate. If you see no such indication, only "Windows," assume it means Windows 9x.

The Windows Registry is arguably the most important, yet least understood, change to the way modern machines are configured and maintained. You won't have to know the low-level details of the Registry for the A+ exam, but you must be able to visualize and remember the essential function of each HKey. We'll discuss the Registry at some length in this chapter, but only from a basic perspective. Understand that programs such as Tweak UI and X-Setup can modify nearly every configurable aspect of Windows, but they can also cause irreparable damage, necessitating a complete reinstallation.

Many of today's home systems come with only an image file of the original installation on a CDROM—a so-called recovery disk.

 Image files are no longer a "perfect" way to reinstall an XP machine. Before you invest in software to create image files, do some investigation. We've found many instances where image files failed completely. They're still a good option, but be aware that they're not infallible.

In some instances, the only way to recover a machine is from the command line. If you think you don't need to know about DOS and command-line syntax, other than for the exam, you'd be well advised to explore Chapter 15 ("Windows NT, 2000, and XP") and the Windows 2000/XP Recovery Console, along with the information on Troubleshooting discussed in Chapter 16.

A so-called recovery disk (OEM Setup disks), or original installation image, wipes out any and all user-created information. This information includes such things as documents, financial management data, business records, client histories, address books, online bookmarks, personal photographs, email, and so forth. Be sure to have current, valid backups of data files before making changes.

Windows 95 began the basic changeover from a 16-bit operating system to a 32-bit OS. Many people tend to assume this change to 32-bit operation was the most important. Actually, the more important change was the development of the Windows Registry. Windows 3.x used a primitive Registry (REG.DAT) to keep track of objects, but from Windows 95 all the way through into Windows NT and XP, the Registry is what holds all the versions together.

The hidden SYSTEM.DAT and USER.DAT files make up the Windows 9x Registry, but they're only part of the overall configuration system. Initialization files (.INI files) continue to provide backward compatibility for older applications, as well as necessary settings for current applications. Even the Registry Repair utility (SCANREGW.EXE), which makes daily backups of the Registry (and should not be confused with the Registry Editor), requires its own .INI file. (ScanReg was a manual utility in Windows 95, meaning that it was not run automatically at startup.)

Registry Backup Files

ScanReg runs automatically during the Windows 98 startup (it isn't automatic in Windows 95), or when Windows 98 shuts down improperly. This utility, ordinarily located in the \Windows folder, is a somewhat simple Registry analysis program designed to check for problems in the Registry files. Those files include the two .DAT files, but also the SYSTEM.INI and

WIN.INI files. The default number of five backups is configured in the SCANREG.INI file (also in the \Windows folder), with the line MaxBackupCopies=5. You can change this to any other number by editing the .INI file with a text editor (such as NotePad).

The Registry Repair utility isn't included in Windows Me/NT/2000/XP (note that it's not in Windows Me). In fact, the entire concept of making an automated daily backup of the Registry changed, becoming part of the overall system backup strategy (System Restore). Windows XP uses an optional checkbox to include System Files in a *restore point* (a calendar date). As always, there are workarounds for this new "feature." (One person's feature is another person's problem.) Basically, don't count on having a workable Registry for Windows XP if the system fails.

The Windows 98 Startup process includes checking the Registry files for various problems. After the files have been scanned, ScanReg uses Microsoft's compression utility (similar to PKZip, or WinZip) to create a .CAB file. Each day, ScanReg creates a new .CAB file, stored in the location described by the line BackupDirectory=[folder], where [folder] is normally C:\WINDOWS\SYSBCKUP, but can be changed.

After the files have been compressed, they're given an incremental name: rb000.cab, rb001.cab, rb002.cab, and so forth. When the maximum number has been reached (specified by the .INI file line), Windows overwrites the first .CAB file with the next day's backup.

To restore a corrupted Registry, you can use the **scanreg /restore** command, but only from a DOS command line. Otherwise, to extract only a single file, you can use WinZip or any other archive program that handles .CAB files. For more information, see the Microsoft support forum at http://support.microsoft.com/default.aspx?scid=KB;EN-US;Q183887&.

An important component of the A+ exam has to do with understanding the way in which Windows loads, and the typical Startup problems. We cover these problems again in Chapter 16, but remember that this book is designed as a compressed review before you take the test. You should have a solid, hands-on experience with the Registry and the command line by now. If you don't, we strongly recommend that you use additional preparation resources, some of which we've listed in the "Need to Know More?" section at the end of this chapter.

.INI Files

The Microsoft Windows 95 Resource Kit states that "The Registry simplifies the operating system by eliminating the need for AUTOEXEC.BAT,

CONFIG.SYS, and .INI files (except when legacy applications require them)." This is about as true as saying that Congress simplifies the management of the country by eliminating the need for citizens to govern themselves. Initialization files are used routinely in *every* version of Windows, including XP, and both CONFIG.SYS and AUTOEXEC.BAT are alive and well. It's true that neither of the startup files are *as* necessary as before. It's also true that .INI files aren't the *only* way to configure Windows, either. However, they still exist and are used regularly.

To see how a CONFIG.SYS file is still useful, create a Windows 98 Emergency Backup Disk (EBD) and boot the system with that disk. Note the use of menus. Then, re-boot the machine normally and start Windows. Use a text editor to go in and examine the CONFIG.SYS file on the floppy.

Computers are different from other types of machines in that they remember things like user settings, the color of a desktop, or the arrangement of icons. Configuration settings were originally held in the CONFIG.SYS and AUTOEXEC.BAT files. There were a few data files (.DAT) and other configuration files (.CFG), but the text-based initialization files became the method of choice for storing configurations. Microsoft encouraged developers to use .INI files, providing the SYSTEM.INI and WIN.INI files as examples of how it was done.

Unfortunately, problems with this idea were already starting to crop up by the time Windows 3.x hit the market. There were too many .INI files being splattered all over the hard drives. Aside from the number of files, all these critical settings were in text files, making it too easy for anyone to modify them—even if they didn't know what they were doing. Microsoft, along with corporate IT managers, decided that would never do.

Most, but not all of the information that was once in .INI files, is now stored somewhere in the Registry. Even so, Windows itself still creates new .INI files (for example, TELEPHON.INI) that didn't exist under Windows 3.x.

The two important .INI files used by Windows (all versions) are the SYSTEM.INI and WIN.INI files. You may see references to PROGMAN.INI (the Windows 3.x Program Manager) or CONTROL.INI (the older Control Panel). PROGMAN.INI contains a listing of the Program Group files (*.GRP) used within the old Win 3.x Program Manager. Windows provides a converter program to change .GRP to program items on the Start menu.

Always remember that SYSTEM.INI has more to do with hardware configuration, device settings, and memory management. WIN.INI usually stores the way the system looks to the end user. WIN.INI also has the important **LOAD=** and **RUN=** lines, which can be used to start a program automatically. WIN.INI settings are typically stored in the HKEY_USERS or HKEY_CURRENT_CONFIG keys.

Editing Registry Files

For the most part, the Windows 9x Registry combined program configuration details into binary files (as opposed to text files), preventing people from casually changing settings. The operative word is "casual," meaning that less knowledgeable users could no longer open a critical configuration file in Word, saving it again in the proprietary Word format and causing a catastrophic system crash.

Windows 3.x used a combination of the SYSTEM.INI, WIN.INI, and REG.DAT files to keep track of device drivers, environment settings, and *objects* being controlled by Windows. REG.DAT was a binary file, requiring REGEDIT.EXE, a special editor program, to open it and make changes. We'll discuss the Registry Editor console again in Chapter 16, but you should know that RegEdit shows you a virtual presentation of the Registry files. In other words, you aren't opening a single file and seeing the HKeys. Instead, the editor opens many files (somewhat like SYSEDIT.EXE) and presents a blended combination of the data contained in all of them. Again, current lingo calls those underlying files *hives*.

REGEDIT.EXE continued to be the preferred editor for Windows 95, 98, and Me. Windows NT and 2000 use REGEDT32.EXE as their own preferred editor. Windows XP goes back to using REGEDIT.EXE.

Windows 9x still uses the SYSTEM.INI file to load 16-bit drivers. If there's a conflict over two of the same devices, the device listed in the SYSTEM.INI file takes precedence over the one listed in the SYSTEM.DAT Registry file. The System Configuration Editor (SYSEDIT.EXE) utility is a quick way to examine and edit the legacy .INI files, as well as CONFIG.SYS and AUTOEXEC.BAT. This program opens a text-editing window and cascades all the open files.

Objects and Shortcuts

The original Registry database was a little-known tool that managed Object Linking and Embedding (OLE) and the drag-and-drop features in Windows. OLE is a way to place (embed) a document inside another document, using a kind of pointer to data from an outside program's data. (The document is a "client" and the program that creates the document is an "OLE server.")

When a program can embed a piece of itself in the form of an embedded object, that program is said to be an *OLE server*. It's called a server because it provides functional services to the program trying to open the object—the *OLE client*. If you're following all this confusion, you should also see that this is the primitive ancestor to something we're all familiar with today: *shortcuts*.

These kinds of documents are called *compound documents* because you can view or edit the data in the OLE connection (link) without knowing which application created it. (This is also the first inkling of Active Directory.) For example, the [Embedding] section in the WIN.INI file might contain the entry:

```
PBrush=Paintbrush
Picture,C:\Programs\Access\MSPAINT.EXE,picture
```

The example shows how a certain type of OLE picture object found in, say, a Word document (the client) should find MSPAINT.EXE (the server) in the specified location. Furthermore, the line tells Windows that it should use Microsoft Paint to open the picture when the picture's OLE object is double-clicked.

The original database maintained information about the pathname and file-names of OLE servers, the names and extensions of data files, and their associated programs (the original file associations). The file also maintained the *classname* of the objects the OLE servers could edit (such as pictures), and the protocols used by the objects. The CLSID numbers in today's Registry evolved from those old "CLaSs ID" numbers.

Be very careful that you don't buy into a response to a question that asks you whether REG.DAT is one of the current Windows Registry files. SYSTEM.DAT and USER.DAT are the only .DAT files used in the Windows 9x Registry.

Microsoft claimed that OLE would increase the amount of inter-connectivity among computer applications. The company hoped that compound documents would enable users to focus more on the data and documents they were making, rather than worry about how to open and use a particular program. To some extent, HyperText Markup Language (HTML) superseded OLE, though not necessarily by using the same process. The technology behind OLE and Dynamic Data Exchange (DDE) is complex, but you should know what the acronyms stand for.

Microsoft has never given up on the idea that people want to simply click on either a picture or a simple description and go right to work with all the underlying files and data available. Part of the next release of Windows XP (codenamed Longhorn, and possibly slated for 2005) will be a new application programming interface (API) framework. This new interface, together with Active Directory (a network interface), is supposed to allow users to organize and share information more intuitively. Presumably, files will no longer be displayed on their physical location, being organized by context or in some other way defined by users or administrators. Rumor has it that Longhorn may move all your files to a Web storage site, leaving only links to those files on your personal hard drive. Naturally, this would open the door to charging a small "rent" for that Internet storage space (so you can rent the files you think you own).

Pointers

Hardware devices and software applications place references in the Registry, pointing to their program files and the location of additional configuration files. For instance, if a scanner requires a SCANNER.DLL file, the Registry holds the file's location, along with the various configuration switches and options under which the file is working. These consolidated references are also used by utilities such as the Windows Update Manager and the System File Checker (SFC).

The concept of using a pointer (vector) to another object, along with using an icon to represent the pointer, eventually led to the Windows "shortcuts" (.LNK) files. Shortcuts can be created in many ways, but the simplest way is to highlight a program filename, hold down the right mouse button (formally called the properties button), drag it onto the Desktop (or into another folder), and then release the mouse button. A short menu dialog pops up—the Context menu—with one of the choices being "Create Shortcut(s) Here."

Another simple way to create a shortcut on the Desktop is to use the "Send To" menu option on the Context menu. You can open the menu either by right-clicking on an icon, or by selecting the icon and pressing Shift+F10. "Send To" is a default menu option in all versions of Windows later than Windows 3.x.

Keyboard Movement and Shortcut Keys

From the first release of Windows 1.0, certain letters in a graphic menu option have always represented the use of shortcut keys. Pressing the Alt key highlights the first option in any Windows menu. Pressing the underlined letter of an option drops down that main options menu. With the options menu showing, pressing a combination of the Alt key and the underlined letter of an option executes the specific choice without requiring an additional mouse click. The Tab and Arrow keys move focus around various menu options, and Shift-Tab usually moves it in the opposite direction. In some cases (such as AOL), Ctrl+Tab moves the focus through various menu options and dialog boxes.

You should know the classic Windows shortcut keys, in case you have to access a system without a mouse. Ctrl+A selects everything. Ctrl+C copies a selection. Ctrl+V pastes a selection, and Ctrl+X cuts a selection. The F2 key almost always allows editing a selection. F5 is the Explorer's refresh key. Ctrl+S almost always saves a file. Ctrl+Esc brings up the Start Menu. Alt+Tab and Shift+Alt+Tab move you through any open (running) program in a carousel fashion. Alt+Space drops you down the main Application menu, allowing you to close, minimize, or restore a main window. Alf+F4 closes an application, and Ctrl+F4 closes a child window within an application.

Finally, the Windows Explorer has its own menu, with an "Edit" option. In the Files pane, you can press and hold the Ctrl key to select individual, separate files. Or, you can select the first file in a contiguous list, and then press and hold the Shift key before you click on the last file in the list to select all the files in between. The "Edit" option offers the option to "Invert Selection." If you select three files, for example, and then use this option, Explorer de-selects the three files, and reverses the selection to include all the previously unselected files.

Components of the Registry

Windows 9x uses two files, each of which is a Hidden, Read-only, System file (+H +R +S attributes) in the Windows folder. Although a common procedure for making a copy of SYSTEM.DAT includes turning off all the attributes so that DOS can see the file, the Explorer happily copies or moves hidden files with only a brief dialog box asking for confirmation. Be sure that you check a question about SYSTEM.DAT for any reference to which environment is being used.

Practically no one really understands the Windows Registry, but you should know how to identify some of its parts. These files are

➤ *USER.DAT*—Holds user-specific customization settings, such as the Desktop, video resolution, shortcuts, icon sets, and so on. These user settings were formerly held in the WIN.INI file, under Windows 3.x. Multiple users can customize Windows according to their own personal preferences.

➤ *SYSTEM.DAT*—The largest of the two components; stores all the hardware configurations, Windows internal settings, and application settings that were originally held in SYSTEM.INI.

SYSTEM.DAT and USER.DAT are both binary files, and can't be edited with Notepad, the Microsoft Editor (EDIT.COM), WordPad, or any other ASCII editor. The only way to edit the Registry is by using REGEDIT.EXE or a third-party program designed specifically for the purpose.

NOTE Any part (key) of the Registry, or the entire file itself, can be exported to a separate text file. You can use an ASCII editor to make changes to the exported file. The text file can then be imported back into the Registry. This is one way to send various Registry patches and modifications through email or via Internet downloads.

Exporting a particular Registry key before making changes is also a fast way to make a small backup of just the area you're about to modify. When you make a change in the Registry Editor, that change takes place immediately, in most cases, and can't be reverted with an "Undo" feature.

If a computer is configured for multiple users, Windows creates a separate variation of the USER.DAT file for each user. Windows takes the User ID and password information from the Logon dialog box, using it to select the correct .DAT file. Typically, the User ID is part of the filename. For example, Bob Smith's User ID might be BSmith, which would lead to a BSMITH.DAT file. Although USER.DAT is the default file, these other files (if they exist) also become part of the overall Registry.

HKeys

The Windows Explorer lists folders in the left pane, using a + or – symbol to indicate any sub-folders within (below) a given folder. The Registry looks the same, but calls each primary heading a *handle*, with *keys* being the underlying subdivisions. The Computer Management Console in Windows 2000/XP also looks like the Explorer or Registry, but refers to *nodes* at the folder level and *branches* as the subdivisions.

An "HKey" is Microsoft's language for a program *handle* to a *key* that contains configuration information. Looking at the various HKeys in RegEdit is somewhat like looking at a drive in Windows Explorer. Each key looks like a folder icon, and can be expanded or collapsed just like folders and sub-folders.

 You may see a question that asks you what the little + sign is to the left of a folder. If you don't know that this is a one-click way to expand the folder, then we suggest that you postpone taking the exam until after you've installed Windows 9x and played around with it for awhile. Another shortcut key, in the Explorer, is to press Alt+* to expand an entire folder and all its sub-folders. (To revert to single-level expanding, press the minus key, and then press F5 to refresh the view.)

The Windows 9x Registry contains six primary HKeys. Each HKey is like a primary folder located in the root directory of a drive and has many levels of sub-keys that descend like a directory tree. The root directory is called HKEY_CLASSES_ROOT. Realistically, only two of the HKeys contain all the data in the entire Registry. The remaining HKeys are *mirrors* of subsections of the master keys.

A "mirror" is a technical word meaning that whatever happens in one place magically appears in another place at the same time. When you edit a mirror key, the change automatically applies to the original key. Conversely, if you make a change in the master HKey, the change automatically appears in the mirrored "other" HKey. Beyond this very simplistic discussion, we'll leave it to you to research how the HKeys work, according to your interest. The six primary HKeys are

➤ *HKEY_CLASSES_ROOT*—File extensions and applications used for OLE.

➤ *HKEY_USERS*—Data stored in USER.DAT that keeps network information and user configuration options of all users who have logged on to the PC.

➤ *HKEY_CURRENT_USER*—The default (template) HKey that stores settings information specific to the Windows user at the moment. (This is a mirrored key, with additional keys for each user in a multi-user configuration. In that case, "USER" becomes the User ID reference, as previously mentioned.)

➤ *HKEY_LOCAL_MACHINE*—The hardware and software configurations for a computer. (Another mirrored key. Multiple configurations can be stored for the same computer.)

➤ *HKEY_CURRENT_CONFIG*—Printers and display settings for the current, running session.

➤ *HKEY_DYN_DATA*—Dynamic data in RAM having to do with how Windows is running (shown by the System Monitor applet).

The Windows Registry (all versions) is built around two master sections. It then breaks out mirrored copies of sub-sections. The Registry Editor presents all the sections as **HKey_[*SectionName*]**. At the top of the Registry tree is HKey_Classes_Root. The section used for hardware is HKey_Local_Machine.

Although we didn't see any questions asking for a list of all the main HKeys, there may be a reference to the Local Machine key as the location for all the device configurations. Neither did we see anything having to do with **HKey_Dyn_Data**.

The odds are high that questions about the Registry keys will provide the correct names in the response or body of the text. For example, you might be asked to choose or identify an HKey in terms of what it does, and we're fairly confident that you'll have to know only the **Local_Machine** and **Users** keys.

Windows works with and changes the Registry during Startup, during a session, or whenever you install a program. If problems occur during Setup and a hardware device refuses to be recognized, editing the Local_Machine key might help. However, the main problem is that removing software or changing a hardware device doesn't automatically change its entries in the Registry. Information about hardware and software is stored in *many* places within the Registry, and uninstaller programs have varying degrees of success in finding all occurrences and references.

Always make a backup of the Registry, particularly the SYSTEM.DAT file, before you make *any* changes to the system. This includes running an uninstaller program because an incorrect guess on the part of the program can render the system totally inoperable. In Windows Me and Windows 2000/XP, create a Restore Point before making any significant change to the system.

Registry-Protection Files

SYSTEM.NEW is the first version of the Registry. Windows creates this file during Setup, and stores hardware and software configuration information made during the detection phase of the installation. If everything works well and Windows successfully starts without crashing, SYSTEM.NEW is renamed to SYSTEM.DAT.

After Windows is installed and working, the first successful SYSTEM.DAT is renamed to SYSTEM.DA0 and held as a backup of the original Registry. The very first SYSTEM.DAT used when Windows 9x starts from the hard disk is also copied to SYSTEM.1ST in the root directory, as another backup of the clean, first installation.

 We'll remind you, once again, that the Windows 2000/XP Registry is completely different from the Windows 9x Registry. We'll discuss some of the XP Registry files in Chapter 16.

SYSTEM.1ST includes everything up to the original, first reboot of the system. If you replace SYSTEM.DAT with SYSTEM.1ST at any time, and then reboot the computer, you get the "Starting Windows 9x For The First Time" screen and Windows goes through the configuring hardware process, initializing the Control Panel, Start menu, and all the other aspects of a first-time start. Windows then reboots and starts up normally.

Every time Windows starts successfully, it backs up SYSTEM.DAT to SYSTEM.DA0 and USER.DAT to USER.DA0 (overwriting any existing .DA0 files). If something goes wrong, Windows automatically uses the .DA0 files to try to return the computer to the successful previous startup. This is essentially the same process used in Windows NT/2000 (not Windows XP) as the "Last Known Good" hardware profile.

If Windows 9x is unable to start correctly, it tries to start in Safe Mode. If the problem is something that Windows can recognize clearly enough to start the session, the Registry files are *not* copied to the .DA0 names. In some situations you can manually copy the previously good .DA0 files to .DAT names, and start Windows again. However, not all problems are recognized by Windows's limited recovery capabilities.

Don't rely on the .DA0 files as a backup of the Registry. If you do, it's easy to start the computer and create a bad SYSTEM.DAT file, which copies to the SYSTEM.DA0 file along with the bad information. If the computer locks up and is rebooted, the bad SYSTEM.DA0 can copy over the bad SYSTEM.DAT and cause the same problem, leaving two copies of the bad Registry file. Then your only recourse is the SYSTEM.1ST file, which has only original configuration information—no changes that have been made since the original installation.

To be safe, and to provide the most convenient and speedy recovery from inadvertent or random corruption of the Registry, keep the following points in mind:

➤ Always keep backups of the latest successful Registry—SYSTEM.DAT and USER.DAT—somewhere other than in the \Windows folder.

➤ SYSTEM.1ST is a last-resort backup of the first configuration file created following a successful first-time installation on a given computer. If this file doesn't work, you're probably going to have to reinstall everything on the computer (Windows, and all the software that's been added since the last installation).

➤ SYSTEM.1ST is located in the root directory of the bootable partition.

➤ SYSTEM.DAT and USER.DAT are located in the WINDOWS subdirectory.

➤ SYSTEM.DA0 and USER.DA0 are also located in the WINDOWS subdirectory (by default).

SYSTEM.DA0 is not the same as the automated backup copies made with SCANREGW.EXE, the Registry Scanner (Registry Repair utility). Remember that ScanReg creates Cabinet files, which are replaced on a daily basis. If you make a change to the system and it crashes a week later, none of the .CAB files will contain a Registry prior to the change. Another good idea is to copy the most recent, working .CAB file backup to a backup location.

Manual Registry Backups

To copy Registry files from a DOS command line, you must use the ATTRIB command to turn off the hidden, system, and read-only attributes. From within Windows Explorer, you can copy the files without adjusting the attributes. If you use the Explorer to copy the SYSTEM.DAT file, you must be sure to set the View Folder Options to show hidden files. From the main menu bar in the Explorer, choose View | Options | View tab and check the "Show All Files" button.

You should also have the option check box of the Explorer "View" tab set to show that Explorer will *not* "Hide MS-DOS extensions for file types that are registered." There are several files with the name SYSTEM.* and USER.* in the \Windows folder, but only the SYSTEM.DAT and USER.DAT are the current Registry file.

Each succeeding version of Windows uses a slightly different number of steps and check boxes to show all files. We don't list them every time, but you should modify a default installation for Windows 98, Windows 2000, and Windows XP, to show hidden files (and system files). Remember that the main difference is in language. Logically, "Don't hide files" is the same as "Show files."

ERU.EXE

The Emergency Recovery Utility (ERU.EXE) can be used to back up the Registry, but usually not to a floppy disk. SYSTEM.DAT is often larger than 1.4MB and, except for the most minimally configured computer, won't fit on a single floppy. However, ERU can copy specified system files to a different drive or directory, so using an Iomega Zip or Jaz disk will work. You can also copy critical Registry files to a different directory or partition on the hard drive.

Something else to consider is that archiving programs such as WinZip (Niko Mak Computing, Inc.) can spread a single file across multiple floppy disks. This is called "spanning," and you can store a very large SYSTEM.DAT file on multiple floppies by using this process. WinZip is available at **http://www.winzip.com**.

REGEDIT.EXE

REGEDIT.EXE (Registry Editor, or RegEdit) runs from the command line or a custom icon. It combines the Registry hives in a window that looks much like the Explorer, listing HKeys on the left pane, and the information within those keys in the right pane.

Although REGEDIT.EXE is installed to the \Windows folder during setup, Windows doesn't create a Desktop icon or menu entry anywhere on the Start Menu. You can create a shortcut in the %Windir%\Start Menu\Accessories\System Tools folder, which gives you access to the editor from the menu. Keep in mind that this may not be such a good idea if novice users with an adventurous spirit have access to that computer.

%Windir%

We've mentioned system variables in previous chapters, but you're likely to encounter the concept on the Internet whenever you search for problem resolutions. DOS and Windows both store certain variables in the *environment*, which the system uses to provide settings and parameters to other programs. For example, Windows uses the **\Temp** folder to store temporary files during installations. The **TEMP=**(folder) variable tells Windows where that temporary folder is located. Remember that you can open a command-line window or a DOS window, and type **SET** at the command prompt to see the environment, its variables, and their settings. (Type **SET > PRN** and press Enter, to send a report of the environment variables to the printer.)

Variables are often set in AUTOEXEC.BAT files, or in properties-configuration dialog boxes. Variables are also set by Windows itself, or by the installation routine for other software program. The variable name can be anything, and follows the **SET** command. However, when a program references that variable name *outside* the environment, a pair of percent characters surrounds the name. Problem-resolution documents often use this method to reference a folder name or pathname, where the actual information varies according to someone's computer setup. So for example, %SystemRoot% is a global reference to the environment variable that stores the "root" (top) Windows program folder. In most default situations that folder is C:\Windows.

An example of this usage would be where a Web page states, "This program can be found in the %systemroot%\System32 folder." What it means is that you replace %systemroot% with the Windows installation folder on your specific machine. Then the System32 folder is a child folder for wherever the Windows folder happens to be on your system. MSDOS.SYS contains a line that sets a **WinBootDir** variable to some location. This is the Windows start location folder. However, to reference that variable in a batch file or reference manual, we would call it %WinBootDir%. Remember that whatever is inside the percent signs is the variable name. That name is then replaced by its setting, whenever the variable is used (called). For example, "Go to the %temp% folder," might translate to "Go to the d:\windows\temp folder."

Working with the Registry requires a serious amount of caution, as accidental changes can lead to a total reinstallation. Unlike word processors, changes in the Registry take place as soon as the Enter key is pressed. Some important points to remember about changes in the Registry include the following:

▶ The Registry is changed directly by changes to the Control Panel or some other Windows applets.

▶ The Registry is also changed directly by REGEDIT.EXE or a third-party application specifically designed to edit the .DAT files. (Windows 2000 and NT prefer that you work with REGEDT32.EXE.)

▶ Some installation routines use .INF (program INFormation) files to write changes to the Registry automatically.

➤ Changes to the Registry take place immediately and are written to the SYSTEM.DAT and USER.DAT files without requiring use of a typical File | Save option.

➤ The *only* way to undo a change in the Registry is to re-edit the line that was changed, copy a previous version of the .DAT file over the newly changed version, or import a previously saved exported segment. (Exporting a section you're about to edit is a good protection habit to build.)

Unless you know exactly what you're doing, you shouldn't edit the Registry. Use the Control Panel interface to make changes to the system. As always, before you install any new software, or any new hardware device, you should make a safe backup of the existing SYSTEM.DAT file and USER.DAT file, or create a Restore Point.

Bizarre and amazing changes to Windows can occur with the installation of any new component. Sound cards and their drivers are a wonderful example of this. Sometimes, mystical gremlins can knock out a piece of hardware for no apparent reason whatsoever. Backing up the Registry to another directory (such as REG_BACK) or partition is simple to do, and can save you hours (if not days) of time recovering from a corrupted Registry.

Summary—Windows Registry

Most of the Windows questions we found on the operating system exam had to do with general concepts, critical files, and menu navigation steps to arrive at troubleshooting areas. You should understand the basic idea of the Windows Registry and the basics of FAT32 (discussed later in this chapter). The most important points of the preceding section include

➤ Understanding .INI files, and knowing what the WIN.INI and SYSTEM.INI files do

➤ Remembering the two critical Registry files (SYSTEM.DAT and USER.DAT), and knowing that they are hidden files

➤ OLE (Object Linking and Embedding) and .LNK files (shortcuts)

➤ The main list of HKeys, and the fact that the Registry looks a lot like the Explorer folder (or tree) view

➤ Understanding why REGEDIT and REGEDT32, the two Registry editors, exist and what their intended uses are

You should understand the way Windows 98 makes backups of the Registry when it starts, and the various copies of SYSTEM.DAT. In most cases, if you know the main filename, the list of responses to exam questions will give you clues as to the other filenames (see Chapter 1 and the Sample Hardware Test for exam strategies). This also works with the Registry keys, for the most part. If you know the main HKey_Local_Machine and HKey_Users, the exam doesn't try to trip you up with phony names—at least not from what we saw.

Installing Windows 95, 98, and Me

Windows (all versions later than Windows 3.x) provides two types of installation methods—the *upgrade* and *full* versions. An upgrade installation requires the computer to have a licensed copy of Windows previously installed, whereas the full installation doesn't require a previous copy of Windows. Both formats required a logical partition with some amount of free space.

Windows 9x requires 32MB of free space on a FAT32 partition. Windows XP requires 212MB of free space, also on a FAT32 partition. Converting a partition to NTFS takes place after the XP installation files have been copied to the FAT32 partition. If a previous version of Windows doesn't exist on the hard drive, the Windows Update Setup program pauses to ask you to insert a licensed copy of Windows (full version) in the CDROM drive before continuing.

 Even as early as Windows 98, OEM suppliers had access only to the full version of Windows. At the time, computer dealers would make their brand modifications to the original Microsoft Windows and include the operating system on a recovery disk (disk image). Microsoft has been exerting more effort to move vendors away from providing any type of Windows installation capability at all, leaving the customer with only the recovery disk. Who's to say whether this will eventually increase Microsoft's sales figures? You should carefully check with the vendor before you decide to buy a "ready-to-go" computer, as you might uncover a hidden additional cost if you have to purchase an installable version of the operating system.

CDROM Device Drivers

Most PCs have a BIOS-compatible CDROM drive, meaning that the motherboard BIOS will recognize a CD drive during the POST. On older machines, the CDROM drive requires a device driver, loaded with the operating system. Where Windows is running smoothly, it handles the CDROM device with its internal list of device drivers. Many computer vendors don't include any external device driver for the CDROM drive—assuming that Windows will never crash. But if the hard drive totally crashes and you have to reformat the drive, how will you use the CDROM drive to install Windows from a CDROM?

The full installation version of Windows 9x included a bootable 3.5-inch disk for partitioning and formatting, but didn't include the CDROM device drivers. Nowadays, all installation versions come on CDROM disks, with no bootable floppies at all. It's good practice to maintain a separate DOS system disk with the CDROM device driver for the installed drive. Windows 98 provides the Emergency Startup Disk, and you'll find it very useful, even on an XP machine.

The Windows 98SE emergency diskette uses generic CDROM drivers, and generally provides access to most CDROM drives. You can create an EBD from any Windows 98 machine and use it to boot just about any other PC. From there, you can install whichever version of Windows is required.

The best way to ensure that you can reinstall Windows is to re-partition the disk with at least a second partition for the installation files. Partitions can be independently formatted, meaning that if you have a C: and a D: partition, you can reformat the C: drive, if you have to, leaving the D: drive untouched. This is particularly useful for laptop computers, or any other situation where you can't access a bootable CDROM installation disk. A secondary advantage is that using Add/Remove Programs to install various Windows components is a lot faster from a hard disk partition than a CD. (This process works just as well with Windows XP.)

Installation Phases

Nowadays, it's almost impossible to demonstrate a generic installation. For that reason, we'll present a generic Windows 9x installation here, and a generic Windows NT/2000/XP installation in the next chapter.

 With the trend toward removing any installation and configuration control from individual users, purchasing an installation copy of the Windows operating system is becoming increasingly difficult. In many instances the only way to buy a copy of Windows 98 is through the so-called gray market (OEM versions sold at flea markets and swap meets), or online. You'll often be able to purchase an original "recovery" disk or "system disk" from the vendor's online site. However, they aren't always inexpensive.

The four main phases for installing Windows 9x are as follows:

1. The startup and information-gathering phase
2. The hardware detection phase

3. The copying and expanding files phase

4. The final system configuration phase

Startup and Information-Gathering Phase

When SETUP.EXE runs from a DOS prompt, the program searches all local (mounted) drives (volumes) for any previous version of Windows. The program assumes that an existing copy of DOS is on the bootable hard drive. (Windows 2000 introduced bootable CDROM installation.) If a previous version of Windows is found, one of two things happens, depending on whether this was an upgrade or a full installation version of Windows. If it was an upgrade version, Setup pauses, and then suggests running Setup from within Windows. With a full installation version, Setup quits, and then displays an error message that a previous copy of Windows was found. The suggestion to run Setup from within Windows can be bypassed.

It may come in handy to know that Setup looks only for WIN.COM (or sometimes WINVER.EXE) to determine whether a previous version of Windows exists on the drive. If you need to reinstall an upgrade version of Windows 9x, it's less messy and you can save a lot of time by just copying WIN.COM to a C:\WINDOWS directory, and then running the Windows Setup. In fact, you can create a WIN.COM file with any editor. Windows 9x doesn't care what's in the file, only that the filename exists.

If you need to reinstall a Windows 9x system from the full installation version CD, you can just delete or rename WIN.COM to something like WIN.CEM and run Setup. The installation routine won't detect the presence of the previous Windows installation, even though all the files are sitting right there on the hard drive.

As Phase 1 continues, Setup runs the DOS version of SCANDISK.EXE (located on the installation disk). ScanDisk looks at the hard drive to make sure that it's running correctly and that it meets the minimum requirements (such as enough memory, modern CPU, and disk space). If any of the setup requirements is missing, the installation quits.

The rest of Phase 1 checks for extended memory and runs an XMS memory manager if one isn't running. If you don't remember what an XMS manager is, go back and read Chapter 13. Setup installs HIMEM.SYS if no other extended memory manager is found. Setup then checks main memory for any existing terminate-and-stay resident programs (TSRs) that are known to cause problems, and then pauses to warn you before proceeding.

Test-Taking Note

Please observe that you just saw an example of a test-taking strategy. In the previous "Phase 1" paragraph, you encountered the XMS acronym with no spell-out or reference. To introduce some confusion, we suggested that you go back and read another chapter in this book. Immediately following that suggestion, you were given the fact that HIMEM.SYS is an extended memory manager. Aside from the clue of eXtended Memory, the sentence stated that HIMEM.SYS is an "other" extended memory manager. If you use your head, you'll see that XMS apparently refers to extended memory. This is how you can use some of the questions on the exam to respond correctly to other questions.

Windows 9x requires extended memory—XMS. If no other memory management program is loaded, Setup installs HIMEM.SYS, and IO.SYS loads HIMEM every time the system starts. Remember that XMS is different from EMS (expanded memory).

When the GUI starts, the Installation Wizard begins prompting the user for which components to install, and for various networking options. It asks for user information, registration information, and in which directory (on what drive) to install Windows. When all the questions have been answered, the Installation Wizard moves on to the next phase.

Hardware Detection Phase

At this point, Plug and Play and the concept of VxDs (virtual device drivers) come into effect. Setup checks the entire system for hardware and peripherals attached to the computer. It also checks the system resources for I/O addresses, IRQs, and DMAs. This is where Windows begins to build the first Registry.

PnP is a standards specification that attempts to remove IRQ and DMA conflicts among hardware devices. PnP data must be built in to both the ROM BIOS on a motherboard and a BIOS chip on the device. Finally, the operating system must be able to read the BIOS data and work with it for configuration purposes. Three things are necessary for Plug and Play: a chipset BIOS, device compatibility, and a PnP operating system.

PnP devices let Windows know what they are, and which resources they need in order to run. For non-PnP devices, Windows looks at I/O ports and specific memory addresses, compares them against a database of known devices, and then makes a best guess. Otherwise, Windows 9x queries the DMI Pool and CMOS for all installed devices and their configurations. This same hardware detection process is used from the Control Panel under the "Add

New Hardware" option when any new hardware device is added to the computer.

 If the Device Manager shows a question mark indicator for a particular device, it doesn't necessarily mean the device is having a problem. It may only mean that Windows was unable to find the specific driver information in its PnP database.

Copying and Expanding Files Phase

A number of *archiving programs* have been developed over time to pack as many files as possible onto a relatively small floppy disk. These programs (for example, PKZip, Extract, and LHArc) change the form of a file to reduce its size (file compression). Microsoft uses EXTRACT.EXE (found in \Windows\Command\) to return these stored programs back to their original sizes. In other words, you can't use the COPY command to install any version of Windows, because the files on the installation disks are in archived form.

The File Copy phase uses a list of files that was created during the hardware detection phase, depending on which components should be installed. Windows then copies all necessary files to the destination directory and extracts them to their full executable size. Setup then runs various .DLL files, both to create directories that might not exist and to install the selected features and capabilities.

Windows 98 Emergency Boot Disk (EBD)

The Installation Wizard offers the user the option to make a "Startup" disk during the files expansion step of the installation. Technically called the Emergency Boot Disk, the user can make a disk at this time, or bypass the option. If the option is bypassed, you can make a startup disk at any time by using the "Add/Remove Software" applet in Control Panel. The EBD requires a minimum of 1.2MB of storage.

The EBD is designed mainly for troubleshooting the Windows 9x program and system. Many users think that the disk enables them to start their computers in DOS Mode and to access the regular features and configuration of their PCs. This supposition is wrong, although the same thinking might apply to the Recovery Console. When you think DOS, also think Recovery Console. Emergency disks might get you to DOS, but they won't actually load Windows, regardless of what messages show on the monitor.

The "Startup" disk assumes that Windows is available on the hard drive, but isn't starting for some reason. A major difference between the Windows 98

EBD and a Windows XP/2000 start disk is that the EBD can actually boot the computer into a useable DOS operating system. The XP disk provides only the NT Loader, which must have a boot manager either on the hard drive or on an installation CD in a visible drive.

The files on the Windows 98 startup disk (some of which are in a .CAB file) include the bootable system files (COMMAND.COM, IO.SYS, and MSDOS.SYS), along with FDISK, FORMAT, EDIT, SYS.COM, and a few other files for low-level access to partitioning and reformatting. Note that the copies of IO.SYS and MSDOS.SYS are the startup files for Windows 9x, but that they're not the same files that started DOS 6.x and earlier.

One of the CompTIA objectives for the software module of the exam refers to RAMDRIVE.SYS. This is a software driver file that creates a RAM drive—a virtual logical drive created in system memory. The Windows 98 EBD sets up this RAM drive because there isn't enough room on a 1.44MB floppy disk for all the necessary emergency tools and utilities. After the RAM drive has been "mounted" (set up as visible), AUTOEXEC.BAT calls another program to expand the files in the EBD.CAB file.

We strongly encourage you to use a Windows 98 system to create a Startup diskette. Use any working machine, or set up a multiple-boot system on your computer and install Windows 98 on a separate partition. Windows XP and Windows 2000 make this type of setup very easy. After you've created the diskette, go in and examine the CONFIG.SYS file to see an example of a complex configuration file. Do the same for the AUTOEXEC.BAT file. These three tips will give you a well-rounded understanding of DOS, particularly geared toward the types of questions you'll encounter on the exam.

First Restart

Windows 9x keeps track of start and restart events, both during installation and with each new session. During an installation, and following a successful first-time restart of the computer, Windows makes further updates to the configuration of the system through the following process:

1. WINIT.EXE processes three sections of the WINIT.INI file (`arial.win`, `user32.tmp`, and `logo.sys`) to create a combined VMM32.VXD with all the VxDs needed by the specific computer.

2. SYSTEM.DAT is renamed SYSTEM.DA0, and SYSTEM.NEW is renamed SYSYTEM.DAT.

3. The Registry flag (indicator) is set to indicate that this is the first time Windows is being run following a new installation.

4. The "Run Once" module is run to configure printers, MIDI, and PCMCIA devices (on a new computer), and to run any new hardware manufacturers' custom setup programs.

5. If the installation was done over a pre-existing Windows 3.x system, GRPCONV.EXE converts all Program Groups and Program Items from the previous version of Windows to Windows 9x format and renames the files to use Long File Names.

An installation may not necessarily install and configure a printer. If this happens, you can go to the Control Panel and open the Printers icon, and then choose "Add Printer" ("Printers and Faxes" in XP). It's sometimes a good idea to install a Generic Printer and set the printer port (under Device Options) to FILE. This way, you can easily send a print job to a .PRN file and import the results into another application.

Installation Log Files

Windows uses a number of *log files* for tracking the state of applications and the way in which the applications load. These states are generated through error codes, and the log files contain messages written to the files by the error codes. A "good" or successful code can still be understood as an error code. During installation, even with custom choices and settings offered by the Installation Wizard, Windows still fails to install many of the additional utilities that come on the installation disks or CDROM.

The files in the root directory that Windows 9x Setup uses to track installation and successful configuration are

➤ *SETUPLOG.TXT*—Setup sequence and pass/fail

➤ *DETLOG.TXT*—Hardware detection log file

➤ *NETLOG.TXT*—Networking setup log file

➤ *DETCRASH.LOG*—Hardware detection failure/crash log

➤ *BOOTLOG.TXT*—Success/fail boot sequence log

DETLOG.TXT keeps track of what hardware devices are found on the system. BOOTLOG.TXT keeps track of the first startup process and the success or failure of each step.

If the Startup Menu key is pressed (F8 or Ctrl), BOOTLOG.TXT can be changed to reflect the current startup, and the previous version is overwritten. To keep a copy of the original installation startup sequence, copy BOOTLOG.TXT to another name (for example, FIRSTBOOT.TXT).

Windows Setup tracks each phase of an installation and makes success or fail notations in SUWARN.BAT (SetUp WARNings BATch file). Setup also makes notations in the AUTOEXEC.BAT prior to a successful complete installation. Much of the moment-by-moment installation process is tracked in SETUPLOG.TXT and DETCRASH.LOG (detect crash) in case the setup crashes. If the installation and setup are successful, DETCRASH.LOG is deleted.

The Windows 9x Setup can fail at three points:

➤ When insufficient, incorrect, or unavailable system resources are detected during SETUP.EXE in Real Mode

➤ When a crash occurs during the hardware detection phase, creating DETCRASH.LOG

➤ When a device stops working following hardware detection

Setup uses SETUPLOG.TXT to list information about the steps in the installation, including their sequence and the error information returned at the end of the step (whether it completed successfully or why not). In case of a failed setup, Windows uses SETUPLOG.TXT to bypass the steps that completed successfully, and continues only with the steps that failed.

If the installation fails, the process is designed to continue from a restart of the computer. Rather than reformat the drive and reinstall from the beginning, restart the computer and let Windows Setup pick up where it left off, trying to correct the installation problem itself.

Starting Windows 9x

No matter which operating system you use, ROM BIOS runs the POST routine when the computer is first turned on. Everything that applies to a plain DOS computer applies to a Windows computer. The bootstrap loader looks to the boot sector of the Primary, Active partition (the boot partition) for instructions on how to start whatever operating system is installed on that partition.

Windows looks in the boot sector, where it finds IO.SYS. Windows NT and OS/2 can be booted from the *boot track*, making it possible to boot them from a different partition than the Primary, Active one; however, note that Windows NT/2000 still run the NT Loader that looks in the boot track. In Windows 9x, the "Starting Windows 9x..." message is displayed on the screen following the initial POST and parity check, and is written into IO.SYS.

Pressing F8 between the "Starting Windows 9x..." message and the Windows logo splash screen interrupts the boot process and allows you to choose various options from a Startup menu (more on this shortly).

A "splash screen" is jargon for anything that appears on the screen prior to the actual program environment. This can often be a corporate logo, a shareware registration screen, or simply a notification screen that the program is still being prepared to run.

DOS

If you remember the DOS boot sequence, you'll recognize IO.SYS as one of the system files in the DOS startup trio. IO.SYS starts DOS in Real Mode. IO.SYS in Windows 9x does the same thing: It sets up the segment addressing in conventional memory, and loads Real Mode device drivers into the first segment of memory (low memory). IO.SYS then reads MSDOS.SYS (or an existing CONFIG.SYS file).

Windows 9x uses a preliminary hardware profile from the hardware detection phase to attempt to start the computer (for example, interrupts, BIOS serial and parallel ports, and CMOS or BIOS system board identification). After the computer is started for the first time, the Registry tells Windows which settings to use at startup. IO.SYS reads the MSDOS.SYS file to process specific devices, and reads the Registry (SYSTEM.DAT) for device settings.

MSDOS.SYS

Whether or not CONFIG.SYS, AUTOEXEC.BAT, or both exist, IO.SYS reads the MSDOS.SYS file first and reads it again for VxDs and other configuration settings. MSDOS.SYS is a plain ASCII text file that can be edited by DOS's EDIT.COM or Microsoft's WordPad. The two important points to remember are that all attributes are set on the file, making it hidden, system, and read-only, and that the file must stay the same size.

The MSDOS.SYS file tells Windows about different startup options, menus, in which mode to start, and whether the Windows GUI is supposed to start at all following boot up. If you press and hold the Shift key before the Windows splash screen instead of the F8 key, MSDOS.SYS is bypassed and not read at all.

Windows 9x Logo Files

The Windows startup process includes the use of various graphic files known as logo files or splash screens. You might find a question on the exam having to do with these files. (Windows XP uses a different method to generate the Welcome screen.) Three separate files are used during the startup and shutdown process:

➤ *LOGO.SYS*—The image file with the Microsoft Windows logo.

➤ *LOGOW.SYS*—The image file that says, "Windows xx is shutting down."

➤ *LOGOS.SYS*—An image file with text telling you that "It is now safe to turn off your computer."

 Windows uses a separate image file to produce the "Starting Windows for the first time" message during an installation.

If these files are not present in the \Windows folder, the same information is contained within IO.SYS, in text form. Previous to Windows 95, IO.SYS contained the message "Starting MS-DOS…". When you use the Emergency Boot Disk, you'll also see the message "Starting Windows xx…" (where "xx" is the version of Windows). This text message, as well as "You may now turn off your computer" are also built into IO.SYS. If the logo files are accessible to IO.SYS, they'll be used. If not, IO.SYS creates the "Starting Windows" image out of internal components.

 The final shutdown screen is actually one of two graphics image files and can be changed. These files are located initially in your Windows folder. LOGOW.SYS is the one that reads "Please wait while…," and LOGOS.SYS is the one that reads "It is now safe to…" Make backup copies of the files LOGOW.SYS and LOGOS.SYS in a safe place, and then copy the two originals into a temporary folder.

These files are standard bitmaps, so rename the extensions of these duplicates to .BMP. You can use any graphics editor to edit these files, such as Microsoft Paint, Photoshop, or Paint Shop Pro. The files are 256-color windows bitmaps (RGB-encoded, but not RGB color), 320×400. Because the aspect ratio (width/height) of these files are not the standard 4:3, like most computer screens, the bitmaps will appear vertically elongated.

To make your new design conform to this aspect ratio, resize the bitmap to 534×400 while you're working on it. Make sure to resize them back to 320×400 when you're finished. Save your changes, and rename the extensions of your new files back to .SYS. Last, copy the new files back into your Windows folder.

WIN.COM

If MSDOS.SYS is configured to start Windows, it runs WIN.COM and loads Windows. MSDOS.SYS also contains path locations for important Windows files, including where to find the Registry. To enable the F4 short-cut key option of running a previous version of DOS, the directive BootMulti= must have the value 1 (BootMulti=1) in the [Options] section of

MSDOS.SYS. Windows 2000 made this entire process of using different operating systems on the same hard drive much easier.

ATTRIB Problems

ATTRIB is very explicit in its syntax. If you want to change the SHR (System, Hidden, Read-only) attributes of the MSDOS.SYS file, you must include a space between each reference to a specific bit. In other words, enter the command **ATTRIB -S -H -R msdos.sys** and be very sure to include the spaces between -s and -H and -R. Otherwise, you'll get a "Parameter format not correct -shr" error message.

Oddly enough, ATTRIB is not consistent (is anything from Microsoft?) in its capability to modify multiple archive bits. In certain instances, you may get an error message: "Not resetting" a particular archive bit. In other situations, you may get an "Invalid path" error message. Keep in mind that if more than one attribute is set, you may not be able to change the R, H, or S bit. Try changing all the bits at the same time for a particular file.

BootGUI=0

This section may seem to be much ado about nothing, but you should try to set up a Windows 98 machine to boot to DOS without loading the Windows Desktop. Then, figure out how to start Windows. Finally, shut down the machine a couple of times to see whether Windows hangs during the process. If it does, work out why. After you've resolved the problem, re-edit MSDOS.SYS, but don't use Windows to do it. Realize that you'll have practiced most of the critical command-line activities you'll find on the exam. You can do this on an old Pentium 133 test machine, which you can pick up at a flea market for around $100 (or less).

To boot directly into DOS, you must first change the Logo= and BootGUI= options from 1 to 0. Inside the editable area of the file, you'll find various types of information. Most of the listings under the [Options] heading aren't present in the default MSDOS.SYS file, but must be manually created. The complete listing looks something like the following:

```
[Paths]
WinDir=C:\WINDOWS
WinBootDir=C:\WINDOWS
HostWinBootDrv=C

[Options]
Autoscan=0
BootGUI=0
BootKeys=1
BootMenu=1
BootMenuDefault=1
BootMenuDelay=5
```

```
BootMulti=1
BootWin=1
DblSpace=0
DisableLog=1
DoubleBuffer=0
DrvSpace=0
Logo=1
SystemReg=0
WinVer=4.10.2222
;
;The following lines are required
➥for compatibility with
➥other programs.
;Do not remove them (MSDOS.SYS needs
➥to be >1024 bytes).
;xxxxxxxxxxxxxxxxxxxxxxxxxxxxxxxxxx
➥xxxxxxxxxxxxxxxxxxxxxxxxxxxxxxxxxxa
```

In a nutshell, you must turn off the Logo=1 line by making it Logo=0. Additionally, you must change the BootGUI= line to 0. Finally, after Windows 9x has run and then been shut down, the "now safe" text message may have an odd bug where it refuses to go away. In our experience, simply renaming the LOGOS.SYS file to something like LOGOS@.SYS forces Windows to exit to a clean DOS environment. It makes little sense to boot to a DOS environment if running and exiting Windows won't return you to a working DOS environment. One good source for MSDOS.SYS information can be found at http://members.aol.com/axcel216/msdos.htm (as of the writing of this book).

It may also help to start Windows from a batch file. One of the interesting features of batch files is that the system remembers that a batch file was running when it called another program—even with Windows. If you use WIN.COM in a batch file, and have additional command lines (such as CLS to clear the screen) after the WIN command, in many cases this will also help to bypass the glitch with an exit to plain DOS.

Windows Me

Windows Me does not allow booting to DOS (otherwise known as DOS 8.0) or using the Shut Down feature to go to MS-DOS Mode. As with almost anything, this can be overridden if you know what you're doing. Windows Me uses a file called WINBOOT.INI to bypass MSDOS.SYS. The two files must be exactly the same, so you can edit an existing MSDOS.SYS file and copy it over to WINBOOT.INI to modify how Windows Me starts up.

With Windows XP coming preinstalled on most of today's computers, Windows Me—an interim release of Windows, between 98 and 2000—has become a bizarre footnote in history. As far as we can see, one of the failed experiments Microsoft tried in the "Millennium Edition" was to forcibly steal control of the user's computer and disallow any possibility of accidentally corrupting the program. Unfortunately, this also made it almost impossible for knowledgeable

technicians to effect any repairs on a misbehaving operating system. We discuss Windows Me
to a limited degree in this book, but because Microsoft itself has discontinued support, we try
to cover only the most necessary aspects.

We've pointed out how Windows Me redirects the startup process from MSDOS.SYS to
WINBOOT.INI. This is much like the way it "watches" the installation of any new device driver
or application software. Although the installation process is allowed to run in a normal fashion,
modifying WIN.INI, SYSTEM.INI, or other configuration files, Windows Me then steps in and
takes those settings into itself. After the Registry has been modified, Me then comments out
the original configuration lines and bypasses the configuration files. This is one of the main reasons why there were so many crashes when anyone tried to add or remove anything on a
Windows Me system.

Virtual Device Drivers

Remember that Windows 9x was an interim interface that was trying to keep
compatible with 16-bit Windows 3.x and DOS Real Mode applications.
Microsoft was also trying to induce programmers to write programs in the
32-bit Windows NT format. The resulting combination of 16-bit Windows,
DOS, Windows NT, and 32-bit Windows 9x is confusing, which is why
Microsoft changed the name of the operating system to Windows 2000.
Following any Real Mode device drivers, Windows 9x loads any *static* VxDs
required by 16-bit programs.

Virtual device drivers were first introduced in Windows 3.1, where they were
loaded into memory and remained there throughout the session, making
them static (not moving). Windows 9x *dynamic* VxDs can be loaded into
memory and then unloaded when a program terminates, if the VxD is no
longer needed. Just as in Windows 3.1x, the executable Virtual Machine
Manager (VMM) runs, but this time VMM32.VXD includes both a Real
Mode loader and the VMM, as well as common, static VxDs from 16-bit
format (in MRCI2.VXD).

VMM32.VXD is a combination file with many common VxD files bound up
inside it. Typical VxD files are about 80KB, and typical VMM32.VXD files
are about 650KB. The devices found inside this file were once loaded in the
[386Enh] section of the SYSTEM.INI file. Windows 9x first checks the
WINDOWS\SYSTEM\VMM32 directory for any 32-bit VXD files, rather
than the VxDs bound in VMM32.VXD. If it finds any newer files, it loads
them from that folder.

The Windows Update Manager (discussed later in this chapter) can access Internet Web sites for updated .DLLs and .VXD files.

Assuming Windows finds no later-version virtual device drivers in the VMM32 folder, VMM32.VXD loads static device drivers found in the DEVICE= line of the SYSTEM.INI file (which still comes with Windows 9x). The actual devices load from within VMM32, but show in the SYSTEM.INI file for backward compatibility.

The Registry contains entries for every .VXD file and, through its processing, controls VMM32.VXD. The Registry also contains entries for every virtual device driver that isn't directly associated with a piece of hardware. If two devices have a conflict at load time, the VxD in the SYSTEM.INI DEVICE= takes precedence over the one specified by the Registry. If the device can't be found, an error occurs.

As Windows starts up, the following three files are run in the sequence listed here (note the continued use of WIN.COM and SYSTEM.INI):

1. *WIN.COM*—Controls the initial environment checks and loads the core Windows 95 components

2. *VMM32.VXD*—Creates the virtual machine (VM) and installs all VxDs

3. *SYSTEM.INI*—Is read for DEVICE= entries, which may differ from the Registry entries

Final Steps to Loading Windows 9x

To ensure backward compatibility, Windows 9x loads in the same way that Windows 3.x loads. One of the primary differences is that Windows 9x runs DOS programming code under a *virtual* 8086 machine rather than a Real Mode machine. Keep in mind that Windows NT/2000/XP ended all support for this Real Mode (although it's still necessary at the CPU level, to start a machine).

After the installation is complete and Windows 9x starts from the hard disk, it goes back and checks to see whether it has a matching internal 32-bit VxD for any static device drivers in memory. If it does, Windows comments out the original device's line in either CONFIG.SYS or AUTOEXEC.BAT. Windows 9x uses the following steps to start:

1. When the startup process calls WIN.COM, the SYSTEM.INI file is read for Real Mode device drivers, and the SYSTEM.DAT file is read for the rest of the device configurations. In other words, Windows 9x reads both the Windows 3.x .INI files and the Registry .DAT files as it loads. Most of the devices and their configuration are installed from the SYSTEM.DAT file, but SYSTEM.INI is still read first.

2. Following the SYSTEM.INI and SYSTEM.DAT processing, WIN.INI is read for associated resources and environment values such as fonts, wallpaper, associated file extensions, and so on. After WIN.INI has been processed, the USER.DAT file is read.

3. If networking has been enabled, Windows reads the USER.DAT file after the WIN.INI file for Desktop configurations. Sometimes USER.DAT and networking are used on standalone machines to maintain consistencies throughout a corporate environment. At home, networking can be enabled to allow individual family members their own customized Desktop.

4. Finally, the SHELL= line in SYSTEM.INI is run to load EXPLORER.EXE (Windows 9x only), assuming that no other shell has been specified in a default installation. (Windows NT/XP install the Desktop completely differently.)

Loading Device Drivers

We've said that Windows 9x continues to use IO.SYS to begin the startup process and initiate Real Mode. (If the computer is started under a previous version of DOS, IO.SYS is renamed WINBOOT.SYS.) Even in DOS 6.x, IO.SYS had rudimentary capabilities built into it to handle some of the basic directives (command lines) of the CONFIG.SYS file. However, the program wasn't ready to assume full control until Windows 95.

The Windows 9x IO.SYS finally took over from CONFIG.SYS and loads HIMEM.SYS, IFSHLP.SYS, SETVER.EXE, and DBLSPACE.BIN or DRVSPACE.BIN by default, if they exist (see Table 14.1). Additionally, the DOS 7.0 version includes defaults for all the old CONFIG.SYS directives, such as FILES, BUFFERS, COUNTRY, and SETVER.

Table 14.1	The Common Device Directives That Moved from CONFIG.SYS to IO.SYS
DEVICE=	**Description**
DOS=HIGH	IO.SYS does not load EMM386.EXE. (If this expanded memory manager is found in an existing CONFIG.SYS file, the UMB line is added.)
HIMEM.SYS	Real Mode memory manager to access extended memory; part of IO.SYS by default.
IFSHLP.SYS	Installable File System Helper that loads device drivers and allows the system to make file system connections from within Windows to the DOS file management I/O.
SETVER.EXE	To maintain backward compatibility with some older TSRs that won't run under newer versions of COMMAND.COM; optional and usually not necessary.
FILES=	60 (default). Included for compatibility; specifies how many files can be open at any one time during an MS-DOS session; not required by Windows 95 and later.
BUFFERS=	30 (default). Specifies the number of file buffers; used by IO.SYS calls from DOS and Windows 3.x programs.
STACKS=	9,256 (default). The number and size of the stack frames that the CPU uses during prioritization of incoming interrupts; used for backward compatibility; not required by Windows 95 and later.
SHELL=	C:\COMMAND.COM /p indicates which command processor to use (for example, NDOS or DRDOS); not the same as the SHELL= line in SYSTEM.INI. (If the directive is used, but the /p switch is not used, AUTOEXEC.BAT is not processed. /p makes the command processor permanent in the environment.)
FCBS=	4 (default). A very old method of controlling open files (file control blocks); necessary only with DOS programs designed for DOS 2.x and earlier.

NOTE

CONFIG.SYS ordinarily doesn't use a **SHELL=** directive because the default assumption of the system is that COMMAND.COM is used and found on the boot disk. This directive is used primarily to increase the DOS environment space, and in that case, the **/p** switch must be included, as noted in Table 14.1. We discuss the DOS environment in Chapter 12.

To change a DEVICE setting from the default within IO.SYS, create a CONFIG.SYS file and use the same DEVICE= directive, but with a different setting. For example, FILES=100 would override the default FILES directive in IO.SYS and change the default from 60 to 100 possible open files. Some final thoughts to keep in mind regarding IO.SYS:

➤ IO.SYS cannot be edited (unlike MSDOS.SYS).

➤ Directive values in CONFIG.SYS must be set to the default or higher in IO.SYS before their settings can be changed.

➤ EMM386.EXE can be loaded only in CONFIG.SYS for DOS, 16-bit Windows, and Windows 9x.

AUTOEXEC.BAT

Windows 9x specifically disables (with REM, or "remark") SMARTDRV, DBLBUFF.SYS, and MOUSE.SYS from any existing CONFIG.SYS, and disables any incompatible TSRs in an existing AUTOEXEC.BAT file by using an internal "known conflicts" list. It removes WIN and SHARE commands from an existing AUTOEXEC.BAT file, if they exist, and updates the PATH line.

> Before making updates to an existing AUTOEXEC.BAT, Windows copies the file to AUTOEXEC.DOS. One nice thing about having an AUTOEXEC.BAT file on a Windows machine is that it quickly helps to diagnose startup problems. Create a simple AUTOEXEC.BAT file with only the **PAUSE** batch command to pause the screen.
>
> You can use this AUTOEXEC.BAT file to pause the machine before starting Windows. If you see the **Press any key...** message, you know for a fact that the hardware and basic operating system is fine. If Windows won't start, you also know the problem is directly associated with Windows and not some other problem.

Devices loaded from CONFIG.SYS often require ancillary command-line switches in the AUTOEXEC.BAT file. An AUTOEXEC.BAT file is usually required to set the path to something other than the Windows default search path (C:\WINDOWS; C:\WINDOWS\COMMAND). Likewise, you can use the AUTOEXEC.BAT file to set the Temporary (TEMP) directory to something other than C:\WINDOWS\TEMP every time the machine starts.

Networking (on a Windows 9x machine) usually requires an AUTOEXEC.BAT file to run the command for NET START. However, because Windows is designed to handle many networking capabilities itself, it's usually better to create a separate batch file for starting the network and then place that file in the Windows Startup folder. Remember that along with .EXE and .COM, Windows considers files with a .BAT or .PIF extension as executable files. Generally, let Windows try to use one of its own VxDs for everything except the most ornery DOS-based Real Mode programs.

The Installable File System (IFS) Manager

DOS has always had the 8.3 filename structure. Although the creative use of directory and subdirectory names can produce a lot of information about a file, Apple's method of using common English names has been easier for most users. Because of the way the DOS FAT works, the maximum limit for a filename, including all the directory information, is 64 characters. Windows 9x long filenames (LFN) allow up to 255 characters and can include previously illegal characters, such as <space> and the + symbol.

Novell's NetWare NOS created something called the "OS/2 name space" feature, which was designed to resolve conflicts between DOS and Apple computers running on the same network. If an Apple user saved a file as "1997 Third Quart Annual Report" and a DOS user opened and saved that file again, the Apple user might see "1997thir.dqa" as the new filename. NetWare and the OS/2 namespace helped resolve the abrupt cutting off (truncating) of anything after 11 characters.

Windows 9x uses something similar to the OS/2 namespace in that the Installable File System Manager (IFS Manager) works with VFAT (discussed next) to convert long filenames to the 8.3 names required by the underlying 16-bit FAT. IFS Manager also works the other way, in that a request for a short filename goes out to retrieve the correct long filename in the directory listing. The IFS Manager is loaded through a "helper file" called IFSHLP.SYS (in the Windows folder).

Filenaming *conventions* are voluntary ways of naming files. Filenaming *rules*, on the other hand, are statements of what characters may or may not be used in a filename. The exam may confuse you by using the term "convention" to mean "rule."

Remember that in DOS filenames, the <space>, plus, asterisk, question mark, and slashes are not allowed. Even though Windows 9x LFNs allow some of these illegal characters, our feeling is that the exam will test your knowledge of allowable characters rather than whether a certain name is possible under the extended capabilities of the long filename feature.

The Windows 9x IFS (again, Installable File System) is a way to store additional file information about LFNs, while allowing the DOS 16-bit FAT to control the location of the basic file clusters and sectors. Remember that part of a file system's job is to associate human names to a series of numbers that describe the cylinder, track, sectors, and clusters where data is physically stored. The file system is made up of four parts:

➤ IFS helper (IFSHLP.SYS), the Real Mode device driver that works as a go-between with either the VFAT or NTFS device driver to manage file operations

➤ IFS Manager device manager (IFSMGR.VXD, which works out the problems and differences between the file system and virtual device drivers

➤ File system–compatible device drivers (VxD files), which translate access to low-level disk devices, CDROM file systems, and network devices

➤ The block I/O subsystem, which deals directly with physical disks and a controller's firmware

People sometimes refer to FAT32, 32-bit FAT, VFAT, or even HPFS when discussing Windows 9x. "VFAT" stands for "Virtual FAT" and is part of the Installable File System. VFAT was first introduced in Windows for Workgroups 3.11, and then was tightened up in Windows 95. The IFSHELP.SYS driver reference in a CONFIG.SYS file refers to the prototype version of what went on to become the Windows 95 IFS Manager.

On the other hand, HPFS stands for *high-performance file system*, which was engineered into OS/2. Neither Windows 95 nor Windows NT uses nor currently supports the HPFS. Windows NT uses the NT File System (NTFS). For simplicity, we refer to the underlying 16-bit FAT as the *base file system*, the Windows 95 modification as the IFS, and any other file systems by their own names. Windows 95 uses a 32-bit VFAT that works in conjunction with the 16-bit base FAT controlled by DOS 7.0. The "32" in FAT32 refers to this VFAT.

You should understand that DOS was the model for the original file and storage system used with all IBM-compatible PCs. Also understand that a computer must work with both the operating system and various types of device-level program code to take what you write and convert it to something the computer can store. DOS and the File Allocation Table (FAT16) were so prevalent that every PC has built-in support at the lowest levels for this process. Windows NT and Windows 95 changed all that.

We're discussing the Installable File System because everything having to do with long filenames, in all later versions of Windows, requires something more than the most basic, system-level support. VFAT (used with FAT32 partitions) and NTFS (Windows NT/2000/XP) both work with necessary device driver files (.SYS files). The Virtual FAT system uses IFSMGR.VXD and VFAT.SYS. The NT File System uses NTFS.SYS, together with a hidden subfolder (`%SystemRoot%\System Volume Information`) and various tracking files called *metadata* (not on the exam).

The reason all this is so important is that whatever you do with filenames from a DOS prompt or in the Recovery Console doesn't give you any guarantee that the same names will translate back to Windows. It's also why you see two different representations of a filename: the Windows name, and the truncated "real" name. Always remember that Windows is doing a lot of behind-the-scenes work to offer the convenience of so-called descriptive filenames.

It isn't a particularly common problem, but Windows can develop some interesting problems if either the VFAT or NTFS becomes corrupted. Even without corruption, moving a file from one location to another in DOS can disconnect the actual filename from its Windows name. The NTFS is usually a lot better at maintaining its filename database integrity than other file systems, but it still can break.

NTFS is the Windows NT (New Technology) file system, whereas WINS is a Windows Internet naming system used for certain types of network protocols. Although we don't believe you'll see a question on the WINS or HPFS, you should make note of their names and abbreviations.

FAT32

Although Windows 95 was described as an operating system, the technical fact remained that Windows 95 required an underlying DOS 7.0, and used a 16-bit FAT for its file management system for backward compatibility with older DOS and Windows 3.11 systems. A second release of Windows 95 (Operating System Release 2, or B, known as OS/R-B) was only available as an OEM version. OS/R-B included a new 32-bit FAT. In fact, Windows 95 was more of an interface than an operating system. DOS was, and continues to be, the real operating system behind the entire Windows 9x family, with backward compatibility being the driving force.

Windows 95 OS/R-B, Windows 98, and Windows Me all included an option to format a FAT32 partition. FAT32 provides multi-threaded Protected Mode access to the disk through a Virtual File Allocation Table (VFAT) and a faster, more efficient method of disk caching. Windows 2000/XP supports both FAT32 and NTFS.

Always remember that Windows running in conjunction with NTFS can read both NTFS and FAT32 file systems. However, Windows (all versions) in a FAT32 partition cannot read NTFS file data. Consider the compatibility problem when you're setting up multiple operating systems on a single machine (or in certain networking situations). This same problem arises if Windows 2000 is using FAT32, but Windows XP is on an NTFS partition. Finally, FDISK.EXE can remove an NTFS partition by deleting the "Non-DOS" or "Unknown" partition.

VFAT is part of the Windows 9x Virtual Machine Manager (VMM) and uses the underlying FAT16 files structure. FAT32 is an actual enhancement to the underlying, disk-based file management system, being created through FDISK.EXE and taking place long before Windows ever loads. Keep in mind that versions of FDISK are not interchangeable. You must use the program that applies to the operating system you're going to install. FDISK for Windows 9x is not the same as the FDISK for OS/2, even if they have the same name. (Windows XP/2000 use DISKPART.EXE.)

FAT16 uses 16-bit numbers for cluster addressing. The maximum allowable size for a FAT16 partition is 65,536 clusters, or 2 gigabytes. (FAT32 allows for 8GB partitions.) Current systems routinely come installed with huge hard disks far larger than 2GB. However, after a disk has been partitioned as FAT32, it can't be easily changed back to FAT16.

Drive Converter (CVT.EXE)

Windows 98 provides "Drive Converter" as a conversion utility to convert an existing FAT16 to FAT32 without data loss. Windows 95, on the other hand, only allows for a drive to be set up with either FAT16 or FAT32 during the FDISK process. In other words, "Drive Converter" enables a file system conversion after the disk has been previously partitioned. Although the conversion utility allows a drive to be converted, you can't revert back to FAT16 without reformatting the partition. This is the same as converting a FAT32 partition to NTFS: It's a one-way street, on an existing volume.

Viewing a FAT32 or NTFS partition with FDISK will show that the partition is a "Non-DOS" partition. That could mean the partition is a FAT32 or NTFS partition, a Unix partition, or some other type of partition the 16-bit program can't describe. PowerQuest's "Partition Magic" is a much better tool for partitioning disks, viewing partition information, and for modifying partitions without reformatting the entire disk.

Network Redirectors

Applications, the operating system, or both, typically use Interrupt 21 to access the disk and file system. Networking operating system *redirectors* (residing in memory) and CDROM drivers keep an eye on Interrupt 21 and determine whether the file system request is for the base file system or for their own file systems. (Optical disks use a special type of file system.) A redirector grabs a request for the base file system and redirects the request to a different file system. Essentially, a redirector is like an executive secretary, watching the phone and directing calls either to the boss or to someone else in the company.

One problem with this idea is that you must load different device drivers for each system watching over that ever-popular IRQ 21. For example, different networks have their own redirectors, and they often argue about who gets to take the file home to Mom and Dad. Aside from that, PCs have a terrible time connecting to more than two different networks at the same time.

The Windows 9x IFS Manager takes control of all the network redirectors as though they were different file systems. This way, Windows can work with an unlimited number of redirectors, all at the same time. On any given machine, including standalone machines, the DOS file system is "seen" as just another network file system.

If DOS could be magically turned into a network operating system, many problems would go away. The IFS Manager is the magic wand, and acts somewhat like a network redirector to grab all the Interrupt 21 requests from applications that want to access the base file system. The DOS file system is still laying down bits of information in clusters, on sectors, in tracks, and on cylinders. However, the IFS Manager stands between you (the user) and DOS, managing filenames and storage-tracking events.

VFAT

When Windows starts up, the IFS waits for the system files to run all the Real Mode device drivers, and for the drivers to connect to the file system and hardware devices. (Remember that Windows XP supposedly no longer supports Real Mode.) After DOS (or the NT loader) has the computer functioning, Windows steps in and takes control. VMM32 (a Windows startup component) uses a compiled library of internal VxDs to replace whatever Real Mode drivers it finds in memory.

The VxDs in VMM32 are designed specifically to communicate with the IFS Manager, so the DOS file system is *mounted* (connected) in the same sense that a network volume is mounted and recognized by a network operating system. This capability to communicate with the IFS is part of what it means to write a 32-bit application that's 100% Windows compatible.

Truncating to Short Filenames

Windows 9x (not NT/2000/XP) maintains an internal list of all the interrupts that DOS can use (a maximum of 71) and adds a few more. Among the extra interrupts is the way in which an operating system can recognize long filenames. Because DOS itself can't recognize the long name, IFS Manager uses one of the extra interrupts to store an *alias* pointer (similar to a vector), and returns to tell DOS what to do with the file.

IFS Manager takes what you enter as a long filename and splits it apart (parses it) so that part of it can be used as a corresponding short filename (regular DOS 8.3 name). The rest of the name is stored for later rebuilding, and the alias pointer is associated with the various pieces of the filename.

If you have a file called "2005 Fooferaugh + My list of stuff" and another file called "2005 Fooferaugh and Dave's stuff," IFS Manager will truncate the two files to 8.3 names. Theoretically, that would result in two files, both called 2005foof.era at the same time—*totally illegal* by DOS rules, the United Nations Resolution 439 on International Tom Foolery, and a breach of the 1927 Zambian nuclear arms treaty!

When IFS Manager finds two files that will truncate to the same name, it uses the first six characters (minus spaces) and adds a tilde (~) plus incremental numbers (beginning with 1). If any periods are in the long filename, IFS Manager uses the first three characters after the last period as the DOS extension. Otherwise, it uses the next three characters it finds. In our example, the files would be named 2005fo~1.era and 2005fo~2.era for the short DOS name.

Short Names and Aliases

The file system works to find room on the disk, store a filename in the Directory Allocation Table (DAT), and help the disk controller move the hardware around. The DAT is an index for the longer FAT. FAT32 also uses a partition table, with information about the location and size of each partition. The NT System partition (like a boot manager) contains all these various areas. The NT Boot partition is really only where the Windows (NT/2000/XP) files are stored.

Remember that NT (XP and 2000) generates separate partitions, one for starting the computer, and one for loading Windows. The two names are backward, in terms of what you'd intuitively suspect. In situations where a previously installed XP fails completely but the machine provides a start menu, it's the Boot partition (system files) that crashed. The System partition (boot files) can easily remain uncorrupted and generate error messages and a menu.

On the other hand, a virus can corrupt the System partition (with **ntldr** and **NTDETECT.COM**), in which case the system fails to get to the startup menu. However, that doesn't necessarily mean the Boot partition and Windows files have been affected. You can repartition and reformat the XP Boot partition, but you can't easily do anything about the System partition, other than completely repartition the entire hard drive with something like FDISK or Partition Magic.

Along with the short name in the FAT, the parsed long filename is given the pointer to hang onto. When anything calls the file system, IFS Manager goes back to DOS and presents the request. DOS hands IFS Manager the file location information, and IFS Manager looks at the associated alias number to find the rest of the filename. IFS Manager then shows the user the long filename.

By the time the proposed Windows 9x long filename reaches the file system, IFS Manager has parsed it and added a pointer number. Meanwhile, DOS hasn't a clue that anything unusual is happening and still thinks it's running the same as it did back in 1981. DOS dutifully lays down the file, stores what it was told to store in the DAT, and goes back to sleep. The file is stored in clusters all over the disk, and IFS Manager makes sure that anything and everything in Windows sees the filename that it's supposed to see.

When you're in a DOS window, the IFS Manager grabs the DIR command and returns the DOS directory with the long filename to the far right. On the other hand, if you restart the computer in DOS Mode, outside of the entire Windows environment, you eliminate the IFS Manager, along with LFN support. In this situation, the DIR command shows only the short name of the file as it's actually registered in the DAT (again, the Directory Allocation Table).

From a DOS command prompt within Windows you can still use a long name (if you know it) by surrounding the long name with quotation marks. For example, if you type **CD "Program Files"** instead of **CD PROGRA~1**, Windows IFS Manager will put you in the correct folder. This also works for individual files on a command line. (The second, or closing quote, isn't usually necessary.)

Saving Long Filenames (LFNBK.EXE)

As you can see, the only thing keeping track of the long filenames is IFS Manager. If you decide to store all the files from a Windows computer on a network, the long filename data will be stored only if the OS/2 namespace has been enabled. If the namespace isn't enabled, the long filenames are lost in the river of history. This same problem appears if you store files on a floppy disk and copy them over to a 16-bit DOS or Windows machine.

A little-known (and hardly referenced) utility that comes with the Windows 9x CDROM is the LFNBK.EXE utility (for "long file name backup"). LFNBK.EXE is found in the ADMIN\APPTOOLS\LFNBACK folder, along with LFNBK.TXT, which describes the basic operations and switches. Perhaps the program is hard to notice because Microsoft says that it's for experienced users and shouldn't be relied on for day-to-day maintenance.

Using DOS-based file maintenance programs can disassociate the short filename data from the long filename, causing the long filename to be lost forever. Reformatting a hard drive and reinstalling Windows will not keep previous filename data associated with the short filenames held by DOS.

An interesting problem arises when long filenames disappear from the system. Windows stores certain program instructions in various files. Those instructions sometimes make calls to other files, using their specific long filenames. Understand that the actual files do exist on the drive, but only in short-name form. Because Windows is looking for the exact long filename and expecting IFS Manager to have it, Windows can't find the file because it can see only the short name. At that point, Windows fails to run.

NTFS

Many people seem to be talking about how NTFS is the best thing since sliced bread, and that if you have a Windows XP system, there's no question that you should immediately convert the hard drive to the NT File System. Why? At that point, most of those people suddenly become quiet, telling you only that "everybody knows it." So what's different about NTFS?

Think about how Windows NT was originally developed as a network operating system. On the one hand, Microsoft had DOS. On the other hand, the company worked with IBM to build a whole other, 32-bit multi-tasking OS. As far as networks are concerned, the two big items on the wish list are security and resource sharing. DOS has file attributes, but you can't set security permissions at a file level. NT was designed to link individual filenames, not to mention folders and whole drives, to a User ID through additional network attributes. However, the only way to do that would be to use a "new" file management system.

NTFS is especially designed to provide heavy-duty security to disks and file information. Aside from granting or denying someone access rights, NTFS also provides very complex file encryption, making it very difficult to read a file's contents, even if you break into a system. So, there's security and encryption: two big selling points.

A few people might argue that NTFS is faster than VFAT, in terms of file management. It turns out the two systems run at about the same speed. NTFS uses a number of hidden database files, acting like a relational database to keep track of every "transaction" taking place. In other words, DOS basically gets a filename, hands it to the FAT, and the disk controller works with RAM and the CPU to store the data bits. It's very fast. NTFS inserts many layers of rigmarole (technical term) between each of those transactions, making it slower. Fortunately, CPUs and hardware have speeded up substantially, making up the speed differences.

Now consider that any file must be "opened" before the computer can use it. That means that all or part of the file must be copied into RAM. All changes and work take place in RAM, then any data changes move out of memory and are stored to the file again, modifying the file or not, according to need. In between the time data is in memory and it's stored, the computer might lose power. When that happens, files can become corrupted because they weren't properly closed by the operating system. The VFAT and NTFS both use special files, opening and closing them all the time. Therefore, the actual file systems also rely on RAM.

NTFS uses transaction logging and all those hidden database files to prevent (as much as possible) system corruption due to crashes. Only tiny pieces of the basic file system remain open at any given instant. The critical thing to remember is that both VFAT and NTFS are file management systems. They work closely with the underlying base file system, but they're almost like their own special applications.

Regardless of whether you want to install NTFS or not, Windows 2000/XP both begin their Setup process on a FAT32 partition. Even when you indicate to the Setup Wizard that you want an NTFS partition on an unformatted disk, XP and Windows 2000 start with FAT32. After the setup files have been copied, the Setup Wizard then runs a scheduled conversion, changing the FAT32 partition to NTFS.

As far as the real world is concerned, the other critical thing to understand is that NTFS works completely within the Windows GUI. The Recovery Console may look like a DOS environment, but it's really a specialized application in its own right, designed to provide command-line, disk-level access to an NTFS partition. After you convert a partition to NTFS, that's the last time you'll ever see your filenames from a DOS prompt. Be very sure you understand that you cannot boot a computer directly into Windows NT/2000/XP. The NT Loader does many things before Windows offers you access to your system.

Understand further that disk problems, virus infections, file corruption, and partition management all take place outside of Windows. You can only manage NTFS partitions from within Windows (and the Windows Recovery Console), not from a plain DOS command line. Given that Windows 98SE was the last version of DOS, and that FAT32 is a DOS file management system, don't expect to use a Windows 98 EBD to work with a broken NTFS partition.

The only thing you can do when an NTFS partition develops problems is either work with the Recovery Console to see whether you can repair the underlying metadata files, or delete the entire partition (with all your data and programs) and repartition the drive. In our opinion, NTFS is a very stable, well-designed system. However, you should understand how it works and what it entails before you blithely and irrevocably convert a working FAT32 partition to NTFS.

Windows Applets

Many of the tools described in this section can be found under the Start | Accessories | System Tools menu. Microsoft has historically tried to keep end users separate from developers, tech support people, and systems administration. Inevitably, the Internet has opened access to all sorts of specialized tools and utilities that people have developed to make supporting Windows easier. Over time, these in-house, undocumented programs have made their way into the open market, taking on growing status within the tech support community. After a program has become a "must-have" utility for anyone involved with troubleshooting a system, Microsoft eventually comes around to formally putting it into a new release of their software, giving it a user interface, menus, name, and some supporting help.

Oddly enough, Windows 9x doesn't always install some of the more useful utilities that come on the installation CDROM. Among these extra utilities are the Accessibility options for people with disabilities, the LOGVIEW program, and the Emergency Recovery Utility (ERU.EXE), which can back up the Registry files. Although the Accessibility options are important for people who need them, they can be useful for just about anyone. (The Accessibility options are routinely installed during an Express setup.)

Not all the extra utilities are listed in the Windows Setup Wizard, either. For example, the Emergency Recovery Utility is in the OTHER\MISC\ERU folder of the CDROM, and must be manually copied to the hard drive.

Tweak UI

Microsoft technical support has developed a collection of small utility programs ever since Windows 95 was released. Over time, those tools made their way onto the Internet and became known as "Power Toys." This collection is called Tweak UI and provides a central console for changing various settings without going directly into the Registry. Some of these changes, such as turning off the ubiquitous animation and tool tips, can't be accessed through the Control Panel.

Tweak UI was finally included on the Windows 98 installation CDROM in the **\tools\reskit\ powertoy** folder. Note that each version of Windows has its own specific version of the program utilities, so don't use the Windows 95 version on a Windows 98 system.

Tweak UI can be downloaded from the Microsoft Web site, but the tools have gradually become less and less powerful. Windows 2000 incorporates a few of the most innocuous features from the old Tweak UI in the Accessories area of the Start Menu. Windows XP has its own version of Tweak UI (XP Power Toys), but as is often the case, developers decided to "fix" it and make it "better." The best place to find out all about Tweak UI is at the Annoyances.org site, **http://www.annoyances.org**. There, you can download the appropriate version and get tips regarding how to install the program.

Microsoft System Information (MSINFO32.EXE)

The Microsoft System Information utility provides a single interface for several of the older Windows 95 utilities, including the Device Manager and HWDIAG.EXE. MSINFO isn't the same as MSCONFIG (discussed later in this section). Be sure you're not in a fog on the day of the exam, or when you're troubleshooting a problem machine: It's easy to type the wrong letters, and then scratch your head wondering why Windows can't find what you're looking for. Don't forget the "32" in MSINFO32.EXE.

The Microsoft System Information utility acts as a central control panel for several other troubleshooting and debugging tools. From the Tools menu option, you can check the Registry and make a backup copy to a .CAB file (Windows 9x only). Remember that this was the almost undocumented ERU.EXE. There are also menu options for the System File Checker, the System Configuration Utility (MSCONFIG), Dr. Watson (a trap for system errors and system snapshots), the Version Conflict manager, ScanDisk, and more.

The utility runs out of MSINFO32.EXE, and can be found either through Start | Accessories | System Tools | System Information, or in the C:\Program Files\Common Files\Microsoft Shared\MSINFO sub-folder. This utility is also a precursor to the Windows 2000 and Windows XP Computer Management tool, which opens the System Information applet.

If you purchase and install Norton Utilities, you'll find a System Information option on the context menu when you right-click on the "My Computer" icon. This is the Norton System Information, not to be confused with the Microsoft System Information, and provides a comprehensive view of the machine's hardware, memory, and networking status. The utility has a Reports button for printing out any view.

System File Checker (SFC.EXE)

Windows 95 tech support people were able to use a Registry Checker (ScanReg, SCANREGW.EXE) utility, available for download from the Microsoft site (if you knew about it), to analyze a corrupted Windows Registry and to attempt to fix it. Windows 98 incorporated the System File Checker to work in a similar fashion on overall system files.

This utility (not available in Windows 95 or Me, but in XP/2000) checks through the critical system files on a machine by taking a snapshot of each file whenever a program calls any of the files. DOS used something called a checksum to keep a database of how many bits a file should contain. Some of the original, simple virus checkers used a database made up of the filename, how many bits the file comprised, and the time and date of the original file. SFC checks these system files against a similar database each time a file is run. According to Microsoft, System File Checker tracks over 512 different file types (by extension).

If the System File Checker finds a difference between a current file and the description of that file in its database, it offers to either restore any file that has changed, or to update its database to reflect a new version of the file.

Windows Me dropped the System File Checker and replaced it with two new features called System File Protection and System Restore. System File Protection protects various critical system files from being modified by other programs. SFC makes it possible (theoretically) to bring back a previous system configuration.

Be very careful that you don't confuse System File Checker with System Restore! SFC compares files installed by a program other than Windows against the original files that come with Windows. It's used to fix a problem where someone other than Microsoft overwrites an important Windows file (for example, with a bad .DLL).

System Restore, on the other hand, is essentially the Windows Me/2000/XP backup tool. It's also Microsoft's way of helping you to back up the Registry for these versions of Windows. Windows 9x uses SCANREGW.EXE, ERU.EXE, or you can manually back up SYSTEM.DAT and USER.DAT. System Restore creates incremental backups called "restore points," meaning a calendar date, and we'll discuss it at length in Chapter 16.

Dr. Watson (DRWATSON.EXE)

Dr. Watson is designed to send trouble reports back to technical support people. The program runs in the background and watches for system errors. At that point, it creates a log file containing technical information about what took place. The snapshot of the error should identify which program had a problem, along with a possible detailed description of the cause.

Sometimes it will even offer a problem resolution suggestion. Hardly anyone outside of Microsoft uses it, but you must know the program for the exam.

Disk Cleanup (CLEANMGR.EXE)

Somewhat similar to DeFrag, Disk Cleanup "cleans up" the hard drive by removing or compressing files you don't need. The program runs through the files on a hard drive, flagging those that are out of date, or that haven't been used in a long time, warning you when the drive is getting filled up. At that point, you can make decisions as to what you'd like to do with those files (available through Start I Accessories I System Tools). You can check the "View" tab to examine all the files that will be removed. (Note that in Windows XP, the path is Start I All Programs I System Tools.)

Microsoft System Configuration (MSCONFIG.EXE)

The System Configuration utility (not available in Windows 95 or Windows 2000) helps you specify which processes you want to run during Startup. Aside from the Startup tab, you can also view the CONFIG.SYS, AUTOEXEC.BAT, SYSTEM.INI, and WIN.INI files, all from one Console. Check boxes allow you to edit individual lines in the various initialization files.

The "Startup" tab (Windows 9x) is similar to the "Service" tab in Windows XP. Basically, the tab lists everything that Windows loads from locations other than the DOS configuration files. It includes a check box in front of each item, and you can decide which items to allow Windows to load. Unchecking a box doesn't affect the underlying file or program, so this is a quick way to determine whether an application or service is causing a Startup problem.

You can find several Web sites with complete listings of every Windows XP/2000 service, and descriptions of every Startup program for all the versions of Windows. Our purpose isn't to help you learn how to use MSCONFIG, but to let you know that it's an important diagnostics tool. Always remember that viruses, adware, and spyware are all programs. Many times you'll find documented programs with MSCONFIG that indicate a Startup problem is coming from such a program.

There's a great freeware program that not only replaces MSCONFIG, but provides better and more functionality. You can find CodeStuff "Starter" version 5.x at **http://codestuff.tripod.com/news.shtml**. The program works in Windows 2000, adding in a very useful and helpful diagnostics tool.

The "General" tab provides button options for a Normal startup; for a Diagnostic startup, with an interactive processing of individual drivers and devices; or for a Selective Startup. Using the Selective Startup, you can disable each of the main tabs, one at a time, to quickly determine which area is causing the problem. After you've determined that the Startup Group, for instance, is the culprit, you can then disable individual items until you find the specific problem.

This utility also can be accessed through the Tools option of the System Information utility. Another option is to press Start and choose the Run option, and then type MSCONFIG in the Run dialog box. (Remember, it won't work in Windows 2000, and you'll have to use a third-party utility.)

Exiting certain utilities produces a dialog box asking you whether you want to reboot your computer. If you choose OK, you'll most likely have a complete, cold reboot, restarting the entire machine. In most cases, you can choose to reboot later, or say No to the dialog box. If you then choose Start | Log Off (regardless of whether or not you have networking options installed), Explorer shuts down and restarts, applying the changes you've made.

Another way to accomplish a Desktop refresh is to click the mouse anywhere in an open area of the Desktop and press the F5 (refresh) key. Finally, you can press Ctrl+Alt+Del to bring up the Task Manager; click to select Explorer, and choose End Task. This shuts down the Explorer (and the Desktop shell). After a moment, the Explorer restarts, applying any changes you made.

If you choose to use the Shut Down option of the Start menu, and you want to restart your computer without going through a full reboot, you can hold down the Shift key while you click on OK. This restarts Windows 98 without a cold boot.

Windows Update Manager (WUPDMGR.EXE)

The Update Manager tries to keep Windows current, with the latest software drivers, patches, bug fixes, and incremental release updates (service packs). Under the supposition that most computers will be always connected to the Internet in some fashion, accessing the Update Manager produces an automatic attempt to access the Internet and go directly to Microsoft's Web site. (In some instances, the Update Manager might also try to go to an application's vendor support site to accomplish the same thing.)

After the machine is connected, the Update Manager examines the Registry, working through all the software and hardware configurations along with the associated files being used in those settings. The Update Manager then compares the files it finds on your hard drive with the information held in the update database on the Web site, downloading appropriate updated files into the locations pointed to in the Registry keys.

After various files have been flagged (marked) for updating, the Web site provides links to various other locations on the site where these updated files can be found and downloaded. The Update Manager then helps install and/or uninstall various files. Following an Update Manager session, the program creates a history log (file) of the activities and file modifications that took place during the session. Through this history log, you can remove previous updates and return the machine to original configurations in the event it becomes necessary.

Maintenance Wizard (TUNEUP.EXE)

Windows 3.x introduced various macros (automated series of steps). Third-party developers soon began to create small programs that made it easier (in theory) to use these macros. IBM created something called REXX in OS/2 as something more than a batch language, but less than a full-blown programming language. Microsoft did something similar with the slimmed-down version Visual Basic used for Office macros.

DOS users were skilled at creating small batch files containing all the various programs, switches, and file locations involved in certain maintenance tasks. For instance, to copy any changed files from a directory to a floppy disk, a batch file would store the various switches used by XCOPY.EXE, along with whichever directories were to be examined. However, it was left to third-party developers to figure out how to time the batch files to the system clock.

Over time it became quite clear that the average user had no intention of, nor interest in, learning a complex programming language for anything. To bring the ease of automated task steps down to Earth, Microsoft introduced the Maintenance Wizard and Task Scheduler. The Maintenance Wizard stores not only the time of day, but also the number of times a particular maintenance task should be performed, and walks the user through such mundane tasks as defragmenting the hard drive, getting rid of old and unwanted files, and running ScanDisk (Windows 9x only).

The Task Scheduler is the annoying little icon that sits in the Tray forevermore, after it's been run one time. To get a consolidated view of scheduled maintenance tasks without going through the Task Scheduler, right-click on a drive icon in the Explorer. Choose Properties from the Context Menu, and then choose the Tools tab. Finally, you can run each of these tasks by selecting Start | Accessories | System Tools, and picking each tool from the resulting menu.

Windows Me

The year 2000 came and went, and the world didn't come to an end. With the release of Windows 95, Microsoft decided to stop using a version number in the name of the operating system, choosing instead to use a year reference. As Windows 98 continued to change through updates and fixes, it too eventually required a full version release, becoming Windows Millennium Edition (Me). This was where things really started getting confusing.

At one time, both Windows Me and Windows 2000 were fully supported versions on the open market. Based on the logic of the names, one would think that Me and 2000 are essentially the same thing. In fact, Me and 2000 are very different systems. We'll discuss Windows 2000 in the next chapter, but the release of Windows Me was based on a marketing assessment where Microsoft believed the home market was ready to abandon applications based on Windows 3.1 architecture and move to NT. Windows NT was still too restrictive, but a transition system moving toward NT could be very viable. That system would become Windows Me.

Windows Me was primarily featured as an enhanced home networking system. Although you didn't hear it from us, rumor has it that Microsoft wanted to capitalize on the changeover from the 20th to the 21st century, and rushed Me to the market as a sort of pre-release for what later became Windows 2000.

 NOTE We discuss Me from a troubleshooting perspective in Chapter 16. This version of Windows was so unstable and filled with problems that Microsoft effectively stopped supporting it. We would encourage you to strongly advise anyone with a problematic machine running Me to either revert to Windows 98SE, or upgrade to Windows 2000 or XP.

For the first time, Windows Me got rid of (theoretically) support for virtual machines running in Real Mode. If you remember, Real Mode is a reference to the original XT computers, and addressing real memory with direct addresses. The CONFIG.SYS and AUTOEXEC.BAT configuration files, having always been necessary for any hardware or software expecting to find a basic, 16-bit DOS machine, vanished. Because Me eliminated support for this type of virtual machine, all references to the configuration files disappeared. (Not that there'd be a problem, or anything.)

Windows Me no longer even processed a CONFIG.SYS or AUTOEXEC.BAT in any fashion during the Startup. Additionally, there was no longer any way to get to a DOS machine, under Windows Me, from a default installation. The only way to get to DOS was with an Emergency Boot Disk created after Windows Me was installed.

Perhaps one of the most bizarre aspects of Microsoft's definition of "consistency" was that FORMAT.COM suddenly lost the capability of installing the critical DOS system files with the /s switch. You could right-click on a floppy drive icon to format a disk, but not to transfer system files. Even more strangely, you could run FORMAT A: /s from the \Windows\Command subfolder (from a DOS window) and it would work again.

Windows 95 automated the process of checking to see whether real device drivers could be replaced with virtual device drivers. If a VxD could do whatever the original driver was designed to do, a knowledgeable user could comment out the driver from the CONFIG.SYS file, reboot the machine, and see whether the device still worked. Windows Me took more control over this process, going through any existing CONFIG.SYS file and assigning what Microsoft thought were the appropriate VxDs. After the file was stripped of all its device drivers, Me then went through the AUTOEXEC.BAT file and moved all configuration switches into the Registry.

Both the CONFIG.SYS and AUTOEXC.BAT files could continue to reside on the hard drive, and Me would leave them there in the event it found one of the pesky buggers during an update installation. However, after Windows Me was installed, it would modify the filenames and their locations, keeping an eye on any new hardware installations. If an installation searched for either of the files, Me would intercept the search and hand off its own location to the installation routine. The device's installation routine commands were allowed to modify the older files, and then Me would wait for a reboot.

The next time the Windows Me machine started up, Me went through the changed configuration files, placing SET commands in the AUTOEXEC.BAT file, and adjusting the installation according to what Microsoft thinks the way things ought to be. In more than a few instances, Windows Me made the wrong choices and many programs, games, and devices the home computer user wanted very much to use failed to run. (Not that there was a problem, or anything.)

There is very little on the low-level specifics of Me in the current A+ exam, though the exam seems to be continually evolving. The primary change in Windows Me was the elimination of Real Mode support and enhanced networking setup management. Other than that, Windows Me essentially hid many of the configuration utilities from the casual user.

Summary—Windows 9x

For the most part, the exam folds together Windows 98, Windows 2000, and Windows XP, making no particular distinction between them at a low level. Questions relating to Windows 9x and Windows XP/2000 generally specify each of the two main families, and questions about Windows NT likewise indicate that they are specific to NT. Keep track of the following points:

➤ Windows 98 introduced the Active Desktop, a way of seeing file and disk information in a World Wide Web format. You should understand the feature and how to activate or deactivate it from the Desktop Properties menu (Web tab).

➤ Microsoft System Information (MSINFO32.EXE) had its roots in the old Microsoft Diagnostics (MSD.EXE) tool. Understand how to run the program from the File | Run command line, as well as how to navigate to the System Tools accessories. Note that Windows XP uses the same concept in its Computer Management tool, discussed in Chapter 15.

➤ Be aware of tools such as the Registry Checker, System File Checker (SFC), Defrag, and Scandisk.

➤ MSCONFIG (the System Configuration Utility) has gone a long way in making startup configurations and optional startup items manageable. You should understand the program and run it on your own, using a Windows 9x machine. It was not available in Windows 95, NT, or 2000, but is available in Windows 98, Me, and XP.

We don't think you'll see many questions directly related to Windows Me, but you'll want to remember that the Millennium Edition was truly a hybrid release of 16/32-bit Windows and NT. The main thing to remember about Me is that if you encounter a machine with many problems and the installed OS is Windows Me, do whatever you can to convert the installation either forward to Windows XP/2000 or backward to Windows 98SE.

Exam Prep Questions

Question 1

Windows maintains filenames through which of the following? (Check all that apply)

❑ A. LFNs

❑ B. VFAT

❑ C. FAT32

❑ D. DAT

Answers B, C, and D are correct. Choice A, the Windows Long File Names (LFNs), are not a maintenance process. After names have been created, Windows uses the Virtual FAT (VFAT), the underlying 32-bit File Allocation Table (FAT32), and the Directory Allocation Table (DAT) to maintain the address locations for the data in the file's clusters.

Question 2

The Windows Registry is made up of which set of files?

○ A. USER.BAT, SYSTEM.BAT, SYSTEM.INI, WINDOWS.INI

○ B. SYSTEM.INI, WIN.INI, HKEY.DAT, REG32.DAT

○ C. USER.DAT, SYSTEM.DAT

○ D. SYSTEM.INI, WIN.INI

Answer C is correct. Note that this kind of question is tricky because it doesn't tell you which version of Windows is being questioned. Although Windows 9x may still use the original initialization files from Windows 3.x, the SYSTEM.INI and WIN.INI files are not part of the Registry. Therefore, choices A, B, and D are all incorrect. A .BAT file is a batch file extension and the Registry files are in binary format.

Question 3

> Where will Windows look before finding a 32-bit virtual device driver to replace a static VxD?
>
> ○ A. SYSTEM.INI
> ○ B. WIN.INI
> ○ C. VMM32.DLL
> ○ D. KRNL328.EXE

Answer A is correct. Note the use of "before" in the question, along with a reference to a static device driver. The first place Windows 9x will look for these static VxDs is in the SYSTEM.INI file. Answer B is incorrect because the WIN.INI file maintains user configuration settings, not device driver. Answers C and D are incorrect because Windows doesn't look in either .DLL or .EXE files for device drivers.

Question 4

> The best way to back up the system registration files is with the _____ utility.
>
> ○ A. BACKUP.EXE
> ○ B. ERU.EXE
> ○ C. REGEDT32.EXE
> ○ D. LFNBK.EXE

Answer B is correct. ERU.EXE is the Emergency Repair Utility program specifically designed to back up the Windows Registry, sometimes called the system registration files. Once again, this is a tricky question because it uses the formal "system registration" rather than the "Registry." Answer A is incorrect because the DOS Backup program is designed to back up entire file areas. Answer C is incorrect because it refers to the version of REGEDIT.EXE designed for Windows 2000 and NT. Answer D is incorrect because it refers to a utility for backing up Long File Names.

Question 5

> FAT32 has the advantage over FAT16 for which of the following main reasons? (Check all that apply)
>
> ❑ A. Partitions larger than 2GB
>
> ❑ B. Multiple 2GB partitions
>
> ❑ C. Variable cluster sizes
>
> ❑ D. The non-active bootable file system

Answers A and C are correct. FAT16 is limited to a maximum file size of 2GB, either in one file or a single partition size. FAT32 uses larger, 32-bit addresses in the FAT to provide access to partitions larger than 2GB. FAT32 also provides adjustable cluster sizes, making storage of small files more efficient. Answer B is technically correct but functionally incorrect in that although FAT32 can easily support many 2GB partitions, this is no more an advantage than FAT16, NTFS, or HPFS file systems. There is no such term as that referenced by answer D.

Question 6

> Which of the following files would you work with to get a copy of the Registry?
>
> ○ A. SYSTEM.DAT
>
> ○ B. 042952.CAB
>
> ○ C. RB003.CAB
>
> ○ D. EBD.CAB

Answer C is correct. Although this might seem to be an obscure question, notice that three of the four responses include a .CAB extension. That should clue you in to the one special area where Cabinet files apply, other than an installation. The question asks about the Registry, hoping to distract you with the wrong answer A. system.dat is one of the Registry files, but it isn't "the" Registry. Answer B is incorrect, being a made-up filename. Answer D is incorrect because it applies to the Windows 98 Emergency Boot Disk archive file. Try to remember: Registry, backup, Cabinet (.CAB), and "RB" for Registry Backup.

Question 7

> Which two of the following files are text files?
>
> ❑ A. CONFIG.SYS
> ❑ B. SYSTEM.INI
> ❑ C. USER.DAT
> ❑ D. SYSTEM.DAT

Answers A and B are correct. You should have a solid understanding of the most common file extensions. You should also know that .INI (initialization files) are always plain text files. Answer C is incorrect, and you should know that not only is a .DAT extension used to store binary data, for the most part, but that the two primary Windows 9x Registry files are binary files. Answer D is the other binary Registry file. The distraction relies on the fact that the Registry Editor opens up both files, but that only SYSTEM.INI is a text file.

Question 8

> Every time Windows starts it halts with an error message that it can't load **msvc32i.MFC** or one of its modules. You can press OK to pass through the error. Which of the following Consoles would best provide you with diagnostics and repair functionality?
>
> ○ A. Microsoft System Information
> ○ B. The Computer Administration Console
> ○ C. Control Panel
> ○ D. Microsoft System Configuration

Answer D is correct. The problem with this question is that instead of offering you program filenames, you're having to choose from those names in the Title bar that nobody ever reads. The question refers to a startup error, but not a complete crash. Something is giving Windows gas during the startup process. Answer B is wrong, and you should know that there's a Computer Management console, but not Computer Administration (although there's Administrative Tools). Answer C is incorrect, and you should likewise know that the Control Panel isn't where you'd normally go when Windows is telling you it can't "load" (read "start") something. That leaves a hard choice between "information" versus "configuration."

If something isn't starting correctly, wouldn't that apply to how the system was configured, rather than a report of what devices were installed? Answer

A is incorrect because MSINFO32.EXE produces a listing of such things as IRQs, hardware services, devices, and what modules are in memory. MSCONFIG.EXE offers the "Startup" tab as a place to go to try and see what Windows thinks it should load during that startup. (By the way, this MFC module causes problems in XP, and is the result of downloading an adware program, "Client Man." If you're experiencing this problem, go to the Web and do a search on Client Man or clientman for a solution.)

Question 9

Which file can you safely remove from the user's desktop without causing a Load problem at a future date?

- ○ A. DeFrag.exe
- ○ B. DeFrag~1.com
- ○ C. DeFrag.lnk
- ○ D. DeFrag.diz

Answer C is correct. Although it might seem as if this is a DOS extension question, you're actually being tested on the concept of Windows shortcuts and their .LNK extension. The red herring in the question has to do with "a load problem." Who knows what it really means, but it presumably has something to do with running a program sometime in the future. You must understand that shortcuts are stored in their own files, and that those files are really only a convenience for the user. Answers A and B should be readily understood as wrong because .EXE and .COM files are programs. They load, and would maybe be a problem if they were missing. Answer D is incorrect, even if you don't know that a .DIZ file is usually just a shareware file description. The elegant troubleshooting technique is never to delete an unrecognizable file.

Question 10

Marilyn is the Executive Vice President of the Chamber of Commerce, and uses a Pentium 4 machine with 256MB of RAM to manage a number of spreadsheets. She's been storing the year's financial data on the desktop as shortcuts. The Registry has been keeping track of those spreadsheets in which key?

- ○ A. HKEY_LOCAL_MACHINE
- ○ B. HKEY_USERS
- ○ C. HKEY_CLASSES_ROOT
- ○ D. HKEY_LOCAL_CONFIG

Answer B is correct. This is a classic example of how you can be given all the information you need, but none of it helps unless you have a pretty good sense of how the Registry (all Windows versions) is organized. You don't need the detail information, but you must remember the summary of what each key handles. Answer A is incorrect because the Local Machine key stores hardware settings. Answer C is wrong because the Root is the top branch of the entire Registry. Answer D is wrong because it doesn't exist. (Trust your visual memory and instincts. If it looks weird, it is.) Answer B is correct, and you should have a clue in the "users" reference. The question is a scenario type of question, and all the junk about the person's name, title, or kind of machine means nothing. What matters is the shortcuts, the reference to the desktop, and the concept of display settings. Windows provides personalized appearance settings to each logged-in user, and those personal settings are the "user's" settings, stored in the USER or CURRENT_CONFIG keys.

Need to Know More?

 Lee "Tutor's" Doing and Fixing Windows site
`http://home.earthlink.net/~leetutor/index.html`
Created by Lee Reynolds. An excellent site for reference material
on almost any Microsoft system utility included with any version
of Windows.

 Sysinternals Web site
`http://www.sysinternals.com/`
Created and developed by Mark Russinovich and Bryce Cogswell
(copyright Sysinternals LLC). Includes many freeware utilities to
enhance Windows troubleshooting. The Sysinternals Web site
provides you with advanced utilities, technical information, and
source code related to Windows 9x, Windows Me, and Windows
NT/2000 internals that you won't find anywhere else.

 Annoyances.org
`http://www.annoyances.org`
This site is one of the best places on the Web for discussion boards
and quick response to any type of Windows question. The site also
provides downloadable versions of Tweak UI and other very helpful tools for making Windows easier to deal with.

 Chellis, Perkins, and Streb. *MCSE Networking Essentials Study
Guide*. San Francisco, CA: Sybex Network Press, 1996. ISBN:
0-7821-1971-9. This book goes into more detail than you'll need for
the certification exam but is a good place to start if you're consider-
ing a career as a network engineer.

 Derfler, Frank J. *PC Magazine Guide to Connectivity*. New York, NY:
Ziff Davis, 1995. ISBN: 1-56276-274-5. This book is easy to read
and provides a good introduction to networking.

 Microsoft Windows 98 Resource Kit. Redmond, WA: Microsoft Press,
1998. ISBN: 1-57231-644-0. This is the definitive resource for all
Windows 98 questions. It assumes that you have a good working
knowledge of Windows.

 Tidrow, Rob. *Windows 95 Registry Troubleshooting*. Indianapolis, IN:
New Riders, 1996. ISBN: 1-56205-556-9. This book goes into more
detail than you'll need for the certification exam, but if you really
want to get into it, this is your source.

Windows NT, 2000, and XP

. . . .

Terms you'll need to understand:

✓ Multitasking and the Virtual Machine (VM)

✓ Network server and local machines (clients)

✓ End user and network administrator

✓ Logging on to a network

✓ Load and initialize (a program)

Concepts you'll need to master:

✓ User mode and Kernel mode

✓ Modular programming and development

✓ Operating system layers surrounding a kernel

✓ Security: granting and blocking access rights

✓ User and Group accounts and profiles

✓ Loader programs (NT Loader)

✓ Booting from multiple operating systems

✓ Volume sets, mirroring, and RAID

Before we begin our discussion of Windows NT, 2000, and XP, we'd like you to think about a couple of important points. Prior to the integration between Microsoft's home-user operating system (Windows 9x) and the enterprise networking versions of Windows (Windows NT), A+ certification was focused on supporting individual computers. True, the exam took into account low-level support for client machines in an enterprise network, but those support issues were mostly limited to the same ones found on home and personal systems.

We've attempted to keep this book as thin as possible, choosing only those topics we think will best help you remember the avalanche of facts, acronyms, numbers, and problem-solving techniques you'll encounter on the exam. We'll use Windows 98SE and Windows XP in specific references to navigational paths, utility names, and the combination applets Microsoft now calls "consoles." We'll use notes and tips as best we can, to reference how Windows 98 and XP differ from Windows NT and Windows 2000. In other words, just because we say that disk partitioning is done by FDISK.EXE or under the Computer Management tool, that in no way means that those are the only tools and their locations. This book would easily grow to more than a thousand pages if we covered every individual name for each command, and all their differences in every existing operating system.

As you read through this chapter and the next one, focus on the fact that the A+ exam has been designed as an entry-level benchmark for first-tier tech support personnel. You can develop an entire career path in full-fledged network administration, enterprise systems integration, computer security, email administration, and other aspects of Windows. However, A+ certification isn't about those career paths. Some of you are taking the exam as part of a global certification program. Others of you, the readers we're primarily addressing, are entering the IT field at the start of a new career.

To those readers who've been in the business since Windows 3.x and DOS, many of the complexities surrounding today's 32-bit operating systems are relatively easy to see as being fixes or evolutions from the past. For those of you whose introduction to computers began with Windows 95 or Windows 98 (or even Windows XP), we think there are several ways to approach the A+ exam. Many preparation books go through every feature of all the operating systems currently in existence. Many other books try to highlight specific questions on the exam, and then give the correct response to those questions in a very long list, expecting you to take the exam on rote memory.

We've said in the introductory chapters that our approach is to provide you with a foundation for the underlying concepts involving hardware and the PC operating system. We've found that when someone has a contiguous story line, they'll be far more prepared to associate individual facts to that story. They can then more easily extract correct responses to any type of question. To that end, we're going to go over how Windows became Windows NT, and then evolved into Windows 2000 and Windows XP. We also stress, again, that you should have a significant amount of hands-on experience with Windows 98 and Windows XP, at the very least, as well as Windows 2000 before you take the exam.

Finally, Microsoft has repeatedly chosen (for no discernable reason) to change the names of important features, tools, and problem-solving utilities. Although the company claims that consistency is the key to making Windows successful, we've seen decreasing evidence of that consistency. We've tried to point out how certain tools and utilities are the same things, but we can't list every single example of Microsoft's made-up words, terms, and other make-believe language. On the other hand, if you know the essential concept behind a tool, you should be able to recognize it, regardless of what name it has in any particular operating system. This book is designed to remind you of those things you'll likely encounter on the exam, not to explain operating systems from the ground up.

This is a very long chapter, mostly because Windows NT/XP is completely different from every version of Windows prior to XP. We recommend that you set aside two days for the chapter, reading the first half involving the principles of NT in the first day. The second half of the chapter begins with "Windows XP" and is a quick review of specific tools and utilities you should remember. If you're already well versed in Windows XP, spend the time on the first half of the chapter to build a context for what you know in relation to Windows NT and 2000 (both are listed objectives for the exam). If you can't easily visualize navigational routes in XP, use the second half of the chapter to keep track of those tools you must remember for the exam.

A Simple History of Windows NT

Windows NT was Microsoft's venture into large-scale, enterprise operating systems. Enterprise installations must have stability, security, scalability, and sophisticated networking capabilities. When we talk about scalability, we mean that a smaller system can grow to meet more complex demands involving many people, computers, and locations. Neither Windows 3.1 nor Windows 9x were originally designed to meet any of these requirements, having been primarily developed for the consumer market and individual computers. Although they did offer small-scale peer-to-peer networking, it was more as an optional feature than a basic foundation for national and international business operations. Windows NT was Microsoft's competitive response to Novell's Netware, which dominated the corporate desktop networking market at the time.

Windows 9x ran a completely separate virtual machine for each application. You've seen how you can open an MS-DOS window at the same time as you're working in a word processor and the Explorer. All three of these events are understood by Windows to be individual sessions. A session is just another name for a virtual machine. By isolating every session from each other, Windows 9x was able to provide much more stability, thereby reducing the chances of any single software program causing an entire system crash.

We'll spend a lot of time in this chapter examining Windows NT. The reason is that Windows 2000 (Win 2000, W2K or, simply, 2K) and Windows XP are entirely based on Windows NT. If you understand the general theory of NT and how it differs from DOS, you'll also understand most of the underlying concepts behind Windows XP. (Not that you'll be able to fix anything in XP, but we'll cover the various administrative and troubleshooting tools here and in the following chapter.)

A Word About Pre-emptive Multitasking

In cooperative multitasking, the CPU has no control over a given program, and that program can completely take over the CPU. If the program doesn't give back that control, too bad. A single program can "steal" the CPU, along with all the memory resources, and keep other programs from getting any attention. In *pre-emptive* multitasking, the operating system stays in control of any individual program when it tries to access both the resources and the central processor.

Basically, Windows 9x retains control of the CPU, using its own decision-making procedures to give running programs access to the CPU. The philosophy is that the CPU must be protected at all times. This control is given on a *conditional* basis. In other words, at any given time, Windows 9x can pre-empt a program from performing a destructive function. By acting first and taking control of the virtual machine, Windows 9x can suspend the program's operations, along with any access to resources that program had (including the CPU). This also prevents any individual program from hogging the processor.

In theory, if one program crashes in a pre-emptive multitasking operating system, it won't affect any of the other virtual machines. For example, if a 16- or 32-bit program crashes within Windows 9x, the operating system can shut down that specific virtual machine, leaving the other processes running untouched. You've probably seen those error messages where you're told that a program has performed an illegal function. Windows 9x gives you the option of either shutting down that specific session or getting more detail as to what happened. In this instance, Windows has pre-empted any further operation of that program, but your overall system hasn't crashed. NT takes more control of not only programs, but also the system services we'll discuss in this chapter.

Windows 9x also supports 32-bit *multi-threaded* multitasking, as long as the program has been written with the appropriate programming threads. It went a long way toward stability, but was still far short of enterprise networking and security requirements. Because of its origins as a simple interface, as well as its need for backward compatibility in a mostly non-technical home or office environment, Windows 9x could never become a large-scale networking OS. Windows NT, on the other hand, was developed from the ground up, specifically to meet enterprise requirements and with little concern for backward compatibility. Microsoft's primary focus was security, and that focus is still the foundation in Windows XP.

 In a nutshell, a program can be like an online discussion group, where many "threads" of conversations are taking place at the same time. Multi-threaded programs include a sort of sub-program with instructions that tell the operating system how to work with the main programming instructions most efficiently. In a way, a multi-threaded program is like a device controller, with localized instructions that act as an assistant manager to the operating system's executive management decisions. Multi-threaded multitasking allows an individual program to sort of "help out" with the delegation of resources.

Windows Versions

Windows NT may appear to have been built on the features and capabilities of Windows 95, but it's actually the other way around. Originally, NT used quite a different interface and underlying structure than "Windows." Windows 95 was the first home version of Windows to take on the appearance of NT. That look and feel then went on to become Windows 98, and Millennium Edition (Me). The interface culminated in Windows 2000, and then became the more graphics-intensive XP interface. The thing to remember is that there are essentially only two system-level designs: DOS (and Windows 9x) versus NT. The two are quite distinct from each other, but often use similar command names.

Windows Me was a hybrid hodgepodge of DOS, Windows 95/98, and Windows NT, all thrown together in an attempt to convert the home user to Microsoft's fully integrated networking operating system (regardless of whether individual users needed the added features). Windows 2000 is actually different from Windows XP, in that it's much more like NT (installing to the \WINNT folder). Windows XP now looks more like earlier versions of Windows, as far as the user is concerned (going back to installing in the \Windows folder). However, both XP and Windows 2000 are essentially the next evolution of Windows NT.

Windows NT and 2000 provided the technical core for Windows XP, but they didn't always offer as many tools, Wizards, and integrated consoles as the consumer market versions of Windows. An important difference is that Windows 9x and XP store individual configuration settings under the \Windows folder. NT/2000 make extensive use of the \Documents and Settings folder to store user configurations, data, and other important settings. You can see another link to NT with the \My Documents folder built into Windows 9x. The Registry looks the same in all three versions, but be aware of the \WINNT installation folder, and the \Documents and Settings configuration folder.

It's now become almost impossible for entry-level technicians or home users to really effect any repairs on a serious XP problem. The machine either works or it doesn't. Fortunately, XP is more stable than many other versions of Windows, although Windows 98SE is still a strong contender. When XP fails to the point where last-known-good settings don't work, the most likely option is to go back to an earlier configuration with System Restore, or do an in-place reinstall (repair the operating system). Understand that System Restore presupposes that you can get into Windows in the first place. When even that fails, you have few repair options beyond a reinstall, or using the Recovery Console.

NT Versions 3.1 and 4.0

NT 3.1 was Microsoft's first release of its own version of a multitasking network operating system. Version 1.x and 2.x were part of the joint project with IBM's OS/2. By the time NT was ready for release, IT administrators had concluded that nobody installs a "point-zero" release until all the bugs were worked out. Microsoft, always with an eye on marketing, decided to release NT 3.1 so that technicians would "think" it was actually a secondary, fixed version of NT. The interface for Windows NT 3.1 looked almost exactly like 16-bit Windows 3.1, but when you opened up an object on the desktop, the menus were all different. This made for a nicely confusing situation.

NT 3.x was an early example of how separating device drivers from their underlying hardware could cause serious compatibility problems. Because of this, Microsoft began publishing a book with lists of all the specific devices that had been tested successfully for compatibility with NT. This *hardware compatibility list* (the HCL) was routinely updated on the Internet.

Windows NT 4.0 began the real divergence between IBM and Microsoft. IBM's OS/2 Warp made a momentary splash on the market, but NT was starting to gain a foothold in corporate America. On the home front, although Windows 95 was able to support 32-bit applications, it was still, at its core, a 16-bit operating system. The main problem with NT was that it did a poor job of supporting all those 16-bit applications that home users continued to run.

Windows XP is more like Windows NT 5.1 and it is as different from Windows 2000 (NT 5.0) as Windows 3.1 was from 3.0. Rumor has it that Bill Gates wanted people to "experience" a computer, rather than simply "use" a computer. Tying the product name to the calendar year was becoming problematic, and so Windows finally became the Windows eXPerience, or Windows XP.

> Other Microsoft productivity applications will take on the XP name, with developmental tools being renamed with a .NET extension. Apparently Microsoft believes that programmers will develop applications based on the sharing concepts of the World Wide Web (remember the Active Desktop in Windows 98?). End users should have no idea what the underlying technology is, knowing only that they can sit down and get to work—just like they can on the Internet.

NT Workstation and NT Server

Client/server networking is a network where individual PCs act as clients to a central file server. The client machines are often referred to as *local* machines, and the file server (or servers) is often referred to as a *remote* machine because it's often quite a distance away from the local machines. We've also said that Windows NT was designed from its inception to be a network operating system that could run on many hardware platforms (portability). As a result, Windows NT, Windows 2000, and XP come in both a server version (remote) and a workstation version (local). The server version that complements Windows XP clients is now known as Windows Server 2003.

> Remember that we're talking about Windows NT, but everything pretty much applies the same way to Windows 2000 and XP. For simplicity's sake, we sometimes mention only NT. Generally, you can replace "NT" with the XP or 2000 in your mind.

Both versions of NT share the same core operating system code (within modules). NT, like Windows 9x, also uses a Registry, although it's put together quite differently. During startup, NT checks with the system registration (the technical term for the Registry) to learn whether the system should be run as either a workstation (client) or a server.

Here's an example of where Microsoft assigns the same name, "Registry," to two very different ways of doing things. Perhaps the company believes this will further the cause of consistency. The Windows NT/XP Registry has almost no relationship at all to the Windows 9x Registry, although both systems use REGEDIT.EXE as an editor and have similarly appearing HKeys. We'll take a closer look at the Registry files and "hives" in Chapter 16, "Troubleshooting."

The server versions of NT and XP have additional administrative tools, as well as disk-level enhancements. Aside from the administrative tools, Windows NT uses a distinct disk and file management structure: NTFS. We've seen how Windows 9x can use either a FAT16 (16-bit file allocation table) or a FAT32 (32-bit FAT) at the disk level. The NT File System, somewhat related to the OS/2 High Performance File System (HPFS), is a completely redesigned networking file management system. Windows XP and 2000 offer you the option of using FAT32 or NTFS during the installation phase, or converting a volume from FAT32 to NTFS at a later time.

You may find a question on the exam that asks you whether the Registry is like a relational database. Technically speaking, the Registry is nothing whatsoever like a database. The Registry is a grouping of complex files (hives) that store all sorts of settings and configurations. Those files are gathered together and presented in an illusion of a continuous application inside the Registry Editor. Microsoft hopes to convince people that the visual representation of the Registry is like a hierarchical tree (or database), regardless of the traditional use of the word "database."

VFAT and NTFS, discussed in Chapter 14, introduce a separation between disk-level file management and the operating system. The original FAT is a very small (and simple) index of file locations, like a flat-file database. BIOS and disk controllers have a link to FAT16, whereas only Windows can manage FAT32 and NTFS systems. NTFS uses a number of hidden files to manage file information. As such, NTFS is very much like a relational database, using transaction logging to provide not only powerful security features, but also to reduce the chances of corrupted files resulting from system failures, crashes, and improper program termination.

NT Architecture

Internally, Windows NT uses a *modular* design (or modular architecture). DOS is made up of many separate program files, as opposed to NT's use of separate *components*. The difference is that each component in NT manages a separate conceptual function of the overall operating system. One of the problems with updating DOS was that the three basic system files all had to be modified to work with each other. Then, all the ancillary tools and utility programs also had to be modified whenever there was a change to the system files.

Modular design is a way to upgrade individual parts of the operating system without the expense of having to upgrade the entire OS and all its ancillary files. Each module in Windows NT is completely independent of every other module. None of them share any specific program code. The way the modules work together is with *system calls*. Dynamic Link Libraries are outside the main operating system, and can be called from a given component. These .DLL files aren't really called modules, because they're entirely separate files, and not a section of the basic operating system's body of programming code.

Modular Design

We know that a computer program is a series of very exact statements, where each statement leads to the next statement. A series of statements is often called a *routine*. No statement has to necessarily be the next line of code because a computer can read very fast and find the next statement wherever it's located in the program (like the Find feature in a word processor). When a statement tells the computer to go to another statement that isn't next in line, we could say the program is making a *call*. The program calls system functions and memory functions, but when it asks the computer to run another whole set of instructions before it returns to where the program left off, we say the main routine is calling a sub-routine.

Originally, programming was done in a long line of sequential statements. Whenever anyone had to modify the program, they would insert a call to a subroutine and write the entire modification somewhere else in the program. Sometimes those sub-routines had to be modified, in which case someone would insert another call to a new sub-routine. Programs can often be hundreds of thousands, or even millions of lines long, and after a while, all the modifications calling other modifications became known as *spaghetti code,* referring to the total mess of tangled references.

Although spaghetti code calls up a reasonable image for the old way of programming, it became too expensive to continue the practice of inserting calls to sub-routines in such a disorganized fashion. Modular design is a formal set of practices designed to make the individual components of a program easier to work with. Each module is a separate component that can be connected with other modules (routines). Any component, or module, can be added, modified, or replaced without affecting the rest of the components. Integrated design is where there is no clear distinction or separation between the parts of a program.

Modular software design was introduced as a way to keep the related parts of a program all in one area. Main routines were kept separate from sub-routines, and modifications were done in an organized fashion. The programs are still very long, but at least they tend to follow an orderly progression of references.

User Mode

Not only does NT use modular design, but the operating system is also divided into two overall concepts: the *Kernel Mode* and *User Mode*.

Applications (and virtual machines) run in User Mode, and have no direct access to either the microkernel (or just "the kernel") or the hardware abstraction layer (HAL). For example, a 16-bit virtual machine process is an application—the implementation of a program. A database, running inside an MS-DOS window (that is, on the DOS VM), is also considered to be an application. There are really two separate applications, even though you only see what seems to be a single process.

Unlike Windows 9x and DOS, NT exerts many levels of low-level control to prevent the database application from ever having any access to the actual computer system, even though the database appears to be running on the real machine. Earlier versions of Windows could only watch the events taking place on the virtual machine. If that machine crashed, so to speak, then Windows could step in and pre-empt the virtual machine from taking down the main (real) system. NT watches everything: not only the VM, but each program running on that virtual machine. It also watches every other event taking place on the actual, real computer. NT is sort of the CPU's body-guard.

User Mode is divided into sub-systems. Each sub-system communicates with the Executive layer (the NT Executive). The Executive is part of the Kernel Mode. As you can see in Figure 15.1, the two important components of the User Mode are the Win32 sub-system and the Security sub-system. Applications connect to the operating system partly through each sub-system. The sub-systems then place calls to the Executive, which in turn places calls to individual system services modules. (Sure it's confusing, but stick with us. It'll become clearer as we proceed.)

Let's suppose you want to open Microsoft Word. When you (the user) make the request in User Mode, NT uses the Security sub-system to verify that you're allowed to open the program—that you have the proper security rights. These rights are given to you as part of configuring the system security. (We'll take a look at security later in this chapter.) If you're authorized to open the application, NT then uses the Win32 sub-system to discuss your request with the Executive layer. Understand that both sub-systems are constantly sending messages back and forth. We're trying to keep things relatively simple, so it may look as if we're saying all this happens in a linear fashion. It doesn't.

Kernel Mode

User Mode is where you (a person) interact with Windows. Kernel Mode is where all the really complicated computer stuff takes place. Figure 15.1 demonstrates why it's so complicated. Microsoft isn't particularly keen on explaining exactly how each component, layer, and level works, but we've tried to give you a general sense of how they all interact.

The kernel is where NT gives critical components of the operating system direct access to system hardware and the CPU. By the way: We speak of the *privileges* of a given module, as in Kernel Mode being more privileged than User Mode. When components of the OS are running in User Mode, they do not have direct access to the system hardware. Therefore, we say they run in a less privileged, or non-privileged mode. Because the kernel does have direct access to the hardware, we say it's more privileged, and anything running in Kernel Mode is also more privileged.

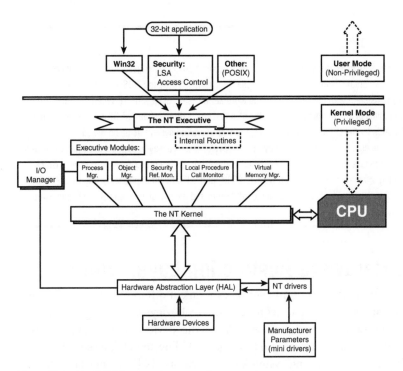

Figure 15.1 The NT/XP layers and components.

The NT kernel (which is the same technology as the XP and Windows 2000 kernel) is responsible for communicating with the CPU. Essentially, the kernel is the gateway through which all other events must pass before they can get to the central processor. The NT Executive is another sort of gateway, acting as the liaison between you and your applications, and the operating system kernel.

In a way, Kernel Mode is sort of the underlying management system. User Mode, on the other hand, is where applications (such as word processors, spreadsheets, printers, digital cameras) and login security connect with that management system. In other words, what you see and how you interact with Windows XP takes place mostly in the User Mode area. Then, whatever you ask the computer to do, those instructions filter through the Executive layer and travel to other places within the operating system. When a device responds to your instructions, being a piece of hardware, it filters its response back through the Hardware Abstraction Layer (the HAL) to get to the kernel. So basically, the NT kernel, or core, pretty much runs the entire shebang.

A Kernel

DOS was known as an *open* operating system because any knowledgeable person could access the fundamental system files. Some people refer to IO.SYS as the DOS kernel, but this is not really consistent with the definition of the word *kernel* as it's used with NT. When the underlying system files of an operating system—the files that speak directly with the BIOS—are placed out of bounds by the OS developers, we refer to that operating system as being based on a kernel. A kernel uses *metadrivers*, created by the OS developers, as a way to connect third-party device driver software to the operating system and motherboard. The prefix *meta* comes from Greek, meaning *after* or *beyond*. Windows NT, 2000, and XP are differentiated from DOS, 16-bit Windows, and Windows 9x in that Microsoft terminated the use of an open OS and began using a kernel.

The Hardware Abstraction Layer (HAL)

The Hardware Abstraction Layer takes a look at different kinds of hardware, and disguises the actual (concrete or real) device, turning it into an *abstraction*—a sort of pretend version of the device. It then presents that abstraction (a virtual reference) to the kernel. The actual device isn't allowed to talk with the operating system's core anymore. NT watches how the virtual device acts, and if it doesn't get kinky or anything, NT then transmits the real, concrete instructions and allows them to go through. It's almost like a very fast, trial run-through of an event before the actual event is allowed to take place.

Microsoft uses only its own device drivers to communicate with the kernel, not the manufacturer's. Device manufacturers may create auxiliary files that contain parameter settings or other minor modifications. Those "mini drivers" connect to the main NT driver software, which then communicate with the HAL.

NT uses this method to prevent badly written device drivers from bringing down the entire system. The problem is that Microsoft must then take on the responsibility of writing all driver software, for every possible type of peripheral device. An important troubleshooting step is to ensure that all hardware devices attached to the system have the latest driver updates, either from Microsoft, or as mini driver updates from the manufacturer.

The Executive Layer

Okay, so the kernel is responsible for managing everything going to the CPU. It also controls each processor in a multi-processor system (for example, Itanium chips). The kernel is also somewhat like a command interpreter (COMMAND.COM), in that it must reside in main memory. Because the kernel is the fundamental control structure for the CPUs, it can never be removed from main memory in any type of memory paging. Remember that COMMAND.COM routinely moves large parts of its programming in and out of memory, making for the distinction between the its transient and resident parts. (See Chapters 12 and 13.)

System Services

The system service modules (shown in Figure 15.1) interact with each other, and with the kernel. When an application makes a request to do something, one of the User Mode sub-systems "contacts" the Executive. The Executive then routes the request to one of its own system services modules. The modules include

➤ The Process Manager

➤ The Object Manager

➤ The Security Reference Monitor (discussed in more detail later in this chapter)

➤ The Local Procedure Call Monitor

➤ The Virtual Memory Manager

➤ The I/O Manager

Of these modules, the I/O Manager is unusual in that it connects directly with the kernel. This is the module responsible for such things as access to a disk drive, printing a file, or working with the mouse. Understand that the Executive contains a number of internal programming routines to enable each module to "talk" with the other sub-modules in the layer. It's as if the

Executive has six secretaries, each responsible for handling a particular type of work. The I/O "secretary" has special authority to talk directly with the kernel, whereas the other sub-systems still have to go through additional channels of communication.

An NT Example Model

Another way of looking at all this might be a military base. Let's suppose that the kernel is the command center. Now suppose you want to come onto the base, so you arrive at the main gate. You're an application, or a piece of hardware that wants to do something on the computer (the military base). The User Mode security sub-system stops you, and demands to see your credentials. After you prove you're legitimate, you're asked to state your business. Whatever that business is, the sub-system takes a look at it and decides which part of the base you should go to. Everything is mostly happening in User Mode, up to this point.

The "you" in this story could just as easily be a DOS virtual machine, or an Excel spreadsheet, or an email coming from Outlook. The main gate sub-systems call the Executive layer and talk over whether you're allowed to proceed. The Executive checks with the security sub-system to see if you're listed (if you have a profile and Security ID), and what you're allowed to do. When the authorization comes back to the main gate, the User Mode sub-systems tell the Executive to prepare any modules you'll need. At that point, you're allowed to pass into the military base (Kernel Mode). Now let's suppose you need a Jeep to travel around on the base.

The Jeep would be like a hardware device, and that request goes back to Win32, and then through all the same processes involving the Executive. The difference is that instead of your request coming from outside the system, you (the application) are already inside the system. Even so, the security sub-systems check the Access Control List (ACL) to see whether the application's user (you) is allowed to have a Jeep (whether you can access the piece of hardware on the network). This time, the Jeep might be a print request coming from a spreadsheet (that you're using) and designated for a network printer. When security determines you have access to the printer (therefore, so does the application you're using), the Executive then talks with the I/O manager module about passing the print job along.

The I/O manager has a direct connection to the hardware manager—the HAL. You've been cleared to use a printer (the Jeep), and so the system calls up the garage to order you a Jeep. However, the Jeep itself has to be authorized to travel around the base. The Hardware Abstraction layer calls up the central garage for a driver (a device driver). The military (Microsoft) trains drivers in a basic fashion, but each driver might go through additional, special training (mini-drivers) for things like half-tracks, missile carriers, and other vehicles (devices).

You, personally, are not going to be allowed to drive the Jeep anywhere on the base. In the same way, the actual device isn't going to be allowed to access the system directly (using the manufacturer's driver). Only Microsoft (the military base) drivers can access the kernel. You've got papers (security rights). Those papers authorize the driver to contact the HAL and pass the print job to the kernel. At that point, the command center checks with everyone else to make sure you're legitimate. If that's cleared, then finally the command center passes along the print job to the CPU. Understand that everything else going on with Excel, or your mouse, or the monitor, is going through the same steps.

Ultimately, Windows NT is all about checking every single event taking place inside the computer before it gets to the CPU for processing. The CPU is the "Base Commander," so to speak, and must be protected at all times, according to Microsoft. It doesn't matter if that protection is from user configuration settings or from badly written software programs. Essentially, the operating system (surrounding the kernel) is supposed to make sure that the CPU never shuts down or locks up. Finally, the entire system is supposed to be thoroughly protected against unauthorized access, either through a virus or a security hack.

NT Security

Let's suppose we were to set up a computer in a building somewhere, and then we installed some kind of software on that machine. After we've configured a particular machine, we *deploy* (spread out) a networking strategy and install many additional computers and devices. NT networking strategy is based on *workgroups* (people) and *domains* (territories). Each grouping makes up a type of security definition. In other words, groups and domains make it possible to enforce security on the network by assigning access rights to individuals (several of whom can join together in a group) or geographic areas (for example, the East Coast region and the West Coast offices).

After a machine has been set up and all the software has been installed, it's ready to be used by a person. In the case of a file server, the machine is ready to be used by other machines. However, even file servers have to be managed (administered) by a person. As we talk about NT security, we refer to an *end user* as the person doing day-to-day work on a local computer. We refer to the *network administrator* as the person in charge of giving network access to end users.

Microsoft designed Windows NT to be used in government installations, as well as multinational corporate environments. One of the reasons the following discussion of security is so complicated is that NT is a C-2–compliant operating system, as defined by the National Computer Security Council (NCSC). NCSC security levels are then specified in the U.S. Department of Defense Trusted Computer Systems Evaluation Criteria, known as the Orange Book. C-2 allows NT to be used by the Department of Defense, along with other government agencies. That doesn't make the ensuing discussion any easier to understand, but we thought you'd like to know.

Security Account Manager (SAM)

In a small workgroup deployment, each individual machine is considered an equal to every other machine, much like peer-to-peer networking. Each machine stores its own *Security Account Manager (SAM)* database (Sam isn't related to Hal). One big difference between a local or standalone machine and a network setup is that many times the workstation actually stores security data right on the hard drive. In larger installations, much of the programming information and security data is stored on a file server, and then "distributed" to the individual computers.

You should be able to see the Security Account Manager module within the Executive services, in Figure 15.1, shown previously. Workgroups make sense in situations where someone can easily go around to each local PC and adjust who has access to what. Larger environments, often covering many buildings, introduce the problem of managing hundreds or thousands of users. It would be nearly impossible for the few IT professionals to be constantly running around to each PC, whenever an employee needed access to a new or different network resource.

This kind of environment calls for distributed applications, where central file servers hold various programs and send session copies over the backbone to whoever needs that application at any given time. In such a large-scale setting, the server might have a network version of Office XP, for example. An individual employee calls up a copy of Word into memory on their local PC (the one on their desk), instead of having the program actually installed on his or her own hard drive.

Consider that a file server can identify another computer by examining data on the hard drive, or even by looking at a network card address on a card in that specific machine. But how does the network know whether you're at your desk or at someone else's desk and computer? Certain security configurations store passwords and User ID information on a computer's hard drive. If you try to use a different computer, you won't be able to log on to the network. Domains and more complex security store your authorization data on the network itself, thereby allowing you to use any available machine.

Distributed applications are set up with the Windows NT domain structure. Every computer in a domain uses a *Central Domain* SAM database. Windows NT file servers coordinate these domain Security Account Managers (the SAM). Domains enable an individual network administrator to assign such things as resource sharing, login names, passwords, and other rights to access something on the network from a single machine.

User ID

Networks use a logon name as the *user identification* (User ID). The User ID is the set of characters that define a specific individual to the operating system. The typical way to ensure that people are who they say they are is for end users to invent a password. First-time users are given an initial User ID and password by the network administrator during the setup process. Then, after the person has taken the responsibility for their own computer, they create their own personal password. In other words, the User ID stays the same, but the password changes.

Making Up Passwords

Passwords are the only real protection you have in terms of keeping your identity secure on a network. In many corporate environments, your password allows you access to information that can have legal ramifications. Rather than making up something fairly logical as a password, such as your initials or birthday, a better password is a certain phrase you remember. For instance, you might like the phrase, "I'm a little teapot," so you can easily remember it. Why not make your password IALTP? This acronym makes no sense whatsoever on its own, but each letter stands for the words in a phrase you particularly like and can remember. This sort of password is difficult to crack by an illegal user, yet very easy to remember (and type) as a phrase. If you like short phrases and your password must be longer, make a rule that you type your password twice in a row, as in IALTP IALTP.

Today's computer espionage relies heavily on human nature, and the fact that most corporations with sensitive data are also large enough that few employees know who works for the company. Regardless of the types of passwords anyone uses, the most common way to break into a system is to simply call up an employee and tell them there's a work emergency and the caller doesn't remember a vital piece of logon information. Given the stress and pressures in a typical environment, many people give out important network security information without thinking about it at all. Try not to keep your User IDs and passwords taped to the computer monitor, and don't casually give out logon information to anyone who asks for it.

The Logon Procedure

The first step to working with a networked computer is to *log on* to the network (with the *logon* procedure or logon command). Network computers have to recognize a human being to understand what that person is or isn't allowed to do. The list of these privileges is called a *user account*, and the end user's account information determines which areas and resources on the network that person has access to.

Understand that Windows XP and 2000 begin with the assumption that every PC is a network computer, regardless of whether it's a home system or business machine. However, on a home computer, you have the option of leaving the password blank. You're the Administrator, by default, but you can choose to create a sort of virtual network within the single computer, and set up individual users (members of the family, for instance). The logon procedure is a fundamental part of the overall security perspective designed into Windows NT/2000/XP.

The logon procedure in Windows NT begins with pressing the Ctrl+Alt+Del. Originally, this was the way to restart a machine with a warm boot (see Chapter 12). In Windows 9x, the keystrokes were reassigned to the Task Manager, calling up TASKMAN.EXE to show programs running in memory at that moment. Pressing Ctrl+Alt+Del on an NT machine calls up an NT Logon Information dialog box (generally called WinLogon).

Local Security Authorization (LSA)

Within the logon dialog box, you select the option indicating you want to log on to the network, then enter your User ID and password. When you've entered your information, NT begins the Local Security Authorization (LSA) process, which runs the *logon authentication package*. The LSA is one of the sub-systems between the end user and the Kernel mode. (Refer to Figure 15.1.)

The logon name identifies you as part of a workgroup or a domain, and the authentication package compares what you entered against the SAM database. (Keep in mind that a workgroup has a local Security Account Management database right on the machine you're using, whereas a domain setup transmits the authentication package over the network to the Central Domain SAM database on a remote file server.)

 In large corporations, different User IDs can be assigned to seek out completely different sets of remote file servers. This is an example of situations in which both the User ID and the password might change. However, the more common procedure is for the network administrator to keep a single User ID for you and add or remove different servers according to your changing work requirements.

Security Access Token (SAT)

If the logon authentication package matches, NT creates a logon *session* and passes specific account information to the Local Security Authority. The LSA creates a *security access token (SAT)*. This token is like an electronic ID badge that the system moves through the network in a similar fashion to how you would use a plastic badge to move around a building. If the information in the logon package doesn't match the SAM, a dialog box pops up displaying a "Logon failure" warning. The Local Security Authority generates the SAT (token) following a successful logon procedure. This token has its own properties.

Security Identification (SID)

The SAT contains the end user's *security identification* (security ID, or SID). It also contains the SID for any groups to which the end user belongs, as well as various network privileges (user rights) assigned to that person. Again, the token is like an electronic security badge, with descriptions of what you're allowed to use. If it isn't listed, then you're prevented from accessing a network resource.

 The SID is a permanent account identifier, based on a hashing algorithm. After the SID is generated it stays the same even when the account name and/or password is changed. The only way to change the SID itself is to delete the User account and then re-create it.

The security access token (SAT), on the other hand, is generated following a successful logon procedure. Additionally, any rights or privileges the network administrator changes take effect in the SAT only after the end user has logged off the network and begins the logon process the next time. It's like getting a new badge every time you log onto the network. The Security ID is your master identification name. The Security Authorization Token lists what rights you have on the network at any given time.

Windows NT provides a way for every logon session to be stored, much like any history log. This *session log* can then be audited, which means that a network administrator can review the log for information about what was done by the end user. Only Administrators have access to the security logs under the Event Viewer.

The User Process

Finally, the logon process calls the Win32 sub-system (in the User Mode), which creates a *user process*. Win32 then connects the SAT to that process. The Win32 sub-system then creates the end user's Desktop from the person's profile (held in HKEY_CURRENT_USER). This may sound pretty complicated, but imagine the people who dreamed up all this stuff in the first place!

Network Security Philosophy

Why is it so complicated just to sit down and type a letter? The reason has to do with two basic philosophies of network security. Peer-to-peer networks have generally tended to begin with the premise that individual people should control their own machines, relying on honor and character when giving every user full access to the entire network. Client/server networks tend to be based on a more skeptical perspective, taking total control over the network and allowing individual users only specific privileges. NT, much like NetWare, begins with the assumption that no one has access to anything. It then creates user profiles where specific access is granted, little by little.

Session Manager (SMSS)

Windows NT runs the Session Manager (SMSS.EXE), which starts the User Mode sub-systems and services for the individual end user. When the SMSS is successfully in place, NT runs a boot-time Check Disk (not anything at all like the old DOS CHKDSK.EXE) on every partition, to verify partition integrity. (Actually, Check Disk in NT is much like ScanDisk, only it needed a different name because NT was way cooler than everything else.)

NT then sets up a swap file, giving it a different (and cooler) name. This swap file is called the *paging file* (pagefile.sys), and works pretty much the way that any other swap file is used for virtual memory disk swapping (paging). After the paging file has been set up, NT runs the Win32 sub-system to set up the User mode and control user input at the keyboard and monitor. (See Chapter 13 for more on virtual memory and swap files.)

Win32 and LSA

Essentially, Win32 starts WINLOGON.EXE, which runs the Local Security Authority (LSASS.EXE) that pops up the Logon dialog box. At that point, even though you'll see a logon dialog box, the startup process is still continuing with system services loading in the background.

When we talk about multitasking, one event is in the foreground, taking the computer's focus and interacting directly with the user. Other events (such as system services, printing, or the Windows Messenger, for example) are in the background, running on the system out of sight from the user and behind the window on the screen.

Last Known Good

After an end user has successfully logged on, the startup is considered to be "good," and the HKEY_LOCAL_MACHINE\System\LastKnownGood Registry sub-key is updated to point to the particular key containing the hardware configuration that was just used to start NT.

Each time NT has a successful startup, the hardware profile and associated pass/fail error codes are recorded in a particular file. "Last Known Good" accesses this file in the event of a crash on startup, and allows you to choose whether you want to use that last profile. This safety feature was carried over to Windows 9x, and, as we've seen, the Registry makes an automatic copy of itself, along with a first-time startup file, each time a successful startup takes place.

Windows XP modifies this process, and we discuss the XP Registry in the next chapter. However, whether you see Last Known Good, something about last known settings, or a reference to starting Windows with any previous configuration, remember that Windows is storing a workable set of configuration settings in the Registry.

A situation where the last known hardware profile might not be the appropriate selection could arise when a laptop computer connects through a docking station. The last time the user logged on, he was using an additional piece of hardware (the docking station). If he tries to log on with a direct cable connection to the NIC, "Last Known Good" might generate a problem. The optional hardware configuration menu item was available in Windows NT, but removed in Windows 2000 and XP.

The Security Reference Monitor

The Security Reference Monitor takes charge of verifying whether an *access request* to an object (such as sending a document to a printer and accessing that printer) is allowed, and whether the requesting process has permission to perform an operation on the object. (Remember the Jeep in the military base example?) In other words, part of your account profile gives you certain user rights. These rights grant you and your machine permission to do stuff (technical term). That "stuff" might be something like your wanting to save a file (a process) to a disk (an object) somewhere. When you and your machine request access to disk space on a file server, the Security Reference Monitor checks to see whether you have permission to access that disk.

Access Control List (ACL)

The Security Reference Monitor generates the audit messages we just mentioned (session logs), and to come up with these particular messages, it looks in the *access control list (ACL)*. The access control list is made up of *access masks*. These masks are just a complicated way of saying that each object has a list detailing which end users and workgroups can mess with (another technical term) the object. Remember how we said NT's hardware abstraction layer disguises an actual piece of hardware? In a way, the HAL is treating every piece of hardware like an object. Filled with an overblown sense of its own importance, NT chooses to call each entry on the access control list an *access control entry (ACE)*.

There are three types of access masks: specific (specific to an object), standard (objects within a group), and generic (pointers to both specific and standard masks). A specific access mask can have up to 16 properties used to describe a specific object. A mask is nothing more than a complicated way of saying "the list of things that describe an object." Your driver's license is a specific access mask for you, the specific object. In this case, your driver's license could have 16 places to put some descriptive information, like your hair color, your weight, or the color of your eyes.

Entities, Attributes, and Masks

An *entity* is a single thing. That thing exists in some fashion, and we human beings understand its existence by observing its attributes. An apple is an entity and it has many attributes. Some of the apple's attributes include seeds, a core, leaves, red skin, sour or sweet taste, worms, and so on. A 2 is also an entity, but in this case the 2 is an *abstraction*. You can't point to a 2, but can only point to the influence of *two-ness* on other entities. For instance, two apples are not the same thing as the two-ness of the "pair" of apples. Pair-ness is an attribute of 2.

A concrete entity is something you can perceive directly with your senses. An abstract entity is something you can perceive only with your mind. A 2 has attributes in exactly the same way that an apple or a file has attributes. Some of the attributes of a 2 include the actual symbol we use to describe the two-ness of things (2 or II), its even-ness, and the fact that it contains a 1 and a 1. The 1 is also an entity, with attributes of singleness, oddness, unit, and individuality.

In an object-oriented computer world, we try to consolidate various associated attributes into a single entity. Then we call the entity an object. An entity is the same thing as an object. Because attributes are often abstract, the entities themselves are even more abstract (high-level or low-level abstractions). The computer world is being created in an ongoing way, and each programmer or developer sees sets of attributes in his or her own way. NT is a world of abstractions, and Microsoft has chosen to assign names to things based on what it considers to be similarities. In one world, a description is a list of attributes assigned to an entity. In the NT world, Microsoft changed the word "description" to the word "mask" and proclaimed it good. This would be the philosophy of Microsoftism, or a Microsoftian way of understanding reality.

If you think about how the security monitor actually works, you can see how NT also creates a sort of end user object out of whoever is using an NT workstation. Part of the network operating system assigns attributes to the living, people-type objects, whereas another part of the operating system is busy assigning attributes to the hardware and file resource objects. Just as you would have an account profile that tells NT what you're allowed to do, so does every object have an access mask (description) that tells NT what groups of people can mess with that object.

In the NT world, an object might be a printer, a modem, a word processor application, a folder, or even a file within a folder. The network administrator builds an access mask for every object, and lists those descriptions in the access control list—the ACL we were just talking about.

The Security Reference Monitor is like a hall monitor in school, constantly interrupting the flow of requests and asking to see a pass. The pass is the listing that gives someone the permission (rights) to be in the hall. The pass also details why that person is in the hall, and where he can and can't go. The hall monitor looks on a list (the ACL) to see whether the information on the pass (the security access token) matches that list.

Finally, you should be aware of the fact that *blocked* access takes precedence over *granted* access. NT always finds that a user has been blocked before it checks to see whether the user has permission to access an object. In other words, NT starts with the assumption that a user is blocked, and then looks to see whether there are access privileges. The thing that's interesting about this is that if an end user has individual access rights to a folder, but that end user is logged onto the network as part of a blocked group, the group rights take precedence over the individual rights (not unlike communism). In a situation where a group is denied access to an object, all the users within that group are also denied access, regardless of their rights when they're logged in as individuals.

To sum it all up in the simplest possible terms and to make all of this exceptionally easy to remember, we could say that the SRM from the LSA looks at the SAT for the SID. If the SAT compared to the ACL's ACE doesn't match, the SRM and ACL deny the SAT's SID access. See? Nothing could be simpler. Oh, and don't forget the User mode working alongside the Kernel mode, talking through the Executive layer with the Win32 sub-system to get the micro kernel to fool around with the system services. And just think, you don't even have to try to install an NT system.

The preceding paragraph was ironic.

Accounts and Profiles

User accounts and profiles are ways for the network to understand end users and what kind of privileges they have. An *account* is basically another way of talking about a *user profile*. Consider this: If you were to open a savings account, you would put money into your account. The bank would assign you an account number. At the same time, the bank could look at how you seem to be similar to many other people, and they might create a profile for people like you. The bank could try to tailor different kinds of accounts for every individual person in the world, but it's a lot less work (and expense) to tailor its services to a smaller number of profiles.

Given the flagrant disregard for common understanding of language in the computer industry, networking reverses the way accounts and profiles are used. In a networking environment, an *account* is a generic category for end users who fit into a typical pattern. A *profile*, on the other hand, is the specific services to which an individual end user has access. In the backward world of computer-speak, you would go into a bank and open a checking profile. If you seem to be similar to lots of other people, the bank would then create an account for groups of people like you.

Administrator

The Administrator account is a default account, meaning that it's been set up within the operating system and will always be there. Every installation of NT/2000/XP must have someone in charge of managing the networking events and the operating system. That person has rights to the Administrator account. The Administrator account can't be removed, and it grants permissions to that person (or group of people) to make changes within the operating system itself. If you choose to leave the password blank during a standalone installation, any user can log on as the Administrator and make any changes to the system.

Both Windows XP Home edition and Professional have a default Administrator account. However, in the Home edition, all users on an individual PC have Administrator rights. XP Professional allows different levels of security and administration to separate users on the same machine. XP Pro Administrators can set up a standalone machine that blocks or allows other users' access rights to configuration settings and areas within the computer system.

User

The User account is another generic account, installed by default. The basic User account is more like a template because when the Administrator opens a New User dialog box, the initial User account template forms the basis for whatever modifications the administrator will make. Those modifications then become the template for each new user the Administrator wants to set up. Saving that information creates a specific User account, and the next time a new account is opened, the template comes up with blank spaces to fill in. The templates can be saved with different names, making it a simple task to set up different types of accounts.

User accounts, which can be used for both groups and individuals, contain the varying information making up the profile for that user. Keep in mind that a "user," as we're using it in "User account," could mean more than one person. The bottom line is that each User account has different rights, depending on what network resources the Administrator assigns. Also remember that a profile determines what the user or group can or cannot do on the system.

Essentially, you (being an Administrator) would open up the first User account and set it up with description lines. Then you might save that account under a different name, making an Accounting Users template, for example. When the company hires someone new for the Accounting Department, you would put her into the Accounting Users account, and then edit her profile to give her specific access to network resources. If there was no special difference in her access rights, the Accounting Users group would need to add only the one new name.

Guest

A default installation also creates a third type of account called the Guest account (initially disabled). The reason for this is that it's not at all unusual for a corporation to have many file servers and applications, all designed to produce whatever work the company does. In all that technology, there's usually a standard word processor and spreadsheet application. The files being created each day by those two applications are stored on various disks with some amount of security and privacy. But what happens when a visitor wants to borrow a computer to type a memo to his or her secretary back at the home office?

The Guest account provides a way for someone who isn't an end user (with an assigned User account) to use network resources in a very restricted fashion. The network administrator has control over all accounts and all resources, and can set the default rights to the Guest account.

Windows NT/2000/XP provides three default accounts: Administrator, User, and Guest. (The default installation setup disables the Guest account.) After a User account has been set up, the administrator uses the operating system security features to grant rights and permissions to each account in terms of accessing network resources. Every account generates its own security access token (SAT) which identifies the account to every object at every access request.

Managing User Accounts

The Windows 9x Explorer is a dulled-down version of the NT Explorer and is mostly used for file maintenance tasks, such as copying, moving, deleting files, and creating folders and subfolders. NT introduced the NT File System (NTFS), which expands the Explorer's capabilities. Not only can the Explorer be used for folder and file maintenance, but on an NTFS partition, it also can be used to view and set object permissions and to configure *auditing* on files and folders. In other words, on a FAT32 partition, the Explorer shows only such things as file attributes, last modified date, and size. An NTFS partition adds more information, and gives the Explorer added capabilities to assign access rights to individual files and folders.

You can imagine what it would be like if you were setting up an NT network in a corporation with 5,000 employees and you had to create a User account for each person, and then assign rights and access to individual folders and files every time. To aid in this process, many end users can be assigned to a single group. This is what we were describing when we discussed the Accounting Users a moment ago.

After a group has been defined, the profile information for that group is automatically assigned to any individual user joined to that group. Suppose you get a job in the IT department of the A+ Corporation. The network administrator has probably set up a "Totally Cool Group" for everyone in the IT department. One of the privileges of that group is that anyone assigned to the Totally Cool Group has the right to assign other users to groups, or to assign object access to end users. All your boss has to do is enter you into the system and assign you to the group, and you take on all the rights and privileges of being Totally Cool. It's a lot like the cliques in high school when you stop to think about it.

Another example would be where a group of people in the real world is in charge of developing and writing a business course. Each person in this bunch (group) already has his or her own user account, but they're working together on a special project. The whole group might need access to parts of the network they ordinarily wouldn't be allowed to use.

A management person temporarily assigned to the project would have access to things that other employees would not. When the project group has been set up, NT automatically gives anyone involved in that particular project the rights and permissions allowed while that particular project is under way. (The Administrator can delete the group at the end of the project.) Note that if the management person is logged in to the project group, he has only whatever rights are assigned to that group. To regain his special management rights would require logging out of the project group, and then logging back in under his personal User ID.

NT establishes certain groups at the time it's installed. Each of these groups has certain default rights and permissions. The default groups are

➤ Administrators (NT Server)

➤ Operators—based on operations defined as Account, Backup, Print, or Server

➤ Power Users

➤ Users

➤ Guests

NT Workstation uses local groups. NT Servers use a combination of both local and global groups. A *local group* is specific to a local machine (your own PC), whereas a *global group* can be set up across an entire domain. Any end user assigned to a global group can go to any machine on the network and log on under that group name, gaining access to all the resources assigned to the global group anywhere in the domain.

Policies Versus Profiles

Windows for Workgroups (WFW) 3.11 used simple peer-to-peer networking. NT is much more sophisticated. In the old days, part of managing a network was to set certain *policies*, or general rules as to how people could interact with the overall network. The term "policies" has fallen into disuse, being replaced by the concept of group rights, domain management, and systems administration templates.

Windows 3.x introduced an almost undocumented feature whereby the PROGMAN.INI file could be opened (in a text editor) and a [Restrictions] heading could be inserted at a blank line. These restrictions included NoRun=, NoClose=, NoSaveSettings=, NoFileMenu=, and EditLevel=. Depending on the numeric values (0–4) entered after the equal sign, an administrator could prevent users from running certain programs, saving modified settings, or even accessing the main menu's File option.

Windows 95 began making the restrictions more sophisticated, introducing the optional Policy Editor. (Optional means that the Policy Editor [POLEDIT.EXE] was not automatically installed during Setup.) The restrictions broadened to include restricted access to the Control Panel, customization limits for the Desktop, and restrictions on network access configuration changes. An example would be the Administrator setting the policy for the MS-DOS environment where certain types of programs could not be run at all.

Policies are an *exclusive* authorization process, meaning that out of all possible ways an end user might get into trouble, certain global areas can be excluded. Profiles, on the other hand, are more like an *inclusive* authorization process, meaning that the systems administrator has to figure out ahead of time what an end user may need to accomplish. Given that work environments are constantly adapting to meet changing conditions, an inclusive process tends to carry with it a much greater burden (overhead) on the corporate network administrators as they run around adding rights and permissions they hadn't thought of previously.

Starting Windows NT

Windows NT is a portable operating system, meaning that it can be installed on systems using an Alpha CPU or an Intel CPU, among others. Therefore, the way NT starts up is different for each platform. We'll focus on the Intel environment, given that it's the most typical environment for an A+ technician to be working with. We'll also reference only the most basic landmarks, and leave out the hundreds of services and additional files that are opened and closed during the process.

 If you understand the way NT starts up, you'll also understand how Windows 2000 and XP do the same thing. Understand that the startup process is not the same thing as the Start Menu and the options available on that menu, such as a different OS or the F8 Safe Mode key. Also remember that NT uses a small, separate startup partition, and then looks at the boot partition for the main operating system files. The boot partition doesn't have to be the same as the so-called system partition, which boots the computer.

There are 17 steps in the startup process, and we're pretty sure that within the year, anyone shopping in a supermarket will be required to know all 17

steps before they can purchase a pint of milk. The first step, as it is for any other computer, is the POST. At the end of the POST, the BIOS hands off to the NT loader (different from the DOS bootstrap loader), which looks for something in the boot sector of a disk.

NT, like any other operating system, looks for the Master Boot Record (MBR). Instructions in the MBR tell the operating system to look for a bootable partition and to load the NT boot sector from that partition. In DOS, the location of the boot sector was restricted to an Active, Primary partition. OS/2 didn't have this restriction and could load from a so-called non-bootable partition. NT puts certain critical files on an Active, Primary partition, but can load the rest of the operating system from any other type of partition, including an extended partition.

Boot and System Partitions

Windows NT (also XP and W2000) creates a small *system partition* (bootable) at the front of the disk, and this partition contains the boot loader (NTLDR) that tells the operating system where to find the system files. The system files (\WINNT for Windows 2000, or the \Windows folder for XP) are installed on a *boot partition* (backwards naming again), which is the volume that contains the required files needed to load NT. The system partition must be on a disk that BIOS can find. Understand that the boot partition can be on the same disk as the system partition, but it doesn't have to be. (The overall NT/XP system files can even be on an extended partition's logical drive.)

In some instances where XP has completely crashed, you can see the different partitions used during the boot process. For example, regardless of what you may have heard, the upgrade versions of Windows 2000 and XP are not bootable CDROMs. However, if a hard drive has a previously installed system that's crashed, you can place the upgrade CDROM in the drive and the system will appear to boot from the disk. In fact, the system is starting the boot process from the boot manager partition, and then looking for the NT system files. When it fails to find or load XP from the hard drive, it then looks at all mounted volumes. Assuming the CDROM drive is working, the boot process finds the basic startup files on the upgrade disk, and then offers you the option of repairing or reinstalling XP/2000.

Be sure that you understand this concept of a system partition (bootable) being separate from the boot partition (working files). This system partition is why XP is so easily installed with multiple operating systems. Windows NT/2000/XP no longer can be started with a single floppy disk. The Emergency Repair Disk, or a so-called bootable floppy diskette, contains only the loader files necessary for NT to try and find the system files. If you were to create a DOS boot disk, using FORMAT A: /S, and install the DOS system files, the boot process would bypass NTLDR and boot to DOS. On the other hand, the NT/XP startup diskette contains no actual system files. Remember, the loader's only job is to go out and find the NT system files (first using BOOT.INI, if it exists).

The NT Loader (NTLDR)

After the information in the boot sector goes into memory, it loads the NT *boot loader* (again, the NTLDR) into memory. The boot loader switches the processor into 32-bit mode, and starts a *mini file system* to support either a FAT32 or NTFS volume. At that point, the system reads a BOOT.INI file, displaying a menu of the available operating systems to the end user. (A specific configuration line in the .INI file defines how long the options list stays displayed.)

The BOOT.INI file displays a list of any other operating systems available on the disk (that NT can understand). "Operating system," in this case, means only bootable system files. Installing an upgrade version of XP on a bootable DOS disk formatted with only the three DOS system files will generate a menu option to load Windows 9x (or even just plain DOS), even though the fully functioning OS doesn't exist.

Also remember that a new installation for XP/2000 must begin with a FAT32 partition. NTFS is installed during a scheduled conversion partway through the process, if the user chooses to use the NT File System, even when the NTFS option takes place on a newly formatted hard disk.

Following the BOOT.INI display, NT boot loader then runs NTDETECT.COM to detect and prepare a list (profile) of the currently installed hardware. This list of hardware is passed back to the NT Loader. In Windows NT (only), the process pauses allowing the user to pick the Last Known Good hardware profile. Windows 2000/XP doesn't have the same pause or option anymore. However, XP/2000 does examine the lastknowngood Registry entry for a hardware profile. (Note that in an XP crash, you'll get a startup menu option to use previously working settings.)

NT Loader then brings the NT kernel (NTOSKRNL.EXE) into memory, and passes the hardware profile to the kernel. At this point, the kernel loads, *but does not initialize*, all the hardware device drivers associated with the hardware profile. The kernel then attempts to take control of the hardware devices. When all device drivers have been initialized and their companion devices are under control, the kernel then loads and initializes a second group of drivers. (This is step 11, by the way, for anyone who's counting.)

The landmarks in a boot process include the pre-booting events of the POST and the boot process itself. Following these two steps, there's a distinction between the *load* events and *initialization* events. This is

Microsoftian for getting something into memory (loading). After that something is in memory, it's connected to a piece of hardware or software and made to start running (initialized).

Finally, there's the logon procedure, which continues forward while the services load in the background. The short version of loading Windows NT/2000/XP is as follows:

1. *NTLDR.COM*—Acts as a bootstrap loader for the basic operating system. This begins the NT hardware detection phase, switches the CPU into 32-bit mode, and loads a mini file system that can work with either a FAT or NTFS file management system.

2. *BOOT.INI*—Contains a pointer listing any other operating systems available, along with a configuration statement as to how long the options list will display.

3. *BOOTSECT.DOS*—Multiple boots (see the following section, "Multiple Boot Options").

4. *NTDETECT.COM*—Identifies current hardware components installed on the machine and prepares a list of that configuration. This is where the spacebar option takes place, allowing different hardware profiles to be loaded.

5. *NTBOOTDD.SYS*—Used with SCSI and ATA controller devices, where an adapter is not using BIOS.

6. *NTOSKRNL.EXE*—Loads the operating system kernel and creates the current Registry hardware key. Along with the kernel, the file loads (not initializes) device drivers and loads (not initializes) the Session Manager.

7. *HAL.DLL*—A dynamic link library that generates the hardware abstraction layer, interfacing between the operating system and the specific hardware.

8. *SYSTEM*—Opens the Registry and reads the operating system configuration, initializing the device drivers loaded previously by NTSOSKRL.EXE, and then loads any additional device drivers found in the Registry.

9. *SMSS.EXE*—Initializes the Session Manager, executes any boot-time command files (like the old AUTOEXEC.BAT), and then loads basic services and sets up the so-called page file (swap file). The program creates links to the file system that can be used by DOS commands and then starts the Win32 I/O subsystem and begins the logon process.

10. *WINLOGON.EXE*—The specific program file that generates the logon process and starts the Local Security Authority (LSA).

11. *LSASS.EXE*—The program file for the LSA, providing all the security-checking done by the system.

Although we've listed the primary files in this startup process, Windows uses countless other .DLL files, device drivers, helper files, and system files to load and run the system.

Multiple Boot Options

Back when IBM was developing OS/2 (which looked a whole lot like DOS), the company developed a little program that would allow a machine to have more than one operating system installed. This program gave the user a menu listing each bootable OS. The IBM Boot Manager was one of those rare moments of elegance where the program was designed to do one single thing and do it perfectly. You'll still find that program packaged with PowerQuest's PartitionMagic, but we should remember that Microsoft's Windows NT was originally part of the OS/2 joint development effort.

Windows NT (not XP/2000) provides a paused screen during the startup process, to ask you whether you want to use the same hardware profile that worked the last time (Last Known Good). It also offers you a menu of any other available operating system from which you might want to boot. Windows XP/2000 no longer offer the previous hardware profile, but the BOOT.INI file continues to generate a menu with all available, bootable operating systems. (This internalization of a multiple boot process began showing up in DOS 5.0, where you could boot to different configurations. At that time, you were restricted to DOS as the operating system, but NT 3.x introduced multiple operating system capabilities.)

Windows XP installs fairly easily to a system with other operating systems. The boot partition is very similar to IBM's Boot Manager, still found in PowerQuest's Partition Magic. When you convert a partition to NTFS, DOS can no longer read any file information from that partition. Therefore, if you install Windows XP/2000 on a system with Windows 9x, keep in mind that you'll be able to see the files on the Windows 9x partition when you're in XP, but you won't even see the NTFS "drive" in the Windows 9x Explorer.

RAID

The word "redundant" means an unnecessary repetition. The word "array" means a lineup. A *Redundant Array of Inexpensive Disks (RAID)* is essentially where a network file server uses extra disks to keep multiple copies of data.

In these situations, the data itself is more valuable than the cost of the disks. That's why the disks are termed inexpensive. (Making repeated copies of the valuable data isn't actually unnecessary; still, that's what the computer people called it, using the word "redundant.") The concept of RAID data protection has been around long enough that there are now six different levels of protection (0 through 5). Each level indicates a higher degree of protection.

RAID Level 0 (RAID 0) is the no-fault-tolerance process of using 64KB block storage areas in a striped set. Striped sets mean using multiple partitions all of the same size. Striped partitions are partitions of equal size on one or more physical disks, joined into a logical area called a set.

Striped sets provide no fault tolerance and can be set up to use anywhere from 2 to 32 partitions on one or more physical disks. Striped sets with parity combine 3 to 32 partitions, where one of the partitions is used as the parity stripe. Striped sets with parity do provide fault tolerance, and are also known as RAID 5.

RAID 1 is the most common form of RAID at the moment and is often used in disk mirroring and disk duplexing. Level 1 provides positive fault tolerance, but at the cost of a 50% reduction in resources. Disk duplexing means using two disks to store data two times. The idea is that if one disk fails, the other has the same information, and the system can continue. RAID 1 is available only on NT Server machines.

Some high-end gaming machines install a server version of XP, along with multiple hard drives, to take advantage of RAID 1 for certain performance gains. This isn't the same thing as using a second physical disk for swap files and virtual memory. Moving the swap file to a different disk is not using RAID.

RAID 2 is similar to striped sets, but the data is moved at a bit level, rather than in 64KB blocks. One of the disks in RAID 2 is set aside for data recovery. This method of data protection is currently unavailable through Windows NT.

RAID 3 is disk striping with parity, with data being moved at the bit level rather than the block level. RAID 4 is disk striping at the block level, with one disk reserved for parity recovery. RAID 5 is also block-level disk striping, but the parity information is evenly spread across all the disks in the array, as opposed to being on only one disk. This removes the typical single-stripe bottleneck of parity writing.

Windows XP supports RAID Levels 1 and 5 on the Server version (Windows Server 2003, at the time of this writing), along with RAID 0 on both the Server and Workstation versions. You'll likely be tested (if at all) on only the most basic differences between RAID 0, 1, and 5.

NT Error Messages

At this point, you've probably sensed that Windows NT is a somewhat complex operating system. We've heard stories of people who've actually taken seminars lasting weeks so that they might understand only a few of the intricacies of the system. Naturally, we fully expect you to have a complete and thorough understanding of everything involved with NT in 25 or 30 pages. No, we're kidding. All we can do is give you a broad overview of the most likely way in which an A+ technician will come in contact with NT. You probably won't deal with server installations, but will spend most of your time working with workstations. The errors we discuss in this section are related to the startup process.

Someone once told us about a young man who wanted to become one of the world's great writers. When he was asked to define what he meant by great, he said, "I want to write stuff that the whole world will read; stuff that people will react to on a truly emotional level; stuff that will make them scream, cry, and howl in pain and anger!" He now works as an operating systems developer, writing error messages.

We'll cover the various startup floppy diskettes in Chapter 16. For the moment, understand that Windows 9x (and DOS) can use a bootable floppy to start the computer. Windows NT/2000/XP use a floppy diskette as only the first part of a boot process, and can't actually boot the machine into a workable environment. Although we might refer to a startup disk, these disks are extremely simplistic, offering only the basic NT loader and hardware detector. They can do very little to start a completely crashed system.

Be sure to have an installation copy of XP/2000 readily available (in a system binder). Also be sure to understand that an installation copy is not at all the same thing as a recovery disk, which is usually an image of a fully installed retail computer. A recovery disk rarely offers the option of doing an in-place repair (reinstall). Microsoft is making an effort to demand that OEM vendors include a recovery disk, but not an installation disk for Windows XP.

NT Detect

Of the thousands of error messages generated during Windows NT operations, certain messages are fairly common for workstations, and we'd like to at least reference them at this point. The first error message we'll mention is "NT Detect Failed."

NTDETECT.COM is responsible for the hardware detection phase of the startup process. The file is located in the root folder of the boot drive, and if it becomes corrupted or is missing, you can try using a startup floppy. If this solves the problem, copy NTDETECT.COM from the floppy to the root folder on the hard drive. Another possibility would be to boot the system from an installation CDROM, and then choose the Repair Windows option.

You can do a simple copy to put NTLDR, NTDETECT.COM, and the BOOT.INI files on a floppy diskette. Always remember that the COPY command is not sufficient to place the three DOS (Windows 9x) system files on a diskette and make it bootable. These three NT startup files are not system files, but rather, exactly what we're saying they are: startup files. An NT startup diskette is not bootable.

Missing Kernel

Another common error message is "The kernel file is missing from the disk." One way to solve this problem is to strike the machine repeatedly with a five-pound sledgehammer. This is not a recommended procedure for the corporate environment. A better strategy would be to understand that the NTLDR file is missing or has become corrupted. Like NTDETECT.COM, this file is in the root folder of the boot drive and can be copied over from a bootable floppy disk or an Emergency Repair Disk.

Missing BOOT.INI

Sometimes NT is feeling so poorly that it can't even give you an error message telling you what's wrong. An example of this is where the machine starts Windows NT but does not display the startup menu (where you choose to Start Windows 2000, for example). In this problem scenario, the menu does not display, nor does the waiting time take place.

In this situation, the BOOT.INI file is missing from the root folder of the boot drive. You might recall that after the NT Loader has finished loading, the system reads the BOOT.INI file to display the available operating system selections. To fix this, see whether the system will start. If it does, copy the BOOT.INI file from the machine's startup diskette to the root folder of the bootable disk.

If NT or Windows 2000 can't find a BOOT.INI file, the system will load from the first partition on the first disk it finds (according to the CMOS boot order setting). NTLDR will look in the \WINNT folder for Windows 2000 system files, or \Windows folder for Windows XP. One way to avoid many problems is to partition a clean disk with a small (500MB) bootable DOS partition at the front of the disk. You can do this with a Windows 98SE Emergency Boot Disk. Then partition a second partition as Active, Primary, and use it to install XP (or Windows 2000).

Format the first partition as a FAT32 DOS partition, leaving only the three system files installed from the Windows 98 bootable disk. Install Windows on the second partition. If the system totally crashes (and you choose not to use NTFS), it will still boot to DOS from the first partition. At that point you can often find a good copy of the BOOT.INI file, NTLDR, and NTDETECT.COM on one of the other partitions. You might also find it useful to make another small partition for DOS utilities, such as FORMAT.COM, FDISK.EXE, SMARTDRV.EXE, and a CONFIG.SYS file and AUTOEXEC.BAT file for CDROM support drivers.

Missing Files

Another common type of error message comes up as "Windows NT could not start because the following file is missing or corrupt," with a listing of some particularly obscure file name. Below the allegedly missing file is the statement "Please reinstall a copy of the above file." For some strange reason, people seem to make the assumption that when NT says a file is missing, then, by golly, a file must be missing! After all, the machine is a self-aware consciousness, right?

One of the critical lines in the BOOT.INI file is the line pointing to the location of the system files partition. You would think that NT could figure out where to find its own files, wouldn't you? This is a classic instance of an error message that gives you all kinds of interesting information, none of which has any bearing on the actual problem.

To resolve the problem, try to boot the machine from the startup floppy. If that works, replace the BOOT.INI file on the bootable hard drive. If the same error message keeps coming up, try using an installation disk to repair the installation. Essentially, the BOOT.INI file is pointing to an XP installation on a disk other than the C: drive, and/or Windows is in some folder other than the C:\Windows folder. If the BOOT.INI file is missing, Windows is hard-coded to look in C:\Windows. If that doesn't exist on this particular problem computer, NTLDR will continue trying to load Windows, asking for every single system file necessary.

Another common instance where you can find yourself copying file after file in response to an "NT can't find" error is during a crashed installation. If at all possible, the best way to recover from a failed installation is to reformat the partition you're trying to use for the installation, and then begin the entire process over again from scratch. This is another reason why having a bootable DOS partition and a second partition with formatting and partitioning utilities is an excellent idea. If you have the DOS utilities on an extended partition, it makes it even easier to reformat the "C:" drive, and totally remove all the hidden temporary installation files XP uses. Be sure that the system has CDROM support in the event that you don't have a bootable XP installation CDROM.

Bootable and Emergency Repair Disks

Two important hardware tools you'll want to understand are a *bootable floppy disk* and a so-called *Emergency Repair Disk* (often referred to as an ERD). The bootable floppy disk is far too small to hold the entire Windows NT (XP and 2000) operating system, but it can hold the key files necessary to begin a startup process. If NT can boot from a floppy disk, you'll at least have a general idea of the most likely next step. If all the workstations in an environment have been set up the same way, the bootable floppy disk then can use a generic hardware profile to start all those machines.

We'll take another look at bootable disks and startup disks in Chapter 16. You should know that you can boot a computer into DOS, Windows 95, Windows 98, and Windows Me. However, Windows NT, 2000, and XP no longer will start from a floppy disk. NT repair disks and the Windows Recovery Console assume a mostly working underlying operating system. NT startup disks can start the machine only if the loader files have become corrupted. If the actual operating system has a problem, the only way to start the system is with a repair reinstallation (an in-place reinstall), a complete reinstallation, or by restoring a backup.

You should know that Windows NT/2000 (not XP) offers an option to create an Emergency Repair Disk through the Backup program. From the Start menu, choose Programs I Accessories I System Tools, and then the "Backup" Wizard. One of the main button options is to create the disk.

Windows XP changed the name of the ERD to the Automated System Recovery (ASR) diskette. It's the same idea, using the same navigational steps. Choose All Programs I Accessories I System Tools, and then select "Backup." Here's where Microsoft made it more difficult and less intuitive for the end user, always in their desire to make running a computer something completely different from supporting computer problems. In the Backup Wizard, you'll have to choose the "Advanced Mode" from a not-so-visible hyperlink, buried inside an informational paragraph.

If you don't choose Advance Mode, you'll have the option of picking what to back up. One of those options lets you select only the System Settings.

However, in Advance Mode, you'll get a button option to start the "Automated System Recovery Wizard." In theory, this will give you a way to start the system. In fact, it doesn't work so well.

All things considered, it's a whole lot easier to just copy the important files to a floppy diskette and keep an installation CDROM in the back pocket of your jeans at all times. (No! We're kidding! Keep the CDROM in your *front* pocket, so it won't be quite as bent when you need to use it.) Remember, the important files, yet again, are NTLDR, NTDETECT.COM, and BOOT.INI.

Windows XP

Windows 2000 joined the usability of Windows 98 with the security, stability, scalability, and networking of NT. Realistically, Windows Me was the end of the DOS-based Windows 9x product line, and the first real attempt to join NT with DOS. However, although Windows 2000 looked like the next evolution of Windows Me, it was actually the next upgrade from NT 4.0. (The internal version number for Windows 2000 is 5.0, which became 5.1 for Windows XP.) Microsoft has indicated that Windows XP is their primary Windows 98 upgrade product.

Like Windows 2000, Windows XP comes in two consumer versions: the *Home* and the *Professional* editions. (The enterprise versions, such as Windows Server 2003, are beyond the scope of this book.) Although both versions operate in the same way, XP Professional provides additional functionality required in corporate installations. Windows XP has a redesigned desktop, which can be returned to the Windows 98/2000 look by using the "Classic Start Menu" Taskbar configuration option. We'll quickly review the main areas you should know about in terms of troubleshooting, diagnostics, and problem-solving, including

➤ Control Panel

➤ Administrative Tools

➤ Device Manager (System)

➤ The Desktop (Display options)

➤ Start Menu and Taskbar

➤ Accessories

➤ Network Connections

➤ User Accounts

➤ The Windows Recovery Console

Once again, we want to stress the point that there's no way we can teach you Windows XP or Windows 2000 in a book designed to be your final review before taking the exam. CompTIA expects that you'll have a substantial amount of experience with these two versions of Windows, as well as with Windows 9x and DOS. Although the test isn't focused on DOS as an operating system, the Recovery Console and Command Line (CMD.EXE) are outgrowths of the DOS environment. Remember that many of the commands (and how they work) are very similar to the old DOS commands. When you know how one command line works, you'll pretty much know how the other one works.

We think the DOS command line is a lot faster than the Windows Recovery Console. Not only that, but Recovery Console must be installed as a separate application, and you'll be required to have an Administrator password before you can enter it. Finally, the Recovery Console restricts access to the entire system (without certain SET commands). For all these reasons, and given that so many of the Recovery Console commands work so similarly to DOS 7.0 commands, you might find that working with the MS-DOS Mode command prompt on a Windows 98 machine is much easier, if you're learning DOS.

Use a Windows 98 machine to learn the standard startup options such as Safe Mode, and to see the difference between starting at a command line from the F8 start menu and using the command line from within Windows. You can also open a command window through XP's Start I Run dialog box, and then expand the window. However, without configuring the screen font, you won't have a full-screen command environment. In many instances, that full screen makes it a whole lot easier to see what's going on in DOS.

The Control Panel

Every version of Windows since Windows 95 uses the Start button to open the Windows Start menu (not the same thing as the text-based startup menu). The Windows 2000 Start menu looks much the same as Windows 98. Windows XP introduced major changes to that Start menu, and, by default, removes the standard Desktop icons (such as My Computer, Network Neighborhood, and so on). "Classic" view returns some of those icons to the Desktop.

A number of navigational pathways begin with a right-click on the My Computer icon and selecting the Properties menu. Windows XP moved "My Computer" to the Start menu, as a menu option. It works the same as in earlier versions of Windows, but you can return the icon to the Desktop with the "Classic style" option. The exam will probably only refer to "My Computer" and not ask you how to get to it.

The Control Panel is still the central configuration and management area for Windows, and you should know the two basic ways to reach it. In Windows 9x/2000, click on Start | Settings | Control Panel. Windows XP places the Control Panel as a main menu item on the Start menu. In any version of Windows, you can also choose Start | Run and enter CONTROL (control.exe) to open the Control Panel. The thing to remember is that Control Panel refers to Settings.

To diagnose problems with Windows, you need to think in a few main categories: hardware device drivers, access to the computer (passwords and user information), system settings and configuration (Control Panel), and network problems. We've tried to keep our discussion in some sort of order, but as you know, you can get to almost any of the tools and utilities through other tools and routes. We've listed the topics, but that doesn't mean they're linked in any particular hierarchy or order.

Understand that utilities used to be individual programs, such as Format and Smart Drive. Over the years, third-party developers have put together "suites" of utility programs. For example, Norton Utilities is still a number of individual commands, but offers the Norton Commander as a central starting point for each of the underlying programs. Microsoft has gradually incorporated related utilities into these types of suites, and the Control Panel is an early example. Windows 2000 introduced the term "console" as the name for these central starting points. A console (using the .MSC file extension) is just another name for a really fancy menu with drop-down lists, buttons, and icons that provide access to individual tools.

 One of the more peculiar utility suites is MSINFO32.EXE, the Microsoft System Information tool. Although this looks like a basic information window, one of the main menu options is "Tools." In Windows 98, the Tools option included access to many of the other important utilities, including such things as System File Checker, the Update Manager, Dr. Watson, System Configuration (MSCONFIG.EXE), and so forth. Windows XP offers the same console, with the same Tools menu option. However, the XP version is much more limited, offering only System Restore as an important option. Dr. Watson is still another of the five menu choices, but once again, XP is somewhat less easy than Windows 98, in terms of easy access.

The Event Viewer

Stop errors are generated between the point where the NTLDR has begun loading the operating system and the Welcome or Logon screen. A typical problem-solving situation might involve trying to uncover what events took place prior to the problem, and how those events took place. First-tier support handles the basic detective work in terms of describing the "crime scene."

That being said, one of the important troubleshooting utilities you should know about is the *Event Viewer*. The Event Viewer is part of the Computer Management utility console. The files listed under the Event Viewer are log files, and although the tools may be fairly easy to use, interpreting the results isn't always so simple. No special permissions are necessary to view the System and Application logs; however, only a member of the Administrator group can view the Security log.

You can access the Event Viewer in different ways, but the most likely path is through the Control Panel | Administrative Tools, and then the Computer Management (compmgmt.msc) shortcut. Windows XP considers .MSC files (console files) to be executable, and will bring up the main console window. The Computer Management console looks much like a typical Explorer window (with a tree view), and works the same way. Branches can be expanded, with the right-side pane showing individual tools or data.

The information in the Security log file is generated by the audit policy and audit messages managed through the Security Reference Monitor. Security events include such things as failed passwords, failed ID names, inappropriate access attempts, or any other breach of system security as defined by the network administrators.

Typically, the event logs present lines and symbols indicating whether an application or system process was started successfully. An exclamation point indicates a warning of a possible problem, and other symbols help differentiate other types of events. The Event Viewer is one of the first places you'll go to find out what may have caused a stop error. That being said, NT must have successfully started in the first place if you're able to use it. But who ever said that Windows was logical? Realistically, the Event Viewer and Device Manager are diagnostics tools designed to figure out why some part of Windows was unable to load but most of the system loaded and is limping along. Chapter 16 covers problems more related to when Windows completely fails to start.

We'll mention here (because there isn't another logical place to do so) that Startup programs often show up in the system Registry in four primary locations. Keep in mind that using MSCONFIG (from the Run box) is another way to find Startup programs, and that a few sneaky ones might show up in a WIN.INI file. The keys in the Registry are

➤ HKEY_LOCAL_MACHINE\SOFTWARE\Microsoft\Windows\ CurrentVersion\Run

➤ HKEY_LOCAL_MACHINE\SOFTWARE\Microsoft\Windows\ CurrentVersion\RunServices

➤ HKEY_USERS\.DEFAULT\SOFTWARE\Microsoft\Windows\ CurrentVersion\Run

➤ HKEY_CURRENT_USER\SOFTWARE\Microsoft\Windows\ CurrentVersion\Run

Administrative Tools

The Control Panel provides a central access point to all the operating system configuration areas. When the system is part of a network installation, you may have to have Administrator rights to access the Control Panel, but we'll assume you have access to the entire system. The XP Administrative Tools console contains the Computer Management console, as well as shortcuts to the Event Viewer, Local Security Policies, Performance Monitor, and Services. Each of these are also available through the Computer Management console.

Computer Management Console

Those of us who began working with PCs back in the DOS days remember having to use the command line to do pretty much anything at all. Formatting and partitioning was done through specific commands (FORMAT.COM and FDISK.EXE respectively). We couldn't move files, originally, and could only copy them and then delete them from their source location. DOS eventually added a MOVE command, but Windows made it possible to do even such simple things in a single step. The Computer Management console provides a way to do many of these old command-line tasks. However, the only way to use it is from within Windows.

The console looks like an Explorer window, and provides access to both information about various configuration settings and, in some instances, the actual configuration tools. For example, the Storage branch opens up to include Disk Defragmentation and Disk Management. Under Disk Management, you have all the options to view and change partition information.

To manage volumes and partitions, use Start | Control Panel | Administrative Tools | Computer Management, and open the Storage branch to get to Disk Management. This area provides information from within Windows about all the disks Windows can access. The tool offers rudimentary partitioning tools, but you'll do much better with PowerQuest's Parition Magic if you have to do anything involving partition maintenance.

Device Manager

We discuss the Device Manager in various locations throughout this book, and you'll see it again in Chapter 16. You'll use the Device Manager to examine how Windows sees individual hardware devices, and to install and manage driver updates. Remember that Device Manager deals with hardware and device drivers. You should know that the Computer Management console also contains a branch for the Device Manager. Although this is one way to get to the Device Manager, the more likely route is either by right-clicking on the My Computer icon, or by choosing the Control Panel | System application. (The System icon actually opens up the System Properties console.)

Windows 9x and 2000 provide access to the Device Manager through the System Properties console from the Control Panel. For no apparent reason, Windows XP makes it a bit more difficult to find this important utility. Click Control Panel | System, and then go to the "Hardware" tab, and choose the Device Manager button in the middle of the dialog box. Once again, we'd like to reassure you that in almost all the questions you'll see on the exam, you probably won't have to make up these navigational pathways from memory. You'll most likely be given a question that asks about a problem; then each response will provide a particular pathway. The critical thing to remember is that tools and utilities are associated with specific types of problems. Device Manager links with *devices* (hardware).

Printers are such a big deal that you'll find them under their own heading in just about every version of Windows. In Windows 9x/2000, go to the Start | Settings menu to access Printer settings. Windows XP shows you "Printers and Faxes" on the main Start menu. XP also provides printer settings in the main Control Panel window. Almost all other hardware devices are managed through the Device Manager.

The Computer Management tool and the Recovery Console provide access to disk operations, such as formatting and partitioning. Visual settings, such as screen resolution, display adapters, video card settings, themes, and skins are all related to the Display console.

User information, passwords, network cards, and Internet access are all related to Networking, Internet Options, Passwords, or User Accounts (Control Panel). If you can remember these main relationships, you'll more than likely be able to figure out a specific set of navigational steps. For example, a question about printers might offer various pathways coming from the Desktop, or from System Properties. Try to remember that printers are their own area, and most likely won't be found under Display (Desktop) menus.

Remember that devices, visual settings, system configuration, and networking are four broad categories. They're handled (respectively) by the Device Manager, Display Properties (right-click the Desktop), Control Panel, and sub-systems within the Control Panel having to do with Internet, Network, and Users.

The Desktop (Display Properties)

Windows 3.x used the desktop model as a sort of gathering place for icons, and provided very little real functionality. Windows 95 began setting up the Desktop as the main work area, completely removing any surrounding empty space. The Desktop has continued to evolve, becoming something called a "namespace," which is a thoroughly complicated concept involving virtual abstractions and other such nonsense. You should know that the Desktop is part of the Explorer, just as the Start menu is really a representation of an actual folder on the hard drive.

 You can right-click on any Start menu item to get to a Properties menu, just like any other shortcut. You can also drag and drop shortcuts, filenames, and .LNK files to and from the Start menu. Finally, you can right-click on a Start menu sub-listing and sort the items alphabetically. The only thing you must do from the Explorer is create new Start menu options or categories.

The Windows Desktop looked pretty much the same from Windows 95 all the way through to Windows 2000. Microsoft has the idea that everyone will eventually be connected to the Internet all the time, and that everyone likes the way Web browsers work. Windows 98 introduced Web View and Active Desktop as part of this strategy. Active Directory is yet another scheme to put more barriers between the work you do and the underlying storage and location of your data (files). The important thing to know about the Desktop is that you can right-click anywhere on an empty area to reach the Display Properties console

Try to remember that the Display Properties tabs have stayed pretty much the same from Windows 95 all the way through to Windows XP. The one big difference in XP is that the "Background" tab (Windows 9x/2000) changed to become "Themes" in Windows XP. Themes and skins are really only fancy ways of talking about pictures and colors that you use for a background. None of it really affects the work you're doing, but you should remember that this is one of the main places to go to configure the screen resolution.

Problems with video cards (as a piece of hardware) can usually be investigated through the Device Manager. However, if Windows successfully recognizes the video card, you'll more likely go to the "Settings" tab on the Display Properties dialog box to make configuration changes. Choose the "Advanced" button to examine the video adapter settings (Adapter button), and to troubleshoot (Troubleshoot button) problems with the monitor.

The Windows XP style setting under the "Appearance" tab of the Display Properties offers limited color customization. However, this is the place to go to change the "Windows and Buttons" area to "Windows Classic style" or "Windows XP style." For some strange reason, you can't make many customizations to the Windows colors under the default XP style. Note that the visual appearance of "Classic style" is not the same thing as the "Classic Start menu" option on the Taskbar properties dialog box that returns the My Computer icon to the Desktop.

Start Menu, Taskbar, and Task Manager

As you know, the classic (Windows 9x/2000) Start menu rose up in a column out of the Start button. It was divided horizontally into sections, and pretty much any computer had the same menu options. In a never-ending pattern of symbolism over substance, Microsoft seems to have chosen visual customization as the thing most users really want. Although this might be useful for someone who's never seen Windows before, it doesn't take long before people start wishing for speed and access rather than pretty colors and animated cartoon characters. The XP Start menu not only is a whole lot more confusing than previous versions, but it changes according to usage patterns.

The important thing to remember about the Start menu is that it's the easiest place to go to configure the Startup folder. Obviously, it's also the location of the Programs (or All Programs) option, which opens out to all the applications you'll be using on the computer. Another thing to remember is that in the real world, Windows XP and 2000 offer a much more substantial Help feature. The new .HTML format now provides actual links to tools that work, rather than simply descriptions of how to use those tools. In the real world, you can often get useful support from Windows Help. (Note that you probably won't have the Help option as a navigational pathway to utilities on the exam.)

The Start menu also holds the "Run" option. Regardless of how Microsoft tries to hide, bury, or disguise the underlying programming language, everything on the computer must have some kind of program before it can do anything. Most technical books (ours included) offer you the options of running the actual program file for the utilities and tools you should know. Many people will follow Microsoft's graphic pathway to get to a command line. However, an A+ technician will more likely use the Run option to enter CMD.EXE or COMMAND to get to a command line.

The Start | Run dialog box provides a place to enter a command-line statement. In Windows 9x/2000, this option opens up a "shell" to DOS, or the underlying NT command environment. Type **EXIT** to return to Windows. Windows XP provides a similar DOS-like environment, also creating a shell application for using such commands as **COPY**, **DIR**, **ATTRIB**, and so on. Remember that the command line is not the same thing as the Recovery Console. The only way to get to the Recovery Console is from the boot manager, before any part of Windows loads.

Windows 95 introduced the Taskbar as a consolidated area (typically at the bottom of the screen) used to list open programs and to present the System Tray. Remember that the main Taskbar shows icon buttons for applications that you open and close during your work session. The System Tray is almost the same thing, showing only program icons for those applications running in the background. Programmers don't follow any particular standard to place an icon in the tray, but you should know how to right-click, double-click, or left-click on an icon to either generate a menu or close the program. You may find a question regarding the loudspeaker icon and how to remove or restore it to the tray. Just remember that it's the volume control, and you can access it through the Multimedia applet in the Control Panel (Sounds and Audio Devices, in XP).

People seem to forget that the right-click option applies to the Taskbar, just as it does for all the other objects in Windows (95 through XP). The Windows 98 Taskbar provided somewhat simple features such as adding new, customized toolbars, and the Quick Launch toolbar for often-used programs. Another nice (but rarely remembered) feature is the capability to tile several open applications either vertically or horizontally.

To tile Word and Excel, as an example, when both applications are open, hold down the Control key and click once on each application's Taskbar icon. After you've selected the applications you want to tile, right-click on the Taskbar, or on any of the icon buttons, and select the tile option from the pop-up menu. This is a simple way to copy material from one application to another, with both work areas showing next to each other.

Windows 9x provided a "Taskbar & Start Menu" item under the Start | Settings menu option. The "Start Menu" is a shortcut to the underlying Start Menu folder (\Windows folder in 9x and XP, and \Documents and Settings in Windows 2000). Oddly enough, Windows XP now provides these configuration options through the less-intuitive process of right-clicking on the Taskbar, and then choosing Properties. Here, you can configure the look and feel of the Taskbar and Start menu, or you can access the Start Menu folder to change what appears on the actual menu after you click the Start button.

Note also that every version of Windows *prior* to XP provided access to the Task Manager (TASKMAN.EXE) if you pressed Ctrl+Alt+Del. These keystrokes now bring up the Logon screen in Windows XP/2000. To reach the Task Manager you have to right-click on the Taskbar, and then choose Task Manager from the pop-up menu. Remember that the Task Manager is the primary location for a listing of everything currently running during a Windows session. In Windows XP/2000, that includes the various system services, as well as any open application.

 Many times, the first confirmation that a system has a virus is that an unusual program shows on the Task Manager listing. Most Internet antivirus sites provide information about what to look for in the task list, depending on the particular virus. Some of the more obscure stop errors or startup problems can come from a badly written spyware or adware program. These types of pests also will often show part of their programming in the task list.

Accessories

Before you take the exam, be sure to spend some time in Windows 98, Windows 2000, and Windows XP, taking notes as you click through the Start | Programs menu options. Many of the important utility suites and consoles are available as options on the Accessories menu. The important ones to remember are almost always under Start | Programs | Accessories | System Tools. You should be familiar with

➤ Backup

➤ System Restore

➤ System Information

➤ Disk Cleanup

➤ Disk Defragmenter

➤ Scheduled Tasks (The Task Scheduler)

➤ Command Prompt

We discuss the System File Checker in Chapter 14, and we'll take a look at System Restore in the next chapter. You should also understand that we've listed the XP names for these utilities, but any differences are minor, in relation to other versions of Windows. That being said, the exam will most likely ask you conceptual questions having to do with what each program does. In other words, don't spend too much time worrying that you won't remember how to get to System Restore. Instead, focus your attention on remembering that System Restore is a way to back up the Registry, and to create a sort of snapshot of the computer's configuration.

Network Connections

CompTIA began testing on simple networking principles, but you should remember that A+ certification is quite different from a complete network certification of some type. Many A+ candidates get lost in worries over all the complexities of installing a network card, configuring MAC addresses, and wiring problems. The important thing to remember is that you should be familiar with the main terms and concepts having to do with networking, not how to be a network engineer.

Windows XP introduced a more sophisticated set of Wizards to make installing and configuring a simple network easier than in previous versions of Windows. The two most important places to remember are available through the Control Panel: Network Connections and Internet Options. Both these locations offer a listing of "tasks" that you'll most likely want to run, and each task generates a Wizard to walk you through the process.

Think about yourself in relation to some thoroughly inexperienced computer user. To the average person, running the "Create a New Connection" Wizard opens up a series of incomprehensible dialog boxes. Setting up a simple dial-up connection is a relative no-brainer. However, this is also the place where you'll set up a small home network. At that point, you'll be asked about IP addresses, Ethernet cards, and all the basic terms associated with a network. The exam isn't interested in testing you on how to find the IP address configuration location for every version of Windows. Instead, A+ certification means that you have an understanding of what an IP address means, why you would need one, and where to go to begin figuring out why the system can't connect to the network.

 Earlier versions of Windows required a fairly sophisticated knowledge of network configuration utilities and tools. As with much of today's technology, most manufacturers now work with Microsoft developers to join forces in making these types of drudge-work tasks easier and simpler. Plug and Play has gone a long way in taking over almost all the details of installing a small network. As such, you should focus on how to get to the Connection Wizard, and where in the Control Panel (or other locations) to go to run some simple diagnostics on a network connection.

Networking and User Accounts

Not every computer is designed to connect to a network. As strange as it may seem to Microsoft, many people continue to buy a computer as a standalone machine, using only an Internet connection of some type. Windows 2000 joined the concepts of network security to the home interface. Before that, Windows 95 introduced the idea to the home market that individual members of a family could use a single computer with different settings. One way or another, the relevant versions of Windows all provide ways to configure a computer with different user settings in the Control Panel.

You'll want to keep an eye out for anything having to do with User Information, Passwords, Network, or User Accounts. Remember that the hardware aspect of networking involves NICs, wires (or wireless hardware), and the Device Manager. However, the hardware is only half of the situation. The other half is to somehow tell the computer who is using the machine. As we discussed earlier in this chapter, the computer determines who is using the system and how Windows will appear to that user in some sort of user profile.

The types of questions you'll find on the exam have to do with where to go to set or change passwords for individual users. You should know something about passwords, and you should also know that a user configuration determines what that person can or can't do to the machine. In other words, the reason you should remember the concepts having to do with security is that everything about allowing a person access to some part of the computer falls under the heading of computer security. Remember that an Administrator is the master of the universe, and can completely lock someone out of a machine.

User configurations are stored in the Windows Registry (usually under the HKEY_USERS location). Understand that this is only part of the story, and that along with the user's preferences, Windows also stores certain hardware and software settings and configurations. Note that although Microsoft goes to some effort to demand that everyone using a computer must have a password, you can leave the password area blank to eliminate the need to enter a username and password on a standalone machine (not a domain client). Windows XP requires at least one person's name (the Administrator) during an installation, along with a machine name. However, a blank password tells the computer to simply move right into a Windows session from the Welcome screen, without asking for any further information.

Setting up a Windows XP machine with only one user, as a standalone machine, changes the way certain security areas work, and the way various keystrokes take effect. For example, a single machine with one Administrator user, set up to have no password protection at all, reverts Ctrl+Alt+Del to the old Task Manager keystrokes. When the machine has more than one username, the Administrator can select a logon name and either check or uncheck the box indicating that users must use a password to log on to the machine. Passwords are set up in the User Accounts applet under the Control Panel.

The Windows Recovery Console

Although we'll examine the Windows Recovery Console again in Chapter 16, you should know that it isn't installed automatically during a Windows Setup process. Contrary to what some people might think, the Recovery Console is not a command-line environment, but rather a special application in its own right. One clue to this is the fact that the cursor doesn't blink. A second clue is that the installation procedure uses its own Setup routine, run from a command line. In fact, the only place where you'll find an approximation of a real command-line environment in XP/2000 is when you run CMD.EXE in the Start | Run box.

Many preparation guides and other study books having to do with A+ certification provide an entire listing of every Recovery Console command. In our opinion, it's easier to learn the basics and essentials of DOS, and play around with what ends up being mostly the same commands as a real command line. That means running a Windows 9x machine and starting it in the MS-DOS Mode. Another way is to boot Windows 9x to the text startup menu and run a command line only. (Yet another way, on a Windows 98 machine, is to rename WIN.COM to something else. It's not elegant, but it'll sure stop Windows from loading! Just remember what you renamed the file so you can name it back to its original name.)

We've covered the real essentials in Chapters 12 and 13, but you should know that a few commands are specific to Windows XP/2000. For example, older systems provided an undocumented switch to fix a corrupted boot record (FDISK /MBR). By the most astonishing coincidence, Windows Recovery Console now provides a command by the name of fixmbr. When you look closely at the actual command, you should see that the programmer is telling you that it will "fix the MBR" (Master Boot Record). Keep in mind that program developers also like to remember the names of their programs, and what the programs do. Most command filenames actually tell you what purpose they serve (an exception being FDISK).

Be sure to remember that the Windows Recovery Console is not installed automatically during a typical installation process. After Windows XP/2000 has been successfully installed, you must run a second installation routine to put the Recovery Console on a local hard drive. When Windows XP fails to boot, you can run the Recovery Console from a bootable installation CDROM, but you must enter an Administrator password (if there is one) before you can access the command line. You cannot boot a Windows XP/2000 machine from floppy disks when the operating system isn't working. However, you can download a set of disk images from the Microsoft Web site and create a set of six floppy diskettes that will start the Recovery Console. You'll likely not find a question on the exam relating to this type of problem, but you should remember that the Recovery Console is an entirely separate (although related) application that's part of Windows 2000 and Windows XP.

Windows Product Activation (WPA)

Windows XP is the first operating system to feature Windows Product Activation (WPA) technology, designed to cut down on software piracy. Microsoft estimates that close to 80% of the machines running Windows are doing so in violation of the licensing agreement. The new activation procedure creates a unique ID for a specific machine, based on an analysis of the hardware on that machine. The ID is then matched to the Product Key.

The user has a set number of days (for example, 30 days) to activate Windows XP, after which the system won't work. After it is activated, Windows XP works only with the exact computer defined by the identification code. This prevents the OS from being installed on *any* another computer. In fact, if you make a significant change in your system (adding new hardware) Windows XP may very well stop working until you go through another activation procedure. Activation can be accomplished over the Internet, where the authenticity of the license is checked and the copy of XP is unlocked. For buyers who are not connected to the Internet, Microsoft provides an activation process via the phone.

 WPA is becoming one of the most controversial "features" of almost any Microsoft product. If you don't activate your machine within the allotted time, it's impossible to get the system up and running for an activation. Microsoft includes the SYSPREP utility on the XP installation disk, which allows you to reset the activation period three times. When the grace period is up, the only solution is a complete reinstallation. Any applications and data added to the machine since the installation are wiped out. Don't let the activation period slide by.

Summary—Windows NT/XP

In a very simplistic fashion, Windows networking can be split into two categories: enterprise or business installations, and home installations. You should understand the design structure of these operating systems, but you needn't focus too deeply on the complex fashion in which they might be applied to a large corporate setting.

Given that Windows 2000 and XP grew out of Windows NT, security and stability are at the foundation of how these systems work. If you understand the way the OS clamps down on security, you may be able to see where a home or small business network uses a reduced or basic application of many configuration settings. Conceptually, you should understand the following points:

➤ NT and Windows 2000/XP are modular-design operating systems. Understand the essence of Kernel mode and User mode, and how the kernel protects the OS from mistakes or attacks by the end user.

➤ Spend some time getting to know the hardware abstraction layer (HAL), and have a picture of how the operating system takes over much of the device management process.

➤ You should understand the concept of Windows Services, although you won't be tested on specific services and how they load. You should know that the loading process is part of the overall startup process.

➤ Understand that the Registry looks much like the Windows 9x Registry, in terms of the HKeys. If you're comfortable with the division of HKey handles, you should be able to choose correct responses to these types of questions.

➤ Have a fairly good idea of the main acronyms used by Windows NT and 2000/XP. Remember that the LSA is the Local Security Authorization. Note the Security Account Management (SAM) database, the Security Access Token (SAT), and Security Identification (SID).

➤ You should know about the Access Control List (ACL) and how a network grants "rights" to users. A home computer may have an administrative ID and password, or it may not. Depending on the level of security, you may or may not be able to access some of the administrative tools.

➤ Keep a working knowledge of the default User accounts. These are pretty much the same in Windows NT and 2000/XP. Remember the Administrator, User, and Guest accounts and understand the concept of user groups.

➤ Be somewhat familiar with the startup process, following the logic of what ought to load before something else can load. Pay particular attention to the NT Loader because the NTLDR file is a major troubleshooting villain in NT/2000/XP.

➤ Be sure you understand what a "Last Known Good" hardware profile means, and that it's different from the last "known good" Registry file (the last working version of the Registry).

➤ Make sure you know that the NT File System works on an NTFS partition. This should connect, in your mind, with the FAT16 and FAT32 DOS partitions. You should also at least recognize that the High Performance File System (HPFS) was created for IBM's OS/2.

➤ Have a working knowledge of RAID and the various levels (0–5), along with the term "fault tolerance." You won't necessarily have to know exactly how many volumes and sets are specified by each level, but you should be able to recognize that the terms striped set, disk mirroring, and duplexing, for instance, refer to data backup and protection.

The more time and experience you've had actually getting around in Windows, the better you'll be able to visualize the menu paths necessary to reach various tools. Keep in mind, though, that given the format of the exam, you'll almost always be asked to choose a response where the navigation path is already listed. In other words, you should be able to read a response and visualize each cascading menu, but you shouldn't have to create a path from memory.

You'll almost always find at least one question pertaining to bootable disks, ERDs, and emergency startup disks. If you can't visualize the differences, then skim back over Chapter 14 and the preceding section of this chapter. We'll discuss them again in Chapter 16.

Practice Exam Questions

Question 1

> Which of the following two modules are used in the Windows NT Kernel mode?
> - A. The Executive assistant and Security Options layer
> - B. The Hardware Abstraction layer and Executive layer
> - C. The User Applications layer and Hardware Abstraction layer
> - D. The Executive layer and Local Security Authority layer

Answer B is correct. The Kernel mode is divided into two layers. The lower layer is the hardware abstraction layer (HAL), and the higher layer is the Executive layer. Answer A is incorrect because there is no Executive Assistant or Security Options layer. Answer C is incorrect because it confuses a User Applications layer with the User mode and the Applications layer. Answer D is incorrect because the Local Security Authority is part of the Security Reference Monitor module within the Executive layer.

Question 2

> A Windows XP network can be divided into _____, _____, and _____.
> - A. computers, stars, base topologies
> - B. groups, profiles, accounts
> - C. users, groups, domains
> - D. domains, directories, profiles

Answer C is correct. NT networks are commonly divided into individual users, groups of objects, and large domains of groups. Answer A is incorrect in the use of base topologies, and because star topologies are architecture types rather than network divisions. Answer B is incorrect because profiles and accounts are associated with both groups and users. Answer D is incorrect because networks aren't commonly divided into directories and profiles.

Question 3

Which two tools or utilities would you use to troubleshoot a Windows 2000 computer that failed to successfully boot?

- ❑ A. A bootable system disk
- ❑ B. The emergency repair utility
- ❑ C. A systems information disk
- ❑ D. An emergency repair disk

Answers A and D are correct. NT and Windows 2000 both provide an opportunity to create a bootable system disk and an emergency repair disk. (Windows XP no longer calls it an ERD, and uses the Automated System Restore process.) The emergency repair disk is customized to a specific machine, but both disks can be tried with a machine that fails to boot. Answer B is incorrect because it refers to the ERU.EXE utility in Windows 9x, which is used to back up a Registry. Answer C is incorrect because there is no such disk.

Question 4

What are the requirements for an employee to gain access to a printer in the Accounting domain?

- ○ A. An access code
- ○ B. A user account
- ○ C. A group identification
- ○ D. A guest account

Answers B is correct. Windows networks require a User ID (identification), set up through a user account. Answer A is incorrect because an access code is usually applied to an entryway of some sort and is much too broad a term to be applied to the operating system. Answer C is incorrect because a group identification means nothing in terms of specific access configurations. It's too generic. Answer D is incorrect because a Guest account is almost always assigned extremely limited rights and would rarely allow access to Accounting department information.

Question 5

WINLOGON.EXE is the program file that runs the _____ procedure and begins the _____.

- ○ A. logon, Local Security Authority
- ○ B. Windows splash screen, logon process
- ○ C. Session Manager, security logon process
- ○ D. logon, device loading process

Answer A is correct. The WINLOGON program initiates the logon procedure, which then starts the Local Security Authority (LSA). Answer B is incorrect because no program runs the splash screen; the splash screen is called by a program. Answer C is incorrect because the Session Manager is part of the basic NT operating system and loads near the beginning. Answer D is incorrect because devices are loaded and initialized in several places prior to and after the logon process.

Question 6

Which of the following files is responsible for a menu listing that says, "1. Start Windows 2000 Professional"?

- ○ A. NTDETECT.COM
- ○ B. BOOTLDR.INI
- ○ C. NTLDR
- ○ D. BOOT.INI

Answer D is correct. The BOOT.INI file is a hidden text file that lists the names used on the startup menu, the location of the system files, and a time-out period before starting the default operating system. Answer A is incorrect, because NTDETECT.COM examines the hardware configuration on the system, but provides no menus. Answer B is incorrect, being a made-up filename. Answer C is incorrect because the NTLDR file is the basic boot loader used by Windows NT/2000/XP to begin the boot process. It doesn't generate any kind of menu, either.

Question 7

> Which of the following modules is responsible for a problem with a 32-bit sound card?
>
> ○ A. HCL
>
> ○ B. HAL
>
> ○ C. HVAC
>
> ○ D. HMO

Answer B is correct. Although many things might be responsible for sound card problems, the fact that all the responses are a short acronym beginning with "H" indicates that the question is testing you for the Hardware Abstraction Layer. This is the NT layer that steps in between a hardware device and the operating system kernel. Answer A is a serious threat because it refers to the Hardware Compatibility List published by Microsoft, which indicates devices that have been successfully tested on NT. Answers C and D are outright frauds: HVAC stands for Heating, Ventilation, and Air Conditioning, and an HMO is a healthcare maintenance organization. The HAL is an important part of NT, and is directly responsible for many hardware incompatibilities.

Question 8

> What is the best way to reach the System Restore console and set a restore point to the current date?
>
> ○ A. Programs I Settings I Accessories I Backup
>
> ○ B. Programs I Control Panel I System Restore
>
> ○ C. Control Panel I Administrative Tools I System Management
>
> ○ D. Programs I Accessories I System Tools I System Restore

Answer D is correct. One of the distractions in the question has to do with the use of a restore point, and the reference to the current date. Neither of these two ideas has anything to do with the question, really. You should know that System Restore is a part of the Windows Backup feature. When you examine each of the navigational pathways, the wrong choices all have a fairly obvious problem: either that they don't exist, or they make little sense. Answer A is incorrect because Programs I Setting was available only in Windows 9x, and those versions of Windows didn't use System Restore. Answer B is incorrect because the Control Panel is never directly off the Programs menu. Answer C is incorrect because Administrative Tools have more to do with managing configurations and settings than with backups. Secondly, there's no such icon as "System Management" under Administrative Tools. There's a Computer Management, and System Tools, but not the made-up option.

Question 9

Your client has just purchased a new 19" LCD panel monitor. Prior to this, she was using a 14" color CRT. Windows 2000 loads correctly but everything on the screen is very large. What two ways do you have available to verify that the new monitor is using the correct video card?

- ❏ A. Control Panel I System I Hardware I Device Manager I Display
- ❏ B. Display Properties I Settings I Appearance I Display Resolution
- ❏ C. Display Properties I Settings I Advanced
- ❏ D. Control Panel I System I Advanced I Display Settings

Answers A and C are correct. The question brings up something to do with hardware. As such, you should immediately be looking for something to do with the Device Manager. Answer A has a long and confusing list of options, but it's the only response that includes the Device Manager, making it a likely choice. The remaining responses aren't so easy to figure out. However, Answer B is incorrect because there's no such option, anywhere on a main menu, as "Display Resolution." Secondly, you should have a fairly good sense that the tab on the Display Properties dialog box includes separate tabs for Settings and Appearance. Appearance isn't under Settings. Answer D is difficult, but if you remember that the System Properties under Control Panel lists all the hardware devices, then you should have a good idea that there's no "Advanced" option. However, we see "Advanced" in at least two of the responses. Try to remember that "Settings I Advanced" is a common location for information about video cards or display adapters.

Question 10

Which of the following programs would you use to test whether a particular startup option was causing a problem during the Windows Startup process?

- ○ A. MSINFO32
- ○ B. MSCONFIG
- ○ C. MSDIAGS
- ○ D. DRWATSON

Answer B is correct. Although we don't go into great detail in this chapter about the System Configuration Utility, you must know the name of the program, what it does, and why you would use it. Answer A is a legitimate program, but it isn't correct because it provides system information. The clue is in the "info" part of the program name. Answer C is incorrect because it's a made-up program based on an older Windows 95 Hardware Diagnostics (HWDIAGS) program. Answer D is also a legitimate program, but the wrong one for the question. Dr. Watson takes a snapshot of the system at a given point, and then generates a report that you can send to tech support personnel. MSCONFIG (answer B) is the only program that provides a listing of everything in the Startup process. Note that MSCONFIG was not available in Windows 2000. Also note that the question doesn't specify Windows 2000.

Question 11

What's the best way to run ScanDisk on a Windows XP system installed with Service Pack 1?

- ○ A. Select All Programs I Accessories I System Tools I Disk Cleanup
- ○ B. Choose Start I Run, then enter **SCANDISK**, and press Enter
- ○ C. All of the above
- ○ D. None of the above

Answer D is correct. This is a nicely tricky question that doesn't really give you any clues at all as to the correct response. The first thing to reject is the use of the Service Pack reference. It's a false alarm designed to get you even more paranoid about some additional difference in operating systems. The most important point to remember is that Windows NT/2000/XP doesn't use ScanDisk, but uses Check Disk instead (CHKDSK.EXE). Setting that aside, you should also know that Disk Cleanup (in answer A) is a console utility that offers several ways to clean up a disk, with a highlight on removing unwanted or unused files. ScanDisk is a sector-by-sector analysis of a hard disk to check for failing storage areas. It was never used to "clean" a disk. Answer B is bogus because the program doesn't exist on an XP system, except under the outside possibility that the system was upgraded from Windows 9x.

Need to Know More?

 Annoyances.org
http://www.annoyances.org
This is a leading Web site for well-supported discussion groups separated into each version of Windows. The site is maintained by Creative Element, and linked to O'Reilly & Associates, Inc. (www.oreilly.com), an excellent source for extensive coverage of Windows. The site also provides a download link for the various versions of Tweak UI, and a discussion of the pros and cons of different releases of the program.

Boyce, Mark, *et al. Windows NT Workstation 4.0 Advanced Technical Manual.* Indianapolis, IN: Que Publishing, 1996. ISBN: 0-7897-0863-9. This is a "golden oldie" but still a great reference.

Forkner, Jim. *The No BS Guide to Windows NT 4.0.* San Francisco, CA: No Starch Press, 1997. ISBN: 1-886411-14-X. Short, sweet, and to the point.

Stanek, William. *Windows XP Professional, Administrators Pocket Manual.* Redmond, WA: Microsoft Press, 2001. ISBN: 0-7356-1381-8. Fast answers if you are running a network.

Microsoft Windows NT Server Resource Kit: For Windows NT Server Version 4.0. Redmond, WA: Microsoft Press, 1996. ASIN: 1572313447. You cannot do much with a Microsoft Operating System without a Resource Kit. The NT kits are out of print, but available. If you think you might tangle with NT, be sure to have a kit.

Microsoft Windows NT Server Resource Kit Version 4.0, Supplement Two. Redmond, WA: Microsoft Press (1997). ASIN: 1572316268. Supplement to the NT Resource Kit.

Microsoft Windows 2000 Professional Resource Kit. Redmond, WA: Microsoft Press, 2000. The Windows 2000 kits are still in print. Again, if you are going to be working with 2000, be sure to have one.

Microsoft Windows XP Professional Resource Kit Second Edition. Redmond, WA: Microsoft Press, 2003. ISBN: 0735619743. The Windows XP kits are still in print. Again, if you are going to be working with XP, be sure to have one.

Pearce, Eric. *Windows NT in a Nutshell.* Sebastol, CA: O'Reilly & Associates, 1997. ISBN: 1-56592-251-4. This is a very good "how to" book for day-to-day operation of Windows NT.

Troubleshooting

Terms you'll need to understand:

- ✓ Boot, POST, bootstrap loader, connectivity
- ✓ Interactive Startup menu, OS Selection menu, Context menu
- ✓ Safe Mode, normal mode
- ✓ Registry, hive
- ✓ Emergency Boot Disk (EBD), Emergency Recovery Disk (ERD), disk image
- ✓ Console (integrated utility tools applet)
- ✓ Firewall

Concepts you'll need to master:

- ✓ Hardware and configuration profiles
- ✓ Multi-boot configuration (multiple operating systems on one machine)
- ✓ Registry Editor (REGEDIT.EXE, REGEDT32.EXE), hives
- ✓ File management systems (FAT16, FAT32, NTFS)
- ✓ Partitions, System and Boot partition, Windows system files
- ✓ System Restore versus in-place re-install, recovery, repair
- ✓ Network connectivity, Connection Wizard
- ✓ Types of viruses, and ActiveX scripts

In many cases, your first contact with a problem PC will be when the person using it says, "*I don't know what the problem is. Everything was working just fine yesterday, and now it…* (fill in the exam question)." Startup problems are among the most common situations you'll encounter, where the operating system won't boot up, or Windows won't start. Another common problem is where an unknown computer requires some sort of identification, repair, or optimization. Often, a written problem description will be taped to the box.

Realistically, the typical strategy for fixing almost any computer these days, seems to be reformatting the hard drive and reinstalling an original disk image created by the computer vendor. These so-called recovery disks can be a menace to anyone who isn't aware of their function. They aren't designed to recover anything! They're designed to reset the hard drive to its original pre-installed state. In a way, these recovery disks are to applications what a system reset (re-boot) is to RAM. Anything that hasn't been saved in a safe location is wiped out when the machine is returned to its factory condition. "Recovery" (sometimes a setup disk) means the original OEM installation, with no user-created data or added software (programs and device drivers) at all.

In the following discussion, we break out Windows troubleshooting into five main categories:

➤ Boot problems—When the machine can't get past the bootstrap or NT Loader steps.

➤ Startup problems—The Windows startup process fails before arriving at the Desktop.

➤ System failures—Events where DOS or Windows loads, but one of its components fails or becomes unstable.

➤ Installation problems—Problems and instability arising out of hardware or software incompatibilities

➤ System vulnerability—Viruses, file corruption, service packs, and security problems

We'll also discuss hardware and connectivity problems that tend to relate more to Windows than the underlying hardware itself. Connectivity problems refer to situations in which a machine has booted up and an operating system is present, but the machine isn't connecting to the network. In other words, we'll use this chapter for problems taking place between the time the power is switched on and when the operating system takes over. Specific hardware troubleshooting is covered in the first half of this book.

Throughout the book, we've discussed various things that can go wrong and typical ways to fix them. Once again, this is not a comprehensive book about computer technology, nor is it a technical repair manual. It's a compressed review of PC technology, with A+ certification as the primary goal. This chapter is meant to help with the types of troubleshooting questions you're likely to encounter on the exam, and the typical diagnostics tools used in repairing those problems.

We've been referring to Windows 95, 98, and Me, as "Windows 9x." We're going to use another generic reference to Windows NT, 2000, and XP, for the sake of convenience. When you see references to "an NT kernel" machine or system, we mean a machine running one or more of the three versions of Windows that are based on the NT operating system kernel. Replace "NT kernel" with Windows NT/2000/XP.

Preparing for the Software Module

Over the years, readers have asked us how to know whether or not they're ready for the exam. Understanding an operating system is a seriously complex undertaking. To know how to troubleshoot, diagnose, and repair OS problems is even more daunting. Many of you are already in the IT field, taking the exam as part of an ongoing certification program. Others of you are skilled computer users entering the IT field at the start of a new career. We all know it isn't possible for us to teach one operating system, much less five, in a book designed to be a final review.

Use a Practice Machine

In our opinion, the best way to get ready for the Software module is to put together an inexpensive practice machine (a test machine). We've run Windows XP on as little as a Pentium III (400MHz, 256MB RAM). A 30-day activation period shouldn't be a problem, but even if it is, you'll learn a tremendous amount by having to reinstall XP a few times. Nowadays, computers are commodity items, and you might have access to a flea market or secondhand store where a PIII or a Celeron costs very little. In other situations, you might have an older computer, or a secondary machine sitting around at home. We don't recommend using your primary computer for studying, as you'll be reformatting and partitioning the hard drive. Neither do we recommend using a laptop, as they're not as easy to "play with" as a desktop.

If at all possible, try to put together a practice machine. Buy, beg, or borrow a copy of Windows 98 SE (full version), and Windows 2000 and Windows XP (Home or Professional, either works). Try to use the *upgrade* versions of the latter two, not the full installation versions (you'll learn more). Windows 98 SE is important because it offers features that are unavailable in Windows 95. Windows Me is too unstable to provide much help. Windows NT might be good, but not many people have access to it. If you do have a copy, install it on the test machine as one of multiple operating systems in a multi-boot configuration.

Install Windows 98, then make an emergency boot disk (EBD). Test the disk, then boot to the floppy. Use FDISK to wipe out the hard drive, then create two FAT32 partitions, one Primary and one Extended. Format the C: drive with only the three DOS system files (FORMAT C: /S). Set up a single logical drive on the Extended partition. Reboot the floppy, then reboot the system and see if you have access to the CDROM.

If not, then figure out how to make the hard drive bootable with CDROM access. That'll test your skills with CONFIG.SYS and AUTOEXEC.BAT, as well as your understanding of device drivers. Examine the Windows 98 EBD and figure out the important lines in the CONFIG.SYS file that provide CD access and the RAM drive. Create simple CONFIG.SYS and AUTOEXEC.BAT files necessary to boot to the C: drive with CDROM support. Don't just copy the files from the floppy. Test the boot process, then copy the two configuration files you created to a backup floppy.

Use FDISK.EXE to re-partition the drive into three FAT32 partitions (one Primary, one Extended with two logical volumes), and make the machine bootable to the C: drive. Re-install Windows 98 to the C: drive, then copy the DOS files (usually in C:\Windows\Command) to the E: partition. Place copies of the backup CONFIG.SYS and AUTOEXEC.BAT files on the E: drive, and write a small batch file so that you can quickly reformat the C: drive and make it fully bootable (with CD support).

The batch file should copy the DOS configuration files to the C: drive, along with SmartDrive. Use the PATH environment variable to leave the CD driver file on the E: drive. Use only one of the CD device drivers, rather than copying every one of them from the Windows 98 EBD. The intent is to be able to reformat the C: drive with only the three DOS system files, then run the batch file to provide CDROM support with as few actual program files as possible.

Boot to the floppy and reformat the C: drive as bootable. Use the batch file and reboot the system to gain access to the CDROM. If it doesn't work, figure out why. Install Windows 2000 on the C: drive. Test the installation, checking the OS Selection menu to see that you have both Windows 98 and Windows 2000 as options. Modify the BOOT.INI file in Windows 2000 to change the way the initial selection menu appears. Change the "Windows

98" option to read "Plain DOS 7.0." Figure out how to change the "System" attribute (s) when Windows 2000 is running. (Try it again in Windows XP.)

Install Windows XP to the logical D: drive on the Extended partition, leaving it as FAT32. Don't use an Administrator password. Turn off Windows Messenger. Manually install the Windows Recovery Console. Run a conversion on the Windows XP partition, making the D: drive an NTFS partition. Examine what happens when you boot to different operating systems and try to work with files on the NTFS partition. Boot to DOS and use the DIR D: command. Figure out what files you're seeing, and which drive DOS thinks is the D: drive.

Convert the NTFS partition back to FAT32. When you discover you can't, use the DOS files on the E: drive to reformat the D: partition, then reinstall Windows XP. Find and use SMARTDRV.EXE and the winnt.exe Setup program to install XP from a DOS prompt. Run the DIR command often during these various tasks and watch what happens to the drive letter assignments.

All of these tasks are basic to installing an operating system. It doesn't matter that you won't be installing any applications or games; Windows has enough of them that you can run the system and see how it works. You're primarily interested in the startup menus, navigational pathways, and how to reconfigure the OS Select menu: the one that says, *"Please select the operating system to start."* Simply figuring out how to boot to DOS with CDROM support will show you volumes of information about the command line environment. (This is why the upgrade versions of Windows XP/2000 are much better for you in your preparation.)

When you've accomplished all these tasks, you're ready to take the A+ software exam module. Again, install the Recovery Console and play around in it. You'll see that it's an application, not an operating system. However, your experiences with the Windows 98 EBD and setting up a bootable hard drive with only the three DOS 7.0 system files will go a long way toward helping you with questions about the Recovery Console. (Avoid using an Administrator password, for convenience sake.)

Windows XP Upgrade Version—Clean Install

As you know, XP comes in both a Home and Professional edition. It also offers upgrade and full installation packaging. (Again, we recommend that you use the upgrade version in your exam preparation.) You can perform a clean install of the upgrade version without first having to install a previous operating system. You'll have to create or copy over an AUTOEXEC.BAT and CONFIG.SYS file containing CDROM drivers. Remember, you'll have only a simple DOS bootable hard disk, so even with BIOS-level CDROM support, there won't be operating system drive support.

The easy way is to simply use a Windows 98 SE emergency boot disk. Create the two startup files, using CD driver files that work. The Win98 disk includes versions for many types of computers, and you should find one that works. Otherwise, make sure you have the correct drivers for the working system you'll be upgrading.

You'll also have to have a copy of SMARTDRV.EXE. The program must be the same version as the DOS system files. Copy it from the Windows 98 SE folder so you can put it on the destination drive. Windows XP will run Setup without the resident portion of Smart Drive (cache) in memory, but the *Copying Files* phase is extremely slow.

Format the destination partition (for example, Drive C:) as a bootable partition. Stick with FAT32 for the moment. When using an upgrade version, you'll need a valid copy of an earlier version of Microsoft windows. That copy can be a CDROM disk. When the system boots to the newly formatted hard drive, run smartdrv /v (the verbose switch) to get a confirmation report that it's running. Log on to the CD drive with the XP installation disk. Go to the i386 folder and enter winnt at the DOS prompt to begin the Setup program. Setup will stop at some point, when it can't find the End User License Agreement (EULA). At that point, remove the XP installation disk and place the previous Windows version disk in the CDROM drive. Press Enter, and XP will read the EULA from that disk, then proceed to the rest of the installation.

Some machines generate a "CDR101: Not ready reading drive [*x*]. Abort, Retry, Fail?" error (where [*x*] is the CD drive). Many technicians and support sites say the error indicates that the CDROM drive is going bad, or there's a problem with scratches on the disk. Before you tear out all your hair trying to replace a supposed bad drive, try rebooting without loading Smart Drive. Log onto the drive, then run a **DIR** command. It seems that in some instances, Smart Drive interferes with the DOS read functions. If it's successful, then load Smart Drive and the error should be resolved.

Windows Product Activation (WPA)

We mentioned WPA in Chapter 15, "Windows NT, 2000, and XP," but there are a number of interesting problems you may encounter. One problem has to do with system image files. Suppose you have thirty days from installation before the system will stop working. You install the system, configure it, and install a number of user applications. In fact, you might even create some data, store pictures and e-mail, and do various other things to the system. After you've got it "perfect," you create a disk image backup.

A few days or weeks later, you activate Windows, either via the Internet or with a phone call to Microsoft. Everything seems fine. Sometime after activation, the entire system crashes and you want to set it back to its original condition. You get out your CDROM and restore the hard drive from the backup image. However, the image file was never activated, and the 30-day grace period has long-since expired. Sadly, there's an expression in the technical community for this condition: "You're toast!"

XP Product Activation

We won't get into the growing controversy over Microsoft's policy of preventing software piracy through the new (XP only) activation key system. You should know that XP looks at ten hardware areas, to determine the *identity* of a specific machine. These are the display adapter, SCSI card, IDE adapter, NIC MAC address, amount of RAM, the processor type, the processor serial number, the hard drive, the drive volume and serial number, and any CD or DVD drives. The activation process combines each of these devices in a "hashed" number, and produces a unique machine configuration.

Product Activation requires a second product ID number, different from and in addition to the 25-charactter Product Key found on the installation disk. After the machine has been activated, XP stores the licensing key in two small files under the %systemroot%\system32 folder (**wpa.dbl** and **wpa.bak**). XP deletes these files when it finds any significant changes to the system. You can make a backup of these files prior to any significant hardware changes to the licensed and activated machine. In many instances, you can then copy the backup files over newer or missing files, and avoid a re-activation process. We make no guarantees or other claims at all about this process. We've listed it here for your information only.

You may be tempted to try some of the various activation hacks floating around on the Internet. For the most part, they're urban legends. There was a famous **Reset3.exe** hack developed for beta releases of XP, but you'll likely find yourself having to reformat your hard drive and reinstall XP from scratch if you try it. There isn't any way to get around this latest Microsoft "feature." When an XP machine passes beyond the activation deadline, nothing at all will allow you to run XP. In that case, you'll most likely have to reinstall the entire system (and most likely lose any data on the drive).

Be advised that Microsoft includes the **SYSPREP.EXE** file, in the **\Support\Tools\Deploy.cab** file on the installation CDROM. This is the Windows System Preparation Tool, and you can use it for up to three times to reset (or "reseal") the activation grace period. (OEM vendors use this utility to pre-install XP on a computer and set the activation period to begin the first time a customer starts the computer.) The program requires that you also extract **SETUPD.EXE**.

Startup Function Keys

Windows offers an Interactive Startup menu, with various options for how to load the operating system. We'll discuss this menu again later in this chapter, but you should know the function key to use for each operating system. By default, certain function keys are available in DOS, Windows 9x, and Windows 2000/XP. Although each operating system uses the same set of keys, specific keys work differently at startup. System Administrators can disable access to these function keys, either by editing MSDOS.SYS, or with customization utilities such as Tweak UI. Table 16.1 is a listing of the function keys.

Table 16.1	The Startup Function Keys	
Keys	**OS**	**Description**
F5	DOS	Bypass all the commands in your CONFIG.SYS and AUTOEXEC.BAT files when the text "Starting MS-DOS..." appears.
F8	DOS	Steps through each individual command in the AUTOEXEC.BAT and CONFIG.SYS files. To carry out all remaining startup commands, press **ESC**.
Ctrl-F5	DOS	Bypasses all the commands in your CONFIG.SYS and AUTOEXEC.BAT files and does not load DRVSPACE.BIN.
Ctrl-F8	DOS	Bypasses loading DRVSPACE.BIN, and provides interactive Y/N for individual commands in CONFIG.SYS and AUTOEXEC.BAT files. To carry out all remaining startup commands, press **ESC**. To bypass all remaining startup commands, press F5.
F4	Windows 95	Starts the previous version of MS-DOS or Windows 3.1 if it was installed before.
F5	Windows 95	Starts in Safe Mode. Very few drivers are loaded and no backup of the Registry is made, preventing the use of a corrupt copy. The screen resolution is VGA 640×480, 16 colors, and network is not supported.
F6	Windows 95	Starts in Safe Mode with network support.
F8	Windows 95, 98, SE, Me, 2000, XP	Displays the Windows Interactive Startup menu. In Windows 98 and Me, the F8 key is still functional, but there is no "Starting Windows..." prompt, so it's hard to know exactly when to press it. Use the Ctrl key.

(continued)

Table 16.1	The Startup Function Keys *(continued)*	
Keys	**OS**	**Description**
Ctrl	Windows 98, Me	Hold the Ctrl key down while your computer is booting to pause at the Windows 98 and Windows Me Interactive Startup menu.
Shift+F8	Windows 95, 98	Interactive startup process, where the system asks for confirmation for each line in CONFIG.SYS.SYS and AUTOEXEC.BAT.
Shift	Windows 3x, 95	Holding the Shift key down during Startup prevents all programs in the Startup group (folder) from loading.
Shift (Restart)	Windows 98	If you choose Restart during a Windows 98 shutdown, holding the Shift key while clicking on "Okay" avoids restarting the machine from a cold boot. This option restarts the Windows Explorer shell.
Shift	Windows 2000, XP	You can bypass the Startup folders during logon by holding down the Shift key. First, type your password at login, then hold down the Shift key and continue holding Shift until the login process completes.

You can quickly refresh the Desktop by logging off as the current user, then logging back on under the same User ID. If the machine has been configured for only a single user, you can still use the Log Off option on the Start menu, to accomplish an Explorer reset. (The Desktop is part of Explorer.) Remember that you also can press F5 from the Desktop to refresh the Explorer. In some situations this can accomplish changes to the Registry without having to completely reboot the machine.

The F8 Key

When an NT kernel system is configured with more than one operating system, Windows 2000 and XP both generate an initial text menu asking you to choose which operating system you want to load. The system pauses prior to loading any operating system and produces a menu. We'll refer to this menu as the "OS Selection" menu. We're making up the menu title for simplicity sake; there isn't an actual title. The F8 key (noted at the bottom of the screen) accesses the Interactive Startup menu.

The OS Selection menu is generated through the BOOT.INI file, and includes a "timeout" period before the default operating system loads automatically. You can modify the menu listings, which OS to make as the default, and the timeout period. On systems with only a single operating system, the OS Selection menu doesn't appear. You'll have to be fast with your fingers to know how to pause the normal startup process so as to get to the Interactive Start menu.

Last Known Good (LKG)

Windows NT introduced a pause prior to loading Windows, to ask you what you wanted to do. This selection menu included the "Last Known Good" (LKG) option. We discussed "Last Known Good" in Chapter 15, "Windows NT, 2000, and XP," but there's some confusion you should know about. Windows NT Startup always offered the feature as a way to revert the computer to the last successful configuration settings used to start Windows. Windows 2000 and Windows XP no longer offer the option by default, but they still have the feature. It's now an Interactive Startup menu option, prior to loading Windows.

When Windows XP/2000 have a problem starting, they both generate the Interactive Startup menu, and "Last Known Good" shows up at that time. However, if you press the F8 key to start Windows in the interactive mode, the LKG option once again shows up on the menu. On a multi-boot system, you must first choose which OS you want to start, then choose the option. You're then asked to once again choose which operating system will use the "Last Known Good" settings.

"Last Known Good" is one way to try to repair a system that won't start. Often, this type of problem develops after you've installed a new hardware device. Shut down the machine and remove the new device. Try LKG to see if you can boot the machine.

Windows XP/2000 offer three relatively quick ways to recover from a problem with a bad hardware installation. "Last Known Good" is the only option available prior to actually starting Windows. If Windows actually starts (either normally or in Safe Mode) you can also use the "Add Hardware" option in the Control Panel, or "Add/Remove Software Programs." Thirdly, you can try System File Checker (SFC) to revert to the original device drivers and support files installed on the system. Windows XP (only) offers the "Device Rollback" option in the Device Manager (discussed later in this chapter).

System Restore (also discussed later in this chapter) is a backup program, designed to capture a healthy system at various times. Although you can use System Restore to repair a hardware or application installation problem, it's really more of a complete restoration of the computer, rather than a tool to correct a single mistake or problem.

Repair the Operating System

Another menu option that magically shows up either on the OS Selection menu or when Windows fails to start, is an offer to Repair Windows. Windows has become so complicated that often the only way to "fix" the system is to do an in-place installation—a reinstall. We discuss this again, later in this chapter, but you should be very familiar with the changing Startup menus you're likely to encounter when Windows starts under different conditions.

Repairing an already-installed version of Windows 2000 or XP requires having the installation CD handy. Always understand that Window NT/2000/XP use two partitions to "boot" the system. Counter-intuitively, the System partition contains the bootable NT Loader file (ntldr). NT Loader then searches for the Windows "system" files on the Boot partition. The Boot partition is the logical drive with the \Windows or \WINNT folder and subfolders containing all the system files.

The reason you should work with the upgrade versions of Windows 2000 and XP is that you'll get an immediate and direct understanding of how Windows loads when you don't have the luxury of booting from a bootable installation CD. Windows XP/2000 can crash completely, or maybe develop corrupted system files, but the computer can still start and present the OS Selection menu or Interactive Startup menu. As long as the System partition isn't corrupted, that's enough to run NTLDR, which then searches all mounted volumes (including a CD in the CD drive) for the Widows "boot" files.

If the System partition becomes corrupted, you can run ntldr from a floppy diskette. However, you must also have ntdetect.com and the boot.ini file for the specific machine and its configuration on that floppy. We'll discuss the Emergency Repair Disk again in this chapter.

Boot Problems

During the very first initialization process, a machine can't display anything to the monitor, and you can't enter anything from the keyboard. We discussed the power-on self-test (POST) in Chapter 13, "Booting, Startup Files, and Memory," and included a listing of the error signals in the "Beep Codes" section. If the machine can't get past the initialization, the most likely problem involves either a bad power supply or a failed motherboard.

Sometimes, a machine has actually booted up, but the monitor is turned off or broken. In some instances, the monitor's image controls have been dimmed down to point where you can't see anything on the screen. Check the brightness controls and monitor indicator lights, but in a worst case, you might have to try a different monitor. When we refer to the process of using a different piece of equipment that we know works, we speak of *switching out* the problem piece of equipment. After the machine has passed the POST, but before ROM BIOS hands off to the operating system, the most common area where you'll encounter the next set of problems is with the CMOS.

Two typical messages about a missing operating system are "Bad or missing command interpreter" and "Non-system disk or disk error." These errors might show up on any DOS or Windows machine, and indicate that you should try to reinstall the system files. On Windows 9x machines, you can try to run SYS.COM from an EBD. On an NT or 2000 system, try using an Emergency Repair Disk (ERD). Windows XP no longer offers the ERD, but you can use either a bootable installation CD or a manually created start disk (discussed later in this chapter).

"No fixed disk present" Error

Among the various error messages that can provide wonderful bursts of adrenaline to your system, this particular error is right up there with "Invalid media type." At least with the invalid media error, you know you have a hard drive in the box, and that the operating system noticed it. "No fixed disk present" means that as far as the motherboard is concerned, you have no hard drive at all. Note that this is at the motherboard level, long before you get to CMOS and the operating system.

The most common cause for this type of problem is a bad cable or its connectors. Turn off all power and disconnect all peripheral devices from the computer. Open the case and check that the drive cables are securely attached. These connectors sometimes are hard to seat, and they may have been improperly connected. Check that the power supply connections going to the drive are secure and haven't broken. (Certain Maxtor drives seem to have this problem, for no apparent reason.)

If the problem persists, try changing the power connector, using one from a different cable. Or, use a different IDE cable entirely. You'll likely be in a total panic condition, since this error generally shows up an hour before you're about to do something critical with the computer.

"Invalid media type" Error

This is a good place to point out that having an old computer to play with is a really, really good idea! If you haven't had a chance to play with some of these catastrophic problems, errors, and system crashes, do so before you sit for the exam. Even a 486 is workable, but an old Pentium machine is great. You don't need a huge hard drive, just a CDROM drive and a floppy disk drive. This is the time to play with FDISK and see what happens when you "accidentally" do certain things.

After you partition a disk, you're required to designate Primary and/or Extended partitions. You then must choose an Active partition on which to install a bootable operating system. When that's been done, you exit FDISK. However, you still have to format (logical formatting) the partitions with some type of file system. Suppose you forget to format what you thought was the C: drive? When you remove the bootable floppy from the drive and restart the machine, you'll get this "invalid media type" error. It means the disk contains no operating system and no file system. It's an empty disk and the system can't figure out what to do with it.

On the other hand, if you ever get this type of error on a system that was previously working, we'll offer you our condolences in advance. If you get this error, chances are you'll probably have to reinstall the entire system. Either the drive is broken, or a virus wiped out the file system and boot track. Presumably you or the end user have an up-to-date backup...right? This error is different from "invalid or missing system files." In the latter case, you can sometimes use SYS.COM to reinstall the system files (DOS and Windows 9x only).

Some error messages indicate that the CMOS has been configured to seek a bootable operating system from the A: drive, and someone left a non-bootable floppy disk in the drive bay. However, the error will almost always say something about "replace disk" and "press any key." Windows XP/2000 usually bypass a non-system DOS disk in the A: drive, if there's a CD in the CDROM drive, because NTLDR is smart enough to search for NT kernel files.

CMOS Problems

CMOS errors are often generated after someone changes the computer's configuration settings. This situation can lead to anything from being unable to boot the machine, to a short pause at the POST screen. When the change causes only a short pause, it's usually because CMOS found the change and made automatic reconfigured the system to adjust. The machine typically will continue booting after you press a listed function key (often F1).

Incorrect or damaged CMOS and BIOS settings can often cause problems. For information about the correct CMOS and BIOS settings for the computer, either refer to the system's documentation or contact the manufacturer. Also contact the computer manufacturer (usually a visit to their Web site) to find out about the latest BIOS updates, availability, and how to install the latest BIOS on the machine.

Sometimes a machine can have a hardware password stored in the CMOS, in which case it will prompt the user for that password after the POST. Some PCs also offer separate passwords: one to access the machine, and the other for general access to the operating system. Mostly, a default configuration leaves the password setting as None or Disabled. If all machine passwords are disabled, the POST automatically hands off to the operating system.

If the user chooses to set a password and then forgets it, the recommended way to recover the system is to remove the CMOS battery long enough for the loss of power to clear the chip. Another way is to reconfigure a jumper on the motherboard to clear the chip. These steps clear all CMOS settings and require reconfiguring the CMOS when the battery is replaced or the jumper is reset. In the field, some technicians have been known to use a screwdriver to short-circuit the CMOS jumper and clear the chip. However, although this could be the only available option on the exam, it isn't a good idea in the real world.

Finally, an important setting in CMOS is the order in which the machine checks its drives for an operating system. Keep in mind that a *default* setting is the value that will be set if no manual configuration change takes place, or when a cleared CMOS receives power for the first time. The default in most PCs is that the system will search (seek) first in Drive A: and then Drive C:. Other settings include completely disabling the checking of Drive A:, checking for a bootable CDROM, checking for a bootable SCSI drive, and even checking additional attached drives.

In the event that the C: drive becomes disabled, the system can sometimes be booted from the A: drive (to DOS). However, if seeking Drive A: has been disabled, there's no other way to access the hard drive. Understand that booting to DOS will not provide any access at all to an NTFS partition. The partition simply disappears, excepting that FDISK will list a "Non-DOS partition."

CMOS Error Messages

CMOS settings are stored in a sort of file. Checksum validation works with CMOS memory much the way that it works with files. (Checksum is discussed in Chapter 8, "Peripherals: Storage Devices," under the "Cyclical Redundancy Checking [CRC]" heading.) *Checksum validation* begins by adding a number to a file when it's created and stored (written). The number is appended to (added onto) the file, and a copy is stored for later checking. When the file is read, the same process runs again, in reverse. The file CRC compared with the stored number should make a match. If the file number doesn't match the stored number, a *checksum error* occurs. The CMOS settings file itself has a stored checksum.

If no operating system is found, CMOS returns an error message to the screen and pauses the system. There are many CMOS errors, but some of the important ones to know include

➤ *CMOS checksum failure*—A checksum failure indicates that the CMOS memory itself is corrupted. This can happen with a bad battery or a loose connection to the battery. If changing and checking the battery doesn't solve the problem, it might be a motherboard going bad. Checksum errors may also indicate a virus.

➤ *CMOS display type mismatch*—This error indicates that the video settings don't apply to the actual monitor installed on the system. The first step is to re-enter CMOS and verify that the correct monitor has been selected.

➤ *CMOS memory size mismatch*—This error appears on many machines when more memory has been added. Auto-detection usually reconfigures the CMOS, with a pause during the POST to make sure that what CMOS saw matches reality.

➤ *CMOS device mismatch error*—Displays and hard disks are considered devices, and any one of the attached devices can generate this error. Most likely, the actual physical device attached to the machine is incorrectly listed in CMOS.

NTLDR Is Missing

When you start an NT kernel system, you may receive an "NTLDR is missing, Press any key to restart..." error message. This problem may occur if the machine is using outdated BIOS, or if one or more of the following Windows boot files are missing or damaged:

➤ ntldr

➤ ntdetect.com

➤ boot.ini

Verify that the machine is using current BIOS, or repair the Windows installation. Microsoft recommends that you fully back up your data on a regular basis, as the best defense against losses. Backups are a fundamental part of any disaster recovery plan. (You do have a disaster recovery plan, don't you?)

You can format a plain, non-bootable floppy disk and copy onto it the three files listed in the previous bullet points. Again, these files won't boot the system, but if the System partition is corrupted, you may be able to start Windows from the Boot partition.

Ultimately, when the boot process fails, you'll most likely be left with a complete lock-up, a blank screen, an automatic reboot, or a blue error screen (the so-called blue screen of death). Even the screen can provide you with some diagnostics information. For example, if the system boots to a *blank* screen, it often means there's a video problem, or a video driver set to the wrong resolution. On the other hand, if the system boots to a *blue* screen, the problem is often due to an incorrect device driver or a hardware failure. Each blue screen lists an error message (a stop error), pointing to a specific problem. Grab a bottle of aspirin, then check the Windows 2000 or XP Resource Kit, or go to the Microsoft Support Web site for the meaning of specific error messages.

We cannot guarantee that any of the Web sites referenced in this book will continue to be available online. We've tried to choose those sites that appear to have some longevity and stability. If a site is no longer accessible, use any search engine to query the Internet for specific problems.

You can do an Internet search for almost any type of error message. There are a number of Web sites with in-depth listings of every Windows error message. There are also various downloadable, standalone databases with explanations for nearly every error code. Always remember Microsoft's own support site (**www. support.microsoft.com**).

Another place you wouldn't ordinarily think of, in terms of help, is the "Groups" tab on the Google site. The Internet is a large world, and we tend to mostly use a search engine to find whatever we're looking for on a Web site. However, another area of the Web contains the many newsgroups that people put together, to discuss any conceivable topic you can imagine. Don't limit yourself to only the main "Web" tab, on Google, but use the same search criteria from the "Groups" tab. You'll often find very good information about the most obscure Windows problems imaginable.

Windows Registry Files—Hives

The preceding bootup problems are the first of the five categories we listed at the start of this chapter. However, before we get into the next four diagnostics and repair categories, let's take another look at the Windows Registry. We first discussed the System Registry in Chapter 14, saying that it was made up of two critical files. That's true for Windows 95, 98, and Me, and the two files are SYSTEM.DAT and USER.DAT.

Microsoft and CompTIA like to refer to the Registry as a database of some kind, often calling it a hierarchical structure, meaning that it starts at the top of each HKey node, then expands downward into individual branches. When you see the word "hierarchy," think "pyramid" and you should be okay. The fact is that a database uses records and fields to store information having some type of pattern. The Registry uses fields, but that's about it.

The Windows Registry is really a group of individual files that store configuration-settings information. Windows 3.x used REG.DAT and the two important .INI files, SYSTEM.INI and WIN.INI. REG.DAT was a binary file, with only a few obscure settings. Windows 9x became much more sophisticated, and the binary SYSTEM.DAT and USER.DAT files took over almost all the work of storing configuration settings.

Windows NT introduced the term "hives" to mean "files." In its never-accomplished quest for consistency, Microsoft has invented terms, then changed them or changed the meaning of those same terms. When you see the word "hive," think of "files." Windows 2000, having grown out of NT, used more than two binary files to store configuration information, but at that point, Microsoft began to be less expansive in explaining exactly which files. Windows XP now routinely refers to the Registry as the System State, and the underlying storage files as *hives*.

The supporting files for all hives except HKEY_CURRENT_USER are in the %Systemroot%\System32\Config folder.

The Registry Editor

It didn't used to be all that important that you understood exactly what was taking place when you started the Registry Editor. Now, with Windows XP and so many individual configuration files (hives), you should have a better concept of what you're seeing in the editor. Windows 2000 gave us REGEDT32.EXE, and Microsoft proposed that this should be the preferred editor for the Registry. However, all versions of Windows continue to include REGEDIT.EXE as the Registry Editor application file.

Understand that the Registry has only two "real" HKeys. The remaining keys are mirrors of sections of the main keys, as we discussed in Chapter 14. However, the editor does show both the main keys and the mirrors as HKeys, and you'll have to know all their names. REGEDT32 opens up a console window with each HKey in a separate child window. Why? Nobody knows, and although the program is still available, few people use it. Windows XP went back to using REGEDIT.EXE as the Registry Editor program.

You open the Registry Editor by choosing Start | Run and entering regedit in the dialog box. The program goes out to those certain mysterious folders and files and begins opening each hive. When all the files have been opened,

REGEDIT organizes the information into the HKey structure, then lists each key as a node under the "My Computer" heading.

Each node has a small + or – sign that works just like the Explorer. When you expand an HKey, the underlying nodes and sub-nodes eventually open out to a configuration "record," and you can view or edit the specific settings. Many books offer ways to enhance Windows through the use of Registry changes (patches). In some instances, you're asked to create a field in a particular location, then use certain settings. (Check the "Need to Know More?" section at the end of this chapter, and the listing for David Karp's *Windows XP Annoyances*.)

One important thing to remember about the Registry Editor is that it acts as a consolidation area to provide access to some number of files, stored somewhere on the hard drive. Those files—the hives—contain settings data in binary form. Although you can use REGEDT32.EXE to open the editor (in Windows 2000/XP), the more likely program is REGEDIT.EXE. Review the "HKeys" section in Chapter 14 for a listing of the Registry nodes.

Startup Problems

A Windows startup problem isn't the same thing as a system failure. We've said that Startup begins after the operating system boot loader has found the Windows system files. A successful Startup ends with the Desktop, first going through the Logon dialog box, if the machine has been configured for multiple users or as a network client. When the computer can't properly generate the Desktop, we're calling that part of the troubleshooting process Startup problems.

System instability (where Windows becomes unstable and acts erratically) is that point after Startup, where a different set of troubleshooting events takes place. In many instances, Windows can almost start, but not quite. If that's the case, it tries to start in Safe Mode. If the system starts, and generates the Desktop, then crashes, we're calling it a system failure.

Safe Mode—The Interactive Startup Menu

Windows 95 introduced Safe Mode as a way to run a bare-bones instance of the operating system. Safe Mode is one of the options listed on the Interactive Startup menu. Understand that we're calling the text menu containing a list of startup options the Interactive Startup menu, to conveniently discuss a menu that doesn't ordinarily appear unless there's a problem. You can edit MSDOS.SYS to always start the computer with this menu, but the default is to automatically start Windows after the boot loader finds the system files.

 Use Table 16.1 at the beginning of this chapter to remember which function key to press to bring up the Interactive Startup menu. "Safe Mode" is an option on that menu. There isn't a Safe Mode menu.

A sneaky way to force Safe Mode on a Windows 9x machine is to rename the WIN.COM file to something else, then restart the machine. (NT kernel systems don't use WIN.COM to start Windows.) Let's say you rename it to WEN.COM. Windows won't start because it can't find the .COM loader file necessary to begin the startup process. You'll end up at a plain DOS prompt. You can then type WEN /D:M to force Windows into Safe Mode. (If you can't remember what to type, WIN /? or in this case, WEN /? will give you a list of all the Windows startup switches.) Remember to rename wen.com back to win.com, or the system will never start normally. (Type ren wen.com win.com and press Enter.)

All versions of Windows provide access to the Interactive Startup menu, and all versions of Windows have a Safe Mode. If you can't start the computer in Safe Mode, the odds are you'll have to restore a backup, reinstall, or "repair" Windows. In Safe Mode, Windows uses only basic files and drivers (mouse, monitor, keyboard, disks, base video, default system services, and *no network connections*).

You can choose "Safe Mode with Networking," which loads the essential services and drivers to start networking. You can also choose "Safe Mode with Command Prompt," which is exactly the same as Safe Mode except it starts a DOS command prompt instead.

Interactive Startup Options

The Windows 9x startup menu is slightly different from the Windows XP/2000 "Advanced Options Menu," but both menus offer pretty much the same choices. We'll list the generic options in the first set of bullets, then list the Windows XP/2000 options in a second set of bullets.

➤ *Start Windows Normally*—Provides the options of starting the machine at a command line and waiting for the user to start Windows.

➤ *Safe Mode*—Starts Windows in the most basic configuration with VGA graphics (16 colors, 640×480).

➤ *Safe Mode with Networking*—Starts Windows using only basic files and drivers, plus network connections.

➤ *Safe Mode with Command Prompt*—After logging on, once again using only basic files and drivers, the system stops at a command prompt. The GUI is not loaded.

➤ *Enable Boot Logging*—Logs all drivers and services that were loaded (or not loaded) to the BOOTLOG.TXT (or NTBTLOG.TXT for NT kernel machines) file, located in the %windir% directory. Safe Mode, Safe Mode with Networking, and Safe Mode with Command Prompt use the boot log to list all drivers and services being loaded.

➤ *Enable VGA Mode*—Starts Windows 2000 using the standard VGA driver. This is useful if you have installed a new video driver and Windows 2000 is not starting properly. The basic video driver is also used when you start Windows 2000 in Safe Mode, Safe Mode with Networking, or Safe Mode with Command Prompt.

Be sure that you've run Windows 98, 2000, and XP before you take the exam. Get to the Interactive Startup menu and make a note of the difference. There isn't enough room in this book to go into any great detail about the different options, but you must know the menu options and a summary of what each option does. NT kernel systems provide additional options, including:

➤ *Last Known Good Configuration*—Starts Windows using the hardware configuration and profile from last successful shutdown. "Last Known Good" does not solve problems caused by corrupted or missing drivers or files. Any changes made in the current session will be lost.

➤ *Directory Service Restore Mode*—Used by Windows server versions or domain controllers. (You won't need to know this for the exam.)

➤ *Debugging Mode*—Starts Windows while sending debug information through a serial cable to another computer.

➤ *Return to OS Choices Menu*—This refers to the OS Selection menu on multi-boot systems, where the user chooses which operating system to start.

 If you are using, or have used, Remote Install Services to install Windows XP/2000 on your computer, you may see additional options related to restoring or recovering your system using Remote Install Services.

Last Known Good Revisited

The "Last Known Good" configuration starts the computer using Registry information saved at the last proper shutdown. Windows 9x routinely backs up the Registry when the date changes following a shutdown. Windows 9x also routinely keeps two non-compressed copies of the Registry. Startup uses the .DAT files, and the backup is the .DA0 files. If Windows can't start using the .DAT files stored during last shutdown process, it automatically tries to start with the backup .DA0 Registry files.

Windows NT uses a similar process, but works with different files. After Windows has started successfully and the user chooses to shutdown the machine (Shutdown, in 9x/NT/2000, or Turn off the machine, in XP), NT saves the hardware and configuration settings. Obviously, if Windows was running then those settings are "good." Windows NT (specifically) begins the Startup process with a pause at a blue screen, and provides an option to begin the next session with the previously successful settings.

Windows 2000/XP moved the "Last Known Good" menu option to the so-called Advanced Options Menu, on the assumption that the only time you would need to access previous settings would be in the event of a problem. If you find startup problems after making a major configuration change to the computer, try using the "Last Known Good" option. These kinds of problems might include installing a new device and software driver, or a new software application and then being unable to fully start Windows.

If you can start the computer with "Last Known Good," then chances are that one of the last changes was the cause of the problem. Revert the change by removing or updating the driver, then uninstall the program and restart the machine. Contact the device or software vendor for compatibility information.

 Remember that copies of "good" files are created during a successful and proper Shutdown. When you start the computer using the "Last Known Good" configuration, the configuration does not contain any changes that were made since the last successful startup. Understand that when you successfully log onto the machine, do your work then log off the machine, Windows will overwrite the previous configuration settings and create a new "last known good" set of configuration information. Also remember the System Restore possibility, if you can get into the system at all, even if it's unstable.

Windows 9x Registry Checker

We discussed the ScanReg, the Registry Checker, in Chapter 14, under the "Registry Backup Files" heading. To quickly review it one more time, ScanReg is only available in Windows 98 and Me. To start the Registry Checker, restart your computer, press and hold the Ctrl key, then choose "Command Prompt Only." Type scanreg, then press Enter. To use SCAN-REG to restore a previous version of the Registry, follow these steps:

1. Restart your computer with the bootable EBD disk, in your floppy disk drive. (You won't need to boot with CDROM support.)

2. Type `scanreg /restore` at the command line, then press Enter.

The Registry Checker *requires* extended memory to operate properly. It will not run if you start your computer with the "Safe Mode Command Prompt Only" option. The only exception to this is the `scanreg /restore` command. This is the only ScanReg function that can run without extended memory. This means you cannot use the "Restart in MS DOS Mode" option on the Shutdown menu to run other ScanReg options.

You can also restore a previous copy of the Registry from inside Windows, using the Windows version of ScanReg. SCANREGW.EXE is essentially the same as SCANREG.EXE, excepting that you can double click the file in the Explorer, or use the Start | Run dialog box. (To open a .CAB file and extract files, you'll need an archive extracting program such as WinZip.) You'll often find it easier to simply drag copies of SYSTEM.DAT and USER.DAT to a backup folder—somewhere other than the \Windows folder.

Not only can the Registry Checker be used to back up and restore the Registry files, but the DOS version of ScanReg attempts to go through corrupted system files and make a best guess as to how to fix them. (You'll likely have much better success with a third-party Registry Repair program.) The DOS version of the Registry Checker is SCANREG.EXE. This is the program used to run `scanreg /restore` from a command line, and is also used during the Windows Setup procedure.

Windows NT/2000 Emergency Repair Disk (ERD)

NT kernel versions of Windows don't provide the option of creating an emergency startup disk as did Windows 9x. If you remember, you could go to the Control Panel, in those versions, and choose Add/Remove Software. You could then choose the "Startup" tab and then choose "Create a Startup Disk."

The Windows NT/2000 so-called emergency repair disk does nothing to actually fix or repair Windows. Remember that the NT Loader uses a System partition to begin a two-part startup operation. NTLDR first acts as a basic bootstrap loader, then tries to find the Windows system files (on the Boot partition). The three reasons for the ERD are that NTLDR must exist, it must be able to detect the hardware profile for the machine, and it must be able to find the system files.

If `ntldr`, `ntdetect.com`, and `boot.ini` become corrupted, the Emergency Repair Disk provides a backup for the files on a floppy diskette. Understand, too, that the `boot.ini` file usually contains a folder listing for the Windows system files on a specific machine. Likewise, the `ntdetect.com` file lists the specific hardware configuration for that particular machine.

Windows 2000 (only) provides the following steps for making an Emergency Repair Disk:

1. From the desktop, choose Start | All Programs | Accessories | System tools | "Backup."

2. You are given three options: Backup, Restore, and Emergency Repair Disk.

3. Choose "Emergency Repair Disk" and a wizard will walk you through the process of creating the disk.

Windows XP Automated System Recovery (ASR)

Windows XP no longer offers an ERD, but suggests that you can create something similar by making an Automated System Recovery. We also discuss the ASR in Chapter 15, under the "Bootable and Emergency Repair Disks" heading. Use the following steps to access the Automated System Recovery:

1. From the desktop, choose Start | All Programs | Accessories | System tools | "Backup."

2. Make sure the "Backup Utility Wizard" checkbox is checked (the default).

3. Click on the "Advanced Mode" button in the wizard.

4. Follow the steps that appear on the screen.

The Automated System Recovery is really more of a backup of the system. However, you can make an emergency start disk similar to that for a Windows 2000 machine. Start with a stable, functioning session of Windows XP. Get a 1.44MB floppy disk and follow these steps:

1. Format the 1.44MB floppy disk (full format).

2. Copy the NTLDR (system file), NTDETECT.COM (MS-DOS application), and BOOT.INI (configuration settings) files to the floppy. (Note: if you're using a SCSI disk, you will also have to copy NTBOOTDD.SYS to the floppy).

NTLDR and NTDETECT.COM are hidden files. If you're going to use a command-line window and the **COPY** command, you may have to use the **ATTRIB** command to unhide the files before you can copy them. Another option is a freeware utility called XXCOPY16, available at **www.xxcopy.com**. This utility allows one-step copying of hidden files from a command line.

Remember that you can also go to the Tools | Folder Options | "View" tab, in the Explorer, and uncheck the "Hide protected operating system files," then check the "Show hidden files and folders" boxes.

Selective Startup (MSCONFIG.EXE)

Another way to diagnose and sometimes fix startup problems if to use MSCONFIG.EXE. Choose Start | Run, and type `msconfig` in the "Open" dialog box. This is the Microsoft System Configuration utility we discussed in Chapter 14. Keep in mind that it isn't available in Windows 2000, but you can download the XP version and it'll work fine.

The General tab of the System Configuration Utility offers choices for a Normal startup, a Diagnostic startup, where you can selectively choose device drivers and software, and the Selective startup. The Selective startup has a set of check boxes that let you choose whether or not to process the CONFIG.SYS, AUTOEXEC.BAT, WIN.INI, SYSTEM.INI, or Startup Group. Windows XP is slightly different, and includes a "Services" tab. Table 16.2 demonstrates the four different boot options under "Selective Startup." The table indicates the items each boot option verifies.

Table 16.2 Selective Startup Options of the System Configuration Utility				
Description	Boot A	Boot B	Boot C	Boot D
Process System.ini file	Yes	No	Yes	Yes
Process Win.ini file	No	Yes	Yes	Yes
Load Static VxD	Yes	Yes	No	Yes
Load Startup group items	Yes	Yes	Yes	No

If the Load Startup Group Item is grayed out, the Startup Group has been customized at some point. Click the Startup tab at the top and record the startup items that are checked so you can return to this customized configuration after the installation.

Windows Me Considerations

The System Configuration Utility tool cannot disable a file that has the read-only attribute. Even so, it pretends that it did. To determine whether the System Configuration Utility tool has replaced the file that you are trying to disable, open the file. If the System Configuration Utility did replace the file, you should see the following text at the beginning of the file:

```
rem
rem    *** DO NOT EDIT THIS FILE! ***
rem
rem    This file was created by the System Configuration Utility as
rem    a placeholder for your SYSTEM.INI file. Your actual
rem    SYSTEM.INI file has been saved under the name SYSTEM.TSH.
rem
```

 This is reminiscent of how Windows Me would hide and change basic configuration files on its own, without notifying the computer user.

Windows Me and Fast CPUs

Your computer may stop responding (hang) during the boot process if the computer contains a processor that runs at 850 megahertz (MHz) or faster. When this occurs, the computer hangs before the Windows Millennium Edition (Me) bitmap is displayed. Computers with a Japanese BIOS may be more susceptible to this problem.

A supported fix is now available from Microsoft, but it is only intended to correct the problem described in this article and should be applied only to systems experiencing this specific problem. See the Microsoft Service Link: **http://support.microsoft.com/?id=kb;en-us;Q278844**.

System Failures

Windows 2000 and XP are pretty stable versions of Windows. However, they still crash unexpectedly, or go through mysterious restarts from time to time. We've listed system failures as our third, broad category of problems, meaning that Windows has been successfully running for some time. After the Desktop appears, people use a computer to do regular work. They also install new software and add or change hardware. A system failure indicates that Windows has become unstable after these types of change (or for no reason at all).

There are a number of good Web sites devoted to the increasingly complex issues of troubleshooting Windows 2000/XP. We've included some of the sites we found, under the "Need to Know More?" heading at the end of this chapter. Discussion forums, such as those found on Annoyances.org (`www.annoyances.org`), indicate that system crashes are most often caused by the following situations:

➤ *Corrupted Registry Files*—Editing the Registry, installation routines, or changes to low-level configuration settings can all cause a failure in the Registry. The machine usually becomes unstable and attempts to start in Safe Mode with the next startup.

➤ *Power Supplies and Heat*—An insufficient power supply, especially on machines with multiple expansion cards, drives, or cooling fans, should be upgraded to at least a 350–400W power supply. If the power supply is faulty, it should be replaced (not repaired). Make sure the cooling fan or fans are working, and that there is adequate ventilation around the computer case. Temperature problems are very hard to diagnose. Some of today's computers provide a CPU temperature reading (see the computer's reference manual).

➤ *Sound Cards*—Even though most sound cards can be recognized by the Windows Plug-and-Play database, they continue to cause problems. Before you install drivers and files for an add-on sound card, be sure to back up the Registry.

➤ *USB Hubs*—These seems to be an important reason for system crashes—particularly hotsync cradles for handheld devices (such as Palm, Handspring, Sony, and so on). If the system crashes on a regular basis, try taking out the USB device. If that solves the problem, contact the manufacturer for possible driver updates.

➤ *Loose PCI Cards*—Another reason for continuing crashes may be loose expansion cards. All the way back to the original XTs, loose memory modules were causing trouble. The development of in-line memory modules solved the problem by hardwiring the chips to an IC board (SIMMs and DIMMs). Add-on cards are becoming less necessary, as integrated motherboards and USB devices become more prevalent. Re-seat all the expansion cards and restart the machine. Use the Device Manager to remove the driver information and Windows will rescan the system, reinstalling the devices.

Memory Modules

Most machines will experience unusual stability problems if there's a bad memory chip or module in the system. Commercial hardware analysis software products, such as Smith Micro, Inc.'s *Check-It* (www.smithmicro.com) can do comprehensive tests on all the hardware in a system, including the memory. Otherwise, you'll have to remove each module, one at a time, to see whether it's the cause of the problem. Keep in mind that some computers require memory modules to be installed in pairs. If this is the case (see the computer's reference manual), then be sure to remove and replace the modules in pairs.

Bad memory modules can cause very sneaky problems. For example, you may be able to start the machine and load Windows. Shortly thereafter, you get a strange error message. It could be a page-fault error, or "Windows has performed an illegal operation" message. One suspicious indicator pointing to a RAM module is that the error is hard to re-create. It crops up unexpectedly, or after the system has been running for awhile. Memory is pretty inexpensive, so if you suspect a problem, test the modules and replace them. Keep in mind that overheating can also cause these types of errors, shutting down the CPU.

IBM often provides a downloadable hardware diagnostics utility for their laptops. These programs run a comprehensive test on the machine, including memory modules. Troubleshooting notebook computers is an entire book in itself. Never format the hard drive for a laptop without first making absolutely sure you can boot the system from a floppy, and that you can access the CDROM drive. This requires investigation into all the hardware configuration files and possible DOS startup files. Always make a separate partition on the drive, and store critical files on that partition before you format the main C: drive.

File Management Systems

There may be more than one non-removable disk in the system. If one drive is using NTFS while another is using FAT32, the different file management systems can sometimes be the source of the problem. Try running Check Disk until it shows no errors. Another possible solution is to convert all the drives to NTFS and see whether that solves the problem.

When you install Windows XP, you're given the option of converting a FAT32 file system to NTFS. The two are not compatible! Aside from compatibility issues, many people are familiar with a traditional DOS boot disk, used to start a machine without any operating system. Windows NT/2000/XP are not based on DOS at all. They continue to have a command-line capability that looks like DOS, but it isn't the same. You can't use a DOS boot disk to get into an NTFS partition and do any file manipulation. You can use only the Windows Recovery Console, discussed later in this chapter.

XP Looping Restarts

Services errors are among the more common causes for continuing restarts in XP. When XP runs into a system failure, it tries to automatically restart the machine. You can change this setting from the Control Panel. Choose the "System" icon, and the "Advanced" tab. In the "Startup and Recovery" area, click the "Settings" button. Under "System failure," de-select the "Automatically restarts" option.

You can also choose to write an event to the system log from this window. This gives you a way to see what happened without the constant re-booting. The Event Viewer is also in the Control Panel, under the "Administrative Tools" icon. (You can also choose Start | Run, and enter `eventvwr` in the dialog box.)

Installation Problems

Figuring out why a computer fails to start, or why it crashes in the middle of a session, is a large part of what makes tech support such a joy. Windows routinely throws up globs (technical term) of error messages, offering you the option of choosing a "Details" button as an explanation for the error. The details are lines of hexadecimal addresses, none of which make any sense to most living human beings. There are, however, clues to be found in the particular kind of behavior associated with a crash. For example, foot-long flames shooting from the top of the monitor indicate a fire error of some type. In situations like this, the properly certified A+ technician will generally run screaming out of the building, or call the fire department.

We're using the term "installation problems" to mean situations where someone has installed a new toy (hardware) or a software application, and the machine becomes unstable. "Unstable" could mean anything, but mostly it means that the system locks up, Windows crashes periodically, screen objects look particularly weird, and any number of other symptoms.

Windows XP (only) offers Compatibility Mode for certain types of problems with a particular device or software program. The indication that an older device or program may work with Compatibility Mode is that you get an error message telling you the program requires a previous operating system.

To run the Program Compatibility Wizard: Choose Start | Help and Support | Fixing a problem | Application and software problems | Getting older programs to run on Windows XP. Then click the Program Compatibility Wizard link in the instructions.

An alternative method is to manually configure a program. Find the program file name (or device) in the Explorer. Right-click for the Context menu to get to the Properties dialog box, then choose the Compatibility tab. Check the box marked "Run this program in compatibility mode." Choose the appropriate operating system, then check the "Display Settings" if the program can only use a particular resolution. Finally, click "Apply."

The Device Manager

Most hardware diagnostics and management is done through The Device Manager. If you find a problem device, you have two options: You can remove, disable, or reconfigure the actual device, or you can update the device driver software. If the computer then restarts correctly, that particular device may be the cause of the problem.

We won't go into much detail on the Add/Remove Software Programs console, located in the Control Panel. You should know how to find it, and that it's used when a new software application makes Windows unstable. If the installation routine was written to make it compatible with the Windows Install Shield, you should be able to easily remove the entire program. If it isn't listed in the Add/Remove console, there may be a program-specific Uninstall option in the Start menu's Programs group listing. If that doesn't work, then you'll have to manually remove the program, and somehow find any support files it put on the hard drive. You also may have to edit the Registry to remove all references to the program after it's been removed.

When you install a new piece of hardware, Windows is supposed to be able to detect that something new has been connected to the system. Following a restart, Windows will usually scan the hard drive for a software driver, then try to find a driver on an installation disk. Failing that, Windows will ask you if you have a disk with driver software but you're hiding it just to be mean. (That's the actual error message. Really!) Windows also offers you the option of connecting to the Microsoft Windows Update site.

If you have no device driver disk, you couldn't find a driver on the Update site, and Windows can't find a driver on the system, then the device won't work. However, after the hardware is installed, it may cause a problem. Use the Device Manager to diagnose hardware device problems. You can access the Device Manager in the following ways:

➤ In Windows 9x/NT/2000, move through Start | Settings | Control Panel to the System icon. Double-click "System," and choose the Device Manager tab.

➤ In Windows XP, choose Start | Control Panel | System, then choose the "Hardware" tab. Select the "Device Manager" option button.

➤ In Windows 9x/2000, access the Device Manager using the following steps: Right-click the My Computer icon and choose the Properties option. Choose the "Hardware" tab, then choose the Device Manager.

➤ In Windows 9x/2000, double-click on the My Computer icon, located on the Desktop, and choose the Control Panel icon. Double-click on Control Panel, then double-click on the System icon. Choose the Device Manager tab.

Device Manager Symbols

If a symbol is displayed next to a device (for example, an exclamation point), there may be a problem with the device. To disable a device, click on the device name and choose "Remove." In Windows 2000/XP, right-click on the device name, then click "Disable." The following symbols indicate types of problems:

➤ A black exclamation point (!) on a yellow field indicates the device is in a problem state. Note that a device that is in a problem state can be functioning. There is usually also an associated problem code.

➤ A red "X" indicates a disabled device physically present in the computer and consuming resources, but the device doesn't have a protected-mode driver loaded.

➤ A blue "i" on a white field (found under the Computer properties) on a device resource, indicates that the "Use Automatic Settings" feature is not selected for the device. The resource was manually selected; however, this does not indicate a problem or disabled state.

➤ (Windows Me only) A green question mark "?" means that a compatible driver for this device is installed, indicating the possibility that all the features of the device may not be accessible.

If you disable a device, check that the device is listed on the Windows Hardware Compatibility List (HCL), and that it is correctly installed. If the problem persists, contact the manufacturer to see about a possible version update, or to report the problem.

Device Memory Resources

To check for possible device conflicts, double-click the device name or right-click for the Context menu and choose Properties. Then choose the "Resources" tab. If there does happen to be a device conflict, it should be listed on the Conflicting Device list.

If Windows successfully detected a device and the device is functioning correctly, the "Use Automatic Settings" check box will be selected or grayed out. If not, examine the "Change Setting" option. If the resource settings are based on "Basic Configuration," you may have to change the configuration. To do so, either click a different basic configuration from the list, or manually change the resource settings (you may need the device's reference manual for this).

 This procedure may require you to change the computer's CMOS settings, as well as the BIOS settings. If you make the wrong changes to these setting, you may be unable to start the machine at all.

If the computer starts correctly, the device that you disabled may be the cause of the startup problem. Check to see if the device is listed on the Windows Hardware Compatibility List (HCL), and that it's correctly installed. You also may want to contact the manufacturer.

Device Rollback (XP Only)

Windows XP offers an even better Help and Support feature than previous versions, as part of the default installation. In many instances you can click on active links to arrive at the actual feature. XP includes System File Checker, which tracks the original support files for Windows and all the installed devices. However, you can choose a specific device in the Device Manager and revert, or "roll back" to previous driver software following an update.

To get to the Device Rollback, open the Device Manager, one way or another. Select the device that was recently updated. Right-click for the Context menu, then select the Properties option. Choose the "Driver" tab, then select the "Roll Back Driver" option. (Note that this is the same tab that holds the "Update Driver" option.

SFC—System File Checker

We discussed System File Checker in Chapter 15, but it's worth mentioning it again. When you install Windows (98, Me, 2000, XP) Setup copies onto the hard disk all the necessary program and support files Microsoft includes with Windows. At the same time, the various detection phases examine the particular system and choose particular device drivers and other software for that system. At the end of the process, Setup sets up the System File Checker database, listing information about all the original files on the system.

From that point forward, you have the option of using this feature in the event you install something that overwrites an original file with a different file using the same name. System File Checker (SFC.EXE) examines over 500 file types, checking them against current system files. When it finds a difference it offers you the option of reverting to an original system file.

Run sfc from the Start | Run dialog Window. The problem is that if you choose to automatically replace all changed files, you can easily wipe out a perfectly good and healthy program. On the other hand, SFC offers you the choice to manually select which files to revert, but who knows all those files?

System File Checker (SFC.EXE) examines current system files and checks them against stored copies of the original Windows files. In some cases the tool may be a better way to go than a reinstall, but usually only immediately following a problem installation. If a new program or device causes a crash, try SFC. When many changes have taken place prior to a crash, a better option is to try the System Restore utility. If System Restore isn't an option, then the only remaining option is usually an in-place reinstallation—Repair Windows.

System Backup and Restore

A complete restore, often called a full restore, is not the same thing as a Windows reinstallation. A reinstall will generally fix corrupted system files, or files that have been over-written by some program's installation routine. However, you'll most likely have to then re-install various applications. Even so, the reinstallation should keep any configuration files previously stored on the hard drive. This may be a bad thing, if one of those files is causing the constant crashing.

Windows 2000 Backup

We touched on the Windows XP System Restore in Chapter 15, but we'll go over it again, one more time. Microsoft has always included some form of backup program in Windows and DOS. Usually, the backup feature was either rudimentary or too complicated for the average user to figure out. Windows 98 finally included on a new backup utility developed by Seagate, and it works very well.

Windows 2000, looking much like Windows 98, continued forward with the Backup console. For the most part, you can get to the backup utility through

Programs | Accessories | System Tools | Backup. The Windows 2000 program provides a Wizard on the Welcome tab. (Remember, this is also where you go to create an ERD.) If you choose to not use the Wizard, the remaining tabs reference the three typical tasks included in every backup procedure.

All backups, regardless of what they're called, must include a way to back up all or part of the system. Then the tool must provide a way to restore the backup. Restoring simply means putting whatever is in the backup, back onto the broken system. Remember that a backup will overwrite any later data unless the utility offers an option to prevent this from happening. Finally, a backup program almost always has a way to schedule backups for times when the system isn't being used. Windows typically joins the backup tool with the Task Scheduler.

Windows XP System Restore

The backup tool improved even more in Windows XP, taking on the new, System Restore name. You can access System Restore through the All Programs | Accessories | System Tools | Backup menu path. The actual program is `\Windows\system32\restore\rstrul.exe`. You must have Administrator rights to use the tool.

System Restore, like other backup programs, offers you the option to create a full backup, an incremental backup, or a differential backup. A full backup is just what it sounds like: a complete backup of every selected file on the system; you select all or some of the files. An incremental backup means backing up any files that have changed since the last full backup was run. How does Windows know when the last backup was done? The backup program clears the Archive attribute (A), indicating that the file has been backed up.

A differential (different) backup is similar to an incremental (pieces) backup, in that it looks for changed files (differences in files). Differential backup uses the Archive (A) bit to determine what files have changed since the last full or incremental backup.

Both full and incremental backups offer you the option of selecting what files to back up. Then, after each file has been backed up, the backup process "turns off" the Archive bit. On the other hand, a differential backup doesn't require a list of selected files to back up. Instead, the process looks at every file on the system, checking to see if the Archive bit is on or off. If the bit is on, Windows assumes the file is new or has changed, and backs it up.

In other words, the operating system checks the A (archive) bit on a file and makes a decision. If the bit is on (see Chapter 12, "DOS," for more on the ATTRIB command and attributes), the file is waiting to be backed up.

Understand that the archive bit resets to "on" whenever anything changes in a file, even if you add only a single period to a sentence and save the file. The backup process turns the archive bit off after the file has been backed up. (The xcopy command provides switches that you can use to copy selected files based on the status of the Archive bit.)

System State—The Registry

We've said in Chapter 14 that Windows 9x included the Emergency Recovery Utility (ERU) or ScanReg to backup the few Registry files. Windows XP/2000 use the Windows backup program (System Restore, in XP) to make backups of the Registry. When you reach the selection dialog box, you're given the option to select what files to back up. One of the choices is the "System State."

System State, always remembering Microsoft's fantasy of consistency, is what *used to be known* as backing up the Registry. The system "state" means the condition of all the configuration settings and file locations stored in the Registry hives. If you choose only the System State, the backup utility will back up all the various configuration files making up the Registry.

System Restore creates "restore points," meaning that you're given a calendar from which to pick a point in time. That point is a moment when Windows was running in some condition. The important thing to remember is that if the computer has contracted a virus and you don't know about it, you can easily choose to make a backup of the computer with the virus included. Later, when the virus has begun to wreck the system, you might use System Restore to "restore" the computer from a restore point. However, the backup included the virus, and the cycle begins again.

Restoring a Backup Without Windows

If you've tested everything you can test and the machine continues to crash, then a full restore may be your only remaining option. The restoration can be from either a vendor's original recovery disk, or from a backup of some kind—a disk image on a CD-RW or DVD, a tape backup, a separate backup partition, or an image file on a network server. The problem with a full restoration is that you can't restore a backup unless you have a running copy of Windows. For the most part, this will mean re-formatting the hard drive.

Here's a better solution. Install Windows to a different, temporary directory. When you finally can run the backup program, it will restore Windows to its original folder, preventing the just-installed version from being over-written. In other words, you're installing a temporary copy of Windows only in order to gain access to the backup and restore functions. If this solves the problem, you can then go back and remove the temporary Windows folder, leaving the restored version in place.

 Windows XP Home edition doesn't automatically install the Backup utility. XP Pro installs the utility and places an option the Start menu. For Home edition, you can find Backup on the installation CD under the \ValueAdd folder. It requires a manual installation, and doesn't allow for scheduled backups. However, the program works well in all other situations.

System Maintenance

One of the biggest problems with modern iterations of Windows and the Internet is the number of temporary files accumulated on the hard drive. In Windows 9x, the way you removed those files was to use the Explorer's saved search criteria to create shortcuts for ~*.* and *.TMP files. You could also create Desktop shortcuts for ScanDisk and Defrag. Otherwise, you were left to purchasing commercial third-party software programs designed to clean up the hard drive. Windows offers a utility called Disk Cleanup.

 The Internet Explorer did offer an option of cleaning out temporary files, but it was a manual decision process. Utilities such as Tweak UI can configure Windows 98 to do some automated clearing of temporary files. Various third-party utilities do a very good job of reducing clutter. (Be aware that Windows Washer is a spyware program.)

Disk Cleanup

To reach the cleanup utility, choose Start | Programs | Accessories | System Tools | Disk Cleanup. One of the options under Disk Cleanup is "Select Drive," which reads the drive you select and produces a menu. The menu options are checkboxes asking you which types of files you want to delete. Among the types you can select are: downloaded program files, temporary Internet files, offline Web pages, Recycle Bin, temporary files, temporary offline files, offline files, or catalog files for the Content Indexer.

 The Content Indexer is similar to the Windows 9x Find Fast utility, which would index an entire hard drive and search through the index rather than searching the drive directly. There's an efficiency penalty in that indexing takes place in real time, causing a slight slowdown during the work session.

Other option tabs in the Disk Cleanup utility include "Windows Components" and "Installed Programs." The Windows Components menu offers the option of removing unused components. You're presented with a list of checkboxes, and you tell Disk Cleanup what you want it to get rid of.

The Installed Programs menu is much the same as the Windows Components menu in that it lists all the installed programs on the PC, along with how much space they take. To help you decide what you'd like to remove, the lists can be sorted in several ways, such as by usage frequency, date last used, and names and sizes.

The Windows Recovery Console

After you've tried Safe Mode and it doesn't seem to be working, one of your last options before re-installing a Windows 2000 or XP machine is to enter the Recovery Console. The Recovery Console requires the same password as the Windows Administrator password. If a password isn't necessary to get into Windows, neither is a password necessary to open the Recovery Console. Otherwise, you have three chances to enter the correct password.

Recovery Console is actually a standalone application, but it reads password information from XP/2000. This can be a problem if a vendor sets up an administrative password and you don't know it. In that case you may have to reinstall Windows. Although passwords are an important feature, remember that a password isn't required on a single-user machine (if it's a standalone system). With no password, Windows starts automatically whenever you turn on the machine, proceeding to the Desktop.

Installing Recovery Console

The Recovery Console can run from the Windows installation CD, or you can choose to install it right on the hard drive. In the latter case, Windows will include an option to use the Recovery Console on the OS Selection menu. To install the Recovery Console on the hard drive, place the installation disk in the CDROM drive. Choose Start | Run, and enter [*drive:*]\i386\winnt32.exe /cmdcons (where [*drive*] is the CDROM drive letter. The application requires approximately 7MB of hard disk space. Recovery Console then installs to the c:\Cmdcons folder.

Generally, you'll run Recovery Console from the installation CD only if there's a problem starting Windows. During a problematic Startup, the OS Selection menu provides an added option to run the Recovery Console to repair Windows. Again, if you have multiple operating systems, you'll have to choose which OS you want to start or try to repair.

By default, the Windows Recovery Console allows access to only the following folders (if you try to access other folders, you receive an "Access Denied" error message):

➤ The root folder (typically `c:\`)

➤ The %SystemRoot% folder (`c:\Window` or `c:\WINNT`), and the subfolders of the currently logged Windows installation

➤ The `Cmdcons` folder

➤ Removable media drives such as CDROM drives

The various restrictions in the Recovery Console can be changed with environment variable settings. You'll have to create the variables each time you enter the Recovery Console, because they're not stored in the normal environment. However, you could create a small batch file that sets the variables as follows:

➤ Set `AllowAllPaths=True`—Removes the default restriction of providing access only to certain directories.

➤ Set `AllowWildCards=True`—Enables the use of the * and ? wildcards with such commands as ATTRIB, DIR, COPY, and so on.

➤ Set `NoCopyPrompt=True`—Removes a warning prompt during the copy process when a file overwrites another file by with same name.

➤ Set `AllowRemovableMedia=True`—Allows access to floppy drives and other types of removable storage.

The SET command may be disabled in some situations. If you have Administrator rights, start the Local Security Settings console with **secpol.msc** (*Security Policies*) in the Run dialog box. Choose the Security Settings | Local Policies | Security Options menu area. Double-click the "Recovery Console: Allow floppy copy and access to all drives and folders" option. Click "Enabled" and then Okay. Close the Local Security Settings console and re-start the Recovery Console, then try setting the variables again.

Recovery Console and Recovery Disks

Many people get a computer with only the OEM recovery disk as a "repair" tool. This leads to an interesting problem where the vendor has set up an administrative password prior to making the disk image. The end user might go into the newly installed XP and change or remove the system administrative password, but that won't change the Recovery Console setting. Now suppose that user wants to use the Recovery Console. In many instances, there's no way to even call up or install the option because the user also has no Windows XP installation disk of any kind. (Vendors are tending to no longer supply original Windows installation disks with factory-shipped computers, these days.)

You can download disk images for 6 floppy disks from the Microsoft support site. These disks act as the floppy version of an XP startup. In some cases, these disks will offer an option to repair the system. At that point, Recovery Console loads from the floppy disks. However, the old administrative password doesn't work because it's not the same one used by the vendor. There's really no way to get around this without having a true installation disk and reinstalling Windows.

Recovery Console Commands

Some of the familiar DOS commands available at the Recovery Console include ATTRIB, CD, CHKDSK, COPY, DIR, DEL, FORMAT, MD, RD, and REN. You can also type HELP and get a complete list of commands, just like at the DOS prompt, or you can use *[command]* /? for the typical short form of the command. (You can also type Help *[command]* to get help for a specific command.) Table 16.3 lists the commands available in the Recovery Console. We discuss only some of the more common commands following the table.

Table 16.3 Commands Available in Recovery Console				
Attrib	dir	format	ren	Batch
disable	help	rmdir (rd)	Bootcfg	diskpart
listsvc	set	ChDir (cd)	enable	logon
systemroot	chkdsk	exit	map	type
cls	expand	mkdir (md)	copy	fixboot
more	delete (del)	fixmbr	net use	

CHKDSK

XP refers to a disk in need of this type of maintenance as being "dirty." The NT Check Disk tool is similar to the Windows 9x ScanDisk utility. It isn't the same as the original DOS ChkDsk. You can run Check Disk from the Recovery console to clean up lost clusters, unlinked and cross-linked files, and various other file problems.

You can also run Check Disk during any XP session. It's no different than running ScanDisk from a Windows 9x machine. Open "My Computer," then right-click on the drive icon for the drive you want to check. Open the Context menu, go to the Properties dialog box, then click on the "Tools" tab.

The tab is divided into three areas, and the one you want is "Error Checking." Click the "Check Now" button. Alternately, you can choose Start | Run, then enter chkdsk in the dialog line.

Whether you use ChkDsk from within XP or from the Recovery Console, the syntax for the command is

```
chkdsk [volume:][[Path] FileName] [/f] [/v] [/r] [/x] [/i] [/c] [/l[:size]]
```

Most of the options apply to an NTFS file system, and you can get help by using the standard chkdsk /? at the prompt. The most likely switch will be the drive letter (and colon). The /F switch tells the program to fix any problems it finds. (The drive must be locked for it to work.)

> You may have to run Check Disk several times before all errors have been resolved.

Like ScanDisk, and the Check Disk before it, repaired problem files are stored in the root directory. The files begin with FILE, then have a 4-digit number and a .CHK extension. For example, you might see FILE0000.CHK, FILE0001.CHK, and so on. There's nothing you can do with these files, in terms of returning them to their original condition. However, the files exist so that you can possibly extract absolutely critical information they might contain. In other words, if you lose some data to a cross-linked file that you have no other way of retrieving, you might be able to use a hex editor to go into the .CHK file and copy out that information. Don't expect to use it to retrieve a corrupted copy of your annual budget or your last term paper.

Bootcfg/rebuild

You should know by now that Windows 2000/XP won't start without a valid BOOT.INI file. Therefore, you should have a valid backup of that file on an emergency boot disk, as well as a printed copy in the system binder. If you can't find any copies of the file, you can sometimes rebuild the file by going into the Recovery Console and typing bootcfg/rebuild. Before you run this, make a backup copy of the existing file by typing bootcfg/copy.

ATTRIB

You can *view* the attributes of files such as BOOTLOG.INI by using either the DIR or the ATTRIB command. However, you can only *change* the attributes of a file by using the ATTRIB command, as discussed in Chapter 12. The four main attributes are Hidden (H), System (S), Read-Only (R), and Archive (A). At least one attribute must be set.

Listsvc

This command lists all available services, drivers, and their start types for the current Windows installation. The command may be useful when using the `disable` and `enable` commands. These are extracted from the `%SystemRoot%\System32\Config\SYSTEM` hive. Unpredictable results may occur if the SYSTEM hive becomes damaged or is missing. (Remember that a registry "hive" is a group of keys, sub-keys, and values in the Registry that has a set of supporting files containing backups of its data.)

Disable

This command can be used to disable a system service or a device driver. Use the `listsvc` command to display all services or drivers that can be disabled. `Disable` prints the original start type of the service, then resets the service to SERVICE_DISABLED. Record the old start type in case you need to re-enable the service.

Enable

This command is used to enable a Windows system service or driver. The `enable` command prints the old start type of the service before resetting it to the new value. The values are the same as for `Disable`, excepting that SERVICE_DISABLED is not an option.

Map

Use this command to list drive letters, file system types, partition sizes, and mappings to physical devices.

Diskpart

This is the Windows NT/2000/XP command used to manage the partitions on your hard disk volumes. The command replaces the Windows 9x and DOS `FDISK.EXE` command. If no switches are used, `Diskpart` displays a menu for managing the existing partitions.

 Be very careful with this command. **Diskpart** can damage your partition table if the disk has been upgraded to a dynamic disk configuration. Do not modify the structure of dynamic disks unless you are using the Disk Management tool. Understand that **Diskpart** is compressed as **DISKPART.EX_** on a Windows XP/2000 upgrade installation disk, but that the Setup Wizard will temporarily decompress a copy of the program if you choose to partition a clean hard drive during the installation. **Diskpart**, on the CDROM, isn't ordinarily available from a command line.

Fixboot

This command is the used to write new Windows boot sector code on a boot partition. This command fixes problems where the Windows boot sector is corrupted. The Emergency Repair process also fixes the boot sector. This command overrides the default of writing to the system boot partition.

Fixmbr

This command is similar to an almost undocumented switch with the DOS FDISK command (FDISK /mbr). As a command in the Recovery Console, it's used to repair the master boot record (MBR) of the System partition. This command may work if a virus has damaged the MBR and Windows can't start.

 This command has the potential to damage your partition tables if a virus is present or a hardware problem exists. This command may lead to inaccessible partitions. Microsoft suggests running anti-virus software before using this command.

Logon

The logon command lists all detected installations of Windows, and then requests the local administrator password for the copy of Windows to which you chose to log on. If more than three attempts to log on do not succeed, the console quits and your computer restarts.

Exit

Use EXIT to quit the Recovery Command Console and restart the computer.

System Vulnerability

The last of the five broad categories having to do with Windows problem solving involves software attacks and security. Our primary focus will be viruses, and you should know the basic types of viruses. A virus often comes in two parts. The delivery system is the file or program that carries executable code into memory. The payload is the virus programmer's "intent," so to speak—the damage done to the system.

The majority of viruses tend to attack Windows PCs. This is partly because of the one-size-fits-all philosophy Microsoft uses, whereby everyone uses pretty much the same files and libraries to install and run Windows. Although the philosophy brought computers to the world, that standardization enables a virus programmer to have a very good knowledge of exactly what support programs exist on a target machine. Particularly with Windows 2000/XP, and the increasing vulnerability of ActiveX controls, pay attention to security update notices and service packs.

Viruses

A computer virus is a set of instructions (a program) that tells the PC to execute a series of actions without the owner's consent or knowledge. A virus can operate only by running the instructions held within a program. Even macro and scripting viruses are a series of instructions. The difference between a program virus and a macro virus is that a macro virus uses an application—Microsoft Word, Microsoft Excel, or Netscape, for example—rather than the operating system as the command interpreter.

Macro viruses can be stored in files with any extension. Most modern applications can recognize their own files by information stored in the header of the file. A Microsoft Word document might have the default .DOC extension or an .XYZ extension. Regardless of the extension, it's still a Word document and is capable of running macros. Macro viruses are spread through file transfers and email. However, only the program that interprets the macro commands can execute them.

One of the more arguable "features" of later versions of Windows is the default to hide file extensions. The theory seems to be that file extensions are a leftover from the obsolete bad-old days. Users, in theory, want only to know the main filename and work with the computer. File extensions and associations are a fundamental part of using a PC. Many times, the extension is the only way you'll have any idea of what type of attachment you're about to download. Even then, virus programmers can embed code in a delivery file with an innocent extension.

A virus program usually waits for an event to take place and then executes its instructions (the payload). The operative word here, is "execute." A virus is a small program of some kind. One way or another, there must be some kind of executable code. The trigger event might be a specific date and time on the system clock, or a set of keystrokes, or it could be an autorun macro designed to automatically run when an application opens. A virus may also work by attaching itself to a particular host program. When the host program is executed, it runs the virus code. Each virus program has its own program code, called a *signature*.

 NOTE Many email messages are clogging the Internet, warning of deadly email viruses. Opening and reading a text email message provides no opportunity to execute a binary program. Only the attachments that come with email messages can be potential virus carriers. That being said, Outlook is particularly vulnerable to diabolical ways programmers use to embed attachments or scripted viruses in an email message. Always use a firewall with Outlook, or use another email client.

Types of Viruses

A virus is classified according to how the virus is transmitted and how it infects the computer. No matter which kind of virus is involved, it can't be spread by coughing on a machine or by placing a PC too close to another PC (or a VCR). Another common myth (with no basis in reality) is that viruses can enter a PC through some sort of sub-band channel of a modem connection. Viruses are computer programs: pure and simple.

The main categories of viruses are as follows:

➤ *Boot sector*—Overwrites the disk's original boot sector with its own code. Every time the PC boots up, the virus is executed.

➤ *Master boot sector*—Overwrites the master boot sector's partition table on the hard disk. These viruses are difficult to detect because many disk examination tools don't allow you to see the partition sector (head 0, track 0, sector 0) of a hard disk.

➤ *Macro viruses*—Written in the macro language of applications, such as a word processor or spreadsheet. Macro viruses infect files (not the boot sector or partition table) and can reside in memory when the specific application's document is accessed. Usually, an autorun feature in the application triggers a macro, much as an AUTOEXEC.BAT file triggers the virus. Otherwise, the virus runs by user actions, such as certain keystrokes or menu choices.

➤ *Scripted viruses*—Use JavaScript, ActiveX controls, or other such scripting languages to introduce instructions to the machine through the operating system. Scripted viruses use Internet functionality as the command processor, and can be written as plain text commands that will run from email messages, graphics files, or any other area where the virus programmer hides them.

Scripted Viruses

ActiveX controls allow Web developers to create interactive, dynamic Web pages. An ActiveX control is a component object embedded in a Web page. It can run automatically when the page is viewed, or most browsers can be configured to prompt the user whenever an ActiveX control is about to run. People who write viruses may embed malicious or destructive programming code in an ActiveX control.

Java Scripts also allow Web developers to create interactive, dynamic Web pages. JavaScript provides a bit more general capability than ActiveX, running as small applications from the Web site. Java applets, much like the old Windows 3x applets, are small programs embedded in HTML pages. Remember that HTML stands for Hypertext Markup Language, and is mostly a plain-text format language. Setting a Web browser's security configuration options can prevent both ActiveX and Java scripts.

VBScript (Visual Basic Script), or VBS, is a script written in a script programming language designed for local PCs. Where JavaScript is designed to be "pushed" from a Web site, Visual Basic is designed to be run as an application on a local hard drive. VBScript and JavaScript viruses both make use of Microsoft's Windows Scripting Host to infect a machine. Because Windows Scripting Host is available on Windows 98 and Windows 2000, these viruses can be activated if a user simply double-clicks on a file with a .VBS or .JS extension in the Explorer.

As Microsoft updates its scripting languages and develops new tools, Windows becomes ever more vulnerable. The latest rash of viruses spread around the world so fast that they made news headlines. In most cases, these were scripted viruses taking advantage of the ubiquitous Outlook email client and standard Microsoft scripting tools. Windows XP includes a rudimentary firewall, but you should always keep XP updated with the latest security patches and have a good firewall on your machine. (We discuss firewalls again in a moment.)

Stealth Viruses

Two common types of stealth viruses are the Trojan and the Worm. A Trojan is a destructive program disguised as a game or other useful program. Users download a program that looks like it will meet some particular need, but when they run it, the virus enters their system. In many cases, the program containing the virus actually does what the victim had hoped it would do.

A *Worm*, coming from the Write Once, Read Many (WORM) acronym, propagates across computers by duplicating itself in memory, then duplicating itself again and again. The Worm writes itself to the infected machine one time, then copies itself again and again, eventually filling up an entire disk. Some Worms can even transfer themselves to other machines through links between the two machines. MSN Messenger (Windows Messenger), and Windows Remote Desktop offer new and improved pathways for virus programmers to spread their work.

Example Script Trojan Horse

There was a virus not long ago that arrived in an email message. The Subject line read: Scene from last weekend, with the Message line reading: "Please do not forward!!" This email carried an attachment named: scenes.zip. The attached .ZIP file contained a Rich Text Format (.RTF) document named SCENES.WRI (a Microsoft Write or WordPad extension). If the document was opened, there were two icons representing two embedded objects (remember OLE?). Both icons appeared to be placeholders for an image file, but the actual embedded object was an executable program detected by Sophos AntiVirus as Troj/Senecs.

The object labeled SCENE2.JPG was an actual image. However, the object identified in the document as SCENES1.JPG was actually named "Copy of RESULT.EXE" and was an executable file. This file contained a number of files, including a JPEG image and a mass mailing script, along with other malicious programming code. Note that while it may seem as though an image file was carrying a virus, it wasn't an actual image file; the extension was renamed.

When the embedded executable was opened, it inserted and ran a Visual Basic Script (VBS) file, which attempted to send the SCENES.ZIP file to all the contacts listed in the Microsoft Outlook address book on that machine. Troj/Senecs also inserted two additional Trojan horses: Troj/Optix-03-C and Troj/WebDL-E. Troj/Optix-03-C was a backdoor virus that ran in the background as a server process, allowing a remote user (using a client program) to gain access and control over the machine.

Firewalls

A firewall isn't really an antiviral program so much as a way to prevent unauthorized programs from finding their way onto a computer. Firewalls can be either hardware based or software based, and they're designed to put a security layer between computers. Remember that networks (including the Internet) are made up of computers connected with each other in some fashion. Most often, firewalls are installed on home computers with always-on connections (such as DSL or cable modems), or on networks. Network firewalls put the security layer between the local network and an ultra-network like the Internet.

Windows XP includes the Internet Connection Firewall, a basic firewall. To set it up, choose Start | Control Panel | Network Connections. Click on the LAN, or High-Speed Internet connection that you want to protect. Under Network Tasks, click "Change settings of this connection." On the "Advanced" tab, choose the "Internet Connection Firewall" option. This is where you can enable or disable the firewall at the "Protect my computer and network by limiting or preventing access to this computer from the Internet" selection.

The problem with the firewall included with XP is that it only "keeps an eye" on incoming information—files coming into the machine from outside. It doesn't do anything to guard against infected files moving from inside the computer out to the network. Neither does it do a very good job of protecting the increasingly more sophisticated security attacks spreading around the Web. Finally, the firewall can cause problems on Virtual Private Networks (VPNs) and client machines, interfering with file sharing and printing.

A much better strategy is to use a third-party firewall such as Zone Labs' "Zone Alarm" (www.zonelabs.com), Symantec's Internet Security suite, or Ositis WinProxy, to name a few. Zone Alarm has become popular because you can download a free copy for a single-user machine. The commercial (pay money) version includes additional features and functionality. Third-party firewalls protect both incoming and outgoing information, and enable you to remain connected without having your computer "show" to anyone searching for a system to attack.

 You can find a pretty interesting system to stop Internet pop-ups at **www.sankey.ws/proxomitron.html**. "Proxomitron" installs a sort of proxy server on a standalone machine, setting up something like a firewall. It then checks all incoming calls to the Internet Explorer against your own custom configuration.

How Viruses Work

Viruses of different types work in different ways. Some viruses keep the same code and attach to programs or load into memory. Newer viruses are aware of antivirus programs, so they make an effort to change their code while continuing to do their damage.

Functional characteristics of viruses include the following:

➤ *Memory-resident viruses*—Load themselves in memory, take control of the operating system, and attach themselves to executable files (for example, .EXE, .COM, and .SYS). These viruses often change the file attribute information and the file size, time, and date information.

 Viruses can't attach to .BAT files because these files are text-based lists of commands. A virus may, however, be attached to a program file *called* by a batch file.

➤ *Nonresident file viruses*—Infect other programs when an infected program is run. They don't remain in memory, so they don't infect the system. These viruses often change the file attribute information and the file size, time, and date information. Like memory-resident viruses, nonresident viruses attach themselves to executable files.

> *Multipartite viruses*—Combine the characteristics of memory-resident, nonresident file and boot sector viruses.

 Remember that COMMAND.COM is a program. If a virus attaches itself to the main command interpreter, executing any of the DOS internal commands (for example, **DIR**, **DEL**, or **MD**) will cause the virus to execute. Inserting a disk infected with a boot sector virus in drive A: and running a simple **DIR** command often causes the virus to be copied to the hard drive's boot sector.

> *Polymorphic viruses*—Modify their appearance and change their *signatures* (their program code) periodically (for example, by changing the order of program execution). This allows the virus to escape signature-scanning detection methods.

> *Stealth viruses*—Hide their presence. All viruses try to conceal themselves in some way, but stealth viruses make a greater effort to do so. This type of virus can infect a program by adding bytes to the infected file. It then subtracts the same number of bytes from the directory entry of the infected file, making it appear as if no change has taken place.

 It seems that the exam capitalizes on the bizarre and complex names and acronyms used in the PC world. If you know only that polymorphic and multipartite are weird names that you don't hear much at all, you'll have a tool for deciphering any questions that throw these terms at you. Keep in mind that the most deadly viruses tend to affect the boot sector, Master Boot Record, and partition table.

Viruses in Image Files

As of 2004, it hasn't been possible to actually embed executable code in an image file. These image files are typically known as .JPG, .BMP, .PNG files, and so forth. Although representatives from the McAfee corporation say that it could happen in the future, it can't be done at the moment. You can, however, rename an attachment file with an image extension, as we mentioned previously. The file will still be an executable file, or a macro document, even though the extension says it's not.

A secret image embedded within another image is sometimes called *spy code*. Messages can be embedded within images in this fashion—and even password protected—giving rise to modern-day secret messages that can be sent as email attachments. These are not viruses in that they do not contain executable code.

Spyware and Adware

Technically speaking, spyware is the jargon name given to any technology that gathers information about a person or organization without their knowledge. Spyware is typically a program that secretly gathers information about the user and relays that information to advertisers or other interested parties. Spyware is often attached to an interesting, useful, or entertaining piece of software or freeware that you download from the Internet. It might be a game, such as Snood, or it might be a utility designed to make your desktop look pretty. Whatever application carries the spyware, when the PC connects to the Internet, the spyware sends out whatever information it's been designed to gather.

In a most strict and formal use of the word, programs that are installed on a computer with the user's knowledge are not gathering information without that person's knowledge. To that extent, if the user fully understands that data is being collected and what that data is, spyware walks a narrow line between advertising and a virus. Spyware can gather information about email addresses and even find and transmit passwords and credit card numbers.

Spyware is similar to a Trojan horse in that users unwittingly install the program when they install something else. Because these are independent, executable programs, they can monitor keystrokes, scan files on the hard drive, catalog applications such as word processors, install other spyware programs, read cookies, change the default home page on the Web browser, or anything else a program can do. The problem is that there isn't an easy way to see that the computer is being controlled or affected. All that happens is that the spyware sends information back to the author, who then either uses it for marketing purposes or sells it to someone else.

 There are a number of free programs on reliable sites such as the Ziff-Davis (**http://www.zdnet.com**) site, designed to check your system for spyware. Spychecker (**www.spychecker.com**) is also a reputable Web site, devoted to helping people find and remove spyware and adware. You can easily download freeware programs to keep your system from becoming clogged with this type of software junk.

Windows XP includes many automation features, such as Windows Update, that assume an always-on Internet connection. In some instances, a virus or adware program can even use XP to dial up the Internet through a modem. One user discovered his computer was continually connecting to the Internet, even when he wasn't home. The problem was very difficult to diagnose, but you should be aware that XP seems determined to make every PC look the same (internally) and become self-sufficient. Perhaps that's the hidden message in that movie where the alien keeps saying, "XP...phone home!"

Hardware Problems

One of the most common problems uncovered during the boot process is a piece of hardware that the Device Manager doesn't recognize. A bad keyboard will generate a beep code and often, a message to the monitor. Keyboards are inexpensive enough that if you can't switch out the keyboard, replacing it is a reasonable way to solve the problem.

If the machine seems to be running okay, you'll probably hear the cooling fan making some amount of noise, and some indicator lights should be showing on the faceplate. A bad monitor doesn't have a cooling fan, so without sophisticated testing equipment, the only way to test a video connection is to switch out the monitor.

Master/Slave Jumpers

Another problem is where a new drive of some kind has been added to one of the controllers on the motherboard. For example, you might have a hard drive attached to one IDE controller and then attach a second drive to the same controller. If you weren't paying attention to jumpers, you might discover that the system doesn't recognize the second hard drive.

Most drives have a configuration setting for Primary Only, Primary Second Available, and Second (or terminology to that effect). The typical default setting for a new drive is to make it the Primary Only (master) drive. If the original hard drive is configured as a Primary Only drive, then when you add a second drive the controller doesn't even see it because it's being told there's only one drive on the controller interface. Additionally, even if the first drive was configured to see a second drive, the new drive is probably set to Primary Only.

 The default IRQ for a primary IDE fixed disk controller is IRQ 14. The secondary controller takes IRQ 15 by default. Note that jumpering an additional drive on the same controller isn't generally an IRQ problem, but rather a jumper switch problem.

Jumper settings are the first thing to check when a new drive isn't being recognized. Make sure you've opened up access to the new drive by changing the first drive's jumper switches. You'll also have to set the jumpers on the second drive to make it a secondary drive (or slave). The second thing to look for is a bad power supply at the cable connections. When all else fails, switch out the new drive with a drive that you know is good, and verify that any power connectors are working and in good condition.

A good place to have electronic testing equipment is where you're having possible troubles with power connectors and cables. If nothing else, a multimeter can verify that a connection is providing a complete circuit between one location and another.

Circuitry Failures

It's not often that you'll come across a machine where the entire mother-board has been fried (technical term). It happens, though, and in those instances, it might be more cost-effective to buy a new computer. You should already know that integrated circuits are delicate and can be short-circuited with a blast of static electricity (electrostatic discharge [ESD]). Another way to fry a motherboard is when a bad power supply sends a high voltage discharge through the electronics of the entire system, melting many of the components.

Lightning is another source of high voltage, and when lightning discharges to a nearby ground point, it's called a *proximity strike*. If a powerful storm is moving through the area, it's a very good idea to disconnect all computers from the building's wiring structure. Not only should you disconnect the power cords, but you should remember that any modems are connected to the building's telephone wiring.

In the hardware section, we touched on *hot swapping*, one of the features of USB. You also know that a computer constantly polls a keyboard, waiting for any activity coming from that keyboard. Because of the constant interplay between the motherboard and the various devices attached to that mother-board, it's never a good idea to unplug a device or plug in a new device while the power is on. The universal serial bus is one of the first technologies that safely allows you to add and remove devices without turning off the main power supply.

Some computer reference manuals indicate that you don't need to turn off the machine to attach or detach a device. Laptop computers often use portable floppy drives or detachable CDROM drives. Desktop machines can run into trouble with keyboards, scanners, removable storage devices, and even a mouse. Anything that attaches to the motherboard can cause an electronic pulse to run through the motherboard and its components.

Although you would think the reference manual would tell you the truth about the machine, it's a rare instance where the machine will recognize a new device without a cold boot (machine reset). It may be possible to attach a new device with the machine running, but you can get into real trouble when you detach a device in this manner. Unless you're working with a USB device, the recommended method is still to turn off the machine before you plug in or unplug any piece of hardware.

Connectivity Problems

Up until this point, we've mostly discussed troubleshooting procedures for either a standalone machine or a network machine. However, one of the biggest headaches to deal with is when a machine has started successfully but won't connect to a network. In this scenario, the two possible causes are the network card itself or the way that the NIC is interfacing with the operating system.

You can use the Device Manager to go in and look at the type of card Windows thinks is installed in the machine. However, the only way to know for sure what type of card is installed is to open the machine and actually look at the card. Older cards had no way of telling you whether they were working or not, so unless the card has LED indicators, you'll have to first switch out the card to prove whether or not it's working. Keep in mind that when you install another card, you'll have to reconfigure most of the network settings.

Windows 9x introduced a Network Neighborhood icon on the Desktop, which became My Network Places in Windows 2000, then Network Connections, in Windows XP. Right-clicking on the network icon (whatever it's called) and selecting Properties opens up much of the configuration information. A more thorough way to check the network configuration is through the Control Panel.

The Windows 2000 Control Panel includes a Network and Dial-up Connections icon, which includes a Make New Connection option. Windows XP includes the Connection Wizard, under the Network Connections icon option. There can be more than one connection, and assuming networking has already been set up and there is an active connection, the Windows Tray usually displays a small icon that looks like two computers talking with each other.

Double-clicking the icon brings up a status and activity dialog box that shows the connection status, duration, and speed of a good connection. A second box shows connection activity in terms of real-time packets sent and received. Right-clicking on the icon brings up a menu of options, such as configuring the network and NICs, and includes a second button that allows you to disable a specific network connection.

Network Card Configuration Problems

Assuming you've been lucky and the NIC has onboard LEDs to indicate that the card is in good working condition, the second aspect of connectivity is how the card is configured within Windows. We're only going to touch lightly on the entire concept of installing a NIC and configuring connections, but you should know how to get to the places where you might be asked to find out any existing information.

Begin with the Start | Settings | Network and Dial-up Connections menus. You're given a choice of all the available connections or networks that have been set up for that computer. When you highlight any of the available networks, you'll be given a screen with icons representing each network and a Make New Connections Wizard.

Double-click on any of the existing network connections to produce a window that tells you the connection, status duration speed, activity, and properties. The Properties option opens the Network Configure window, where you can add or configure a new protocol, NIC, or client. Note that these options are the same as when you double-click the icon on the Taskbar, which we mentioned a moment ago.

Another way to get to the same place is to right-click on My Network Places (Windows 98 and 2000) or Network Neighborhood (Windows 95). The Properties option takes you to the Network and Dial-up Connections window, where you can examine the configurations for the local machine's network installation.

We discussed PING and TRACEROUTE (also known as TRACERT) in Chapter 10, "Basic Networking." Be sure to remember these diagnostics commands. Another command is PATHPING, which is very similar to tracing the route a packet takes between a source and destination computer. The primary difference is that PATHPING sends multiple Echo Request messages to each router between a source and destination over a period of time, instead of only the single request. PATHPING then calculates an overall analysis of how network traffic is moving through the multiple routers between the two machines.

Summary—Troubleshooting

We've reached the end of our overall review of personal computers. At this point, we would recommend that you leaf through the book, going back and checking yourself against all the previous practice questions. If you've forgotten the underlying knowledge captured by any of those questions, take the time to re-read the chapter or skim the headings.

If you feel good about your understanding of each topic we've covered, then by all means proceed to the Software Sample Test. We haven't provided a listing of the main points in this chapter because *everything* in the chapter is important. You should know all the topics, and each of the techniques discussed under each section.

Finally, we'd like you to remember two of the most widely used system errors in the entire computer industry: the IATC error, and the id10t error. Many tech support people have encountered these problems, falling victim to the same errors themselves, from time to time. Idiot At The Controls (IATC) indicates that what appears to be a system error is actually the result of some dumb set of operator actions. The closely related ID10T error is found in situations where a caffeine-frazzled support person slaps his or her forehead, realizing they've missed something obvious and totally self-evident.

Everyone has to start somewhere, and regardless of how advanced your understanding of computers may be, you too, were once a beginner. Never forget that to the person whose computer you're working on, the data is far more important than the machine and application software. If it's at all possible, repair the system before you reinstall the hard drive.

Exam Prep Questions

Question 1

> Which one of the following options would you choose to resolve a problem when starting Windows XP?
>
> ○ A. Last Known Configuration
>
> ○ B. Last Known Boot
>
> ○ C. Last Known System
>
> ○ D. Last Known Good

Answer D is correct. Windows NT/2000/XP maintain a record of a successful startup and configuration in the Last Known Good configuration. Answers A, B, and C are all bogus menu options. Note, however, that "Last Known" shows up in all the responses, so you need only remember that "Good" is legitimate.

Question 2

> Which two of the following are indications that a virus has possibly infected the computer?
>
> ❏ A. CMOS memory size mismatch error
>
> ❏ B. CMOS checksum error
>
> ❏ C. Insufficient space on Drive D: error
>
> ❏ D. GUI image failure error

Answers B and C are correct. A checksum failure indicates that a file has changed between the time it was read into memory and written back to disk, a common first indicator of a virus. Another common indicator is when files begin to unexpectedly fill up a disk. Answer A is incorrect because this is an indication that physical memory has been changed by the addition or removal of memory modules. The error listed in answer D doesn't exist.

Question 3

Which menu would you choose in order to connect a user to a different printer on a network?

○ A. Start | Programs | Accessories | System Tools

○ B. Start | Settings | Accessories | Printers

○ C. Start | Programs | Settings | Control Panel

○ D. Start | Settings | Control Panel

Answer D is correct. Although the faster way to access this menu would be through the Start | Settings | Printers option, you can also get to the Printers icon through the Control Panel under the Start menu route. Answer A is incorrect because printers are not configured or added from the System Tools menu. Answer B is incorrect because the Settings menu does not include an Accessories option. Answer C is incorrect because the Programs menu does not include a Settings menu. (Note that Windows XP uses Start | Control Panel | Printers and Faxes.)

Question 4

A checksum error is also a file _____ error used as part of the _____ validation.

○ A. IRQ, CMOS

○ B. CRC, CMOS

○ C. CPU, BIOS

○ D. System, FAT

Answer B is correct. CMOS errors are generated by the CMOS chip and settings file. A checksum error means that the stored file has become corrupted in some fashion, and the CPU is using a Cyclical Redundancy Check (CRC) process to compare the existing file size with the size it's supposed to be. Answer A is incorrect because IRQs are interrupt requests taking place during bus transfers and never generate CRC errors. Answer C is incorrect because the BIOS either works or generates a possible "Incompatible BIOS" message, and is never used to validate anything. BIOS connects the motherboard with the rest of the system. Answer D is wrong but you'll have to know that checksum errors relate to files and CMOS, not to system errors and FAT "validation." ScanDisk (Windows 9x) and ChkDsk (NT systems) examine the FAT (or NTFS) to verify that it has no errors and isn't corrupted.

Question 5

> Choose the two best responses that indicate critical boot-up files for a Windows XP Professional Edition computer.
>
> ❏ A. NTDETECT.EXE
>
> ❏ B. BOOTINI.COM
>
> ❏ C. NTDETECT.COM
>
> ❏ D. NTLDR

Answers C and D are correct. The reference to which version of Windows XP is a red herring, designed to send you off on a sidetrack. All that matters is that the system is an XP (therefore also NT/2000) computer. Try to remember that .EXE files are compiled, executable files. COM files are small, and can be quickly created. Answer A is incorrect because it refers to the wrong extension. Answer B is incorrect because the actual file is BOOT.INI. This is an initialization file, not a command file.

Question 6

> Which of the following is not a type of virus?
>
> ○ A. Multipartite
>
> ○ B. Boot sector
>
> ○ C. Polymorphic
>
> ○ D. Passive host

Answer D is correct. This is one of those questions that tries to scare you with complicated technical sounding words. Even if you don't remember the real names for virus technologies, take a close look at the responses. "Passive" means to do nothing. "Host" refers to caring for or managing something. You know that a virus is an "active" weapon, and that it attacks a host. A "passive host" makes no sense as a virus causing actions. Answers A, B, and C are all types of viruses with various characteristics, as discussed under the "Types of Viruses" and "How Viruses Work" topic headings.

Question 7

Windows XP has become unstable, and you've run a series of diagnostics tests on the machine. As you narrow down the possible problems you're left with the probability that one of the system services is the culprit. Which of the following would best describe your next course of action?

- ○ A. Run MSINFO32 and choose the Services tab to disable a service.
- ○ B. Run Recovery Console and choose the **listsvc** command.
- ○ C. Run Recovery Console and run the **service disable /on** command.
- ○ D. Boot to a command prompt and run **set ServiceLogging=True**.

Answer B is correct. Remember that this is a scenario question, so you'll want to break it down to only the essential components. It's an XP machine, so you should see immediately that answer D is wrong. Windows NT, 2000, and XP can't boot to a command prompt. Aside from that, a SET command only creates a variable. It doesn't do anything in its own right. Answer A is wrong because MSINFO is the Microsoft System Information console, and reports out the machine's hardware settings. Answers B and C both refer to the Recovery Console, and something about services. The question asks about services, making these to the best candidates. Answer C is incorrect because "service_disabled" is a status listing, generated by LISTSVC to indicate if a service is enabled or disabled. The Recovery Console has no "service" command. In fact, only answer B contains a legitimate Recovery Console command, regardless of how you would use it. LISTSVC offers a report of the running services, and the option to enable or disable any particular service.

Question 8

Why would you run CHKDSK? [Choose two]
- ❑ A. Drive C: is reported as being dirty.
- ❑ B. Drive C: is reported as being fragmented.
- ❑ C. Drive C: is reported as having cross-linked files.
- ❑ D. Drive C: is showing as an unmounted volume.

Answers A and C are correct. CheckDisk is to an NT kernel system as ScanDisk is to a Windows 9x system. The term "dirty" (answer A) applies to a volume with some kind of problem. That problem can easily be cross-linked files as referred to in answer C. Answer B is incorrect because you would use DEFRAG to defragment the disk. Answer D is completely wrong because an unmounted volume means that Windows can't even "see" the drive. Therefore the response is a contradiction in terms: Windows can't show something it doesn't see.

Question 9

Which of the following would you use to repair a Windows XP installation that has contracted a virus through the downloading of an Outlook attachment?

○ A. System File Checker

○ B. Recovery Console

○ C. Device Manager

○ D. System Restore

Answer D is correct. This type of question actually offers you some help. Note the repetition of the word "system." When someone is trying to confuse you, they'll often introduce two things that sound alike, hoping that you won't notice the difference. The odds are that answers B and C are wrong because they each are completely different from A and D. Answer C is definitely wrong because the Device Manager handles hardware problems and device drivers. The likelihood of the question asking about a corrupted device driver is slim. Answers A, B, and D are plausible.

Think about the purpose of the exam, and the focus of the question. A virus has thoroughly screwed up the machine. If you use System File Checker, you would have to know which file or files were corrupted, and overwrite them with the original installation files. The Recovery Console might possibly handle the problem if the master boot record (MBR) had been corrupted and you could use the `fixmbr` command. However, System Restore (answer D) would enable you to revert the entire system to a restore point prior to the Outlook download. Of the three, answers A and B are much less useful than answer D, making them the incorrect choices.

Question 10

Which file is not unnecessary on a Windows Emergency Boot Disk?

○ A. io.sys

○ B. ntldr

○ C. ntdetect.com

○ D. ramdrive.sys

Answer A is correct. The EBD is the emergency startup disk that can be created only in Windows 9x versions. NT kernel systems (NT/2000/XP) can provide a sort of "helper" disk that might start Windows, but won't necessarily boot the system. Answers B (ntldr) and C (ntedetect.com) are both files used on an NT kernel system start disk, not the EBD. So they're out. The catch in the question has to do with language: "not unnecessary." That means that a file *is* necessary! (Always read the question carefully.) RAMDRIVE.SYS, referred to in answer D, creates a RAM drive, but that drive isn't necessary for anything other than making a storage area for additional DOS utilities found in the EBD.CAB file. However, IO.SYS (answer D) is a critical DOS system file, and is absolutely necessary to boot the machine from the floppy emergency diskette.

Need to Know More?

http://www.annoyances.org

Annoyances.org—Web site devoted to problem-solving with Windows 9x, 2000 and XP.

http://support.microsoft.com

The Microsoft technical support site, with their Knowledge Base and every other type of support capability. If you can't remember the "support" part of the address, use http://www.microsoft.com and click on the "Support" tab.

http://www.google.com

Google, Inc.

You've surely heard of and used Google for all kinds of searches. Don't discount it for resolving problems, troubleshooting, and research. Enter **troubleshooting XP** and you'll find some great sites. However, you may not have been using the "Groups" tab, off the main window. This is a comprehensive search of user groups, news groups, and "alt." groups. Here's where you'll find entirely different ideas for fixes, problems, solutions, and analysis.

http://www.kellys-korner-xp.com/xp_resources.htm

Kelly's Korner

This is a great site for a comprehensive listing of Microsoft Knowledge Base articles on many aspects of Windows XP. The home page for Win98 is at http://www.kellys-korner.com, and the home page for WinXP is at http://www.kellys-korner-xp.com.

http://www.labmice.net/troubleshooting/boot_problems.htm

Labmice.net—wholly owned, operated, and edited by Bernie Klinder

http://www.labmice.net/windowsxp/default.htm

Windows XP Resource Center

http://aumha.org/index.htm

Windows Support Center, James A. Eshelman, Proprietor & Webmaster

http://aumha.org/kbstrtup.htm

Startup Problems

http://www.pacs-portal.co.uk/startup_content.htm
Using MSCONFIG.EXE and the various Start Group options:
"A central resource for PC users and Tech Support staff alike who are concerned about the poor performance of their PCs due to the number of programs that run at system start-up."—Paul Collins, Webmaster
http://www.pacs-portal.co.uk/startup_pages/startup_full.htm
An alphabetic listing of the more than 1,400 items that can run at startup in the various versions of Windows.

http://www.symantec.com/avcenter/vinfodb.html
Symantec Security Response: Virus Search & Threats encyclopedia.

http://vil.nai.com/vil/default.asp
McAfee Security AVERT (Anti-Virus Emergency Response Team) virus listings.

Karp, David A. *Windows XP Annoyances, 1st Edition*. Sebastopol, CA: O'Reilly & Associates, 2002. ISBN: 0-596-00416-8. All O'Reilly books are well written and don't get caught up in corporate mythology. These books give you the straight scoop, by authors who've actually spent a lot of time with the product they're discussing. This book, and the previous *Windows 98 Annoyances*, offers a very good explanation of the Windows Registry.

Brooks, Charles J. *A+ Training Guide, 5th Edition*. Indianapolis, IN: Que Certification, 2003. ISBN: 0-7897-3044-8. This book is a valuable resource for reference material on Windows security and policies.

Mueller, Scott. *Upgrading and Repairing PCs, 14th Edition*. Indianapolis, IN: Que Publishing, 2002. ISBN: 0-7897-2745-5. This is one of our favorites! If you are going to have only one reference book, give this one serious consideration.

Bigelow, Stephen. *Troubleshooting, Maintaining, and Repairing Personal Computers, 5th Edition*. New York, NY: McGraw-Hill Osborne Media, 2001. ISBN: 0-0721-3272-8. Detailed information from a break-fix standpoint.

Freedman, Alan. *Computer Desktop Encyclopedia, 9th Edition*. New York, NY: McGraw-Hill Osborne Media, 2001. ISBN: 0-0721-9306-9. Great for a fast look-up or refresher.

Karney, James. *Upgrade and Maintain Your PC, 3rd Edition*. Indianapolis, IN: Hungry Minds, 1998. ISBN: 1-55828-585-7.

Messmer, Hans-Peter. *The Indispensable PC Hardware Book, 4th Edition*. Addison-Wesley Publishing Company, 2001. ISBN: 0-201-596-164. This is a comprehensive, up-to-date reference book that covers far more than you will need to know for the exam.

Minasi, Mark. *The Complete PC Upgrade and Maintenance Guide, 12th Edition*. San Francisco, CA: Sybex Network Press, 2002. ISBN: 0-782-140-750. This is considered one of the best reference books available. In fact, Minasi's book was instrumental in the formulation of the first A+ exam.

Rosch, Winn. *Hardware Bible, 6th Edition*. Indianapolis, IN: Sams Publishing, 2003. ISBN: 0-7897-2859-1. This is a well-organized reference book that covers software issues as well as hardware.

Operating System Practice Exam

Give yourself 90 minutes to complete this exam. Sit at a table or desk, and try to make the surface as empty and clean as you can. Lay down a piece of paper and a pencil and spend 5 minutes writing down the things you most want to have handy (from the Cram Sheet and your notes). Remember that you're allowed a blank sheet of paper and a pencil in the exam room, but you are not allowed to bring anything else in with you. This paper can hold last-minute cram points you scribble down, or it can be used to break apart complex lists of possible responses to questions.

From the time you complete your notes on the blank sheet of paper, you have 90 minutes to complete the test. Take your time, and imagine you're shipwrecked on a desert island, having all the time in the world. Read every word carefully, and then read the whole question a second time before you look at the responses.

Read each response on its own, and don't try to fit it in with the question. When you've read each response as though it were a random fact, go back and read the question one more time.

This particular sample test (more so than the hardware test) has been particularly designed with many devious test-taking tricks in mind. You'll find diversions, a lot of misdirection, red herrings, and confusing terminology. Don't worry! We provide ample strategic and psychological help in the ensuing answer key. If you do well on this sample, congratulate yourself! You should have very few problems with the actual exam. Each question is designed for a general understanding of Windows and DOS software. There aren't any questions that depend on low-level programming knowledge, or that cover features and functions that only a software engineer would be expected to know.

Start your timer, and begin the exam now.

Question 1

The **DIR** command shows the following file: An HRS   SYSTEM.DAT in the Recovery Console. What would allow you to use the **COPY** command to make a backup of the file in the **C:\windows\Backup** folder?

- ○ A. **COPY SYSTEM.DAT C:**
- ○ B. **ATTRIB SYSTEM.DAT > C:**
- ○ C. **ATTRIB -s -r -h SYSTEM.DAT**
- ○ D. **ATTRIB -shra SYSTEM.DAT**

Question 2

When you type the _____ command, you see a listing that includes WinBootDir=C:\Windows in the _____.

- ○ A. PATH, environment
- ○ B. SET, Path
- ○ C. SET, environment
- ○ D. PATH, settings

Question 3

During the POST, which of the following areas provides the programming necessary to access the primary, bootable partition?

- ○ A. ROM BIOS
- ○ B. CMOS
- ○ C. DOS
- ○ D. Windows

Question 4

You are upgrading Windows 98 to Windows XP. What should you do with regard to SMARTDRV?

- ○ A.   Disable SMARTDRV.
- ○ B.   Load SMARTDRV.
- ○ C.   Change the settings for SMARTDRV to Protected Mode.
- ○ D.   Activate the write-through option for SMARTDRV.

Question 5

A user complains that he has connected his Windows 2000 workstation to the network, but cannot find any other devices on the network. What would be the best thing to do first?

- ○ A.   Remove the NIC and start over.
- ○ B.   Replace the patch cable with a known good cable.
- ○ C.   Check the card link status light.
- ○ D.   Reinstall the drivers for the NIC.

Question 6

You have a Windows 2000 Upgrade version of the CDROM. The system installed well, but now there's a problem you think you can fix with the Recovery Console. You start the machine to run the Repair function, but it isn't listed on the menu. How do you get into the Recovery Console when the installation disk is loaded in the CDROM drive?

- ○ A.   Run i386.exe from the **e:\winnt** folder.
- ○ B.   Run winnt.exe with the **/cmdcons** switch.
- ○ C.   Run cmdcons.exe from the **%systemroot%** folder.
- ○ D.   Run rcvycons.exe from the **e:\i386** folder.

Question 7

Your customer has just purchased a used IBM Thinkpad with a CDROM and a 1.44MB floppy disk. The system has an old copy of Windows Me installed. You've been asked to reformat the hard drive and install Windows XP on the machine. Which two areas would you examine to determine whether you will have to do anything other than reformat the drive?

☐ A. **c:\windows\drivers**

☐ B. CMOS

☐ C. CONFIG.SYS

☐ D. ROM BIOS

Question 8

Windows 98 provides a way to create a bootable emergency startup disk. A client has a Pentium 4 laptop computer, with an 8GB hard drive partitioned into a single volume. The CDROM drive isn't working. During a troubleshooting session you boot the system with the startup disk and you notice the following drives when you run various **DIR** commands: the C: drive, D: drive, and E: drive. Which file is causing the third drive to appear?

○ A. MSDOS.SYS

○ B. BTCDROM.SYS

○ C. RAMDRIVE.SYS

○ D. DRVSPACE.BIN

Question 9

One of your friends has a copy of Windows XP Professional installed on a Pentium III system. When he tried to start the system he was unable to get beyond the Administrator login and Welcome screen. Which of the following is the cause of the problem?

○ A. The ntldr file is missing from the boot partition.

○ B. WPA has locked the system.

○ C. Windows is attempting to connect to the Windows Update site to register the system.

○ D. SFC has detected a difference in the NT32.dll file.

Question 10

A friend has just upgraded her home computer to Windows 2000 and complains about needing to log on with a username and password. What could you do to help?

- ○ A. Nothing. Windows 2000 security requires a username and password.
- ○ B. Disable networking if it is a standalone computer.
- ○ C. Log on as Administrator and uncheck the "Users Must Enter A Username And Password To Use This Computer" password requirement box in the Users and Passwords dialog box.
- ○ D. Change the password to blank.

Question 11

A user of a Windows 98 peer-to-peer networked computer has loaded one of his favorite DOS-based programs but cannot print from it to the network printer. What is the most likely reason?

- ○ A. The DOS print drivers are not loaded.
- ○ B. DOS program support has not been enabled.
- ○ C. The printer is not supported in DOS.
- ○ D. The printer port has not been captured for DOS applications.

Question 12

Which file was created by SCANREGW.EXE?

- ○ A. rb000.cab
- ○ B. FILE0001.CHK
- ○ C. USER.DA0
- ○ D. SYSTEM.DA0

Question 13

Shutting down Windows normally requires the use of the Start I Shutdown, or the Start I Turn Off the Machine option. A Windows 98 user was working on a report when the building experienced a short power failure. What will that user most likely see when he turns on his machine following the blackout?

- ○ A. A Windows error message prompting him to use DeFrag on his hard drives.
- ○ B. A blue screen with hexadecimal error codes.
- ○ C. A message telling him that Windows is running ScanDisk.
- ○ D. Nothing. Windows will start normally.

Question 14

You shut down Windows to an MS-DOS command line. The prompt shows **C:\WINDOWS**. When you run TYPE Listing.txt and press Enter, you receive an "Invalid filename(s)" error. Why?

- ○ A. The **TYPE** command is not in the search path.
- ○ B. Listing.txt isn't in the search path.
- ○ C. Listing.txt isn't in the **c:\windows** folder.
- ○ D. **TYPE** is an invalid program name.

Question 15

HIMEM.SYS is reported missing or corrupted as Windows 98 loads. What will happen?

- ○ A. Nothing. Windows 98 does not require HIMEM.SYS.
- ○ B. Windows 98 will load in Safe Mode.
- ○ C. Windows 98 will fail to load.
- ○ D. Windows 98 will load, but will have access to only the first 1MB of RAM memory.

Question 16

Windows XP fails to recognize a digital camera connection. Which of the following would most likely be the problem area?

○ A. The HAL

○ B. The Access Control List

○ C. The I/O module

○ D. The kernel

Question 17

Windows XP seems to be taking longer than usual to load. You decide to run MSCONFIG to do some preliminary diagnostics. Which of the following would you examine?

○ A. The System Startup folder

○ B. System Resources

○ C. The System Services tab

○ D. The Prefetch tab

Question 18

How would you start a Windows XP computer in Safe Mode if no other operating systems were present?

○ A. Press an arrow key immediately following the POST, and select Safe Mode.

○ B. Hold down the Ctrl key during the logon screen.

○ C. Press F8 during the initial OS menu.

○ D. Select Start | Run, then type **CMD** to enter Command Mode, and then type **Safe**.

Question 19

Windows hangs at the "It is now safe to turn off your computer" message. Which file could you rename that might offer a way to determine the cause of the hangup?

○ A. IO.SYS

○ B. LOGOS.SYS

○ C. MSDOS.SYS

○ D. SYSTEM.DAT

Question 20

ATTRIB -H C:*.SYS /S will cause which of the following to occur?

○ A. Archive all .SYS files on Drive C:.

○ B. Hide all .SYS files in the root directory.

○ C. Unhide all .SYS files in the root directory.

○ D. Unhide all .SYS files on Drive C:.

Question 21

The CONFIG.SYS file contains the line **LASTDRIVE=F**. The system uses a CDROM, one primary partition, and three logical DOS drives. A loaded CDROM disk does which of the following?

○ A. Install a program

○ B. Become the G: drive

○ C. Become the F: drive

○ D. Nothing at all

Question 22

To bypass the execution of a line in a configuration file, which two of the following choices are used?

❑ A. **REM**

❑ B. :

❑ C. ;

❑ D. //

Question 23

FDISK has been used to partition a disk into three volumes. You copy FDISK.EXE and FORMAT.COM onto the D: drive of a working Windows laptop. You then copy various device drivers and system utilities to the E: drive. Windows has become corrupted on the C: drive and you want to reformat the drive. You start the system at a command prompt and log into the D: drive to run the format command. This procedure is incorrect because it will wipe out the hard drive, and all user data.

○ A. True

○ B. False

Question 24

Which files are required by Windows Me to load? (Choose the two best answers)

❑ A. IO.SYS

❑ B. autoexec.bat

❑ C. MSDOS.SYS

❑ D. CONFIG.SYS

Question 25

One of your friends has just loaded Windows XP on a home system. You want to show her how to get into Safe Mode in case she gets into trouble. What do you do?

○ A. Press F2 at the startup menu.

○ B. Press F8 when the "Please Select the Operating System to Start" menu appears.

○ C. Hold the Shift key while the system is booting up.

○ D. Restart the machine and hold the F5 key while clicking the "Restart" icon.

Question 26

One of your clients has decided to install a new USB hub on his machine. He's running a Windows 2000 machine, and for some reason it has begun to randomly crash. What would be the best diagnostics pathway to follow?

- ○ A. Go into the Device Manager and determine whether the USB port needs to be updated.
- ○ B. Examine the hub's version number to determine whether there's a USB conflict.
- ○ C. Remove each device from the hub to see which device is causing the problem.
- ○ D. Remove the hub and see whether the machine repeats the crash problem.

Question 27

The best command to use to shut down an MS-DOS window and return to Windows 98SE is

- ❑ A. Quit
- ❑ B. Exit
- ❑ C. WIN
- ❑ D. Start I Shut down I Restart

Question 28

Which command would you use to create a bootable floppy disk from Command Mode?

- ○ A. **Format a: /u /s**
- ○ B. **Format a: /u**
- ○ C. **Format a: /boot**
- ○ D. **Format a:**

Question 29

Why would you want to enter the File Associations area of the Windows Explorer?

○ A. To change the settings for default DOS filenames

○ B. To double-click on a .WZH data file

○ C. To unhide file extensions for hidden system files

○ D. To determine why Windows was failing to load a particular .EXE file

Question 30

HIMEM.SYS is an _____ driver that provides access to _____ memory.

○ A. EMS, high

○ B. XMS, expanded

○ C. XMS, extended

○ D. EMS, extended

Question 31

Which of the following files are executable? (Choose the three best answers)

❑ A. .EXE

❑ B. .BAT

❑ C. .INI

❑ D. .COM

Question 32

How can you verify what services are running under Windows 2000?

○ A. Go to My Computer I Control Panel I Administrative Tools I Computer Management I Services and Applications, and select the Services icon.

○ B. Go to My Computer I Control Panel I Administrative Tools I Computer Management, and select the Event Viewer.

○ C. Hold down the Ctrl, Alt, and Del keys, and select Task Manager.

○ D. Go to Start I Settings I Control Panel, and select the System icon.

Question 33

Which command will list all files in the directory where the third character of the extension is the underscore character?

○ A. **DIR *._**

○ B. **DIR ??_.***

○ C. **DIR *.?_**

○ D. **DIR *.??_**

Question 34

One of your friends is using a Windows 2000 machine, and the system won't start. When you examine the startup process you receive the following error message: "NT Detect Failed." What seems to be the problem?

○ A. The system is unable to determine a hardware configuration.

○ B. The system cannot find the NTLDR system file.

○ C. Windows system files have become corrupted.

○ D. A virus has wiped out the BOOT.INI file.

Question 35

Which file is used to control the Windows XP boot process?

○ A. NTOSKRNL.EXE

○ B. NTLDR

○ C. SMSS.EXE

○ D. NTBOOTDD.SYS

Question 36

Which of the following cannot be changed by a polymorphic virus?

○ A. The boot sector

○ B. The master boot record

○ C. The master cylinder

○ D. The partition table

Question 37

Windows 98 has been set up on the C: drive. Examining the drive properties, you discover that installed programs are using 3.7GB of a 4GB partition. The system has a D: partition with 500MB of free space. When the user tries to run America Online, he receives an "Out of memory" error message. Which of the following solutions would best apply, to resolve this problem?

○ A. Right-click on the "My Computer" icon and examine the Performance tab and Virtual Memory settings.

○ B. Right-click on the Desktop and examine the Settings tab.

○ C. Propose that the user delete some of the older programs that may not be in use anymore.

○ D. Re-partition the drive without the extra D: partition.

Question 38

You've just received a problem computer where the customer indicates that she's tried to install a 40GB hard drive as a second drive and it was bad. She's brought the machine in and asked for a refund on the drive, and that you install a working replacement drive. Before you exchange the drive and return the one that isn't working to the manufacturer, what should you check? (Choose all that apply)

❑ A. That the CMOS settings have been properly set to the second drive's configuration

❑ B. The second drive's jumper settings

❑ C. That the LBA compatibility can read the second drive

❑ D. The correct IRQ settings for the secondary master IDE controller

Question 39

During a Windows XP upgrade installation process, you boot to a Windows 98 emergency startup disk and run FDISK to partition the C: drive into a single, primary, active partition. Following that process, you remove all disks from all drive bays and reboot the system. You receive the following error: "Invalid media type." Why?

○ A. You loaded Windows 98 system files on an XP system.

○ B. The XP installation disk is looking for a valid media license file for the upgrade.

○ C. The partition contains the wrong file system.

○ D. The partition contains no file system.

Question 40

A user has set a hardware password in CMOS and then forgotten it. What would you do to gain access to the system?

- ○ A. Use one of the password-breaking programs available on the Internet.
- ○ B. Remove battery power to CMOS to clear it, reconnect the battery, and then reconfigure the CMOS.
- ○ C. Go to Start I Settings I Control Panel I Users and Passwords, and check the No Password Required option.
- ○ D. Run the FIXBIOS.EXE program to reinstall the master password.

Question 41

There is no beep code at system startup. What is the most likely problem?

- ○ A. The speaker is disconnected.
- ○ B. There is no beep code for a normal system start.
- ○ C. The system clock is not working.
- ○ D. A memory module failed the POST.

Question 42

Windows crashes during Startup, allowing only Safe Mode. Which file would you use to determine at what point and for what reason the system was failing?

- ○ A. SETUPLOG.TXT
- ○ B. DETLOG.TXT
- ○ C. DETCRASH.TXT
- ○ D. BOOTLOG.TXT

Question 43

Which of the following files would you modify to start Windows at a DOS prompt without ever showing the Desktop?

○ A. LOGO.SYS

○ B. MSDOS.SYS

○ C. WIN.INI

○ D. USER.DAT

Question 44

Which of the following would you use to create a single 7GB partition on the C: drive?

○ A. FAT16

○ B. NTSF

○ C. FAT32

○ D. VFAT

Question 45

You can only start the system in a DOS command line. Nothing seems to be working and it looks like you'll have to manually back up many MS Word files the user has created since his last backup. You issued the command **CD My Documents from the C:\>** prompt and received a "Too many parameters - documents" error. What is the correct command?

○ A. **CD mydoc*.***

○ B. **CD mydocu~1**

○ C. **DIR my*.* /V**

○ D. **CD my doc***

Question 46

Which of the following programs would you use to diagnose various Windows problems and generate a report of a system error?

○ A. SFC.EXE

○ B. MSINFO32.EXE

○ C. DRWATSON.EXE

○ D. DRDIAGS.EXE

Question 47

What are two ways to find out which programs are running during a Windows XP session?

❑ A. Right-click on the Taskbar and select the Task Manager.

❑ B. Choose Start I All Programs I Accessories I System Tools I System Information.

❑ C. Choose Start I Control Panel I Taskbar Properties.

❑ D. Right-click on the Desktop and select System Tray.

Question 48

Your little brother wandered into your room while you were out and did something to your computer. Although you can start Windows XP Pro, you're getting many errors, programs aren't loading, and you have no idea what he did. How would you most easily fix the problem?

○ A. Run SCANREGW **/r** from the Start I Run dialog box.

○ B. Start the System File Checker (SFC) and repair file damage.

○ C. Select a restore point using System Restore from the System Tools.

○ D. Perform an in-place repair installation using the XP installation CDROM.

Question 49

A 15GB hard drive has been partitioned into one Primary partition, with an extended partition containing three logical volumes. The system has a second SCSI drive, and you want to partition it as a single extended partition to be used by Windows Virtual Memory management. What drive letter will the SCSI drive show in the Explorer?

○ A. F:

○ B. H:

○ C. E:

○ D. G:

Question 50

Which two files must be on a Windows NT/XP boot disk?

❑ A. SYSTEM.DAT

❑ B. NTLDR

❑ C. BOOTINI.COM

❑ D. BOOT.INI

Question 51

A user tries to open Adobe Photoshop but the program won't open. Which of the following would be the best troubleshooting options?

○ A. Go to Start I Programs I Accessories I System Tools I System Information.

○ B. Use the Network Security tab under System Tools to check the user's rights.

○ C. Choose the Control Panel and go into the Event Viewer.

○ D. Select the application executable file and press Shift-F10 to examine the program's properties.

Question 52

ROM BIOS is responsible for providing low-memory addressing and vector addresses. Windows uses PAGEFILE.SYS or 386SPART.PAR to manage which type of memory?

- ○ A. Segments F000h through FFFFh high memory
- ○ B. Expanded memory paging
- ○ C. Upper memory blocks
- ○ D. Virtual memory swapping

Question 53

One of your past clients calls you with a problem involving repeated XP crashes. He sent the machine into a local repair shop to have a sound card installed. Everything was working fine, but now the system often crashes. What's the most likely cause of the problem?

- ○ A. The sound card isn't loading the correct 32-bit multimedia extensions.
- ○ B. NTDETECT.COM has failed to load.
- ○ C. The system resources must be reconfigured.
- ○ D. The sound card isn't seated properly.

Question 54

You've been asked to install a security service pack to the corporate machines over the course of the next few days. Several employees have developed virus symptoms and the IT manager is throwing a fit. What's the most likely reason the machines became infected?

- ○ A. The proxy server failed to activate the virus alert function call.
- ○ B. A bug in the firewall allowed the original XP installation to connect with the virus.
- ○ C. An employee's Security Access Token expired and opened a backdoor to the network.
- ○ D. The XP local security manager contained a bug in the original installation.

Question 55

How would you change the drive letter assigned to the CDROM in a Windows 2000 system?

- ○ A. Change the load order in the SYSTEM.INI file so that the proper drive letter is assigned.
- ○ B. Change the drive assignment in CMOS.
- ○ C. Use REGEDIT.EXE to open the Registry. Highlight the **HKEY_LOCAL_MACHINE**, and select the CDROM subkey.
- ○ D. Select the CDROM drive properties on the Device Manager I Settings tab. Set the Start Drive Letter and End Drive Letter.

Question 56

A user wants to change his default printer on an NT workstation. How would you do this?

- ○ A. Go to Start I Programs I Accessories I Printer Tools, and select the Print First check box.
- ○ B. Select the properties for the printer that the user wants in the Printer window, and choose Set As Default.
- ○ C. Configure the existing default printer as Secondary, and set the desired printer as Primary.
- ○ D. Provide the desired printer with a lower IP address.

Question 57

You're experiencing a problem with files in the Explorer. Windows XP seems to be running poorly and when you do some investigation you find that the D: drive is listed as being dirty. Which of the following utilities would you use?

- ○ A. SCANDSKW.EXE
- ○ B. CHKDSK.EXE
- ○ C. DEFRAG.EXE
- ○ D. DISKPART.EXE

Question 58

You're called into someone's office because she's trying to save a very important spreadsheet. Each time she clicks on the Save icon, a window pops up with an "Out of memory" error. You examine the Taskbar and discover many open programs. What is the most likely cause for the error?

- ❑ A. Windows has run out of disk space.
- ❑ B. Windows has run out of resources.
- ❑ C. The spreadsheet program has taken over all memory.
- ❑ D. The system has insufficient RAM to run the spreadsheet program.

Question 59

A user complains that Lotus Notes is continually failing to sound the various alarms he has set for scheduled meetings. You examine the system and find that the alarm features are working properly, and that the user has correctly entered the scheduled times in their appropriate fields. What would be another area to check?

- ○ A. The system time icon in the notification tray
- ○ B. The CMOS settings
- ○ C. BIOS version and date
- ○ D. The Lotus Notes application data folder under the user's network file space

Question 60

Every time you try to start Windows XP you get a "Windows XP could not start because the following file is missing or corrupt." You find the file on the CD installation disk and copy it to the hard drive, but the next time Windows starts up, it provides the same error message for a different file. What would be a better way to resolve this problem?

- ○ A. Reinstall Windows.
- ○ B. Repair XP with an in-place installation.
- ○ C. Check the Boot.ini file.
- ○ D. Run NTDetect.com.

Question 61

From an MS-DOS command line, which command would you issue to find out why a CDROM drive fails to appear in the Explorer?

○ A. **LASTDRIVE**

○ B. **SET**

○ C. **TYPE AUTOEXEC.BAT**

○ D. **PATH MSCDEX.EXE**

Question 62

The Windows Me default installation process removes which file reference from a CONFIG.SYS file?

○ A. EMM386.EXE

○ B. MSCDROM.SYS

○ C. IFSHLP.SYS

○ D. MSDOS.SYS

Question 63

One of your friends has been running Windows 2000 and has decided to upgrade to Windows XP Home Edition. The installation went off without a hitch, and the machine has been running well for a couple of months. It was activated, but now the system has crashed. When you try to examine the system, you can't get anything to work at all. Your own system is running Windows 98 and you decide to try an emergency startup disk. The machine boots up and you try to examine the C: drive, only to discover that the **DIR** command fails. Why?

○ A. The system has a corrupted Windows folder.

○ B. The system is using Extended DOS partitioning.

○ C. The system uses a FAT32.

○ D. The system uses NTFS.

Question 64

How would you print a copy of the SYSTEM.INI file from a computer that can boot only to a plain DOS command line?

- ❑ A. **type c:\windows\system.ini > lpt1**
- ❑ B. **type c:\windows\system.ini > printer**
- ❑ C. **dir c:\windows\system.ini > prn**
- ❑ D. **run c:\windows\system.ini > lpt1**

Question 65

Which of the following is not a valid wildcard in Windows Me?

- ○ A. The **?** mark.
- ○ B. The ***** mark.
- ○ C. The **~** mark.
- ○ D. Windows Me does not use wildcards.

Question 66

IO.SYS must be located in the _____ of the _____ and _____ partition:

- ○ A. boot sector, active, logical
- ○ B. boot sector, primary, active
- ○ C. boot track, first cylinder, formatted
- ○ D. boot sector, master cylinder, primary

Question 67

Which of the following keys is not displayed by the **REGEDIT** command?

- ○ A. HKEY_USERS
- ○ B. HKEY_CLASSES_ROOT
- ○ C. HKEY_LOCAL_SECURITY
- ○ D. HKEY_CURRENT_CONFIG

Question 68

Two folders exist on the C: drive: the **C:\Windows\system32** folder and the **C:\Windows\Command** folder. You logged in to the System32 folder to look for a VxD, and now you want to check to see whether Smart Drive is in the Command folder. Which of the following two actions would allow you to do so?

- ❑ A. **CD..\COMMAND**
- ❑ B. **CD COMMAND**
- ❑ C. **DIR Smar*.* /s**
- ❑ D. **DIR c:\Windows\smar*.* /s**

Question 69

You want to find out whether a computer has any Excel spreadsheets on the hard drive. From the Windows Desktop you press F3 and enter which of the following?

- ○ A. *.DOC
- ○ B. *.XLS
- ○ C. "Excel" (with quotes)
- ○ D. None of the above

Question 70

After Windows 98 completes a normal Startup process, a strange icon appears in the system tray. Running the program seems to indicate that it's a 16-bit DOS application of some kind. Which two files would you examine to find out how the program was being loaded?

- ❑ A. SYSTEM.DAT
- ❑ B. SYSTEM.INI
- ❑ C. WIN.INI
- ❑ D. WIN.DAT

Operating System
Practice Exam
Answer Key

. . . .

1. C

2. C

3. A

4. B

5. C

6. B

7. B and D

8. C

9. B

10. C

11. D

12. A

13. C

14. C

15. C

16. A

17. C

18. C

19. B

20. D

21. D

22. A and C

23. B

24. A and C

25. B

26. D

27. B

28. A

29. B

30. C

31. A, B, and D

32. A

33. D

34. A

35. B

36. C

37. A

38. A and B

39. D

40. B

41. A

42. D

43. B

44. C

45. B

46. C

47. A and B

48. C

49. D

50. B and C

51. C

52. D

53. D

54. B

55. D

56. B

57. B

58. B

59. B

60. C

61. C

62. A

63. D

64. A

65. C

66. B

67. C

68. A and D

69. B

70. A and C

Question 1

Answer C is correct. The COPY command in DOS and Recovery Console can't see a file with the Hidden and/or System attribute set. You would first have to turn off those two attributes before you could copy the file. Answer A is incorrect because it attempts to copy a hidden file. Answer B is incorrect because ATTRIB only shows the file, much as using a DIR command produces only a listing. Answer D is more sophisticated, yet still incorrect because you can't adjust multiple attribute settings with a single plus or minus sign. Each attribute must be individually set with its own sign. Note that with three responses referring to the ATTRIB command, you should have a clear warning that there's a link between the COPY command and the attributes. Also note that answer A is different from the other three. In most cases, this is a clue that it's the wrong answer.

Question 2

Answer C is correct. The clue in this question has to do with the equal sign after WinBootDir=. The responses all refer to environment variables, with two of the choices including the word "environment." You should already know that PATH is a standard environment variable, so even if you didn't remember that SET is the command used to set those variables, you're well on your way to resolving this question. Answer A is incorrect because typing any variable name does not produce a "listing." It only shows that variable's setting. Answer B is incorrect because you can't type SET within the Path. Answer D is incorrect, but a hard choice. However, it still offers you a strong clue. If you type PATH, why would you see WinBootDir=? You might possibly see the c:\windows folder listed in the resulting report of the settings for the search path.

Question 3

Answer A is correct. The BASIC firmware programming searches for a boot-strap loader in the Master Boot Record on a bootable partition. This is a very tricky question because all the responses could technically, possibly, be correct. However, answer B is contextually incorrect because we don't ordinarily refer to the CMOS as containing programming. The CMOS also isn't an immediate part of the power-on self-test routine. Answers C and D are incorrect because during the POST, no operating system has been loaded at all. The critical point of the question is "during the POST"—not after, along with, following, or before.

Question 4

Answer B is correct. Although you could use rote memory for this question, a better way would be for you to try to do a clean install from a command-line environment on a test machine. If you've installed upgrades to XP only from within a previous version of Windows, you might easily miss the connection with SmartDrive. Additionally, Windows 9x disables the cache program, whereas Windows XP installs much faster with the SmartDrive loaded into memory. The two hard choices are between answers A and B, where you have to actually know the correct answer. The other two options offer internal clues as to why they're wrong. Answer C is incorrect because SmartDrive has no particular settings for any type of specific mode, and certainly not "Protected Mode." Answer D is incorrect because a write-through option is a type of caching, which would require that the program be loaded with certain switches. Although this might possibly be correct, the response is far less relevant than either A or B. Additionally, answer D assumes SmartDrive is already loaded, and the question is asking whether or not it should be loaded in the first place.

Question 5

Answer C is correct. A link status light on the NIC would indicate that the physical connection to the network is okay and that the card is functioning. Absence of a link status light could point to a physical problem with the card or cable, or a missing driver. Answer A is incorrect because without a network interface card, the user can't connect to a network. Answer D is incorrect because although physically reinstalling the card might be useful, this is not what you would do first, given that response C offers you the link status LED. Answer B is incorrect because although the next step in the process may be to replace the patch cord, the question asks, "What would be the best thing to do first?"

Question 6

Answer B is correct. Once again, we would strongly encourage you to run a clean installation of Windows 2000 or XP from a blank, formatted, bootable hard disk. We suggest using an upgrade version, rather than a full version, so that you don't have the easy way out of using a bootable CDROM. The upgrade versions are not bootable, and so you must spend more time learning how to get around in the command-line environment. You should know that the winnt.exe program is the text-based setup program for Windows NT/2000/XP. You should also know that the i386 folder is where the installation files are stored. Answer D is incorrect because there's no such file as "rcvycons.exe." Answer C is incorrect because Recovery Console is clearly not installed on the hard drive, referenced by the SystemRoot variable. Otherwise, it would show up as a Repair option at startup time. Answer A is incorrect and offers a clue. The i386 folder is one you'll often refer to, use, and look for. It isn't a program. If you know that, you might also have a clue to the correct use of winnt.exe listed in answer B.

Question 7

Answers B and D are correct. Be very careful with the amount of misdirection in this question. Work out the hardware configuration in your imagination, and pay special attention to the CDROM drive. You should also know that many laptops, nowadays, don't come with a pre-installed floppy drive. However, the CDROM drive is the critical one. In almost all cases, and regardless of the CMOS access to an optical drive, the CD drive will require something to provide device driver software. The question makes no reference to which type of XP you're to install, whether it's the full edition on a bootable CD, or an upgrade version. Answer B is correct because you would definitely want to know if the laptop has CDROM support within the CMOS. Likewise, answer D is correct because the BIOS would also have to support the drive.

Answer A could be correct, but not absolutely so. Although a computer might have a folder for drivers as listed, nothing about the question indicates that this is so. Therefore, because the folder isn't an absolute, default installation in every instance of Windows Me, it's a misdirection.

Answer C is an extremely sophisticated trick option. In almost every version of Windows, you might require a CONFIG.SYS file to install CDROM drivers. That file might not be totally necessary, given that Windows would take over running the drive following a startup. However, this question explicitly refers to Windows Me, which was the only version of Windows that went to great lengths to remove configuration settings from a CONFIG.SYS file. Learn it; know it!

Question 8

Answer C is correct. Once again, watch out for misdirection and skullduggery! There's a lot of blather about the hardware configuration in this question, but a glance at the responses indicates this is going to be about software and device drivers. Note also that the real question asks about three drive letters. The clue is the link between drive letters and .SYS file drivers. Finally, the actual question asks why a drive letter appears. At this point you can go back and check the hardware and partitioning. Notice the specific reference to a single volume, making it the C: drive. Yet three drives are listed. The CDROM should be drive D:.

The very first words of the question indicate Windows 98. Why? Because the Win 98 emergency boot disk includes RAMDRIVE.SYS and boots the system to support a CDROM as well as a virtual RAM drive. Answer A is incorrect because MSDOS.SYS doesn't create drive letters. Answer B is incorrect because although it's a CDROM driver, it would only be responsible for a second drive, not the third. Answer D is incorrect because DRVSPACE.BIN is a hidden file DOS uses to store compressed file information. Print a directory listing of a Windows 98 emergency boot disk; then boot a system to that disk.

Question 9

Answer B is correct. Whenever you see hardware listings on a software question, you can almost count on the fact that they're there to get you going in the wrong direction. All that matters is that this question involves Windows XP. Answer A is incorrect because the system would generate a boot-time error, and never get to the Welcome screen. Answer C is incorrect because the system would show the Desktop before running the Update Manager. Answer D is incorrect because System File Checker is a utility that's run from within Windows. If you know that WPA stands for Windows Product Activation, you should see a red flag go up in your imagination as soon as you read the response. We spend a lot of time on this "feature" in Chapter 15, and there's a reason for doing so. If you have a second machine to play with, load XP on the system and set the CMOS date past the activation period. Then see what you'll have to do to get into the machine. Try it! You'll like it. (Not!)

Question 10

Answer C is correct. Windows 2000 provides a check box in the Users and Passwords dialog box so that the username and password function can be bypassed in standalone situations where security is not an issue (standalone computers only, not those configured as part of a domain). Answer A is incorrect because although Windows 2000 is designed as a network operating system, it does not *require* a username and password. Answer B is incorrect because Windows 2000 passwords are a separate issue from networking capabilities. Disabling networking does nothing to resolve the password problem. Answer D is incorrect because configuring a blank password does not necessarily remove the initial logon dialog box if there is more than one username set up on the machine. The question doesn't make it clear how many users there are on the system.

Question 11

Answer D is correct. Windows 98 asks whether the printer will be used for DOS applications during setup. If you respond yes, all the settings are made automatically. However, if the printer was not configured for DOS initially, you must go back to the Printer I Properties I Detail dialog box and select Capture Printer Port to enable DOS printing. Answer A is incorrect because although applications use printer drivers and DOS has a printer device driver, nothing uses "print drivers." Answer B is incorrect because the program is apparently working and the complaint is only that the user cannot print. Answer C is incorrect because Windows printer support is the issue, not DOS printer support. The program is running in a virtual DOS machine and Windows 98 is controlling the surrounding peripherals, including the printer.

Question 12

Answer A is correct. The program in question should be recognizable as having something to do with "scanning" and "registry (Windows)" if you've done any work at the command line in Windows. Even if you haven't, answer B is incorrect and you should be familiar with the type of file from seeing the results of ScanDisk on a drive with cross-linked files. Answers C and D should be readily recognizable as some type of actual Registry files. Answer A is correct because the Windows 9x Registry scanner creates daily backups of the Registry files in the Microsoft archive format (Cabinet files with a .CAB extension).

Question 13

Answer C is correct. Note the attempt to fool you into thinking that this question may apply to Windows 9x and NT. However, the actual question clearly states that the system is running Windows 98 and was improperly shut down. If you haven't spent time on a Win 98 machine, we would suggest you do so. Crash the system a few times to see what happens. You'll become very familiar with the automated ScanDisk process. Answer A is incorrect because DEFRAG is used to optimize a disk, not recover from errors. Answer B is incorrect because blue screens and error codes almost always apply to events taking place during an NT/2000/XP startup process. Answer D is incorrect because only DOS and Windows 95 machines made no attempt to automate cleanup following crashes or other file problems.

Question 14

Answer C is correct. There's no way around it: You're going to have to play with the DOS command line and the Recovery Console, which amounts to a very similar environment. Note that the error indicates something to do with a filename, not media types, drive letters, or commands. Something is wrong with the filename. Answer A is incorrect because it refers only to the TYPE command, and not a filename. Answer B is incorrect because the search path is used only to point DOS to folders containing commands. Answer D is incorrect because it refers only to the TYPE command and program names. Answer C is the only choice that lists both the filename and its containing folder. Even if you're very unfamiliar with explicit DOS error messages, you should be able to work out the correct answer if you understand what a search path means, and how a command differs from a filename. Windows always installs a rudimentary search path and includes its own system folder (c:\windows, in this case) in that path.

Question 15

Answer C is correct. Windows 98 requires HIMEM.SYS and a minimum of 4MB of extended memory. HIMEM.SYS is a memory manager that allows access to all memory above the first 1MB of conventional memory. Answer

A is incorrect because if HIMEM.SYS is missing or fails, Windows cannot access anything more than 1MB of memory and will fail to load. Answer B is incorrect because to reach Safe Mode, Windows must have been able to access extended memory in the first place. Answer D is incorrect because Windows cannot load at all without HIMEM.SYS.

Question 16

Answer A is correct. This is another one of those questions that's both tricky and ambiguous. The first approach is to get rid of any obviously wrong responses. Answer B (the ACL) refers to networks and user rights, and you should just know it. Answer C is incorrect because the I/O module deals with input and output after a device is working. It might be right, but check it against the other responses. Answer D is technically correct, but the kernel pretty much manages everything in NT/2000/XP, and isn't restricted to hardware problems. So your choice is between the I/O and the Hardware Abstraction Layer. Of the two, a device recognition problem would show up far more immediately as a result of a HAL problem than an I/O module.

Question 17

Answer C is correct. This question relies on your experience with the Microsoft System Configuration Utility. If you've run only Windows 2000 you won't be familiar with the tool. You must have some experience with XP or Windows 98 before taking the exam. Aside from that, you should know that a problem involving time delays is going to involve the length of time something is taking to load, or the number of things being loaded into memory. Answer A might be a good candidate, except that answer C directly refers to Services. Answer B is incorrect because MSCONFIG has no tab for "System Resources." Answer D is a sneaky way to go after more sophisticated technicians who are familiar with XP's use of the Prefetch cache. However, it too has no listing on the MSCONFIG dialog box. The final decision comes down to the fact that MSCONFIG shows what programs are being loaded during the Startup from many locations. The tab is not exclusive to the Startup folder. Therefore, only answer C meets all the question's requirements.

Question 18

Answer C is correct. This is a brute force memory question. You simply must know the main ways to get to Safe Mode from the various versions of Windows. Answer A is incorrect because none of the versions uses the arrow key to get into Safe Mode. Answer B is incorrect because it refers to Windows 98. Answer D is totally bogus, because you want to get into Safe Mode, which is an entire mode of Windows. You can't be in normal mode and also be in Safe Mode, both at the same time.

Question 19

Answer B is correct. This question might seem to be based on obscure knowledge of arcane details, but it isn't. With Windows having now been on the market for a number of years, this problem is well documented. Aside from that, you should have some experience with how any operating system generates any messages to the screen. It doesn't matter if the message is "Starting windows…" or a splash screen. The best approach to this question is to go over what you know of each response and think about what's left. Answer A is incorrect because it clearly refers to a startup and system file, not a closing file. Answer C is the same, and refers to startup. Answer D is incorrect, and clearly refers to the overall Registry. The problem being examined has to do with the point where Windows is ready to shut down. Something is preventing that final process. The only option left is answer B. Even so, you should know about the logo files that create all the pretty pictures during startup and shutdown events in Windows.

Question 20

Answer D is correct. The /s switch tells ATTRIB to operate on all subdirectories. The c:*.sys tells ATTRIB to operate on all .SYS files on Drive C:, beginning at the root directory. The -H switch tells ATTRIB to turn the hidden attribute off or to unhide the file. Answer A is incorrect because the archive attribute is set with the /+A switch. Answer B is incorrect because the /-H switch uses the minus sign, not the plus sign (hide). Answer C is incorrect because the /s switch extends the reach of the command beyond the root directory. Know the ATTRIB command. Learn it and play with it. It's there in DOS, and it's there in the Recovery Console. Don't rely on the Windows Explorer Property menu to adjust attributes.

Question 21

Answer D is correct. This is a really sneaky question, and relies on the fact that Windows 2000/XP automatically open up the system to Drive Z:. The LASTDRIVE command isn't a common command on modern machines. However, it was a very common command on other machines, and not everyone is running XP on every computer. When the command doesn't exist at all, it uses a default to the E: drive on Windows 9x and DOS machines. Remember that Windows XP doesn't ordinarily have it, and defaults to the Z: drive. This machine has a CONFIG.SYS file and the LASTDRIVE directive does exist. It explicitly configures the machine so that it sees all drives up to the F: drive, and no others.

Work out the drive letters. A: and B: are floppies, C: is the primary partition. Three additional logical drives, DOS or otherwise, would become D:, E:, and F:, respectively. The CDROM would be the next drive, letter G:. However, LASTDRIVE is limiting the machine to the F: drive, so the system can't see drive G:. Therefore, answer D is the only correct response. Answer A is totally bogus. Answer C would require that one drive can supercede or override another drive, and that's just not possible. Answer B is logically correct, but the system won't see it without a change to the LASTDRIVE statement.

Question 22

Answers A and C are correct. REM (an abbreviation of remark) is used in DOS to bypass a line (comment out or remark out) in batch files and configuration files such as CONFIG.SYS and AUTOEXEC.BAT. Windows uses the semicolon (;) to bypass lines in .INI files, which are also configuration files. Answer B is incorrect because the colon is used to signify drive letters. Answer D is incorrect because paired forward slashes are commonly used as a directory statement in networking operating systems and the Internet.

Question 23

Answer B is correct. Be very careful with "scenario" questions. Although it's true that pertinent details show up in the story part of the question, they're almost always secondary. Your best strategy is to find the direct, actual question and read that first. That will set your mind straight as to what you're being asked to resolve. In this case, the real question begins with a command prompt and the D: drive. The next big clue has to do with reformatting a drive. Your final clue is the term "wipe out." The question plays on the common use of the words "hard drive" to mean "fixed disk." A drive is not a disk! The FORMAT program affects only a logical drive—a partition. It wipes out an entire disk only when that disk has been partitioned into a single volume covering the entire disk. In this instance, we know there's a D: and an E: drive. Therefore a format process applied to the C: drive would only re-format that single partition.

Question 24

Answers A and C are correct. This question is a nice way to build the panic adrenaline in a lot of people. Who's familiar with Windows Me anymore? The real trick to getting this one correct has to do with the list of responses. Notice that every one of them refers to a DOS file, particularly with the inclusion of the two DOS configuration files. It doesn't matter whether the question asks about Windows 95, 98, 98SE, or Me. All of them are Windows 9x, and all of them run on top of DOS. You must learn that answers B and D refer to optional DOS configuration files, not mandatory files! Note that the question refers to files being required. If you haven't done so, we strongly urge you to read the section in Chapter 1 that deals with exam questions and how they can mess you up.

Question 25

Answer B is correct. This goes back to knowing how to get into Safe Mode. Remember the keys and write them down on the blank sheet of paper in the exam room. Answer B is the only response that deals with Windows XP. There is a clue in the responses, in that only Windows NT/2000 and XP offer a standard option to select an operating system. Other systems can be specially configured for multiple boots, but the question doesn't refer at all to special configurations. It speaks only of Windows XP, and implies that nothing special was done during the installation process.

Question 26

Answer D is correct. This question seems to be a hardware question. Something about a device is trashing the system. Do you worry about the technology of a USB hub, or worry about how Windows handles devices? Answer B is incorrect because it focuses more on hardware analysis. Answers

C and D are good possibilities. However, take a look at answer A and a reference to the Device Manager. This could easily go along with a software question problem. Upon further analysis, answer A refers to updating an I/O port, which is highly unlikely. The dilemma revolves around answers C and D. The question states that a new hub is causing a problem, not a new device. Answer D is the only response that simply pulls out the hub and checks whether the problem continues. Answer C would require removing each device, and then restarting the machine a number of times to see about the ongoing crash. Answer B is wrong because a USB version conflict might slow things down, but not crash the system.

Question 27

Answer B is correct. This should be a no-brainer if you've ever opened a command-line window. However, if you're used to clicking the close box "X" on the corner of the window, then you're likely to get confused with this question. Answer A is a bogus option. There is no "quit" command in either DOS or the Recovery Console. Alt+Q (Quit) can sometimes show up on a menu within an application. Answer C is incorrect because it would call WIN.COM and try to start the entire Windows system. Answer D is incorrect because it would shut down all of Windows, not only the DOS session. Next time you shut down a Windows 9x system and restart in MS-DOS mode, type EXIT (upper- or lowercase, it doesn't matter) at the supposedly all-black screen. See what happens.

Question 28

Answer A is correct. Once again, you must be familiar with command-line options and events. It won't matter if you're in DOS or the Recovery Console, you're going to have to deal with these problems. If all you've ever done is used the Explorer to format a disk, you would be well advised to either postpone your exam or do some hurry-up work with basic text commands. Answer B is incorrect because it would only format the disk (unconditionally) and fail to transfer the system files. The disk would not boot the system. Answer C is incorrect because there is no /boot switch for FORMAT.COM. Answer D is much like answer B, in that it would simply format the disk and not transfer the system files. It would also most likely format the disk by using the default "quick format" program option.

Question 29

Answer B is correct. File associations rely on the continuing use of file extensions, regardless of whether or not Windows tries to remove extensions from the user's view. By default, all versions of Windows (other than 3.x) install with file extensions hidden. You're supposed to be able to double-click on a filename and run the program that controls that file. It might be a program (application file), or the program's data file. Answer A is incorrect because you would use the Folder Options of the Explorer to change settings. Answer C is incorrect because you would likewise use Folder Options to deal with file extensions visibility. Answer D is incorrect because file extensions are data files, and not primary program files. If Windows failed to load an executable (application) file, it would have far more to do with a problem involving that entire program. Answer B is the only response that refers to using the double click to do something with a data file. It doesn't matter whether you've never heard of a ".WZH" file (AvniTech Solutions "WhizFolders").

Question 30

Answer C is correct. This question relies on your technical understanding of various types of memory (see Chapter 13). Answer A is incorrect because EMS refers to expanded memory, and HIMEM.SYS is an extended memory (XMS) driver. Likewise, answers B and D are incorrect for the same reason. The key to this question is to always remember that EMS and expanded memory are the same. Remember the X-10 trick, where it sounds like EXTENded memory, and starts with the letter X, the Roman numeral for "10."

Question 31

Answers A, B, and D are correct. Files with .BAT, .EXE, and .COM extensions are all considered executable. Although Windows considers .PIF files to be executable, files ending in .INI (answer C) are Windows configuration files and can't be executed from a command line. However, you can run an .INI file by double-clicking on it within the Explorer. Be careful that you don't confuse "run" with "executable." An executable file is a program file. Running a file from the Explorer is very different from entering the filename in the Start | Run dialog box, or trying to execute it from the MS-DOS environment. Windows is actually using the File Associations feature to actually run NOTEPAD.EXE first, when you double click the filename. NotePad then opens the .INI file.

Question 32

Answer A is correct. Windows 2000, NT, and XP all provide many services that help other programs run. On a Windows 2000 machine, the status of these services is listed under the Services icon in Computer Management. (In XP the path is Control Panel | Administrative Tools | Services.) Answer B is incorrect because it would be used to find out why something failed to work properly. Answer C is incorrect because it would be used to find out what programs were currently in memory. Answer D is incorrect because the System icon is used to check the devices installed on the system and to check the percentage of Windows resources remaining.

Question 33

Answer D is correct. The ? wild card is used to represent a single, unknown character. The question indicates a three-character extension, so DIR *.??_ is correct. DIR ??_.* (answer B) is wrong because it will find all files with the underscore characteras the third character in the main filename, not the extension. Answer A is incorrect because DIR *._ will find any file with a single underscore extension. The question indicates a three-character extension, not a single character. DIR *.?_ (answer C) will find any file with a two-character extension ending with an underscore. Be sure you play around with the DIR command in either a DOS window or the Recovery Console. It's one of the most used commands at the command line, in every Microsoft operating system.

Question 34

Answer A is correct. You must be sure to know the critical startup files for a Windows NT/2000/XP system. These are not the DOS and Windows 9x system files. Understand what each file does (see Chapters 15 and 16). The question refers to an NT Detect error. NT Detect is the specific hardware detection process that takes place during each startup for Windows 2000 and XP. Answer B is incorrect because NTLDR installs the kernel. Answer C is incorrect because the error message in the question refers to a specific file.

Answer D is incorrect because the BOOT.INI file determines where Windows will find its own system files.

Question 35

Answer B is correct. The Window NT Loader file (NTLDR) controls the boot process for Windows NT, Windows 2000, and Windows XP. Answer A is incorrect because only after the NT Loader is installed does it then load NTOSKRNL.EXE, the operating system kernel. Answer C is incorrect because SMSS.EXE loads the Session Manger. Answer D is incorrect because NTBOOTDD.SYS is an optional file used to mount a removable hard drive or SCSI drive.

Question 36

Answer C is correct. Be careful! This question doesn't ask what can be changed! It asks what *can't* be changed. If you got this wrong on that basis, then go back and read Chapter 1 to learn about trick questions. A polymorphic virus or any other type of virus cannot make changes to the master cylinder (answer C), because a cylinder is a single track located in the same place on every platter making up a hard drive. Although a cylinder is made up of tracks and each track contains sectors and clusters, a virus program can affect only one of those sectors or clusters, not the whole cylinder (in this context).

A virus is a set of program instructions and, as such, can make programming changes anywhere on a system where other program or instruction data can be stored. The boot sector (answer A), Master Boot Record (answer B), and partition table (answer D) all contain data that can be changed. Therefore all three are incorrect responses because they can be changed. The question asks what *can't* be changed.

Question 37

Answer A is correct. Yikes! If you got this right, then by all means, go take the exam. This question first begins with an "out of memory" problem. That might refer to RAM, but almost always refers to either Windows resources or the swap files (virtual memory). Nowadays, most machines have ample RAM to handle just about anything, so it's a memory management issue. The configuration shows that the C: drive is approaching full status, so a red flag should go up in your mind. The D: drive has plenty of space. You should also know that AOL is a large application and resource hog. Taking the scenario, all together, it looks like this is definitely a resource or virtual memory problem.

Answer B is incorrect because the Desktop controls only the overall display settings for the monitor, wallpaper, screen savers, and so forth. Answer C is incorrect because the user has a 500MB partition sitting empty. There's no reason to delete programs unless the entire drive has just about reached its storage capacity. Answer D is incorrect because a re-partitioning would wipe out the entire drive unless you used a third-party application. Windows XP allows dynamic repartitioning, but this is a Windows 98 machine. Virtual memory is a low-level system property and setting, and shows up under either the My Computer option or the System properties through the Control Panel. The Virtual Memory area would allow moving the swap file to the wide-open D: drive.

Question 38

Answers A and B are correct. Watch out for the misleading reference to hardware specifics and so forth. They might mean something, but often they're just a distraction. This is going to deal with a hard drive, and the question is included because you might find a hardware question in the software exam, either by accident, or just to mess you up. Go for the process of elimination on this one. Answer C is clearly wrong because there's no such thing as "LBA compatibility." Answer D is incorrect, but not as obviously. IRQ settings are almost always generated by Windows, and this is about a possible bad hard drive. It's a possibility, but an unlikely one. That leaves two other options, and the question already tells us there's more than one response. If CompTIA indicates more than a single response, they don't lie about it. There's always more than one response, and it isn't a trick to get you to only choose a single response. Drive configurations almost always end up either in the CMOS or the jumper settings. Who knows? The drive may actually be bad. But the correct response is to check both answer A and answer B.

Question 39

Answer D is correct. This question relies on your having played around with FDISK and FORMAT when you're either in a rush or very tired. It's a common oversight error, and you should be familiar with it. Always remember that FDISK and partitioning alone are not enough to prepare a disk for an operating system. Each partitioned volume must be logically formatted. If you walk through each step in the question, you discover that the system was never formatted. Therefore it has no file system, whether that would be FAT16, FAT32, or NTFS. Neither the boot disk nor the installation disk has any way of understanding the sectors and clusters on the hard drive. Answer A is incorrect because the system booted to Windows 98. There isn't an XP system, yet. Answer B is incorrect because there's no such thing as "media license file." There's an end user license agreement (EULA), but that's different. Answer C is incorrect because the Format process hasn't been run to install any file system at that point.

Question 40

Answer B is correct. Any program that requires an operating system to be loaded can't access the CMOS chip. Applications such as password analysis tools work only after a PC has been configured. This problem is at the hard drive level, and doesn't allow the user to boot to anything. As such, answers A, C, and D are incorrect because they all refer to a program or a program (Window) option. There is no generic, master password for CMOS, and the password is contained within the chip itself. The best way to clear the password is to clear the CMOS by removing all power to the chip. If the system has CMOS jumpers, there may be a "clear" jumper that will reset the CMOS back to its default settings (with no password).

Question 41

Answer A is correct. The POST always generates beep codes. Regardless of the number of beeps generated, there will always be at least one. If no beeps are heard, the most likely problem is that the speaker is disconnected or broken. Although you may think this is a hardware question, always remember that the Power On Self-Test is part of the boot process, and therefore part of the operating system startup process.

Question 42

Answer D is correct. This is another really sneaky question, and relies on fooling IT professionals who routinely install many Windows systems.

Answer C refers to a log file generated when the installation fails during the preliminary stages. Be careful! The question explicitly states that the system is entering into Safe Mode. That can happen only following a successful installation, and after Windows has removed the installation crash detection log. Safe Mode offers an option to "boot with logging," which creates a BOOTLOG.TXT log file to examine errors in loading and unloading driver files. Answer A is incorrect because Windows has no SETUPLOG.TXT file. Even if it did, the log might apply to a new install and setup, not a running machine. Answer B is incorrect because it refers to the hardware detection file, and not crash errors. Answer C is incorrect even though it looks correct. The file looks like it would log a "detected crash" or something. In fact, it only logs an installation setup that crashes partway through. You have to read the question very carefully! If you can run Safe Mode, you've successfully passed the installation phase.

Question 43

Answer B, true, is correct. The MSDOS.SYS file began offering certain configuration settings to replace the old CONFIG.SYS file with the introduction of Windows 95. One of the important lines is `BootGUI= (0 or 1)`. This line has a significant determining factor as to whether Windows starts with the Desktop or starts at a command line. Answer A is incorrect because it's one of the Microsoft logo files that presents the splash screen picture during Startup. Answer C is incorrect because the WIN.INI file (primarily used in Windows 3.x) is a legacy configuration file for how the Desktop might look. Answer D is incorrect because although USER.DAT is the Registry file responsible for user configurations, it stores Desktop configurations and has no setting option to begin Windows at a command line.

Question 44

Answer C is correct. Here's another one of those questions that depends on your forgetting your glasses or contacts on the day of the exam. It also plays on any possible dyslexia you might have. Your best bet is to start by eliminating what you know won't work. Answer D is incorrect because the VFAT has nothing to do with partitioning, but rather has to do with long filenames. That leaves you with FAT16 and FAT32. However, if you didn't read the responses carefully, you might also think that answer B is a possibility.

Answer B is incorrect because there isn't any NTSF file system, only an NTFS system. Between the remaining two, you should understand that FAT16 is limited to a 2GB partition (see Chapter 8 and hard drives). Answer A is incorrect for that reason, leaving only answer C and the 8GB FAT32 system (which is larger than the 7GB called for in the question).

Question 45

Answer B is correct. Once again, we can't emphasize enough that you must be familiar with the basic DOS commands. They work the same way in the Recovery Console. The CD command (change directory) moves you up and down through file folders. However, the command takes no switches at all. Whatever text follows the CD, RD, and MD commands must be a single contiguous string. DOS tries to parse any spaces as a possible parameter setting. Answer A is incorrect because the underlying DOS name for the long filename is an abbreviated version of the actual directory name. DOS tries to find a "mydoc"-something file, with an extension and return a "file not found" error.

Answer C is incorrect because it shows only that the directory exists. The /V switch shows the full long filename below the true DOS name. It won't make the change to the folder. Answer D also returns a "too many parameters" error because of the space. Remember that underlying filenames in DOS use the ~ contraction unless otherwise configured in Windows. This is probably a Windows 9x system because it boots to DOS.

Question 46

Answer C is correct. Who really uses Dr. Watson? Even so, CompTIA will probably have a question on the utility, so you'd better know what it does and that it exists. Answer A is incorrect because the System File Checker (SFC) is designed to compare versions of .DLL files with the original copies Windows installed on the disk. Answer B is incorrect because the question refers to a system error and a report. Although MSINFO32 is a great diagnostics tool, it doesn't trap for errors and doesn't generate a diagnostics report. Answer D is incorrect because it's a bogus filename. Microsoft provides the Dr. Watson utility as a way for the system to take a snapshot of the system during an error, and then send a report of that snapshot to Microsoft tech support.

Question 47

Answers A and B are correct. As soon as you see a reference to programs running, you should think Task Manager. Windows 9x uses the Ctrl+Alt+Del keystrokes to call up the Task Manager. Those keys are used on a Windows 2000/XP networked system to call up the logon screen. You should know that answer C is incorrect in any version of Windows because the control panel doesn't have a separate Task Manager or Taskbar applet. You should also know that answer D is incorrect because right-clicking on the Desktop calls up the visual settings. There's no such tab as "System Tray" on the Desktop settings. There are two responses, so if you know what doesn't work, you can easily figure out the correct response, even if you can't visualize the specific steps during the exam.

Question 48

Answer C is correct. This is another scenario question. The story indicates that the XP machine was running, but now it isn't. The issue of XP Home or Professional is irrelevant, and is only there as a distraction. You should recognize that answer A is wrong immediately, because SCANREGW is a Windows 9x utility and doesn't exist in Windows NT/XP.

Answer D is almost always a last resort, and surely isn't an "easy" solution to anything. Answers B and C might be reasonable candidates, but the System File Checker normally handles changes made to system files. The odds are that an individual messing around on a computer wouldn't program a new version of a .DLL file and overwrite a critical file by the same name. Between the remaining answers C and D, System Restore (answer C) is the easiest first step to return an XP installation to a previous, working condition. Remember that although System Restore may not be turned on, the question offers the option as though it's routinely backing up the computer. Don't over-analyze the responses.

Question 49

Answer D is correct. This is another question designed to pound FDISK into your head before you take the exam. Run the partitions in your mind, and write them down on the blank scratch paper you'll have. The question indicates two physical disks. It doesn't matter how large they are. The first disk has a primary partition (C:), and three logical drives in the extended partition

(D:, E:, and F:). The second physical disk is formatted as a single, extended partition, and would presumably become the G: drive. The real "gotcha" in the question relates to how the Explorer lists the drive.

We didn't cover this extensively in the main body of the book, but you should know that Windows lists all Primary partitions in descending order, with the first IDE controller ahead of the second controller, and then a SCSI controller. Extended partitions are listed next, with the first controller's extended partitions ahead of the second controller's. After all hard drives, Windows lists slave drives such as CDROM drives. Following that, Windows lists removable drives. And following that, Windows lists network drives, aliased and mapped drives, and substituted drives (made with the SUBST) command.

Question 50

Answers B and D are correct. There's no way around it. You're going to have to remember what critical files must be on the Windows NT/2000/XP start-up disk. However, there are some clues in the responses. Answer A is incorrect because it refers to one of the Windows 9x Registry files. Answer C should be unfamiliar to you because it's a bogus filename. Always trust your instincts. If you've really used a lot of filenames before, you'll have a pretty good subconscious sense of how a particularly important filename just doesn't look right. Aside from that, you'll probably never see a file that ends in "ini" followed by an executable extension like "com" or "exe." That leaves only answers B and D, and the question tells you that there are two correct responses. Should we remind you to check Chapter 1 again, for question strategies? What the heck; why not.

Question 51

Answer C is correct. Here's a nice way to get you wandering off into panic and anxiety by getting you thinking about Adobe Photoshop. It's a scenario question, so remember that the likelihood is that the specific program name is irrelevant. However, you should know that Photoshop is an application. Answer D is clearly incorrect because knowing what a program's properties show doesn't help in terms of opening the program, for the most part. Answer B might be an option, but the "troubleshooting" reference indicates that the question is probably testing you on something coming from the Start menu. Put B on hold. An application has little to do with the underlying hardware configuration, so answer A is unlikely. We already gave you a question earlier in the exam that indicated the Event Viewer is directly linked to problems with applications, so you should have found answer C either with elimination or by remembering a previous question. These are both valid strategies in any exam. Compare the response in answer B (on hold) with the one in response C, and then ponder the fact that A+ certification has more to do with troubleshooting event problems than network rights and permissions.

Question 52

Answer D is correct. This question tries to short-circuit your mind with complex terminology and hexadecimal addresses. Don't be distracted! Remember to always examine the question for the real, most basic question essentials. Examine the responses and note that this is definitely a memory question of some kind. Notice that the question itself refers to both PAGEFILE.SYS and 386PART.PAR, both of which you should know are swap files. If you don't, then examine your own system, checking for an extremely large hidden file in the root folder. Answer D is the only response having to do with virtual memory and swap files. Answer A is incorrect because it refers to a video area in conventional memory, and nobody really expects you to remember segment addresses. Answer B is incorrect because BIOS and Windows don't use expanded memory on a Windows machine. Answer C is incorrect because it refers to a way for DOS to place very specific file information in a very small area of conventional memory (see Chapter 13). The first sentence of the question has no bearing on the actual question. It's merely a distraction.

Question 53

Answer D is correct. If you missed this one, go back and skim over Chapter 16, "Troubleshooting." There aren't that many hardware reasons for Windows crashes, but a badly seated PCI card is a common one. Answer A is incorrect because there's no such thing as "32-bit multimedia extensions" in relation to a piece of hardware. It's there to get you worrying about MMX technology. Answer B is incorrect because the system wouldn't even start. This system is starting, but then crashing. Answer C is incorrect because "system resources" aren't a configurable option. Once again the process of elimination comes to the rescue.

Question 54

Answer B is correct. Watch out for those scenarios. Remember that they're there to distract you. Who cares what the IT manager is doing? The real question has to do with viruses. Looking over the responses, you should see that they all have references to security and networking. What's the best way to secure a network from unauthorized hackers? A firewall. Answer A is incorrect because a proxy server doesn't have a "virus alert function call." Even if it did, and it activated that call, it would only alert someone and not prevent anything. Totally bogus option! Answer C is incorrect because it's also bogus, distracting you with the term "backdoor." The SAT has to do with providing the network with identification information about individual users. Answer D is incorrect because the local security manager (not authority, as in LSA), if it existed, would be a possible red-herring reference to Windows user security management, passwords, and resource access. Answer B is the only response that uses language to reference a common problem with Windows and viruses. It isn't a great response, but the exam often has these types of shaky response options. Just be careful.

Question 55

Answer D is correct. Remember that for the most part, questions relating to Windows NT and Windows 2000 will have very similar options to Windows XP. Don't get panicked because you're not an NT expert. And don't panic if you're not familiar with Windows 2000, although you should at least try to fool around with an installed Windows 2000 system. Drive letters are assigned by the operating system during the boot process. Answer B is incorrect because CMOS controls only the order in which the system looks at drives. Windows 2000 provides a way to reassign drive letters from within the operating system by selecting the device (in this case, a CDROM drive) in the Device Manager and then choosing the appropriate start and end drive letters. Answer A is incorrect because SYSTEM.INI has no control over assigning drive letters. Answer C is incorrect because the Registry contains configuration settings for the hardware device, not drive letter assignments.

Question 56

Answer B is correct. Again, you're being distracted by the restriction to a Windows NT station. This printer problem applies to almost every version of Windows. The question has no reference to a network, so it's a standard, standalone system. Setting the default printer for a Windows NT workstation is done in the same way as in Windows 2000 and Windows 9x. Right-click on the printer in the Printers folder, and select Set As Default. Answer A presents a fictitious menu path and there is no "Print First" check box in Windows. Answer C is incorrect because changing a printer involves making a printer the default, not the primary or secondary printer. Answer D is incorrect because although a network printer may have an IP address, the relative priority of a network resource has nothing at all to do with the many-digit IP address number and the IP address has no bearing on whether a printer is the default printer.

Question 57

Answer B is correct. Way back when, DOS used Check Disk to test for file integrity, cross-linked files, and to reconcile the FAT with the actual file locations. Answer A is incorrect because later versions of DOS, on through Windows Me, used ScanDisk as a complete replacement for Check Disk. SCANDSKW.EXE is the Windows version of the program, and can run from the Explorer. SCANDISK.EXE is the command-line version of the same program.

Answer C is incorrect because a "dirty" disk is a specific term used by Windows NT/2000/XP to indicate a problem with file integrity. DEFRAG is only a way to optimize the storage of the files on a disk, not a way to check the disk for location problems. Answer D is incorrect because it refers to the XP version of FDISK, and is used to re-partition a disk, not to resolve a "dirty" error.

Question 58

Answer B is correct. This is yet another very sneaky trick question. References to the Taskbar and lots of open programs should give you a clue that the system resources are being overloaded. The "out of memory" error points to either System Resources or a Virtual Memory (swap file) problem. Here's where it gets tricky. There are two responses, either of which is a legitimate cause for the problem. Answer C is incorrect because no other programs would run at all, or they would stay minimized if the spreadsheet took every piece of memory. Answer D is incorrect because it isn't "likely" that a machine has insufficient RAM. Even if it did, the "out of memory" error wouldn't show up only during a Save operation. "Likely" is the key to this question, and this type of question in general. Note that the question specifically points you to a crowded Taskbar. The implication is that the user has been running the system quite well, up until this moment. Although the disk could have run out of space, answer A is less "likely" than answer B. Therefore, answer A is incorrect.

Question 59

Answer B is correct. Once again, nobody cares what program is running on what machine in an exam like the A+ exam. All that matters is that alarms aren't running correctly. Alarms mean time, and sure enough, the responses all point to something involving the system clock. Answer A might be a place to check, but all it would give you would be the system time. Answer C is incorrect because an out-of-date BIOS chip would have a lot more problems than missed alarm notifications. Answer D is incorrect because it would show you only that Lotus Notes was installed on the machine. The reason the question is a tricky question is that checking the CMOS settings, on its own, wouldn't do anything. However, the Windows time in the system tray isn't necessarily accurate, depending on how Windows power management and hardware power management have been configured.

Of all the responses, only checking the CMOS settings for the date and time the hardware is holding might show you that the CMOS battery is dying. The real clue to this question is in the inclusion of the word "continually" along with the failing alarms. The implication is that the user starts the system, then notices the time of day is wrong and double-clicks on the time to reset it to a correct time. When he starts the machine the next day, the time is wrong again. It's not a fair question, really, but then again, neither are many of the real exam questions.

Question 60

Answer C is correct. This question separates out people who haven't had to deal with broken Windows NT/2000/XP systems from those who routinely have to fix startup crashes. We cover this topic in Chapter 15, because it's a common problem resulting from a bad or missing BOOT.INI file. Answer A might be possible, but you should never automatically reinstall Windows without first doing some simple troubleshooting. Answer B is reasonable, and would solve the problem for the most part, but again, it refers to a re-installation as the immediate fix. Answer D is incorrect because it refers to the hardware detection taking place prior to each Startup. Running the program would do nothing. Answer C is correct because the BOOT.INI file contains the pointer for all the Windows system files. The question indicates that each time the system tries to start, it can't find yet another file.

Question 61

Answer C is correct. We're quite proud of this question, as it should generate a nice "deer in the headlights" expression for many of our readers. Examine the question. You know you're in a DOS mode. The question indicates that somehow you'll be able to figure out why a CD drive isn't showing up on the system. It doesn't matter that it doesn't show up in Explorer. You could try to run a DIR command on the drive and it still wouldn't show up. The few possibilities, besides a broken drive, would be that the drive isn't correctly connected to the controller or that some type of device drivers are missing. Answer A is incorrect. Issuing the LASTDRIVE environment command on its own would only show how many drives the system can recognize, not give you a reason for a missing CD drive. Answer B is likewise incorrect because it would show only the environment. Answer D is incorrect because PATH is also an environment command, and would change the search pattern to a folder called MSCDEX.EXE.

Response D offers you a clue to how to resolve the problem in the question. MSCDEX.EXE is a generic CDROM driver. Even if you didn't remember the correct spelling, you should be readily familiar with the file. Given that all three other responses are environment statements, the only "useful" response would be to type something out and look at it. AUTOEXEC.BAT is a configuration file, and if the CD drive requires device drivers and configuration settings, that would be a highly probable place to start. Skim Chapters 12 and 13 for a review of the DOS environment.

Question 62

Answer A is correct. Here again you're being conned into breaking out in hives over a Windows Me question. The question refers to a CONFIG.SYS file, which you know is a DOS configuration file. You also know that Windows 9x requires a memory manager. Strategy indicates a process of elimination. Answer D is incorrect because MSDOS.SYS is a system file, not to mention a required file on any DOS and Windows 9x machine. Answer C is incorrect because it loads the Windows helper file and is an obscure driver file that nobody knows much about. CompTIA may be unfair in some cases, but they're never mean-spirited. Answer B is incorrect because although it looks like a CD driver, the question refers to a Me "default" installation. That means that every copy of Windows Me would encounter this file. Have you ever encountered it?

The fact is that all versions of Windows 9x require HIMEM.SYS. That's why it was hard-coded into the MSDOS.SYS file as a load line. Likewise, no version of Windows 9x allows an expanded memory manager during installation. To use expanded memory for a legacy 16-bit program, you have to configure a .PIF file or Windows shortcut (using the impossible-to-find MSDOS.Pif file) properties for a DOS environment. Windows Me is only a red herring. The question relies on your understanding of how Windows 9x handles CONFIG.SYS files (see Chapter 13).

Question 63

Answer D is correct. Here's yet another distracting scenario question (we can't warn you enough about them!). What's the real question? "Why isn't the DIR command working?" That's it, pure and simple. Two of the responses indicate something to do with file systems, so make a note. Answer A is incorrect because although you might not be able to access the Windows folder, the implication is that the folder somehow controls the function of the DIR command. It doesn't. Answer B is incorrect because many hard disks are routinely partitioned into extended partitions. A particular partition doesn't affect the DIR command. However, partitions do relate to file systems, which makes three responses having to do with file systems.

The question explicitly indicates a Windows 98 boot disk, meaning the system has booted into DOS 7, and the DIR command expects to see DOS-type files. Answer C is wrong, because FAT32 is easily recognizable by 16-bit DOS. The only remaining response has to do with NTFS, which is entirely different from DOS and FAT16 and FAT32. Answer D is correct because DOS can't read an NTFS partition. However, the Recovery Console version of DOS (not the Windows 98 COMMAND.COM) can run a DIRectory listing on an NTFS partition.

Question 64

Answer A is correct. This question once again plays on your basic understanding of the command-line interface. Note that every response includes the ">" redirector symbol, so you don't need to know how it works. It's obviously a critical whatchamacallit, so ignore it. Two of the responses start with the TYPE command. Answer C is incorrect because the DIR command only lists filenames. It doesn't list file contents! The result would be to send the name of the file to the printer. Answer D is completely bogus because DOS has no run command. Even if it did, it would presumably try to "run" the printer with the system.ini program. Answer B is incorrect, but requires that you know that DOS has no "printer" device name (see Chapter 11). You get a clue to the possible device names by the repetition of LPT1 and the reference to PRN, which should strike your subconscious memory. Therefore, answer A is the correct response because it would type the contents of the System.ini file to the screen, then redirect (with the > symbol) the results to the LPT1 printer port.

Question 65

Answer C is correct. Have we helped you overcome your anxiety over Windows Me? If not, here's another way to make you familiar with how you can be fooled into a nervous breakdown for no reason at all. Parse the question, and realize that you're being asked about "wildcards." In fact, you're being asked to choose something that won't work, rather than what will work. Answer D is incorrect, right off the bat, because Windows Me runs over DOS and the Explorer always uses wildcards, in every version of Windows. Answer C is a legitimate DOS character, but it isn't a wildcard character. You should know from Chapter 12 that there are only two DOS wildcards: the asterisk and the question mark. That's it. Period. Therefore, answers A and B are valid wildcards. The only character (mark) that is *not* a valid wildcard in any version of DOS or Windows is the tilde referenced in answer C.

Question 66

Answer B is correct. These are "list" questions, and are relatively easy to figure out if you simply state the sentence each time with a different response. Just fill in the blanks. You have a clue about IO.SYS, in that it's a critical system file for DOS and Windows 9x. It must be on the drive somewhere. If you know that it's a system file and required to boot the computer, then the fact that the word "boot" shows up in every response is helpful. This question is asking you about the boot sector, and the master boot record. Answer A is incorrect because there are only logical drives, not logical partitions. Answer C is incorrect because every partition must be formatted, otherwise it would generate an "invalid media type" error. Answer D is incorrect because a "master cylinder" tends to show up in a car engine, not a hard drive. You should know that answer B is correct because the system files must be in the boot sector of the Primary, Active partition on a bootable hard drive. (Floppy disks can't be partitioned.)

Question 67

Answer C is correct. The only thing to watch out for on this question is that you're asked to choose what does *not* appear. Answer A, HKEY_USERS, answer B, HKEY_CLASSES_ROOT, and answer D, HKEY_CURRENT_CONFIG are three of the six keys displayed in the Registry Editor (REGEDIT). Answer C is correct because there is no HKEY_LOCAL_SECURITY key. Therefore it wouldn't appear. Be careful because there is a Local Security Authority, and you could inadvertently wander off into a brain fog if you're not careful. As we've said, you won't have to know the spellings and details for the individual HKeys, but you're going to have to do what you can to remember their names fairly closely. This is a question designed to show you how the exam can use HKeys without going into any details on them.

Question 68

Answers A and D are correct. This was another question designed to completely ruin your life if you've rarely used a command line. If you have used a command line a lot, then you've almost absolutely encountered the dot and dot-dot command option. (In Windows 98, NT/2000, and XP, you also have the dot-dot-dot option.) The question trips you up, even if you're a skilled DOS technician, by throwing in the /s switch. Answer B is incorrect because using a space after the CD command drops you lower on the tree, into a "command" child folder of the System32 folder (the logged, default folder). SmartDrive might be there, but not on a typical system. Answer C is incorrect because the DIR command would show a listing for the System32 folder and any subfolders. It wouldn't show the entire drive. We want to see what's in the c:\windows\command folder, which is clearly not below the current directory.

Answer A is correct because it uses the dot-dot option to move up to the parent folder first (c:\windows), then down to the command subfolder (c:\windows\command). From there you would run a DIR command and find the SmartDrive utility. Answer D is also correct because the DIR command uses the complete pathname for c:\Windows as the starting point. The /s switch would list every file that began with the letters SMAR-something, in all subfolders of c:\windows.

Question 69

Answer B is correct. This question is for all you folks who don't believe Windows uses anything involving DOS anymore. In that case, you should be thoroughly experienced and skilled in using the Windows Explorer to find files on the system. If you use only the main menu bar and choose the Tools | Find option, then you're way too dependent on the mouse. The F3 command from anywhere on the Desktop or in the Explorer calls up the Find: All Files dialog box in Windows 9x, and the Search Results dialog in Windows XP/2000. Even if you're not familiar with the .XLS extension, you must know that .DOC refers to document files (typically Word). Answer A is incorrect because it would search for those .DOC files. Answer D is incorrect, but it's there to play on your fears of not knowing a shortcut key. Don't be fooled. The responses "look" legitimate, so they probably are legitimate.

Answer C is incorrect because you can't enter an application name anywhere in Windows to search for its data files. Although Excel uses the .XLS extension by default, there isn't anything to prevent you from assigning a .ABC extension other than tradition, elegance, and consistent naming conventions. Answer B is correct because the Windows Explorer routinely uses DOS wildcards to find extensions, files, programs, and any other type of file management. Other options within the dialog window offer date range selections, and the option to search subfolders. This is what you type in the Name: dialog box, in Windows 9x, and the "All or parts of the filename:" area in Windows XP.

Question 70

Answers A and C are correct. This is a really tricky way to get you completely off the track. Parse the question and understand that the only thing that matters is how a program is being loaded. Answer D is incorrect, right off the bat, because no version of Windows uses a WIN.DAT file to load anything. It isn't a default or normal file on a routine system. Answer A is correct, and you should know that programs are routinely loaded from the Windows Startup folder, with references in the main Windows 9x Registry file (SYSTEM.DAT). So you're left with two responses to account for: B and C.

We recommend that you use the Start | Run box to run SYSEDIT on your machine. Examine the System.ini and Win.ini files, and see how they're organized. Do whatever you can to remember that "system" (SYSTEM.INI) stores system settings and is similar to the SYSTEM.DAT Registry file. If you can remember that SYSTEM.DAT is like SYSTEM.INI, then it should be easier to remember that WIN.INI is like USER.DAT. Otherwise, use rote memory to store the fact that LOAD= and RUN= are two lines available in the WIN.INI file to start a program directly, bypassing the Windows Startup folder.

System.ini uses the [386Enh] section to install many drivers. However, the WIN.INI file contains a "Load=" line and a "Run=" line. This is where Windows 3.x stored references to programs loaded when Windows started up. Those lines still exist and are still valid. An old 16-bit program could easily use either of those lines to put a program into memory, and drop an icon into the System tray. It isn't likely, but you're being tested on a well-known initialization line in an equally well-known configuration file. Remember that "System" refers to system files, and "WIN.INI" stores user configurations. A program that runs during a startup is more likely to show an icon as a user setting than as a hardware configuration.

PART 3

Appendixes

Using the PrepLogic Practice Tests, Preview Edition Software

This Exam Cram 2 includes a special version of PrepLogic Practice Tests—a revolutionary test engine designed to give you the best in certification exam preparation. PrepLogic offers sample and practice exams for many of today's most in-demand and challenging technical certifications. This special Preview Edition is included with this book as a tool to use in assessing your knowledge of the Exam Cram 2 material while also providing you with the experience of taking an electronic exam.

This appendix describes in detail what PrepLogic Practice Tests, Preview Edition is, how it works, and what it can do to help you prepare for the exam. Note that although the Preview Edition includes all the test simulation functions of the complete, retail version, it contains only a single practice test. The Premium Edition, available at www.PrepLogic.com, contains the complete set of challenging practice exams designed to optimize your learning experience.

Exam Simulation

One of the main functions of PrepLogic Practice Tests, Preview Edition is exam simulation. To prepare you to take the actual vendor certification exam, PrepLogic is designed to offer the most effective exam simulation available.

Question Quality

The questions provided in the PrepLogic Practice Tests, Preview Edition are written to highest standards of technical accuracy. The questions tap the content of the Exam Cram 2 chapters and help you review and assess your knowledge before you take the actual exam.

Interface Design

The PrepLogic Practice Tests, Preview Edition exam simulation interface provides you with the experience of taking an electronic exam. This enables you to effectively prepare for taking the actual exam by making the test experience a familiar one. Using this test simulation can help eliminate the sense of surprise or anxiety you might experience in the testing center because you will already be acquainted with computerized testing.

Effective Learning Environment

The PrepLogic Practice Tests, Preview Edition interface provides a learning environment that not only tests you through the computer, but also teaches the material you need to know to pass the certification exam. Each question comes with a detailed explanation of the correct answer and often provides reasons the other options are incorrect. This information helps to reinforce the knowledge you already have and also provides practical information you can use on the job.

Software Requirements

PrepLogic Practice Tests, Preview Edition requires a computer with the following:

➤ Microsoft Windows 98, Windows Me, Windows NT 4.0, Windows 2000, or Windows XP

➤ A 166MHz or faster processor is recommended

➤ A minimum of 32MB of RAM

➤ As with any Windows application, the more memory, the better your performance

➤ 10MB of hard drive space

Installing PrepLogic Practice Tests, Preview Edition

Install PrepLogic Practice Tests, Preview Edition by running the setup program on the PrepLogic Practice Tests, Preview Edition CD. Follow these instructions to install the software on your computer:

1. Insert the CD into your CDROM drive. The Autorun feature of Windows should launch the software. If you have Autorun disabled, click Start and select Run. Go to the root directory of the CD and select setup.exe. Click Open, and then click OK.

2. The Installation Wizard copies the PrepLogic Practice Tests, Preview Edition files to your hard drive; adds PrepLogic Practice Tests, Preview Edition to your Desktop and Program menu; and installs test engine components to the appropriate system folders.

Removing PrepLogic Practice Tests, Preview Edition from Your Computer

If you elect to remove the PrepLogic Practice Tests, Preview Edition product from your computer, an uninstall process has been included to ensure that it is removed from your system safely and completely. Follow these instructions to remove PrepLogic Practice Tests, Preview Edition from your computer:

1. Select Start, Settings, Control Panel.

2. Double-click the Add/Remove Programs icon.

3. You are presented with a list of software installed on your computer. Select the appropriate PrepLogic Practice Tests, Preview Edition title you want to remove. Click the Add/Remove button. The software is then removed from your computer.

Using PrepLogic Practice Tests, Preview Edition

PrepLogic is designed to be user friendly and intuitive. Because the software has a smooth learning curve, your time is maximized because you start practicing almost immediately. PrepLogic Practice Tests, Preview Edition has two major modes of study: Practice Test and Flash Review.

Using Practice Test mode, you can develop your test-taking abilities as well as your knowledge through the use of the Show Answer option. While you are taking the test, you can expose the answers along with a detailed explanation of why the given answers are right or wrong. This enables you to better understand the material presented.

Flash Review is designed to reinforce exam topics rather than quiz you. In this mode, you are shown a series of questions but no answer choices. Instead, you are given a button that reveals the correct answer to the question and a full explanation for that answer.

Starting a Practice Test Mode Session

Practice Test mode enables you to control the exam experience in ways that actual certification exams do not allow:

➤ *Enable Show Answer Button*—Activates the Show Answer button, allowing you to view the correct answer(s) and full explanation(s) for each question during the exam. When not enabled, you must wait until after your exam has been graded to view the correct answer(s) and explanation.

➤ *Enable Item Review Button*—Activates the Item Review button, allowing you to view your answer choices, marked questions, and to facilitate navigation between questions.

➤ *Randomize Choices*—Randomize answer choices from one exam session to the next. Makes memorizing question choices more difficult, therefore keeping questions fresh and challenging longer.

To begin studying in Practice Test mode, click the Practice Test radio button from the main exam customization screen. This enables the options detailed in the preceding list.

To your left, you are presented with the option of selecting the preconfigured Practice Test or creating your own Custom Test. The preconfigured test has a fixed time limit and number of questions. Custom Tests enable you to configure the time limit and the number of questions in your exam.

The Preview Edition included with this book includes a single preconfigured Practice Test. Get the compete set of challenging PrepLogic Practice Tests at www.PrepLogic.com and make certain you're ready for the big exam.

Click the Begin Exam button to begin your exam.

Starting a Flash Review Mode Session

Flash Review mode provides you with an easy way to reinforce topics covered in the practice questions. To begin studying in Flash Review mode, click the Flash Review radio button from the main exam customization screen. Select either the preconfigured Practice Test or create your own Custom Test.

Click the Best Exam button to begin your Flash Review of the exam questions.

Standard PrepLogic Practice Tests, Preview Edition Options

The following list describes the function of each of the buttons you see. Depending on the options, some of the buttons are grayed out and inaccessible or missing completely. Buttons that are appropriate are active. The buttons are as follows:

➤ *Exhibit*—This button is visible if an exhibit is provided to support the question. An exhibit is an image that provides supplemental information necessary to answer the question.

➤ *Item Review*—This button leaves the question window and opens the Item Review screen. From this screen you can see all questions, your answers, and your marked items. You also see correct answers listed here when appropriate.

➤ *Show Answer*—This option displays the correct answer with an explanation of why it is correct. If you select this option, the current question is not scored.

➤ *Mark Item*—Check this box to tag a question you need to review further. You can view and navigate your Marked Items by clicking the Item Review button (if enabled). When grading your exam, you are notified if you have marked items remaining.

➤ *Previous Item*—View the previous question.

➤ *Next Item*—View the next question.

➤ *Grade Exam*—When you have completed your exam, click to end your exam and view your detailed score report. If you have unanswered or marked items remaining you are asked whether you would like to continue taking your exam or view your exam report.

Time Remaining

If the test is timed, the time remaining is displayed on the upper-right corner of the application screen. It counts down minutes and seconds remaining to complete the test. If you run out of time, you are asked whether you want to continue taking the test or end your exam.

Your Examination Score Report

The Examination Score Report screen appears when the Practice Test mode ends—as the result of time expiration, completion of all questions, or your decision to terminate early.

This screen provides you with a graphical display of your test score with a breakdown of scores by topic domain. The graphical display at the top of the screen compares your overall score with the PrepLogic Exam Competency Score.

The PrepLogic Exam Competency Score reflects the level of subject competency required to pass this vendor's exam. Although this score does not directly translate to a passing score, consistently matching or exceeding this score does suggest you possess the knowledge to pass the actual vendor exam.

Review Your Exam

From the Your Score Report screen, you can review the exam that you just completed by clicking on the View Items button. Navigate through the items, viewing the questions, your answers, the correct answers, and the explanations for those questions. You can return to your score report by clicking the View Items button.

Get More Exams

Each PrepLogic Practice Tests, Preview Edition that accompanies your Exam Cram 2 contains a single PrepLogic Practice Test. Certification students worldwide trust PrepLogic Practice Tests to help them pass their IT certification exams the first time. Purchase the Premium Edition of PrepLogic Practice Tests and get the entire set of all new challenging Practice Tests for this exam. PrepLogic Practice Tests—Because You Want to Pass the First Time.

Contacting PrepLogic

If you would like to contact PrepLogic for any reason, including information about our extensive line of certification practice tests, we invite you to do so. Please contact us online at www.preplogic.com.

Customer Service

If you have a damaged product and need a replacement or refund, please call the following phone number:

800-858-7674

Product Suggestions and Comments

We value your input! Please email your suggestions and comments to the following address:

feedback@preplogic.com

License Agreement

YOU MUST AGREE TO THE TERMS AND CONDITIONS OUTLINED IN THE END USER LICENSE AGREEMENT ("EULA") PRESENTED TO YOU DURING THE INSTALLATION PROCESS. IF YOU DO NOT AGREE TO THESE TERMS, DO NOT INSTALL THE SOFTWARE.

What's on the CD

This appendix is a brief rundown of what you'll find on the CDROM that comes with this book. For a more detailed description of the PrepLogic Practice Tests, Preview Edition exam simulation software, see Appendix A, "Using the PrepLogic Practice Tests, Preview Edition Software."

PrepLogic Practice Tests, Preview Edition

PrepLogic is a leading provider of certification training tools. Trusted by certification students worldwide, PrepLogic is, we believe, the best practice exam software available. In addition to providing a means of evaluating your knowledge of the Exam Cram 2 material, PrepLogic Practice Tests, Preview Edition features several innovations that help you to improve your mastery of the subject matter.

For example, the practice tests enable you to check your score by exam area or domain to determine which topics you need to study more. Another feature enables you to obtain immediate feedback on your responses in the form of explanations for the correct and incorrect answers.

PrepLogic Practice Tests, Preview Edition exhibits most of the full functionality of the Premium Edition but offers only a fraction of the total questions. To get the complete set of practice questions and exam functionality, visit www.PrepLogic.com and order the Premium Edition for this and other challenging exam titles.

Again for a more detailed description of the PrepLogic Practice Tests, Preview Edition features, see Appendix A.

Acronym Glossary

AC (alternating current)
Changes from a positive voltage to a negative voltage during one cycle. The most common example is household electricity, which is 110 volts at 60 hertz in the United States.

ADC (analog-to-digital converter)
An electronic device, usually packaged in a chip, that converts analog signals, such as speech, to a digital bit stream.

AGP (accelerated graphics port)
Provides the video controller card with a dedicated path to the CPU. Found on newer PCs.

ALU (arithmetic logic unit)
An area inside a CPU that handles simple arithmetic and logic instructions.

AM (amplitude modulation)
A type of radio transmission.

AMD (Advance Micro Devices)
A corporation specializing in microprocessor chip manufacturing.

ANSI (American National Standards Institute)
One of several organizations that develop standards for the information technology industry.

AOL (America OnLine)
An international private networking system, providing online services to paid subscribers.

API (application programming interface)
Provides a set of uniform building blocks that many programmers can use when building an application (see MAPI).

ASCII (American Standard Code for Information Interchange)
Specifies a seven-bit pattern used for communications between computers and peripherals.

ASPI (Advanced SCSI Programming Interface)

A protocol for a program or device to interface with the SCSI bus (see SCSI).

AT (Advanced Technology)

IBM's name for its 80286 PC form factor, which it introduced in 1984.

AT&T (American Telephone and Telegraph)

One of the world's largest communications providers, originally Bell Telephone Company (1878).

ATA (Advanced Technology Attachment)

The ANSI standard for IDE drives.

ATAPI (ATA packet interface)

A specification for attaching additional drives to an ATA connector. The ANSI standard for EIDE drives.

ATC (advanced transfer cache)

Intel's wide-bit (128-bit, 256-bit) transfer bus used with L-2 cache memory in Net Burst technology (Pentium 4).

ATX (Advanced Technology Xtensions)

A system board form factor that incorporates an accelerated graphics port. It is designed for the Pentium II and is mounted vertically.

Basic (Beginner's All-Purpose Symbolic Instruction Code)

A free popular programming language developed in the 1960s at Dartmouth College, used as part of the original foundation for DOS.

BBS (bulletin board service)

Online access locations where users post information and where other users can read or download information.

BDOS (Basic DOS)

One of the original system files in CP/M, the other being BIOS (not the same thing as the ROM BIOS chip on a motherboard).

BIOS (Basic Input Output System)

A set of detailed instructions for PC startup that usually are stored in ROM on the system board.

BNC (bayonet nut connector)

A type of connecting hardware used with network cables and interface cards.

CAD (computer aided design)

Drawing programs used in engineering and architectural settings.

CAV (constant angular velocity)

A reference to maintaining an optical disk's steady rotational speed by transferring data to a small buffer.

CCD (charge-coupled device)

A semiconductor that is sensitive to light and is used for imaging in scanners, video cameras, and digital still cameras.

CCP (console command processor)

The original command interpreter used in CP/M.

CD (Compact Disc [Disk])

A plastic disk measuring 4.75 inches in diameter that is capable of storing 1GB of digital information, although 650MB is more typical.

CDC (Control Data Corporation)

One of the original developers of the IDE specification.

CDROM (Compact Disk [Disc] Read-Only Memory)

A compact disk (see CD) used to store information one time only, but which can be read many times.

CD-RW (Compact Disc, Read-Write)

A compact disk that can be written to and read from. Technically, the RW does not stand for re-writeable.

CGA (Color Graphics Adapter)

An IBM video standard that provides low-resolution text and graphics.

CGI (common gateway interface)

An Internet scripting language.

CHS (cylinder/head/sector)

The table of physical addresses used to find information on a hard disk. Large Block Addressing (LBA) uses both Physical (P-CHS) and Logical (L-CHS) parameter numbers.

CISC (complex instruction set computer)

Pronounced "sisk" (rhymes with *disk*), a way of handling instructions within a chip.

CLV (constant linear velocity)

Technology by which an optical disk maintains a correct speed by using reference data to adjust spindle motor speed.

CMA (common monochrome adapter)

IBM's original PC monitor, also known as monochrome display adapter (MDA).

CMOS (Complementary Metal Oxide Semiconductor)

The type of chip commonly used to store the BIOS for a PC. It is usually backed up with a small battery for times when the PC's power is off.

CMY (cyan, magenta, yellow)

The three primary colors of reflective light used in paint, ink, and other indirect sources of color. CMY is used in LCD color monitors.

COBOL (COmmon Business-Oriented Language)

A high-level programming language commonly used on mainframe and minicomputers.

CompTIA (Computing Technology Industry Association)

A nonprofit organization made up of over 6,000 member companies that developed the A+ certification program.

CP/M (Control Program for Microcomputers)

The first operating system developed for microcomputers.

CPU (central processing unit)

The main chip where instructions are executed.

CRC (cyclical redundancy check)

A method used to verify data.

CRT (cathode ray tube)

The picture tube of a monitor.

CSMA/CD (Carrier Sense, Multiple Access, Collision Detection)

A method of preventing or limiting packet collisions on an Ethernet cable. Collisions can jam the cable, halting or severely reducing data transfers.

DAC (Digital-to-Analog Converter)

An electronic device that converts digital signals to analog.

DASD (direct access storage device)

The original technical name given by the IBM PC Institute for a disk drive subsystem.

DAT (digital audio tape)

Used in small cassettes for storing backup information (also refers to a Directory Allocation Table). DAT has been replaced by DLT.

DC (direct current)

Electricity that flows in only one direction. The power supply in a PC converts alternating current from the wall socket to direct current at voltages needed by PC components.

DDE (Dynamic Data Exchange)

A message protocol within Windows that allows applications to exchange data automatically.

DDR (double data rate)

Usually associated with DDR SDRAM.

DEC (Digital Equipment Corporation)

One of the original corporations involved with the development of PCs.

DHTML (Dynamic HyperText Markup Language)

Like HTML, except that information can be changed, based upon data gathered at a Web site. For example, user location can be captured to change the contents of a Web page.

DIMM (dual inline memory module)

A narrow printed circuit board that holds DRAM memory chips on both sides of the board, rather than only one side of the board (see SIMM).

DIN (Deutsche Institut fur Normung)

The German Standards Institute, which developed standards for many of the connectors used in PCs.

DIP (dual inline package)

A common rectangular chip housing with leads on both of its long sides.

DLT (digital linear tape)

A form of tape backup unit used for network file servers.

DMA (direct memory access)

Specialized circuitry, often including a dedicated microprocessor, that allows data transfer between memory locations without using the CPU.

DMF (distributed media format)

Microsoft's proprietary 1.7MB formatting method for distribution disks.

DMI (Desktop Management Interface)

A specification created by the Desktop Management Task Force. The DMI Pool is made up of the various resources the BIOS and a PnP OS understand and manage on the system, somewhat like the OSI layers.

DNS (domain name system)

A DNS server works to convert numeric IP addresses to readable format.

DOS (Disk Operating System)

The most widely used single-user operating system in the world. Quick and Dirty Operating System (QDOS) was the original model for DOS.

dpi (dots per inch)

Written in lowercase, a measure of resolution mostly applied to printers and scanners.

DRAM (Dynamic RAM)

The most common type of computer memory.

DS (double sided)

Description of a storage method used with disks (see HD).

DS/DL (double sided, double layer)

A storage format for DVDs.

DS/SL (double sided, single layer)

A storage format for DVDs.

DSL (digital subscriber line)

A high-speed Internet connection system.

DSSS (Direct Sequence Spread Spectrum)

Relates to the IEEE 802.11a and 802.11g wireless networking standard, where transmitters send multiple copies of addressed data packets across a wide band of frequencies (see FHSS).

DUV (deep ultra violet)

Light used in the lithographic process of etching signal traces. DUV wavelengths can only go as small as 100 nanometers.

DVD (digital versatile disk)

An optical storage disk much like a compact disk (CD) using a different method for storing data. DVDs have storage capacities of 10GB or more, depending upon the type of laser used to write data and the number of layers making up the disk.

DVD-R (Digital Versatile Disk, Recordable)

An optical storage disk that can be written to by the consumer. Usually the R refers to Read, or Read-Only. A more typical acronym for a recordable disk would be DVD-RW.

DVI (digital video interface)

A specification proposed by Intel for video connectors. DVI-A for analog, and DVI-D for digital signals.

EB (exabyte)

1,024 petabytes, 1 million terabytes. 5 exabytes would store every word ever spoken by all human beings.

ECC (error correction code)

Tests for memory errors, which it corrects on the fly.

ECP (electronic control package)

Not the same as the enhance capabilities port for parallel interfaces, the electronic control package is the circuitry used by a laser printer to communicate with its CPU and control panel.

ECP (Enhanced Capabilities Port)

The IEEE 1284 standard for enhanced parallel ports that are compatible with the Centronics parallel port.

EDO (extended data output)

A type of memory that approaches the speed of SRAM by overlapping internal operations.

EEMS (Enhanced EMS)

An enhancement of the Enhanced Memory Specification (EMS). EEMS was developed by AST, Inc. together with Ashton-Tate, Inc. The Enhanced memory management driver is the EMM386.EXE file, no longer used by Windows.

EEPROM (Electrically Erasable Programmable Read-Only Memory)

Holds data without power. It can be erased and overwritten from within the computer or externally with an electrical charge. EEPROM chips are used mostly for BIOS. Flash memory chips are similar, but are mostly used for data storage.

EGA (enhanced graphics adapter)

A medium-resolution IBM text and graphics standard. It was superseded by today's VGA standard.

EIDE (Enhanced Integrated Drive Electronics)

An extension of the IDE interface that is compatible with more devices and offers increased transfer rates.

EISA (Extended Industry Standard Architecture)

Expands the 16-bit ISA bus to 32 bits and provides bus mastering.

ELD (electro-luminescent display)

A type of video display used in notebook computers.

EMI (ElectroMagnetic Interference)

An adverse effect caused by electromagnetic waves emanating from an electrical device.

EMS (Expanded Memory Specification)

The expanded memory specification developed by Lotus, Intel, and Microsoft prior to the development of extended memory (XMS).

EP (ElectroPhotographic)

The EP drum in a laser printer is sensitive to light and stores a magnetic image prior to attracting toner particles.

EPP (Enhanced Parallel Port)

Part of the IEEE 1284 specification for a high-speed printer port capable of bi-directional speeds approaching 2MB per second.

EPROM (Erasable Programmable Read-Only Memory)

A type of ROM that uses ultraviolet light to erase and reprogram the chip, instead of using an electrical charge to reprogram an EEPROM chip.

ESD (ElectroStatic Discharge)

Electrical current moving from an electrically charged object to an approaching conductive object.

ESDI (Enhanced Small Device Interface)

An interface specification for hard drive controllers (see IDE).

EUV (extreme ultra violet)

Light used in the lithographic process of etching signal traces. EUV wavelengths can only go as small as 10–14 nanometers.

FAT (file allocation table)

The part of DOS that keeps track of where data is stored on a disk (see NTFS).

FC PGA (Flipped Chip Pin Grid Array)

A configuration of CPU connector pins where the chip is turned upside down.

FCB (file control block)

Used in the CP/M file management system (still found on many Windows systems).

FDDI (Fiber Distributed-Data Interface)

Used in fiber optics for transmission of large bursts of high-speed data.

FH (firmware hub)

Part of Intel's 800-series chipset hub architecture (see GMCH).

FHSS (frequency hopping spread spectrum)

Relates to the IEEE 802.11b mobile computing standard where transmitters broadcast over many frequencies, hopping from one to another in a pattern (see DSSS).

FIFO (first in, first out)

Applied to buffering, usually in a modem buffer. The first data to enter the buffer is also the first data to leave the buffer.

FLOPS (FLoating point unit Operations Per Second)

A measure of CPU speed that replaced Millions of Instructions Per Second (MIPS).

FM (frequency modulation)

A type of radio transmission.

FORTRAN (FORmula TRANslator)

Designed by John Backus for IBM in the late 1950s, FORTRAN is the oldest high-level programming language.

FPM (fast page memory)

A type of memory that uses addressing pages.

FPU (Floating-Point Unit)

Commonly called a math coprocessor, it was available as an optional chip for Intel CPUs up to and including the 80386. The unit was internally integrated in the 80486 and Pentium processors. The FPU is still an important part of a CPU.

FTM (flat technology monitor)

A monitor with a flat face in front (not the same as a flat panel display or LCD panel used in notebooks).

GB (gigabyte)

1,024 megabytes, 1 million kilobytes.

GIF (Graphics Interchange Format)

A proprietary file format for bitmap graphics, owned by Unisys, and made popular by CompuServe (online service), often used in Web page designs. Because of legal demands, GIF has been replaced with the free PNG format (Ping's Not Gif) developed by the Linux and GNU (GNU's Not Unix) community of open-source (free) developers.

GMCH (Graphics and Memory Controller Hub)

Part of the Intel 800–series chipset hub architecture, along with the I/O Controller Hub (IOCH), and the Firmware Hub (FH).

GUI (graphic user interface)

Implemented with OS/2 and Windows, it incorporates icons, pull-down menus, and the use of a mouse.

HAL (Hardware Abstraction Layer)

One of the foundation layers of Windows NT and Windows 2000, used to isolate system hardware from the operating system kernel.

HAZMAT (HAZardous MATerials)

Chemical compounds that can cause public health dangers (see MSD).

HD (high density)

Description of data density on a disk (DS, HD).

HDTV (High-Definition TeleVision)

A standard for displaying high-resolution television images.

HMA (high memory area)

Part of the first 1MB of system memory, HMA is above the first 640MB application area of conventional memory.

HPFS (High Performance File System)

The preferred file management system for OS/2, and the original model for the Windows NTFS.

HT Technology (hyper-threading technology)

Intel Pentium 4 chips allow multiple execution threads to take place simultaneously inside the CPU, similar to having multiple processors directly inside a single chip housing. HT Technology is an Intel feature-set brand name.

HTML (HyperText Markup Language)

A standard for defining, formatting, and linking documents on the World Wide Web (see XML).

Hz (Hertz)

A unit named in honor of Heinrich Rudolf Hertz (German physicist) measuring cycles per second. MHz is millions (mega) of Hertz (cycles per second).

I/O (Input/Output)

An acronym used to reference any place where data is moving into or out of something.

IBM (International Business Machines)

The corporation that developed the first personal computer (PC).

IC (integrated circuit)

An arrangement of circuit traces and electronic components often placed on a so-called integrated circuit card or board.

IDE (Integrated Drive Electronics)

A popular hardware interface used to connect hard drives to a PC.

IEEE (Institute of Electrical and Electronic Engineers)

An organization with an overall membership of over 300,000 members that is highly involved in setting standards.

IFS (Installable File System)

1. A Windows file management component, not the same as the FAT or NTFS.

2. The image formation system in a laser printer.

InterNIC (Internet Network Information Center)

A committee funded by the National Science Foundation to provide specifications for the Internet.

IOCH (I/O Controller Hub)

One of Intel's ways of bringing together memory and CPU bus operations in the 800-series chipset that uses hub architecture (see GMCH).

IP (Internet Protocol)

An IP address is a series of numbers and periods, and the address is used by many networks. The protocol is the set of rules for that addressing.

IR (InfraRed)

A frequency of light in the short wave spectrum.

IRQ (Interrupt ReQuest)

A hardware interrupt generated by a device that requires service from the CPU. The request is transmitted through one of 8 to 16 physical lines on the system board, with one device typically allowed per line.

ISA (Industry Standard Architecture)

An expansion bus commonly used on PCs. It provides a data path of 8 to 16 bits and is sometimes referred to as an AT bus because of its use in the first IBM AT computers.

ISDN (Integrated Services Digital Network)

A specification for digital transmission of data over analog phone lines.

ISM (Industrial, Scientific, Medical)

An FCC-regulated radio spectrum with less regulation than other bands (such as AM and FM radio stations). Used for 802.11 wireless networking, cell phones, and other consumer electronics.

ISO (International Organization for Standardization)

An umbrella group for many of the international standards committees, such as ANSI.

ISP (Internet Service Provider)

Usually a business involved in providing Internet connections and Web hosting.

JPEG (Joint Photographic Experts Group)

A compression format used for graphic files, resulting in the common .JPG extension. The .JPG and .JPEG extension both usually refer to the same file format.

KB (kilobyte)

1,024 bytes.

LAN (local area network)

Standard acronym for most networks (see WAN).

LBA (logical block addressing)

Used to overcome early BIOS and IDE controller limitations in recognizing hard drives larger than 512MB.

LCD (Liquid Crystal Display)

A type of computer display panel using liquid crystals to pass or block light.

LDAP (Lightweight Directory Access Protocol)

A query language used by Windows NT, 2000, and XP to manage access requests.

LED (Light-Emitting Diode)

A small electrical device that generates light when current passes through it.

LIM (Lotus/Intel/Microsoft)

Three companies that jointly developed a standard for memory management above 640K (expanded memory).

LPX (Low-Profile eXtensions)

A thin, "low" AT form factor used in small desktop cases.

LSA (Local Security Authority)

A module in Windows NT and Windows 2000 acting as the interface between User Mode and Kernel Mode.

LUN (Logical Unit Number)

The identification (ID) number assigned to a device on a SCSI interface.

MAPI (Messaging Application Programming Interface)

Built into Windows as a way for different email programs to work together.

MB (megabytes)

1,024 kilobytes, 1 million bytes.

MB/s (megabytes per second)

A data transfer rate of 1 million bytes per second.

Mbps (megabits per second)

A data transfer rate of 1 million bits per second.

MBR (Master Boot Record)

The first sector on a bootable partition.

MCA (MicroChannel Architecture)

A proprietary 32-bit expansion bus developed by IBM. The bus requires specially designed cards that are not interchangeable with other popular bus designs.

MDA (monochrome display adapter)

The first IBM standard for monochrome video displays for text (evolved to become the CGA color adapter).

MDRAM (Multibank Dynamic Random Access Memory)

A type of video memory that uses many 32KB DRAM chips to form an interleaved array of graphics memory banks.

MFM (modified frequency modulation)

A system used for magnetic encoding, used on older PCs and floppy disks (see RLL).

MICR (magnetic ink character recognition)

Used in some scanners to capture a magnetic pattern information.

MIF (Management Information Format)

The DMI pool creates MIF files to store device configuration information used by other modules making up the DMI specification.

MIME (Multi-purpose Internet Mail Extensions)

A specification used to translate binary files to the text-based email transfer protocol used by the Internet.

MIPS (Millions of Instructions Per Second)

A unit of measure to gauge the speed of a CPU (see FLOPS).

MMDS (Multi-channel Multi-point Distribution Services)

A form of broadband Internet connection using line-of-sight transmission towers.

MMU (memory management unit)

A component of a microprocessor (CPU) used to direct data traffic to various internal areas.

MMX (MultiMedia eXtensions)

An expanded CPU instruction set optimized for multimedia applications, introduced with the early Pentium chips.

modem (MOdulator-DEModulator)

A device for sending data over telephone lines.

MPEG (Moving Picture Experts Group)

Pronounced m-peg, a type of video compression.

MSCDEX (Microsoft CD EXtensions)

The MSCDEX.EXE generic software driver for CDROM drives.

MSD Sheet (material safety data)

Usually written as MSDS; a required description of each and every hazardous material (HAZMAT) used in a business location. (Not to be confused with MSD.EXE, the Microsoft Diagnostics program utility.)

NCSC (National Computer Security Council)

A government agency that defines levels of security for computer systems. Windows NT is C-2 compliant.

NIC (network interface card)

Provides the physical connection of a PC to the cable of a local area network.

NLX (InteLeX form factor)

A trademark of the InteLex Corporation (probably Intel Extended or Extensions), the NLX was a form factor designed to follow the LPX motherboard form factor. NLX is a standard supported by Intel and IBM, and has mostly been replaced by the ATX form factor.

NOS (network operating system)

An operating system used to connect many computers together. NOS is used to distinguish an operating system written for networks, as opposed to DOS, which is a disk operating system written for standalone computers.

NRZI (Non Return to Zero Inverted)

A signaling process using changing voltage states to generate binary numbers in a USB cable. NRZI is also used to synchronize both a sending and a receiving clock.

NT (New Technology)

Windows NT is a multitasking operating system that became Windows 2000, then Windows XP.

NTFS (New Technology File System)

A file system specifically available to Windows NT, 2000, and XP. NTFS and FAT32 are the typical choices used to format a Windows partition.

NTSC (National Television Standards Committee)

The committee responsible for setting video standards in the United States. NTSC signals are composite signals used with television and VCRs and are different than RGB signals on a computer monitor.

OEM (original equipment manufacturer)

Many products are included in a ready-to-sell PC, including the operating system. OEM distinguishes a product specifically created, built, or manufactured by a company from the overall, final product. The Microsoft Windows operating system is a Microsoft product. The OEM version of Windows has been modified by the company selling a complete computer system.

OS/2 (Operating System 2)

IBM's second generation, single-user, multitasking operating system, developed for PCs. The last successful version was OS/2 Warp (version 3.x).

OSI (Open Systems Interconnection)

The OSI layers (the OSI model) describe the way various parts of a network operating system work with hardware and software.

PAL (Phase Alternating Line)

The predominant television specification used in Europe.

PARC (Palo Alto Research Center)

The Xerox development center where laser printers, the mouse, and the GUI were developed.

PAT (partition allocation table)

The first sector on a fixed disk, containing partition information and locations for that disk.

PB (petabyte)

1,024 terabytes, 1 million giga-bytes, 1 billion megabytes. 2 petabytes would hold the contents of all U.S. academic research libraries.

PCB (printed circuit board)

A board where electrical pathways are etched on the board, as opposed to using wires.

PCI (Peripheral Component Interconnect)

A specification developed by Intel and other industry leaders for an expansion bus that provides a high-speed data path between the CPU and peripherals (evolved to become PCI-X).

PCL (printer control language)

Formatting commands used by a printer during the print process.

PCMCIA (Personal Computer Memory Card Industry Association)

A nonprofit industry association that standardized the 16-bit socket, allowing portable computers to uti-lize credit card–size expansion cards. Sometimes known as "peo-ple can't memorize computer industry acronyms."

PDA (personal digital assistant)

A handheld device (for example, Palm, Pocket PC) used to track schedules, appointments, notes, and other personal information.

PDP (plasma display panel)

A type of video display sometimes used in notebook computers (also referred to as gas plasma panels).

PGA (pin grid array)

An arrangement of connection pins on a microprocessor. When the pins are in a set of staggered rows, they are called a staggered pin grid array (SPGA).

PIC (programmable interrupt con-troller)

An improvement added to the sec-ond series Pentium chips, designed to provide IRQ management capa-bilities to the operating system.

PIF (Program Information File)

A proprietary format file used by Windows to store configuration settings for a Real Mode (DOS) virtual machine session. The Explorer still uses PIF files for File Associations, although the file extensions are permanently hidden.

PIO (Programmed Input/Output)

Five modes used in the ATA speci-fication (see ATA).

PnP (Plug 'n' Play, Plug and Play)

An Intel standard that specifies how hardware components can be automatically configured when added to a PC. The standard requires support from the BIOS, the device, and the operating system.

POSIX (Portable Operating System Interface for Unix)

An operating system used in many government offices.

POST (Power On Self-Test)

A series of built-in tests performed by the BIOS at system startup, prior to loading an operating system. The POST generates beep codes.

PROM (Programmable Read-Only Memory)

This type of ROM requires a special machine to write instructions to a chip one time only, and the chip cannot be changed (see EPROM).

QDOS ("Quick and Dirty" Operating System)

The original version of the disk operating system (DOS), developed by Tim Paterson for the 8086 chip.

QIC (quarter-inch cartridge)

A recordable tape format used in tape backup machines.

RADAR (Radio Detecting/Detection And Ranging)

Radio waves generated by a source to bounce back from an object for the purpose of revealing the object's shape.

RAID (Redundant Array of Inexpensive Disks)

Used in networking as a form of data protection. There are six levels of RAID (0 through 5).

RAM (random access memory)

The computer's main workspace. Data stored in RAM can be accessed directly without requiring that information be read from a capacitor or transistor on a memory chip.

RAMDAC (Random Access Memory Digital-to-Analog Converter)

A component used with graphics cards and video subsystems to convert binary information to analog images.

RDRAM (Rambus Dynamic Random Access Memory)

A special type of DRAM memory chip developed by the Rambus corporation.

Rexx (Restructured Extended Executor)

A batch language developed for OS/2, with many more powerful commands than those in DOS.

RGB (red, green, blue)

The three primary colors of light used in color monitors (see also CMY).

RIMM (Rambus Inline Memory Module)

A memory module composed of Rambus memory chips on a printed circuit board.

RISC (reduced instruction set computer)

Computers using processors designed to run limited numbers of instructions very quickly.

RLE (run-length encoding)

A compression format used for graphic files, commonly used to compress Windows logo files. These files have an .RLE extension.

RLL (run length limited)

A system of magnetic encoding used with modern hard drives (see MFM).

ROM (Read-Only Memory)

A memory chip that permanently stores instructions and data. Data can be read from but not written to.

RPM (revolutions per minute)

The speed at which a disk revolves around a spindle.

SAA (System Application Architecture)

A user interface standard developed by IBM. The SAA was eventually replaced by Microsoft's API.

SAM (Security Accounts Manager)

A security module in Windows NT, 2000, and XP.

SASI (Shugart Associates Systems Interface)

Developed by Alan Shugart as part of the original floppy disk drive system.

SAT (Security Access Token)

A token created for each user on a Windows NT, 2000, or XP network. The SAT carries identification information across the network.

SCSI (Small Computer System Interface)

A hardware interface that provides for connecting up to seven devices to the motherboard (see also IDE).

SDRAM (Synchronous Dynamic Random Access Memory)

SDRAM is a DRAM chip with an internal synchronizing clock designed to reduce interrupt requests to the CPU.

SEC (single edge connector)

A chip packaging design used with printed circuit boards, having a single, edge connector.

SECAM (SEquential Couleur Avec Memoire)

A French video standard adopted by the Eastern bloc countries of the former Soviet Union.

SEP (single edge processor)

A type of packaging for a microprocessor with a single edge connector.

SGRAM (synchronous graphics RAM)

A type of video memory that uses an internal clock to synchronize graphics memory to the motherboard clock.

SID (security identification)

The Security ID is part of the security access token in Windows NT and Windows 2000.

SIMM (single inline memory module)

A narrow printed circuit board that holds memory chips. The connector is integrated into the edge of the board so it can easily be added to sockets on the system board. This module uses DRAM chips on one side of the board.

SMI (System Management Interrupt)

Used for power conservation and management.

SONAR (Sound Navigation and Ranging)

Sound signals generated by a source to bounce back from an object for the purpose of revealing the object's shape.

SONET (Synchronous Optical NETwork)

A protocol used for fiber optics cable data transfers.

SPARC (Scalable Processor ARChitecture)

A 32-bit and 64-bit microprocessor architecture created by Sun Microsystems, Inc., designed to run on RISC chips; usually used on Unix systems, or the Sun Solaris operating system.

SPGA (staggered pin grid array)

Microprocessor connection pin configuration (see PGA).

SPI (SCSI parallel interface)

Pronounced "spy," a subdivision of the SCSI-3 specification.

SPP (standard parallel port)

The original parallel port controller, assigned the LPT or PRN device abbreviation name.

SQL (structured query language)

A query language used to request information from a database.

SRAM (Static RAM)

A type of memory chip that uses transistors instead of capacitors to store data with no capacitor leakage. Static RAM is usually much faster than Dynamic RAM (DRAM), but is often more expensive. CMOS and secondary cache memory typically use SRAM chips.

SS (single sided)

Description of a storage method used with disks (see DS).

SS/DL (single sided, double layer)

A storage format for DVDs.

SS/SL (single sided, single layer)

A storage format for DVDs.

SSFDC (Solid State Floppy Disk Card)

The original name for the SmartMedia flash memory card.

ST (Shugart Technology, Inc.)

The ST-506/412 interface was the accepted standard for all PC hard disks and stood as the basis for the ESDI and IDE hard drive controller interfaces.

STP (shielded twisted pair)

A type of twisted-pair wire used in networking and telephony. The shielding is an outer wrap, usually metallic, which helps to prevent electromagnetic interference.

SVGA (Super Video Graphics Array)

The SVGA video standard provides a higher resolution than VGA, providing 16 million colors and resolutions up to 1,600×1,200 pixels.

TB (terabytes)

1,024 gigabytes, 1 million megabytes, 1 billion kilobytes. 10 terabytes would hold a printout of the entire U.S. Library of Congress. Estimates indicate that the human mind can hold approximately 15 terabytes of information.

TCP/IP (transport control protocol/Internet protocol)

Formerly named transport control *program*, the transport protocol coordinates packet information for the many IP packets and addresses in an online transmission.

TIFF (Tagged Image File Format)

A compression format used for bitmap image files, resulting in a .TIF extension that can be read by both PCs and Macintosh systems.

TSR (Terminate: Stay Resident)

A type of program that stays in memory (resident) even when it has stopped running (terminated). A TSR can be called up through the use of a "hot key," and runs in its own DOS window. TSRs were replaced by the Widows GUI, where many programs could run at the same time, leaving minimized icons on a Desktop. A TSR is similar to a program running in the background from the System Tray.

UART (Universal Asynchronous Receiver Transmitter)

A chip that transmits and receives data through the serial port, mostly used with dial-up modems.

UDMA (Ultra DMA)

The way Direct Memory Access (DMA) was speeded up in the Ultra ATA specification. Also called UDMA/33 (see ATA).

ULSI (Ultra Large-Scale Integration)

A type of manufacturing for microprocessor chips with hundreds of thousands of transistors.

UMB (upper memory block)

An area of the first megabyte of memory, above the first 640MB but below the high memory area.

UPS (uninterruptible power supply)

Provides battery backup power when the main power fails or moves to an unacceptable level. A UPS can also have a built-in line conditioner, used to stabilize the voltage entering the computer.

URL (universal resource locator)

An Internet address, typically presented as a domain name in the common www.address.com format.

USB (Universal Serial Bus)

A serial transfer specification that allows 127 devices to be daisy-chained to a cable.

UTP (unshielded twisted pair)

A type of twisted-pair wire used in networking where there is no special shielding against electromagnetic interference (see STP).

UV (UltraViolet)

A frequency of light in the long wave spectrum (see IR).

VCR (video cassette recorder)

A device used to record NTSC signals from television inputs. VCRs are gradually being replaced by Digital Video Recorders (DVRs).

VDD (Virtual Device Driver)

A software file acting as an interface between a device running in Real Mode and the surrounding Windows shell. VxD files are Virtual "something" (the *x*) Drivers where the device name abbreviation replaces the *x*.

VDM (virtual DOS machine)

Provides a 16-bit DOS session under a graphical operating system such as Windows or OS/2.

VDT (video display terminal)

Any video device used to display video information (also called a console).

VESA (Video Electronics Standards Association)

An organization composed of PC vendors that is dedicated to improving video and multimedia standards (see VL Bus).

VFAT (Virtual File Allocation Table)

A 32-bit file system used in Windows for Workgroups and Windows 95. The Virtual FAT is faster than the DOS FAT and provides for long filenames. VFAT and NTFS require loader files that act in a similar fashion to device drivers or memory managers.

VGA (Video Graphics Array)

The IBM video standard that has become the minimum standard for PC displays. It provides 16 colors at 640×480 resolution.

VHD (very high density)

Found in SCSI connectors providing high data transfer rates.

VID (Voltage IDentification)

The voltage ID pins that work with a voltage regulator module (VRM) to control voltages on a microprocessor.

VL Bus (VESA Local bus)

A type of VESA bus interface (see VESA).

VLSI (very large-scale integration)

A type of manufacturing for microprocessor chips with hundreds of thousands of transistors.

VM (Virtual Machine)

Programming microcode in a CPU that creates a representation (or emulation) of an 8086 processor and computer. Windows works with the CPU to generate a Virtual DOS Machine.

VME

1. VERSA Module Eurocard, part of the VMEbus, a competing architecture to the PCI bus.

2. Virtual Mode Extensions, an obscure function of Pentium chip architecture allowing for better control of Virtual DOS Machines (VDMs) and virtualized interrupts.

VMM (Virtual Machine Manager)

The Windows software that manages the Real Mode VMs. Windows XP no longer supports Real Mode.

VRAM (Video RAM)

Differs from common RAM in that it utilizes two ports (dual-ported) to simultaneously refresh the video screen and receive data for the next screen.

VRM (voltage regulator module)

An electronic component that can provide varying levels of voltage to another component (see VID).

VxD (virtual device driver)

Runs in the most privileged CPU mode and allows low-level interaction with hardware and internal Windows functions (see VDD).

WAN (wide area network)

Typically used for very large networks, often where multiple geographic locations are included (see LAN).

WORM (Write Once, Read Many)

1. A compact disk that can be written to one time and then read from many times.

2. A type of virus, installed (written) on a disk one time, but read many times to corrupt the system.

WOSA (Windows Open Services Architecture)

Part of the Windows technology used in conjunction with Active Directory.

WRAM (Windows RAM)

Windows RAM is not at all connected to Microsoft Windows. WRAM is a type of dual-ported video memory with large block addressing.

WWW (World Wide Web)

A subdivision of the Internet that uses HTML formatting. Other areas of the Internet include Gopher and FTP (File Transfer Protocol).

WYSIWYG ("What You See Is What You Get")

Refers to the capability to display text and graphics on a monitor with the same fonts and size relationships as will be printed in the final document.

XGA (eXtended Graphics Adapter)

The first IBM video adapter to use VRAM.

XML (eXtensible Markup Language)

A type of Internet markup language, extended from HTML, used for managing data rather than formatting text.

XMS (eXtended Memory Specification)

Any physical memory beyond the first 1MB of conventional memory. XMS (HIMEM.SYS) is common on modern PCs. EMS (EMM386.EXE) is rarely used with Windows.

XT (eXtended Technology)

The first IBM PC with a hard drive. It used the same 8088 processor (then the 8086) and 8-bit expansion bus as the original PC.

YB (yottabyte)

1,024 zettabytes.

ZB (zettabyte)

1,024 exabytes.

ZIF (zero-insertion force)

A socket that uses a lever to grasp the pins of a chip after it is inserted. This eliminated bent pins and became very popular for mounting CPUs.

Index

PR (Processor Rating) numbers, 193, 196-198

slots/sockets, 206-208

amplitude, 81

amps (current), 224

analog information versus digital information (electronics), 220-221

ANSI (American National Standards Institute), 274

answers

hardware test answer keys, 491-514

multiple choice question strategies, 469

practice exams, showing in, 878

software test answer keys, 839-871

anti-aliasing, 336

Appearance tab (Display Properties dialog box), 737

Apple Desktop Buses (ADB), 386

applets (Windows 9x), 571

CLEANMGR.EXE (Disk Cleanup), 680

DRWATSON.EXE (Dr. Watson), 679

MSCONFIG.EXE (Microsoft System Configuration), 680-681

MSINFO32.EXE (Microsoft System Information), 678

SYS.EXE (System File Checker), 679

TUNEUP.EXE (Maintenance Wizard), 682-683

Tweak UI, 677

WUPDMGR.EXE (Windows Update Manager), 681

Application layer (OSI model), 407

applications, 521

architectures

dual-pipeline, 89

superscalar, 184

Windows NT, 701

areal density, 293

arithmetic logic units (ALU), 120, 126

arrays, RAID, 312

Arrow keys, navigating Windows menu options, 642

ASCII (American Standard Code for Information Interchange) character sets, 121-122

ASR (Automated System Recovery), 729, 775-776

assigning IRQ, 47

associating files, 607-608

Asynchronous DRAM chips, 139

asynchronous memory, 79, 99

asynchronous operations, examples of, 37

AT (Advanced Technology)

connectors, 23

form factors, 24

Baby AT motherboards, 27

development of, 22-23

keyboard serial connectors, 449

ATA

drive controllers, IRQ 14, 154-155

specifications, 299-303. *See also* Fast ATA; Ultra ATA

ATA-2 specifications, 303

ATA-3 specifications. *See* Fast ATA specifications

ATA-4 specifications. *See* Ultra ATA specifications

ATA-5 specifications. *See* Ultra ATA/66 specifications

ATA-6 specifications (hard drives), 292. *See also* Ultra ATA/100 specifications

ATA-7 specifications. *See* Ultra ATA/133 specifications

ATA/ATAPI-7 specifications (hard drives), 292

ATAboy2 specifications (hard drives), 293

ATC (Advanced Transfer Cache), 206

backside buses, 148

Net Burst technology, 191

ATTRIB *.* /s >PRN command, 543

ATTRIB -H -R C:\Windows\System.DAT command, 543

ATTRIB command, 519, 661, 791

ATTRIB.EXE command (DOS), 541-543

attributes, defining, 714

ATX (Advanced Technology eXtension) form factors, 27-30

audio, streaming, 183

AUTOEXEC.BAT files, 572-574

DOS environment variables, setting, 535

SET TEMP=, 538

updating, 667

Windows Me, 683-684

Automated System Recovery (ASR), 729, 775-776

auxiliary cooling fans, 29

B

baby AT motherboards, 27

backpanes (networks), 399

backside buses, 145, 148, 167. *See also* dedicated memory buses

backslash (\), directories, 539

backups

differential versus incremental backups, 785

restoration strategies, 786-787

tape backups, 312

DLT, 313

LTO specifications, 314

platters, clusters, 284, 288
platters, cylinders, 284-285, 293-294
platters, defragmenting, 285
platters, reformatting, 285
platters, tracks, 284-287, 293-294
platters, zone bit recording, 287
RAMAC, 270
read-write heads, 278-279
SCSI specifications, 307-309
troubleshooting, 801-802
hot-swapping, 311
SCSI specifications, 301
SCSI-1 specifications, 309
SCSI-12 specifications, 310
Serial ATA specifications, 306
sliders, 278-280
spindle motors, 278-279
spindles, 278-279
testing access, 557
U2W (Ultra2 Wide) SCSI specifications, 311
Ultra ATA specifications, 304-305
Ultra ATA/66 specifications, 305
Ultra ATA/100 specifications, 306
Ultra ATA/133 specifications, 306
Ultra SCSI specifications, 310-311
Ultra Wide SCSI specifications, 311
Ultra2 SCSI specifications, 311
Ultra3 SCSI specifications, 311
XCHS, 291
logical drives, 272, 551, 554-555
extended partitions, 553
naming, 550
volume labels, 552, 556
Zip drives, daisy-chaining peripheral
devices, 384
drop ceilings, cable shielding, 456
DRWATSON.EXE (Dr. Watson) applet, 679
DSL (Digital Subscriber Line), 411
DSSS (direct sequence spread spectrum),
IEEE 802.11g standard, 417
dual-pipeline architectures, 89
Duplex ST connectors, fiber optic cable networks, 426. See also ST connectors
DVD, 318
drives, 319-320
tracks, size of, 319
DVD-R disks, 314
DVD-ROM disks, 314
DVD-RW disks, 314
DVI-A connectors, 439
DVI-D connectors, 439
dynamic VxD (Virtual Device Drivers), 663

E

EBD (Emergency Boot Disks), 655-656
ECC (error correction code), 112
ECHO command (DOS), 574
ECHO ^L >PRN command (DOS), 541
ECP (electronic control package). *See* main
logic assembly
ECP (extended capabilities ports), 441
edge connectors, 44
EDIT.COM, 122
editing
device driver settings, 666
logo files, 660
Windows 9x Registry, 649-650
Windows 9x Registry files
OLE, 640-641
pointers, 642
REGEDIT.EXE, 640
EDO (Extended Data Out)
DRAM ports, 105
memory, 98-99
EEPROM (electrically erasable programmable
ROM), 74
EIA-232 standard (serial connectors), 444
EISA (Extended Industry Standard
Architecture) buses, 44, 61
electricity, 222
AC capacitors, 229-230
ballasts, 232
charges, 223-224
circuits
closed, 225
short, 226
current
AC, 223
amps, 224
charges, 223-224
DC, 223
defining, 222
ohms, 226
DC capacitors, 228
electronic components
capacitors, 227-232
fuses, 226
potentiometers, 227
power supplies, 231-232
resistors, 226-227
switches, 226
EMI, 232
ESD
circuit boards, 235
ESD kits, 234-235
Hindenburg, 234

O

How can we make this index more useful? Email us at indexes@quepublishing.com

How can we make this index more useful? Email us at indexes@quepublishing.com

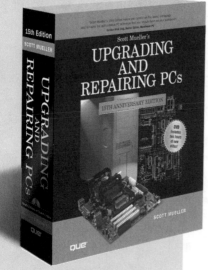

Your Guide to Information Technology Training and Reference

www.informit.com

Que has partnered with **InformIT.com** to bring technical information to your desktop. Drawing on Que authors and reviewers to provide additional information on topics you're interested in, **InformIT.com** has free, in-depth information you won't find anywhere else.

Articles

Keep your edge with thousands of free articles, in-depth features, interviews, and information technology reference recommendations – all written by experts you know and trust.

Online Books

Answers in an instant from **InformIT Online Books'** 600+ fully searchable online books. Sign up now and get your first 14 days **free**.

POWERED BY

Catalog

Review online sample chapters and author biographies to choose exactly the right book from a selection of more than 5,000 titles.

As an **InformIT** partner, **Que** has shared the knowledge and hands-on advice of our authors with you online. Visit **InformIT.com** to see what you are missing.